Introduction to Statistical Relational Learning

Adaptive Computation and Machine Learning

Thomas Dietterich, Editor
Christopher M. Bishop, David Heckerman, Michael I. Jordan, and Michael Kearns, Associate Editors

Bioinformatics: The Machine Learning Approach
Pierre Baldi and Søren Brunak, 1998

Reinforcement Learning: An Introduction
Richard S. Sutton and Andrew G. Barto, 1998

Graphical Models for Machine Learning and Digital Communication
Brendan J. Frey, 1998

Learning in Graphical Models
Michael I. Jordan, ed., 1998

Causation, Prediction, and Search, 2nd Edition
Peter Spirtes, Clark Glymour, and Richard Scheines, 2001

Principles of Data Mining
David Hand, Heikki Mannila, and Padhraic Smyth, 2001

Bioinformatics: The Machine Learning Approach, 2nd Edition
Pierre Baldi and Søren Brunak, 2001

Learning with Kernels: Support Vector Machines, Regularization, Optimization, and Beyond
Bernhard Schölkopf and Alexander J. Smola, 2001

Learning Kernel Classifiers: Theory and Algorithms
Ralf Herbrich, 2001

Introduction to Machine Learning
Ethem Alpaydin, 2004

Gaussian Processes for Machine Learning
Carl Edward Rasmussen and Christopher K. I. Williams, 2005

Semi-Supervised Learning
Olivier Chapelle, Bernhard Schölkopf, and Alexander Zien, eds. 2006

The Minimum Description Length Principle
Peter D. Grünwald, 2007

Introduction to Statistical Relational Learning
Lise Getoor and Ben Taskar, eds., 2007

Introduction to Statistical Relational Learning

edited by
Lise Getoor
Ben Taskar

The MIT Press
Cambridge, Massachusetts
London, England

Typeset by the authors using LATEX 2$_\varepsilon$
Printed and bound in the United States of America

Library of Congress Cataloging-in-Publication Data
Introduction to statistical relational learning / edited by Lise Getoor, Ben Taskar.
p.   cm.
Includes bibliographical references and index.
ISBN 978-0-262-07288-5 (hardcover : alk. paper)
1. Relational databases. 2. Machine learning–Statistical methods 3. Computer algorithms. I. Getoor, Lise. II. Taskar, Ben.
QA76.9.D3I68 2007   006.3'1–dc22   2007000951
10 9 8 7 6 5 4 3 2 1

Contents

Series Foreword

The goal of building systems that can adapt to their environments and learn from their experience has attracted researchers from many fields, including computer science, engineering, mathematics, physics, neuroscience, and cognitive science. Out of this research has come a wide variety of learning techniques that have the potential to transform many scientific and industrial fields. Recently, several research communities have converged on a common set of issues surrounding supervised, unsupervised, and reinforcement learning problems. The MIT Press series on Adaptive Computation and Machine Learning seeks to unify the many diverse strands of machine learning research and to foster high quality research and innovative applications.

Thomas Dietterich

Preface

The goal of this book is to bring together important research at the intersection of statistical, logical and relational learning. The material in the collection is aimed at graduate students and researchers in machine learning and artificial intelligence. While by no means exhaustive, the articles introduce a wide variety of recent approaches to combining expressive knowledge representation and statistical learning.

The idea for this book emerged from a series of successful workshops addressing these issues:

- *Learning Statistical Models from Relational Data (SRL2000)* at the National Conference on Artificial Intelligence, AAAI-2000, organized by Lise Getoor and David Jensen.

- *Learning Statistical Models from Relational Data (SRL2003)* at the International Joint Conference on Artificial Intelligence, (IJCAI-2003), organized by Lise Getoor and David Jensen.

- *Statistical Relational Learning and its Connections to Other Fields (SRL2004)* at the International Conference on Machine Learning, (ICML2004), organized by Tom Dietterich, Lise Getoor and Kevin Murphy.

- *Probabilistic, Logical and Relational Learning - Towards a Synthesis*, Dagstuhl Seminar 2005, organized by Luc De Raedt, Thomas Dietterich, Lise Getoor and Stephen Muggleton.

- *Open Problems in Statistical Relational Learning (SRL2006)* at the International Conference on Machine Learning, (ICML2006), organized by Alan Fern, Lise Getoor, and Brian Milch.

We would like to thank all of the participants at these workshops for their intellectual contributions and also for creating a warm and welcoming research community coming together from several distinct research areas.

In addition, there have been several other closely related workshops, including the series of workshops on Multi-Relational Data Mining held in conjunction with the Knowledge Discovery and Data Mining Conference beginning in 2002 organized by Sašo Džeroski, Luc De Raedt, Stefan Wrobel, and Hendrik Blockeel.

This volume contains invited contributions from leading researchers in this new research area. Each chapter has been reviewed by at least two anonymous reviewers. We are very grateful to all the authors for their high quality contributions and to all the reviewers for helping to clarify and improve this work.

In addition to thanking the workshop participants, book contributors and reviewers, we would like to thank our advisors: Daphne Koller, our PhD advisor; Stuart Russell, Lise Getoor's MS advisor; and Michael Jordan, Ben Taskar's Postdoctoral advisor. Lise Getoor would also like to thank David Jensen; besides being one of the people responsible for the name "Statistical Relational Learning," David has been a great mentor, workshop co-organizer and friend. We would also like to thank Tom Dietterich, Pedro Domingos, and David Heckerman, who have been very encouraging in developing this book. Luc De Raedt, Kristian Kersting, Stephen Muggleton, Sašo Džeroski and Hendrik Blockeel have been especially encouraging members from the inductive logic programming and relational learning community. Lise would also like to thank her inquisitive graduate students, members of the LINQs group at the University of Maryland, College Park, for their participation in this project. Finally, on a more personal note, Lise would like to thank Pete for his unwavering support and Ben would like to thank Anat for being his rock.

1 Introduction

Lise Getoor and Ben Taskar

We outline the major themes, problems and approaches that define the subject of the book: statistical relational learning. While the problems of statistical learning and relational representation and reasoning have a fairly long history on their own in Artificial Intelligence research, the synthesis of the approaches is currently a burgeoning field. We briefly sketch the background and the recent developments presented in the book.

1.1 Overview

The vast majority of statistical learning literature assumes the data is represented by points in a high-dimensional space. For any particular isolated task, such as learning to detect a face in an image or classify an email message as spam or not, we can usually construct the relevant low-level features (e.g., pixels, filters, words, URLs) and solve the problem using standard tools for the vector representation. While extremely useful for development of elegant and general algorithms and analysis, this abstraction hides the rich logical structure of the underlying data that is crucial for solving more general and complex problems. We may like to detect not only a face in an image but to recognize that, for example, it is the face of a tall woman who is spiking a volleyball or a little boy jumping into a puddle, etc. Or, in the case of email, we might want to detect that an email message is not only not-spam but is a request from our supervisor to meet tomorrow with three colleagues or an invitation to the downstairs neighbor's birthday party next Sunday, etc. We are ultimately interested in not just answering an isolated yes/no question, but in producing and manipulating structured representations of the data, involving objects described by attributes and participating in relationships, actions, and events. The challenge is to develop formalisms, models, and algorithms that enable effective and robust reasoning about this type of object-relational structure of the data.

Dealing with real data, like images and text, inevitably requires the ability to handle the uncertainty that arises from noise and incomplete information (e.g., occlusions, misspellings). In relational problems, uncertainty arises on many levels. Beyond uncertainty about the attributes of an object, there may be uncertainty about an object's type, the number of objects, and the identity of an object (what kind, which, and how many entities are depicted or written about), as well as relationship membership, type, and number (which entities are related, how, and how many times). Solving interesting relational learning tasks robustly requires sophisticated treatment of uncertainty at these multiple levels of representation.

In this book, we present the growing body of work on a variety of statistical models that target relational learning tasks. The goal of these representations is to express probabilistic models in a compact and intuitive way that reflects the relational structure of the domain and, ideally, supports efficient learning and inference. The majority of these models are based on combinations of graphical models, probabilistic grammars, and logical formulae.

1.2   Brief History of Relational Learning

Early work on machine learning often focused on learning deterministic logical concepts. Methods were typically noise and mostly applied to "toy" domains. One of the earliest relational learning systems is Winston's arch learning system [49]. This online-style system was trained using a sequence of instances labeled as positive and negative examples of arches. The system maintained a "current" hypothesis, represented as a semantic network. When a new example was presented, the system made a prediction using the current hypothesis. If the prediction was correct, no changes were made to the hypothesis. If it was incorrect, then the set of differences between the current hypothesis and the example was identified. If the example was a positive instance, the differences were used to generalize the concept; if the example was a negative instance, it was used to specialize the concept. Following this there were a number of more advanced relational learning systems [8, 18, 45], but all used a similar logic-based representation for the concepts.

This approach of machine learning (ML) fell out of vogue for many years because of problems handling noise and large-scale data. During that time, the ML community shifted attention to statistical methods that ignored relational aspects of the data (e.g., neural networks, decision trees, and generalized linear models). These methods led to major boosts in accuracy in many problems in low-level vision and natural language processing [11, 28]. However, their focus was on the propositional or attribute-value representation.

The major exception has been the inductive logic programming (ILP) community. The ILP community has concentrated its efforts on learning (deterministic) first-order rules from relational data [27, 30]. Initially the ILP community focused its attention solely on the task of program synthesis from examples and background knowledge. However, recent research has tackled the discovery of useful rules from larger databases [9]. These rules are often used for prediction and may have a probabilistic interpretation. The ILP community has had successes in a number of application areas including discovery of 2D structural alerts for mutagenicity/carcinogenicity [22], 3D pharmacophore discovery for drug design [10], and analysis of chemical databases [7].

1.3 Emerging Trends

Recently, both the ILP community and the statistical ML community have begun to incorporate aspects of the complementary technology. Many ILP researchers are developing stochastic and probabilistic representations and algorithms [31, 21, 6]. In more traditional ML circles, researchers who have in the past focused on attribute-value or propositional learning algorithms are exploring methods for incorporating relational information [5, 32, 4]. It is our hope that this trend will continue, and that the work presented in this book will provide a bridge connecting relational and statistical learning.

Among the strong motivations for using a relational model is its ability to model dependencies between related instances. Intuitively, we would like to use our information about one object to help us reach conclusions about other, related objects. For example, in web data, we should be able to propagate information about the topic of a document to documents it has links to and documents that link to it. These, in turn, would propagate information to yet other documents. Many researchers have proposed a process along the lines of this relational "influence propagation" idea [3, 44, 32]. Chakrabarti et al. [3] describe a relaxation labeling algorithm that makes use of the neighboring link information. The algorithm begins with the labeling given by a text-based classifier constructed from the training set. It then uses the estimated class of neighboring documents to update the distribution of the document being classified. The intuitions underlying these procedural systems can be given declarative semantics using probabilistic graphical models [46, 15, 47].

1.4 Statistical Relational Learning

We refer to this emerging area of research as *statistical relational learning* (SRL). SRL research attempts to represent, reason, and learn in domains with complex relational and rich probabilistic structure. Other terms that have been used recently include probabilistic logic learning and multi-relational data mining. Many of the tasks known as structured prediction problems also overlap greatly with problems addressed by SRL research.

The majority of proposed SRL systems can be distinguished along several dimensions. The most common representation formalisms are based on either logic (e.g., rule-based formalisms) or frame-based (e.g., objected-oriented) formalisms.

The probabilistic semantics are mostly based on graphical models or stochastic grammars; early SRL approaches were often defined in terms of directed graphical models (e.g., Bayesian networks) whereas recently there has been a growing interest in undirected models (e.g., Markov networks). The directed models can represent complex generative models while the undirected models can represent non-causal dependencies. Other alternatives, such as dependency networks [19] and mixed directed and undirected models,6 are also possible.

The logical interpretation for most SRL languages (e.g., probabilistic relational models, Bayesian logic programs, relational Markov networks) is often in terms of least Hebrand models and the probabilistic semantics is most often in terms of a possible worlds semantics. Some of the early approaches, such as knowledge-based model construction (KBMC) [48], relied on procedural semantics. There are other possibilities, described in greater deal in the upcoming chapters.

The semantics of many of the SRL systems is given in terms of an unrolled or ground graphical model. Thus, one approach to doing inference in these models is to perform the appropriate probabilistic inference in the base-level model. One simple KBMC-style optimization is to make use of the query in the construction of the network. Rather than constructing the entire base-level model, the construction may be made more efficient by constructing only the portion of the network required to answer the query. But this doesn't exploit any of the inherent structure in the probabilistic model. Pfeffer et al. [38] observe that in many cases the models can be decomposed into loosely coupled systems, and show how the interfaces between the components can be used to encapsulate inference within the components. This allows the reuse and caching of inferences and can lead to significant improvements in efficiency during inference. More general approaches, such as first-order variable elimination [41, 1], combine variable elimination with unification and allow a lifted inference to be performed (see chapter 15 for details).

Not surprisingly, learning is a fundamental component in any SRL approach. The power of the structured representation is the hierarchical nature of the statistical models. The advantage of the hierarchical models, and what distinguishes them from "flat" statistical models, is parameter sharing or parameter tying. Parameter sharing occurs when potentially distinct parameters of the model are constrained to be the same. A simple example occurs in a hidden Markov model: because of the Markovian assumption, the parameters determining the next state are the same at each time instance, hence we do not require distinct parameters indexed by specific values of t, we simply have one set of parameters $\theta_{t+1|t}$.

This parameter tying not only gives us a compact model for rich classes of distributions but is also what enables robust parameter estimation to even be feasible. Unlike traditional ML scenarios, where the learning system is given as input a sequence of i.i.d. observations, the input to an SRL learning algorithm is most often just a single, richly connected, instance. If there were no parameter sharing, this instance would be of little use for performing statistical inference. But, because the same parameters are used in multiple places in the model, we can still extract meaningful statistics from the data to use in our statistical inference procedures.

Model selection is a challenging SRL problem. Similar to work in propositional graphical models, many approaches make use of some type of heuristic search through the model space. Methods for scoring propositional graphical models have been extended for SRL learning [12, 13]. The search can make use of certain biases defined over the model space, such as allowing dependencies only among attributes of related instances according to the entity relationship model or the use of binding patterns to constrain clauses to consider adding to the probabilistic rules.

Certain common issues arise repeatedly, in different guises, in a number of the SRL systems. One of the most common issues is feature construction and aggregation. The rich variety in structure combined with the need for a compact parameterization gives rise to the need to construct relational features or aggregates [12] which capture the local neighborhood of a random variable. Because it is infeasible to explicitly define factors over all potential neighborhoods, aggregates provide an intuitive way of describing the relational neighborhood. Common aggregates include taking the mean or mode of some neighboring attribute, taking the min or the max, or simply counting the number of neighbors. More complex, domain-specific aggregates are also possible. Aggregation has also been studied as a means for propositionalizing a relational classification problem [25, 23, 26] Within the SRL community, Perlich and Provost [36, 37] have studied aggregation extensively and Popescul and Ungar [42] have worked on statistical predicate invention.

Structural uncertainty is another common issue that researchers have begun investigating. Many of the early SRL approaches consider the case where there is a single logical interpretation, or relational skeleton, which defines the set of random variables, and there is a probability distribution over the instantiations of the random variables. Structural uncertainty supports uncertainty over the relational interpretation. Koller and Pfeffer [24] introduced several forms, including number uncertainty, where there is a distribution over the number of related objects. Getoor et al. [16] studied learning models with structural uncertainty, and showed how these representations could be supported by a probabilistic logic-based system [14]. Pasula and Russell [35] studied identity uncertainty, a form of structural uncertainty which allows modeling uncertainty about the identity of a reference. Most of these models rely on a closed world assumption to define the semantics for the models. More recently, Milch et al. [29] have investigated the use of nonparametric models which allow an infinite number of objects and support an open-world model (see the chapter 13 for details). Other recent flexible approaches include the infinite relational models of Kemp et al. [20] and Xu et al. [50].

1.5   Chapter Map

The book begins with several introductory chapters providing tutorials for the material which many of the later chapters build upon. chapter 2 is on graphical models and covers the basics of representation, inference, and learning in both directed and undirected models. Chapter 3 by Džeroski describes ILP. ILP, unlike many other ML approaches, has traditionally dealt with multi-relational data. The learned models are typically described by sets of relational rules called *logic programs*, and the methods can make use of logical background knowledge. Chapter 4 by Sutton and McCallum covers conditional random fields (CRFs), a very popular class of models for structured supervised learning. An advantage of CRFs is that the models are optimized for predictive performance on only the subset of variables of interest. The chapter provides a tutorial on training and inference in CRFs, with particular attention given to the important special case of linear CRFs. The chapter concludes with a discussion of applications to information extraction.

Then next set of chapters describes several frame-based SRL approaches. Chapter 5 provides an introduction to probabilistic relational models (PRMs). PRMs are directed graphical models which can capture dependencies among objects and uncertainty over the relational structure. In addition to describing the representation, the chapter describes algorithms for inference and learning. Chapter 6 describes Markov relational networks (RMNs), which are essentially CRFs lifted to the relational setting. A particularly relevant advantage of RMNs over PRMs is that acyclicity requirements do not hinder modeling complex, non-causal correlations concisely; however, as in the non-relational case, this comes at the price of more expensive parameter estimation. Another advantage of RMNs, like CRFs, is that they are well suited to discriminative training. Algorithms for inference and learning are given. Chapter 7, by Heckerman et al., describes a graphical language for probabilistic entity-relationship models (PERs). One of the contributions of this chapter is its discussion of the relationship between PERs, PRMs, and plate models. Plate models [2, 17] were introduced in the statistics community as a graphical representation for hierarchical models. They can represent the repeated, shared, or tied parameters in a hierarchical graphical model. PERs synthesize these approaches. The chapter describes a directed version of PERs, DAPERs, and gives a number of illustrative examples. Chapter 8, by Neville and Jensen, describes relational dependency networks (RDNs). RDNs extend propositional dependency networks to relational domains, and, like dependency networks, have some advantages over directed graphical models and undirected models. This chapter describes the representation, inference, and learning algorithms and presents results on several data sets.

The next four chapters describe logic-based formalisms for SRL. An introductory chapter, chapter 9 by Cussens, surveys this area, describing work on some of the early logic-based formalisms such as Poole's work on probabilistic Horn abduction [39] and independent choice logic [40], Ngo and Haddawy's work on probabilistic knowledge bases [34] and Sato's work on the PRISM system [43], and Ng and Subrahmanian's work on probabilistic logic programming [33]. Cussens compares and contrasts these approaches and describes some of the common representational issues, making connections to approaches described in later chapters. Chapter 10, by Kersting and De Raedt, describes Bayesian logic programs (BLPs). Their approach combines Bayesian networks and logic programs to "upgrade" them to a representation which overcomes the propositional nature of Bayesian networks and the purely logical nature of logic programs. This chapter gives an introduction to BLPs, describing both a Bayesian logic programming tool and a graphical representation for them. Chapter 11, by Muggleton and Pahlavi, describes stochastic logic programs (SLPs). SLPs were originally introduced as a means of extending the expressiveness of stochastic grammars to the level of logic programs. The chapter provides several example programs and describes both parameter estimation and structure learning. Chapter 12, by Domingos and Richardson, describes Markov logic. Markov logic combines Markov networks and first-order logic. First-order logic formulae are given weights; the formulae define a log-linear model with a feature for each grounding of the logical formulae with the appropriate weights. The relationship between many of the other SRL approaches and Markov logic networks (MLNs) is discussed, along with several common SRL tasks such as collective inference, link prediction, and object identification. Inference and learning in MLNs are presented.

Many of the approaches discussed so far have assumed, either implicitly or explicitly, several practical assumptions (the closed-world assumption, domain closure, unique names) about the underlying logical interpretation in order to define the underlying semantics. Chapter 13, by Milch et al. describes BLOG, a system especially tailored toward cases in which these assumptions are not appropriate. BLOG models define stochastic processes for generating worlds; inference in these models is done via a sampling process. Chapter 14, by Pfeffer, describes IBAL, a functional programming language for probabilistic AI. IBAL supports a rich decision-theoretic framework which includes probabilistic reasoning and utility maximization. The chapter describes the syntax and semantics for the IBAL, along with a sophisticated inference algorithm which exploits both lazy evaluation and memoization for efficient inference.

One of the issues that comes up in many of the approaches is the need to perform effective inference in large scale probabilistic models. Many of the approaches can make use of "lifted" inference, inference which is done at level of the first-order representation directly, rather than at the propositional level. Chapter 15 describes first-order variable elimination, an algorithm for lifted probabilistic inference, and presents recent results.

One of the issues that comes up in each of the learning algorithms is the need for feature generation and selection. Chapter 16, by Popescul and Ungar, examines this issue in the context of structured generalized linear regression (SGLR). They address the need for an integrated approach to feature generation and selection. Chapter 17, by Davis et al., addresses a related issue, the need for view learning to support feature generation and selection. They describe two approaches and present results on a mammography analysis system.

Chapter 18, by Fern et al. surveys recent work in reinforcement learning in relational domains. There has been a lot of recent work on relational learning within the reinforcement learning setting and our collection does not try to comprehensively cover its scope. Instead we have chosen a representative contribution describing a novel approach to approximate policy iteration which is applicable to very large relational Markov decision problems.

One of the domains which naturally lends itself to SRL techniques is natural language processing. Chapter 19 by Bunescu and Mooney shows how RMNs can be used for information extraction. An advantage of their approach is that inference and learning support "collective information extraction" in which dependencies between extractions are exploited. They present results on extracting protein names from biomedical abstracts. Chapter 20, by Roth and Yih, also investigates SRL approaches for information extraction, specifically for combining named entity and relation extraction. They show how a linear programming formulation can capture the required global inference.

1.6   Outlook

In this introduction we have touched on a number of the common themes and issues that will be developed in greater detail in the following chapters. While a single unified framework has yet to emerge, we believe that the book highlights the commonalities, and clarifies some of the important differences among proposed approaches. Along the way, important representational and algorithmic issues are identified.

Statistical relational learning is a young and exciting field. There are many opportunities to develop new methods and apply the tools to compelling real-world problems. We hope this book will provide an introduction to the field, and stimulate further research, development, and applications.

References

[1]   R. Braz, E. Amir, and D. Roth. Lifted first-order probabilistic inference. In *Proceedings of the International Joint Conference on Artificial Intelligence*, 2005.

[2]   W. Buntine. Operations for learning with graphical models. *Journal of Artificial Intelligence Research*, 3:159–225, 1994.

[3]   S. Chakrabarti, B. Dom, and P. Indyk. Enhanced hypertext categorization using hyperlinks. In *Proceedings of ACM International Conference on Management of Data*, 1998.

[4]   D. Cohn and T. Hofmann. The missing link—a probabilistic model of document content and hypertext connectivity. In *Proceedings of Neural Information Processing Systems*, 2001.

[5]   M. Craven, D. DiPasquo, D. Freitag, A. McCallum, T. Mitchell, K. Nigam, and S. Slattery. Learning to extract symbolic knowledge from the World Wide Web. In *Proceedings of the National Conference on Artificial Intelligence*, 1998.

[6] J. Cussens. Loglinear models for first-order probabilistic reasoning. In *Proceedings of the Conference on Uncertainty in Artificial Intelligence*, 1999.

[7] L. Dehaspe, H. Toivonen, and R.D. King. Finding frequent substructures in chemical compounds. In *International Conference on Knowledge Discovery and Data Mining*, 1998.

[8] T. Dietterich and R. S. Michalski. Inductive learning of structural descriptions: Evaluation criteria and comparative review of selected methods. *Artificial Intelligence*, 16:257–294, 1986.

[9] S. Dzeroski and N. Lavrac, editors. *Relational Data Mining*. Kluwer, Berlin, 2001.

[10] P. Finn, S. Muggleton, D. Page, and A. Srinivasan. Discovery of pharmacophores using the inductive logic programming system Progol. *Machine Learning*, 30(1-2):241–270, 1998.

[11] D. A. Forsyth and J. Ponce. *Computer Vision: A Modern Approach*. Prentice Hall, Upper Saddle River, NJ, 2002.

[12] N. Friedman, L. Getoor, D. Koller, and A. Pfeffer. Learning probabilistic relational models. In *Proceedings of the International Joint Conference on Artificial Intelligence*, 1999.

[13] L. Getoor. *Learning Statistical Models from Relational Data*. PhD thesis, Stanford University, Stanford, CA, 2001.

[14] L. Getoor and J. Grant. PRL: A probabilistic relational language. *Machine Learning Journal*, 62(1-2):7–31, 2006.

[15] L. Getoor, E. Segal, B. Taskar, and D. Koller. Probabilistic models of text and link structure for hypertext classification. In *Proceedings of the IJCAI Workshop on Text Learning: Beyond Supervision*, 2001.

[16] L. Getoor, N. Friedman, D. Koller, and B. Taskar. Learning probabilistic models of link structure. *Journal of Machine Learning Research*, 3:679–707, 2002.

[17] W. Gilks, A. Thomas, and D. Spiegelhalter. A language and program for complex Bayesian modeling. *The Statistician*, 43:169–177, 1994.

[18] F. Hayes-Roth and J. McDermott. Knowledge acquisition from structural descriptions. In *Proceedings of the International Joint Conference on Artificial Intelligence*, 1997.

[19] D. Heckerman, D. Chickering, C. Meek, R. Rounthwaite, and C. Kadie. Dependency networks for inference, collaborative filtering and data visualization. *Journal of Machine Learning Research*, 1:49–75, 2000.

[20] C. Kemp, J. Tenenbaum, T. Griffiths, T. Yamada, and N. Ueda. Learning systems of concepts with an infinite relational model. In *Proceedings of the National Conference on Artificial Intelligence*, 2006.

[21] K. Kersting, L. De Raedt, and S. Kramer. Interpreting Bayesian logic programs. In *Proceedings of the AAAI-2000 Workshop on Learning Statistical Models from Relational Data*, 2000.

[22] R. King, S. Muggleton, A. Srinivasan, and M. Sternberg. Structure-activity relationships derived by machine learning: The use of atoms and their bond connectivities to predict mutagenicity by inductive logic programming. In *Proceedings of the National Academy of Sciences of the United States of America*, volume 93, pages 438–442, 1996.

[23] A. Knobbe, M. deHaas, and A. Siebes. Propositionalisation and aggregates. In *Proceedings of the Fifth European Conference on Principles of Data Mining and Knowledge Discovery*, 2001.

[24] D. Koller and A. Pfeffer. Probabilistic frame-based systems. In *Proceedings of the National Conference on Artificial Intelligence*, 1998.

[25] S. Kramer, N. Lavrac, and P. Flach. Propositionalization approaches to relational data mining. In S. Dzeroski and N. Lavrac, editors, *Relational Data Mining*. Springer-Verlag, New York, 2001.

[26] M. Krogel, S. Rawles, F. Zeezny, P. Flach, N. Lavrac, and S. Wrobel. Comparative evaluation of approaches to propositionalization. In *Proceedings of the International Conference on Inductive Logic Programming*, 2003.

[27] N. Lavrac and S. Dzeroski. *Inductive Logic Programming: Techniques and Applications*. Ellis Horwood, New York, 1994.

[28] C. Manning and H. Schütze. *Foundations of Statistical Natural Language Processing*. MIT Press, Cambridge, MA, 1999.

[29] B. Milch, B. Marthi, S. Russell, D. Sontag, D. Ong, and A. Kolobov. BLOG: Probabilistic models with unknown objects. In *Proceedings of the International Joint Conference on Artificial Intelligence*, 2005.

[30] S. Muggleton, editor. *Inductive Logic Programming*. Academic Press, London, 1992.

[31] S. Muggleton. Learning stochastic logic programs. In *Proceedings of the AAAI-2000 Workshop on Learning Statistical Models from Relational Data*, 2000.

[32] J. Neville and D. Jensen. Iterative classification in relational data. In *Proceedings of the AAAI-2000 Workshop on Learning Statistical Models from Relational Data*, 2000.

[33] R. Ng and V.S. Subrahmanian. Probabilistic logic programming. *Information and Computation*, 101(2):150–201, 1992.

[34] L. Ngo and Peter Haddaway. Answering queries from context-sensitive probabilistic knowledge bases. *Theoretical Computer Science*, 171:147–171, 1997.

[35] H. Pasula and S. Russell. Approximate inference for first-order probabilistic languages. In *Proceedings of the International Joint Conference on Artificial Intelligence*, 2001.

[36] C. Perlich and F. Provost. Aggregation-based feature invention and relational concept classes. In *International Conference on Knowledge Discovery and Data Mining*, 2003.

[37] C. Perlich and F. Provost. Distribution-based aggregation for relational learning with identifier attributes. *Machine Learning Journal*, 62(1-2):65–105, 2006.

[38] A. Pfeffer, D. Koller, B. Milch, and K. Takusagawa. SPOOK: A system for probabilistic object-oriented knowledge representation. In *Proceedings of the Conference on Uncertainty in Artificial Intelligence*, 1999.

[39] D. Poole. Probabilistic Horn abduction and Bayesian networks. *Artificial Intelligence*, 64(1):81–129, 1993.

[40] D. Poole. The independent choice logic for modelling multiple agents under uncertainty. *Artificial Intelligence*, 94(1–2):5–56, 1997.

[41] D. Poole. First-order probabilistic inference. In *Proceedings of the International Joint Conference on Artificial Intelligence*, 2003.

[42] A. Popescul and L. Ungar. Structural logistic regression for link analysis. In *KDD Workshop on Multi-Relational Data Mining*, 2003.

[43] T. Sato. A statistical learning method for logic programs with distribution semantics. In *Proceedings of the International Conference on Inductive Logic Programming*, 1995.

[44] S. Slattery and T. Mitchell. Discovering test set regularities in relational domains. In *Proceedings of the International Conference on Machine Learning*, 2000.

[45] R. Stepp and R. S. Michalski. Conceptual Clustering: Inventing goal-oriented classifications of structured objects. Technical Report 940, University of Illinois, Urbana, 1985.

[46] B. Taskar, E. Segal, and D. Koller. Probabilistic classification and clustering in relational data. In *Proceedings of the International Joint Conference on Artificial Intelligence*, 2001.

[47] B. Taskar, P. Abbeel, and D. Koller. Discriminative probabilistic models for relational data. In *Proceedings of the Conference on Uncertainty in Artificial Intelligence*, 2002.

[48] M. Wellman, J. Breese, and R. Goldman. From knowledge bases to decision models. *Knowledge Engineering Review*, 7(1):35–53, 1992.

[49] P. Winston. Learning structural descriptions from examples. In P. H. Winston, editor, *The Psychology of Computer Vision*, pages 157–209. McGraw-Hill, New York, 1975.

[50] Z. Xu, V. Tresp, K. Yu, and H. Kriegel. Infinite hidden relational models. In *Proceedings of the Conference on Uncertainty in Artificial Intelligence*, 2006.

2 Graphical Models in a Nutshell

Daphne Koller, Nir Friedman, Lise Getoor and Ben Taskar

Probabilistic graphical models are an elegant framework which combines uncertainty (probabilities) and logical structure (independence constraints) to compactly represent complex, real-world phenomena. The framework is quite general in that many of the commonly proposed statistical models (Kalman filters, hidden Markov models, Ising models) can be described as graphical models. Graphical models have enjoyed a surge of interest in the last two decades, due both to the flexibility and power of the representation and to the increased ability to effectively learn and perform inference in large networks.

2.1 Introduction

Graphical models [11, 3, 5, 9, 7] have become an extremely popular tool for modeling uncertainty. They provide a principled approach to dealing with uncertainty through the use of probability theory, and an effective approach to coping with complexity through the use of graph theory. The two most common types of graphical models are Bayesian networks (also called belief networks or causal networks) and Markov networks (also called Markov random fields (MRFs)).

At a high level, our goal is to efficiently represent a joint distribution P over some set of random variables $\mathcal{X} = \{X_1, \ldots, X_n\}$. Even in the simplest case where these variables are binary-valued, a joint distribution requires the specification of 2^n numbers — the probabilities of the 2^n different assignments of values $x_1, \ldots, x_n$. However, it is often the case that there is some structure in the distribution that allows us to factor the representation of the distribution into modular components. The structure that graphical models exploit is the independence properties that exist in many real-world phenomena.

The independence properties in the distribution can be used to represent such high-dimensional distributions much more compactly. Probabilistic graphical models provide a general-purpose modeling language for exploiting this type of structure in our representation. Inference in probabilistic graphical models provides us with the mechanisms for gluing all these components back together in a probabilistically coherent manner. Effective learning, both parameter estimation and model selection, in probabilistic graphical models is enabled by the compact parameterization.

This chapter provides a compact graphical models tutorial based on [8]. We cover representation, inference, and learning. Our tutorial is not comprehensive; for more details see [8, 11, 3, 5, 9, 4, 6].

2.2   Representation

The two most common classes of graphical models are *Bayesian networks* and *Markov networks*. The underlying semantics of Bayesian networks are based on directed graphs and hence they are also called *directed graphical models*. The underlying semantics of Markov networks are based on undirected graphs; Markov networks are also called *undirected graphical models*. It is possible, though less common, to use a mixed directed and undirected representation (see, for example, the work on chain graphs [10, 2]); however, we will not cover them here.

Basic to our representation is the notion of *conditional independence*:

Definition 2.1
Let $\boldsymbol{X}$, $\boldsymbol{Y}$, and $\boldsymbol{Z}$ be sets of random variables. $\boldsymbol{X}$ is *conditionally independent* of $\boldsymbol{Y}$ given $\boldsymbol{Z}$ in a distribution P if

$$P(\boldsymbol{X} = \boldsymbol{x}, \boldsymbol{Y} = \boldsymbol{y} \mid \boldsymbol{Z} = \boldsymbol{z}) = P(\boldsymbol{X} = \boldsymbol{x} \mid \boldsymbol{Z} = \boldsymbol{z})P(\boldsymbol{Y} = \boldsymbol{y} \mid \boldsymbol{Z} = \boldsymbol{z})$$

for all values $\boldsymbol{x} \in Val(\boldsymbol{X})$, $\boldsymbol{y} \in Val(\boldsymbol{Y})$ and $\boldsymbol{z} \in Val(\boldsymbol{Z})$. ∎

In the case where P is understood, we use the notation $(\boldsymbol{X} \perp \boldsymbol{Y} \mid \boldsymbol{Z})$ to say that $\boldsymbol{X}$ is conditionally independent of $\boldsymbol{Y}$ given $\boldsymbol{Z}$. If it is clear from the context, sometimes we say "independent" when we really mean "conditionally independent".

2.2.1   Bayesian Networks

The core of the Bayesian network representation is a directed acyclic graph (DAG) $\mathcal{G}$. The nodes of $\mathcal{G}$ are the random variables in our domain and the edges correspond, intuitively, to direct influence of one node on another. One way to view this graph is as a data structure that provides the skeleton for representing the joint distribution compactly in a factorized way.

Let $\mathcal{G}$ be a BN graph over the variables $X_1, \ldots, X_n$. Each random variable X_i in the network has an associated *conditional probability distribution (CPD)* or *local probabilistic model*. The CPD for X_i, given its parents in the graph (denoted $\mathbf{Pa}_{X_i}$), is $P(X_i \mid \mathbf{Pa}_{X_i})$. It captures the conditional probability of the random variable, given its parents in the graph. CPDs can be described in a variety of ways. A common, but not necessarily compact, representation for a CPD is a table which contains a row for each possible set of values for the parents of the node describing

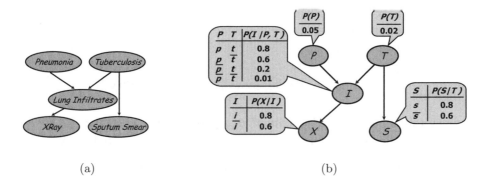

(a)   (b)

Figure 2.1   (a) A simple Bayesian network showing two potential diseases, *Pneumonia* and *Tuberculosis*, either of which may cause a patient to have *Lung Infiltrates*. The lung infiltrates may show up on an *XRay*; there is also a separate *Sputum Smear* test for tuberculosis. All of the random variables are Boolean. (b) The same Bayesian network, together with the conditional probability tables. The probabilities shown are the probability that the random variable takes the value true (given the values of its parents); the conditional probability that the random variable is false is simply 1 minus the probability that it is true.

the probability of different values for X_i. These are often referred to as *table CPD*s, and are tables of multinomial distributions. Other possibilities are to represent the distributions via a tree structure (called, appropriately enough, *tree-structured CPDs*), or using an even more compact representation such as a *noisy-OR* or *noisy-MAX*.

Example 2.1

Consider the simple Bayesian network shown in figure 2.1. This is a toy example indicating the interactions between two potential diseases, pneumonia and tuberculosis. Both of them may cause a patient to have lung infiltrates. There are two tests that can be performed. An x-ray can be taken, which may indicate whether the patient has lung infiltrates. There is a separate sputum smear test for tuberculosis. figure 2.1(a) shows the dependency structure among the variables. All of the variables are assumed to be Boolean. figure 2.1(b) shows the conditional probability distributions for each of the random variables. We use initials P, T, I, X, and S for shorthand. At the roots, we have the prior probability of the patient having each disease. The probability that the patient does not have the disease a priori is simply 1 minus the probability he or she has the disease; for simplicity only the probabilities for the true case are shown. Similarly, the conditional probabilities for the non-root nodes give the probability that the random variable is true, for different possible instantiations of the parents.

Definition 2.2
Let $\mathcal{G}$ be a Bayesinan network graph over the variables $X_1, \ldots, X_n$. We say that a distribution $P_{\mathcal{B}}$ over the same space *factorizes according to* $\mathcal{G}$ if $P_{\mathcal{B}}$ can be expressed as a product

$$P_{\mathcal{B}}(X_1, \ldots, X_n) = \prod_{i=1}^{n} P(X_i \mid \mathbf{Pa}_{X_i}). \qquad (2.1)$$

A *Bayesian network* is a pair $(\mathcal{G}, \boldsymbol{\theta}_{\mathcal{G}})$ where $P_{\mathcal{B}}$ factorizes over $\mathcal{G}$, and where $P_{\mathcal{B}}$ is specified as set of CPDs associated with $\mathcal{G}$'s nodes, denoted $\boldsymbol{\theta}_{\mathcal{G}}$. ∎

The equation above is called the *chain rule for Bayesian networks*. It gives us a method for determining the probability of any complete assignment to the set of random variables: any entry in the joint can be computed as a product of factors, one for each variable. Each factor represents a conditional probability of the variable given its parents in the network.

Example 2.2
The Bayesian network in figure 2.1(a) describes the following factorization:

$$P(P, T, I, X, S) = P(P)P(T)P(I \mid P, T)P(X \mid I)P(S \mid T).$$

Sometimes it is useful to think of the Bayesian network as describing a generative process. We can view the graph as encoding a generative sampling process executed by nature, where the value for each variable is selected by nature using a distribution that depends only on its parents. In other words, each variable is a stochastic function of its parents.

2.2.2 Conditional Independence Assumptions in Bayesian Networks

Another way to view a Bayesian network is as a compact representation for a set of conditional independence assumptions about a distribution. These conditional independence assumptions are called the *local Markov assumptions*. While we won't go into the full details here, this view is, in a strong sense, equivalent to the view of the Bayesian network as providing a factorization of the distribution.

Definition 2.3
Given a BN network structure $\mathcal{G}$ over random variables $X_1, \ldots, X_n$, let *NonDescendants*$_{X_i}$ denote the variables in the graph that are not descendants of X_i. Then $\mathcal{G}$ encodes the following set of conditional independence assumptions, called the *local Markov assumptions*:

> *For each variable X_i, we have that*
>
> $$(X_i \perp \text{NonDescendants}_{X_i} \mid \mathbf{Pa}_{X_i}),$$
>
> *In other words, the local Markov assumptions state that each node X_i is inde pendent of its nondescendants given its parents.* ∎

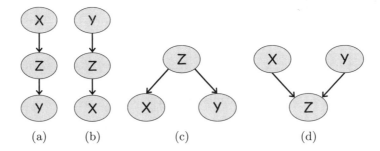

Figure 2.2   (a) An indirect causal effect; (b) an indirect evidential effect; (c) a common cause; (d) a common effect.

Example 2.3
The BN in figure 2.1(a) describes the following local Markov assumptions: $(P \perp T \mid \emptyset), (T \perp P \mid \emptyset), (X \perp \{P, T, S\} \mid I)$, and $(S \perp \{P, I, X\} \mid T)$.

These are not the only independence assertions that are encoded by a network. A general procedure called *d-separation* (which stands for directed separation) can answer whether an independence assertion *must* hold in *any* distribution consistent with the graph $\mathcal{G}$. However, note that other independencies may hold in *some* distributions consistent with $\mathcal{G}$; these are due to flukes in the particular choice of parameters of the network (and this is why they hold in some of the distributions).

Returning to our definition of d-separation, it is useful to view probabilistic influence as a flow in the graph. Our analysis here tells us when influence from X can "flow" through Z to affect our beliefs about Y. We will consider flow allows (undirected) paths in the graph.

Consider a simple three-node path X—Y—Z If influence can flow from X to Y via Z, we say that the path X—Z—Y is *active*. There are four cases:

- **Causal path** $X \to Z \to Y$: active if and only if Z is not observed.
- **Evidential path** $X \leftarrow Z \leftarrow Y$: active if and only if Z is not observed.
- **Common cause** $X \leftarrow Z \to Y$: active if and only if Z is not observed.
- **Common effect** $X \to Z \leftarrow Y$: active if and only if either Z or one of Z's descendants is observed.

A structure where $X \to Z \leftarrow Y$ (as in figure 2.2(d)) is also called a *v-structure*.

Example 2.4
In the BN from figure 2.1(a), the path from $P \to I \to X$ is active if I is not observed. On the other hand, the path from $P \to I \leftarrow T$ is active if I *is* observed.

Now consider a longer path X_1—$\cdots$—X_n. Intuitively, for influence to "flow" from X_1 to X_n, it needs to flow through every single node on the trail. In other words, X_1 can influence X_n if every two-edge path X_{i-1}—X_i—X_{i+1} along the trail allows influence to flow. We can summarize this intuition in the following definition:

Definition 2.4
Let $\mathcal{G}$ be a BN structure, and $X_1 - \ldots - X_n$ a path in $\mathcal{G}$. Let $\boldsymbol{E}$ be a subset of nodes of $\mathcal{G}$. The path $X_1 - \ldots - X_n$ is *active* given evidence $\boldsymbol{E}$ if

- whenever we have a v-structure $X_{i-1} \rightarrow X_i \leftarrow X_{i+1}$, then X_i or one of its descendants is in $\boldsymbol{E}$;
- no other node along the path is in $\boldsymbol{E}$. ■

Our flow intuition carries through to graphs in which there is more than one path between two nodes: one node can influence another if there is any path along which influence can flow. Putting these intuitions together, we obtain the notion of *d-separation*, which provides us with a notion of separation between nodes in a directed graph (hence the term d-separation, for directed separation):

Definition 2.5
Let $\boldsymbol{X}$, $\boldsymbol{Y}$, $\boldsymbol{Z}$ be three sets of nodes in $\mathcal{G}$. We say that $\boldsymbol{X}$ and $\boldsymbol{Y}$ are *d-separated given* $\boldsymbol{Z}$, denoted *d-sep*$_\mathcal{G}(\boldsymbol{X}; \boldsymbol{Y} \mid \boldsymbol{Z})$, if there is no active path between any node $X \in \boldsymbol{X}$ and $Y \in \boldsymbol{Y}$ given $\boldsymbol{Z}$. ■

Finally, an important theorem which relates the independencies which hold in a distribution to the factorization of a distribution is the following:

Theorem 2.6
Let $\mathcal{G}$ be a BN graph over a set of random variables $\mathcal{X}$ and let P be a joint distribution over the same space. If all the local Markov properties associated with $\mathcal{G}$ hold in P, then P factorizes according to $\mathcal{G}$.

Theorem 2.7
Let $\mathcal{G}$ be a BN graph over a set of random variables $\mathcal{X}$ and let P be a joint distribution over the same space. If P factorizes according to $\mathcal{G}$, then all the local Markov properties associated with $\mathcal{G}$ hold in P.

2.2.3   Markov Networks

The second common class of probabilistic graphical models is called a *Markov network* or a *Markov random field*. The models are based on undirected graphical models. These models are useful in modeling a variety of phenomena where one cannot naturally ascribe a directionality to the interaction between variables. Furthermore, the undirected models also offer a different and often simpler perspective on directed models, both in terms of the independence structure and the inference task.

A representation that implements this intuition is that of an undirected graph. As in a Bayesian network, the nodes in the graph of a *Markov network graph* $\mathcal{H}$ represent the variables, and the edges correspond to some notion of direct probabilistic interaction between the neighboring variables.

The remaining question is how to parameterize this undirected graph. The graph structure represents the qualitative properties of the distribution. To represent the distribution, we need to associate the graph structure with a set of parameters, in the same way that CPDs were used to parameterize the directed graph structure. However, the parameterization of Markov networks is not as intuitive as that of Bayesian networks, as the factors do not correspond either to probabilities or to conditional probabilities.

The most general parameterization is a *factor*:

Definition 2.8
Let $\boldsymbol{D}$ be a set of random variables. We define a *factor* to be a function from $Val(\boldsymbol{D})$ to $\mathbb{R}^+$. ∎

Definition 2.9
Let $\mathcal{H}$ be a Markov network structure. A distribution $P_{\mathcal{H}}$ *factorizes* over $\mathcal{H}$ if it is associated with

- a set of subsets $\boldsymbol{D}_1, \ldots, \boldsymbol{D}_m$, where each $\boldsymbol{D}_i$ is a complete subgraph of $\mathcal{H}$;
- factors $\pi_1[\boldsymbol{D}_1], \ldots, \pi_m[\boldsymbol{D}_m]$,

such that

$$P_{\mathcal{H}}(X_1, \ldots, X_n) = \frac{1}{Z} P'(X_1, \ldots, X_n),$$

where

$$P'_{\mathcal{H}}(X_1, \ldots, X_n) = \pi_i[\boldsymbol{D}_1] \times \pi_2[\boldsymbol{D}_2] \times \cdots \times \pi_m[\boldsymbol{D}_m]$$

is an unnormalized measure and

$$Z = \sum_{X_1, \ldots, X_n} P'_{\mathcal{H}}(X_1, \ldots, X_n)$$

is a normalizing constant called the *partition function*. A distribution P that factorizes over $\mathcal{H}$ is also called a *Gibbs distribution* over $\mathcal{H}$. (The naming convention has roots in statistical physics.) ∎

Note that this definition is quite similar to the factorization definition for Bayesian networks: There, we decomposed the distribution as a product of CPDs. In the case of Markov networks, the only constraint on the parameters in the factor is non negativity.

As every complete subgraph is a subset of some clique, we can simplify the parameterization by introducing factors only for cliques, rather than for subcliques. More precisely, let $\boldsymbol{C}_1, \ldots, \boldsymbol{C}_k$ be the cliques in $\mathcal{H}$. We can parameterize P using a set of factors $\pi_1[\boldsymbol{C}_1], \ldots, \pi_k[\boldsymbol{C}_k]$. These factors are called *clique potentials* (in the context of the Markov network $\mathcal{H}$). It is tempting to think of the clique potentials as representing the marginal probabilities of the variables in their scope. However, this is incorrect. It is important to note that, although conceptually somewhat simpler, the parameterization using clique potentials can obscure the structure that is present in the original parameterization, and can possibly lead to an exponential increase in the size of the representation.

It is often useful to consider a slightly different way of specifying potentials, by using a logarithmic transformation. In particular, we can rewrite a factor $\pi[\boldsymbol{D}]$ as

$$\pi[\boldsymbol{D}] = \exp(-\epsilon[\boldsymbol{D}]),$$

where $\epsilon[\boldsymbol{D}] = -\ln \pi[\boldsymbol{D}]$ is often called an *energy function*. The use of the word "energy" derives from statistical physics, where the probability of a physical state (e.g., a configuration of a set of electrons), depends inversely on its energy.

In this logarithmic representation, we have that

$$P_{\mathcal{H}}(X_1, \ldots, X_n) \propto \exp\left[-\sum_{i=1}^{m} \epsilon_i[\boldsymbol{D}_i]\right].$$

The logarithmic representation ensures that the probability distribution is positive. Moreover, the logarithmic parameters can take any real value.

A subclass of Markov networks that arises in many contexts is that of *pairwise Markov networks*, representing distributions where all of the factors are over single variables or pairs of variables. More precisely, a pairwise Markov network over a graph $\mathcal{H}$ is associated with a set of *node potentials* $\{\pi[X_i] : i = 1, \ldots, n\}$ and a set of *edge potentials* $\{\pi[X_i, X_j] : (X_i, X_j) \in \mathcal{H}\}$. The overall distribution is (as always) the normalized product of all of the potentials (both node and edge). Pairwise MRFs are attractive because of their simplicity, and because interactions on edges are an important special case that often arises in practice.

Example 2.5

Figure 2.3(a) shows a simple Markov network. This toy example has random variables describing the tuberculosis status of four patients. Patients that have been in contact are linked by undirected edges. The edges indicate the possibilities for the disease transmission. For example, *Patient* 1 has been in contact with *Patient* 2 and *Patient* 3, but has not been in contact with *Patient* 4. figure 2.3(b) shows the same Markov network, along with the node and edge potentials. We use $P1$, $P2$, $P3$, and $P4$ for shorthand. In this case, all of the node and edge potentials are the same, but this is not a requirement. The node potentials show that the patients are much more likely to be uninfected. The edge potentials capture the intuition that it is most likely for two people to have the same infection state — either both infected, or both not. Furthermore, it is more likely that they are both not infected.

2.2.4   Independencies in Markov Networks

As in the case of Bayesian networks, the graph structure in a Markov network can be viewed as encoding a set of independence assumptions. Intuitively, in Markov networks, probabilistic influence "flows" along the undirected paths in the graph, but is blocked if we condition on the intervening nodes. We can define two sets

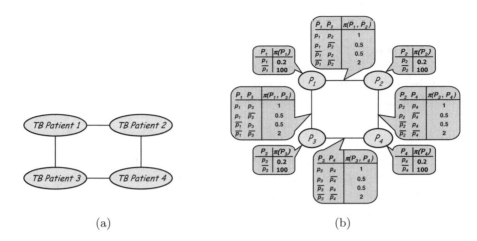

(a)   (b)

Figure 2.3   (a) A simple Markov network describing the tuberculosis status of four patients. The links between patients indicate which patients have been in contact with each other. (b) The same Markov network, together with the node and edge potentials.

of independence assumptions, the local Markov properties and the global Markov properties.

The local Markov properties are associated with each node in the graph and are based on the intuition that we can block all influences on a node by conditioning on its immediate neighbors.

Definition 2.10
Let $\mathcal{H}$ be an undirected graph. Then for each node $X \in \mathcal{X}$, the Markov blanket of X, denoted $\mathcal{N}_{\mathcal{H}}(X)$, is the set of neighbors of X in the graph (those that share an edge with X). We define the *local Markov independencies* associated with $\mathcal{H}$ to be

$$\mathcal{I}_\ell(\mathcal{H}) = \{(X \perp \mathcal{X} - \{X\} - \mathcal{N}_{\mathcal{H}}(X) \mid \mathcal{N}_{\mathcal{H}}(X)) \; : \; X \in \mathcal{X}\}.$$

In other words, the Markov assumptions state that X is independent of the rest of the nodes in the graph given its immediate neighbors. ∎

Example 2.6
The MN in figure 2.3(a) describes the following local Markov assumptions: $(P_1 \perp P_4 \mid \{P_2, P_3\})$, $(P_2 \perp P_3 \mid \{P_1, P_4\})$, $(P_3 \perp P_2 \mid \{P_1, P_4\})$, $(P_4 \perp P_1 \mid \{P_2, P_3\})$.

To define the global Markov properties, we begin by defining active paths in undirected graphs.

Definition 2.11
Let $\mathcal{H}$ be a Markov network structure, and $X_1 — \ldots — X_k$ be a path in $\mathcal{H}$. Let $\boldsymbol{E} \subseteq \mathcal{X}$ be a set of *observed variables*. The path $X_1 — \ldots — X_k$ is *active* given $\boldsymbol{E}$ if none of the X_i's, $i = 1, \ldots, k$, is in $\boldsymbol{E}$. ∎

Using this notion, we can define a notion of *separation* in the undirected graph. This is the analogue of *d-separation*; note how much simpler it is.

Definition 2.12
We say that a set of nodes $\boldsymbol{Z}$ *separates* $\boldsymbol{X}$ and $\boldsymbol{Y}$ in $\mathcal{H}$, denoted $sep_{\mathcal{H}}(\boldsymbol{X};\boldsymbol{Y}\mid\boldsymbol{Z})$, if there is no active path between any node $X\in\boldsymbol{X}$ and $Y\in\boldsymbol{Y}$ given $\boldsymbol{Z}$. We define the *global Markov assumptions* associated with $\mathcal{H}$ to be

$$\mathcal{I}(\mathcal{H}) = \{(\boldsymbol{X}\perp\boldsymbol{Y}\mid\boldsymbol{Z})\ :\ sep_{\mathcal{H}}(\boldsymbol{X};\boldsymbol{Y}\mid\boldsymbol{Z})\}.\ \blacksquare$$

As in the case of Bayesian networks, we can make a connection between the local Markov properties and the global Markov properties. The assumptions are in fact equivalent, but only for positive distributions. (Informally, a distribution is positive if every possible joint instantiation has probability > 0.)

We begin with the analogue to theorem 2.7, which asserts that a Gibbs distribution satisfies the global independencies associated with the graph.

Theorem 2.13
Let P be a distribution over $\mathcal{X}$, and $\mathcal{H}$ a Markov network structure over $\mathcal{X}$. If P is a Gibbs distribution over $\mathcal{H}$, then all the local Markov properties associated with $\mathcal{H}$ hold in P.

The other direction, which goes from the global independence properties of a distribution to its factorization, is known as the *Hammersley-Clifford theorem*. Unlike for Bayesian networks, this direction does not hold in general. It only holds under the additional assumption that P is a positive distribution.

Theorem 2.14
Let P be a positive distribution over $\mathcal{X}$, and $\mathcal{H}$ a Markov network graph over $\mathcal{X}$. If all of the independence constraints implied by $\mathcal{H}$ hold in P, then P is a Gibbs distribution over $\mathcal{H}$.

This result shows that, for positive distributions, the global Markov property implies that the distribution factorizes according to the network structure. Thus, for this class of distributions, we have that a distribution P factorizes over a Markov network $\mathcal{H}$ if and only if all of the independencies implied by $\mathcal{H}$ hold in P. The positivity assumption is necessary for this result to hold.

2.3   Inference

Both directed and undirected graphical models represent a full joint probability distribution over $\mathcal{X}$. We describe some of the main query types one might expect to answer with a joint distribution, and discuss the computational complexity of answering such queries using a graphical model.

The most common query type is the standard *conditional probability query*, $P(\boldsymbol{Y}\mid\boldsymbol{E}=\boldsymbol{e})$. Such a query consists of two parts: the *evidence*, a subset $\boldsymbol{E}$ of random variables in the network, and an instantiation e to these variables; and the *query*, a subset Y of random variables in the network. Our task is to compute $P(Y \mid E = e) = \frac{P(Y,e)}{P(e)}$, i.e., the probability distribution over the values y of Y, conditioned on the fact that $E = e$.

Another type of query that often arises is that of finding the *most probable assignment* to some subset of variables. As with conditional probability queries, we have evidence $E = e$. In this case, however, we are trying to compute the most likely assignment to some subset of the remaining variables. This problem has two variants, where the first variant is an important special case of the second. The simplest variant of this task is the *most probable explanation (MPE)* queries. An MPE query tries to find the most likely assignment to all of the (non-evidence) variables. More precisely, if we let $W = \mathcal{X} - E$, our task is to find the most likely assignment to the variables in W given the evidence $E = e$: $\operatorname{argmax}_w P(w, e)$, where, in general, $\operatorname{argmax}_x f(x)$ represents the value of x for which $f(x)$ is maximal. Note that there might be more than one assignment that has the highest posterior probability. In this case, we can either decide that the MPE task is to return the set of possible assignments, or to return an arbitrary member of that set.

In the second variant, the *maximum a posteriori (MAP)* query, we have a subset of variables Y which forms our query. The task is to find the most likely assignment to the variables in Y given the evidence $E = e$: $\operatorname{argmax}_y P(y \mid e)$. This class of queries is clearly more general than MPE queries, so it might not be clear why the class of MPE queries is sufficiently interesting to consider as a special case. The difference becomes clearer if we explicitly write out the expression for a general MAP query. If we let $Z = \mathcal{X} - Y - E$, the MAP task is to compute: $\operatorname{argmax}_Y \sum_Z P(Y, Z \mid e)$. MAP queries contain both summations and maximizations; in a way, they contain elements of both a conditional probability query and an MPE query. This combination makes the MAP task harder than either of these other tasks. In particular, there are techniques and analysis for the MPE task that do not generalize to the MAP task. This observation, combined with the fact that the MPE case is reasonably common, makes it worthwhile to consider MPE as a separate task. Note that in statistics literature, as well as in some work on graphical models, the term MAP is often used to mean MPE, but the distinction can be made clear from the context.

In principle, a graphical model can be used to answer all of the query types described above. We simply generate the joint distribution, and exhaustively sum out the joint (in the case of a conditional probability query), search for the most likely entry (in the case of an MPE query), or both (in the case of an MAP query). However, this approach to the inference problem is not very satisfactory, as it results in the exponential blowup of the joint distribution that the graphical model representation was precisely designed to avoid.

We assume that we are dealing with a set of factors $\mathcal{F}$ over a set of variables $\mathcal{X}$. This set of factors defines a possibly unnormalized function

$$P_{\mathcal{F}}(\mathcal{X}) = \prod_{\phi \in \mathcal{F}} \phi. \tag{2.2}$$

For a Bayesian network without evidence, the factors are simply the CPDs, and the distribution $P_{\mathcal{F}}$ is a normalized distribution. For a Bayesian network $\mathcal{B}$ with evidence $\boldsymbol{E} = \boldsymbol{e}$, the factors are the CPDs restricted to $\boldsymbol{e}$, and $P_{\mathcal{F}}(\mathcal{X}) = P_{\mathcal{B}}(\mathcal{X}, \boldsymbol{e})$. For a Markov network $\mathcal{H}$ (with or without evidence), the factors are the (restricted) compatibility potentials, and $P_{\mathcal{F}}$ is the unnormalized distribution $P'_{\mathcal{H}}$ before dividing by the partition function. It is important to note, however, that most of the operations that one can perform on a normalized distribution can also be performed on an unnormalized one. Thus, we can marginalize $P_{\mathcal{F}}$ on a subset of the variables by summing out the others. We can also consider a conditional probability $P_{\mathcal{F}}(\boldsymbol{X} \mid \boldsymbol{Y}) = P_{\mathcal{F}}(\boldsymbol{X}, \boldsymbol{Y})/P_{\mathcal{F}}(\boldsymbol{Y})$. Thus, for the purposes of this section, we treat $P_{\mathcal{F}}$ as a distribution, ignoring the fact that it may not be normalized.

In the worst case, the complexity of probabilistic inference is unavoidable. Below, we assume that the set of factors $\{\phi \in \mathcal{F}\}$ of the graphical model defining the desired distribution can be specified in a polynomial number of bits (in terms of the number of variables).

Theorem 2.15
The following decision problems are $\mathcal{NP}$-complete:

- Given a distribution $P_{\mathcal{F}}$ over $\mathcal{X}$, a variable $X \in \mathcal{X}$, and a value $x \in Val(X)$, decide whether $P_{\mathcal{F}}(X = x) > 0$.

- Given a distribution $P_{\mathcal{F}}$ over $\mathcal{X}$ and a number τ, decide whether there exists an assignment $\boldsymbol{x}$ to $\mathcal{X}$ such that $P_{\mathcal{F}}(\boldsymbol{x}) > \tau$.

The following problem is $\#\mathcal{P}$-complete:

- Given a distribution $P_{\mathcal{F}}$ over $\mathcal{X}$, a variable $X \in \mathcal{X}$, and a value $x \in Val(X)$, compute $P_{\mathcal{F}}(X = x)$.

These results seem like very bad news: every type of inference in graphical models is $\mathcal{NP}$-hard or harder. In fact, even the simple problem of computing the distribution over a single binary variable is $\mathcal{NP}$-hard. Assuming (as seems increasingly likely) that the best computational performance we can achieve for $\mathcal{NP}$-hard problems is exponential in the worst case, there seems to be no hope for efficient algorithms for even the simplest type of inference. However, as we discuss below, the worst-case blowup can often be avoided. For all other models, we will resort to approximate inference techniques. Note that the worst-case results for approximate inference are also negative:

Theorem 2.16
The following problem is $\mathcal{NP}$-hard for any $\epsilon \in (0, 1/2)$: Given a distribution $P_{\mathcal{F}}$ over $\mathcal{X}$, a variable $X \in \mathcal{X}$, and a value $x \in Val(X)$, find a number τ, such that $|P_{\mathcal{F}}(X = x) - \tau| \leq \epsilon$.

Fortunately, many types of exact inference can be performed efficiently for a very important class of graphical models (low treewidth) we define below. For a large number of models, however, exact inference is intractable and we resort to approximations. Broadly speaking, there are two major frameworks for probabilistic inference: optimization-based and sampling-based. Exact inference algorithms have been historically derived from the dynamic programming perspective, by carefully avoiding repeated computations. We take a somewhat unconventional approach here by presenting exact and approximate inference in a unified optimization framework. We thus start out by considering approximate inference and then present conditions under which it yields exact results.

2.3.1   Inference as Optimization

The methods that fall into an optimization framework are based on a simple conceptual principle: define a target class of "easy" distributions $\boldsymbol{Q}$, and then search for a particular instance Q within that class which is the "best" approximation to $P_{\mathcal{F}}$. Queries can then be answered using inference on Q rather than on $P_{\mathcal{F}}$. The specific algorithms that have been considered in the literature differ in many details. However, most of them can be viewed as optimizing a target function for measuring the quality of approximation.

Suppose that we want to approximate $P_{\mathcal{F}}$ with another distribution Q. Intuitively, we want to choose the approximation Q to be close to $P_{\mathcal{F}}$. There are many possible ways to measure the distance between two distributions, such as the Euclidean distance (L_2), or the L_1 distance. Our main challenge, however, is that our aim is to avoid performing inference with the distribution $P_{\mathcal{F}}$; in particular, we cannot effectively compute marginal distributions in $P_{\mathcal{F}}$. Hence, we need methods that allow us to optimize the distance (technically, divergence) between Q and $P_{\mathcal{F}}$ without answering hard queries in $P_{\mathcal{F}}$. A priori, this requirement may seem impossible to satisfy. However, it turns out that there exists a distance measure — the relative entropy (or KL-divergence) — that allows us to exploit the structure of $P_{\mathcal{F}}$ without performing reasoning with it.

Recall that the relative entropy between P_1 and P_2 is defined as $\boldsymbol{D}(P_1 \| P_2) = \boldsymbol{E}_{P_1}\left[\ln \frac{P_1(\mathcal{X})}{P_2(\mathcal{X})}\right]$. The relative entropy is always non-negative, and equal to 0 if and only if $P_1 = P_2$. Thus, we can use it as a distance measure, and choose to find an approximation Q to $P_{\mathcal{F}}$ that minimizes the relative entropy. However, the relative entropy is not symmetric — $\boldsymbol{D}(P_1 \| P_2) \neq \boldsymbol{D}(P_2 \| P_1)$. A priori, it might appear that $\boldsymbol{D}(P_{\mathcal{F}} \| Q)$ is a more appropriate measure for approximate inference, as one of the main information-theoretic justifications for relative entropy is the number of bits lost when coding a true message distribution $P_{\mathcal{F}}$ using an (approximate) estimate Q.

However, computing the so-called M-projection Q of $P_{\mathcal{F}}$ — the $\operatorname{argmin}_Q \boldsymbol{D}(P_{\mathcal{F}}\|Q)$ — is actually equivalent to running inference in $P_{\mathcal{F}}$. Somewhat surprisingly, as we show in the subsequent discussion, this does not apply to the so-called I-projection: we can exploit the structure of $P_{\mathcal{F}}$ to optimize $\operatorname{argmin}_Q \boldsymbol{D}(Q\|P_{\mathcal{F}})$ efficiently, *without* running inference in $P_{\mathcal{F}}$.

An additional reason for using relative entropy as our distance measure is based on the following result, which relates the relative entropy $\boldsymbol{D}(Q\|P_{\mathcal{F}})$ with the partition function Z:

Proposition 2.17

$$\ln Z = F[P_{\mathcal{F}}, Q] + \boldsymbol{D}(Q\|P_{\mathcal{F}}), \qquad (2.3)$$

where $F[P_{\mathcal{F}}, Q]$ is the *energy functional* $F[P_{\mathcal{F}}, Q] = \sum_{\phi \in \mathcal{F}} \boldsymbol{E}_Q[\ln \phi] + \boldsymbol{H}_Q(\mathcal{X})$.

This proposition has several important ramifications. Note that the term $\ln Z$ does not depend on Q. Hence, minimizing the relative entropy $\boldsymbol{D}(Q\|P_{\mathcal{F}})$ is equivalent to maximizing the energy functional $F[P_{\mathcal{F}}, Q]$. This latter term relates to concepts from statistical physics, and it is the negative of what is referred to in that field as the *Helmholtz free energy*. While explaining the physics-based motivation for this term is out of the scope of this chapter, we continue to use the standard terminology of energy functional.

In the remainder of this section, we pose the problem of finding a good approximation Q as one of maximizing the energy functional, or, equivalently, minimizing the relative entropy. Importantly, the energy functional involves expectations in Q. As we show, by choosing approximations Q that allow for efficient inference, we can both evaluate the energy functional and optimize it effectively.

Moreover, as $\boldsymbol{D}(Q\|P_{\mathcal{F}}) \geq 0$, we have that $\ln Z \geq F[P_{\mathcal{F}}, Q]$. That is, the energy functional is a *lower bound* on the value of the logarithm of the partition function Z, for any choice of Q. Why is this fact significant? Recall that, in directed models, the partition function Z is the probability of the evidence. Computing the partition function is often the hardest part of inference. And so this theorem shows that if we have a good approximation (that is, $\boldsymbol{D}(Q\|P_{\mathcal{F}})$ is small), then we can get a good lower bound approximation to Z. The fact that this approximation is a lower bound plays an important role in learning parameters of graphical models.

2.3.2   Exact Inference as Optimization

Before considering approximate inference methods, we illustrate the use of a variational approach to derive an exact inference procedure. The concepts we introduce here will serve in discussion of the following approximate inference methods.

The goal of exact inference here will be to compute marginals of the distribution. To achieve this goal, we will need to make sure that the set of distributions $\boldsymbol{Q}$ is expressive enough to represent the target distribution $P_{\mathcal{F}}$. Instead of approximating $P_{\mathcal{F}}$, the solution of the optimization problem transforms the representation of the

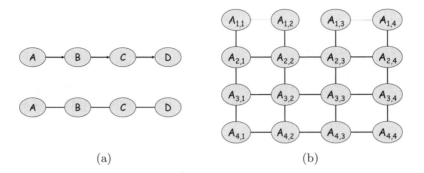

Figure 2.4   (a) Chain-structured Bayesian network and equivalent Markov network (b) Grid-structured Markov network.

distribution from a product of factors into a more useful form Q that directly yields the desired marginals.

To accomplish this, we will need to optimize over the set of distributions $\boldsymbol{Q}$ that include $P_{\mathcal{F}}$. Then, if we search over this set, we are guaranteed to find a distribution Q^* for which $\boldsymbol{D}(Q^* \| P_{\mathcal{F}}) = 0$, which is therefore the unique global optimum of our energy functional. We will represent this set using an undirected graphical model called the clique tree, for reasons that will be clear below.

Consider the undirected graph corresponding to the set of factors $\mathcal{F}$. In this graph, nodes are connected if they appear together in a factor. Note that if a factor is the CPD of a directed graphical model, then the family will be a clique in the graph, so its connectivity is denser then the original directed graph since parents have been connected (moralized). The key property for exact inference in the graph is chordality:

Definition 2.18
Let X_1—X_2—$\cdots$—X_k—X_1 be a loop in the graph; a *chord* in the loop is an edge connecting X_i and X_j for two nonconsecutive nodes X_i, X_j. An undirected graph $\mathcal{H}$ is said to be *chordal* if any loop X_1—X_2—$\cdots$—X_k—X_1 for $k \geq 4$ has a chord.
∎

In other words, the longest "minimal loop" (one that has no shortcut) is a triangle. Thus, chordal graphs are often also called *triangulated*.

The simplest (and most commonly used) chordal graphs are chain-structured (see figure 2.4(a)). What if the graph is not chordal? For example, grid-structured graphs are commonly used in computer vision for pixel-labeling problems (see figure 2.4(b)). To make a graph chordal (triangulate it), *fill-in* edges are added to short-circuit loops. There are generally many ways to do this and finding the least number of edges to fill is $\mathcal{NP}$-hard. However, good heuristic algorithms for this problem exist [12, 1].

We now define a *cluster graph* — the backbone of the graphical data structure needed to perform inference. Each node in the cluster graph is a *cluster*, which is associated with a subset of variables; the graph contains undirected edges that connect clusters whose scopes have some nonempty intersection.

Definition 2.19

A *cluster graph* $\mathcal{K}$ for a set of factors $\mathcal{F}$ over $\mathcal{X}$ is an undirected graph, each of whose nodes i is associated with a subset $\boldsymbol{C}_i \subseteq \mathcal{X}$. A cluster graph must be *family-preserving* — each factor $\phi \in \mathcal{F}$ must be associated with a cluster $\boldsymbol{C}$, denoted $\alpha(\phi)$, such that $Scope[\phi] \subseteq \boldsymbol{C}_i$. Each edge between a pair of clusters $\boldsymbol{C}_i$ and $\boldsymbol{C}_j$ is associated with a *sepset* $\boldsymbol{S}_{i,j} = \boldsymbol{C}_i \cap \boldsymbol{C}_j$. A singly connected cluster graph (a tree) is called a *cluster tree*. ∎

Definition 2.20

Let $\mathcal{T}$ be a cluster tree over a set of factors $\mathcal{F}$. We say that $\mathcal{T}$ has the *running intersection property* if, whenever there is a variable X such that $X \in \boldsymbol{C}_i$ and $X \in \boldsymbol{C}_j$, then X is also in every cluster in the (unique) path in $\mathcal{T}$ between $\boldsymbol{C}_i$ and $\boldsymbol{C}_j$. A cluster tree that satisfies the running intersection property is called a *clique tree*. ∎

Theorem 2.21

Every chordal graph $\mathcal{G}$ has a clique tree $\mathcal{T}$.

Constructing the clique tree from a chordal graph is actually relatively easy: (1) find maximal cliques of the graph (this is easy in chordal graphs) and (2) run a maximum spanning tree algorithm on the appropriate clique graph. More specifically, we build an undirected graph whose nodes are the maximal cliques, and where every pair of nodes $\boldsymbol{C}_i, \boldsymbol{C}_j$ is connected by an edge whose *weight* is $|\boldsymbol{C}_i \cap \boldsymbol{C}_j|$.

Because of this correspondence, we can define a very important characteristic of a graph, which is critical to the complexity of exact inference:

Definition 2.22

The *treewidth* of a chordal graph is the size of the largest clique minus 1. The *treewidth* of an untriangulated graph is the minimum treewidth of all of its triangulations. ∎

Note that the treewidth of a chain in figure 2.4(a) is 1 and the treewidth of the grid in figure 2.4(b) is 4.

2.3.2.1   The Optimization Problem

Suppose we are given a clique tree $\mathcal{T}$ for $P_{\mathcal{F}}$. That is, $\mathcal{T}$ satisfies the running intersection property and the family preservation property. Moreover, suppose we are given a set of potentials $\boldsymbol{Q} = \{\pi_i\} \cup \{\mu_{i,j} : (\boldsymbol{C}_i \text{—} \boldsymbol{C}_j) \in \mathcal{T}\}$, where $\boldsymbol{C}_i$ denotes clusters in $\mathcal{T}$, $\boldsymbol{S}_{i,j}$ denote separators along edges in $\mathcal{T}$, π_i is a potential over $\boldsymbol{C}_i$, and $\mu_{i,j}$ is a potential over $\boldsymbol{S}_{i,j}$. The set of potentials defines a distribution Q according to $\mathcal{T}$ by the formula

$$Q(\mathcal{X}) = \frac{\prod_{\boldsymbol{C}_i \in \mathcal{T}} \pi_i}{\prod_{(\boldsymbol{C}_i - \boldsymbol{C}_j) \in \mathcal{T}} \mu_{i,j}}. \tag{2.4}$$

Note that by construction, $\boldsymbol{Q}$ can represent $P_{\mathcal{F}}$ by simply letting the appropriate potentials π_i equal factors ϕ_i and letting $\mu_{i,j}$ equal 1. However, we will consider a different, more useful, representation.

Definition 2.23
The set of potentials $\boldsymbol{Q}$ is *calibrated* when for each $(\boldsymbol{C}_i - \boldsymbol{C}_j) \in \mathcal{T}$ the potential $\mu_{i,j}$ on $\boldsymbol{S}_{i,j}$ is the marginal of π_i (and π_j). ∎

Proposition 2.24
Let $\boldsymbol{Q}$ be a set of calibrated potentials for $\mathcal{T}$, and let Q be the distribution defined by (2.4). Then $\pi_i[\boldsymbol{c}_i] = Q(\boldsymbol{c}_i)$ and $\mu_{i,j}[\boldsymbol{s}_{i,j}] = Q(\boldsymbol{s}_{i,j})$.

In other words, the potentials correspond to marginals of the distribution Q defined by (2.4). Now if $\boldsymbol{Q}$ is a set of *uncalibrated* potentials for $\mathcal{T}$, and Q is the distribution defined by (2.4), we can construct $\boldsymbol{Q}'$, a set of *calibrated potentials* which represent Q by simply using the appropriate marginals of Q.

Once we decide to focus our attention on calibrated clique trees, we can rewrite the energy functional in a factored form, as a sum of terms each of which depends directly only on one of the potentials in $\boldsymbol{Q}$. This form reveals the structure in the distribution, and is therefore a much better starting point for further analysis. As we shall see, this form will also be the basis for our approximations in subsequent sections.

Definition 2.25
Given a clique tree $\mathcal{T}$ with a set of potentials, $\boldsymbol{Q}$, and an assignment α that maps factors in $P_{\mathcal{F}}$ to clusters in $\mathcal{T}$, we define the *factored energy functional*

$$\tilde{F}[P_{\mathcal{F}}, \boldsymbol{Q}] = \sum_i \boldsymbol{E}_{\pi_i}\left[\ln \pi_i^0\right] + \sum_{\boldsymbol{C}_i \in \mathcal{T}} \boldsymbol{H}_{\pi_i}(\boldsymbol{C}_i) - \sum_{(\boldsymbol{C}_i - \boldsymbol{C}_j) \in \mathcal{T}} \boldsymbol{H}_{\mu_{i,j}}(\boldsymbol{S}_{i,j}), \tag{2.5}$$

where $\pi_i^0 = \prod_{\phi, \alpha(\phi) = i} \phi$. ∎

Before we prove that the energy functional is equivalent to its factored form, let us first understand its form. The first term is a sum of terms of the form $\boldsymbol{E}_{\pi_i}\left[\ln \pi_i^0\right]$. Recall that π_i^0 is a factor (not necessarily a distribution) over the scope $\boldsymbol{C}_i$, that is, a function from $Val(\boldsymbol{C}_i)$ to $\mathbb{R}^+$. Its logarithm is therefore a function from $Val(\boldsymbol{C}_i)$ to $\mathbb{R}$. The clique potential π_i is a distribution over $Val(\boldsymbol{C}_i)$. We can therefore compute the expectation, $\sum_{\boldsymbol{c}_i} \pi_i[\boldsymbol{c}_i] \ln \pi_i^0$. The last two terms are entropies of the distributions — the potentials and messages — associated with the clusters and sepsets in the tree.

Proposition 2.26
If $\boldsymbol{Q}$ is a set of calibrated potentials for $\mathcal{T}$, and Q is defined by by (2.4), then

$$\tilde{F}[P_{\mathcal{F}}, \boldsymbol{Q}] = F[P_{\mathcal{F}}, Q].$$

Using this form of the energy, we can now define the optimization problem. We first need to define the space over which we are optimizing. If Q is factorized according to $\mathcal{T}$, we can represent it by a set of calibrated potentials. Calibration is essentially a constraint on the potentials, as a clique tree is calibrated if neighboring potentials agree on the marginal distribution on their joint subset. Thus, we pose the following constrained optimization procedure:

CTree-Optimize
> **Find** $\boldsymbol{Q}$
> **that maximize** $\tilde{F}[P_{\mathcal{F}}, \boldsymbol{Q}]$

$$\sum_{\boldsymbol{C}_i \backslash \boldsymbol{S}_{i,j}} \pi_i = \mu_{i,j}, \quad \forall(\boldsymbol{C}_i\!-\!\boldsymbol{C}_j) \in \mathcal{T}; \tag{2.6}$$

> **subject to**

$$\sum_{\boldsymbol{C}_i} \pi_i = 1, \qquad \forall \boldsymbol{C}_i \in \mathcal{T}. \tag{2.7}$$

The constraints (2.6) and (2.7) ensure that the potentials in $\boldsymbol{Q}$ are calibrated and represent legal distributions. It can be shown that the objective function is strictly concave in the variables π, μ. The constraints define a convex set (linear subspace), so this optimization problem has a unique maximum. Since $\boldsymbol{Q}$ can represent $P_{\mathcal{F}}$, this maximum is attained when $\boldsymbol{D}(Q\|P_{\mathcal{F}}) = 0$.

2.3.2.2   *Fixed-Point Characterization*

We can now prove that the *stationary points* of this constrained optimization function — the points at which the gradient is orthogonal to all the constraints — can be characterized by a set of *self-consistent equations*.

Recall that a stationary point of a function is either a local maximum, a local minimum, or a saddle point. In this optimization problem, there is a single global maximum. Although we do not show it here, we can show that it is also the single stationary point. We can therefore define the global optimum declaratively, as a set of equations, using standard methods based on Lagrange multipliers. As we now show, this declarative formulation gives rise to a set of equations which precisely corresponds to message-passing steps in the clique tree, a standard inference procedure usually derived via dynamic programming.

Theorem 2.27

A set of potentials $\boldsymbol{Q}$ is a stationary point of CTree-Optimize if and only if there exists a set of factors $\{\delta_{i \to j}[\boldsymbol{S}_{i,j}] : \boldsymbol{C}_i\!-\!\boldsymbol{C}_j \in \mathcal{T}\}$ such that

$$\delta_{i \to j} \propto \sum_{\boldsymbol{C}_i - \boldsymbol{S}_{i,j}} \pi_i^0 \left(\prod_{k \in \mathcal{N}_{\boldsymbol{C}_i} - \{j\}} \delta_{k \to i} \right) \tag{2.8}$$

$$\pi_i \propto \pi_i^0 \left(\prod_{j \in \mathcal{N}_{\boldsymbol{C}_i}} \delta_{j \to i} \right) \tag{2.9}$$

$$\mu_{i,j} = \delta_{j \to i} \times \delta_{i \to j}, \tag{2.10}$$

where $\mathcal{N}_{\boldsymbol{C}_i}$ are the neighboring cliques of $\boldsymbol{C}_i$ in $\mathcal{T}$.

Theorem 2.27 illustrates themes that appear in many approaches that turn variational problems into message-passing schemes. It provides a characterization of the solution of the optimization problem in terms of *fixed-point equations* that must hold when we find a maximal Q. These fixed-point equations define the relationships that must hold between the different parameters involved in the optimization problem. Most importantly, (2.8) defines each $\delta_{i \to j}$ in terms of $\delta_{k \to j}$ *other than* $\delta_{i \to j}$. The other parameters are all defined in a noncyclic way in terms of the $\delta_{i \to j}$'s.

The form of the equations resulting from the theorem suggest an iterative procedure for finding a fixed point, in which we view the equations as assignments, and iteratively apply equations to the current values of the left-hand side to define a new value for the right-hand side. We initialize all of the $\delta_{i \to j}$'s to 1, and then iteratively apply (2.8), computing the left-hand side $\delta_{i \to j}$ of each equality in terms of the right-hand side (essentially converting each equality sign to an assignment). Clearly, a single iteration of this process does not usually suffice to make the equalities hold; however, under certain conditions (which hold in this particular case) we can guarantee that this process converges to a solution satisfying all of the equations in (2.8); the other equations are now easy to satisfy.

2.3.3 Loopy Belief Propagation in Pairwise Markov Networks

We focus on the class of pairwise Markov networks. In these networks, we have a univariate potential $\phi_i[X_i]$ over each variable X_i, and in addition a pairwise potential $\phi_{(i,j)}[X_i, X_j]$ over some pairs of variables. These pairwise potentials correspond to edges in the Markov network. Examples of such networks include our simple tuberculosis example in figure 2.3 and the grid networks we discussed above.

The transformation of such a network into a cluster graph is fairly straightforward. For each potential, we introduce a corresponding cluster, and put edges between the clusters that have overlapping scope. In other words, there is an edge

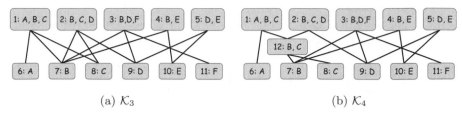

(a) $\mathcal{K}_3$ (b) $\mathcal{K}_4$

Figure 2.5   Two additional examples of generalized cluster graphs for a Markov network with potentials over $\{A, B, C\}$, $\{B, C, D\}$, $\{B, D, F\}$, $\{B, E\}$, and $\{D, E\}$. (a) Bethe factorization. (b) Capturing interactions between $\{A, B, C\}$ and $\{B, C, D\}$.

between the cluster $\boldsymbol{C}_{(i,j)}$ that corresponds to the edge X_i—X_j and the clusters $\boldsymbol{C}_i$ and $\boldsymbol{C}_j$ that correspond to the univariate factors over X_i and X_j.

As there is a direct correspondence between the clusters in the cluster graphs and variables or edges in the original Markov network, it is often convenient to think of the propagation steps as operations on the original network. Moreover, as each pairwise cluster has only two neighbors, we consider two propagation steps along the path $\boldsymbol{C}_i$—$\boldsymbol{C}_{(i,j)}$—$\boldsymbol{C}_j$ as propagating information between X_i and X_j. Indeed, early versions of generalized belief propagation were stated in these terms. This algorithm is known as *loopy belief propagation*, as it uses propagation steps used by algorithms for Markov trees, except that it was applied to networks with loops.

A natural question is how to extend this method to networks that are more complex than pairwise Markov networks. Once we have larger potentials, they may overlap in ways that result in complex interactions among them.

One simple construction creates a bipartite graph. The first layer consists of "large" clusters, with one cluster for each factor ϕ in $\mathcal{F}$, whose scope is $Scope[\phi]$. These clusters ensure that we satisfy the family-preservation property. The second layer consists of "small" univariate clusters, one for each random variable. Finally, we place an edge between each univariate cluster X on the second layer and each cluster in the first layer that includes X; the scope of this edge is X itself. For a concrete example, see figure 2.5(a).

We can easily verify that this is a proper cluster graph. First, by construction it satisfies the family-preserving property. Second, the edges that mention a variable X form a star-shaped subgraph with edges from the univariate cluster with scope X to all the large clusters that contain X. We will call this construction the *Bethe approximation* (for reasons that will be clarified below). The construction of this cluster graph is simple and can easily be automated.

So far, our discussion of belief propagation has been entirely procedural, and motivated purely by similarity to message-passing algorithms for cluster trees. Is there any formal justification for this approach? Is there a sense in which we can view this algorithm as providing an approximation to the exact inference task? In this section, we show that belief propagation can be justified using the energy function formulation. Specifically, the messages passed by generalized belief propagation can be derived from fixed-point equations for the stationary points of an approximate version of the energy functional of (2.3). As we shall see, this formulation provides significant insight into the generalized belief propagation algorithm. It allows us to better understand the convergence properties of generalized belief propagation, and to characterize its convergence points. It also suggests generalizations of the algorithm which have better convergence properties, or that optimize a more "accurate" approximation to the energy functional.

Our construction will be similar to the one in section 2.3.2 for exact inference. However, there are some differences. As we saw, the calibrated cluster graph maintains the information in $P_{\mathcal{F}}$. However, the resulting cluster potentials are not, in general, the marginals of $P_{\mathcal{F}}$. In fact, these cluster potentials may not represent the marginals of any single coherent joint distribution over $\mathcal{X}$. Thus, we can think of generalized belief propagation as constructing a set of *pseudo-marginal distributions*, each one over the variables in one cluster. These pseudo-marginals are calibrated, and therefore locally consistent with each other, but are not necessarily marginals of a single underlying joint distribution.

The energy functional $F[P_{\mathcal{F}}, Q]$ has terms involving the entropy of an entire joint distribution; thus, it cannot be used to evaluate the quality of an approximation defined in terms of (possibly incoherent) pseudo-marginals. However, the factored free energy functional $\tilde{F}[P_{\mathcal{F}}, \boldsymbol{Q}]$ is defined in terms of entropies of clusters and messages, and is therefore well-defined for pseudo-marginals $\boldsymbol{Q}$. Thus, we can write down an optimization problem as before:

CGraph-Optimize

Find Q

that maximize $\tilde{F}[P_{\mathcal{F}}, \boldsymbol{Q}]$

$$\text{subject to} \qquad \sum_{\boldsymbol{C}_i \setminus \boldsymbol{S}_{i,j}} \pi_i = \mu_{i,j}, \quad \forall (\boldsymbol{C}_i \!-\! \boldsymbol{C}_j) \in \mathcal{T}; \tag{2.11}$$

$$\sum_{\boldsymbol{C}_i} \pi_i = 1, \qquad \forall \boldsymbol{C}_i \in \mathcal{T}. \tag{2.12}$$

Importantly, however, unlike for clique trees, $\tilde{F}[P_{\mathcal{F}}, \boldsymbol{Q}]$ is no longer simply a reformulation of the free energy, but rather an approximation of it. Thus, our optimization problem contains two approximations: we are using an approximation, rather than an exact, energy functional; and we are optimizing it over the space of pseudo-marginals, which is a relaxation (a superspace) of the space of all coherent probability distributions that factorize over the cluster graph. The approximate energy functional in this case is a restricted form of an approximation known as the *Kikuchi free energy* in statistical physics.

We noted that the energy functional is a lower bound of the log-partition function; thus, by maximizing it, we get better approximations of $P_{\mathcal{F}}$. Unfortunately, the factored energy functional, which is only an approximation to the true energy functional, is not necessarily also a lower bound. Nonetheless, it is still a reasonable strategy to maximize the approximate energy functional.

Our maximization problem is the natural analogue of CTree-Optimize to the case of cluster graphs. Not surprisingly, we can derive a similar analogue to theorem 2.27.

Theorem 2.28
A set of potentials $\boldsymbol{Q}$ is a stationary point of CGraph-Optimize if and only if for every edge $(\boldsymbol{C}_i\text{—}\boldsymbol{C}_j) \in \mathcal{K}$ there are auxiliary potentials $\delta_{i\to j}(\boldsymbol{S}_{i,j})$ and $\delta_{j\to i}(\boldsymbol{S}_{j,i})$ so that

$$\delta_{i\to j} \propto \sum_{\boldsymbol{C}_i - \boldsymbol{S}_{i,j}} \pi_i^0 \times \prod_{k \in \mathcal{N}_{\boldsymbol{C}_i} - \{j\}} \delta_{k\to i} \tag{2.13}$$

$$\pi_i \propto \pi_i^0 \times \prod_{j \in \mathcal{N}_{\boldsymbol{C}_i}} \delta_{j\to i} \tag{2.14}$$

$$\mu_{i,j} = \delta_{j\to i} \times \delta_{i\to j}. \tag{2.15}$$

This theorem shows that we can characterize convergence points of the energy function in terms of the original potentials and messages between clusters. We can, once again, define a procedural variant, in which we initialize $\delta_{i\to j}$, and then iteratively use (2.13) to redefine each $\delta_{i\to j}$ in terms of the current values of other $\delta_{k\to i}$. theorem 2.28 shows that convergence points of this procedure are related to stationary points of $\tilde{F}[P_{\mathcal{F}}, \boldsymbol{Q}]$.

It is relatively easy to verify that $\tilde{F}[P_{\mathcal{F}}, \boldsymbol{Q}]$ is bounded from above. And thus, this function must have a maximum. There are two cases. The maximum is either an interior point or a boundary point (some of the probabilities in $\boldsymbol{Q}$ are 0). In the former case the maximum is also a stationary point, which implies that it satisfies the condition of theorem 2.28. In the latter case, the maximum is not necessarily a stationary point. This situation, however, is very rare in practice, and can be guaranteed not to arise if we make some fairly benign assumptions.

It is important to understand what these results imply, and what they do not. The results imply only that the convergence points of generalized belief propagation are stationary points of the free energy function They do *not* imply that we can reach these convergence points by applying belief propagation steps. In fact, there is no guarantee that the message-passing steps of generalized belief propagation necessarily improve the free energy objective: a message passing step may increase or decrease the energy functional. (In fact, if generalized belief propagation was guaranteed to monotonically improve the functional, then it would necessarily always converge.)

What are the implications of this result? First, it provides us with a declarative semantics for generalized belief propagation in terms of optimization of a target functional. This declarative semantics opens the way to investigate other computational approaches for optimizing the same functional. We discuss some of these approaches below.

This result also allows us to understand what properties are important for this type of approximation, and subsequently to design other approximations that may be more accurate, or better in some other way. As a concrete example, recall that, in our discussion of generalized cluster graphs, we required the running intersection property. This property has two important implications. First, that the set of clusters that contain some variable X are connected; hence, the marginal over X will be the same in all of these clusters at the calibration point. Second, that there is no cycle of clusters and sepsets all of which contain X. We can motivate this assumption intuitively, by noting that it prevents us from allowing information about X to cycle endlessly through a loop. The free energy function analysis provides a more formal justification. To understand it, consider first the form of the factored free energy functional when our cluster graph $\mathcal{K}$ has the form of the Bethe approximation Recall that in the Bethe approximation graph there are two layers: one consisting of clusters that correspond to factors in $\mathcal{F}$, and the other consisting of univariate clusters. When the cluster graph is calibrated, these univariate clusters have the same distribution as the separators between them and the factors in the first layer. As such, we can combine together the entropy terms for all the separators labeled by X and the associated univariate cluster and rewrite the free energy, as follows:

Proposition 2.29
If $\boldsymbol{Q} = \{\pi_\phi : \phi \in \mathcal{F}\} \cup \{\pi_i(X_i)\}$ is a calibrated set of potentials for $\mathcal{K}$ for a Bethe approximation cluster graph with clusters $\{\boldsymbol{C}_\phi \ : \ \phi \in \mathcal{F}\} \cup \{X_i \ : \ X_i \in \mathcal{X}\}$, then

$$\tilde{F}[P_\mathcal{F}, \boldsymbol{Q}] = \sum_{\phi \in \mathcal{F}} \boldsymbol{E}_{\pi_\phi}[\ln \phi] + \sum_{\phi \in \mathcal{F}} \boldsymbol{H}_{\pi_\phi}(\boldsymbol{C}_\phi) - \sum_i (d_i - 1)\boldsymbol{H}_{\pi_i}(X_i), \qquad (2.16)$$

where $d_i = |\{\phi : X_i \in Scope[\phi]\}|$ is the number of factors that contain X_i.

Note that (2.16) is equivalent to the factored free energy only when $\boldsymbol{Q}$ is calibrated. However, as we are interested only in such cases, we can freely alternate between the two forms for the purpose of finding fixed points of the factored free energy functional. Equation (2.16) is known as the *Bethe free energy*, and again has a history in statistical mechanics. The Bethe approximation we discussed above is a construction in terms of cluster graphs that is designed to match the Bethe free energy.

As we can see in this alternative form, if the variable X_i appears in d_i clusters in the cluster graph, then it appears in an entropy term with a positive sign exactly d_i times. Due to the running intersection property, the number of separators that contain X_i is $d_i - 1$ (the number of edges in a tree with k vertices is $k - 1$), so that X_i appears in an entropy term with a negative sign exactly $d_i - 1$ times. In this case, we say that the *counting number* of X_i is 1. Thus, our approximation does not over- or undercount the entropy of X_i. It is not difficult to show that the counting number result holds for any approximation that satisfies the running intersection property. Thus, one motivation for the running intersection property is that cluster graphs satisfying it provide a better approximation to the free energy functional.

This intuition forms the basis for improved approximations. Specifically, we can construct energy functionals (called *Kikuchi free energy* approximations) that resemble (2.5), in which we introduce additional entropy terms, with both positive and negative signs, in a way that ensures that the counting number for all variables is 1. Somewhat remarkably, the same analysis we performed in this section — defining a set of fixed-point equations for stationary points of the approximate free energy — also leads to message-passing algorithms for these richer approximations. The propagation rules for these approximations, which also fall under the heading of generalized belief propagation, are more elaborate, and we do not discuss them here.

2.3.4   Sampling-Based Approximate Inference

As we discussed above, another approach to dealing with the worst-case combinatorial explosion of exact inference in graphical models is via *sampling-based methods*. In these methods, we approximate the joint distribution as a set of instantiations to all or some of the variables in the network. These instantiations, often called *samples*, represent part of the probability mass.

The general framework for most of the discussion is as follows. Consider some distribution $P(\mathcal{X})$, and assume we want to estimate the probability of some event $\boldsymbol{Y} = \boldsymbol{y}$ relative to P, for some $\boldsymbol{Y} \subseteq \mathcal{X}$ and $\boldsymbol{y} \in Val(\boldsymbol{Y})$. More generally, we might want to estimate the expectation of some function $f(\mathcal{X})$ relative to P; this task is a generalization, as we can choose $f(\xi) = \boldsymbol{1}\{\xi\langle \boldsymbol{Y}\rangle = \boldsymbol{y}\}$. We approximate this expectation by generating a set of M samples, estimating the value of the function or its expectation relative to each of the generated samples, and then aggregating the results.

2.3.4.1   *Markov Chain Monte Carlo Methods*

Markov chain Monte Carlo (abbreviated *MCMC*) is an approach for generating samples from the posterior distribution. As we discussed, we cannot typically sample from the posterior directly; however, we can construct a process which gradually samples from distributions that are closer and closer to the posterior. Intuitively, we define a state graph whose nodes are the states of the system, i.e., possible instantiations $Val(\mathcal{X})$. (This graph is very different from the graphical model that defines the distribution $P(\mathcal{X})$, whose nodes correspond to variables.) We then define a process that randomly traverses this graph, moving from one state to another. This process is defined so that, ultimately (after enough steps), the probability of being in any particular state is the desired posterior distribution.

We begin by describing the general framework of Markov chains, and then describe their application to approximate inference in graphical models. We note that, unlike forward sampling methods (including likelihood weighting), Markov chain methods apply equally well to directed and to undirected models.

A *Markov chain* is defined in terms of a set of states, and a transition model from one state to another. The chain defines a process that evolves stochastically from state to state.

Definition 2.30
A *Markov chain* is defined via a state space $Val(\boldsymbol{X})$ and a *transition probability model*, which defines, for every state $\boldsymbol{x} \in Val(X)$ a *next-state* distribution over $Val(X)$. The *transition probability* of going from $\boldsymbol{x}$ to $\boldsymbol{x}'$ is denoted $\mathcal{T}(\boldsymbol{x} \rightarrow \boldsymbol{x}')$. This transition probability applies whenever the chain is in state $\boldsymbol{x}$. ∎

We note that, in this definition and in the subsequent discussion, we restrict attention to *homogeneous* Markov chains, where the system dynamics do not change over time.

We can imagine a random sampling process that defines a sequence of states $\boldsymbol{x}^{(0)}, \boldsymbol{x}^{(1)}, \boldsymbol{x}^{(2)}, \ldots$. As the transition model is random, the state of the process at step t can be viewed as a random variable $\boldsymbol{X}^{(t)}$. We assume that the initial state $\boldsymbol{X}^{(0)}$ is distributed according to some initial state distribution $P^{(0)}(\boldsymbol{X}^{(0)})$. We can now define distributions over the subsequent states $P^{(1)}(\boldsymbol{X}^{(1)}), P^{(2)}(\boldsymbol{X}^{(2)}), \ldots$ using the chain dynamics:

$$P^{(t+1)}(\boldsymbol{X}^{(t+1)} = \boldsymbol{x}') = \sum_{\boldsymbol{x} \in Val(\boldsymbol{X})} P^{(t)}(\boldsymbol{X}^{(t)} = \boldsymbol{x})\mathcal{T}(\boldsymbol{x} \rightarrow \boldsymbol{x}'). \qquad (2.17)$$

Intuitively, the probability of being at state $\boldsymbol{x}'$ at time $t + 1$ is the sum over all possible states $\boldsymbol{x}$ that the chain could have been in at time t of the probability being in state $\boldsymbol{x}$ times the probability that the chain took a transition from $\boldsymbol{x}$ to $\boldsymbol{x}'$.

As the process converges, we would expect $P^{(t+1)}$ to be close to $P^{(t)}$. Using (2.17), we obtain

$$P^{(t)}(\boldsymbol{x}') \approx P^{(t+1)}(\boldsymbol{x}') = \sum_{\boldsymbol{x} \in Val(\boldsymbol{X})} P^{(t)}(\boldsymbol{x})\mathcal{T}(\boldsymbol{x} \rightarrow \boldsymbol{x}').$$

At convergence, we would expect the resulting distribution $\pi(\boldsymbol{X})$ to be an equilibrium relative to the transition model; i.e., the probability of being in a state is the same as the probability of transitioning into it from a randomly sampled predecessor. Formally:

Definition 2.31
A distribution $\pi(\boldsymbol{X})$ is a *stationary distribution* for a Markov chain $\mathcal{T}$ if it satisfies

$$\pi(\boldsymbol{X} = \boldsymbol{x}') = \sum_{\boldsymbol{x} \in Val(\boldsymbol{X})} \pi(\boldsymbol{X} = \boldsymbol{x})\mathcal{T}(\boldsymbol{x} \rightarrow \boldsymbol{x}'). \quad ∎ \qquad (2.18)$$

We wish to restrict attention to Markov chains that have a unique stationary distribution, which is reached from any starting distribution $P^{(0)}$. There are various conditions that suffice to guarantee this property. The condition most commonly used is a fairly technical one, that the chain be *ergodic*. In the context of Markov chains where the state space $Val(\boldsymbol{X})$ is finite, the following condition is equivalent to this requirement:

Definition 2.32

A Markov chain is said to be *regular* if there exists some number k such that, for every $\boldsymbol{x}, \boldsymbol{x}' \in Val(\boldsymbol{X})$, the probability of getting from $\boldsymbol{x}$ to $\boldsymbol{x}'$ in exactly k steps is greater than 0. ∎

The following result can be shown to hold:

Theorem 2.33

A finite-state Markov chain $\mathcal{T}$ has a unique stationary distribution if and only if it is regular.

Ensuring regularity is usually straightforward. Two simple conditions that guarantee regularity in finite-state Markov chains are:

- It is possible to get from any state to any state using a positive probability path in the state graph.
- For each state $\boldsymbol{x}$, there is a positive probability of transitioning from $\boldsymbol{x}$ to $\boldsymbol{x}$ in one step (a self-loop).

These two conditions together are sufficient but not necessary to guarantee regularity. However, they often hold in the chains used in practice.

2.3.4.2 Markov Chains for Graphical Models

The theory of Markov chains provides a general framework for generating samples from a target distribution π. In this section, we discuss the application of this framework to the sampling tasks encountered in probabilistic graphical models. In this case, we typically wish to generate samples from the posterior distribution $P(\mathcal{X} \mid \boldsymbol{E} = \boldsymbol{e})$. Thus, we wish to define a chain for which $P(\mathcal{X} \mid \boldsymbol{e})$ is the stationary distribution. Clearly, there are many ways of defining such a chain. We focus on the most common approaches.

In graphical models, we define the states of the Markov chain to be instantiations ξ to $\mathcal{X}$, which are compatible with $\boldsymbol{e}$; i.e., all of the states ξ in the Markov chain satisfy $\xi\langle\boldsymbol{E}\rangle = \boldsymbol{e}$. The states in our Markov chain are therefore some subset of the possible assignments to the variables $\mathcal{X}$. In order to define a Markov chain, we need to define a process that transitions from one state to the other, converging to a stationary distribution $\pi(\xi)$ which is the desired posterior distribution $P(\xi \mid \boldsymbol{e})$.

In the case of graphical models, our state space has a factorized structure — each state is an assignment to several variables. When defining a transition model over this state space, we can consider a fully general case, where a transition can go from any state to any state. However, it is often convenient to decompose the transition model, considering transitions that only update a single component of the state vector at a time, i.e., only a value for a single variable. In this case, as in several other settings, we often define a set of transition models $\mathcal{T}_1, \ldots, \mathcal{T}_k$, each with its own dynamics. In certain cases, the different transition models are necessary, because no single transition model on its own suffices to ensure regularity.

In other cases, having multiple transition models simply makes the state space more "connected," and therefore speeds the convergence to a stationary distribution.

There are several ways of combining these multiple transition models into a single chain. One common approach is simply to randomly select between them at each step, using any distribution. Thus, for example, at each step, we might select one of $T_1, \ldots, T_k$, each with probability $1/k$. Alternatively, we can simply cycle over the different transition models, taking each one in turn. Clearly, this approach does not define a homogeneous chain, as the transition model used in step i is different from the one used in step $i + 1$. However, we can simply view the process as defining a single transition model T each of whose steps is an aggregate step, consisting of first taking T_1, then T_2, ..., through T_k.

In the case of graphical models, we define $\boldsymbol{X} = \mathcal{X} - \boldsymbol{E} = \{X_1, \ldots, X_k\}$. We define a multiple transition chain, where we have a *local transition model* T_i for each variable $X_i \in \boldsymbol{X}$. Let $\boldsymbol{U}_i = \mathcal{X} - \{X_i\}$, and let $\boldsymbol{u}_i$ denote an instantiation to $\boldsymbol{U}_i$. The model T_i takes a state $(\boldsymbol{u}_i, x_i)$ and transitions to a state of the form $(\boldsymbol{u}_i, x_i')$. As we discussed above, we can combine the different local transition models into a single global model in various ways.

2.3.4.3 Gibbs Sampling

Gibbs sampling is one simple yet effective Markov chain for factored state spaces, which is particularly efficient for graphical models. We define the local transition model T_i as follows. Intuitively, we simply "forget" the value of X_i in the current state, and sample a new value for X_i from its posterior given the rest of the current state. More precisely, let $(\boldsymbol{u}_i, x_i)$ be a state in the chain. We define

$$T((\boldsymbol{u}_i, x_i) \rightarrow (\boldsymbol{u}_i, x_i')) = P(x_i' \mid \boldsymbol{u}_i). \tag{2.19}$$

Note that the transition probability does not depend on the current value x_i of X_i, but only on the remaining state $\boldsymbol{u}_i$.

The Gibbs chain is defined via a set of local transition models; we use the multistep transition model to combine them. Note that the different local transitions are taken consecutively; i.e., having changed the value for a variable X_1, the value for X_2 is sampled based on the new value. Also note that we are only collecting a single sample for every sequence where each local transition has been taken once.

This chain is guaranteed to be regular whenever the distribution is positive, so that every value of X_i has positive probability given an assignment $\boldsymbol{u}_i$ to the remaining variables. In this case, we can get from any state to any state in at most k local transition steps, where $k = |\mathcal{X} - \boldsymbol{E}|$. Positivity is, however, not necessary; there are many examples of nonpositive distributions where the Gibbs chain is regular. It is also easy to show that the posterior distribution $P(\mathcal{X} \mid \boldsymbol{e})$ is a stationary distribution of this process.

Gibbs sampling is particularly well suited to many graphical models, where we can compute the transition probability $P(X_i \mid \boldsymbol{u}_i)$ very efficiently. In particular, as we now show, this distribution can be done based only on the Markov blanket of X_i. We show this analysis for a Markov network; the extension to Bayesian networks is straightforward. In general, we can decompose the probability of an instantiation as follows:

$$P(x_1 \mid x_2, \ldots, x_n) = \frac{1}{Z} \prod_j \pi_j[C_j] = \frac{1}{Z} \prod_{j\,:\,X_i \in C_j} \pi_j[C_j] \prod_{j\,:\,X_i \notin C_j} \pi_j[C_j].$$

For shorthand, let $\pi_j[x_i, \boldsymbol{u}]$ denote $\pi_j[x_i, \boldsymbol{u}\langle C_j\rangle]$. We can now compute

$$P(x_i' \mid \boldsymbol{u}_i) = \frac{P(x_i', \boldsymbol{u}_i)}{\sum_{x_i''} P(x_i'', \boldsymbol{u}_i)} = \frac{\prod_{C_j \ni X_i} \pi_j[x_i', \boldsymbol{u}_i]}{\sum_{x_i''} \prod_{C_j \ni X_i} \pi_j[(x_i'', \boldsymbol{u}_i)]}. \tag{2.20}$$

This last expression uses only the clique potentials involving X_i, and depends only on the instantiation in $\boldsymbol{u}_i$ of X_i's Markov blanket. In the case of Bayesian networks, this expression reduces to a formula involving only the CPDs of X_i and its children, and its value, again, depends only on the assignment in $\boldsymbol{u}_i$ to the Markov blanket of X_i. It can thus be computed very efficiently.

We note that the Markov chain defined by a graphical model is not necessarily regular, and might not converge to a unique stationary distribution. It turns out that this type of situation can only arise if the distribution defined by the graphical model is nonpositive, i.e., if the CPDs or clique potentials have entries with the value 0.

Theorem 2.34
Let $\mathcal{H}$ be a Markov network such that all of the clique potentials are strictly positive. Then the Gibbs-sampling Markov chain is regular.

2.3.4.4 Building a Markov Chain

As we discussed, the use of MCMC methods relies on the construction of a Markov chain that has the desired properties: regularity, and the target stationary distribution. Above, we described the Gibbs chain, a simple Markov chain that is guaranteed to have these properties under certain assumptions. However, Gibbs sampling is only applicable in certain circumstances; in particular, we must be able to sample from the distribution $P(X_i \mid \boldsymbol{u}_i)$. Although this sampling step is easy for discrete graphical models, there are other types of models where this step is not practical, and the Gibbs chain is not applicable. Unfortunately, it is beyond the scope of this chapter to discuss the Metropolis-Hastings algorithm, a more general method of constructing a Markov chain that is guaranteed to converge to the desired stationary distribution.

2.3.4.5 Generating Samples

The burn-in time for a large Markov chain is often quite large. Thus, the naive algorithm described above has to execute a large number of sampling steps for every usable sample. However, a key observation is that, if $\boldsymbol{x}^{(t)}$ is sampled from π, then $\boldsymbol{x}^{(t+1)}$ is also sampled from π. Thus, once we have run the chain long enough that we are sampling from the stationary distribution (or a distribution close to it), we can continue generating samples from the same trajectory, and obtain a large number of samples from the stationary distribution.

More formally, assume that we use $\boldsymbol{x}^{(0)}, \ldots, \boldsymbol{x}^{(T)}$ as our burn-in phase, and then collect M samples $\boldsymbol{x}^{(T+1)}, \ldots, \boldsymbol{x}^{(T+M)}$. Thus, we have collected a data set $\mathcal{D}$ where $\boldsymbol{x}^m = \boldsymbol{x}^{(T+m)}$, for $m = 1, \ldots, M$. Assume, for simplicity, that $\boldsymbol{x}^{(T+1)}$ is sampled from π, and hence so are all of the samples in $\mathcal{D}$. It follows that for any function f: $\sum_{m=1}^{M} f(\boldsymbol{x}^m)$ is an unbiased estimator for $\boldsymbol{E}_{\pi(\boldsymbol{X})}[f(\boldsymbol{X})]$.

The key problem, of course, is that consecutive samples from the same trajectory are correlated. Thus, we cannot expect the same performance as we would from M independent samples from π. In other words, the variance of the estimator is significantly higher than that of an estimator generated by M independent samples from π, as discussed above.

One solution to this problem is not to collect consecutive samples from the chain. Rather, having collected a sample $\boldsymbol{x}^{(T)}$, we let the chain run for a while, and collect a second sample $\boldsymbol{x}^{(T+d)}$ for some appropriate choice of d. For d large enough, $\boldsymbol{x}^{(T)}$ and $\boldsymbol{x}^{(T+d)}$ are only slightly correlated, and we can view them as independent samples from π. However, the time d required for "forgetting" the correlation is clearly related to the mixing time of the chain. Thus, chains that are slow to mix initially also require larger d in order to produce close-to-independent samples. Nevertheless, the samples do come from the correct distribution for any value of d, and hence it is often better to compromise and use a shorter d than it is to use a shorter burn-in time T. This method thus allows us to collect a larger number of usable samples with fewer transitions of the Markov chain.

In fact, we can often make even better use of the samples generated using this single-chain approach. Although the samples between $\boldsymbol{x}^{(T)}$ and $\boldsymbol{x}^{(T+d)}$ are not independent samples, there is no reason to discard them. That is, using all of the samples $\boldsymbol{x}^{(T)}, \boldsymbol{x}^{(T+1)}, \ldots, \boldsymbol{x}^{(T+d)}$ produces a provably better estimator than using just the two samples $\boldsymbol{x}^{(T)}$ and $\boldsymbol{x}^{(T+d)}$: our variance is always no higher if we use all of the samples we generated rather than a subset. Thus, the strategy of picking only a subset of the samples is useful primarily in settings where there is a significant cost associated with using each sample (e.g., the evaluation of f is costly), so that we might want to reduce the overall number of samples used.

2.3.4.6   Discussion

This description of the use of Markov chains is quite abstract: It contains no specification of the number of chains to run, the metrics for evaluating mixing, techniques for determining the delay between samples that would allow them to be considered independent, and more. Unfortunately, at this point, there is little theoretical analysis that can help answer these questions for the chains that are of interest to us. Thus, the application of Markov chains is more of an art than a science, and often requires significant experimentation and hand-tuning of parameters.

Nevertheless, MCMC methods are, for many probabilistic models, the only technique that can achieve reasonable performance. Specifically, unlike forward sampling methods, it does not degrade when the probability of the evidence is low, or when the posterior is very different from the prior. Furthermore, unlike forward sampling, it applies to undirected models as well as to directed models. As such, it is an important component in the suite of approximate inference techniques.

2.4   Learning

Next, we turn our attention to learning graphical models [4, 6]. There are two variants of the learning task: parameter estimation and structure learning. In the parameter estimation task, we assume that the qualitative dependency structure of the graphical model is known; i.e., in the directed model case, $\mathcal{G}$ is given, and in the undirected case, $\mathcal{H}$ is given. In this case, the learning task is simply to fill in the parameters that define the CPDs of the attributes or the parameters which define the potential functions of the Markov network. In the structure learning task, there is no additional required input (although the user can, if available, provide prior knowledge about the structure, e.g., in the form of constraints). The goal is to extract a Bayesian network or Markov network, structure as well as parameters, from the training data alone. We discuss each of these problems in turn.

2.4.1   Parameter Estimation in Bayesian Networks

We begin with learning the parameters for a Bayesian network where the dependency structure is known. In other words, we are given the structure $\mathcal{G}$ that determines the set of parents for each random variable, and our task is to learn the parameters $\boldsymbol{\theta}_{\mathcal{G}}$ that define the CPDs for this structure. Our learning is based on a particular training set $\mathcal{D} = \{x^1, \ldots, x^m\}$, which, for now, we will assume is *complete* (i.e., each instance is fully observed, there are no missing values). While this task is relatively straightforward, it is of interest in and of itself. In addition, it is a crucial component in the structure learning algorithm described in section 2.4.3.

There are two approaches to parameter estimation: *maximum likelihood estimation (MLE)* and Bayesian approaches. The key ingredient for both is the likelihood function: the probability of the data given the model. This function captures the response of the probability distribution to changes in the choice of parameters. The likelihood of a parameter set is defined to be the probability of the data given the model. For a Bayesian network structure $\mathcal{G}$ the likelihood of a parameter set $\boldsymbol{\theta}_{\mathcal{G}}$ is

$$L(\boldsymbol{\theta}_{\mathcal{G}} : \mathcal{D}) = P(\mathcal{D} \mid \boldsymbol{\theta}_{\mathcal{G}}).$$

2.4.1.1   *Maximum Likelihood Parameter Estimation*

Given the above, one approach to parameter estimation is *maximum likelihood parameter estimation*. Here, our goal is to find the parameter setting $\boldsymbol{\theta}_\mathcal{G}$ that maximizes the likelihood $L(\boldsymbol{\theta}_\mathcal{G} : \mathcal{D})$. For Bayesian networks, the likelihood can be decomposed as follows:

$$
\begin{aligned}
L(\boldsymbol{\theta}_\mathcal{G}, \mathcal{D}) &= \prod_{j=1}^{m} P(x^j : \boldsymbol{\theta}_\mathcal{G}) \\
&= \prod_{j=1}^{m} \prod_{i=1}^{n} P(x_i^j \mid \mathbf{Pa}_{x_i^j} : \boldsymbol{\theta}_\mathcal{G}) \\
&= \prod_{i=1}^{n} \prod_{j=1}^{m} P(x_i^j \mid \mathbf{Pa}_{x_i^j} : \boldsymbol{\theta}_\mathcal{G})
\end{aligned}
$$

We will use $\boldsymbol{\theta}_{X_i \mid \mathbf{Pa}_i}$ to denote the subset of parameters that determine $P(X_i \mid \mathbf{Pa}_i)$. In the case where the parameters are disjoint (each CPD is parameterized by a separate set of parameters that do not overlap; this allows us to maximize each parameter set independently. We can write the likelihood as follows:

$$
L(\boldsymbol{\theta}_\mathcal{G} : \mathcal{D}) = \prod_{i=1}^{n} L_i(\boldsymbol{\theta}_{X_i \mid \mathbf{Pa}_i} : \mathcal{D}),
$$

where the *local likelihood* function for X_i is

$$
L_i(\boldsymbol{\theta}_{X_i \mid \mathbf{Pa}_i} : \mathcal{D}) = \prod_{j=1}^{m} P(x_i^j \mid \mathbf{pa}_i^j : \boldsymbol{\theta}_{X_i \mid \mathbf{Pa}_i}).
$$

The simplest parameterization for the CPDs is as a table. Suppose we have a variable X with parents $\boldsymbol{U}$. If we represent that CPD $P(X \mid \boldsymbol{U})$ as a table, then we will have a parameter $\theta_{x \mid \boldsymbol{u}}$ for each combination of $x \in Val(X)$ and $\boldsymbol{u} \in Val(\boldsymbol{U})$. In this case, we can write the local likelihood function as follows:

$$
\begin{aligned}
L_X(\boldsymbol{\theta}_{X \mid \boldsymbol{U}} : \mathcal{D}) &= \prod_{j=1}^{m} \theta_{x^j \mid \boldsymbol{u}^j} \\
&= \prod_{\boldsymbol{u} \in Val(\boldsymbol{U})} \left[\prod_{x \in Val(X)} \theta_{x \mid \boldsymbol{u}}^{N_{\boldsymbol{u},x}} \right],
\end{aligned}
\tag{2.21}
$$

where $N_{\boldsymbol{u},x}$ is the number of times $X = x$ and $\mathbf{Pa}_i = \boldsymbol{u}$ in $\mathcal{D}$. That is, we have grouped together all the occurrences of $\theta_{x \mid \boldsymbol{u}}$ in the product over all instances.

We need to maximize this term under the constraints that, for each choice of value for the parents $\boldsymbol{U}$, the conditional probability is legal:

$$
\sum \theta_{x \mid \boldsymbol{u}} = 1 \quad \text{for all } \boldsymbol{u}.
$$

These constraints imply that the choice of value for $\theta_{x|\boldsymbol{u}}$ can impact the choice of value for $\theta_{x'|\boldsymbol{u}}$. However, the choice of parameters given different values $\boldsymbol{u}$ of $\boldsymbol{U}$ are independent of each other. Thus, we can maximize each of the terms in square brackets in (2.21) independently.

We can thus further decompose the local likelihood function for a tabular CPD into a product of simple likelihood functions. It is easy to see that each of these likelihood functions is a *multinomial* likelihood. The counts in the data for the different outcomes x are simply $\{N_{\boldsymbol{u},x} : x \in Val(X)\}$. We can then immediately use the MLE parameters for a multinomial which are simply

$$\hat{\theta}_{x|\boldsymbol{u}} = \frac{N_{\boldsymbol{u},x}}{N_{\boldsymbol{u}}},$$

where we use the fact that $N_{\boldsymbol{u}} = \sum_x N_{\boldsymbol{u},x}$.

2.4.1.2   *Bayesian Parameter Estimation*

In many cases, maximum likelihood parameter estimation is not robust, as it over-fits the training data. The Bayesian approach uses a prior distribution over the parameters to smooth the irregularities in the training data, and is therefore significantly more robust. As we will see in section 2.4.3, the Bayesian framework also gives us a good metric for evaluating the quality of different candidate structures.

Roughly speaking, the Bayesian approach introduces a prior over the unknown parameters, allowing us to specify a joint distribution over the unknown parameters and the data instances, and performs Bayesian conditioning, using the data as evidence, to compute a posterior distribution over these parameters.

Consider the following simple example: we want to estimate parameters for a simple network with two variables X and Y, where X is the parent of Y. Our training data consists of observations x^j, y^j for $j = 1, \ldots, m$. In addition, assume that our CPDs are represented as multinomials and we have unknown parameter vectors $\boldsymbol{\theta}_X$, $\boldsymbol{\theta}_{Y|x^0}$, and $\boldsymbol{\theta}_{Y|x^1}$.

The dependencies between these variables are described in the network of figure 2.6. This is the *meta-Bayesian network* that describes our learning setup. This Bayesian network structure immediately reveals several points. For example, the instances are independent given the unknown parameters. In addition, a common assumption made is that the individual parameter variables are a priori independent. That is, we believe that knowing the value of one parameter tells us nothing about another. This is called *parameter independence*. The suitability of this assumption depends on the domain, and it should be considered with care.

If we accept parameter independence, we can draw an important conclusion. Complete data d-separates the parameters for different CPDs. Given the data set $\mathcal{D}$, we can determine the posterior over $\boldsymbol{\theta}_X$ independently of the posterior over $\boldsymbol{\theta}_{Y|X}$. Once we solve each problem separately, we can combine the results. This is the analogous result to the likelihood decomposition for MLE estimation of section 2.4.1.1.

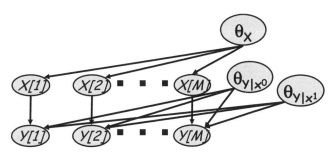

Figure 2.6   The Bayesian network for parameter estimation for a simple two-node Bayesian network.

Consider, for example, the learning setting described in figure 2.6, where we take both X and Y to be binary. We need to represent the posterior $\boldsymbol{\theta}_X$ and $\boldsymbol{\theta}_{Y|X}$ given the data. If we use a Dirichlet prior over $\boldsymbol{\theta}_X$, $\theta_{Y|x^0}$, and $\theta_{Y|x^1}$, then the posterior $P(\boldsymbol{\theta}_X \mid x^1, \ldots, x^M)$ can also be represented as a Dirichlet distribution.

Suppose that $P(\boldsymbol{\theta}_X)$ is a Dirichlet prior with hyperparameters α_{x^0} and α_{x^1}, $P(\boldsymbol{\theta}_{Y|x^0})$ is a Dirichlet prior with hyperparameters $\alpha_{y^0|x^0}$ and $\alpha_{y^1|x^0}$, and $P(\boldsymbol{\theta}_{Y|x^1})$ is a Dirichlet prior with hyperparameters $\alpha_{y^0|x^1}$ and $\alpha_{y^1|x^1}$.

As in decomposition for the likelihood function in section 2.4.1.1, the likelihood terms that involve $\boldsymbol{\theta}_{Y|x^0}$ depend on all the data elements X^j such that $x^j = x^0$ and the terms that involve $\boldsymbol{\theta}_{Y|x^1}$ depend on all the data elements X^j such that $x^j = x^1$ We can decompose the joint distribution over parameters and data as follows:

$$
\begin{aligned}
P(\boldsymbol{\theta}_\mathcal{G}, \mathcal{D}) = P(&\boldsymbol{\theta}_X) L_X(\boldsymbol{\theta}_X : \mathcal{D}) \\
&P(\boldsymbol{\theta}_{Y|x^1}) \prod_{j: x^j = x^1} P(y^j \mid x^n : \boldsymbol{\theta}_{Y|x^1}) \\
&P(\boldsymbol{\theta}_{Y|x^0}) \prod_{j: x^j = x^0} P(y^j \mid x^j : \boldsymbol{\theta}_{Y|x^0})
\end{aligned}
$$

Thus, this joint distribution is a product of three separate joint distributions with a Dirichlet prior for some multinomial parameter and data drawn from this multinomial. We can conclude that the posterior for $P(\boldsymbol{\theta}_X \mid \mathcal{D})$ is Dirichlet with hyperparameters $\alpha_{x^0} + N_{x^0}$ and $\alpha_{x^1} + N_{x^1}$; the posterior for $P(\boldsymbol{\theta}_{Y|x^0} \mid \mathcal{D})$ is Dirichlet with hyperparameters $\alpha_{y^0|x^0} + N_{x^0,y^0}$ and $\alpha_{y^1|x^0} + N_{x^0,y^1}$; and the posterior for $P(\boldsymbol{\theta}_{Y|x^1} \mid \mathcal{D})$ is Dirichlet with hyperparameters $\alpha_{y^0|x^1} + N_{x^1,y^0}$ and $\alpha_{y^1|x^1} + N_{x^1,y^1}$.

The same pattern of reasoning we discussed applied to the general case. Let $\mathcal{D}$ be a complete data set for $\mathcal{X}$, and let $\mathcal{G}$ be a network structure over these variables with table CPDs. If the prior $P(\boldsymbol{\theta}_\mathcal{G})$ satisfies parameter independence, then

$$
P(\boldsymbol{\theta}_\mathcal{G} \mid \mathcal{D}) = \prod_i \prod_{\mathbf{pa}_i} P(\boldsymbol{\theta}_{X_i|\mathbf{pa}_i} \mid \mathcal{D}).
$$

If $P(\boldsymbol{\theta}_{X|\boldsymbol{u}})$ is a Dirichlet prior with hyperparameters $\alpha_{x^1|\boldsymbol{u}}, \ldots, \alpha_{x^K|\boldsymbol{u}}$, then the posterior $P(\boldsymbol{\theta}_{X|\boldsymbol{u}} \mid \mathcal{D})$ is a Dirichlet distribution with hyperparameters $\alpha_{x^1|\boldsymbol{u}} + N_{\boldsymbol{u},x^1}, \ldots, \alpha_{x^K|\boldsymbol{u}} + N_{\boldsymbol{u},x^K}$.

This induces a predictive model in which, for the next instance, we have that

$$P(X_i[m+1] = x_i \mid \boldsymbol{U}[m+1] = \boldsymbol{u}, \mathcal{D}) = \frac{\alpha_{x_i|\boldsymbol{u}} + N_{x_i,\boldsymbol{u}}}{\sum_i \alpha_{x_i|\boldsymbol{u}} + N_{x_i,\boldsymbol{u}}}. \tag{2.22}$$

Putting this all together, we can see that for computing the probability of a new instance, we can use a single network parameterized as usual, via a set of multinomials, but ones computed as in (2.22).

2.4.2 Parameter Estimation in Markov Networks

Unfortunately, for general Markov networks, the likelihood function cannot be decomposed. A notable exception is chordal Markov networks, but we will focus on the general case here. For a network with a set of cliques $\boldsymbol{D}_1, \ldots, \boldsymbol{D}_n$, the likelihood function is given by

$$L(\epsilon, \mathcal{D}) = \prod_{j=1}^{m} \frac{1}{Z} \exp\left[-\sum_{i=1}^{n} \epsilon_i[\boldsymbol{x}_i^j]\right],$$

where $\boldsymbol{x}_i^j$ is the value of the variables $\boldsymbol{D}_i$ in the instance x^j and $Z = \sum_{\boldsymbol{x}} \exp\left[-\sum_{i=1}^{n} \epsilon_i[\boldsymbol{x}_i]\right]$ is the normalization constant. This normalization constant is responsible for coupling the estimation parameters and effectively ruling out a closed-form solution. Luckily, this objective function is concave in ϵ, so we have an unconstrained concave maximization problem, which can be solved by simple gradient ascent or second-order methods.

More concretely, for each $\boldsymbol{u}_i \in Val(\boldsymbol{D}_i)$ we have a parameter $\epsilon_{i,\boldsymbol{u}_i} \in \mathbb{R}$. This is the simplest case of complete parameterization. Often, however, parameters may be tied or clamped to zero. This does not change the fundamental complexity or method of estimation. The derivative of the log-likelihood with respect to $\epsilon_{i,\boldsymbol{u}_i}$ is given by

$$\frac{\partial \log L(\epsilon, \mathcal{D})}{\partial \epsilon_{i,\boldsymbol{u}_i}} = \sum_{j=1}^{m} \left[P(\boldsymbol{u}_i \mid \epsilon) - \boldsymbol{1}\{\boldsymbol{x}_i^j = \boldsymbol{u}_i\}\right] = m P(\boldsymbol{u}_i \mid \epsilon) - N_{\boldsymbol{u}_i}.$$

Note that the gradient is zero when the counts of the data correspond exactly with the expected counts predicted by the model. In practice, a prior on the parameters is used to help avoid overfitting. The standard prior is a diagonal Gaussian, $\epsilon \sim N(0, \sigma^2 I)$, which adds an additional factor of $\frac{\epsilon_{i,\boldsymbol{u}_i}}{\sigma^2}$ to the gradient.

To compute the probability $P(\boldsymbol{u}_i \mid \epsilon)$ needed to evaluate the gradient, we need to perform inference in the Markov network. Unlike in Bayesian networks, where parameters of intractable (large treewidth) graphs can be estimated by simple counting because of local normalization, the undirected case requires inference even during the learning stage. This is one of the prices of the flexibility of global normalization in Markov networks. See further discussion in chapter 4. Because of this added complexity, maximum-likelihood learning of the Markov network structure is much more expensive and much less investigated; we will focus below on Bayesian networks.

2.4.3   Learning the Bayesian Network Structure

Next we consider the problem of learning the *structure* of a Bayesian network. There are three broad classes of algorithms for BN structure learning:

Constraint-based approaches These approaches view a Bayesian network as a representation of independencies. They try to test for conditional dependence and independence in the data, and then find a network that best explains these dependencies and independencies. Constraint-based methods are quite intuitive; they closely follow the definition of Bayesian network. A potential disadvantage of these methods is they can be sensitive to failures in individual independence tests.

Score-based approaches These approaches view a Bayesian network as specifying a statistical model, and then address learning as a *model selection* problem. These all operate on the same principle: We define a hypothesis space of potential models — the set of possible network structures we are willing to consider — and a scoring function that measures how well the model fits the observed data. Our computational task is then to find the highest-scoring network structure. The space of Bayesian networks is a combinatorial space, consisting of a superexponential number of structures — $2^{O(n^2)}$. Therefore, even with a scoring function, it is not clear how one can find the highest-scoring network. There are very special cases where we can find the optimal network. In general, however, the problem is NP-hard, and we resort to heuristic search techniques. Score-based methods consider the whole structure at once, and are therefore less sensitive to individual failures and are better at making compromises between the extent to which variables are dependent in the data and the "cost" of adding the edge. The disadvantage of the score-based approaches is that they are in general not gauranteed to find the optimal solution.

Bayesian model averaging approaches The third class of approaches do not attempt to learn a single structure. They are based on a Bayesian framework describing a distribution over possible structures and try to average the prediction of all possible structures. Since the number of structures is immense, performing this task seems impossible. For some classes of models this can be done efficiently, and for others we need to resort to approximations.

In this chapter, we focus on the second approach, score-based approaches to structure selection. For details about the other approaches, see [8].

2.4.3.1   *Structure Scores*

As discussed above, score-based methods approach the problem of structure learning as an optimization problem. We define a score function that can score each candidate structure with respect to the training data, and then search for a high-scoring structure. As can be expected, one of the most important decisions we must make in this framework is the choice of scoring function. In this subsection, we discuss two of the most obvious choices.

The Likelihood Score   A natural choice for scoring function is the likelihood function, which we used for parameter estimation. This measures the probability of the data given a model; thus, it seems intuitive to find a model that would make the data as probable as possible.

Assume that we want to maximize the likelihood of the model. Our goal is to find both a graph $\mathcal{G}$ and parameters $\boldsymbol{\theta}_{\mathcal{G}}$ that maximize the likelihood. It is easy to show that to find the maximum-likelihood $(\mathcal{G}, \boldsymbol{\theta}_{\mathcal{G}})$ pair, we should find the graph structure $\mathcal{G}$ that achieves the highest likelihood when we use the MLE parameters for $\mathcal{G}$. We therefore define

$$\text{score}_L(\mathcal{G} \; : \; \mathcal{D}) = \ell(\langle \mathcal{G}, \hat{\boldsymbol{\theta}}_{\mathcal{G}} \rangle : \mathcal{D}),$$

where $\ell(\langle \mathcal{G}, \hat{\boldsymbol{\theta}}_{\mathcal{G}} \rangle \; : \; \mathcal{D})$ is the logarithm of the likelihood function, and $\hat{\boldsymbol{\theta}}_{\mathcal{G}}$ are the maximum-likelihood parameters for $\mathcal{G}$. (It is typically easier to deal with the logarithm of the likelihood.)

The problem with the likelihood score is that it *overfits* the training data. It will learn a model that precisely fits the specifics of the empirical distribution in our training set. This model captures both dependencies that are "true" of the underlying distribution, and dependencies that are artifacts of the specific set of instances that were given as training data. It therefore fails to generalize well to new data cases: these are sampled from the underlying distribution, which is not identical to the empirical distribution in our training set.

However it is reasonable to use the maximum-likelihood score when there are additional mechanisms that disallow overcomplicated structures. For example, learning networks with a fixed indegree. Such a limitation can constrain the tendency to overfit when using the maximum-likelihood score.

Bayesian Score   An alternative scoring function is based on Bayesian considerations. Recall that the main principle of the Bayesian approach is that, whenever we have uncertainty over anything, we should place a distribution over it. In this case, we have uncertainty both over structure and over parameters. We therefore define a structure prior $P(\mathcal{G})$ that puts a prior probability on different graph structures, and a parameter prior $P(\boldsymbol{\theta}_{\mathcal{G}} \mid \mathcal{G})$ that puts a probability on a different choice of parameters once the graph is given. By Bayes rule, we have

$$P(\mathcal{G} \mid \mathcal{D}) = \frac{P(\mathcal{D} \mid \mathcal{G})P(\mathcal{G})}{P(\mathcal{D})},$$

where, as usual, the denominator is simply a normalizing factor that does not help distinguish between different structures. Then, we define the *Bayesian score* as

$$\text{score}_B(\mathcal{G} \; : \; \mathcal{D}) = \log P(\mathcal{D} \mid \mathcal{G}) + \log P(\mathcal{G}), \qquad (2.23)$$

The ability to ascribe a prior over structures gives us a way of preferring some structures over others. For example, we can penalize dense structures more than sparse ones. It turns out, however, that this term in the score is almost irrelevant compared to the second term. This first term, $P(\mathcal{D} \mid \mathcal{G})$ takes into consideration our uncertainty over the parameters:

$$P(\mathcal{D} \mid \mathcal{G}) = \int_{\Theta_\mathcal{G}} P(\mathcal{D} \mid \boldsymbol{\theta}_\mathcal{G}, \mathcal{G}) P(\boldsymbol{\theta}_\mathcal{G} \mid \mathcal{G}) d\boldsymbol{\theta}_\mathcal{G}, \qquad (2.24)$$

where $P(\mathcal{D} \mid \boldsymbol{\theta}_\mathcal{G}, \mathcal{G})$ is the likelihood of the data given the network $\langle \mathcal{G}, \boldsymbol{\theta}_\mathcal{G} \rangle$ and $P(\boldsymbol{\theta}_\mathcal{G} \mid \mathcal{G})$ is our prior distribution over different parameter values for the network $\mathcal{G}$. This term is the *marginal likelihood* of the data given the structure, since we marginalize out the unknown parameters.

Note that the marginal likelihood is different from the maximum-likelihood score. Both terms examine the likelihood of the data given the structure. The maximum-likelihood score returns the maximum of this function. In contrast, the marginal likelihood is the average value of this function, where we average based on the prior measure $P(\boldsymbol{\theta}_\mathcal{G} \mid \mathcal{G})$.

Instantiating this further, if we consider a network with Dirichlet priors, such that $P(\boldsymbol{\theta}_{X_i|\mathbf{pa}_i} \mid \mathcal{G})$ has hyperparameters $\{\alpha^\mathcal{G}_{x_i^j|\boldsymbol{u}_i} : j = 1, \ldots, |X_i|\}$, then we have that

$$P(\mathcal{D} \mid \mathcal{G}) = \prod_i \prod_{\boldsymbol{u}_i \in Val(\mathbf{Pa}^\mathcal{G}_{X_i})} \frac{\Gamma(\alpha^\mathcal{G}_{X_i|\boldsymbol{u}_i})}{\Gamma(\alpha^\mathcal{G}_{X_i|\boldsymbol{u}_i} + N_{\boldsymbol{u}_i})} \prod_{x_i^j \in Val(X_i)} \left[\frac{\Gamma(\alpha^\mathcal{G}_{x_i^j|\boldsymbol{u}_i} + N_{x_i^j, \boldsymbol{u}_i})}{\Gamma(\alpha^\mathcal{G}_{x_i^j|\boldsymbol{u}_i})} \right],$$

where $\alpha^\mathcal{G}_{X_i|\boldsymbol{u}_i} = \sum_j \alpha^\mathcal{G}_{x_i^j|\boldsymbol{u}_i}$. In practice, we use the logarithm of this formula, which is more manageable to compute numerically.

The Bayesian score is biased toward simpler structures, but as it gets more data, it is willing to recognize that a more complex structure is necessary. In other words, it trades off fit to data with model complexity. To understand behavior, it is useful to consider an approximation to the Bayesian score that better exposes its fundamental properties.

Theorem 2.35

If we use a Dirichlet parameter prior for all parameters in our network, then, as $M \to \infty$, we have that

$$\log P(\mathcal{D} \mid \mathcal{G}) = \ell(\hat{\boldsymbol{\theta}}_{\mathcal{G}} : \mathcal{D}) - \frac{\log M}{2}\mathrm{Dim}[\mathcal{G}] + O(1),$$

where $\mathrm{Dim}[\mathcal{G}]$ is the number of independent parameters in $\mathcal{G}$.

From this we see that the Bayesian score tends precisely to trade off the likelihood — fit to data — on the one hand, and the model complexity on the other.

This approximation is called the *Bayesian information criterion (BIC) score*:

$$\mathrm{score}_{BIC}(\mathcal{G} \; : \; \mathcal{D}) = \ell(\hat{\boldsymbol{\theta}}_{\mathcal{G}} : \mathcal{D}) - \frac{\log M}{2}\mathrm{Dim}[\mathcal{G}]$$

Our next task is to define the actual priors that are used in the Bayesian score. In the case of the prior of network structures, $P(\mathcal{G})$, note that although this term seems to describe our bias for a certain structure, in fact it plays a relatively minor role. As we can see in theorem 2.35, the logarithm of the marginal likelihood grows linearly with the number of examples, while the prior over structures remains constant. Thus, the structure prior does not play an important role in asymptotic analysis as long as it does not rule out (i.e., assign probability 0) any structure.

In part because of this, it is common to use a uniform prior over structures. Nonetheless, the structure prior can make some difference when we consider small samples. Thus, we might want to encode some of our preferences in this prior. For example, we might penalize edges in the graph, and use a prior

$$P(\mathcal{G}) \propto c^{|\mathcal{G}|},$$

where c is some constant smaller than 1, and $|\mathcal{G}|$ is the number of edges in the graph. In both these choices (the uniform, and the penalty per edge) it suffices to use a value that is proportional to the prior, since the normalizing constant is the same for all choices of $\mathcal{G}$ and hence can be ignored.

It is mathematically convenient to assume that the structure prior satisfies *structure modularity*. This condition requires that the prior $P(\mathcal{G})$ is proportional to a product of terms, where each term relates to one family. Formally,

$$P(\mathcal{G}) \propto \prod_i P(\mathbf{Pa}_{X_i} = \mathbf{Pa}^{\mathcal{G}}_{X_i}),$$

where $P(\mathbf{Pa}_{X_i} = \mathbf{Pa}^{\mathcal{G}}_{X_i})$ denotes the prior probability assigned to choosing the specific set of parents for X_i. Structure priors that satisfy this property do not penalize for global properties of the graph (such as its depth), but only for local properties (such as the number of indegrees).

Next we need to represent our parameter priors. The number of possible structures is superexponential, which makes it difficult to elicit separate parameters for each one.

A simple approach is simply to take some fixed Dirichlet distribution, e.g., $Dirichlet(\alpha, \alpha, \alpha, \ldots, \alpha)$, for every parameter, where α is a predetermined constant. A typical choice is $\alpha = 1$. This prior is often referred to as the *K2 prior*, referring to the name of the system where it was first used.

A more sophisticated approach is called the *BDe prior*. We elicit a prior distribution P' over the entire probability space and an equivalent sample size M' for the set of imaginary samples. We then set the parameters as follows:

$$\alpha_{x_i | \mathbf{pa}_i} = M' \cdot P'(x_i, \mathbf{pa}_i).$$

This choice avoids certain inconsistencies exhibited by the K2 prior. We can represent P' as a Bayesian network, whose structure can represent our prior about the domain structure. Most simply, when we have no prior knowledge, we set P' to be the uniform distribution, i.e., the empty Bayesian network with a uniform marginal distribution for each variable.

The BDe score turns out to satisfy an important property. Two networks are said to be *I-equivalent* if they encode the same set of independence statements. Hence based on observed independencies we cannot distinguish between I-equivalent networks. This suggests that based on observing data cases, we do not expect to distinguish between equivalent networks. The BDe score has the desirable property that I-equivalent networks have the same score, or are *score-equivalent*.

2.4.3.2 Search

We now have a well-defined optimization problem. Our input is

- training set $\mathcal{D}$;
- scoring function (including priors, if needed);
- a set $\mathcal{G}$ of possible network structures (incorporating any prior knowledge).

Our desired output is a network structure (from the set of possible structures) that maximizes the score.

It turns out that, for this discussion, we can ignore the specific choice of score. Our search algorithms will apply unchanged to all three of these scores.

An important property of the scores that affects the efficiency of search is their *decomposability*. A score is decomposable if we can write the score of a network structure $\mathcal{G}$:

$$\text{score}(\mathcal{G} \; : \; \mathcal{D}) = \sum_i \text{FamScore}(X_i \mid \mathbf{Pa}_i^{\mathcal{G}} \; : \; \mathcal{D})$$

All of the scores we have considered are decomposable. Another property that is shared by all these scores is *score equivalence*; if $\mathcal{G}$ is independence-equivalent to $\mathcal{G}'$, then $\text{score}(\mathcal{G} \; : \; \mathcal{D}) = \text{score}(\mathcal{G}' \; : \; \mathcal{D})$.

There are several special cases where structure learning is tractable. We won't go into full details, but two important cases are: (1) learning tree-structured networks and (2) learning networks with known ordering over the variables.

A network is *tree-structured* if each variable has at most one parent. In this case, for decomposable, score-equivalent scores, we can construct an undirected graph, where the weight on an edge $X_i \rightarrow X_j$ is the change in network score if we add X_i as the parent of X_j (note that, because of score-equivalence, this is the same as the change if we add X_j as parent of X_i). We can find a weighted spanning tree of this graph in polynomial time. We can transform the undirected spanning tree into a directed spanning tree by choosing an arbitrary root, and directing edges away from the root.

Another interesting tractable case is the problem of learning a BN structure consistent with some known total order $\prec$ over $\mathcal{X}$ and bounded indegree d. In other words, we restrict attention to structures $\mathcal{G}$ where if $X_i \in \mathbf{Pa}_{X_j}^{\mathcal{G}}$ then $X_i \prec X_j$ and $\left| \mathbf{Pa}_{X_j}^{\mathcal{G}} \right| < d$. For some domains, finding an ordering such as this is relatively straightforward; for example, a temporal flow over the order in which variables take on their values. In this case, for each X_i we can evaluate each possible parent-set of size d from $\{X_1, \ldots, X_{i-1}\}$. This is polynomial in n (but exponential in d).

Unfortunately, the general case, finding an optimally scoring $\mathcal{G}^*$, for bounded degree $d \geq 2$, is $\mathcal{NP}$-hard. Instead of aiming for an algorithm that will always find the highest-scoring network, we resort to heuristic algorithms that attempt to find the best network, but are not guaranteed to do so.

To define the heuristic search algorithm, we must define the search space and search procedure. We can think of a search space as a graph, where each vertex or node is a candidate network structure to be considered, and edges denote possible "moves" that the search procedure can perform. The search procedure defines an algorithm that explores the search space, without necessarily seeing all of it . The simplest search procedure is the greedy one that whenever it is a node chooses to move the neighbor that has the highest score, until it reaches a node that has a better score than all of its neighbors.

To elaborate further, in our case a node in the search space is a complete network structure $\mathcal{G}$ over $\mathcal{X}$. There is a tradeoff in how densely each node is connected with how effective the search will be. If each node has few neighbors, then the search procedure has to consider only few options at each point of the search. Thus, it can afford to evaluate each of these options. However, paths from the initial node to a good one might be long and complex. On the other hand, if each node has many neighbors, there are short paths from each point to another, but we might not be able to pick it, because we don't have time to evaluate all of the options at each step.

A good tradeoff for this problem chooses reasonably few neighbors for each node, but ensures that the "diameter" of the search space remains small. A natural choice of neighbors of a network structure is a set of structures that are identical to it except for small "local" modifications. The most commonly used operators which define the local modifications are

Procedure Greedy-Structure-Search (
    $\mathcal{G}_\emptyset$,   // initial network structure
    $\mathcal{D}$ // Fully observed dataset
    score,   // Score
    $\mathcal{O}$,   // A set of search operators
)
```
1     G_best ← G_∅
2     do
3        G ← G_best
4        Progress ← false
5        for each operator o ∈ O
6           G_o ← o(G)    // Result of applying o on G
7           if G_o is legal structure then
8              if score(G_o : D) > score(G_best : D) then
9                 G_best ← G_o
10                Progress ← true
11    while Progress
12
13    return G_best
```

Figure 2.7 Greedy structure search algorithm, with an arbitrary scoring function $\text{score}(\mathcal{G} : \mathcal{D})$.

- add an edge;
- delete an edge;
- reverse an edge.

In other words, if we consider the node $\mathcal{G}$, then the neighboring nodes in the search space are those where we change one edge, either by adding one, deleting one, or reversing the orientation of one. We only consider operations that result in legal networks (i.e., acyclic networks satisfying any constraints such as bounded indegree).

This definition of search space is quite natural and has several desirable properties. First, notice that the diameter of the search space is at most n^2. That is, there is a relatively short path between any two networks we choose. To see this, note that if we consider traversing a path from $\mathcal{G}_1$ to $\mathcal{G}_2$, we can start by deleting all edges in $\mathcal{G}_1$ that do not appear in $\mathcal{G}_2$, and then we can add the edges that are in $\mathcal{G}_2$ and not in $\mathcal{G}_1$. Clearly, the number of steps we take is bounded by the total number of edges we can have, n^2.

Second, recall that the score of a network $\mathcal{G}$ is a sum of local scores. The operations we consider result in changing only one local score term (in the case of addition or deletion of an edge) or two (in the case of edge reversal). Thus, they result in a local change in the score — the "main" mass of the score remains the same. This implies that there is some sense of "continuity" in the score of neighboring nodes.

The search methods most commonly used are *local search procedures*. Such search procedures are characterized by the following design: they keep a "current" candidate node. At each iteration they explore some of the neighboring nodes, and then decide to make a "step" to one of the neighbors and make it the current candidate. These iterations are repeated until some termination condition. In other words, local search procedures can be thought of as keeping one pointer into the search space and moving it around.

One of the simplest, and often used, search procedures is the *greedy hill-climbing procedure*. The intuition is simple. As the name suggests, at each step we take the step that leads to the largest improvement in the score. The actual details of the procedure are shown in figure 2.7. We pick an initial network structure $\mathcal{G}$ as a starting point; this network can be the empty one, a random choice, the best tree, or a network obtained from some prior knowledge. We compute its score. We then consider all of the neighbors of $\mathcal{G}$ in the space — all of the legal networks obtained by applying a single operator to $\mathcal{G}$ — and compute the score for each of them. We then apply the change that leads to the best improvement in the score. We continue this process until no modification improves the score.

We can improve on the performance of greedy hill-climbing by using more clever search algorithms. Some common extensions are:

- **TABU search:** Keep a list of K most recently visited structures and avoid them, i.e., apply the best move that leads to a structure not on the list. This approach deals with local maxima whose "hill" has fewer than K structures.
- **Random restarts:** Once stuck, apply some fixed number of random edge changes and then restart the greedy search. At the end of the search, select the best structure encountered anywhere on the trajectory. This approach can escape from the basin of one local maximum to another.
- **Simulated annealing:** Evaluate operators in random order. If the randomly selected operator induces an uphill step, move to the resulting structure. (Note: it does not have to be the best of the current neighbors.) If the operator induces a downhill step, apply it with probability inversely proportional to the reduction in score. A *temperature parameter* determines the probability of taking downhill steps. As the search progress, the temperature decreases, and the algorithm becomes less likely to take a downhill step.

2.5   Conclusion

This chapter presented a condensed description of graphical models, including their representation, inference algorithms, and learning algorithms. Many topics have not been covered; we refer the reader to [8] for a more complete description.

References

[1] A. Becker and D. Geiger. A sufficiently fast algorithm for finding close to optimal clique trees. *Artificial Intelligence*, 125(1-2):3–17, 2001.

[2]   W. Buntine. Chain graphs for learning. In *Proceedings of the Conference on Uncertainty in Artificial Intelligence*, 1995.

[3]   R. G. Cowell, A. P. Dawid, S. L. Lauritzen, and D. J. Spiegelhalter. *Probabilistic Networks and Expert Systems*. Springer-Verlag, New York, 1999.

[4]   D. Heckerman. A tutorial on learning with Bayesian networks. Technical Report MSR-TR-95-06, Microsoft Research, Seattle, WA, 1996.

[5]   F. V. Jensen. *Bayesian Networks and Decision Graphs*. Springer-Verlag, New York, 2001.

[6]   M. I. Jordan, editor. *Learning in Graphics Models*. The MIT Press, Cambridge, MA, 1998.

[7]   M. I. Jordan. Graphical models. *Statistical Science (Special issue on Bayesian Statistics)*, 19:140–155, 2004.

[8]   D. Koller and N. Friedman. BNs and beyond, 2007. To appear.

[9]   S. Lauritzen. *Graphical Models*. Oxford University Press, New York, 1996.

[10] S. Lauritzen and N. Wermuth. Graphical models for association between variables, some of which are qualitative and some quantitative. *Annals of Statistics*, 17(1):31–57, 1989.

[11] J. Pearl. *Probabilistic Reasoning in Intelligent Systems*. Morgan Kaufmann, San Mateo, CA, 1988.

[12] K. Shoikhet and D. Geiger. A practical algorithm for finding optimal triangulations. In *Proceedings of the National Conference on Artificial Intelligence*, 1997.

3 Inductive Logic Programming in a Nutshell

Sašo Džeroski

Inductive logic programming (ILP) is concerned with the development of techniques and tools for relational data mining (RDM). Besides the ability to deal with data stored in multiple tables, ILP systems are usually able to take into account generally valid background (domain) knowledge in the form of a logic program. They also use the powerful language of logic programs for describing discovered patterns. This chapter introduces the basics of ILP and RDM. First it introduces the basics of logic programming and relates logic programming terminology to database terminology. It then discusses the major settings for, tasks of, and approaches to ILP and RDM. The tasks of learning relational classification rules, decision trees, and association rules and approaches to solving them are discussed next, followed by relational distance-based approaches. The chapter also briefly discusses recent trends in ILP and RDM research.

3.1 Introduction

From a knowledge discovery in database (KDD) perspective, we can say that inductive logic programming (ILP) is concerned with the development of techniques and tools for relational data mining (RDM). While typical data mining approaches find patterns in a given single table, relational data mining approaches find patterns in a given relational database. In a typical relational database, data resides in multiple tables. ILP tools can be applied directly to such multi-relational data to find patterns that involve multiple relations. This is a distinguishing feature of ILP approaches: most other data mining approaches can only deal with data that resides in a single table and require preprocessing to integrate data from multiple tables (e.g., through joins or aggregation) into a single table before they can be applied.

Integrating data from multiple tables through joins or aggregation can cause loss of meaning or information. Suppose we are given the relation *customer*(*CustID*, *Name*, *Age*, *SpendsALot*) and the relation *purchase*(*CustID*, *ProductID*, *Date*, *Value*, *PaymentMode*), where each customer can make multiple purchases, and we are interested in characterizing customers that spend a lot. Integrating the two relations via a natural join will give rise to a relation *purchase*1 where each row corresponds to a purchase and not to a customer. One possible aggregation would give rise to the relation *customer*1(*CustID, Age, NofPurchases, TotalValue, SpendsALot*). In this case, however, some information has been clearly lost during the aggregation process.

The following pattern can be discovered by an ILP system if the relations *customer* and *purchase* are considered together.

$$customer(CID, Name, Age, yes) \leftarrow$$
$$Age > 30 \land$$
$$purchase(CID, PID, D, Value, PM) \land$$
$$PM = credit\_card \land Value > 100.$$

This pattern says: "a customer spends a lot if she is older than 30, has purchased a product of value more than 100, and paid for it by credit card." It would not be possible to induce such a pattern from either of the relations *purchase*1 and *customer*1 considered on their own.

Besides the ability to deal with data stored in multiple tables directly, ILP systems are usually able to take into account generally valid background (domain) knowledge in the form of a logic program. The ability to take into account background knowledge and the expressive power of the language of discovered patterns are also distinctive for ILP.

Note that data mining approaches that find patterns in a given single table are referred to as *attribute-value* or *propositional learning* approaches, as the patterns they find can be expressed in propositional logic. ILP approaches are also referred to as first-order learning approaches, or relational learning approaches, as the patterns they find are expressed in the relational formalism of first-order logic. A more detailed discussion of the single table assumption, the problems resulting from it, and how a relational representation alleviates these problems can be found in [49] and in (chapter 4 of [15]).

The remainder of this chapter first introduces the basics of logic programming and relates logic programming terminology to database terminology. It then discusses the major settings for, tasks of, and approaches to ILP and RDM. The tasks of learning relational classification rules, decision trees, and association rules and approaches to solving them are discussed in the following three sections. Relational distance-based approaches are covered next. The chapter concludes with a brief discussion of recent trends in ILP and RDM research.

3.2   Logic Programming

We first briefly describe the basic logic programming terminology and relate it to database terminology, then proceed with a more complete introduction to logic programming. The latter discusses both the syntax and semantics of logic programs. While syntax defines the language of logic programs, semantics is concerned with assigning meaning (truth-values) to such statements. Proof theory focuses on (deductive) reasoning with such statements.

For a thorough treatment of logic programming we refer to the standard textbook of Lloyd [31]. The overview below is mostly based on the comprehensive and easily readable text by Hogger [22].

3.2.1   The Basics of Logic Programming

Logic programs consist of clauses. We can think of clauses as first-order rules, where the conclusion part is termed the head and the condition part the body of the clause. The head and body of a clause consist of atoms, an atom being a predicate applied to some arguments, which are called terms. In Datalog, terms are variables and constants, while in general they may consist of function symbols applied to other terms. Ground clauses have no variables.

Consider the clause $father(X, Y) \lor mother(X, Y) \leftarrow parent(X, Y)$. It reads: "if X is a parent of Y, then X is the father of Y or X is the mother of Y" ($\lor$ stands for logical or). $parent(X, Y)$ is the body of the clause, and $father(X, Y) \lor mother(X, Y)$ is the head. $parent$, $father$, and $mother$ are predicates, X and Y are variables, and $parent(X, Y)$, $father(X, Y)$, and $mother(X, Y)$ are atoms. We adopt the Prolog [4] syntax and start variable names with capital letters. Variables in clauses are implicitly universally quantified. The above clause thus stands for the logical formula $\forall X \forall Y : father(X, Y) \lor mother(X, Y) \lor \neg parent(X, Y)$. Clauses are also viewed as sets of literals, where a literal is an atom or its negation. The above clause is then the set $\{father(X, Y), mother(X, Y), \neg parent(X, Y)\}$.

As opposed to full clauses, definite clauses contain exactly one atom in the head. As compared to definite clauses, program clauses can also contain negated atoms in the body. The clause in the paragraph above is a full clause; the clause $ancestor(X, Y) \leftarrow parent(Z, Y) \land ancestor(X, Z)$ is a definite clause ($\land$ stands for logical and). It is also a recursive clause, since it defines the relation $ancestor$ in terms of itself and the relation $parent$. The clause $mother(X, Y) \leftarrow parent(X, Y) \land not\ male(X)$ is a program clause.

A set of clauses is called a clausal theory. Logic programs are sets of program clauses. A set of program clauses with the same predicate in the head is called a predicate definition. Most ILP approaches learn predicate definitions.

A predicate in logic programming corresponds to a relation in a relational database. An n-ary relation p is formally defined as a set of tuples [47], i.e., a subset of the Cartesian product of n domains $D_1 \times D_2 \times \ldots \times D_n$, where a domain (or a type) is a set of values. It is assumed that a relation is finite unless stated otherwise. A relational database (RDB) is a set of relations.

Thus, a predicate corresponds to a relation, and the arguments of a predicate correspond to the attributes of a relation. The major difference is that the attributes of a relation are typed (i.e., a domain is associated with each attribute). For

Table 3.1   Database and logic programming terms

DB terminology	LP terminology
relation name p	predicate symbol p
attribute of relation p	argument of predicate p
tuple $\langle a_1, \ldots, a_n \rangle$	ground fact $p(a_1, \ldots, a_n)$
relation p -	predicate p -
a set of tuples	defined extensionally
	by a set of ground facts
relation q	predicate q
defined as a view	defined intensionally
	by a set of rules (clauses)

example, in the relation $lives\_in(X, Y)$, we may want to specify that X is of type *person* and Y is of type *city*. Database clauses are typed program clauses.

A deductive database (DDB) is a set of database clauses. In DDBs, relations can be defined extensionally as sets of tuples (as in RDBs) or intensionally as sets of database clauses. Database clauses use variables and function symbols in predicate arguments and the language of DDBs is substantially more expressive than the language of RDBs [31, 47]. A deductive Datalog database consists of definite database clauses with no function symbols.

Table 3.1 relates basic database and logic programming terms. For a full treatment of logic programming, RDBs, and DDBs, we refer the reader to [31] and [47].

3.2.2   The Syntax and Semantics of Logic Programs

The basic concepts of logic programming include the language (syntax) of logic programs, as well as notions from model and proof theory (semantics). The syntax defines what are legal sentences/statements in the language of logic programs. Model theory (semantics) is concerned with assigning meaning (truth-values) to such statements. Proof theory focuses on (deductive) reasoning with such statements.

3.2.2.1   *Syntax: The Language*

A first-order *alphabet* consists of variables, predicate symbols, and function symbols (which include constants). A *variable* is a term, and a *function symbol* immediately followed by a bracketed n-tuple of terms is a term. Thus $f(g(X), h)$ is a term when f, g, and h are function symbols and X is a variable – strings starting with lowercase letters denote predicate and function symbols, while strings starting with uppercase letters denote variables. A *constant* is a function symbol of arity 0 (i.e., followed by a bracketed 0-tuple of terms, which is often left implicit). A *predicate symbol* immediately followed by a bracketed n-tuple of terms is called an *atomic formula* or *atom*. For example, $mother(maja, filip)$ and $father(X, Y)$ are atoms.

A *well-formed formula* (also called a sentence or statement) is either an atomic formula or takes one of the following forms: F, (F), $\overline{F}$, $F \vee G$, $F \wedge G$, $F \leftarrow G$, $F \leftrightarrow G$, $\forall X : F$ and $\exists X : F$, where F and G are well-formed formulae and X is a variable. $\overline{F}$ denotes the negation of F, $\vee$ denotes logical disjunction (or), and $\wedge$ logical conjunction (and). $F \leftarrow G$ stands for implication (F if G, $F \vee \overline{G}$) and $F \leftrightarrow G$ stands for equivalence (F if and only if G). $\forall$ and $\exists$ are the universal (for all X F holds) and the existential quantifier (there exists an X such that F holds). In the formulae $\forall X : F$ and $\exists X : F$, all occurrences of X are said to be *bound*. A *sentence* or a *closed formula* is a well-formed formula in which every occurrence of every variable symbol is bound. For example, $\forall Y \exists X father(X, Y)$ is a sentence, while $father(X, andy)$ is not.

The clausal form is a normal form for first-order sentences. A *clause* is a disjunction of *literals* – a *positive literal* is an atom, a *negative literal* the negation of an atom – preceded by a prefix of universal quantifiers, one for each variable appearing in the disjunction. In other words, a clause is a formula of the form $\forall X_1 \forall X_2 ... \forall X_s (L_1 \vee L_2 \vee ...L_m)$, where each L_i is a literal and $X_1, X_2, ..., X_s$ are all the variables occurring in $L_1 \vee L_2 \vee ...L_m$.

A clause can also be represented as a finite set (possibly empty) of literals. The set $\{A_1, A_2, ..., A_h, \overline{B_1}, \overline{B_2}, ..., \overline{B_b}\}$, where A_i and B_i are atoms, stands for the clause $(A_1 \vee ... \vee A_h \vee \overline{B_1} \vee ... \vee \overline{B_b})$, which is equivalently represented as $A_1 \vee ... \vee A_h \leftarrow B_1 \wedge ... \wedge B_b$. Most commonly, this same clause is written as $A_1, ..., A_h \leftarrow B_1, ..., B_b$, where $A_1, ..., A_h$ is called the *head* and $B_1, ..., B_b$ the *body* of the clause. Commas in the head of the clause denote logical disjunction, while commas in the body of the clause denote logical conjunction. A set of clauses is called a *clausal theory* and represents the conjunction of its clauses.

A clause is a *Horn clause* if it contains at most one positive literal; it is a *definite clause* if it contains exactly one positive literal. A set of definite clauses is called a *definite logic program*. A fact is a definite clause with an empty body, e.g., $parent(mother(X), X) \leftarrow$, also written simply as $parent(mother(X), X)$. A *goal* (also called a *query*) is a Horn clause with no positive literals.

A *program clause* is a clause of the form $A \leftarrow L_1, ..., L_m$ where A is an atom, and each of $L_1, ..., L_m$ is a positive or negative literal. A negative literal in the body of a program clause is written in the form *not B*, where B is an atom. A *normal program* (or *logic program*) is a set of program clauses. A *predicate definition* is a set of program clauses with the same predicate symbol (and arity) in their heads.

Let us now illustrate the above definitions with some examples. The clause

$$daughter(X, Y) \leftarrow female(X), mother(Y, X)$$

is a definite program clause, while the clause

$$daughter(X, Y) \leftarrow not\ male(X), father(Y, X)$$

is a normal program clause. Together, the two clauses constitute a predicate definition of the predicate *daughter*/2. This predicate definition is also a normal logic program. The first clause is an abbreviated representation of the formula

$$\forall X \forall Y : daughter(X, Y) \vee \overline{female(X)} \vee \overline{mother(Y, X)}$$

and can also be written in set notation as

$$\{daughter(X, Y), \overline{female(X)}, \overline{mother(Y, X)}\}.$$

The set of *variables* in a term, atom, or clause F is denoted by $vars(F)$. A *substitution* $\theta = \{V_1/t_1, ..., V_n/t_n\}$ is an assignment of terms t_i to variables V_i. Applying a substitution θ to a term, atom, or clause F yields the instantiated term, atom, or clause $F\theta$ where all occurrences of the variables V_i are simultaneously replaced by the term t_i. A term, atom, or clause F is called *ground* when there is no variable occurring in F, i.e., $vars(F) = \emptyset$. The fact $daughter(mary, ann)$ is thus ground.

A clause or clausal theory is called *function-free* if it contains only variables as terms, i.e., contains no function symbols (this also means no constants). The clause $daughter(X, Y) \leftarrow female(X), mother(Y, X)$ is function-free and the clause $even(s(s(X)) \leftarrow even(X)$ is not. A *Datalog clause* (program) is a definite clause (program) that contains no function symbols of nonzero arity. This means that only variables and constants can be used as predicate arguments. The size of a term, atom, clause, or a clausal theory T is the number of symbols that appear in T, i.e., the number of all occurrences in T of predicate symbols, function symbols, and variables.

3.2.2.2   Semantics: Model Theory

Model theory is concerned with attributing meaning (truth-value) to sentences (well-formed formulae) in a first-order language. Informally, the sentence is mapped to some statement about a chosen domain through a process known as interpretation. An *interpretation* is determined by the set of ground facts (ground atomic formulae) to which it assigns the value true. Sentences involving variables and quantifiers are interpreted by using the truth-values of the ground atomic formulae and a fixed set of rules for interpreting logical operations and quantifiers, such as "$\overline{F}$ is true if and only if F is false."

An interpretation which gives the value true to a sentence is said to satisfy the sentence; such an interpretation is called a *model* for the sentence. An interpretation which does not satisfy a sentence is called a *counter-model* for that sentence. By extension, we also have the notion of a model (counter-model) for a set of sentences (e.g., for a clausal theory): an interpretation is a model for the set if and only if it is a model for each of the set's members. A sentence (set of sentences) is *satisfiable* if it has at least one model; otherwise it is *unsatisfiable*.

A sentence F *logically implies* a sentence G if and only if every model for F is also a model for G. We denote this by $F \models G$. Alternatively, we say that G is a *logical* (or *semantic*) *consequence* of F. By extension, we have the notion of *logical implication* between sets of sentences.

A *Herbrand interpretation* over a first-order alphabet is a set of ground facts constructed with the predicate symbols in the alphabet and the ground terms from the corresponding Herbrand domain of function symbols; this is the set of ground atoms considered to be true by the interpretation. A Herbrand interpretation I is a model for a clause c if and only if for all substitutions θ such that $c\theta$ is ground $body(c)\theta \subset I$ implies $head(c)\theta \cap I \neq \emptyset$. In that case, we say c is true in I. A Herbrand interpretation I is a model for a clausal theory T if and only if it is a model for all clauses in T. We say that I is a *Herbrand model* of c, respectively T.

Roughly speaking, the truth of a clause c in a (finite) interpretation I can be determined by running the goal (query) $body(c), not\ head(c)$ on a database containing I, using a *theorem prover* such as Prolog [4]. If the query succeeds, the clause is false in I; if it fails, the clause is true. Analogously, one can determine the truth of a clause c in the *minimal (least) Herbrand model* of a theory T by running the goal $body(c), not\ head(c)$ on a database containing T.

To illustrate the above notions, consider the Herbrand interpretation $i = \{parent(saso, filip), parent(maja, filip), son(filip, saso), son(filip, maja)\}$.
The clause $c = parent(X, Y) \leftarrow son(Y, X)$ is true in i, i.e., i is a model of c. On the other hand, i is not a model of the clause $parent(X, X) \leftarrow$ (which means that everybody is their own parent).

3.2.3 Semantics: Proof Theory

Proof theory focuses on (deductive) reasoning with logic programs. Whereas model theory considers the assignment of meaning to sentences, proof theory considers the generation of sentences (conclusions) from other sentences (premises). More specifically, proof theory considers the *derivability* of sentences in the context of some set of inference rules, i.e., rules for sentence derivation. Formally, an inference system consists of an initial set S of sentences (axioms) and a set R of inference rules.

Using the inference rules, we can derive new sentences from S and/or other derived sentences. The fact that sentence s can be derived from S is denoted $S \vdash s$. A proof is a sequence $s_1, s_2, ..., s_n$, such that each s_i is either in S or derivable using R from S and $s_1, ..., s_{i-1}$. Such a proof is also called a *derivation* or *deduction*. Note that the above notions are of entirely syntactic nature. They are directly relevant to the computational aspects of automated deductive inference.

The set of inference rules R defines the derivability relation $\vdash$. A set of inference rules is *sound* if the corresponding derivability relation is a subset of the logical implication relation, i.e., for all S and s, if $S \vdash s$, then $S \models s$. It is *complete* if the other direction of the implication holds, i.e., for all S and s, if $S \models s$, then $S \vdash s$. The properties of *soundness* and *completeness* establish a relation between the notions of *syntactic* ($\vdash$) and *semantic* ($\models$) *entailment* in logic programming and first-order logic. When the set of inference rules is both sound and complete, the two notions coincide.

Resolution comprises a single inference rule applicable to clausal-form logic. From any two clauses having an appropriate form, resolution derives a new clause as their consequence. For example, the clauses $daughter(X, Y) \leftarrow female(X), parent(Y, X)$ and $female(sonja) \leftarrow$ resolve into $daughter(sonja, Y) \leftarrow parent(Y, sonja)$. Resolution is sound: every resolvent is implied by its parents. It is also refutation complete: the empty clause is derivable by resolution from any set S of Horn clauses if S is unsatisfiable.

3.3 Inductive Logic Programming: Settings and Approaches

Logic programming as a subset of first-order logic is mostly concerned with deductive inference. ILP, on the other hand, is concerned with inductive inference. It generalizes from individual instances/observations in the presence of background knowledge, finding regularities/hypotheses about yet unseen instances.

In this section, we discuss the different ILP settings as well as the different relational learning tasks, starting with the induction of logic programs (sets of relational rules). We also discuss the two major approaches to solving relational learning tasks, namely transforming relational problems to propositional form and upgrading propositional algorithms to a relational setting.

3.3.1 Logical Settings for Concept Learning

One of the most basic and most often considered tasks in machine learning is the task of inductive concept learning (table 3.3.1). Given $\mathcal{U}$, a universal set of objects (observations), a *concept* $\mathcal{C}$ is a subset of objects in $\mathcal{U}$, $\mathcal{C} \subseteq \mathcal{U}$. For example, if $\mathcal{U}$ is the set of all patients in a given hospital, $\mathcal{C}$ could be the set of all patients diagnosed with hepatitis A. The task of *inductive concept learning* is defined as follows: Given instances and non-instances of concept $\mathcal{C}$, find a hypothesis (classifier) H able to tell whether $x \in \mathcal{C}$, for each $x \in \mathcal{U}$.

To define the task of inductive concept learning more precisely, we need to specify $\mathcal{U}$ the space of instances (examples), as well as the space of hypotheses considered. This is done through specifying the languages of examples (L_E) and concept descriptions (L_H). In addition, a coverage relation $covers(H, e)$ has to be specified, which tells us when an example e is considered to belong to the concept represented by hypothesis H. Examples that belong to the target concept are termed positive; those that do not are termed negative. Given positive and negative examples, we want hypotheses that are complete (cover all positive examples) and consistent (do not cover negative examples).

Looking at concept learning in a logical framework, De Raedt [11] considers three settings for concept learning. The key aspect that varies in these settings is

Table 3.2 The task of inductive concept learning

Given:

- a language of examples L_E
- a language of concept descriptions L_H
- a **covers** relation between L_H and L_E, defining when
  an example e is *covered* by a hypothesis H: $covers(H, e)$
- sets of positive P and negative N examples described in L_E

Find hypothesis H from L_H, such that

- **completeness:** H covers all positive examples $p \in P$
- **consistency:** H does not cover any negative example $n \in N$

---

the notion of coverage, but the languages L_E and L_H vary as well. We characterize these for each of the three settings below.

- In *learning from entailment*, the coverage relation is defined as $covers(H, e)$ iff $H \models e$. The hypothesis logically entails the example. Here H is a clausal theory and e is a clause.

- In *learning from interpretations*, we have $covers(H, e)$ iff e is model of H. The example has to be a model of the hypothesis. H is a clausal theory and e is a Herbrand interpretation.

- In *learning from satisfiability*, $covers(H, e)$ iff $H \wedge e \not\models \perp$. The example and the hypothesis taken together have to be satisfiable. Here both H and e are clausal theories.

The setting of learning from entailment, introduced by Muggleton [34], is the one that has received the most attention in the field of ILP. The alternative ILP setting of learning from interpretations was proposed by De Raedt and Džeroski [14]: this setting is a natural generalization of propositional learning. Many learning algorithms for propositional learning have been upgraded to the learning from interpretations ILP setting. Finally, the setting of learning from satisfiability was introduced by Wrobel and Džeroski [50], but has rarely been used in practice due to computational complexity problems.

De Raedt [11] also discusses the relationships among the three settings for concept learning. Learning from finite interpretations reduces to learning from entailment. Learning from entailment reduces to learning from satisfiability. Learning from interpretations is thus the easiest and learning from satisfiability the hardest of the three settings.

As introduced above, the logical settings for concept learning do not take into account background knowledge, one of the essential ingredients of ILP. However, the definitions of the settings are easily extended to take it into account. Given background knowledge B, which in its most general form can be a clausal theory, the definition of coverage should be modified by replacing H with $B \wedge H$ for all three settings.

3.3.2   The ILP Task of Relational Rule Induction

The most commonly addressed task in ILP is the task of learning logical definitions of relations [40], where tuples that belong or do not belong to the target relation are given as examples. From training examples ILP then induces a logic program (predicate definition) corresponding to a view that defines the target relation in terms of other relations that are given as background knowledge. This classical ILP task is addressed, for instance, by the seminal MIS system [44] (rightfully considered as one of the most influential ancestors of ILP) and one of the best known ILP systems FOIL [40].

Given is a set of examples, i.e., tuples that belong to the target relation p (positive examples) and tuples that do not belong to p (negative examples). Given are also background relations (or background predicates) q_i that constitute the background knowledge and can be used in the learned definition of p. Finally, a hypothesis language, specifying syntactic restrictions on the definition of p, is also given (either explicitly or implicitly). The task is to find a definition of the target relation p that is consistent and complete, i.e., explains all the positive and none of the negative tuples.

Formally, given is a set of examples $E = P \cup N$, where P contains positive and N negative examples, and background knowledge B. The task is to find a hypothesis H such that $\forall e \in P : B \wedge H \models e$ (H is complete) and $\forall e \in N : B \wedge H \not\models e$ (H is consistent), where $\models$ stands for logical implication or entailment. This setting, introduced by Muggleton [34] (and discussed in the previous section), is thus also called learning from entailment.

In the most general formulation, each e, as well as B and H, can be a clausal theory. In practice, each e is most often a ground example (tuple), B is a relational database (which may or may not contain views), and H is a definite logic program. The semantic entailment ($\models$) is in practice replaced with syntactic entailment ($\vdash$) or provability, where the resolution inference rule (as implemented in Prolog) is most often used to prove examples from a hypothesis and the background knowledge. In learning from entailment, a positive fact is explained if it can be found among the answer substitutions for h produced by a query $? - b$ on database B, where $h \leftarrow b$ is a clause in H. In learning from interpretations, a clause $h \leftarrow b$ from H is true in the minimal Herbrand model of B if the query $b \wedge \neg h$ fails on B.

As an illustration, consider the task of defining relation $daughter(X, Y)$, which states that person X is a daughter of person Y, in terms of the background knowledge relations $female$ and $parent$. These relations are given in table 3.3. There are two positive and two negative examples of the target relation $daughter$. In the hypothesis language of definite program clauses it is possible to formulate the following definition of the target relation:

$$daughter(X, Y) \leftarrow female(X), parent(Y, X),$$

which is consistent and complete with respect to the background knowledge and the training examples.

Table 3.3 A simple ILP problem: learning the *daughter* relation. Positive examples are denoted by $\oplus$ and negative by $\ominus$

Training examples		Background knowledge	
$daughter(mary, ann)$.	$\oplus$	$parent(ann, mary)$.	$female(ann)$.
$daughter(eve, tom)$.	$\oplus$	$parent(ann, tom)$.	$female(mary)$.
$daughter(tom, ann)$.	$\ominus$	$parent(tom, eve)$.	$female(eve)$.
$daughter(eve, ann)$.	$\ominus$	$parent(tom, ian)$.	

In general, depending on the background knowledge, the hypothesis language, and the complexity of the target concept, the target predicate definition may consist of a set of clauses, such as

$$daughter(X, Y) \leftarrow female(X), mother(Y, X),$$
$$daughter(X, Y) \leftarrow female(X), father(Y, X),$$

if the relations *mother* and *father* were given in the background knowledge instead of the *parent* relation.

The hypothesis language is typically a subset of the language of program clauses. As the complexity of learning grows with the expressiveness of the hypothesis language, restrictions have to be imposed on hypothesized clauses. Typical restrictions are the exclusion of recursion and restrictions on variables that appear in the body of the clause but not in its head (so-called new variables).

Declarative bias [38] explicitly specifies the language of hypotheses (clauses) considered by the ILP system at hand. This is input to the learning system (and not hard-wired in the learning algorithm). Various types of declarative bias have been used by different ILP systems, such as argument types and input/output modes, parameterized language bias (e.g., maximum number of variables, literals, depth of variables, arity, etc.), clause templates, and grammars. For example, a suitable clause template for learning family relationships would be $P(X, Y) \leftarrow Q(X, Z), R(Z, Y)$. Here P, Q, and R are second order variables that can be replaced by predicates, e.g., *grandmother*, *mother*, and *parent*. The same template can be used to learn the notions of grandmother and a grandfather.

3.3.3   Other Tasks of Relational Learning

Initial efforts in ILP focused on relational rule induction, more precisely on concept learning in first-order logic and synthesis of logic programs; cf. [34]. An overview of early work is given in the textbook on ILP by Lavrač and Džeroski [30]. Representative early ILP systems addressing this task are CIGOL [36], FOIL [40], GOLEM [37], and LINUS [29]. More recent representative ILP systems are PROGOL [35] and ALEPH [46].

State-of-the-art ILP approaches now span most of the spectrum of data mining tasks and use a variety of techniques to address these. The distinguishing features of using multiple relations directly and discovering patterns expressed in first-order logic are present throughout: the ILP approaches can thus be viewed as upgrades of traditional approaches. Van Laer and De Raedt [48] (chapter 10 of [15]) present a case study of upgrading a propositional approach to classification rule induction to first-order logic. Note, however, that upgrading to first-order logic is non-trivial: the expressive power of first-order logic implies computational costs and much work is needed in balancing the expressive power of the pattern languages used and the computational complexity of the data mining algorithm looking for such patterns. This search for a balance between the two has occupied much of the ILP research in the last ten years.

Present ILP approaches to multi-class classification involve the induction of relational classification rules (ICL [48]), as well as first order logical decision trees in TILDE [3] and S-CART [26]. ICL upgrades the propositional rule inducer CN2 [6]. TILDE and S-CART upgrade decision tree induction as implemented in C4.5 [41] and CART [5]. A nearest-neighbor approach to relational classification is implemented in RIBL [21] and its successor RIBL2.

Relational regression approaches upgrade propositional regression tree and rules approaches. TILDE and S-CART, as well as RIBL2, can handle continuous classes. FORS [23] learns decision lists (ordered sets of rules) for relational regression.

The main nonpredictive or descriptive data mining tasks are clustering and discovery of association rules. These have been also addressed in a first-order logic setting. The RIBL distance measure has been used to perform hierarchical agglomerative clustering in RDBC , as well as k-means clustering (see section 3.7). Section 3.6 describes a relational approach to the discovery of frequent queries and query extensions, a first-order version of association rules.

With such a wide arsenal of RDM techniques, there is also a variety of practical applications. ILP has been successfully applied to discover knowledge from relational data and background knowledge in the areas of molecular biology (including drug design, protein structure prediction, and functional genomics), environmental sciences, traffic control, and natural language processing. An overview of such applications is given by Džeroski [19] and (chapter 14 in [15]).

3.3.4   Transforming ILP Problems to Propositional Form

One of the early approaches to ILP, implemented in the ILP system LINUS [29], is based on the idea that the use of background knowledge can introduce new attributes for learning. The learning problem is transformed from relational to attribute-value form and solved by an attribute-value learner. An advantage of this approach is that data mining algorithms that work on a single table (and this is the majority of existing data mining algorithms) become applicable after the transformation.

This approach, however, is feasible only for a restricted class of ILP problems. Thus, the hypothesis language of LINUS is restricted to function-free program clauses which are typed (each variable is associated with a predetermined set of values), constrained (all variables in the body of a clause also appear in the head), and nonrecursive (the predicate symbol in the head does not appear in any of the literals in the body).

The LINUS algorithm, which solves ILP problems by transforming them into propositional form, consists of the following three steps:

- The learning problem is transformed from relational to attribute-value form.

- The transformed learning problem is solved by an attribute-value learner.

- The induced hypothesis is transformed back into relational form.

The above algorithm allows for a variety of approaches developed for propositional problems, including noise-handling techniques in attribute-value algorithms, such as CN2 [7], to be used for learning relations. It is illustrated on the simple ILP problem of learning family relations. The task is to define the target relation $daughter(X, Y)$, which states that person X is a daughter of person Y, in terms of the background knowledge relations $female$, $male$, and $parent$.

Table 3.4   Nonground background knowledge for learning the *daughter* relation

Training examples		Background knowledge		
$daughter(mary, ann)$.	$\oplus$	$parent(X, Y) \leftarrow$	$mother(ann, mary)$.	$female(ann)$.
$daughter(eve, tom)$.	$\oplus$	$mother(X, Y)$.	$mother(ann, tom)$.	$female(mary)$.
$daughter(tom, ann)$.	$\ominus$	$parent(X, Y) \leftarrow$	$father(tom, eve)$.	$female(eve)$.
$daughter(eve, ann)$.	$\ominus$	$father(X, Y)$.	$father(tom, ian)$.	

All the variables are of the type *person*, defined as $person = \{ann,\ eve,\ ian,\ mary,\ tom\}$. There are two positive and two negative examples of the target relation. The training examples and the relations from the background knowledge are given in table 3.3. However, since the LINUS approach can use nonground background knowledge, let us assume that the background knowledge from table 3.4 is given.

Table 3.5 Propositional form of the *daughter* relation problem

	Variables		Propositional features							
C	X	Y	$f(X)$	$f(Y)$	$m(X)$	$m(Y)$	$p(X,X)$	$p(X,Y)$	$p(Y,X)$	$p(Y,Y)$
$\oplus$	*mary*	*ann*	*true*	*true*	*false*	*false*	*false*	*false*	*true*	*false*
$\oplus$	*eve*	*tom*	*true*	*false*	*false*	*true*	*false*	*false*	*true*	*false*
$\ominus$	*tom*	*ann*	*false*	*true*	*true*	*false*	*false*	*false*	*true*	*false*
$\ominus$	*eve*	*ann*	*true*	*true*	*false*	*false*	*false*	*false*	*false*	*false*

The first step of the algorithm, i.e., the transformation of the ILP problem into attribute-value form, is performed as follows. The possible applications of the background predicates on the arguments of the target relation are determined, taking into account argument types. Each such application introduces a new attribute. In our example, all variables are of the same type *person*. The corresponding attribute-value learning problem is given in table 3.5, where f stands for *female*, m for *male*, and p for *parent*. The attribute-value tuples are generalizations (relative to the given background knowledge) of the individual facts about the target relation.

In table 3.5, *variables* stand for the arguments of the target relation, and *propositional features* denote the newly constructed attributes of the propositional learning task. When learning function-free clauses, only the new attributes (propositional features) are considered for learning.

In the second step, an attribute-value learning program induces the following if-then rule from the tuples in table 3.5:

$Class = \oplus$ **if** $[female(X) = true] \wedge [parent(Y,X) = true]$

In the last step, the induced if-then rules are transformed into clauses. In our example, we get the following clause:

$daughter(X,Y) \leftarrow female(X), parent(Y,X).$

The LINUS approach has been extended to handle determinate clauses [16, 30], which allow the introduction of determinate new variables (which have a unique value for each training example). There also exist a number of other approaches to propositionalization, some of them very recent: an overview is given by Kramer et al. [28] (chapter 11 of [15]).

Let us emphasize again, however, that it is in general not possible to transform an ILP problem into a propositional (attribute-value) form efficiently. De Raedt [12] treats the relation between attribute-value learning and ILP in detail, showing that propositionalization of some more complex ILP problems is possible, but results in attribute-value problems that are exponentially large. This has also been the main reason for the development of a variety of new RDM and ILP techniques by upgrading propositional approaches.

3.3.5 Upgrading Propositional Approaches

ILP/RDM algorithms have many things in common with propositional learning algorithms. In particular, they share the learning as search paradigm, i.e., they search for patterns valid in the given data. The key differences lie in the representation of data and patterns, refinement operators/generality relationships, and testing coverage (i.e., whether a rule explains an example).

Van Laer and De Raedt [48] explicitly formulate a recipe for upgrading propositional algorithms to deal with relational data and patterns. The key idea is to keep as much of the propositional algorithm as possible and upgrade only the key notions. For rule induction, the key notions are the refinement operator and coverage relationship. For distance-based approaches, the notion of distance is the key one. By carefully upgrading the key notions of a propositional algorithm, an RDM/ILP algorithm can be developed that has the original propositional algorithm as a special case.

The recipe has been followed (more or less exactly) to develop ILP systems for rule induction, well before it was formulated explicitly. The well-known FOIL [40] system can be seen as an upgrade of the propositional rule induction program CN2 [7]. Another well-known ILP system, PROGOL [35], can be viewed as upgrading the AQ approach [33] to rule induction.

More recently, the upgrading approach has been used to develop a number of RDM approaches that address data mining tasks other than binary classification. These include the discovery of frequent Datalog patterns and relational association rules [9] (chapter 8 of [15]), [8], the induction of relational decision trees (structural classification and regression trees [27] and first-order logical decision trees [3]), and relational distance-based approaches to classification and clustering ([25], chapter 9 of [15], [21]). The algorithms developed have as special cases well-known propositional algorithms, such as the APRIORI algorithm for finding frequent patterns; the CART and C4.5 algorithms for learning decision trees; k-nearest neighbor classification, hierarchical and k-medoids clustering. In the following two sections, we briefly review how the propositional approaches for association rule discovery and decision tree inducion have been lifted to a relational framework, highlighting the key differences between the relational algorithms and their propositional counterparts.

3.4 Relational Classification Rules

The first and still most commonly addressed problem in ILP is the one of learning logic programs (sets of relational rules for binary classification). This section first describes the covering algorithm for inducing sets of rules, then the induction of individual rules. In particular, we discuss how the space of rules/clauses is structured and searched.

3.4.1 The Covering Approach to Relational Rule Induction

From a data mining perspective, the task described above is a binary classification task, where one of two classes is assigned to the examples (tuples): $\oplus$ (positive) or

Table 3.6   Top-down (general-to-specific) search of refinement graphs

---

hypothesis $H := \emptyset$
repeat {covering}
    clause $c := p(X_1, ...X_n) \leftarrow$
    repeat {specialization}
        build the set S of all refinements of c
        $c :=$ the best element of S (according to a heuristic)
    until stopping criterion is satisfied ($B \cup H \cup \{c\}$ is consistent)
    add c to H
    delete all examples from P entailed by $B \cup H \cup \{c\}$
until stopping criterion is satisfied
        ($B \cup H \cup \{c\}$ is complete)

$\ominus$ (negative). Classification is one of the most commonly addressed tasks within the data mining community and includes approaches for rule induction. Rules can be generated from decision trees [41] or induced directly [33, 6].

ILP systems dealing with the classification task typically adopt the covering approach of rule induction systems (table 3.6). In a main loop, a covering algorithm constructs a set of clauses. Starting from an empty set of clauses, it constructs a clause explaining some of the positive examples, adds this clause to the hypothesis, and removes the positive examples explained. These steps are repeated until all positive examples have been explained (the hypothesis is complete).

In the inner loop of the covering algorithm, individual clauses are constructed by (heuristically) searching the space of possible clauses, structured by a specialization or generalization operator. Typically, search starts with a very general rule (clause with no conditions in the body), then proceeds to add literals (conditions) to this clause until it only covers (explains) positive examples (the clause is consistent).

When dealing with incomplete or noisy data, which is most often the case, the criteria of consistency and completeness are relaxed. Statistical criteria are typically used instead. These are based on the number of positive and negative examples explained by the definition and the individual constituent clauses.

3.4.2   Structuring the Space of Clauses

Having described how to learn sets of clauses by using the covering algorithm for clause/rule set induction, let us now look at some of the mechanisms underlying single clause/rule induction. In order to search the space of relational rules (program clauses) systematically, it is useful to impose some structure upon it, e.g., an ordering. One such ordering is based on θ-subsumption, defined below.

A substitution $\theta = \{V_1/t_1, ..., V_n/t_n\}$ is an assignment of terms t_i to variables V_i. Applying a substitution θ to a term, atom, or clause F yields the instantiated term, atom, or clause $F\theta$ where all occurrences of the variables V_i are simultaneously replaced by the term t_i. Let c and c' be two program clauses. Clause c θ-subsumes c' if there exists a substitution θ, such that $c\theta \subseteq c'$ [39].

To illustrate the above notions, consider the clause $c = daughter(X, Y) \leftarrow parent(Y, X)$. Applying the substitution $\theta = \{X/mary, Y/ann\}$ to clause c yields

$$c\theta = daughter(mary, ann) \leftarrow parent(ann, mary).$$

Clauses can be viewed as sets of literals: the clausal notation $daughter(X, Y) \leftarrow parent(Y, X)$ thus stands for $\{daughter(X, Y), \neg parent(Y, X)\}$ where all variables are assumed to be universally quantified, $\neg$ denotes logical negation, and the commas denote disjunction. According to the definition, clause c θ-subsumes c' if there is a substitution θ that can be applied to c such that every literal in the resulting clause occurs in c'. Clause c θ-subsumes $c' = daughter(X, Y) \leftarrow female(X), parent(Y, X)$ under the empty substitution $\theta = \emptyset$, since $\{daughter(X, Y), \neg parent(Y, X)\}$ is a proper subset of $\{daughter(X, Y), \neg female(X), \neg parent(Y, X)\}$. Furthermore, under the substitution $\theta = \{X/mary, Y/ann\}$, clause c θ-subsumes the clause $c' = daughter(mary, ann) \leftarrow female(mary), parent(ann, mary), parent(ann, tom)$.

θ-subsumption introduces a syntactic notion of generality. Clause c is at least as general as clause c' ($c \leq c'$) if c θ-subsumes c'. Clause c is more general than c' ($c < c'$) if $c \leq c'$ holds and $c' \leq c$ does not. In this case, we say that c' is a specialization of c and c is a generalization of c'. If the clause c' is a specialization of c, then c' is also called a refinement of c.

Under a semantic notion of generality, c is more general than c' if c logically entails c' ($c \models c'$). If c θ-subsumes c', then $c \models c'$. The reverse is not always true. The syntactic, θ-subsumption-based, generality is computationally more feasible. Namely, semantic generality is in general undecidable. Thus, syntactic generality is frequently used in ILP systems.

The relation $\leq$ defined by θ-subsumption introduces a lattice on the set of reduced clauses [39]: this enables ILP systems to prune large parts of the search space. θ-subsumption also provides the basis for clause construction by top-down searching of refinement graphs and bounding the search of refinement graphs from below by using a bottom clause (which can be constructed as least general generalizations, i.e., least upper bounds of example clauses in the θ-subsumption lattice).

3.4.3 Searching the Space of Clauses

Most ILP approaches search the hypothesis space of program clauses in a top-down manner, from general to specific hypotheses, using a θ-subsumption-based specialization operator. A specialization operator is usually called a refinement operator [44]. Given a hypothesis language $\mathcal{L}$, a refinement operator ρ maps a clause c to a set of clauses $\rho(c)$ which are specializations (refinements) of c: $\rho(c) = \{c' \mid c' \in \mathcal{L}, \ c < c'\}$.

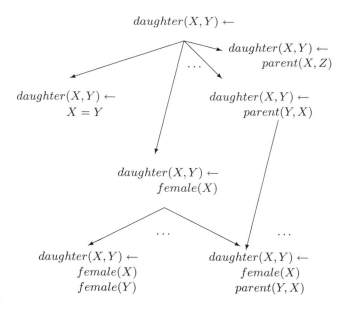

Figure 3.1   Part of the refinement graph for the family relations problem.

A refinement operator typically computes only the set of minimal (most general) specializations of a clause under θ-subsumption. It employs two basic syntactic operations:

- apply a substitution to the clause, and
- add a literal to the body of the clause.

The hypothesis space of program clauses is a lattice, structured by the θ-subsumption generality ordering. In this lattice, a refinement graph can be defined as a directed, acyclic graph in which nodes are program clauses and arcs correspond to the basic refinement operations: substituting a variable with a term, and adding a literal to the body of a clause.

Figure 3.1 depicts a part of the refinement graph for the family relations problem defined in table 3.3, where the task is to learn a definition of the *daughter* relation in terms of the relations *female* and *parent*.

At the top of the refinement graph (lattice) is the clause with an empty body $c = daughter(X, Y) \leftarrow$. The refinement operator ρ generates the refinements of c, which are of the form $\rho(c) = \{daughter(X, Y) \leftarrow L\}$, where L is one of following literals:

- literals having as arguments the variables from the head of the clause: $X = Y$ (applying a substitution X/Y), $female(X)$, $female(Y)$, $parent(X, X)$, $parent(X, Y)$, $parent(Y, X)$, and $parent(Y, Y)$, and

- literals that introduce a new distinct variable Z ($Z \neq X$ and $Z \neq Y$) in the clause body: $parent(X, Z)$, $parent(Z, X)$, $parent(Y, Z)$, and $parent(Z, Y)$.

This assumes that the language is restricted to definite clauses, hence literals of the form *not L* are not considered; and nonrecursive clauses, hence literals with the predicate symbol *daughter* are not considered.

The search for a clause starts at the top of the lattice, with the clause $d(X, Y) \leftarrow$ that covers all examples (positive and negative). Its refinements are then considered, then their refinements in turn, and this is repeated until a clause is found which covers only positive examples. In the example above, the clause $daughter(X, Y) \leftarrow female(X), parent(Y, X)$ is such a clause. Note that this clause can be reached in several ways from the top of the lattice, e.g., by first adding $female(X)$, then $parent(Y, X)$, or vice versa.

The refinement graph is typically searched heuristically levelwise, using heuristics based on the number of positive and negative examples covered by a clause. As the branching factor is very large, greedy search methods are typically applied which only consider a limited number of alternatives at each level. Hill-climbing considers only one best alternative at each level, while beam search considers n best alternatives, where n is the beam width. Occasionally, complete search is used, e.g., A^* best-first search or breadth-first search. This search can be bound from below by using so-called bottom clauses, which can be constructed by least general generalization [37] or inverse resolution/entailment [35].

3.5 Relational Decision Trees

Decision tree induction is one of the major approaches to data mining. Upgrading this approach to a relational setting has thus been of great importance. In this section, we first look into what relational decision trees are, i.e., how they are defined, then discuss how such trees can be induced from multi-relational data.

3.5.1 Relational Classification, Regression, and Model Trees

Without loss of generality, we can say the task of relational prediction is defined by a two-place target predicate $target(ExampleID, ClassVar)$, which has as arguments an example ID and the class variable, and a set of background knowledge predicates/relations. Depending on whether the class variable is discrete or continuous, we talk about relational classification or regression. Relational decision trees are one approach to solving this task.

An example of a relational decision tree is given in figure 3.3. It predicts the maintenance action A to be taken on machine M ($maintenance(M, A)$), based on parts the machine contains ($haspart(M, X)$), their condition ($worn(X)$), and ease of replacement ($irreplaceable(X)$). The target predicate here is $maintenance(M, A)$,

Figure 3.2 A relational regression tree for predicting the degradation time *LogHLT* of a chemical compound C (target predicate $degrades(C, LogHLT)$).

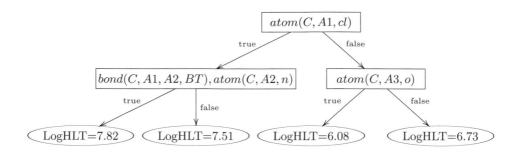

the class variable is A, and background knowledge predicates are $haspart(M, X)$, $worn(X)$, and $irreplaceable(X)$.

Relational decision trees have much the same structure as propositional decision trees. Internal nodes contain tests, while leaves contain predictions for the class value. If the class variable is discrete/continuous, we talk about relational classification/regression trees. For regression, linear equations may be allowed in the leaves instead of constant class-value predictions: in this case we talk about relational model trees.

The tree in figure 3.3 is a relational classification tree, while the tree in figure 3.2 is a relational regression tree. The latter predicts the degradation time (the logarithm of the mean half-life time in water [18]) of a chemical compound from its chemical structure, where the latter is represented by the atoms in the compound and the bonds between them. The target predicate is $degrades(C, LogHLT)$, the class variable $LogHLT$, and the background knowledge predicates are $atom(C, AtomID, Element)$ and $bond(C, A_1, A_2, BondType)$. The test at the root of the tree $atom(C, A1, cl)$ asks if the compound C has a chlorine atom $A1$ and the test along the left branch checks whether the chlorine atom $A1$ is connected to a nitrogen atom $A2$.

As can be seen from the above examples, the major difference between propositional and relational decision trees is in the tests that can appear in internal nodes. In the relational case, tests are queries, i.e., conjunctions of literals with existentially quantified variables, e.g., $atom(C, A1, cl)$ and $haspart(M, X), worn(X)$. Relational trees are binary: each internal node has a left (yes) and a right (no) branch. If the query succeeds, i.e., if there exists an answer substitution that makes it true, the yes branch is taken.

It is important to note that variables can be shared among nodes, i.e., a variable introduced in a node can be referred to in the left (yes) subtree of that node. For example, the X in $irreplaceable(X)$ refers to the machine part X introduced in the root node test $haspart(M, X), worn(X)$. Similarly, the $A1$ in $bond(C, A1, A2, BT)$ refers to the chlorine atom introduced in the root node $atom(C, A1, cl)$. One cannot

Table 3.7   A decision list representation of the relational decision tree in figure 3.3

$maintenance(M, A) \leftarrow haspart(M, X), worn(X),$
    $irreplaceable(X)\, !,\ A = send\_back$
$maintenance(M, A) \leftarrow haspart(M, X), worn(X), !,$
    $A = repair\_in\_house$
$maintenance(M, A) \leftarrow A = no\_maintenance$

---

refer to variables introduced in a node in the right (no) subtree of that node. For example, referring to the chlorine atom $A1$ in the right subtree of the tree in figure 3.2 makes no sense, as going along the right (no) branch means that the compound contains no chlorine atoms.

The actual test that has to be executed in a node is the conjunction of the literals in the node itself and the literals on the path from the root of the tree to the node in question. For example, the test in the node $irreplaceable(X)$ in figure 3.3 is actually $haspart(M, X), worn(X), irreplaceable(X)$. In other words, we need to send the machine back to the manufacturer for maintenance only if it has a part which is both worn and irreplaceable. Similarly, the test in the node $bond(C, A1, A2, BT), atom(C, A2, n)$ in figure 3.2 is in fact $atom(C, A1, cl), bond(C, A1, A2,\ BT), atom(C, A2, n)$. As a consequence, one cannot transform relational decision trees to logic programs in the fashion "one clause per leaf" (unlike propositional decision trees, where a transformation "one rule per leaf" is possible).

Table 3.8   A decision list representation of the relational regression tree for predicting the biodegradability of a compound, given in figure 3.2

$degrades(C, LogHLT) \leftarrow atom(C, A1, cl),$
    $bond(C, A1, A2, BT), atom(C, A2, n), LogHLT = 7.82, !$
$degrades(C, LogHLT) \leftarrow atom(C, A1, cl),$
    $LogHLT = 7.51, !$
$degrades(C, LogHLT) \leftarrow atom(C, A3, o),$
    $LogHLT = 6.08, !$
$degrades(C, LogHLT) \leftarrow LogHLT = 6.73.$

Table 3.9   A logic program representation of the relational decision tree in figure 3.3

$a(M) \leftarrow haspart(M, X), worn(X), irreplaceable(X)$
$b(M) \leftarrow haspart(M, X), worn(X)$
$maintenance(M, A) \leftarrow not\ a(M), A = no\_aintenance$
$maintenance(M, A) \leftarrow b(M), A = repair\_in\_house$
$maintenance(M, A) \leftarrow a(M), not\ b(M), A = send\_back$

Relational decision trees can be easily transformed into first-order decision lists, which are ordered sets of clauses (clauses in logic programs are unordered). When applying a decision list to an example, we always take the first clause that applies and return the answer produced. When applying a logic program, all applicable clauses are used and a set of answers can be produced. First-order decision lists can be represented by Prolog programs with cuts (!) [4]: cuts ensure that only the first applicable clause is used.

A decision list is produced by traversing the relational regression tree in a depth-first fashion, going down left branches first. At each leaf, a clause is output that contains the prediction of the leaf and all the conditions along the left (yes) branches leading to that leaf. A decision list obtained from the tree in figure 3.3 is given in table 3.7. For the first clause (*send_back*), the conditions in both internal nodes are output, as the left branches out of both nodes have been followed to reach the corresponding leaf. For the second clause, only the condition in the root is output: to reach the *repair_in_house* leaf, the left (yes) branch out of the root has been followed, but the right (no) branch out of the *irreplaceable*(X) node has been followed. A decision list produced from the relational regression tree in figure 3.2 is given in table 3.8.

Generating a logic program from a relational decision tree is more complicated. It requires the introduction of new predicates. We will not describe the transformation process in detail, but rather give an example. A logic program, corresponding to the tree in figure 3.3, is given in table 3.9.

3.5.2   Induction of Relational Decision Trees

The two major algorithms for inducing relational decision trees are upgrades of the two most famous algorithms for inducting propositional decision trees. SCART [26, 27] is an upgrade of CART [5], while TILDE [3, 13] is an upgrade of C4.5 [41]. According to the upgrading recipe, both SCART and TILDE have their propositional counterparts as special cases. The actual algorithms thus closely follow

Table 3.10   The TDIDT part of the SCART algorithm for inducing relational decision trees

---

procedure DIVIDEANDCONQUER*(TestsOnYesBranchesSofar, DeclarativeBias, Examples)*

if TERMINATIONCONDITION*(Examples)*
then
    NewLeaf = CREATENEWLEAF*(Examples)*
    return *NewLeaf*
else
    PossibleTestsNow = GENERATETESTS*(TestsOnYesBranchesSofar, DeclarativeBias)*
    BestTest = FINDBESTTEST*(PossibleTestsNow, Examples)*
    $(Split_1, Split_2)$ = SPLITEXAMPLES*(Examples, TestsOnYesBranchesSofar, BestTest)*
    LeftSubtree = DIVIDEANDCONQUER*(TestsOnYesBranchesSofar $\land$ BestTest, Split_1)*
    RightSubtree = DIVIDEANDCONQUER*(TestsOnYesBranchesSofar, Split_2)*
    return [*BestTest, LeftSubtree, RightSubtree*]

CART and C4.5. Here we illustrate the differences between SCART and CART by looking at the TDIDT (top-down induction of decision trees) algorithm of SCART (table 3.10).

Given a set of examples, the TDID algorithm first checks if a termination condition is satisfied, e.g., if all examples belong to the same class c. If yes, a leaf is constructed with an appropriate prediction, e.g., assigning the value c to the class variable. Otherwise a test is selected among the possible tests for the node at hand, examples are split into subsets according to the outcome of the test, and tree construction proceeds recursively on each of the subsets. A tree is thus constructed with the selected test at the root and the subtrees resulting from the recursive calls attached to the respective branches.

The major difference in comparison to the propositional case is in the possible tests that can be used in a node. While in CART these remain (more or less) the same regardless of where the node is in the tree (e.g., $A = v$ or $A < v$ for each attribute and attribute value), in SCART the set of possible tests crucially depends on the position of the node in the tree. In particular, it depends on the tests along the path from the root to the current node, more precisely on the variables appearing in those tests and the declarative bias. To emphasize this, we can think of a GENERATETESTS procedure being separately employed before evaluating the tests. The inputs to this procedure are the tests on positive branches from the root to the current node and the declarative bias. These are also inputs to the top level TDIDT procedure.

The declarative bias in SCART contains statements of the form *schema(CofL, TandM)*, where *CofL* is a conjunction of literals and *TandM* is a list of type and mode declarations for the variables in those literals. Two such statements, used in the induction of the regression tree in figure 3.2 are as follows: *schema((bond(V, W, X, Y), atom(V, X, Z)), [V:chemical:"+", W:atomid:"+", X:atomid:"−", Y:bondtype:"−", Z:element: "="])*, and *schema(bond (V, W, X, Y), [V: chemical:"+", W:atomid:"+", X:atomid:"−", Y:bondtype: "="])*. In the lists, each variable in the conjunction is followed by its type and mode declaration: "+" denotes that the variable must be bound (i.e., appear in *TestsOnYesBranchesSofar*), − that it must not be bound, and = that it must be replaced by a constant value.

Assuming we have taken the left branch out of the root in figure 3.2, *TestsOnYesBranchesSofar = atom(C, A1, cl)*. Taking the declarative bias with the two schema statements above, the only choice for replacing the variables V and W in the schemata are the variables C and $A1$, respectively. The possible tests at this stage are thus of the form $bond(C, A1, A2, BT), atom(C, A2, E)$, where E is replaced with an element (such as cl - chlorine, s - sulphur, or n - nitrogen), or of the form $bond(C, A1, A2, BT)$, where BT is replaced with a bond type (such as *single*, *double*, or *aromatic*). Among the possible tests, the test $bond(C, A1, A2, BT), atom(C, A2, n)$ is chosen.

The approaches to relational decision tree induction are among the fastest multi-relational data mining approaches. They have been successfully applied to a number of practical problems. These include learning to predict the biodegradability of chemical compounds [18] and learning to predict the structure of diterpene compounds from their nuclear magnetic resonance spectra [17].

3.6   Relational Association Rules

The discovery of frequent patterns and association rules is one of the most commonly studied tasks in data mining. Here we first describe frequent relational patterns (frequent Datalog patterns) and relational association rules (query extensions). We then look into how a well-known algorithm for finding frequent itemsets has been upgraded to discover frequent relational patterns.

3.6.1   Frequent Datalog Queries and Query Extensions

Dehaspe and colleagues [8], [9] (chapter 8 of [15]) consider patterns in the form of Datalog queries, which reduce to SQL queries. A Datalog query has the form $? - A_1, A_2, \ldots A_n$, where the A_i's are logical atoms.

An example Datalog query is

$$? - person(X), parent(X, Y), hasPet(Y, Z).$$

This query on a Prolog database containing predicates *person*, *parent*, and *hasPet* is equivalent to the SQL query

> SELECT PERSON.ID, PARENT.KID, HASPET.AID
> FROM PERSON, PARENT, HASPET
> WHERE PERSON.ID = PARENT.PID
> AND PARENT.KID = HASPET.PID

on a database containing relations PERSON with argument ID, PARENT with arguments PID and KID, and HASPET with arguments PID and AID. This query finds triples (x, y, z), where child y of person x has pet z.

Datalog queries can be viewed as a relational version of itemsets (which are sets of items occurring together). Consider the itemset {*person, parent, child, pet*}. The market-basket interpretation of this pattern is that a person, a parent, a child, and a pet occur together. This is also partly the meaning of the above query. However, the variables X, Y, and Z add extra information: the person and the parent are the same, the parent and the child belong to the same family, and the pet belongs to the child. This illustrates the fact that queries are a more expressive variant of itemsets.

To discover frequent patterns, we need to have a notion of frequency. Given that we consider queries as patterns and that queries can have variables, it is not immediately obvious what the frequency of a given query is. This is resolved by specifying an additional parameter of the pattern discovery task, called the key. The key is an atom which has to be present in all queries considered during the discovery process. It determines what is actually counted. In the above query, if $person(X)$ is the key, we count persons; if $parent(X, Y)$ is the key, we count (parent,child) pairs; and if $hasPet(Y, Z)$ is the key, we count (owner,pet) pairs. This is described more precisely below.

Submitting a query $Q = ? - A_1, A_2, \ldots A_n$ with variables $\{X_1, \ldots X_m\}$ to a Datalog database $\mathbf{r}$ corresponds to asking whether a grounding substitution exists (which replaces each of the variables in Q with a constant), such that the conjunction $A_1, A_2, \ldots A_n$ holds in $\mathbf{r}$. The answer to the query produces answering substitutions $\theta = \{X_1/a_1, \ldots X_m/a_m\}$ such that $Q\theta$ succeeds. The set of all answering substitutions obtained by submitting a query Q to a Datalog database $\mathbf{r}$ is denoted $answerset(Q, \mathbf{r})$.

The absolute frequency of a query Q is the number of answer substitutions θ for the variables in the key atom for which the query $Q\theta$ succeeds in the given database, i.e., $a(Q, \mathbf{r}, key) = |\{\theta \in answerset(key, \mathbf{r}) | Q\theta \text{ succeeds w.r.t. } \mathbf{r}\}|$. The relative frequency (support) can be calculated as $f(Q, \mathbf{r}, key) = a(Q, \mathbf{r}, key)/|\{\theta \in answerset(key, \mathbf{r})\}|$. Assuming the key is $person(X)$, the absolute frequency for our query involving parents, children, and pets can be calculated by the following SQL statement:

```
SELECT count(distinct *)
FROM SELECT PERSON.ID
    FROM PERSON, PARENT, HASPET
    WHERE PERSON.ID = PARENT.PID
    AND PARENT.KID = HASPET.PID
```

Association rules have the form $A \rightarrow C$ and the intuitive market-basket interpretation "customers that buy A typically also buy C." If itemsets A and C have supports f_A and f_C, respectively, the confidence of the association rule is defined to be $c_{A \rightarrow C} = f_C/f_A$. The task of association rule discovery is to find all association rules $A \rightarrow C$, where f_C and $c_{A \rightarrow C}$ exceed prespecified thresholds (minsup and minconf).

Association rules are typically obtained from frequent itemsets. Suppose we have two frequent itemsets A and C, such that $A \subset C$, where $C = A \cup B$. If the support of A is f_A and the support of C is f_C, we can derive an association rule $A \rightarrow B$, which has confidence f_C/f_A. Treating the arrow as implication, note that we can derive $A \rightarrow C$ from $A \rightarrow B$ ($A \rightarrow A$ and $A \rightarrow B$ implies $A \rightarrow A \cup B$, i.e., $A \rightarrow C$).

Relational association rules can be derived in a similar manner from frequent Datalog queries. From two frequent queries $Q_1 = ? - l_1, \ldots l_m$ and $Q_2 = ? - l_1, \ldots l_m, l_{m+1}, \ldots l_n$, where Q_2 θ-subsumes Q_1, we can derive a relational association rule $Q_1 \rightarrow Q_2$. Since Q_2 extends Q_1, such a relational association rule is named a query extension.

A query extension is thus an existentially quantified implication of the form $? - l_1, \ldots l_m \rightarrow ? - l_1, \ldots l_m, l_{m+1}, \ldots l_n$ (since variables in queries are existentially quantified). A shorthand notation for the above query extension is $? - l_1, \ldots l_m \rightsquigarrow l_{m+1}, \ldots l_n$. We call the query $? - l_1, \ldots l_m$ the body and the subquery $l_{m+1}, \ldots l_n$ the head of the query extension. Note, however, that the head of the query extension does not correspond to its conclusion (which is $? - l_1, \ldots l_m, l_{m+1}, \ldots l_n$).

Assume the queries $Q_1 = ? - person(X), parent(X, Y)$ and $Q_2 = ? - person(X),$ $parent(X, Y), hasPet(Y, Z)$ are frequent, with absolute frequencies of 40 and 30, respectively. The query extension E, where E is defined as $E = ? - person(X),$ $parent(X, Y) \rightsquigarrow hasPet(Y, Z)$, can be considered a relational association rule with a support of 30 and confidence of $30/40 = 75\%$. Note the difference in meaning between the query extension E and two obvious, but incorrect, attempts at defining relational association rules. The clause $person(X), parent(X, Y) \rightarrow hasPet(Y, Z)$ (which stands for the logical formula $\forall XYZ : person(X) \wedge parent(X, Y) \rightarrow hasPet(Y, Z)$) would be interpreted as follows: "if a person has a child, then this child has a pet." The implication $? - person(X), parent(X, Y) \rightarrow ? - hasPet(Y, Z)$, which stands for $(\exists XY : person(X) \wedge parent(X, Y)) \rightarrow (\exists YZ : hasPet(Y, Z))$ is trivially true if at least one person in the database has a pet. The correct interpretation of the query extension E is: "if a person has a child, then this person also has a child that has a pet."

3.6.2   Discovering Frequent Queries: WARMR

The task of discovering frequent queries is addressed by the RDM system WARMR [8]. WARMR takes as input a database $\mathbf{r}$, a frequency threshold $minfreq$, and declarative language bias $\mathcal{L}$. $\mathcal{L}$ specifies a *key* atom and input-output modes for predicates/relations, discussed below.

WARMR upgrades the well-known APRIORI algorithm for discovering frequent patterns, which performs levelwise search [1] through the lattice of itemsets. APRIORI starts with the empty set of items and at each level l considers sets of items of cardinality l. The key to the efficiency of APRIORI lies in the fact that a large frequent itemset can only be generated by adding an item to a frequent itemset. Candidates at level $l + 1$ are thus generated by adding items to frequent itemsets obtained at level l. Further efficiency is achieved using the fact that all subsets of a frequent itemset have to be frequent: only candidates that pass this test get their frequency to be determined by scanning the database.

In analogy to APRIORI, WARMR searches the lattice of Datalog queries for queries that are frequent in the given database $\mathbf{r}$. In analogy to itemsets, a more complex (specific) frequent query Q_2 can only be generated from a simpler (more general) frequent query Q_1 (where Q_1 is more general than Q_2 if Q_1 θ-subsumes Q_2; see section 3.4.2 for a definition of θ-subsumption). WARMR thus starts with the query $? - key$ at level 1 and generates candidates for frequent queries at level $l + 1$ by refining (adding literals to) frequent queries obtained at level l.

Table 3.11 An example specification of declarative language bias settings for WARMR

warmode_key(person(-)).
warmode(parent(+, -)).
warmode(hasPet(+, cat)).
warmode(hasPet(+, dog)).
warmode(hasPet(+, lizard)).

Suppose we are given a Prolog database containing the predicates *person*, *parent*, and *hasPet*, and the declarative bias in table 3.11. The latter contains the key atom *parent*(X) and input-output modes for the relations *parent* and *hasPet*. Input-output modes specify whether a variable argument of an atom in a query has to appear earlier in the query ($+$), must not ($-$) or may, but need not ($\pm$). Input-output modes thus place constraints on how queries can be refined, i.e., what atoms may be added to a given query.

Given the above, WARMR starts the search of the refinement graph of queries at level 1 with the query $? - person(X)$. At level 2, the literals $parent(X, Y)$, $hasPet(X, cat)$, $hasPet(X, dog)$, and $hasPet(X, lizard)$ can be added to this query, yielding the queries $? - person(X), parent(X, Y)$, $? - person(X), hasPet(X, cat)$, $? - person(X), hasPet(X, dog)$, and $? - person(X), hasPet(X, lizard)$. Taking the first of the level 2 queries, the following literals are added to obtain level 3 queries: $parent(Y, Z)$ (note that $parent(Y, X)$ cannot be added, because X already appears in the query being refined), $hasPet(Y, cat)$, $hasPet(Y, dog)$, and $hasPet(Y, lizard)$.

While all subsets of a frequent itemset must be frequent in APRIORI, not all subqueries of a frequent query need be frequent queries in WARMR. Consider the query $? - person(X), parent(X, Y), hasPet(Y, cat)$ and assume it is frequent. The subquery $? - person(X), hasPet(Y, cat)$ is not allowed, as it violates the declarative bias constraint that the first argument of *hasPet* has to appear earlier in the query. This causes some complications in pruning the generated candidates for frequent queries: WARMR keeps a list of infrequent queries and checks whether the generated candidates are subsumed by a query in this list. The WARMR algorithm is given in table 3.12.

WARMR upgrades APRIORI to a multi-relational setting following the upgrading recipe (see section 3.3.5). The major differences are in finding the frequency of queries (where we have to count answer substitutions for the key atom) and the candidate query generation (by using a refinement operator and declarative bias). WARMR has APRIORI as a special case: if we only have predicates of zero arity (with no arguments), which correspond to items, WARMR can be used to discover frequent itemsets.

More importantly, WARMR has as special cases a number of approaches that extend the discovery of frequent itemsets with, e.g., hierarchies on items [45], as well as approaches to discovering sequential patterns [2], including general epi-

Table 3.12   The WARMR algorithm for discovering frequent Datalog queries.

Algorithm WARMR(**r**, $\mathcal{L}$, *key*, *minfreq*; Q)
Input: Database **r**; Declarative language bias $\mathcal{L}$ and *key* ;
      threshold *minfreq*;
Output: All queries $Q \in \mathcal{L}$ with frequency $\geq$ *minfreq*

1. Initialize level $d := 1$
2. Initialize the set of candidate queries $\mathcal{Q}_1 := \{ \text{?- } key\}$
3. Initialize the set of (in)frequent queries $\mathcal{F} := \emptyset$; $\mathcal{I} := \emptyset$
4. While $\mathcal{Q}_d$ not empty
5.   Find frequency of all queries $Q \in \mathcal{Q}_d$
6.   Move those with frequency below *minfreq* to $\mathcal{I}$
7.   Update $\mathcal{F} := \mathcal{F} \cup \mathcal{Q}_d$
8.   Compute new candidates:
      $\mathcal{Q}_{d+1} = \text{WARMRgen}(\mathcal{L}; \mathcal{I}; \mathcal{F}; \mathcal{Q}_d)$)
9.   Increment d
10. Return $\mathcal{F}$

Function WARMRgen($\mathcal{L}; \mathcal{I}; \mathcal{F}; \mathcal{Q}_d$);

1. Initialize $\mathcal{Q}_{d+1} := \emptyset$
2. For each $Q_j \in \mathcal{Q}_d$, and for each refinement $Q_j' \in \mathcal{L}$ of Q_j:
    Add Q_j' to $\mathcal{Q}_{d+1}$, unless:
      (i) Q_j' is more specific than some query $\in \mathcal{I}$, or
      (ii) Q_j' is equivalent to some query $\in \mathcal{Q}_{d+1} \cup \mathcal{F}$
3. Return $\mathcal{Q}_{d+1}$

---

sodes [32]. The individual approaches mentioned make use of the specific properties of the patterns considered (very limited use of variables) and are more efficient than WARMR for the particular tasks they address. The high expressive power of the language of patterns considered has its computational costs, but it also has the important advantage that a variety of different pattern types can be explored without any changes in the implementation.

WARMR can be (and has been) used to perform propositionalization, i.e., to transform MRDM problems to propositional (single table) form. WARMR is first used to discover frequent queries. In the propositional form, examples correspond to answer substitutions for the key atom and the binary attributes are the frequent queries discovered. An attribute is true for an example if the corresponding query succeeds for the corresponding answer substitution. This approach has been applied with considerable success to the tasks of predictive toxicology [10] and genome-wide prediction of protein functional class [24].

3.7   Relational Distance-Based Methods

To upgrade distance-based approaches to learning, including prediction and clustering, it is necessary to upgrade the key notion of a distance measure from the propositional to the relational case. Such a measure could then be used within

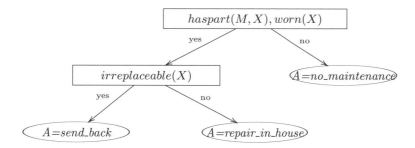

Figure 3.3   A relational decision tree, predicting the class variable A in the target predicate $maintenance(M, A)$.

standard statistical approaches, such as nearest-neighbor prediction or hierarchical agglomerative clustering. In their system RIBL, Emde and Wettschereck [21] propose a relational distance measure. Below we first briefly discuss this measure, then outline how it has been used for relational classification and clustering [25].

3.7.1   The RIBL Distance Measure

Propositional distance measures are defined between examples that have the form of vectors of attribute values. They essentially sum up the differences between the examples' values along each of the dimensions of the vectors. Given two examples $x = (x_1, \ldots, x_n)$ and $y = (y_1, \ldots, y_n)$, their distance might be calculated as

$$\text{distance}(x, y) = \sum_{i=1}^{n} \text{difference}(x_i, y_i)/n,$$

where the difference between attribute values is defined as

$$\text{difference}(x_i, y_i) = \begin{cases} |x_i - y_i| & \text{if continuous,} \\ 0 & \text{if discrete and } x_i = y_i, \\ 1 & \text{otherwise} \end{cases}$$

In a relational representation, an example (also called instance or case) can be described by a set of facts about multiple relations. A fact of the target predicate of the form $target(ExampleID, A_1, ..., A_n)$ specifies an instance through its ID and properties, and additional information can be specified through background knowledge predicates. In table 3.13, the target predicate *member(PersonID,A,G,I,MT)* specifies information on members of a particular club, which includes age, gender, income, and membership type. The background predicates $car(OwnerID, CT, TS, M)$ and $house(OwnerID, DistrictID, Y, S)$ provide information on property owned by club members: for cars this includes car type, top speed, and manufacturer; for houses the district, construction year, and size. Additional information is available on districts through the predicate $district(DistrictID, P, S, C)$, i.e., the popularity, size, and country of the district.

Table 3.13   Two examples on which to study a relational distance measure

---

member($person1$, 45, $male$, 20, $gold$)
member($person2$, 30, $female$, 10, $platinum$)

car($person1$, $wagon$, 200, $volkswagen$)
car($person1$, $sedan$, 220, $mercedesbenz$)
car($person2$, $roadster$, 240, $audi$)
car($person2$, $coupe$, 260, bmw)

house($person1$, $murgle$, 1987, 560)
house($person1$, $montecarlo$, 1990, 210)
house($person2$, $murgle$, 1999, 430)

district($montecarlo$, $famous$, $large$, $monaco$)
district($murgle$, $famous$, $small$, $slovenia$)

The basic idea behind the RIBL [21] distance measure is as follows. To calculate the distance between two objects/examples, their properties are taken into account first (at depth 0). Next (at depth 1), objects immediately related to the two original objects are taken into account, or more precisely, the distances between the corresponding related objects. At depth 2, objects related to those at depth 1 are taken into account, and so on, until a user-specified depth limit is reached.

In our example, when calculating the distance between $e_1 = member(person1, 45, male, 20, gold)$ and $e_2 = member(person2, 30, female, 10, platinum)$, the properties of the persons (age, gender, income, membership type) are first compared and differences between them calculated and summed (as in the propositional case). At depth 1, cars and houses owned by the two persons are compared, i.e., distances between them are calculated. At depth 2, the districts where the houses reside are taken into account when calculating the distances between houses. Before beginning to calculate distances, RIBL collects all facts related to a person into a so-called case. The case for $person1$ generated with a depth limit of 2 is given in figure 3.4.

Let us calculate the distance between the two club members according to the distance measure. $d(e_1, e_2) = 1/5 \cdot (d(person1, person2) + d(45, 30) + d(male, female) + d(20, 10) + d(gold, platinum))$. With a depth limit of 0, the identifiers $person1$ and $person2$ are treated as discrete values, $d(person1, person2) = 1$ and we have $d(e_1, e_2) = (1 + (45 - 30)/100 + 1 + (20 - 10)/50 + 1)/5 = 0.67$; the denominators 100 and 50 denote the highest possible differences in age and income.

To calculate $d(person1, person2)$ at level 1, we collect the facts directly related to the two persons and partition them according to the predicates. Thus we have

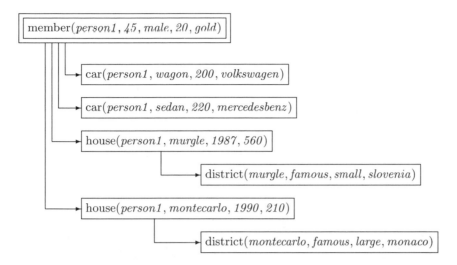

Figure 3.4 All facts related to member($person1, 45, male, 2000000, gold$) constructed with respect to the background knowledge in table 3.13 and a depth limit of 2.

$$F_1, car = \{car(person1, wagon, 200, volkswagen),$$
$$car(person1, sedan, 220, mercedesbenz)\}$$
$$F_2, car = \{car(person2, roadster, 240, audi),$$
$$car(person2, coupe, 260, bmw)\}$$
$$F_1, house = \{house(person1, murgle, 1987, 560),$$
$$house(person1, montecarlo, 1990, 210)\}$$
$$F_2, house = \{house(person2, murgle, 1999, 430)\}.$$

Then $d(person1, person2) = (d(F_1, car, F_2, car) + d(F_1, house, F_2, house))/2$.

Distances between sets of facts are calculated as follows. We take the smaller set of facts (or the first, if they are of the same size): for $d(F_1, house, F_2, house)$, we take $F_2, house$. For each fact in this set, we calculate its distance to the nearest element of the other set, e.g., $F_1, house$, summing up these distances (the house of *person2* is closer to the house of *person1* in *murgle* then to the one in *montecarlo*). We add a penalty for the possible mismatch in cardinality and normalize with the cardinality of the larger set:

$$d(F_1, house, F_2, house) =$$
$$[1 + min($$
$$d(house(person2, murgle, 1999, 430), house(person1, murgle, 1987, 560)),$$
$$d(house(person2, murgle, 1999, 430), house(person1, montecarlo, 1990, 210)))]/2$$
$$= 0.5 \cdot [1 + min((0 + (1999 - 1987)/100 + |430 - 560|/1000)/3,$$
$$(1 + (1999 - 1990)/100 + (430 - 210)/1000)/3)]$$
$$= 0.5 + 0.5 \cdot min(0.25/3, 1.31/3) = 13/24.$$

For calculating $d(F_1, car, F_2, car)$, we take F_1, car and note that both cars of *person1* are closer to the *audi* of *person2* than to the *bmw*. We thus have $d(F_1, car, F_2, car) = 0.5 \cdot [min_{c \in F_2, car} d(car(person1, wagon, 200, volkswagen), c) + 0.5 \cdot min_{c \in F_2, car} d(car(person1, sedan, 220, mercedesbenz), c)] = 0.5 \cdot [(1 + |200 - 240|/100 + 1)/3, (1 + |220 - 240|/100 + 1)/3] = 11/15$. Thus, at level 1, $d(person1, person2) = 0.5 \cdot (13/24 + 11/15) = 0.6375$ and $d(e_1, e_2) = (0.6375 + (45 - 30)/100 + 1 + (20 - 10)/50 + 1)/5 = 0.5975$.

Finally, at level 2, the distance between the two districts is taken into account when calculating $d(F_1, house, F_2, house)$. We have $d(murgle, montecarlo) = (0 + 1 + 1)/3 = 2/3$. However, since the house of *person2* is closer to the house of *person1* in *murgle* then to the one in *montecarlo*, the value of $d(F_1, house, F_2, house)$ does not change as it equals $0.5 \cdot [1 + min((0 + (1999 - 1987)/100 + |430 - 560|/1000)/3, 0.5 \cdot [1 + min((2/3 + (1999 - 1990)/100 + (430 - 210)/1000)/3)] = 0.5 + 0.5 \cdot min(0.25/3, (2/3 + 0.31)/3) = 13/24$. $d(e_1, e_2)$ is thus the same at level 1 and level 2 and is equal to 0.5975.

We should note here that the RIBL distance measure is not a metric [42]. However, some relational distance measures that are metrics have been proposed recently [43]. Designing distance measures for relational data is still a largely open and lively research area. Since distances and kernels are strongly related, this area is also related to designing kernels for structured data.

3.7.2   Relational Distance-Based Learning

Once we have a relational distance measure, we can easily adapt classical statistical approaches to prediction and clustering, such as the nearest-neighbor method and hierarchical agglomerative clustering, to work on relational data. This is precisely what has been done with the RIBL distance measure.

The original RIBL [21] addresses the problem of prediction, more precisely classification. It uses the k-nearest neighbor method in conjunction with the RIBL distance measure to solve the problem addressed. RIBL was successfully applied to the practical problem of diterpene structure elucidation [17], where it outperformed propositional approaches as well as a number of other relational approaches.

RIBL2 [25] upgrades the RIBL distance measure by considering lists and terms as elementary types, much like discrete and numeric values. Edit distances are used for these, while the RIBL distance measure is followed otherwise. RIBL2 has been used to predict mRNA signal structure and to automatically discover previously uncharacterized mRNA signal structure classes [25].

Two clustering approaches have been developed that use the RIBL distance measure [25]. RDBC uses hierarchical agglomerative clustering, while FORC adapts the k-means approach. The latter relies on finding cluster centers, which is easy for numeric vectors but far from trivial in the relational case. FORC thus uses the k-medoids method, which defines a cluster center as the existing case/example that has the smallest sum of squared distances to all other cases in the cluster and only uses distance information.

3.8 Recent Trends in ILP and RDM

Hot topics and recent advances in ILP and RDM mirror the hot topics in data mining and machine learning. These include scalability issues, ensemble methods, and kernel methods.

Scalability issues do indeed deserve a lot of attention when learning in a relational setting, as the complexity of learning increases with the expressive power of the hypothesis language. Scalability methods for ILP include classical ones, such as sampling or turning the loop of hypothesis evaluation inside out (going through each example once) in decision tree induction. Methods more specific to ILP, such as query packs, have also been considered.

Boosting was the first ensemble method to be used on top of a relational learning system. This was followed by bagging. More recently, methods for learning random forests have been adapted to the relational setting.

Kernel methods have become the mainstream of research in machine learning and data mining in recent years. The development of kernel methods for learning in a relational setting has thus emerged as a natural research direction. Significant effort has been devoted to the development of kernels for structured/relational data, such as graphs and sequences.

The latest developments in ILP and RDM are discussed in a special issue of *SIGKDD Explorations* [20]. Besides the topics mentioned above, the hottest research topic in ILP and RDM is the study of probabilistic representations and learning methods. A variety of these have been recently considered. A comprehensive survey of such methods is presented in this book.

References

[1] R. Agrawal, H. Mannila, R. Srikant, H. Toivonen, and A. I. Verkamo. Fast discovery of association rules. In U. Fayyad, G. Piatetsky-Shapiro, P. Smyth,

and R. Uthurusamy, editors, *Advances in Knowledge Discovery and Data Mining*, pages 307–328. AAAI Press, Menlo Park, CA, 1996.

[2] R. Agrawal and R. Srikant. Mining sequential patterns. In *Proceedings of the Eleventh International Conference on Data Engineering*, 1995.

[3] H. Blockeel and L. De Raedt. Top-down induction of first order logical decision trees. *Artificial Intelligence*, 101: 285–297, 1998.

[4] I. Bratko. *Prolog Programming for Artificial Intelligence*, 3rd edition. Addison-Wesley, Harlow, UK, 2001.

[5] L. Breiman, J. H. Friedman, R. A. Olshen, and C. J. Stone. *Classification and Regression Trees*. Wadsworth, Belmont, CA, 1984.

[6] P. Clark and R. Boswell. Rule induction with CN2: Some recent improvements. In *Proceedings of the Fifth European Working Session on Learning*, 1991.

[7] P. Clark and T. Niblett. The CN2 induction algorithm. *Machine Learning*, 3(4): 261–283, 1989.

[8] L. Dehaspe and H. Toivonen. Discovery of frequent datalog patterns. *Data Mining and Knowledge Discovery*, 3(1): 7–36, 1999.

[9] L. Dehaspe and H. Toivonen. Discovery of relational association rules. In [15], pages 189–212, 2001.

[10] L. Dehaspe, H. Toivonen, and R. D. King. Finding frequent substructures in chemical compounds. In *Proceedings of the Fourth International Conference on Knowledge Discovery and Data Mining*, 1998.

[11] L. De Raedt. Logical settings for concept learning. *Artificial Intelligence*, 95: 187–201, 1997.

[12] L. De Raedt. Attribute-value learning versus inductive logic programming: the missing links. In *Proceedings of the Eighth International Conference on Inductive Logic Programming*, 1998.

[13] L. De Raedt, H. Blockeel, L. Dehaspe, and W. Van Laer. Three companions for data mining in first order logic. In [15], pages 105–139, 2001.

[14] L. De Raedt and S. Džeroski. First order jk-clausal theories are PAC-learnable. *Artificial Intelligence*, 70: 375–392, 1994.

[15] S. Džeroski and N. Lavrač, editors. *Relational Data Mining*. Springer-Verlag, Berlin, 2001.

[16] S. Džeroski, S. Muggleton, and S. Russell. PAC-learnability of determinate logic programs. In *Proceedings of the Fifth ACM Workshop on Computational Learning Theory*, 1992.

[17] S. Džeroski, S. Schulze-Kremer, K. Heidtke, K. Siems, D. Wettschereck, and H. Blockeel. Diterpene structure elucidation from ^{13}C NMR spectra with inductive logic programming. *Applied Artificial Intelligence*, 12: 363–383, 1998.

[18] S. Džeroski, H. Blockeel, B. Kompare, S. Kramer, B. Pfahringer, and W. Van Laer. Experiments in predicting biodegradability. In *Proceedings of the*

International Workshop on Inductive Logic Programming, 1999.

[19] S. Džeroski. Relational data mining applications: An overview. In [15], pages 339–364, 2001.

[20] S. Džeroski and L. De Raedt, editors. *SIGKDD Explorations*, Special Issue on Multi-Relational Data Mining, 5(1), 2003.

[21] W. Emde and D. Wettschereck. Relational instance-based learning. In *Proceedings of the Thirteenth International Conference on Machine Learning*, 1996.

[22] C. Hogger. *Essentials of Logic Pogramming*. Clarendon Press, Oxford, UK, 1990.

[23] A. Karalič and I. Bratko. First order regression. *Machine Learning* 26: 147-176, 1997.

[24] R.D. King, A. Karwath, A. Clare, and L. Dehaspe. Genome scale prediction of protein functional class from sequence using data mining. In *Proceedings of the Sixth International Conference on Knowledge Discovery and Data Mining*, 2000.

[25] M. Kirsten, S. Wrobel, and T. Horváth. Distance based approaches to relational learning and clustering. In [15], pages 213–232, 2001.

[26] S. Kramer. Structural regression trees. In *Proceedings of the Thirteenth National Conference on Artificial Intelligence*, 1996.

[27] S. Kramer and G. Widmer. Inducing classification and regression trees in first order logic. In [15], pages 140–159, 2001.

[28] S. Kramer, N. Lavrač, and P. Flach. Propositionalization approaches to relational data mining. In [15], pages 262–291, 2001.

[29] N. Lavrač, S. Džeroski, and M. Grobelnik. Learning nonrecursive definitions of relations with LINUS. In *Proceedings of the Fifth European Working Session on Learning*, 1991.

[30] N. Lavrač and S. Džeroski. *Inductive Logic Programming: Techniques and Applications*. Ellis Horwood, Chichester, UK, 1994. Freely available at `http://www-ai.ijs.si/SasoDzeroski/ILPBook/`.

[31] J. Lloyd. *Foundations of Logic Programming*, 2nd edition. Springer-Verlag, Berlin, 1987.

[32] H. Mannila and H. Toivonen. Discovering generalized episodes using minimal occurrences. In *Proceedings of the Second International Conference on Knowledge Discovery and Data Mining*, 1996.

[33] R. Michalski, I. Mozetič, J. Hong, and N. Lavrač. The multi-purpose incremental learning system AQ15 and its testing application on three medical domains. In *Proceedings of the Fifth National Conference on Artificial Intelligence*, 1986.

[34] S. Muggleton. Inductive logic programming. *New Generation Computing*, 8(4): 295–318, 1991.

[35] S. Muggleton. Inverse entailment and Progol. *New Generation Computing*, 13: 245–286, 1995.

[36] S. Muggleton and W. Buntine. Machine invention of first-order predicates by inverting resolution. In *Proceedings of the Fifth International Conference on Machine Learning*, 1988.

[37] S. Muggleton and C. Feng. Efficient induction of logic programs. In *Proceedings of the First Conference on Algorithmic Learning Theory*, 1990.

[38] C. Nedellec, C. Rouveirol, H. Ade, F. Bergadano, and B. Tausend. Declarative bias in inductive logic programming. In L. De Raedt, editor, *Advances in Inductive Logic Programming*, pages 82–103. IOS Press, Amsterdam, 1996.

[39] G. Plotkin. A note on inductive generalization. In B. Meltzer and D. Michie, editors, *Machine Intelligence 5*, pages 153–163. Edinburgh University Press, Edinburgh, 1969.

[40] J. R. Quinlan. Learning logical definitions from relations. *Machine Learning*, 5(3): 239–266, 1990.

[41] J. R. Quinlan. *C4.5: Programs for Machine Learning*. Morgan Kaufmann, San Mateo, CA, 1993.

[42] J. Ramon. *Clustering and Instance Based Learning in First Order Logic*. PhD Thesis. Katholieke Universiteit Leuven, Belgium, 2002.

[43] J. Ramon and M. Bruynooghe. A polynomial time computable metric between point sets. *Acta Informatica*, 37(10): 765–780.

[44] E. Shapiro. *Algorithmic Program Debugging*. MIT Press, Cambridge, MA, 1983.

[45] R. Srikant and R. Agrawal. Mining generalized association rules. In *Proceedings of the Twenty-first International Conference on Very Large Data Bases*, 1995.

[46] A. Srinivasan. The Aleph manual. Technical Report, Computing Laboratory, Oxford University, Oxford, UK, 2000.

[47] J. Ullman. *Principles of Database and Knowledge Base Systems*, volume 1. Computer Science Press, Rockville, MI, 1988.

[48] V. Van Laer and L. De Raedt. How to upgrade propositional learners to first order logic: A case study. In [15], pages 235–261, 2001.

[49] S. Wrobel. Inductive logic programming for knowledge discovery in databases. In [15], pages 74–101, 2001.

[50] S. Wrobel and S. Džeroski. The ILP description learning problem: Towards a general model-level definition of data mining in ILP. In *Proceedings Fachgruppentreffen Maschinelles Lernen*. University of Dortmund, Germany, 1995.

4 An Introduction to Conditional Random Fields for Relational Learning

Charles Sutton and Andrew McCallum

Conditional random fields (CRFs) combine the modeling flexibility of graphical models with the ability to use rich, nonindependent features of the input. In this tutorial, we review modeling, inference, and parameter estimation in CRFs, both on linear chains and on general graphical structures. We discuss differences between generative and discriminative modeling, latent-variable conditional models, and practical aspects of CRF implementations. Finally, we present a case study applying a loopy CRF to a relational problem in natural language processing.

4.1 Introduction

Relational data has two characteristics: first, statistical dependencies exist between the entities we wish to model, and second, each entity often has a rich set of features that can aid classification. For example, when classifying web documents, the page's text provides much information about the class label, but hyperlinks define a relationship between pages that can improve classification [55]. Graphical models are a natural formalism for exploiting the dependence structure among entities. Traditionally, graphical models have been used to represent the joint probability distribution $p(\mathbf{y}, \mathbf{x})$, where the variables $\mathbf{y}$ represent the attributes of the entities that we wish to predict, and the input variables $\mathbf{x}$ represent our observed knowledge about the entities. But modeling the joint distribution can lead to difficulties when using the rich local features that can occur in relational data, because it requires modeling the distribution $p(\mathbf{x})$, which can include complex dependencies. Modeling these dependencies among inputs can lead to intractable models, but ignoring them can lead to reduced performance.

A solution to this problem is to directly model the conditional distribution $p(\mathbf{y}|\mathbf{x})$, which is sufficient for classification. This is the approach taken by *conditional random fields* (CRFs) [24]. A CRF is simply a conditional distribution $p(\mathbf{y}|\mathbf{x})$ with an associated graphical structure. Because the model is conditional, dependencies among the input variables **x** do not need to be explicitly represented, affording the use of rich, global features of the input. For example, in natural language tasks, useful features include neighboring words and word bigrams, prefixes and suffixes, capitalization, membership in domain-specific lexicons, and semantic information from sources such as WordNet. Recently there has been an explosion of interest in CRFs, with successful applications including text processing [55, 37, 48, 49], bioinformatics [47, 25], and computer vision [18, 23].

This chapter is divided into two parts. First, we present a tutorial on current training and inference techniques for CRFs. We discuss the important special case of linear-chain CRFs, and then we generalize these to arbitrary graphical structures. We include a brief discussion of techniques for practical CRF implementations.

Second, we present an example of applying a general CRF to a practical relational learning problem. In particular, we discuss the problem of *information extraction*, that is, automatically building a relational database from information contained in unstructured text. Unlike linear-chain models, general CRFs can capture long-distance dependencies between labels. For example, if the same name is mentioned more than once in a document, all mentions probably have the same label, and it is useful to extract them all, because each mention may contain different complementary information about the underlying entity. To represent these long-distance dependencies, we propose a *skip-chain CRF*, a model that jointly performs segmentation and collective labeling of extracted mentions. On a standard problem of extracting speaker names from seminar announcements, the skip-chain CRF has better performance than a linear-chain CRF.

4.2   Graphical Models

4.2.1   Definitions

We consider probability distributions over sets of random variables $V = X \cup Y$, where X is a set of *input variables* that we assume are observed, and Y is a set of *output variables* that we wish to predict. Every variable $v \in V$ takes outcomes from a set $\mathcal{V}$, which can be either continuous or discrete, although we discuss only the discrete case in this chapter. We denote an assignment to X by **x**, and we denote an assignment to a set $A \subset X$ by $\mathbf{x}_A$, and similarly for Y. We use the notation $\mathbf{1}_{\{x=x'\}}$ to denote an indicator function of x which takes the value 1 when $x = x'$ and 0 otherwise.

A graphical model is a family of probability distributions that factorize according to an underlying graph. The main idea is to represent a distribution over a large number of random variables by a product of local functions that each depend on only a small number of variables. Given a collection of subsets $A \subset V$, we define an *undirected graphical model* as the set of all distributions that can be written in the form

$$p(\mathbf{x}, \mathbf{y}) = \frac{1}{Z} \prod_A \Psi_A(\mathbf{x}_A, \mathbf{y}_A), \tag{4.1}$$

for any choice of *factors* $F = \{\Psi_A\}$, where $\Psi_A : \mathcal{V}^n \to \Re^+$. (These functions are also called *local functions* or *compatibility functions*.) We will occasionally use the term *random field* to refer to a particular distribution among those defined by an undirected model. To reiterate, we will consistently use the term *model* to refer to a family of distributions, and *random field* (or more commonly, distribution) to refer to a single one.

The constant Z is a normalization factor defined as

$$Z = \sum_{\mathbf{x}, \mathbf{y}} \prod_A \Psi_A(\mathbf{x}_A, \mathbf{y}_A), \tag{4.2}$$

which ensures that the distribution sums to 1. The quantity Z, considered as a function of the set F of factors, is called the *partition function* in the statistical physics and graphical models communities. Computing Z is intractable in general, but much work exists on how to approximate it.

Graphically, we represent the factorization (4.1) by a *factor graph* [21]. A factor graph is a bipartite graph $G = (V, F, E)$ in which a variable node $v_s \in V$ is connected to a factor node $\Psi_A \in F$ if v_s is an argument to Ψ_A. An example of a factor graph is shown graphically in figure 4.1 (right). In that figure, the circles are variable nodes, and the shaded boxes are factor nodes.

In this chapter, we will assume that each local function has the form

$$\Psi_A(\mathbf{x}_A, \mathbf{y}_A) = \exp\left\{ \sum_k \theta_{Ak} f_{Ak}(\mathbf{x}_A, \mathbf{y}_A) \right\}, \tag{4.3}$$

for some real-valued parameter vector θ_A, and for some set of *feature functions* or *sufficient statistics* $\{f_{Ak}\}$. This form ensures that the family of distributions over V parameterized by θ is an exponential family. Much of the discussion in this chapter actually applies to exponential families in general.

A *directed graphical model*, also known as a Bayesian network, is based on a directed graph $G = (V, E)$. A directed model is a family of distributions that factorize as

$$p(\mathbf{y}, \mathbf{x}) = \prod_{v \in V} p(v | \pi(v)), \tag{4.4}$$

where $\pi(v)$ are the parents of v in G. An example of a directed model is shown in figure 4.1 (left).

We use the term *generative model* to refer to a directed graphical model in which the outputs topologically precede the inputs, that is, no $x \in X$ can be a parent of an output $y \in Y$. Essentially, a generative model is one that directly describes how the outputs probabilistically "generate" the inputs.

Figure 4.1　The naive Bayes classifier, as a directed model (left), and as a factor graph (right).

4.2.2　Applications of Graphical Models

In this section we discuss a few applications of graphical models to natural language processing (NLP). Although these examples are well-known, they serve both to clarify the definitions in the previous section, and to illustrate some ideas that will arise again in our discussion of CRFs. We devote special attention to the hidden Markov model (HMM), because it is closely related to the linear-chain CRF.

4.2.2.1　Classification

First we discuss the problem of *classification*, that is, predicting a single class variable y given a vector of features $\mathbf{x} = (x_1, x_2, \ldots, x_K)$. One simple way to accomplish this is to assume that once the class label is known, all the features are independent. The resulting classifier is called the *naive Bayes classifier*. It is based on a joint probability model of the form

$$p(y, \mathbf{x}) = p(y) \prod_{k=1}^{K} p(x_k|y). \tag{4.5}$$

This model can be described by the directed model shown in figure 4.1 (left). We can also write this model as a factor graph, by defining a factor $\Psi(y) = p(y)$, and a factor $\Psi_k(y, x_k) = p(x_k|y)$ for each feature x_k. This factor graph is shown in figure 4.1 (right).

Another well-known classifier that is naturally represented as a graphical model is logistic regression (sometimes known as the *maximum entropy classifier* in the NLP community). In statistics, this classifier is motivated by the assumption that the log probability, $\log p(y|\mathbf{x})$, of each class is a linear function of $\mathbf{x}$, plus a normalization constant. This leads to the conditional distribution:

$$p(y|\mathbf{x}) = \frac{1}{Z(\mathbf{x})} \exp\left\{ \lambda_y + \sum_{j=1}^{K} \lambda_{y,j} x_j \right\}, \tag{4.6}$$

where $Z(\mathbf{x}) = \sum_y \exp\{\lambda_y + \sum_{j=1}^{K} \lambda_{y,j} x_j\}$ is a normalizing constant, and λ_y is a bias weight that acts like $\log p(y)$ in naive Bayes. Rather than using one vector per class, as in (4.6), we can use a different notation in which a single set of weights is shared across all the classes. The trick is to define a set of *feature functions* that are nonzero only for a single class. To do this, the feature functions can be defined as $f_{y',j}(y, \mathbf{x}) = \mathbf{1}_{\{y'=y\}} x_j$ for the feature weights and $f_{y'}(y, \mathbf{x}) = \mathbf{1}_{\{y'=y\}}$ for the bias weights. Now we can use f_k to index each feature function $f_{y',j}$, and λ_k to index its corresponding weight $\lambda_{y',j}$. Using this notational trick, the logistic regression model becomes:

$$p(y|\mathbf{x}) = \frac{1}{Z(\mathbf{x})} \exp \left\{ \sum_{k=1}^{K} \lambda_k f_k(y, \mathbf{x}) \right\}. \tag{4.7}$$

We introduce this notation because it mirrors the usual notation for CRFs.

4.2.2.2 *Sequence Models*

Classifiers predict only a single class variable, but the true power of graphical models lies in their ability to model many variables that are interdependent. In this section, we discuss perhaps the simplest form of dependency, in which the output variables are arranged in a sequence. To motivate this kind of model, we discuss an application from NLP, the task of *named-entity recognition* (NER). NER is the problem of identifying and classifying proper names in text, including locations, such as *China*; people, such as *George Bush*; and organizations, such as the *United Nations*. The NER task is, given a sentence, first to segment which words are part of entities, and then to classify each entity by type (person, organization, location, and so on). The challenge of this problem is that many named entities are too rare to appear even in a large training set, and therefore the system must identify them based only on context.

One approach to NER is to classify each word independently as one of either PERSON, LOCATION, ORGANIZATION, or OTHER (meaning not an entity). The problem with this approach is that it assumes that given the input, all of the named-entity labels are independent. In fact, the named-entity labels of neighboring words are dependent; for example, while *New York* is a location, *New York Times* is an organization.

This independence assumption can be relaxed by arranging the output variables in a linear chain. This is the approach taken by HMMs [42]. An HMM models a sequence of observations $X = \{x_t\}_{t=1}^{\mathrm{T}}$ by assuming that there is an underlying sequence of *states* $Y = \{y_t\}_{t=1}^{\mathrm{T}}$ drawn from a finite state set S. In the named-entity example, each observation x_t is the identity of the word at position t, and each state y_t is the named-entity label, that is, one of the entity types PERSON, LOCATION, ORGANIZATION, and OTHER.

To model the joint distribution $p(\mathbf{y}, \mathbf{x})$ tractably, an HMM makes two independence assumptions. First, it assumes that each state depends only on its immediate predecessor, that is, each state y_t is independent of all its ancestors $y_1, y_2, \ldots, y_{t-2}$ given its previous state y_{t-1}. Second, an HMM assumes that each observation variable x_t depends only on the current state y_t. With these assumptions, we can specify an HMM using three probability distributions: first, the distribution $p(y_1)$

over initial states; second, the transition distribution $p(y_t|y_{t-1})$; and finally, the observation distribution $p(x_t|y_t)$. That is, the joint probability of a state sequence **y** and an observation sequence **x** factorizes as

$$p(\mathbf{y}, \mathbf{x}) = \prod_{t=1}^{T} p(y_t|y_{t-1}) p(x_t|y_t), \tag{4.8}$$

where, to simplify notation, we write the initial state distribution $p(y_1)$ as $p(y_1|y_0)$. In NLP, HMMs have been used for sequence labeling tasks such as part-of-speech tagging, named-entity recognition, and information extraction.

4.2.3   Discriminative and Generative Models

An important difference between naive Bayes and logistic regression is that naive Bayes is *generative*, meaning that it is based on a model of the joint distribution $p(y, \mathbf{x})$, while logistic regression is *discriminative*, meaning that it is based on a model of the conditional distribution $p(y|\mathbf{x})$. In this section, we discuss the differences between generative and discriminative modeling, and the advantages of discriminative modeling for many tasks. For concreteness, we focus on the examples of naive Bayes and logistic regression, but the discussion in this section actually applies in general to the differences between generative models and CRF.

The main difference is that a conditional distribution $p(\mathbf{y}|\mathbf{x})$ does not include a model of $p(\mathbf{x})$, which is not needed for classification anyway. The difficulty in modeling $p(\mathbf{x})$ is that it often contains many highly dependent features, which are difficult to model. For example, in named-entity recognition, an HMM relies on only one feature, the word's identity. But many words, especially proper names, will not have occurred in the training set, so the word-identity feature is uninformative. To label unseen words, we would like to exploit other features of a word, such as its capitalization, its neighboring words, its prefixes and suffixes, its membership in predetermined lists of people and locations, and so on.

To include interdependent features in a generative model, we have two choices: enhance the model to represent dependencies among the inputs, or make simplifying independence assumptions, such as the naive Bayes assumption. The first approach, enhancing the model, is often difficult to do while retaining tractability. For example, it is hard to imagine how to model the dependence between the capitalization of a word and its suffixes, nor do we particularly wish to do so, since we always observe the test sentences anyway. The second approach, adding independence assumptions among the inputs, is problematic because it can hurt performance. For example, although the naive Bayes classifier performs surprisingly well in document classification, it performs worse on average across a range of applications than logistic regression [7].

Furthermore, even when naive Bayes has good classification accuracy, its probability estimates tend to be poor. To understand why, imagine training naive Bayes on a data set in which all the features are repeated, that is,

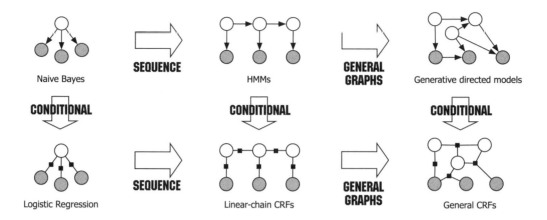

Figure 4.2 Diagram of the relationship between naive Bayes, logistic regression, HMMs, linear-chain CRFs, generative models, and general CRFs.

$\mathbf{x} = (x_1, x_1, x_2, x_2, \ldots, x_K, x_K)$. This will increase the confidence of the naive Bayes probability estimates, even though no new information has been added to the data. Assumptions like naive Bayes can be especially problematic when we generalize to sequence models, because inference essentially combines evidence from different parts of the model. If probability estimates at a local level are overconfident, it might be difficult to combine them sensibly.

Actually, the difference in performance between naive Bayes and logistic regression is due *only* to the fact that the first is generative and the second discriminative; the two classifiers are, for discrete input, identical in all other respects. Naive Bayes and logistic regression consider the same hypothesis space, in the sense that any logistic regression classifier can be converted into a naive Bayes classifier with the same decision boundary, and vice versa. Another way of saying this is that the naive Bayes model (4.5) defines the same family of distributions as the logistic regression model (4.7), if we interpret it generatively as

$$p(y, \mathbf{x}) = \frac{\exp \left\{ \sum_k \lambda_k f_k(y, \mathbf{x}) \right\}}{\sum_{\tilde{y}, \tilde{\mathbf{x}}} \exp \left\{ \sum_k \lambda_k f_k(\tilde{y}, \tilde{\mathbf{x}}) \right\}}. \tag{4.9}$$

This means that if the naive Bayes model (4.5) is trained to maximize the conditional likelihood, we recover the same classifier as from logistic regression. Conversely, if the logistic regression model is interpreted generatively, as in (4.9), and is trained to maximize the joint likelihood $p(y, \mathbf{x})$, then we recover the same classifier as from naive Bayes. In the terminology of Ng and Jordan [36], naive Bayes and logistic regression form a *generative-discriminative pair*.

The principal advantage of discriminative modeling is that it is better suited to including rich, overlapping features. To understand this, consider the family of naive Bayes distributions (4.5). This is a family of joint distributions whose conditionals all take the "logistic regression form" (4.7). But there are many other joint models, some with complex dependencies among $\mathbf{x}$, whose conditional distributions also have the form (4.7). By modeling the conditional distribution directly, we can remain agnostic about the form of $p(\mathbf{x})$. This may explain why it has been observed that CRFs tend to be more robust than generative models to violations of their independence assumptions [24]. Simply put, CRFs make independence assumptions among $\mathbf{y}$, but not among $\mathbf{x}$.

Another way to make the same point is due to Minka[34]. Suppose we have a generative model p_g with parameters θ. By definition, this takes the form

$$p_g(\mathbf{y}, \mathbf{x}; \theta) = p_g(\mathbf{y}; \theta) p_g(\mathbf{x}|\mathbf{y}; \theta). \tag{4.10}$$

But we could also rewrite p_g using Bayes rule as

$$p_g(\mathbf{y}, \mathbf{x}; \theta) = p_g(\mathbf{x}; \theta) p_g(\mathbf{y}|\mathbf{x}; \theta), \tag{4.11}$$

where $p_g(\mathbf{x}; \theta)$ and $p_g(\mathbf{y}|\mathbf{x}; \theta)$ are computed by inference, i.e., $p_g(\mathbf{x}; \theta) = \sum_{\mathbf{y}} p_g(\mathbf{y}, \mathbf{x}; \theta)$ and $p_g(\mathbf{y}|\mathbf{x}; \theta) = p_g(\mathbf{y}, \mathbf{x}; \theta)/p_g(\mathbf{x}; \theta)$.

Now, compare this generative model to a discriminative model over the same family of joint distributions. To do this, we define a prior $p(\mathbf{x})$ over inputs, such that $p(\mathbf{x})$ could have arisen from p_g with some parameter setting. That is, $p(\mathbf{x}) = p_c(\mathbf{x}; \theta') = \sum_{\mathbf{y}} p_g(\mathbf{y}, \mathbf{x}|\theta')$. We combine this with a conditional distribution $p_c(\mathbf{y}|\mathbf{x}; \theta)$ that could also have arisen from p_g, that is, $p_c(\mathbf{y}|\mathbf{x}; \theta) = p_g(\mathbf{y}, \mathbf{x}; \theta)/p_g(\mathbf{x}; \theta)$. Then the resulting distribution is

$$p_c(\mathbf{y}, \mathbf{x}) = p_c(\mathbf{x}; \theta') p_c(\mathbf{y}|\mathbf{x}; \theta). \tag{4.12}$$

By comparing (4.11) with (4.12), it can be seen that the conditional approach has more freedom to fit the data, because it does not require that $\theta = \theta'$. Intuitively, because the parameters θ in (4.11) are used in both the input distribution and the conditional, a good set of parameters must represent both well, potentially at the cost of trading off accuracy on $p(\mathbf{y}|\mathbf{x})$, the distribution we care about, for accuracy on $p(\mathbf{x})$, which we care less about.

In this section, we have discussed the relationship between naive Bayes and logistic regression in detail because it mirrors the relationship between HMMs and linear-chain CRFs. Just as naive Bayes and logistic regression are a generative-discriminative pair, there is a discriminative analogue to HMMs, and this analogue is a particular type of CRF, as we explain next. The analogy between naive Bayes, logistic regression, generative models, and CRFs is depicted in figure 4.2.

4.3   Linear-Chain Conditional Random Fields

In the previous section, we have seen advantages both to discriminative modeling and sequence modeling. So it makes sense to combine the two. This yields a linear-chain CRF, which we describe in this section. First, in section 4.3.1, we define linear-

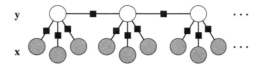

Figure 4.3 Graphical model of an HMM-like linear-chain CRF.

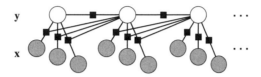

Figure 4.4 Graphical model of a linear-chain CRF in which the transition score depends on the current observation.

chain CRFs, motivating them from HMMs. Then, we discuss parameter estimation (section 4.3.2) and inference (section 4.3.3) in linear-chain CRFs.

4.3.1 From HMMs to CRFs

To motivate our introduction of linear-chain CRFs, we begin by considering the conditional distribution $p(\mathbf{y}|\mathbf{x})$ that follows from the joint distribution $p(\mathbf{y}, \mathbf{x})$ of an HMM. The key point is that this conditional distribution is in fact a CRF with a particular choice of feature functions.

First, we rewrite the HMM joint (4.8) in a form that is more amenable to generalization. This is

$$p(\mathbf{y}, \mathbf{x}) = \frac{1}{Z} \exp \left\{ \sum_t \sum_{i,j \in S} \lambda_{ij} \mathbf{1}_{\{y_t = i\}} \mathbf{1}_{\{y_{t-1} = j\}} + \sum_t \sum_{i \in S} \sum_{o \in O} \mu_{oi} \mathbf{1}_{\{y_t = i\}} \mathbf{1}_{\{x_t = o\}} \right\}, \tag{4.13}$$

where $\theta = \{\lambda_{ij}, \mu_{oi}\}$ are the parameters of the distribution, and can be any real numbers. Every HMM can be written in this form, as can be seen simply by setting $\lambda_{ij} = \log p(y' = i | y = j)$ and so on. Because we do not require the parameters to be log probabilities, we are no longer guaranteed that the distribution sums to 1, unless we explicitly enforce this by using a normalization constant Z. Despite this added flexibility, it can be shown that (4.13) describes exactly the class of HMMs in (4.8); we have added flexibility to the parameterization, but we have not added any distributions to the family.

We can write (4.13) more compactly by introducing the concept of *feature functions*, just as we did for logistic regression in (4.7). Each feature function has the form $f_k(y_t, y_{t-1}, x_t)$. In order to duplicate (4.13), there needs to be one feature $f_{ij}(y, y', x) = \mathbf{1}_{\{y=i\}} \mathbf{1}_{\{y'=j\}}$ for each transition (i, j) and one feature $f_{io}(y, y', x) = \mathbf{1}_{\{y=i\}} \mathbf{1}_{\{x=o\}}$ for each state-observation pair (i, o). Then we can write an HMM as

$$p(\mathbf{y}, \mathbf{x}) = \frac{1}{Z} \exp \left\{ \sum_{k=1}^{K} \lambda_k f_k(y_t, y_{t-1}, x_t) \right\}. \tag{4.14}$$

Again, (4.14) defines exactly the same family of distributions as (4.13), and therefore as the original HMM equation (4.8).

The last step is to write the conditional distribution $p(\mathbf{y}|\mathbf{x})$ that results from the HMM (4.14). This is

$$p(\mathbf{y}|\mathbf{x}) = \frac{p(\mathbf{y}, \mathbf{x})}{\sum_{\mathbf{y}'} p(\mathbf{y}', \mathbf{x})} = \frac{\exp \left\{ \sum_{k=1}^{K} \lambda_k f_k(y_t, y_{t-1}, x_t) \right\}}{\sum_{\mathbf{y}'} \exp \left\{ \sum_{k=1}^{K} \lambda_k f_k(y_t', y_{t-1}', x_t) \right\}}. \tag{4.15}$$

This conditional distribution (4.15) is a linear-chain CRF, in particular one that includes features only for the current word's identity. But many other linear-chain CRFs use richer features of the input, such as prefixes and suffixes of the current word, the identity of surrounding words, and so on. Fortunately, this extension requires little change to our existing notation. We simply allow the feature functions $f_k(y_t, y_{t-1}, \mathbf{x}_t)$ to be more general than indicator functions. This leads to the general definition of linear-chain CRFs, which we present now.

Definition 4.1
Let Y, X be random vectors, $\Lambda = \{\lambda_k\} \in \Re^K$ be a parameter vector, and $\{f_k(y, y', \mathbf{x}_t)\}_{k=1}^{K}$ be a set of real-valued feature functions. Then a *linear-chain conditional random field* is a distribution $p(\mathbf{y}|\mathbf{x})$ that takes the form

$$p(\mathbf{y}|\mathbf{x}) = \frac{1}{Z(\mathbf{x})} \exp \left\{ \sum_{k=1}^{K} \lambda_k f_k(y_t, y_{t-1}, \mathbf{x}_t) \right\}, \tag{4.16}$$

where $Z(\mathbf{x})$ is an instance-specific normalization function

$$Z(\mathbf{x}) = \sum_{\mathbf{y}} \exp \left\{ \sum_{k=1}^{K} \lambda_k f_k(y_t, y_{t-1}, \mathbf{x}_t) \right\}. \tag{4.17}$$

We have just seen that if the joint $p(\mathbf{y}, \mathbf{x})$ factorizes as an HMM, then the associated conditional distribution $p(\mathbf{y}|\mathbf{x})$ is a linear-chain CRF. This HMM-like CRF is pictured in figure 4.3. Other types of linear-chain CRFs are also useful, however. For example, in an HMM, a transition from state i to state j receives the same score, $\log p(y_t = j | y_{t-1} = i)$, regardless of the input. In a CRF, we can allow the score of the transition (i, j) to depend on the current observation vector, simply by adding a feature $\mathbf{1}_{\{y_t=j\}} \mathbf{1}_{\{y_{t-1}=1\}} \mathbf{1}_{\{x_t=o\}}$. A CRF with this kind of transition feature, which is commonly used in text applications, is pictured in figure 4.4.

To indicate in the definition of linear-chain CRF that each feature function can depend on observations from any time step, we have written the observation argument to f_k as a vector $\mathbf{x}_t$, which should be understood as containing all the components of the global observations **x** that are needed for computing features at time t. For example, if the CRF uses the next word x_{t+1} as a feature, then the feature vector $\mathbf{x}_t$ is assumed to include the identity of word x_{t+1}.

Finally, note that the normalization constant $Z(\mathbf{x})$ sums over all possible state sequences, an exponentially large number of terms. Nevertheless, it can be computed efficiently by forward-backward, as we explain in section 4.3.3.

4.3.2 Parameter Estimation

In this section we discuss how to estimate the parameters $\theta = \{\lambda_k\}$ of a linear-chain CRF. We are given i.i.d. training data $\mathcal{D} = \{\mathbf{x}^{(i)}, \mathbf{y}^{(i)}\}_{i=1}^{N}$, where each $\mathbf{x}^{(i)} = \{x_1^{(i)}, x_2^{(i)}, \dots x_T^{(i)}\}$ is a sequence of inputs, and each $\mathbf{y}^{(i)} = \{y_1^{(i)}, y_2^{(i)}, \dots y_T^{(i)}\}$ is a sequence of the desired predictions. Thus, we have relaxed the i.i.d. assumption within each sequence, but we still assume that distinct sequences are independent. (In section 4.4, we will see how to relax this assumption as well.)

Parameter estimation is typically performed by penalized maximum likelihood. Because we are modeling the conditional distribution, the following log-likelihood, sometimes called the *conditional log-likelihood*, is appropriate:

$$\ell(\theta) = \sum_{i=1}^{N} \log p(\mathbf{y}^{(i)} | \mathbf{x}^{(i)}). \tag{4.18}$$

One way to understand the conditional likelihood $p(\mathbf{y}|\mathbf{x}; \theta)$ is to imagine combining it with some arbitrary prior $p(\mathbf{x}; \theta')$ to form a joint $p(\mathbf{y}, \mathbf{x})$. Then when we optimize the joint log-likelihood

$$\log p(\mathbf{y}, \mathbf{x}) = \log p(\mathbf{y}|\mathbf{x}; \theta) + \log p(\mathbf{x}; \theta'), \tag{4.19}$$

the two terms on the right-hand side are decoupled, that is, the value of θ' does not affect the optimization over θ. If we do not need to estimate $p(\mathbf{x})$, then we can simply drop the second term, which leaves (4.18).

After substituting in the CRF model (4.16) into the likelihood (4.18), we get the following expression:

$$\ell(\theta) = \sum_{i=1}^{N} \sum_{t=1}^{T} \sum_{k=1}^{K} \lambda_k f_k(y_t^{(i)}, y_{t-1}^{(i)}, \mathbf{x}_t^{(i)}) - \sum_{i=1}^{N} \log Z(\mathbf{x}^{(i)}), \tag{4.20}$$

Before we discuss how to optimize this, we mention regularization. It is often the case that we have a large number of parameters. As a measure to avoid overfitting, we use *regularization*, which is a penalty on weight vectors whose norm is too large. A common choice of penalty is based on the Euclidean norm of θ and on a *regularization parameter* $1/2\sigma^2$ that determines the strength of the penalty. Then the regularized log likelihood is

$$\ell(\theta) = \sum_{i=1}^{N} \sum_{t=1}^{T} \sum_{k=1}^{K} \lambda_k f_k(y_t^{(i)}, y_{t-1}^{(i)}, \mathbf{x}_t^{(i)}) - \sum_{i=1}^{N} \log Z(\mathbf{x}^{(i)}) - \sum_{k=1}^{K} \frac{\lambda_k^2}{2\sigma^2}. \tag{4.21}$$

The notation for the regularizer is intended to suggest that regularization can also be viewed as performing maximum a posteriori estimation of θ, if θ is assigned a Gaussian prior with mean 0 and covariance $\sigma^2 I$. The parameter σ^2 is a free parameter which determines how much to penalize large weights. Determining the best regularization parameter can require a computationally intensive parameter sweep. Fortunately, often the accuracy of the final model does not appear to be sensitive to changes in σ^2, even when σ^2 is varied up to a factor of 10. An alternative choice of regularization is to use the ℓ_1 norm instead of the Euclidean norm, which corresponds to an exponential prior on parameters [17]. This regularizer tends to encourage sparsity in the learned parameters.

In general, the function $\ell(\theta)$ cannot be maximized in closed form, so numeric optimization is used. The partial derivatives of (4.21) are

$$\frac{\partial \ell}{\partial \lambda_k} = \sum_{i=1}^{N} \sum_{t=1}^{T} f_k(y_t^{(i)}, y_{t-1}^{(i)}, \mathbf{x}_t^{(i)}) - \sum_{i=1}^{N} \sum_{t=1}^{T} \sum_{y,y'} f_k(y, y', \mathbf{x}_t^{(i)}) p(y, y' | \mathbf{x}^{(i)}) - \sum_{k=1}^{K} \frac{\lambda_k}{\sigma^2}.$$
(4.22)

The first term is the expected value of f_k under the empirical distribution:

$$\tilde{p}(\mathbf{y}, \mathbf{x}) = \frac{1}{N} \sum_{i=1}^{N} \mathbf{1}_{\{\mathbf{y}=\mathbf{y}^{(i)}\}} \mathbf{1}_{\{\mathbf{x}=\mathbf{x}^{(i)}\}}.$$
(4.23)

The second term, which arises from the derivative of $\log Z(\mathbf{x})$, is the expectation of f_k under the model distribution $p(\mathbf{y}|\mathbf{x};\theta)\tilde{p}(\mathbf{x})$. Therefore, at the unregularized maximum likelihood solution, when the gradient is zero, these two expectations are equal. This pleasing interpretation is a standard result about maximum-likelihood estimation in exponential families.

Now we discuss how to optimize $\ell(\theta)$. The function $\ell(\theta)$ is concave, which follows from the convexity of functions of the form $g(\mathbf{x}) = \log \sum_i \exp x_i$. Convexity is extremely helpful for parameter estimation, because it means that every local optimum is also a global optimum. Adding regularization ensures that ℓ is strictly concave, which implies that it has exactly one global optimum.

Perhaps the simplest approach to optimize ℓ is steepest ascent along the gradient (4.22), but this requires too many iterations to be practical. Newton's method converges much faster because it takes into account the curvature of the likelihood, but it requires computing the Hessian, the matrix of all second derivatives. The size of the Hessian is quadratic in the number of parameters. Since practical applications often use tens of thousands or even millions of parameters, even storing the full Hessian is not practical.

Instead, current techniques for optimizing (4.21) make approximate use of second-order information. Particularly successful have been quasi-Newton methods such as BFGS [3], which compute an approximation to the Hessian from only the first derivative of the objective function. A full $K \times K$ approximation to the Hessian still requires quadratic size, however, so a limited-memory version of BFGS is used, due to Byrd et al. [6]. As an alternative to limited-memory BFGS, conjugate gradient is another optimization technique that also makes approximate use of second-order information and has been used successfully with CRFs. Either can be thought of as a black-box optimization routine that is a drop-in replacement for vanilla gradient ascent. When such second-order methods are used, gradient-based optimization is much faster than the original approaches based on iterative scaling in Lafferty et al. [24], as shown experimentally by several authors [49, 61, 26, 35]. Recently, stochastic gradient methods, which make updates based on subsets of the training instances, have been shown to be highly effective [58], and may be an attractive alternative to second-order methods, which tend to evaluate the gradient over all the training instances before making an update.

Finally, it is important to remark on the computational cost of training. Both the partition function $Z(\mathbf{x})$ in the likelihood and the marginal distributions $p(y_t, y_{t-1}|\mathbf{x})$ in the gradient can be computed by forward-backward, which uses computational complexity $O(TM^2)$. However, each training instance will have a different partition function and marginals, so we need to run forward-backward for each training instance for each gradient computation, for a total training cost of $O(TM^2NG)$, where N is the number of training examples, and G the number of gradient computations required by the optimization procedure. For many data sets, this cost is reasonable, but if the number of states is large, or the number of training sequences is very large, then this can become expensive. For example, on a standard named-entity data set, with eleven labels and 200,000 words of training data, CRF training finishes in under two hours on current hardware. However, on a part-of-speech tagging data set, with forty-five labels and 1 million words of training data, CRF training requires over a week.

4.3.3   Inference

There are two common inference problems for CRFs. First, during training, computing the gradient requires marginal distributions for each edge $p(y_t, y_{t-1}|\mathbf{x})$, and computing the likelihood requires $Z(\mathbf{x})$. Second, to label an unseen instance, we compute the most likely (Viterbi) labeling $\mathbf{y}^* = \arg\max_{\mathbf{y}} p(\mathbf{y}|\mathbf{x})$. In linear-chain CRFs, both inference tasks can be performed efficiently and exactly by variants of the standard dynamic-programming algorithms for HMMs. In this section, we briefly review the HMM algorithms, and extend them to linear-chain CRFs. These standard inference algorithms are described in more detail by Rabiner [42].

First, we introduce notation which will simplify the forward-backward recursions. An HMM can be viewed as a factor graph $p(\mathbf{y}, \mathbf{x}) = \prod_t \Psi_t(y_t, y_{t-1}, x_t)$ where $Z = 1$, and the factors are defined as

$$\Psi_t(j, i, x) \stackrel{\text{def}}{=} p(y_t = j|y_{t-1} = i)p(x_t = x|y_t = j). \qquad (4.24)$$

If the HMM is viewed as a weighted finite-state machine, then $\Psi_t(j, i, x)$ is the weight on the transition from state i to state j when the current observation is x.

Now, we review the HMM forward algorithm, which is used to compute the probability $p(\mathbf{x})$ of the observations. The idea behind forward-backward is to first rewrite the naive summation $p(\mathbf{x}) = \sum_{\mathbf{y}} p(\mathbf{x}, \mathbf{y})$ using the distributive law:

$$p(\mathbf{x}) = \sum_{\mathbf{y}} \prod_{t=1}^{T} \Psi_t(y_t, y_{t-1}, x_t) \tag{4.25}$$

$$= \sum_{y_{\mathrm{T}}} \sum_{y_{\mathrm{T}-1}} \Psi_{\mathrm{T}}(y_{\mathrm{T}}, y_{\mathrm{T}-1}, x_{\mathrm{T}}) \sum_{y_{\mathrm{T}-2}} \Psi_{\mathrm{T}-1}(y_{\mathrm{T}-1}, y_{\mathrm{T}-2}, x_{\mathrm{T}-1}) \sum_{y_{\mathrm{T}-3}} \cdots \tag{4.26}$$

Now we observe that each of the intermediate sums is reused many times during the computation of the outer sum, and so we can save an exponential amount of work by caching the inner sums.

This leads to defining a set of *forward variables* α_t, each of which is a vector of size M (where M is the number of states) which stores one of the intermediate sums. These are defined as

$$\alpha_t(j) \stackrel{\mathrm{def}}{=} p(\mathbf{x}_{\langle 1 \ldots t \rangle}, y_t = j) \tag{4.27}$$

$$= \sum_{\mathbf{y}_{\langle 1 \ldots t-1 \rangle}} \Psi_t(j, y_{t-1}, x_t) \prod_{t'=1}^{t-1} \Psi_{t'}(y_{t'}, y_{t'-1}, x_{t'}), \tag{4.28}$$

where the summation over $\mathbf{y}_{\langle 1 \ldots t-1 \rangle}$ ranges over all assignments to the sequence of random variables $y_1, y_2, \ldots, y_{t-1}$. The alpha values can be computed by the recursion

$$\alpha_t(j) = \sum_{i \in S} \Psi_t(j, i, x_t) \alpha_{t-1}(i), \tag{4.29}$$

with initialization $\alpha_1(j) = \Psi_1(j, y_0, x_1)$. (Recall that y_0 is the fixed initial state of the HMM.) It is easy to see that $p(\mathbf{x}) = \sum_{y_{\mathrm{T}}} \alpha_{\mathrm{T}}(y_{\mathrm{T}})$ by repeatedly substituting the recursion (4.29) to obtain (4.26). A formal proof would use induction.

The backward recursion is exactly the same, except that in (4.26), we push in the summations in reverse order. This results in the definition

$$\beta_t(i) \stackrel{\mathrm{def}}{=} p(\mathbf{x}_{\langle t+1 \ldots \mathrm{T} \rangle} | y_t = i) \tag{4.30}$$

$$= \sum_{\mathbf{y}_{\langle t+1 \ldots \mathrm{T} \rangle}} \prod_{t'=t+1}^{\mathrm{T}} \Psi_{t'}(y_{t'}, y_{t'-1}, x_{t'}), \tag{4.31}$$

and the recursion

$$\beta_t(i) = \sum_{j \in S} \Psi_{t+1}(j, i, x_{t+1}) \beta_{t+1}(j), \tag{4.32}$$

which is initialized $\beta_{\mathrm{T}}(i) = 1$. Analogously to the forward case, we can compute $p(\mathbf{x})$ using the backward variables as $p(\mathbf{x}) = \beta_0(y_0) \stackrel{\mathrm{def}}{=} \sum_{y_1} \Psi_1(y_1, y_0, x_1) \beta_1(y_1)$.

By combining results from the forward and backward recursions, we can compute the marginal distributions needed for the gradient (4.22). Applying the distributive law again, we see that

$$p(y_{t-1}, y_t | \mathbf{x}) = \Psi_t(y_t, y_{t-1}, x_t)$$
$$\left(\sum_{\mathbf{y}_{\langle 1...t-2 \rangle}} \prod_{t'=1}^{t-1} \Psi_{t'}(y_{t'}, y_{t'-1}, x_{t'}) \right)$$
$$\left(\sum_{\mathbf{y}_{\langle t+1...T \rangle}} \prod_{t'=t+1}^{T} \Psi_{t'}(y_{t'}, y_{t'-1}, x_{t'}) \right), \quad (4.33)$$

which can be computed from the forward and backward recursions as

$$p(y_{t-1}, y_t | \mathbf{x}) \propto \alpha_{t-1}(y_{t-1}) \Psi_t(y_t, y_{t-1}, x_t) \beta_t(y_t). \quad (4.34)$$

Finally, to compute the globally most probable assignment $\mathbf{y}^* = \arg\max_{\mathbf{y}} p(\mathbf{y}|\mathbf{x})$, we observe that the trick in (4.26) still works if all the summations are replaced by maximization. This yields the Viterbi recursion:

$$\delta_t(j) = \max_{i \in S} \Psi_t(j, i, x_t) \delta_{t-1}(i). \quad (4.35)$$

Now that we have described the forward-backward and Viterbi algorithms for HMMs, the generalization to linear-chain CRFs is fairly straightforward. The forward-backward algorithm for linear-chain CRFs is identical to the HMM version, except that the transition weights $\Psi_t(j, i, x_t)$ are defined differently. We observe that the CRF model (4.16) can be rewritten as

$$p(\mathbf{y}|\mathbf{x}) = \frac{1}{Z(\mathbf{x})} \prod_{t=1}^{T} \Psi_t(y_t, y_{t-1}, \mathbf{x}_t), \quad (4.36)$$

where we define

$$\Psi_t(y_t, y_{t-1}, \mathbf{x}_t) = \exp \left\{ \sum_k \lambda_k f_k(y_t, y_{t-1}, \mathbf{x}_t) \right\}. \quad (4.37)$$

With that definition, the forward recursion (4.29), the backward recursion (4.32), and the Viterbi recursion (4.35) can be used unchanged for linear-chain CRFs. Instead of computing $p(\mathbf{x})$ as in an HMM, in a CRF the forward and backward recursions compute $Z(\mathbf{x})$.

A final inference task that is useful in some applications is to compute a marginal probability $p(y_t, y_{t+1}, \ldots y_{t+k} | \mathbf{x})$ over a range of nodes. For example, this is useful for measuring the model's confidence in its predicted labeling over a segment of input. This marginal probability can be computed efficiently using constrained forward-backward, as by Culotta and McCallum[12].

4.4   CRFs in General

In this section, we define CRFs with general graphical structure, as they were introduced originally [24]. Although initial applications of CRFs used linear chains, there have been many later applications of CRFs with more general graphical structures. Such structures are especially useful for relational learning, because they allow relaxing the i.i.d. assumption among entities. Also, although CRFs have typically been used for across-network classification, in which the training and testing data are assumed to be independent, we will see that CRFs can be used for within-network classification as well, in which we model probabilistic dependencies between the training and testing data.

The generalization from linear-chain CRFs to general CRFs is fairly straightforward. We simply move from using a linear-chain factor graph to a more general factor graph, and from forward-backward to more general (perhaps approximate) inference algorithms.

4.4.1   Model

First we present the general definition of a CRF.

Definition 4.2
Let G be a factor graph over Y. Then $p(\mathbf{y}|\mathbf{x})$ is a CRF if for any fixed $\mathbf{x}$, the distribution $p(\mathbf{y}|\mathbf{x})$ factorizes according to G.

Thus, every conditional distribution $p(\mathbf{y}|\mathbf{x})$ is a CRF for some, perhaps trivial, factor graph. If $F = \{\Psi_A\}$ is the set of factors in G, and each factor takes the exponential family form (4.3), then the conditional distribution can be written as

$$p(\mathbf{y}|\mathbf{x}) = \frac{1}{Z(\mathbf{x})} \prod_{\Psi_A \in G} \exp \left\{ \sum_{k=1}^{K(A)} \lambda_{Ak} f_{Ak}(\mathbf{y}_A, \mathbf{x}_A) \right\}. \tag{4.38}$$

In addition, practical models rely extensively on parameter tying. For example, in the linear-chain case, often the same weights are used for the factors $\Psi_t(y_t, y_{t-1}, \mathbf{x}_t)$ at each time step. To denote this, we partition the factors of G into $\mathcal{C} = \{C_1, C_2, \ldots C_P\}$, where each C_p is a *clique template* whose parameters are tied. This notion of clique template generalizes that in Taskar et al. [55], Sutton et al. [54], and Richardson and Domingos [43]. Each clique template C_p is a set of factors which has a corresponding set of sufficient statistics $\{f_{pk}(\mathbf{x}_p, \mathbf{y}_p)\}$ and parameters $\theta_p \in \Re^{K(p)}$. Then the CRF can be written as

$$p(\mathbf{y}|\mathbf{x}) = \frac{1}{Z(\mathbf{x})} \prod_{C_p \in \mathcal{C}} \prod_{\Psi_c \in C_p} \Psi_c(\mathbf{x}_c, \mathbf{y}_c; \theta_p), \tag{4.39}$$

where each factor is parameterized as

$$\Psi_c(\mathbf{x}_c, \mathbf{y}_c; \theta_p) = \exp\left\{\sum_{k=1}^{K(p)} \lambda_{pk} f_{pk}(\mathbf{x}_c, \mathbf{y}_c)\right\}, \qquad (4.40)$$

and the normalization function is

$$Z(\mathbf{x}) = \sum_{\mathbf{y}} \prod_{C_p \in \mathcal{C}} \prod_{\Psi_c \in C_p} \Psi_c(\mathbf{x}_c, \mathbf{y}_c; \theta_p). \qquad (4.41)$$

For example, in a linear-chain CRF, typically one clique template $C = \{\Psi_t(y_t, y_{t-1}, \mathbf{x}_t)\}_{t=1}^{T}$ is used for the entire network.

Several special cases of CRFs are of particular interest. First, *dynamic conditional random fields* [54] are sequence models which allow multiple labels at each time step, rather than single labels as in linear-chain CRFs. Second, *relational Markov networks* [55] are a type of general CRF in which the graphical structure and parameter tying are determined by an SQL-like syntax. Finally, *Markov logic networks* [43, 50] are a type of probabilistic logic in which there are parameters for each first-order rule in a knowledge base.

4.4.2   Applications of CRFs

CRFs have been applied to a variety of domains, including text processing, computer vision, and bioinformatics. In this section, we discuss several applications, highlighting the different graphical structures that occur in the literature.

One of the first large-scale applications of CRFs was by Sha and Pereira [49], who matched state-of-the-art performance on segmenting noun phrases in text. Since then, linear-chain CRFs have been applied to many problems in NLP, including named-entity recognition [30], feature induction for NER [28], identifying protein names in biology abstracts [48], segmenting addresses in webpages [13], finding semantic roles in text [45], identifying the sources of opinions [8], Chinese word segmentation [38], Japanese morphological analysis [22], and many others.

In bioinformatics, CRFs have been applied to RNA structural alignment [47] and protein structure prediction [25]. Semi-Markov CRFs [46] add somewhat more flexibility in choosing features, which may be useful for certain tasks in information extraction and especially bioinformatics.

General CRFs have also been applied to several tasks in NLP. One promising application is to perform multiple labeling tasks simultaneously. For example, Sutton et al. [54] show that a two-level dynamic CRF for part-of-speech tagging and noun phrase chunking performs better than solving the tasks one at a time. Another application is to *multilabel classification*, in which each instance can have multiple class labels. Rather than learning an independent classifier for each category, Ghamrawi and McCallum [16] present a CRF that learns dependencies between the categories, resulting in improved classification performance. Finally, the skip-chain CRF, which we present in section 4.5, is a general CRF that represents long-distance dependencies in information extraction.

An interesting graphical CRF structure has been applied to the problem of proper noun coreference, that is, of determining which mentions in a document, such as *Mr. President* and *he*, refer to the same underlying entity. McCallum and Wellner [31] learn a distance metric between mentions using a fully connected CRF in which inference corresponds to graph partitioning. A similar model has been used to segment handwritten characters and diagrams [11, 40].

In some applications of CRFs, efficient dynamic programs exist even though the graphical model is difficult to specify. For example, McCallum et al[33] learn the parameters of a string-edit model in order to discriminate between matching and nonmatching pairs of strings. Also, there is work on using CRFs to learn distributions over the derivations of a grammar [44, 9, 51, 57]. A potentially useful unifying framework for this type of model is provided by case-factor diagrams [27].

In computer vision, several authors have used grid-shaped CRFs [18, 23] for labeling and segmenting images. Also, for recognizing objects, Quattoni et al. [41] use a tree-shaped CRF in which latent variables are designed to recognize characteristic parts of an object.

4.4.3   Parameter Estimation

Parameter estimation for general CRFs is essentially the same as for linear-chains, except that computing the model expectations requires more general inference algorithms. First, we discuss the fully observed case, in which the training and testing data are independent, and the training data is fully observed. In this case the conditional log-likelihood is given by

$$\ell(\theta) = \sum_{C_p \in \mathcal{C}} \sum_{\Psi_c \in C_p} \sum_{k=1}^{K(p)} \lambda_{pk} f_{pk}(\mathbf{x}_c, \mathbf{y}_c) - \log Z(\mathbf{x}). \qquad (4.42)$$

It is worth noting that the equations in this section do not explicitly sum over training instances, because if a particular application happens to have i.i.d. training instances, they can be represented by disconnected components in the graph G.

The partial derivative of the log-likelihood with respect to a parameter λ_{pk} associated with a clique template C_p is

$$\frac{\partial \ell}{\partial \lambda_{pk}} = \sum_{\Psi_c \in C_p} f_{pk}(\mathbf{x}_c, \mathbf{y}_c) - \sum_{\Psi_c \in C_p} \sum_{\mathbf{y}'_c} f_{pk}(\mathbf{x}_c, \mathbf{y}'_c) p(\mathbf{y}'_c | \mathbf{x}). \qquad (4.43)$$

The function $\ell(\theta)$ has many of the same properties as in the linear-chain case. First, the zero-gradient conditions can be interpreted as requiring that the sufficient statistics $F_{pk}(\mathbf{x}, \mathbf{y}) = \sum_{\Psi_c} f_{pk}(\mathbf{x}_c, \mathbf{y}_c)$ have the same expectations under the empirical distribution and under the model distribution. Second, the function $\ell(\theta)$ is concave, and can be efficiently maximized by second-order techniques such as conjugate gradient and L-BFGS. Finally, regularization is used just as in the linear-chain case.

Now, we discuss the case of *within-network classification*, where there are dependencies between the training and testing data. That is, the random variables **y** are partitioned into a set $\mathbf{y}^{tr}$ that is observed during training and a set $\mathbf{y}^{tst}$ that is unobserved during training. It is assumed that the graph G contains connections between $\mathbf{y}^{tr}$ and $\mathbf{y}^{tst}$.

Within-network classification can be viewed as a kind of *latent variable* problem, in which certain variables, in this case $\mathbf{y}^{tst}$, are not observed in the training data. It is more difficult to train CRFs with latent variables, because optimizing the likelihood $p(\mathbf{y}^{tr}|\mathbf{x})$ requires marginalizing out the latent variables $\mathbf{y}^{tst}$. Because of this difficultly, the original work on CRFs focused on fully observed training data, but recently there has been increasing interest in training latent-variable CRFs [41, 33].

Suppose we have a CRF with inputs **x** in which the output variables **y** are observed in the training data, but we have additional variables **w** that are latent, so that the CRF has the form

$$p(\mathbf{y}, \mathbf{w}|\mathbf{x}) = \frac{1}{Z(\mathbf{x})} \prod_{C_p \in \mathcal{C}} \prod_{\Psi_c \in C_p} \Psi_c(\mathbf{x}_c, \mathbf{w}_c, \mathbf{y}_c; \theta_p). \tag{4.44}$$

The objective function to maximize during training is the marginal likelihood

$$\ell(\theta) = \log p(\mathbf{y}|\mathbf{x}) = \log \sum_{\mathbf{w}} p(\mathbf{y}, \mathbf{w}|\mathbf{x}). \tag{4.45}$$

The first question is how even to compute the marginal likelihood $\ell(\theta)$, because if there are many variables **w**, the sum cannot be computed directly. The key is to realize that we need to compute $\log \sum_{\mathbf{w}} p(\mathbf{y}, \mathbf{w}|\mathbf{x})$ not for any possible assignment **y**, but only for the particular assignment that occurs in the training data. This motivates taking the original CRF (4.44), and clamping the variables Y to their observed values in the training data, yielding a distribution over **w**:

$$p(\mathbf{w}|\mathbf{y}, \mathbf{x}) = \frac{1}{Z(\mathbf{y}, \mathbf{x})} \prod_{C_p \in \mathcal{C}} \prod_{\Psi_c \in C_p} \Psi_c(\mathbf{x}_c, \mathbf{w}_c, \mathbf{y}_c; \theta_p), \tag{4.46}$$

where the normalization factor is

$$Z(\mathbf{y}, \mathbf{x}) = \sum_{\mathbf{w}} \prod_{C_p \in \mathcal{C}} \prod_{\Psi_c \in C_p} \Psi_c(\mathbf{x}_c, \mathbf{w}_c, \mathbf{y}_c; \theta_p). \tag{4.47}$$

This new normalization constant $Z(\mathbf{y}, \mathbf{x})$ can be computed by the same inference algorithm that we use to compute $Z(\mathbf{x})$. In fact, $Z(\mathbf{y}, \mathbf{x})$ is easier to compute, because it sums only over **w**, while $Z(\mathbf{x})$ sums over both **w** and **y**. Graphically, this amounts to saying that clamping the variables **y** in the graph G can simplify the structure among **w**.

Once we have $Z(\mathbf{y}, \mathbf{x})$, the marginal likelihood can be computed as

$$p(\mathbf{y}|\mathbf{x}) = \frac{1}{Z(\mathbf{x})} \sum_{\mathbf{w}} \prod_{C_p \in \mathcal{C}} \prod_{\Psi_c \in C_p} \Psi_c(\mathbf{x}_c, \mathbf{w}_c, \mathbf{y}_c; \theta_p) = \frac{Z(\mathbf{y}, \mathbf{x})}{Z(\mathbf{x})}. \qquad (4.48)$$

Now that we have a way to compute ℓ, we discuss how to maximize it with respect to θ. Maximizing $\ell(\theta)$ can be difficult because ℓ is no longer convex in general (intuitively, log-sum-exp is convex, but the difference of two log-sum-exp functions might not be), so optimization procedures are typically guaranteed to find only local maxima. Whatever optimization technique is used, the model parameters must be carefully initialized in order to reach a good local maximum.

We discuss two different ways to maximize ℓ: directly using the gradient, as in Quattoni et al. [41]; and using expectation maximization (EM), as in McCallum et al. [33]. To maximize ℓ directly, we need to calculate its gradient. The simplest way to do this is to use the following fact. For any function $f(\lambda)$, we have

$$\frac{df}{d\lambda} = f(\lambda) \frac{d \log f}{d\lambda}, \qquad (4.49)$$

which can be seen by applying the chain rule to $\log f$ and rearranging. Applying this to the marginal likelihood $\ell(\Lambda) = \log \sum_{\mathbf{w}} p(\mathbf{y}, \mathbf{w}|\mathbf{x})$ yields

$$\frac{\partial \ell}{\partial \lambda_{pk}} = \frac{1}{\sum_{\mathbf{w}} p(\mathbf{y}, \mathbf{w}|\mathbf{x})} \sum_{\mathbf{w}} \frac{\partial}{\partial \lambda_{pk}} \big[p(\mathbf{y}, \mathbf{w}|\mathbf{x}) \big] \qquad (4.50)$$

$$= \sum_{\mathbf{w}} p(\mathbf{w}|\mathbf{y}, \mathbf{x}) \frac{\partial}{\partial \lambda_{pk}} \big[\log p(\mathbf{y}, \mathbf{w}|\mathbf{x}) \big]. \qquad (4.51)$$

This is the expectation of the fully observed gradient, where the expectation is taken over $\mathbf{w}$. This expression simplifies to

$$\frac{\partial \ell}{\partial \lambda_{pk}} = \sum_{\Psi_c \in C_p} \sum_{\mathbf{w}'_c} p(\mathbf{w}'_c|\mathbf{y}, \mathbf{x}) f_k(\mathbf{y}_c, \mathbf{x}_c, \mathbf{w}'_c) - \sum_{\Psi_c \in C_p} \sum_{\mathbf{w}'_c, \mathbf{y}'_c} p(\mathbf{w}'_c, \mathbf{y}'_c|\mathbf{x}_c) f_k(\mathbf{y}'_c, \mathbf{x}_c, \mathbf{w}'_c).$$
$$(4.52)$$

This gradient requires computing two different kinds of marginal probabilities. The first term contains a marginal probability $p(\mathbf{w}'_c|\mathbf{y}, \mathbf{x})$, which is exactly a marginal distribution of the clamped CRF (4.46). The second term contains a different marginal $p(\mathbf{w}'_c, \mathbf{y}'_c|\mathbf{x}_c)$, which is the same marginal probability required in a fully-observed CRF. Once we have computed the gradient, ℓ can be maximized by standard techniques such as conjugate gradient. In our experience, conjugate gradient tolerates violations of convexity better than limited-memory BFGS, so it may be a better choice for latent-variable CRFs.

Alternatively, ℓ can be optimized using EM. At each iteration j in the EM algorithm, the current parameter vector $\theta^{(j)}$ is updated as follows. First, in the E-step, an auxiliary function $q(\mathbf{w})$ is computed as $q(\mathbf{w}) = p(\mathbf{w}|\mathbf{y}, \mathbf{x}; \theta^{(j)})$. Second, in the M-step, a new parameter vector $\theta^{(j+1)}$ is chosen as

$$\theta^{(j+1)} = \arg\max_{\theta'} \sum_{\mathbf{w}'} q(\mathbf{w}') \log p(\mathbf{y}, \mathbf{w}'|\mathbf{x}; \theta'). \tag{4.53}$$

The direct maximization algorithm and the EM algorithm are strikingly similar. This can be seen by substituting the definition of q into (4.53) and taking derivatives. The gradient is almost identical to the direct gradient (4.52). The only difference is that in EM, the distribution $p(\mathbf{w}|\mathbf{y}, \mathbf{x})$ is obtained from a previous, fixed parameter setting rather than from the argument of the maximization. We are unaware of any empirical comparison of EM to direct optimization for latent-variable CRFs.

4.4.4   Inference

In general CRFs, just as in the linear-chain case, gradient-based training requires computing marginal distributions $p(\mathbf{y}_c|\mathbf{x})$, and testing requires computing the most likely assignment $\mathbf{y}^* = \arg\max_{\mathbf{y}} p(\mathbf{y}|\mathbf{x})$. This can be accomplished using any inference algorithm for graphical models. If the graph has small treewidth, then the junction tree algorithm can be used to exactly compute the marginals, but because both inference problems are NP-hard for general graphs, this is not always possible. In such cases, approximate inference must be used to compute the gradient. In this section, we mention various approximate inference algorithms that have been used successfully with CRFs. Detailed discussion of these are beyond the scope of this chapter.

When choosing an inference algorithm to use within CRF training, the important thing to understand is that it will be invoked repeatedly, once for each time that the gradient is computed. For this reason, sampling-based approaches which may take many iterations to converge, such as Markov chain Monte Carlo (MCMC), have not been popular, although they might be appropriate in some circumstances. Indeed, contrastive divergence [19], in which an MCMC sampler is run for only a few samples, has been successfully applied to CRFs in vision [18].

Because of their computational efficiency, variational approaches have been most popular for CRFs. Several authors [55, 54] have used loopy belief propagation. Belief propagation is an exact inference algorithm for trees which generalizes the forward-backward. Although the generalization of the forward-backward recursions, which are called *message updates*, are neither exact nor even guaranteed to converge if the model is not a tree, they are still well-defined, and they have been empirically successful in a wide variety of domains, including text processing, vision, and error-correcting codes. In the past five years, there has been much theoretical analysis of the algorithm as well. We refer the reader to [63] for more information.

4.4.5   Discussion

This section contains miscellaneous remarks about CRFs. First, it is easily seen that the logistic regression model (4.7) is a CRF with a single output variable. Thus, CRFs can be viewed as an extension of logistic regression to arbitrary graphical structures.

Linear-chain CRFs were originally introduced as an improvement to the *maximum-entropy Markov model* (MEMM) [32], which is essentially a Markov model in which the transition distributions are given by a logistic regression model. MEMMs can exhibit the problems of label bias [24] and observation bias [20]. Both of these problems can be readily understood graphically: the directed model of an MEMM implies that for all time steps t, the observation x_t is marginally independent of the labels y_{t-1}, y_{t-2}. and so on—an independence assumption which is usually strongly violated in sequence modeling. Sometimes this assumption can be effectively avoided by including information from previous time steps as features, and this explains why MEMMs have had success in some NLP applications.

Although we have emphasized the view of a CRF as a model of the conditional distribution, one could view it as an objective function for parameter estimation of joint distributions. As such, it is one objective among many, including generative likelihood, pseudolikelihood [4], and the maximum-margin objective [56, 2]. Another related discriminative technique for structured models is the averaged perceptron, which has been especially popular in the natural language community [10], in large part because of its ease of implementation. To date, there has been little careful comparison of these, especially CRFs and max-margin approaches, across different structures and domains.

Given this view, it is natural to imagine training directed models by conditional likelihood, and in fact this is commonly done in the speech community, where it is called maximum mutual information training. However, it is no easier to maximize the conditional likelihood in a directed model than an undirected model, because in a directed model the conditional likelihood requires computing $\log p(\mathbf{x})$, which plays the same role as $Z(\mathbf{x})$ in the CRF likelihood. In fact, training is more complex in a directed model, because the model parameters are constrained to be probabilities—constraints which can make the optimization problem more difficult. This is in stark contrast to the joint likelihood, which is much easier to compute for directed models than undirected models (although recently several efficient parameter estimation techniques have been proposed for undirected factor graphs, such as Abbeel et al. [1] and Wainwright et al. [60]).

4.4.6   Implementation Concerns

There are a few implementation techniques that can help both training time and accuracy of CRFs, but are not always fully discussed in the literature. Although these apply especially to language applications, they are also useful more generally.

First, when the predicted variables are discrete, the features f_{pk} are ordinarily chosen to have a particular form:

$$f_{pk}(\mathbf{y}_c, \mathbf{x}_c) = \mathbf{1}_{\{\mathbf{y}_c = \tilde{\mathbf{y}}_c\}} q_{pk}(\mathbf{x}_c). \tag{4.54}$$

In other words, each feature is nonzero only for a single output configuration $\tilde{\mathbf{y}}_c$, but as long as that constraint is met, then the feature value depends only on the input observation. Essentially, this means that we can think of our features as depending only on the input $\mathbf{x}_c$, but that we have a separate set of weights for each output configuration. This feature representation is also computationally efficient, because computing each q_{pk} may involve nontrivial text or image processing, and it need be evaluated only once for every feature that uses it. To avoid confusion, we refer to the functions $q_{pk}(\mathbf{x}_c)$ as *observation functions* rather than as features. Examples of observation functions are "word x_t is capitalized" and "word x_t ends in *ing*."

This representation can lead to a large number of features, which can have significant memory and time requirements. For example, matching state-of-the-art results on a standard natural language task, [49] uses 3.8 million features. Not all of these features are ever nonzero in the training data. In particular, some observation functions q_{pk} are nonzero only for certain output configurations. This point can be confusing: One might think that such features can have no effect on the likelihood, but actually they do affect $Z(\mathbf{x})$, so putting a negative weight on them can improve the likelihood by making wrong answers less likely. In order to save memory, however, sometimes these *unsupported features*, that is, those which never occur in the training data, are removed from the model. In practice, however, including unsupported features typically results in better accuracy.

In order to get the benefits of unsupported features with less memory, we have had success with an ad hoc technique for selecting only a few unsupported features. The main idea is to add unsupported features only for likely paths, as follows: first train a CRF without any unsupported features, stopping after only a few iterations; then add unsupported features $f_{pk}(\mathbf{y}_c, \mathbf{x}_c)$ for cases where $\mathbf{x}_c$ occurs in the training data, and $p(\mathbf{y}_c|\mathbf{x}) > \epsilon$. McCallum[28] presents a more principled method of feature selection for CRFs.

Second, if the observations are categorical rather than ordinal, that is, if they are discrete but have no intrinsic order, it is important to convert them to binary features. For example, it makes sense to learn a linear weight on $f_k(y, x_t)$ when f_k is 1 if x_t is the word *dog* and 0 otherwise, but not when f_k is the integer index of word x_t in the text's vocabulary. Thus, in text applications, CRF features are typically binary; in other application areas, such as vision and speech, they are more commonly real-valued.

Third, in language applications, it is sometimes helpful to include redundant factors in the model. For example, in a linear-chain CRF, one may choose to include both edge factors $\Psi_t(y_t, y_{t-1}, \mathbf{x}_t)$ and variable factors $\Psi_t(y_t, \mathbf{x}_t)$. Although one could define the same family of distributions using only edge factors, the redundant node factors provide a kind of backoff, which is useful when there is too little data.

In language applications, there is always too little data, even when hundreds of thousands of words are available.

Finally, often the probabilities involved in forward-backward and belief propagation become too small to be represented within numeric precision. There are two standard approaches to this common problem. One approach is to normalize each of the vectors α_t and β_t to sum to 1, thereby magnifying small values. A second approach is to perform computations in the logarithmic domain, e.g., the forward recursion becomes

$$\log \alpha_t(j) = \bigoplus_{i \in S} \big(\log \Psi_t(j, i, x_t) + \log \alpha_{t-1}(i) \big), \tag{4.55}$$

where $\oplus$ is the operator $a \oplus b = \log(e^a + e^b)$. At first, this does not seem much of an improvement, since numeric precision is lost when computing e^a and e^b. But $\oplus$ can be computed as

$$a \oplus b = a + \log(1 + e^{b-a}) = b + \log(1 + e^{a-b}), \tag{4.56}$$

which can be much more numerically stable, particularly if we pick the version of the identity with the smaller exponent. CRF implementations often use the log-space approach because it makes computing $Z(\mathbf{x})$ more convenient, but in some applications, the computational expense of taking logarithms is an issue, making normalization preferable.

4.5   Skip-Chain CRFs

In this section, we present a case study of applying a general CRF to a practical natural language problem. In particular, we consider a problem in *information extraction*, the task of building a database automatically from unstructured text. Recent work in extraction has often used sequence models, such as HMMs and linear-chain CRFs, which model dependencies only between neighboring labels, on the assumption that those dependencies are the strongest.

But sometimes it is important to model certain kinds of long-range dependencies between entities. One important kind of dependency within information extraction occurs on repeated mentions of the same field. When the same entity is mentioned more than once in a document, such as *Robert Booth*, in many cases all mentions have the same label, such as SEMINAR-SPEAKER. We can take advantage of this fact by favoring labelings that treat repeated words identically, and by combining features from all occurrences so that the extraction decision can be made based on global information. Furthermore, identifying all mentions of an entity can be useful in itself, because each mention might contain different useful information. However, most extraction systems, whether probabilistic or not, do not take advantage of this dependency, instead treating the separate mentions independently.

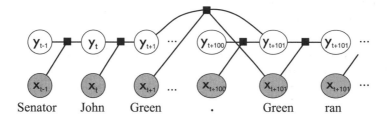

Figure 4.5 Graphical representation of a skip-chain CRF. Identical words are connected because they are likely to have the same label.

To perform collective labeling, we need to represent dependencies between distant terms in the input. But this reveals a general limitation of sequence models, whether generatively or discriminatively trained. Sequence models make a Markov assumption among labels, that is, that any label y_t is independent of all previous labels given its immediate predecessors $y_{t-k} \ldots y_{t-1}$. This represents dependence only between nearby nodes—for example, between bigrams and trigrams—and cannot represent the higher-order dependencies that arise when identical words occur throughout a document.

To relax this assumption, we introduce the *skip-chain CRF*, a conditional model that collectively segments a document into mentions and classifies the mentions by entity type, while taking into account probabilistic dependencies between distant mentions. These dependencies are represented in a skip-chain model by augmenting a linear-chain CRF with factors that depend on the labels of distant but similar words. This is shown graphically in figure 4.5.

Even though the limitations of n-gram models have been widely recognized within NLP, long-distance dependencies are difficult to represent in generative models, because full n-gram models have too many parameters if n is large. We avoid this problem by selecting which skip edges to include based on the input string. This kind of input-specific dependence is difficult to represent in a generative model, because it makes generating the input more complicated. In other words, conditional models have been popular because of their flexibility in allowing overlapping features; skip-chain CRFs take advantage of their flexibility in allowing input-specific model structure.

4.5.1 Model

The skip-chain CRF is essentially a linear-chain CRF with additional long-distance edges between similar words. We call these additional edges *skip edges*. The features on skip edges can incorporate information from the context of both endpoints, so that strong evidence at one endpoint can influence the label at the other endpoint.

When applying the skip-chain model, we must choose which skip edges to include. The simplest choice is to connect all pairs of identical words, but more generally we can connect any pair of words that we believe to be similar, for example, pairs of

Table 4.1   Input features $q_k(\mathbf{x}, t)$ for the seminars data. In the above w_t is the word at position t, T_t is the part-of-speech tag at position t, w ranges over all words in the training data, and T ranges over all part-of-speech tags returned by the Brill tagger. The "appears to be" features are based on hand-designed regular expressions that can span several tokens.

$w_t = w$
w_t matches `[A-Z][a-z]+`
w_t matches `[A-Z][A-Z]+`
w_t matches `[A-Z]`
w_t matches `[A-Z]+`
w_t matches `[A-Z]+[a-z]+[A-Z]+[a-z]`
w_t appears in list of first names,
last names, honorifics, etc.
w_t appears to be part of a time followed by a dash
w_t appears to be part of a time preceded by a dash
w_t appears to be part of a date
$T_t = T$
$q_k(\mathbf{x}, t + \delta)$ for all k and $\delta \in [-4, 4]$

words that belong to the same stem class, or have small edit distance. In addition, we must be careful not to include too many skip edges, because this could result in a graph that makes approximate inference difficult. So we need to use similarity metrics that result in a sufficiently sparse graph. In the experiments below, we focus on named-entity recognition, so we connect pairs of identical capitalized words.

Formally, the skip-chain CRF is defined as a general CRF with two clique templates: one for the linear-chain portion, and one for the skip edges. For a sentence $\mathbf{x}$, let $\mathcal{I} = \{(u, v)\}$ be the set of all pairs of sequence positions for which there are skip edges. For example, in the experiments reported here, $\mathcal{I}$ is the set of indices of all pairs of identical capitalized words. Then the probability of a label sequence $\mathbf{y}$ given an input $\mathbf{x}$ is modeled as

$$p_\theta(\mathbf{y}|\mathbf{x}) = \frac{1}{Z(\mathbf{x})} \prod_{t=1}^{T} \Psi_t(y_t, y_{t-1}, \mathbf{x}) \prod_{(u,v) \in \mathcal{I}} \Psi_{uv}(y_u, y_v, \mathbf{x}), \qquad (4.57)$$

where Ψ_t are the factors for linear-chain edges, and Ψ_{uv} are the factors over skip edges. These factors are defined as

$$\Psi_t(y_t, y_{t-1}, \mathbf{x}) = \exp\left\{ \sum_k \lambda_{1k} f_{1k}(y_t, y_{t-1}, \mathbf{x}, t) \right\} \qquad (4.58)$$

$$\Psi_{uv}(y_u, y_v, \mathbf{x}) = \exp\left\{ \sum_k \lambda_{2k} f_{2k}(y_u, y_v, \mathbf{x}, u, v) \right\}, \qquad (4.59)$$

where $\theta_1 = \{\lambda_{1k}\}_{k=1}^{K_1}$ are the parameters of the linear-chain template, and $\theta_2 = \{\lambda_{2k}\}_{k=1}^{K_2}$ are the parameters of the skip template. The full set of model parameters is $\theta = \{\theta_1, \theta_2\}$.

As described in section 4.4.6, both the linear-chain features and skip-chain features are factorized into indicator functions of the outputs and observation functions, as in (4.54). In general the observation functions $q_k(\mathbf{x}, t)$ can depend on arbitrary positions of the input string. For example, a useful feature for NER is $q_k(\mathbf{x}, t) = 1$ if and only if x_{t+1} is a capitalized word.

The observation functions for the skip edges are chosen to combine the observations from each endpoint. Formally, we define the feature functions for the skip edges to factorize as

$$f'_k(y_u, y_v, \mathbf{x}, u, v) = \mathbf{1}_{\{y_u = \tilde{y}_u\}} \mathbf{1}_{\{y_v = \tilde{y}_v\}} q'_k(\mathbf{x}, u, v), \qquad (4.60)$$

This choice allows the observation functions $q'_k(\mathbf{x}, u, v)$ to combine information from the neighborhood of y_u and y_v. For example, one useful feature is $q'_k(\mathbf{x}, u, v) = 1$ if and only if $x_u = x_v =$ "Booth" and $x_{v-1} =$ "Speaker:." This can be a useful feature if the context around x_u, such as "Robert Booth is manager of control engineering...," may not make clear whether or not Robert Booth is presenting a talk, but the context around x_v is clear, such as "Speaker: Robert Booth." [1]

Because the loops in a skip-chain CRF can be long and overlapping, exact inference is intractable for the data we consider. The running time required by exact inference is exponential in the size of the largest clique in the graph's junction tree. In junction trees created from the seminars data, 29 of the 485 instances have a maximum clique size of 10 or greater, and 11 have a maximum clique size of 14 or greater. (The worst instance has a clique with 61 nodes.) These cliques are far too large to perform inference exactly. For reference, representing a single factor that depends on 14 variables requires more memory than can be addressed in a 32-bit architecture. Instead, we perform approximate inference using loopy belief propagation, which was mentioned in section 4.4.4. We use an asynchronous tree-based schedule known as tree-based representation (TRP) [59].

4.5.2   Results

We evaluate skip chain CRFs on a collection of 485 email messages announcing seminars at Carnegie Mellon University. The messages are annotated with the seminar's starting time, ending time, location, and speaker. This data set is due to Freitag [15], and has been used in much previous work.

Often the fields are listed multiple times in the message. For example, the speaker name might be included both near the beginning and later on, in a sentence like "If you would like to meet with Professor Smith..." As mentioned earlier, it can be

---

1. This example is taken from an actual error made by a linear-chain CRF on the seminars data set. We present results from this data set in section 4.5.2.

Table 4.2   Comparison of F_1 performance on the seminars data. The top line gives a dynamic Bayes net that has been previously used on this data set. The skip-chain CRF beats the previous systems in overall F1 and on the speaker field, which has proved to be the hardest field of the four. Overall F1 is the average of the F1 scores for the four fields.

System	stime	etime	location	speaker	overall
BIEN Peshkin and Pfeffer [39]	96.0	**98.8**	87.1	76.9	89.7
Linear-chain CRF	**97.5**	97.5	**88.3**	77.3	90.2
Skip-chain CRF	96.7	97.2	88.1	**80.4**	**90.6**

Table 4.3   Number of inconsistently mislabeled tokens, that is, tokens that are mislabeled even though the same token is labeled correctly elsewhere in the document. Learning long-distance dependencies reduces this kind of error in the speaker and location fields. Numbers are averaged over five folds.

Field	Linear-chain	Skip-chain
stime	12.6	17
etime	3.2	5.2
location	6.4	0.6
speaker	30.2	4.8

useful to find both such mentions, because different information can occur in the surrounding context of each mention: for example, the first mention might be near an institutional affiliation, while the second mentions that Smith is a professor.

We evaluate a skip-chain CRF with skip edges between identical capitalized words. The motivation for this is that the hardest aspect of this data set is identifying speakers and locations, and capitalized words that occur multiple times in a seminar announcement are likely to be either speakers or locations.

Table 4.1 shows the list of input features we used. For a skip edge (u, v), the input features we used were the disjunction of the input features at u and v, that is,

$$q'_k(\mathbf{x}, u, v) = q_k(\mathbf{x}, u) \oplus q_k(\mathbf{x}, v), \tag{4.61}$$

where $\oplus$ is binary or. All of our results are averaged over five-fold cross-validation with an 80/20 split of the data. We report results from both a linear-chain CRF and a skip-chain CRF with the same set of input features.

We calculate precision and recall as[2]

---

2. Previous work on this data set has traditionally measured precision and recall per document, that is, from each document the system extracts only one field of each type. Because the goal of the skip-chain CRF is to extract all mentions in a document, these

$$P = \frac{\text{\# tokens extracted correctly}}{\text{\# tokens extracted}}$$

$$R = \frac{\text{\# tokens extracted correctly}}{\text{\# true tokens of field}}.$$

As usual, we report $F_1 = (2PR)/(P + R)$.

Table 4.2 compares a skip-chain CRF to a linear-chain CRF and to a dynamic Bayes net used in previous work [39]. The skip-chain CRF performs much better than all the other systems on the SPEAKER field, which is the field for which the skip edges would be expected to make the most difference. On the other fields, however, the skip-chain CRF does slightly worse (less than 1% absolute F1).

We expected that the skip-chain CRF would do especially well on the speaker field, because speaker names tend to appear multiple times in a document, and a skip-chain CRF can learn to label the multiple occurrences consistently. To test this hypothesis, we measure the number of *inconsistently mislabeled* tokens, that is, tokens that are mislabeled even though the same token is classified correctly elsewhere in the document. Table 4.3 compares the number of inconsistently mislabeled tokens in the test set between linear-chain and skip-chain CRFs. For the linear-chain CRF, on average 30.2 true speaker tokens are inconsistently mislabeled. Because the linear-chain CRF mislabels 121.6 true speaker tokens, this situation includes 24.7% of the missed speaker tokens.

The skip-chain CRF shows a dramatic decrease in inconsistently mislabeled tokens on the speaker field, from 30.2 tokens to 4.8. Consequently, the skip-chain CRF also has much better recall on speaker tokens than the linear-chain CRF (70.0 R linear chain, 76.8 R skip chain). This explains the increase in F1 from linear-chain to skip-chain CRFs, because the two have similar precision (86.5 P linear chain, 85.1 skip chain). These results support the original hypothesis that treating repeated tokens consistently especially benefits recall on the SPEAKER field.

On the LOCATION field, on the other hand, where we might also expect skip-chain CRFs to perform better, there is no benefit. We explain this by observing in table 4.3 that inconsistent misclassification occurs much less frequently in this field.

4.5.3 Related Work

Recently, Bunescu and Mooney [5] have used a relational Markov network to collectively classify the mentions in a document, achieving increased accuracy by learning dependencies between similar mentions. In their work, however, candidate phrases are extracted heuristically, which can introduce errors if a true entity is

---

metrics are inappropriate, so we cannot compare with this previous work. Peshkin and Pfeffer [39] do use the per-token metric (personal communication), so our comparison is fair in that respect.

not selected as a candidate phrase. Our model performs collective segmentation and labeling simultaneously, so that the system can take into account dependencies between the two tasks. The skip-chain CRF itself has also been presented elsewhere [52].

As an extension to our work, Finkel et al. [14] augment the skip-chain model with richer kinds of long-distance factors than just over pairs of words. These factors are useful for modeling exceptions to the assumption that similar words tend to have similar labels. For example, in named-entity recognition, the word *China* is as a place name when it appears alone, but when it occurs within the phrase *The China Daily*, it should be labeled as an organization. Because this model is more complex than the original skip-chain model, Finkel et al. estimate its parameters in two stages, first training the linear-chain component as a separate CRF, and then heuristically selecting parameters for the long-distance factors. Finkel et al. report improved results both on the seminars data set that we consider in this chapter, and on several other standard information extraction data sets.

Finally, the skip-chain CRF can also be viewed as performing extraction while taking into account a simple form of coreference information, since the reason that identical words are likely to have similar tags is that they are likely to be coreferent. Thus, this model is a step toward joint probabilistic models for extraction and data mining as advocated by McCallum and Jensen [29]. An example of such a joint model is the one of Wellner et al. [62], which jointly segments citations in research papers and predicts which citations refer to the same paper.

4.6 Conclusion

CRFs are a natural choice for many relational problems because they allow both graphically representing dependencies between entities, and including rich observed features of entities. In this chapter, we have presented a tutorial on CRFs, covering both linear-chain models and general graphical structures. Also, as a case study in CRFs for collective classification, we have presented the skip-chain CRF, a type of general CRF that performs joint segmentation and collective labeling on a practical language understanding task.

The main disadvantage of CRFs is the computational expense of training. Although CRF training is feasible for many real-world problems, the need to perform inference repeatedly during training becomes a computational burden when there are a large number of training instances, when the graphical structure is complex, when there are latent variables, or when the output variables have many outcomes. One focus of current research [1, 53, 60] is on more efficient parameter estimation techniques.

Acknowledgments

We thank Tom Minka and Jerod Weinman for helpful conversations, and we thank Francine Chen and Benson Limketkai for useful comments. This work was supported in part by the Center for Intelligent Information Retrieval; in part by the Defense Advanced Research Projects Agency (DARPA), the Department of the Interior, NBC, Acquisition Services Division, under contract number NBCHD030010; and in part by the Central Intelligence Agency, the National Security Agency, and the National Science Foundation under NSF grants #IIS-0427594 and #IIS-0326249. Any opinions, findings and conclusions or recommendations expressed in this material are the authors' and do not necessarily reflect those of the sponsors.

References

[1] P. Abbeel, D. Koller, and A. Y. Ng. Learning factor graphs in polynomial time and sample complexity. In *Proceedings of the Conference on Uncertainty in Artificial Intelligence*, 2005.

[2] Y. Altun, I. Tsochantaridis, and T. Hofmann. Hidden Markov support vector machines. In *Proceedings of the International Conference on Machine Learning*, 2003.

[3] D. Bertsekas. *Nonlinear Programming*. Athena Scientific, Nashua, NH, 2nd edition, 1999.

[4] J. Besag. Efficiency of pseudolikelihood estimation for simple gaussian fields. *Biometrika*, 64(3):616–618, 1977.

[5] R. Bunescu and R. J. Mooney. Collective information extraction with relational Markov networks. In *Proceedings of the Annual Meeting of the Association for Computational Linguistics*, 2004.

[6] R. Byrd, J. Nocedal, and R. Schnabel. Representations of quasi-Newton matrices and their use in limited memory methods. *Mathematical Programming*, 63(2):129–156, 1994. ISSN 0025-5610.

[7] R. Caruana and A. Niculescu-Mizil. An empirical comparison of supervised learning algorithms using different performance metrics. Technical Report TR2005-1973, Cornell University, Ithica, NY, 2005.

[8] Y. Choi, C. Cardie, E. Riloff, and S. Patwardhan. Identifying sources of opinions with conditional random fields and extraction patterns. In *Proceedings of Human Language Technology Conference and North American Chapter of the Association for Computational Linguistics*, 2005.

[9] S. Clark and J. Curran. Parsing the WSJ using CCG and log-linear models. In *Proceedings of the Annual Meeting of the Association for Computational Linguistics*, 2004.

[10]   M. Collins. Discriminative training methods for hidden Markov models: Theory and experiments with perceptron algorithms. In *Proceedings of the Conference on Empirical Methods in Natural Language Processing*, 2002.

[11]   P. Cowans and M. Szummer. A graphical model for simultaneous partitioning and labeling. In *Tenth International Workshop on Artificial Intelligence and Statistics*, 2005.

[12]   A. Culotta and A. McCallum. Confidence estimation for information extraction. In *Proceedings of Human Language Technology Conference and North American Chapter of the Association for Computational Linguistics*, 2004.

[13]   A. Culotta, R. Bekkerman, and A. McCallum. Extracting social networks and contact information from email and the web. In *Proceedings of the Conference on Email and Anti-Spam*, 2004.

[14]   J. Finkel, T. Grenager, and C. Manning. Incorporating non-local information into information extraction systems by Gibbs sampling. In *Proceedings of the Annual Meeting of the Association for Computational Linguistics*, 2005.

[15]   D. Freitag. *Machine Learning for Information Extraction in Informal Domains.* PhD thesis, Carnegie Mellon University, Pittsburgh, 1998.

[16]   N. Ghamrawi and A. McCallum. Collective multi-label classification. In *Proceedings of the Conference on Information and Knowledge Management*, 2005.

[17]   J. Goodman. Exponential priors for maximum entropy models. In *Proceedings of Human Language Technology Conference and North American Chapter of the Association for Computational Linguistics*, 2004.

[18]   X. He, R. S. Zemel, and M. Á. Carreira-Perpiñián. Multiscale conditional random fields for image labelling. In *IEEE Computer Society Conference on Computer Vision and Pattern Recognition*, 2004.

[19]   G. Hinton. Training products of experts by minimizing contrastive divergence. Technical Report 2000-004, Gatsby Computational Neuroscience Unit, London, 2000.

[20]   D. Klein and C. Manning. Conditional structure versus conditional estimation in NLP models. In *Proceedings of the Conference on Empirical Methods in Natural Language Processing*, 2002.

[21]   F. Kschischang, B. Frey, and H. Loeliger. Factor graphs and the sum-product algorithm. *IEEE Transactions on Information Theory*, 47(2):498–519, 2001.

[22]   T. Kudo, K. Yamamoto, and Y. Matsumoto. Applying conditional random fields to Japanese morphological analysis. In *Proceedings of the Conference on Empirical Methods in Natural Language Processing*, 2004.

[23]   S. Kumar and M. Hebert. Discriminative fields for modeling spatial dependencies in natural images. In *Proceedings of Neural Information Processing Systems*, 2003.

[24] J. Lafferty, A. McCallum, and F. Pereira. Conditional random fields: Probabilistic models for segmenting and labeling sequence data. *Proceedings of the International Conference on Machine Learning*, 2001.

[25] Y. Liu, J. Carbonell, P. Weigele, and V. Gopalakrishnan. Segmentation conditional random fields (SCRFs): A new approach for protein fold recognition. In *Proceedings of the ACM International Conference on Research in Computational Molecular Biology*, 2005.

[26] R. Malouf. A comparison of algorithms for maximum entropy parameter estimation. In *Proceedings of the Conference on Natural Language Learning*, 2002.

[27] D. McAllester, M. Collins, and F. Pereira. Case-factor diagrams for structured probabilistic modeling. In *Proceedings of the Conference on Uncertainty in Artificial Intelligence*, 2004.

[28] A. McCallum. Efficiently inducing features of conditional random fields. In *Proceedings of the Conference on Uncertainty in Artificial Intelligence*, 2003.

[29] A. McCallum and D. Jensen. A note on the unification of information extraction and data mining using conditional-probability, relational models. In *IJCAI'03 Workshop on Learning Statistical Models from Relational Data*, 2003.

[30] A. McCallum and W. Li. Early results for named entity recognition with conditional random fields, feature induction and web-enhanced lexicons. In *Proceedings of the Conference on Natural Language Learning*, 2003.

[31] A. McCallum and B. Wellner. Conditional models of identity uncertainty with application to noun coreference. In *Proceedings of Neural Information Processing Systems*, 2005.

[32] A. McCallum, D. Freitag, and F. Pereira. Maximum entropy Markov models for information extraction and segmentation. In *Proceedings of the International Conference on Machine Learning*, 2000.

[33] A. McCallum, K. Bellare, and F. Pereira. A conditional random field for discriminatively-trained finite-state string edit distance. In *Proceedings of the Conference on Uncertainty in Artificial Intelligence*, 2005.

[34] T. Minka. Discriminative models, not discriminative training Technical Report MSR-TR-2005-144, Microsoft Research, October 2005. ftp://ftp.research.microsoft.com/ pub/tr/TR-2005-144.pdf .

[35] T. P. Minka. A comparsion of numerical optimizers for logistic regression. Technical report, Dept. of Statistics, Carnegie Mellon University, Pittsburgh, 2003.

[36] A. Ng and M. Jordan. On discriminative vs. generative classifiers: A comparison of logistic regression and naive Bayes. In *Proceedings of Neural Information Processing Systems*, 2002.

[37] F. Peng and A. McCallum. Accurate information extraction from research papers using conditional random fields. In *Proceedings of Human Language Technology Conference and North American Chapter of the Association for Computational Linguistics*, 2004.

[38] F. Peng, F. Feng, and A. McCallum. Chinese segmentation and new word detection using conditional random fields. In *Proceedings of the International Conference on Computational Linguistics*, 2004.

[39] L. Peshkin and A. Pfeffer. Bayesian information extraction network. In *Proceedings of the International Joint Conference on Artificial Intelligence*, 2003.

[40] Y. Qi, M. Szummer, and T. Minka. Diagram structure recognition by Bayesian conditional random fields. In *Proceedings of the International Conference on Computer Vision and Pattern Recognition*, 2005.

[41] A. Quattoni, M. Collins, and T. Darrell. Conditional random fields for object recognition. In *Proceedings of Neural Information Processing Systems*, 2005.

[42] L. Rabiner. A tutorial on hidden Markov models and selected applications in speech recognition. *Proceedings of the IEEE*, 77(2):257 – 286, 1989.

[43] M. Richardson and P. Domingos. Markov logic networks. *Machine Learning*, 62(1-2):107–136, 2006.

[44] S. Riezler, T. King, R. Kaplan, R. Crouch, J. Maxwell, and M. Johnson. Parsing the *Wall Street Journal* using a lexical-functional grammar and discriminative estimation techniques. In *Proceedings of the Annual Meeting of the Association for Computational Linguistics*, 2002.

[45] D. Roth and W. Yih. Integer linear programming inference for conditional random fields. In *Proceedings of the International Conference on Machine Learning*, 2005.

[46] S. Sarawagi and W. Cohen. Semi-Markov conditional random fields for information extraction. In *Proceedings of Neural Information Processing Systems*, 2005.

[47] K. Sato and Y. Sakakibara. RNA secondary structural alignment with conditional random fields. *Bioinformatics*, 21:237–242, 2005.

[48] B. Settles. Abner: An open source tool for automatically tagging genes, proteins, and other entity names in text. *Bioinformatics*, 21(14):3191–3192, 2005.

[49] F. Sha and F. Pereira. Shallow parsing with conditional random fields. In *Proceedings of Human Language Technology Conference and North American Chapter of the Association for Computational Linguistics*, 2003.

[50] P. Singla and P. Domingos. Discriminative training of Markov logic networks. In *Proceedings of the National Conference on Artificial Intelligence*, 2005.

[51] C. Sutton. Conditional probabilistic context-free grammars. Master's thesis, University of Massachusetts, Amherst, 2004. URL `publications/cscfg.pdf`.

`http://www.cs.umass.edu/ ~casutton/publications.html.`

[52]   C. Sutton and A. McCallum. Collective segmentation and labeling of distant entities in information extraction. Technical Report TR # 04-49, University of Massachusetts, 2004. Presented at *ICML Workshop on Statistical Relational Learning and Its Connections to Other Fields*.

[53]   C. Sutton and A. McCallum. Piecewise training of undirected models. In *Proceedings of the Conference on Uncertainty in Artificial Intelligence*, 2005.

[54]   C. Sutton, K. Rohanimanesh, and A. McCallum. Dynamic conditional random fields: Factorized probabilistic models for labeling and segmenting sequence data. In *Proceedings of the International Conference on Machine Learning*, 2004.

[55]   B. Taskar, P. Abbeel, and D. Koller. Discriminative probabilistic models for relational data. In *Proceedings of the Conference on Uncertainty in Artificial Intelligence*, 2002.

[56]   B. Taskar, C. Guestrin, and D. Koller. Max-margin Markov networks. In *Proceedings of Neural Information Processing Systems*, 2004.

[57]   P. Viola and M. Narasimhan. Learning to extract information from semi-structured text using a discriminative context free grammar. In *Proceedings of the ACM International Conference on Information Retrieval*, 2005.

[58]   S.V.N. Vishwanathan, N. Schraudolph, M. Schmidt, and K. Murphy. Accelerated training of copnditional random fields with stochastic meta-descent. In *Proceedings of the International Conference on Machine Learning*, 2006.

[59]   M. Wainwright, T. Jaakkola, and A. Willsky. Tree-based reparameterization for approximate estimation on graphs with cycles. In *Proceedings of Neural Information Processing Systems*, 2001.

[60]   M. Wainwright, T. Jaakkola, and A. Willsky. Tree-reweighted belief propagation and approximate ML estimation by pseudo-moment matching. In *Ninth Workshop on Artificial Intelligence and Statistics*, 2003.

[61]   H. Wallach. Efficient training of conditional random fields. MSc thesis, University of Edinburgh, 2002.

[62]   B. Wellner, A. McCallum, F. Peng, and M. Hay. An integrated, conditional model of information extraction and coreference with application to citation graph construction. In *Proceedings of the Conference on Uncertainty in Artificial Intelligence*, 2004.

[63]   J. Yedidia, W. T. Freeman, and Y. Weiss. Constructing free energy approximations and generalized belief propagation algorithms. Technical Report TR2004-040, Mitsubishi Electric Research Laboratories, Cambridge, MA, 2004.

5 Probabilistic Relational Models

Lise Getoor, Nir Friedman, Daphne Koller, Avi Pfeffer and Ben Taskar

Probabilistic relational models (PRMs) are a rich representation language for structured statistical models. They combine a frame-based logical representation with probabilistic semantics based on directed graphical models (Bayesian networks). This chapter gives an introduction to probabilistic relational models, describing semantics for attribute uncertainty, structural uncertainty, and class uncertainty. For each case, learning algorithms and some sample results are presented.

5.1 Introduction

Over the last decade, Bayesian networks have been used with great success in a wide variety of real-world and research applications. However, despite their success, Bayesian networks are often inadequate for representing large and complex domains. A Bayesian network for a given domain involves a prespecified set of random variables, whose relationship to each other is fixed in advance. Hence, a Bayesian network cannot be used to deal with domains where we might encounter a varying number of entities in a variety of configurations. This limitation of Bayesian networks is a direct consequence of the fact that they lack the concept of an "object" (or domain entity). Hence, they cannot represent general principles about multiple similar objects which can then be applied in multiple contexts.

Probabilistic relational models (PRMs) [13, 18] extend Bayesian networks with the concepts of objects, their properties, and relations between them. In a way, they are to Bayesian networks as relational logic is to propositional logic. A PRM specifies a template for a probability distribution over a database. The template includes a relational component that describes the relational schema for our domain, and a probabilistic component that describes the probabilistic dependencies that hold in our domain. A PRM has a coherent formal semantics in terms of probability distributions over sets of relational logic interpretations. Given a set of ground objects, a PRM specifies a probability distribution over a set of interpretations involving these objects (and perhaps other objects as well). A PRM, together with a particular database of objects and relations, defines a probability distribution over the attributes of the objects.

In this chapter, we describe the semantics for PRMs with different types of uncertainty, and at the same time we describe the basic learning algorithms for PRMs. We propose an algorithm for automatically constructing or learning a PRM from an existing database. The learned PRM describes the patterns of interactions between attributes. In the learning problem, our input contains a relational schema that specifies the basic vocabulary in the domain — the set of classes, the attributes associated with the different classes, and the possible types of relations between objects in the different classes. The training data consists of a fully specified instance of that schema in the form of a relational database. Once we have learned a PRM, it serves as a tool for exploratory data analysis and can be used to make predictions and complex inferences in new situations. For additional details, including proofs of all of the theorems, see [9].

5.2 PRM Representation

The two components of PRM syntax are a logical description of the domain of discourse and a probabilistic graphical model template which describes the probabilistic dependencies in the domain. Here we describe the logical description of the domain as a relational schema, although it can be transformed into either a frame-based representation or a logic-based syntax is a relatively straightforward manner. Our probabilistic graphical component is depicted pictorially, although it can also be represented in a logical formalism; for example in the probabilistic relational language of [10]. We begin by describing the syntax and semantics for PRMs which have the simplest form of uncertainty, *attribute uncertainty*, and then move on to describing various forms of *structural uncertainty*.

5.2.1 Relational Language

The relational language allows us to describe the kinds of objects in our domain. For example, figure 5.1(a) shows the schema for a simple domain that we will be using as our running example. The domain is that of a university, and contains professors, students, courses, and course registrations. The classes in the schema are **Professor**, **Student**, **Course**, and **Registration**.

More formally, a schema for a relational model describes a set of *classes*, $\mathcal{X} = \{X_1, \ldots, X_n\}$. Each class is associated with a set of *descriptive attributes*. For example, professors may have descriptive attributes such as popularity and teaching ability; courses may have descriptive attributes such as rating and difficulty.

The set of descriptive attributes of a class X is denoted $\mathcal{A}(X)$. Attribute A of class X is denoted $X.A$, and its space of values is denoted $\mathcal{V}(X.A)$. We assume here that value spaces are finite. For example, the **Student** class has the descriptive

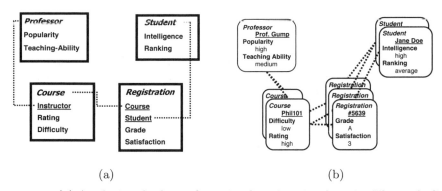

(a)   (b)

Figure 5.1   (a) A relational schema for a simple university domain. The underlined attributes are reference slots of the class and the dashed lines indicate the types of objects referenced. (b) An example instance of this schema. Here we do not show the values of the reference slots; we simply use dashed lines to indicate the relationships that hold between objects.

attributes *Intelligence* and *Ranking*. The value space for Student.*Intelligence* in this example is {*high, low*}.

In addition, we need a method for allowing an object to refer to another object. For example we may want a course to have a reference to the instructor of the course. And a registration record should refer both to the associated course and to the student taking the course.

The simplest way of achieving this effect is using *reference slots*. Specifically, each class is associated with a set of reference slots. The set of reference slots of a class X is denoted $\mathcal{R}(X)$. We use $X.\rho$ to denote the reference slot ρ of X. Each reference slot ρ is typed, i.e., the schema specifies the range type of object that may be referenced. More formally, for each ρ in X, the *domain type* $\mathrm{Dom}[\rho]$ is X and the *range type* $\mathrm{Range}[\rho]$ is Y for some class Y in $\mathcal{X}$. For example, the class Course has reference slot *Instructor* with range type Professor, and class Registration has reference slots *Course* and *Student*. In figure 5.1(a) the reference slots are underlined.

There is a direct mapping between our representation and that of relational databases. Each class corresponds to a single table and each attribute corresponds to a column. Our descriptive attributes correspond to standard attributes in the table, and our reference slots correspond to attributes that are foreign keys (key attributes of another table).

For each reference slot ρ, we can define an *inverse slot* ρ^{-1}, which is interpreted as the inverse function of ρ. For example, we can define an inverse slot for the *Student* slot of Registration and call it *Registered-In*. Note that this is not a one-to-one relation, but returns a *set* of Registration objects. More formally, if $\mathrm{Dom}[\rho]$ is X and $\mathrm{Range}[\rho]$ is Y, then $\mathrm{Dom}[\rho^{-1}]$ is Y and $\mathrm{Range}[\rho^{-1}]$ is X.

Finally, we define the notion of a *slot chain*, which allows us to compose slots, defining functions from objects to other objects to which they are indirectly related. More precisely, we define a *slot chain* $\rho_1, \ldots, \rho_k$ to be a sequence of slots (inverse or otherwise) such that for all i, $\text{Range}[\rho_i] = \text{Dom}[\rho_{i+1}]$. For example, Student.*Registered-In.Course.Instructor* can be used to denote a student's instructors. Note that a slot chain describes a *set* of objects from a class.[1]

The relational framework we have just described is motivated primarily by the concepts of relational databases, although some of the notation is derived from frame-based and object-oriented systems. However, the framework is a fully general one, and is equivalent to the standard vocabulary and semantics of relational logic.

5.2.2   Schema Instantiation

An *instance* $\mathcal{I}$ of a schema is simply a standard relational logic interpretation of this vocabulary. It specifies: for each class X, the set of objects in the class, $\mathcal{I}(X)$; a value for each attribute $x.A$ (in the appropriate domain) for each object x; and a value y for each reference slot $x.\rho$, which is an object in the appropriate range type, i.e., $y \in \text{Range}[\rho]$. Conversely, $y.\rho^{-1} = \{x \mid x.\rho = y\}$. We use $\mathcal{A}(x)$ as a shorthand for $\mathcal{A}(X)$, where x is of class X. For each object x in the instance and each of its attributes A, we use $\mathcal{I}_{x.A}$ to denote the value of $x.A$ in $\mathcal{I}$. For example, figure 5.1(b) shows an instance of the schema from our running example. In this (simple) instance there is one Professor, two Classes, three Registrations, and two Students. The relations between them show that the professor is the instructor in both classes, and that one student ("Jane Doe") is registered only for one class ("Phil101"), while the other student is registered for both classes.

5.2.3   Probabilistic Model

A PRM defines a probability distribution over a set of instances of a schema. Most simply, we assume that the set of objects and the relations between them are fixed, i.e., external to the probabilistic model. Then, the PRM defines only a probability distribution over the attributes of the objects in the model. The *relational skeleton* defines the possible instantiations that we consider; the PRM defines a distribution over the possible worlds consistent with the relational skeleton.

Definition 5.1

A *relational skeleton* σ_r of a relational schema is a partial specification of an instance of the schema. It specifies the set of objects $\sigma_r(X_i)$ for each class and the relations that hold between the objects. However, it leaves the values of the attributes unspecified. ∎

Figure 5.2(a) shows a relational skeleton for our running example. The relational skeleton defines the random variables in our domain; we have a random variable for

---

1. It is also possible to define slot chains as *multi-sets* of objects; here we have found it sufficient to make them sets of objects, but there may be domains where multi-sets are desirable.

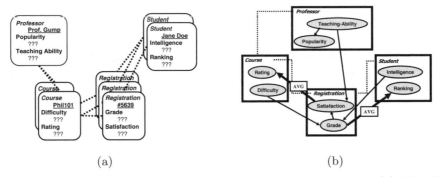

Figure 5.2   (a) The relational skeleton for the university domain. (b) The PRM dependency structure for our university example.

each attribute of each object in the skeleton. A PRM then specifies a probability distribution over *completions* $\mathcal{I}$ of the skeleton.

A PRM consists of two components: the qualitative dependency structure, $\mathcal{S}$, and the parameters associated with it, $\theta_{\mathcal{S}}$. The dependency structure is defined by associating with each attribute $X.A$ a set of *parents* $\mathrm{Pa}(X.A)$. These correspond to *formal* parents; they will be instantiated in different ways for different objects in X. Intuitively, the parents are attributes that are "direct influences" on $X.A$. In figure 5.2(b), the arrows define the dependency structure.

We distinguish between two types of formal parents. The attribute $X.A$ can depend on another probabilistic attribute B of X. This formal dependence induces a corresponding dependency for individual objects: for any object x in $\sigma_r(X)$, $x.A$ will depend probabilistically on $x.B$. For example, in figure 5.2(b), a professor's *Popularity* depends on her *Teaching-Ability*. The attribute $X.A$ can also depend on attributes of related objects $X.\boldsymbol{K}.B$, where $\boldsymbol{K}$ is a slot chain. In figure 5.2(b), the grade of a student depends on Registration.*Student.Intelligence* and Registration.*Course.Difficulty*. Or we can have a longer slot chain, for example, the dependence of student satisfaction on Registration.*Course.Instructor.Teaching-Ability*.

In addition, we can have a dependence of student ranking on Student.*Registered-In.Grade*. To understand the semantics of this formal dependence for an individual object x, recall that $x.\boldsymbol{K}$ represents the *set* of objects that are $\boldsymbol{K}$-relatives of x. Except in cases where the slot chain is guaranteed to be single-valued, we must specify the probabilistic dependence of $x.A$ on the multiset $\{y.B \ : \ y \in x.\boldsymbol{K}\}$. For example, a student's rank depends on the grades in the courses in which he or she are registered. However each student may be enrolled in a different number of courses, and we will need a method of compactly representing these complex dependencies.

The notion of *aggregation* from database theory gives us an appropriate tool to address this issue: $x.A$ will depend probabilistically on some aggregate property of this multiset. There are many natural and useful notions of aggregation of a set: its mode (most frequently occurring value); its mean value (if values are numerical);

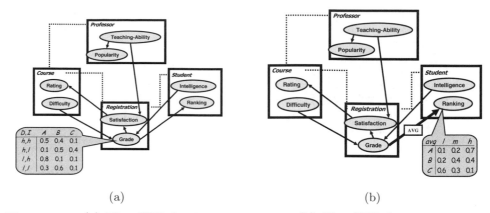

(a)   (b)

Figure 5.3 (a) The CPD for Registration.*Grade* (b) The CPD for an aggregate dependency of Student.*Ranking* on Student.*Registered-In.Grade*.

its median, maximum, or minimum (if values are ordered); its cardinality; etc. In the preceding example, we can have a student's ranking depend on her grade point average (GPA), or the average grade in her courses (or in the case where the grades are represented as letters, we may use median; in our example we blur the distinction and assume that average is defined appropriately).

More formally, our language allows a notion of an aggregate γ; γ takes a multiset of values of some ground type, and returns a summary of it. The type of the aggregate can be the same as that of its arguments. However, we allow other types as well, e.g., an aggregate that reports the size of the set. We allow $X.A$ to have as a parent $\gamma(X.\boldsymbol{K}.B)$; the semantics is that for any $x \in X$, $x.A$ will depend on the value of $\gamma(x.\boldsymbol{K}.B)$. In our example PRM, there are two aggregate dependencies defined, one that specifies that the ranking of a student depends on the average of her grades and one that specifies that the rating of a course depends on the average satisfaction of students in the course.

Given a set of parents Pa$(X.A)$ for $X.A$, we can define a local probability model for $X.A$. We associate $X.A$ with a conditional probability distribution (CPD) that specifies $P(X.A \mid \text{Pa}(X.A))$. We require that the CPDs are legal. Figure 5.3 shows two CPDs. Let $\mathbf{U}$ be the set of parents of $X.A$, $\mathbf{U} = \text{Pa}(X.A)$. Each of these parents U_i — whether a simple attribute in the same relation or an aggregate of a set of $\boldsymbol{K}$ relatives — has a set of values $\mathcal{V}(U_i)$ in some ground type. For each tuple of values $\mathbf{u} \in \mathcal{V}(\mathbf{U})$, we specify a distribution $P(X.A \mid \mathbf{u})$ over $\mathcal{V}(X.A)$. This entire set of parameters comprises $\theta_{\mathcal{S}}$.

Definition 5.2
A *probabilistic relational model (PRM)* Π for a relational schema $\mathcal{R}$ is defined as follows. For each class $X \in \mathcal{X}$ and each descriptive attribute $A \in \mathcal{A}(X)$, we have:

- a set of *parents* Pa$(X.A) = \{U_1, \ldots, U_l\}$, where each U_i has the form $X.B$ or $\gamma(X.\boldsymbol{K}.B)$, where $\boldsymbol{K}$ is a slot chain and γ is an aggregate of $X.\boldsymbol{K}.B$;

■ a legal *conditional probability distribution (CPD)*, $P(X.A \mid \text{Pa}(X.A))$. ■

5.2.4   PRM Semantics

As mentioned in the introduction, PRMs define a distribution over possible worlds. The possible worlds are instantiations of the database that are consistent with the relational skeleton. Given any skeleton, we have a set of random variables of interest: the attributes $x.A$ of the objects in the skeleton. Formally, let $\sigma_r(X)$ denote the set of objects in skeleton σ_r whose class in X. The set of random variables for σ_r is the set of attributes of the form $x.A$ where $x \in \sigma_r(X_i)$ and $A \in \mathcal{A}(X_i)$ for some class X_i. The PRM specifies a probability distribution over the possible joint assignments of values to all of these random variables.

For a given skeleton σ_r, the PRM structure induces a *ground* Bayesian network over the random variables $x.A$.

Definition 5.3
A PRM Π together with a skeleton σ_r defines the following ground Bayesian network:

■ There is a node for every attribute of every object $x \in \sigma_r(X)$, $x.A$.

■ Each $x.A$ depends probabilistically on parents of the form $x.B$ or $x.\boldsymbol{K}.B$. If $\boldsymbol{K}$ is not single-valued, then the parent is the aggregate computed from the set of random variables $\{y \mid y \in x.\boldsymbol{K}\}$, $\gamma(x.\boldsymbol{K}.B)$.

■ The CPD for $x.A$ is $P(X.A \mid \text{Pa}(X.A))$. ■

As with Bayesian networks, the joint distribution over these assignments is factored. That is, we take the product, over all $x.A$, of the probability in the CPD of the specific value assigned by the instance to the attribute given the values assigned to its parents. Formally, this is written as follows:

$$P(\mathcal{I} \mid \sigma_r, \mathcal{S}, \theta_\mathcal{S}) = \prod_{x \in \sigma_r} \prod_{A \in \mathcal{A}(x)} P(\mathcal{I}_{x.A} \mid \mathcal{I}_{\text{Pa}(x.A)})$$
$$= \prod_{X_i} \prod_{A \in \mathcal{A}(X_i)} \prod_{x \in \sigma_r(X_i)} P(\mathcal{I}_{x.A} \mid \mathcal{I}_{\text{Pa}(x.A)}). \tag{5.1}$$

This expression is very similar to the chain rule for Bayesian networks. There are three primary differences. First, our random variables are the attributes of a set of objects. Second, the set of parents of a random variable can vary according to the relational context of the object — the set of objects to which it is related. Third, the parameters are shared; the parameters of the local probability models for attributes of objects in the same class are identical.

5.2.5   Coherence of Probabilistic Model

As in any definition of this type, we have to take care that the resulting function from instances to numbers does indeed define a *coherent* probability distribution, i.e., where the sum of the probability of all instances is 1. In Bayesian networks, where the joint probability is also a product of CPDs, this requirement is satisfied if the dependency graph is acyclic: a variable is not an ancestor of itself. A similar condition is sufficient to ensure coherence in PRMs as well.

5.2.5.1   Instance Dependency Graph

We want to ensure that our probabilistic dependencies are acyclic, so that a random variable does not depend, directly or indirectly, on its own value. To do so, we can consider the graph of dependencies among attributes of objects in the skeleton, which we will call the *instance dependency graph*, G_{σ_r}.

Definition 5.4
The *instance dependency graph* G_{σ_r} for a PRM Π and a relational skeleton σ_r has a node for each descriptive attribute of each object $x \in \sigma_r(X)$ in each class $X \in \mathcal{X}$. Each $x.A$ has the following edges:

1. Type I edges: For each formal parent of $x.A$, $X.B$, we introduce an edge from $x.B$ to $x.A$.

2. Type II edges: For each formal parent $X.\boldsymbol{K}.B$, and for each $y \in x.\boldsymbol{K}$, we define an edge from $y.B$ to $x.A$. ∎

Type I edges correspond to intra-object dependencies and type II edges correspond to inter-object dependencies. We say that a dependency structure $\mathcal{S}$ is *acyclic* relative to a relational skeleton σ_r if the instance dependency graph G_{σ_r} over the variables $x.A$ is acyclic. In this case, we are guaranteed that the PRM defines a coherent probabilistic model over complete instantiations $\mathcal{I}$ consistent with σ_r:

Theorem 5.5
Let Π be a PRM whose dependency structure $\mathcal{S}$ is acyclic relative to a relational skeleton σ_r. Then Π and σ_r define a coherent probability distribution over instantiations $\mathcal{I}$ that extend σ_r via (5.1).

5.2.5.2   Class Dependency Graph

The instance dependency graph we just described allows us to check whether a dependency structure $\mathcal{S}$ is acyclic relative to a fixed skeleton σ_r. However, we often want stronger guarantees: we want to ensure that our dependency structure is acyclic for any skeleton that we are likely to encounter. How do we guarantee this property based only on the class-level PRM? To do so, we consider potential dependencies at the class level. More precisely, we define a *class dependency graph*, which reflects these dependencies.

Definition 5.6
The *class dependency graph* G_Π for a PRM Π has a node for each descriptive attribute $X.A$, and the following edges:

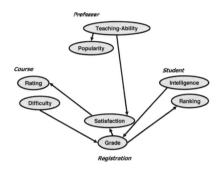

Figure 5.4   The class dependency graph for the school PRM.

1. Type I edges: For any attribute $X.A$ and any of its parents $X.B$, we introduce an edge from $X.B$ to $X.A$.

2. Type II edges: For any attribute $X.A$ and any of its parents $X.\boldsymbol{K}.B$ we introduce an edge from $Y.B$ to $X.A$, where $Y = \mathrm{Range}[X.\boldsymbol{K}]$. ∎

Figure 5.4 shows the dependency graph for our school domain.

The most obvious approach for using the class dependency graph is simply to require that it be acyclic. This requirement is equivalent to assuming a stratification among the attributes of the different classes, and requiring that the parents of an attribute precede it in the stratification ordering. As theorem 5.7 shows, if the class dependency graph is acyclic, we can never have that $x.A$ depends (directly or indirectly) on itself.

Theorem 5.7
If the class dependency graph G_Π is acyclic for a PRM Π, then for *any* skeleton σ_r, the instance dependency graph is acyclic.

The following corollary follows immediately:

Corollary 5.8
Let Π be a PRM whose class dependency structure $\mathcal{S}$ is acyclic. For any relational skeleton σ_r, Π, and σ_r define a coherent probability distribution over instantiations $\mathcal{I}$ that extend σ_r via (5.1).

For example, if we examine the PRM of figure 5.2(b), we can easily convince ourselves that we cannot create a cycle in any instance. Indeed, as we saw in figure 5.4, the class dependency graph is acyclic. Note, however, that if we introduce additional dependencies we can create cycles. For example, if we make **Professor**.*Teaching-Ability* depend on the rating of courses she teaches (e.g., if high teaching ratings increase her motivation), then the resulting class dependency graph is cyclic, and there is no stratification order that is consistent with the PRM structure. An inability to stratify the class dependency graph implies that there are skeletons for which the PRM will induce a distribution with cyclic dependencies.

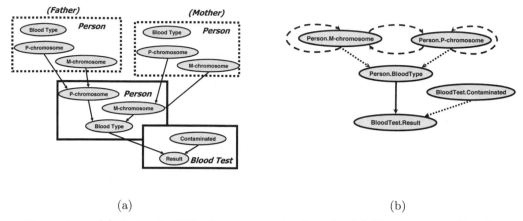

(a)   (b)

Figure 5.5   (a) A simple PRM for the genetics domain. (b) The corresponding dependency graph. Dashed edges correspond to "green" dependencies, dotted edges correspond to "yellow" dependencies, and solid edges correspond to "red" dependencies.

5.2.5.3   Guaranteed Acyclic Relationships

In some important cases, a cycle in the class dependency graph is not problematic, it will not result in a cyclic instance dependency graph. This can be the case when we have additional domain constraints on the form of skeletons we may encounter. Consider, for example, a simple genetic model of the inheritance of a single gene that determines a person's blood type, shown in figure 5.5(a). Each person has two copies of the chromosome containing this gene, one inherited from her mother, and one inherited from her father. There is also a possibly contaminated test that attempts to recognize the person's blood type. Our schema contains two classes: Person and BloodTest. Class Person has reference slots *Mother* and *Father* and descriptive attributes *Gender*, *P-Chromosome* (the chromosome inherited from the father), and *M-Chromosome* (inherited from the mother). *BloodTest* has a reference slot *Test-Of* (not shown explicitly in the figure) that points to the owner of the test, and descriptive attributes *Contaminated* and *Result*.

In our genetic model, the genotype of a person depends on the genotype of her parents; thus, at the class level, we have *Person.P-Chromosome* depending directly on *Person.P-Chromosome*. As we can see in figure 5.5(b), this dependency results in a cycle that clearly violates the acyclicity requirements of our simple class dependency graph. However, it is clear to us that the dependencies in this model are not actually cyclic for any skeleton that we will actually encounter in this domain. The reason is that, in "legitimate" skeletons for this schema, a person cannot be his own ancestor, which disallows the situation of the person's genotype depending (directly or indirectly) on itself. In other words, although the model appears to be cyclic at the class level, we know that this cyclicity is always resolved at the level of individual objects.

Our ability to guarantee that the cyclicity is resolved relies on some prior knowledge that we have about the domain. We want to allow the user to give us information such as this, so that we can make stronger guarantees about acyclicity and allow richer dependency structures in the PRM. In particular, the user can specify that certain reference slots are *guaranteed acyclic*. In our genetics example, *Father* and *Mother* are guaranteed acyclic; cycles involving these attributes may in fact be legal. Moreover, they are mutually guaranteed acyclic, so that compositions of the slots are also guaranteed acyclic. Figure 5.5(b) shows the class dependency graph for the genetics domain, with guaranteed acyclic edges shown as dashed edges.

We allow the user to assert that certain reference slots $\mathcal{R}_{ga} = \{\rho_1, \ldots, \rho_k\}$ are *guaranteed acyclic*; i.e., we are guaranteed that there is a partial ordering $\prec_{ga}$ such that if y is a ρ-relative for some $\rho \in \mathcal{R}_{ga}$ of x, then $y \prec_{ga} x$. We say that a slot chain $\boldsymbol{K}$ is guaranteed acyclic if each of its component ρ's is guaranteed acyclic.

This prior knowledge allows us to guarantee the legality of certain dependency models. We start by building a *colored class dependency graph* that describes the direct dependencies between the attributes.

Definition 5.9
The *colored class dependency graph* G_Π for a PRM Π has the following edges:

1. **Yellow edges:** If $X.B$ is a parent of $X.A$, we have a *yellow* edge $X.B \to X.A$.

2. **Green edges:** If $\gamma(X.\boldsymbol{K}.B)$ is a parent of $X.A$, $Y = \text{Range}[X.\boldsymbol{K}]$, and $\boldsymbol{K}$ is guaranteed acyclic, we have a green edge $Y.B \to X.A$.

3. **Red edges:** If $\gamma(X.\boldsymbol{K}.B)$ is a parent of $X.A$, $Y = \text{Range}[X.\boldsymbol{K}]$, and $\boldsymbol{K}$ is not guaranteed acyclic, we have a red edge $Y.B \to X.A$. ∎

Note that there might be several edges, perhaps of different colors, between two attributes.

The intuition is that dependency along green edges relates objects that are ordered by an acyclic order. Thus, these edges by themselves or combined with intra-object dependencies (yellow edges) cannot cause a cyclic dependency. We must, however, take care with other dependencies, for which we do not have prior knowledge, as these might form a cycle. This intuition suggests the following definition:

Definition 5.10
A (colored) dependency graph is *stratified* if every cycle in the graph contains at least one green edge and no red edges. ∎

Theorem 5.11
If the colored class dependency graph is stratified for a PRM Π, then for *any* skeleton σ_r, the instance dependency graph is acyclic.

In other words, if the colored dependency graph of $\mathcal{S}$ and $\mathcal{R}_{ga}$ is stratified, then for any skeleton σ_r for which the slots in $\mathcal{R}_{ga}$ are jointly acyclic, $\mathcal{S}$ defines a coherent probability distribution over assignments to σ_r.

This notion of stratification generalizes the two special cases we considered above. When we do not have any guaranteed acyclic relations, all the edges in the dependency graph are colored either yellow or red. Then the graph is stratified if and only if it is acyclic. In the genetics example, all the parent relations would be in $\mathcal{R}_{ga}$. The only edges involved in cycles are green edges.

We can also support multiple guaranteed acyclic relations by using different shades of green for each set of guaranteed acyclic relations. Then a cycle is safe as long as it contains at most one shade of green edge.

5.3   The Difference between PRMs and Bayesian Networkss

The PRM specifies a probability distribution using the same underlying principles used in specifying Bayesian networks. The assumption is that each of the random variables in the PRM — in this case the attributes $x.A$ of the individual objects x — is directly influenced by only a few others. The PRM therefore defines for each $x.A$ a set of parents, which are the direct influences on it, and a local probabilistic model that specifies the dependence on these parents. In this way, the PRM is like a Bayesian Network.

However, there are two primary differences between PRMs and Bayesian networks. First, a PRM defines the dependency model at the class level, allowing it to be used for any object in the class. In some sense, it is analogous to a universally quantified statement. Second, the PRM explicitly uses the relational structure of the skeleton, in that it allows the probabilistic model of an attribute of an object to depend also on attributes of related objects. The specific set of related objects can vary with the skeleton σ_r; the PRM specifies the dependency in a generic enough way that it can apply to an arbitrary relational structure.

One can understand the semantics of a PRM together with a particular relational skeleton σ_r by examining the ground Bayesian network defined earlier. The network has a node for each attribute of the objects in the skeleton. The local probability models for attributes of objects in the same class are identical (we can view the parameters as being shared); however, the distribution for a node will depend on the values of its parents, and the parents of each node are determined by the skeleton.

It is important to note the construction of the ground Bayesian Network is just a thought experiment; in many cases there is no need to actually construct this large underlying Bayesian network.

5.4   PRMs with Structural Uncertainty

The previous section gave the syntax and semantics for the most basic type of PRM, a PRM in which there is uncertainty over the the attributes of the objects in the relational skeleton. As discussed in the last section, this is already a significant generalization beyond propositional Bayesian networks. In this section, we propose probabilistic models for the attributes of the objects in a relational model and also for the relational or link structure *itself*. In other words, we model the probability that certain relationships hold between objects. We propose two mechanisms for modeling link uncertainty: *reference uncertainty* and *existence uncertainty*.

The PRM framework presented so far focuses on modeling the distribution over the attributes of the objects in the model. It takes the relational structure itself — the objects and the relational links between entities — to be background knowledge, determined outside the probabilistic model. This assumption implies that the model cannot be used to predict the relational structure itself. A more subtle yet very important point is that the relational structure is informative in and of itself. For example, the links from and to a webpage are very informative about the type of webpage [6], and the citation links between papers are very informative about the paper topics [5].

By making objects and links first-class citizens in the model, our language easily allows us to place a probabilistic model directly over them. In other words, we can extend our framework to define probability distributions over the presence of relational links between objects in our model. By introducing these aspects of the world into the model, and correlating them with other attributes, we can both predict the link structure and use the presence of links to reach conclusions about attribute values.

5.5   Probabilistic Model of Link Structure

In our discussion so far, all relations between attributes are determined by the relational skeleton σ_r; only the descriptive attributes are uncertain. The relational skeleton specifies the set of objects in all classes, as well as all the relationships that hold between them (in other words, it specifies the values for all of the reference slots). Consider the simple university domain of section 5.2 describing professors, courses, students, and registrations. The relational skeleton specifies the complete relational structure in the model: it specifies which professor teaches each course, and it specifies all of the registrations of students in courses. In our simple university example, the relational skeleton (shown in figure 5.2(a)) contains all of the information except for the values for the descriptive attributes.

There is one distinction we will add to our relational schema. It is useful to distinguish between an *entity* and a *relationship*, as in entity-relationship diagrams. In our language, classes are used to represent both entities and relationships. We

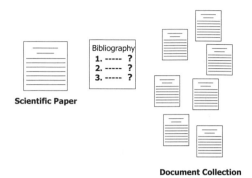

Figure 5.6   Reference uncertainty in a simple citation domain.

introduce $\mathcal{X}_{\mathcal{E}}$ to denote the set of classes that represent entities, and $\mathcal{X}_{\mathcal{R}}$ to denote those that represent relationships. We note that the distinctions are prior knowledge about the domain, and are therefore part of the domain specification. We use the generic term *object* to refer both to entities and to relationships.

5.5.1   Reference Uncertainty

Consider a simple citation domain illustrated in figure 5.6. Here we have a document collection. Each document has a bibliography that references some of the other documents in the collection. We may know the number of citations made by each document (i.e., it is outside the probabilistic model). By observing the citations that are made, we can use the links to reach conclusions about other attributes in the model. For example, by observing the number of citations to papers of various topics, we may be able to infer something about the topic of the citing paper.

figure 5.7(a) shows a simple schema for this domain. We have two classes, **Paper** and **Cites**. The **Paper** class has information about the topic of the paper and the words contained in the paper. For now, we simply have an attribute for each word that is *true* if the word occurs in the page and *false* otherwise. The **Cites** class represents the citation of one paper, the *Cited* paper, by another paper, the *Citing* paper. (In the figure, for readability, we show the **Paper** class twice.) In this model, we assume that the set of objects is prespecified, but relations among them, i.e., reference slots, are subject to probabilistic choices. Thus, rather than being given a full relational skeleton σ_r, we assume that we are given an *object skeleton* σ_o. The object skeleton specifies only the objects $\sigma_o(X)$ in each class $X \in \mathcal{X}$, but not the values of the reference slots. In our example, the object skeleton specifies the objects in class **Paper** and the objects in class **Cites**, but the reference slots of the **Cites** relation, **Cites**.*Cited* and **Cites**.*Citing* are unspecified. In other words, the probabilistic model does not provide a model of the total number of citation links, but only a distribution over their "endpoints." figure 5.7 shows an object skeleton for the citation domain.

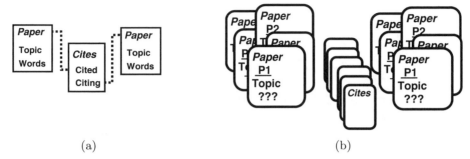

(a)   (b)

Figure 5.7   (a) A relational schema for the citation domain. (b) An object skeleton for the citation domain.

5.5.1.1   *Probabilistic Model*

In the case of reference uncertainty, we specify a probabilistic model for the value of the reference slots $X.\rho$. The domain of a reference slot $X.\rho$ is the set of keys (unique identifiers) of the objects in the class Y to which $X.\rho$ refers. Thus, we need to specify a probability distribution over the set of all objects in Y. For example, for Cites.*Cited*, we must specify a distribution over the objects in class Paper.

A naive approach is to simply have the PRM specify a probability distribution directly over the objects $\sigma_o(Y)$ in Y. For example, for Cites.*Cited*, we would have to specify a distribution over the primary keys of Paper. This approach has two major flaws. Most obviously, this distribution would require a parameter for each object in Y, leading to a very large number of parameters. This is a problem both from a computational perspective — the model becomes very large — and from a statistical perspective — we often would not have enough data to make robust estimates for the parameters. More importantly, we want our dependency model to be general enough to apply over all possible object skeletons σ_o; a distribution defined in terms of the objects within a specific object skeleton would not apply to others.

In order to achieve a general and compact representation, we use the *attributes* of Y to define the probability distribution. In this model, we partition the class Y into subsets labeled $\psi_1, \ldots, \psi_m$ according to the values of some of its attributes, and specify a probability for choosing each partition, i.e., a distribution over the partitions. We then select an object within that partition uniformly.

For example, consider a description of movie theater showings as in figure 5.8(a). For the foreign key Shows.*Movie*, we can partition the class Movie by *Genre*, indicating that a movie theater first selects the genre of movie it wants to show, and then selects uniformly among the movies with the selected genre. For example, a movie theater may be much more likely to show a movie which is a thriller than a foreign movie. Having selected, for example, to show a thriller, the theater then selects the actual movie to show uniformly from within the set of thrillers. In addition, just as in the case of descriptive attributes, the partition choice can

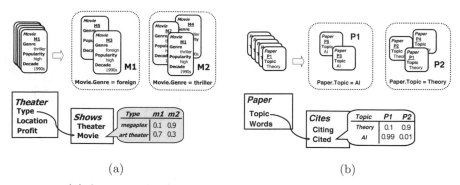

(a)　　　　　　　　　　　　　　　(b)

Figure 5.8　(a) An example of reference uncertainty for a movie theater's showings. (b) A simple example of reference uncertainty in the citation domain

depend on other attributes in our model. Thus, the selector attribute can have parents. As illustrated in the figure, the choice of movie genre might depend on the type of theater. Consider another example in our citation domain. As shown in figure 5.8(b), we can partition the class **Paper** by *Topic*, indicating that the topic of a citing paper determines the topics of the papers it cites; and then the cited paper is chosen uniformly among the papers with the selected topic.

We make this intuition precise by defining, for each slot ρ, a *partition function* Ψ_ρ. We place several restrictions on the partition function which are captured in the following definition:

Definition 5.12

Let $X.\rho$ be a reference slot with domain Y. Let $\Psi_\rho : Y \to \mathrm{Dom}[\Psi_\rho]$ be a function where $\mathrm{Dom}[\Psi_\rho]$ is a finite set of labels. We say that Ψ_ρ is a *partition function* for ρ if there is a subset of the attributes of Y, $\mathcal{P}[\rho] \subseteq \mathcal{A}(Y)$, such that for any $y \in Y$ and any $y' \in Y$, if the values of the attributes $\mathcal{P}[\rho]$ of y and y' are the same, i.e., for each $A \in \mathcal{P}[\rho]$, $y.A = y'.A$, then $\Psi_\rho(y) = \Psi_\rho(y')$. We refer to $\mathcal{P}[\rho]$ as the *partition attributes* for ρ. ∎

Thus, the values of the partition attributes are all that is required to determine the partition to which an object belongs.

In our first example, $\Psi_{\mathsf{Shows}.Movie} : \mathsf{Movie} \to \{foreign, thriller\}$ and the partition attributes are $\mathcal{P}[\mathsf{Shows}.Movie] = \{Genre\}$. In the second example, $\Psi_{\mathsf{Cites}.Cited} : \mathsf{Paper} \to \{AI, Theory\}$ and the partition attributes are $\mathcal{P}[\mathsf{Cites}.Cited] = \{Topic\}$.

There are a number of natural methods for specifying the partition function. It can be defined simply by having one partition for each possible combination of values of the partition attributes, i.e., one partition for each value in the cross product of the partition attribute values. Our examples above take this approach. In both cases, there is only a single partition attribute, so specifying the partition function in this manner is not too unwieldy, but for larger collections of partition attributes or for partition attributes with large domains, this method for defining the partitioning function may be problematic. A more flexible and scalable approach is to define the partition function using a decision tree built over the partition attributes. In this case, there is one partition for each of the leaves in the decision tree.

Each possible value ψ determines a subset of Y from which the value of ρ (the referent) will be selected. For a particular instantiation $\mathcal{I}$ of the database, we use $\mathcal{I}(Y_\psi)$ to represent the set of objects in $\mathcal{I}(Y)$ that fall into the partition ψ.

We now represent a probabilistic model over the values of ρ by specifying a distribution over possible partitions, which encodes how likely the reference value of ρ is to fall into one partition versus another. We formalize our intuition above by introducing a *selector attribute* S_ρ, whose domain is $\text{Dom}[\Psi_\rho]$. The specification of the probabilistic model for the selector attribute S_ρ is the same as that of any other attribute: it has a set of parents and a CPD. In our earlier example, the CPD of $\text{Show}.S_{Movie}$ might have as a parent $\text{Theater}.\textit{Type}$. For each instantiation of the parents, we have a distribution over $\text{Dom}[S_\rho]$. The choice of value for S_ρ determines the partition Y_ψ from which the reference value of ρ is chosen; the choice of reference value for ρ is uniformly distributed within this set.

Definition 5.13

A *probabilistic relational model* Π *with reference uncertainty* over a relational schema $\mathcal{R}$ has the same components as in definition 5.2. In addition, for each reference slot $\rho \in \mathcal{R}(X)$ with $\text{Range}[\rho] = Y$, we have:

- a partition function Ψ_ρ with a set of partition attributes $\mathcal{P}[\rho] \subseteq \mathcal{A}(Y)$;
- a new selector attribute S_ρ within X which takes on values in the range of Ψ_ρ;
- a set of parents and a CPD for S_ρ. ∎

To define the semantics of this extension, we must define the probability of reference slots as well as descriptive attributes:

$$P(\mathcal{I} \mid \sigma_o, \Pi) = \prod_{X \in \mathcal{X}} \prod_{x \in \sigma_o(X)} \prod_{A \in \mathcal{A}(X)} P(x.A \mid \text{Pa}(x.A))$$
$$\prod_{\rho \in \mathcal{R}(X), y = x.\rho} \frac{P(x.S_\rho = \psi[y] \mid \text{Pa}(x.S_\rho))}{|\mathcal{I}(Y_{\psi[y]})|}, \qquad (5.2)$$

where $\psi[y]$ refers to $\Psi_\rho(y)$ — the partition that the partition function assigns y. Note that the last term in (5.2) depends on $\mathcal{I}$ in three ways: the interpretation of $x.\rho = y$, the values of the attributes $\mathcal{P}[\rho]$ within the object y, and the size of $Y_{\psi[y]}$. The above probability is not well-defined if there are no objects in a partition, so in that case we define it to be zero.

5.5.2   Coherence of the Probabilistic Model

As in the case of PRMs with attribute uncertainty, we must be careful to guarantee that our probability distribution is in fact coherent. In this case, the object skeleton does not specify which objects are related to which, and therefore the mapping of formal to actual parents depends on probabilistic choices made in the model. The associated ground Bayesian network will therefore be cumbersome and not particularly intuitive. We define our coherence constraints using an instance dependency graph, relative to our PRM and object skeleton.

Definition 5.14

The *instance dependency graph* for a PRM Π and an object skeleton σ_o is a graph G_{σ_o} with the nodes and edges described below. For each class X and each $x \in \sigma_o(X)$, we have the following nodes:

- a node $x.A$ for every descriptive attribute $X.A$;
- a node $x.\rho$ and a node $x.S_\rho$, for every reference slot $X.\rho$.

The dependency graph contains five types of edges:

- **Type I edges:** Consider any attribute (descriptive or selector) $X.A$ and formal parent $X.B$. We define an edge $x.B \to x.A$, for every $x \in \sigma_o(X)$.
- **Type II edges:** Consider any attribute (descriptive or selector) $X.A$ and formal parent $X.\boldsymbol{K}.B$ where $\text{Dom}[X.\boldsymbol{K}] = Y$. We define an edge $y.B \to x.A$, for every $x \in \sigma_o(X)$ and $y \in \sigma_o(Y)$.
- **Type III edges:** Consider any attribute $X.A$ and formal parent $X.\boldsymbol{K}.B$, where $\boldsymbol{K} = \rho_1, \ldots, \rho_k$, and $\text{Dom}[\rho_i] = X_i$. We define an edge $x.\rho_1 \to x.A$, for every $x \in \sigma_o(X)$. In addition, for each $i > 1$, we add an edge $x_i.\rho_i \to x.A$ for every $x_i \in \sigma_o(X_i)$ and for every $x \in \sigma_o(X)$.
- **Type IV edges:** Consider any slot $X.\rho$ and partition attribute $Y.B \in \mathcal{P}[\rho]$ for $Y = \text{Range}[\rho]$. We define an edge $y.B \to x.S_\rho$ for every $x \in \sigma_o(X)$ and $y \in \sigma_o(Y)$.
- **Type V edges:** Consider any slot $X.\rho$. We define an edge $x.S_\rho \to x.\rho$ for every $x \in \sigma_o(X)$.

We say that a dependency structure $\mathcal{S}$ is *acyclic* relative to an object skeleton σ_o if the directed graph G_{σ_o} is acyclic. ∎

Intuitively, type I edges correspond to intra-object dependencies and type II edges to inter-object dependencies. These are the same edges that we had in the dependency graph for regular PRMs, except that they also apply to selector attributes. Moreover, there is an important difference in our treatment of type II edges. In this case, the skeleton does not specify the value of $x.\rho$, and hence we cannot determine from the skeleton on which object y the attribute $x.A$ actually depends. Therefore, our instance dependency graph must include an edge from every attribute $y.B$.

Type III edges represent the fact that the actual choice of parent for $x.A$ depends on the value of the slots used to define it. When the parent is defined via a slot chain, the actual choice depends on the values of all the slots along the chain. Since we cannot determine the particular object from the skeleton, we must include an edge from every slot $x_i.\rho_i$ potentially included in the chain.

Type V edges represent the dependency of a slot on the attributes defining the associated partition. To see why this dependence is required, we observe that our choice of reference value for $x.\rho$ depends on the values of the partition attributes

$\mathcal{P}[x.\rho]$ of all of the different objects y in Y. Thus, these attributes must be determined before $x.\rho$ is determined. Finally, type V edges represent the fact that the actual choice of parent for $x.A$ depends on the value of the selector attributes for the slots used to define it. In our example, as $\mathcal{P}[\mathsf{Shows}.Movie] = \{\mathsf{Movie}.Genre\}$, the genres of all movies must be determined before we can select the value of the reference slot $\mathsf{Shows}.Movie$.

Based on this definition, we can specify conditions under which (5.2) specifies a coherent probability distribution.

Theorem 5.15
Let Π be a PRM with reference uncertainty whose dependency structure $\mathcal{S}$ is acyclic relative to an object skeleton σ_o. Then Π and σ_o define a coherent probability distribution over instantiations $\mathcal{I}$ that extend σ_o via (5.2).

This theorem is limited in that it is very specific to the constraints of a given object skeleton. As in the case of PRMs without relational uncertainty, we want to learn a model in one setting, and be assured that it will be acyclic for any skeleton we might encounter. We accomplish this goal by extending our definition of class dependency graph. We do so by extending the class dependency graph to contain edges that correspond to the edges we defined in the instance dependency graph.

Definition 5.16
The *class dependency graph* G_Π for a PRM with reference uncertainty Π has a node for each descriptive or selector attribute $X.A$ and each reference slot $X.\rho$, and the following edges:

- **Type I edges:** For any attribute $X.A$ and formal parent $X.B$, we have an edge $X.B \rightarrow X.A$.
- **Type II edges:** For any attribute $X.A$ and formal parent $X.\rho.B$ where $\mathrm{Range}[\rho] = Y$, we have an edge $Y.B \rightarrow X.A$.
- **Type III edges:** For any attribute $X.A$ and formal parent $Y.\boldsymbol{K}.B$, where $\boldsymbol{K} = \rho_1, \ldots, \rho_k$, and $\mathrm{Dom}[\rho_i] = X_i$, we define an edge $X.\rho_1 \rightarrow X.A$. In addition, for each $i > 1$, we add an edge $X.\rho_i \rightarrow X.A$.
- **Type IV edges:** For any slot $X.\rho$ and partition attribute $Y.B$ for $Y = \mathrm{Range}[\rho]$, we have an edge $Y.B \rightarrow X.S_\rho$.
- **Type V edges:** For any slot $X.\rho$, we have an edge $X.S_\rho \rightarrow X.\rho$.

Figure 5.9 shows the class dependency graph for our extended movie example.

While the proof is a bit more complex than in the attribute uncertainty case, the following analogous theorem holds:

Theorem 5.17
Let Π be a PRM with reference uncertainty whose class dependency structure $\mathcal{S}$ is acyclic. For any object skeleton σ_o, Π and σ_o define a coherent probability distribution over instantiations $\mathcal{I}$ that extend σ_o via (5.2).

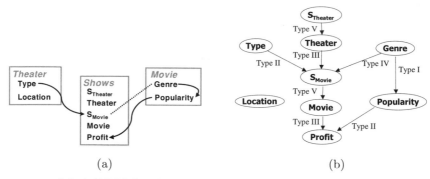

        (a)   (b)

Figure 5.9 (a) A PRM for the movie theater example. The partition attributes are indicated using dashed lines. (b) The dependency graph for the movie theater example. The different edge types are labeled.

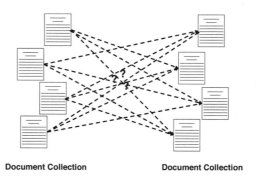

Figure 5.10 Existence uncertainty in a simple citation domain.

5.5.3 Existence Uncertainty

The second form of structural uncertainty we introduce is called *existence uncertainty*. In this case, we make no assumptions about the number of links that exist. The number of links that exist and the identity of the links are all part of the probabilistic model and can be used to make inferences about other attributes in our model. In our citation example above, we might assume that the set of papers is part of our background knowledge, but we want to provide an explicit model for the presence or absence of citations. Unlike the reference uncertainty model of the previous section, we do not assume that the total number of citations is fixed, but rather that each potential citation can be present or absent.

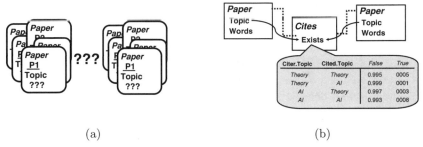

(a)   (b)

Figure 5.11   (a) An entity skeleton for the citation domain. (b) A CPD for the *Exists* attribute of Cites.

5.5.3.1 *Semantics of Relational Model*

The object skeleton used for reference uncertainty assumes that the number of objects in each relation is known. Thus, if we consider a division of objects into entities and relations, the number of objects in classes of both types is fixed. Existence uncertainty assumes even less background information than specified by the object skeleton. Specifically, we assume that the number of relationship objects is not fixed in advance. This situation is illustrated in figure 5.10.

We assume that we are given only an *entity skeleton* σ_e, which specifies the set of objects in our domain only for the entity classes. Figure 5.11(a) shows an entity skeleton for the citation example. Our basic approach is to allow other objects within the model — those in the relationship classes — to be *undetermined*, i.e., their existence can be uncertain. In other words, we introduce into the model all of the objects that can *potentially* exist in it; with each of them, we associate a special binary variable that tells us whether the object actually exists or not. We call entity classes *determined* and relationship classes *undetermined*.

To specify the set of potential objects, we note that relationship classes typically represent many-many relationships; they have at least two reference slots, which refer to determined classes. For example, our Cite class has the two reference slots, *Citing* and *Cited*. Thus the potential domain of the Cites class in a given instantiation $\mathcal{I}$ is $\mathcal{I}(\mathsf{Paper}) \times \mathcal{I}(\mathsf{Paper})$. Each "potential" object x in this class has the form $\mathsf{Cite}[y_1, y_2]$. Each such object is associated with a binary attribute $x.E$ that specifies whether paper y_1 did or did not cite paper y_2.

Definition 5.18

Consider a schema with determined and undetermined classes, and let σ_e be an entity skeleton over this schema. We define the *induced* relational skeleton, $\sigma_r[\sigma_e]$, to be the relational skeleton that contains the following objects:

- If X is a determined class, then $\sigma_r[\sigma_e](X) = \sigma_e(X)$.
- Let X be an undetermined class with reference slots $\rho_1, \ldots, \rho_k$ whose range types are $Y_1, \ldots, Y_k$ respectively. Then $\sigma_r[\sigma_e](X)$ contains an object $X[y_1, \ldots, y_k]$ for all tuples $\langle y_1, \ldots, y_k \rangle \in \sigma_r[\sigma_e](Y_1) \times \cdots \times \sigma_r[\sigma_e](Y_k)$.

The relations in $\sigma_r[\sigma_e]$ are defined in the obvious way: Slots of objects of determined classes are taken from the entity skeleton. Slots of objects of undetermined classes are induced from the object definition: $X[y_1, \ldots, y_k].\rho_i$ is y_i. ∎

To ensure that the semantics of schemata with undetermined classes is well-defined, we need a few tools. Specifically, we need to ensure that the set of potential objects is well-defined and finite. It is clear that if we allow cyclic references (e.g., an undetermined class with a reference to itself), then the set of potential objects is not finite. To avoid such situations, we need to put some requirements on the schema.

Definition 5.19
A set of classes $\mathcal{X}$ is *stratified* if there exists a partial ordering over the classes $\prec$ such that for any reference slot $X.\rho$ with range type Y, $Y \prec X$. ∎

Lemma 5.20
If the set of undetermined classes in a schema is stratified, then given any entity skeleton σ_e the number of potential objects in any undetermined class is finite.

As discussed, each undetermined X has a special *existence* attribute $X.E$ whose values are $\mathcal{V}(E) = \{true, false\}$. For uniformity of notation, we introduce an E attribute for all classes; for classes that are determined, the E value is defined to be always *true*. We require that all of the reference slots of a determined class X have a range type which is also a determined class.

For a PRM with stratified undetermined classes, we define an instantiation to be an assignment of values to the attributes, including the *Exists* attribute, of *all* potential objects.

5.5.3.2 Probabilistic Model

We now specify the probabilistic model defined by the PRM. By treating the *Exists* attributes as standard descriptive attributes, we can essentially build our definition directly on top of the definition of standard PRMs.

Specifically, the existence attribute for an undetermined class is treated in the same way as a descriptive attribute in our dependency model, in that it can have parents and children, and has an associated CPD. figure 5.11(b) illustrates a CPD for the Cites.*Exists* attribute. In this example, the existence of a citation depends on the topic of the citing paper and the topic of the cited paper; e.g., it is more likely that citations will exist between papers with the same topic.

Using the induced relational skeleton and treating the existence events as descriptive attributes, we have set things up so that (5.1) applies with minor changes. There are two important changes to the definition of the distribution:

- We want to enforce that $x.E = false$ if $x.\rho.E = false$ for one of the slots ρ of X. Suppose that X has the slots $\rho_1, \ldots, \rho_k$, we define the *effective* CPD for $X.E$ as follows. Let $\mathrm{Pa}^*(X.E) = \mathrm{Pa}(X.E) \cup \{X.\rho_1.E, \ldots, X.\rho_k.E\}$, and define

$$P^*(X.E \mid \mathrm{Pa}^*(X.E)) = \begin{cases} P(X.E \mid \mathrm{Pa}(X.E)) & \text{if } X.\rho_i.E = true, \forall i = 1, \ldots, k, \\ 0 & \text{otherwise} \end{cases}$$

- We want to "decouple" the attributes of nonexistent objects from the rest of the PRM. Thus, if $X.A$ is a descriptive attribute, we define $\mathrm{Pa}^*(X.A) = \mathrm{Pa}(X.A) \cup \{X.E\}$, and

$$P^*(X.A \mid \mathrm{Pa}^*(X.A)) = \begin{cases} P(X.A \mid \mathrm{Pa}(X.A)) & \text{if } X.E = true, \\ \frac{1}{|\mathcal{V}(X.A)|} & \text{otherwise} \end{cases}$$

It is easy to verify that in both cases $P^*(X.A \mid \mathrm{Pa}^*(X.A))$ is a legal conditional distribution.

In effect, these constraints specify a new PRM Π^*, in which we treat $X.E$ as a standard descriptive attribute. For each attribute (including the *Exists* attribute), we define the parents of $X.A$ in Π^* to be $\mathrm{Pa}^*(X.A)$ and the associated CPD to be $P^*(X.A \mid \mathrm{Pa}^*(X.A))$.

Given an entity skeleton σ_e, a PRM with exists uncertainty Π specifies a distribution over a set of instantiations $\mathcal{I}$ consistent with $\sigma_r[\sigma_e]$:

$$P(\mathcal{I} \mid \sigma_e, \Pi) = P(\mathcal{I} \mid \sigma_r[\sigma_e], \Pi^*) = \prod_{X \in \mathcal{X}} \prod_{x \in \sigma_r[\sigma_e](X)} \prod_{A \in \mathcal{A}(x)} P^*(x.A \mid \mathrm{Pa}^*(x.A)) \tag{5.3}$$

We can similarly define the the class dependency graph for a PRM Π with exists uncertainty using the corresponding notions for the standard PRM Π^*. As there, we require that the class dependency graph G_{Π^*} is acyclic. One immediate consequence of this requirement is that the schema is stratified.

Lemma 5.21

If the class dependency graph G_{Π^*} is acyclic, then there is a stratification of the undetermined classes.

Based on this definition, we can prove the following result:

Theorem 5.22

Let Π be a PRM with existence uncertainty and an acyclic class dependency graph. Let σ_e be an entity skeleton. Then (5.3) defines a coherent distribution on all instantiations $\mathcal{I}$ of the induced relational skeleton $\sigma_r[\sigma_e]$.

5.6   PRMs with Class Hierarchies

Next we propose methods for discovering useful refinements of a PRM's dependency model. We begin by introducing *probabilistic relational models with class hierarchies* (PRMs-CH). PRMs-CH extend PRMs by including class hierarchies over the objects. Subclasses allow us to specialize the probabilistic model for some instances of a class. For example, if we have a class movie in our relational schema, we might consider subclasses of movies, such as documentaries, action movies, British comedies, etc. The popularity of an action movie (a subclass of movies) may depend on its budget, whereas the popularity of a documentary (another subclass of movies) may depend on the reputation of the director. Subclassing allows us to model probabilistic dependencies at the appropriate level of detail. For example, we can have the parents of the popularity attribute in the action movie subclass be different than the parents of the same attribute in the documentary subclass. In addition, subclassing allows additional dependency paths to be represented in the model that would not be allowed in a PRM that does not support subclasses. For example, whether a person enjoys action movies may depend on whether she enjoys documentaries. PRMs-CH provide a general mechanism that allow us to define a rich set of dependencies.

To motivate our extensions, consider a simple PRM for the movie domain. Let us restrict attention to the three classes, Person, Movie, and Vote. We can have the attributes of Vote depending on attributes of the person voting (via the slot Vote.*Voter*) and on attributes of the movie (via the slot Vote.*Movie*). However, given the attributes of all the people and the movie in the model, the different votes are (conditionally) i.i.d.

5.6.1   Class Hierarchies

Our aim is to refine the notion of a class, such as Movie, into finer subclasses, such as action movies, comedy, documentaries, etc. Moreover, we want to allow recursive refinements of this structure, so that we might refine action movies into the subclasses spy movies, car chase movies, and kung-fu movies.

A class hierarchy for a class X defines an IS-A hierarchy for objects from class X. The root of the class hierarchy is simply class X itself. The subclasses of X are organized into an inheritance hierarchy. The leaves of the class hierarchy describe basic classes—these are the most specific characterization of objects that occur in the database. The interior nodes describe abstractions of the base-level classes. The intent is that the class hierarchy is designed to capture useful and meaningful abstractions in a particular domain.

More formally, a hierarchy $H[X]$ for a class X is a rooted directed acyclic graph defined by a subclass relation $\prec$ over a finite set of subclasses $\mathcal{C}[X]$. For $c, d \in \mathcal{C}[X]$, if $c \prec d$, we say that X_c is a *direct subclass* of X_d, and X_d is a *direct superclass* of X_c. The root of the tree is the class X. $Class_\top$ corresponds to the original class X. We define $\prec^*$ to be the transitive closure of $\prec$; if $c \prec^* d$, we say that X_c is a subclass of X_d. For example, figure 5.12 shows the simple class hierarchy for the Movie class.

We denote the sublcasses of the hierarchy by $\mathcal{C}[(|H[X])$. We achieve subclassing for a class X by requiring that there be an additional subclass indicator attribute $X.Class$ that determines the subclass to which an object belongs. Thus, if c is a

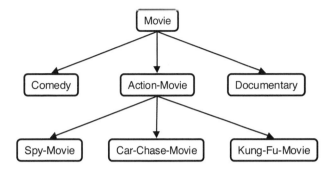

Figure 5.12   A simple class hierarchy for Movie.

subclass, then $\mathcal{I}(X_c)$ contains all objects $x \in X$ for which $x.Class \prec^* c$, i.e., all objects that are in some class which is a subclass of c. In our example, Movie has a subclass indicator variable Movie.*Class* with possible values

$$\{Comedy, Action\text{-}Movie, Documentary, Spy\text{-}Movie, Car\text{-}Chase\text{-}Movie, Kung\text{-}Fu\text{-}Movie\}$$

.

Subclasses allow us to make finer distinctions when constructing a probabilistic model. In particular, they allow us to *specialize* CPDs for different subclasses in the hierarchy.

Definition 5.23

A *probabilistic relational model with subclass hierarchy* is defined as follows. For each class $X \in \mathcal{X}$, we have

- a class hierarchy $H[X] = (\mathcal{C}[X], \prec)$;
- a subclass indicator attribute $X.Class$ such that $\mathcal{V}(X.Class) = \mathcal{C}[(|H[X])$;
- a CPD for $X.Class$;
- for each subclass $c \in \mathcal{C}[X]$ and attribute $A \in \mathcal{A}(X)$ we have either
    - a set of parents $\mathrm{Pa}^c(X.A)$ and a CPD that describes $P(X.A \mid \mathrm{Pa}^c(X.A))$; or
    - an *inherited* indicator that specifies that the CPD for $X.A$ in c is inherited from its direct superclass. The root of the hierarchy cannot have the inherited indicator. ∎

With the introduction of subclass hierarchies, we can refine our probabilistic dependencies. Before each attribute $X.A$ had an associated CPD. Now, if we like, we can specialize the CPD for an attribute within a particular subclass. We can associate a different CPD with the attributes of different subclasses. For example, the attribute Action-Movie.*Popularity* may have a different conditional distribution from the attribute Documentary.*Popularity*. Further, the distribution for each of the attributes may depend on a completely different set of parents. Continuing our earlier example, if the popularity of an action movie depends on its budget, then Action-Movie.*Popularity* would have as parents Action-Movie.*Budget*. However, for documentaries, the popularity depends on the reputation of the director; then Documentary.*Popularity* would have the parent Documentary.*Director.Reputation*.

We define $P(X.A \mid \mathrm{Pa}^c(X.A))$ to be the CPD associated with A in X_d, where d is the most specialized superclass of c (which may be c itself) such that the CPD of $X.A$ in d is not marked with the inherited indicator.

5.6.2   Refined Slot References

At first glance, the increase in representational power provided by supporting subclasses is deceptively small. It seems that little more than an extra constructed type variable has been added, and that the structure that is exploited by the new subclassed CPDs could just as easily have been provided using structured CPDs, such as the tree-structured CPDs or decision graphs [1, 4]. For example, the root node in the tree-structured CPD for attribute $X.A$ can split on the class attribute, $X.Class$, and then the subtrees can define the appropriate specializations of the CPD. In reality, it is not quite so simple; now $X.A$ would need to have as parents the union of all of the parents of its subclasses. However, the representational power is quite similar.

However, the representational power has been extended in a very important way. Certain dependency structures that would have been disallowed in the original framework are now allowed. These dependencies appear circular when examined only at the class level; however, when refined and modeled at the subclass level, they are no longer cyclic. One way of understanding this phenomenon is that, once we have refined the class, the subclass information allows us to disentangle and order the dependencies.

Returning to our earlier example, suppose that we have the classes Voter, Movie, and Vote. Vote has reference slots *Person* and *Movie* and an attribute *Ranking* that gives the score that a person has given for a movie. Suppose we want to model a correlation between a person's votes for documentaries and her votes for action movies. (This correlation might be a negative one.) In the unrefined model, we do not have a way of referring to a person's votes for some particular subset of movies; we can only consider aggregates over a person's entire set of votes. Furthermore, even if we could introduce such a dependence, the dependency graph would show a dependence of Vote.*Rank* on itself.

When we create subclasses of movie, we can also create specializations of any classes that make reference to movies. For example Vote has a reference slot Vote.*Movie*. Suppose we create subclasses of Movie: Comedy, Action-Movie, and Documentary. Then we can create corresponding specializations of Vote: Comedy-Vote, Action-Vote, and Documentary-Vote. Each of these subclasses refers only to a particular category of votes.

The introduction of subclasses of votes provides us with a way of isolating a person's votes on some subset of movies. In particular, we can try to introduce a dependence of Documentary-Vote.*Rank* on Action-Vote.*Rank*. In order to allow this dependency, we need a mechanism for constructing slot chains that restrict the types of objects along the path to belong to specific subclasses. Recall that a reference slot ρ is a function from $\mathrm{Dom}[\rho]$ to $\mathrm{Range}[\rho]$, i.e. from X to Y. We can introduce *refinements* of a slot reference by restricting the types of the objects in the range.

Definition 5.24

Let ρ be a slot (reference or inverse) of X with range Y. Let d be a subclass of Y. A *refined slot reference* $\rho_{\langle d \rangle}$ for ρ to d is a relation between X and Y:

$$\text{For } x \in X, y \in Y, \ y \in x.\rho_{\langle d \rangle} \text{ if } x \in X \text{ and } y \in Y_d, \text{ then } y \in x.\rho. \ \blacksquare$$

Returning to our earlier example, suppose that we have subclasses of Movie: Comedy, Action-Movie, and Documentary. In addition, suppose we also have subclasses of Vote, Comedy-Vote and Action-Vote, and Documentary-Vote. To get from a person to her votes, we use the inverse of slot reference Person.*Votes*. Now we can construct refinements of Person.*Votes*, *Votes*⟨Comedy-Vote⟩, *Votes*⟨Action-Vote⟩, and *Votes*⟨Documentary-Vote⟩.

Let us name these slots *Comedy-Votes* and *Action-Votes*, and *Documentary-Votes*. To specify the dependency of a person's rankings for documentaries on their rankings for action movies we can say that Documentary-Vote.*Rank* has a parent which is the person's action movie rankings: γ(Documentary-Vote.*Person.Action-Votes.Rank*).

5.6.3 Support for Instance-Level Dependencies

The introduction of subclasses brings the benefit that we can now provide a smooth transition from the PRM, a class-based probabilistic model, to models that are more similar to Bayesian networks. To see this, suppose our subclass hierarchy for movies is very "deep" and starts with the general class and ends in the most refined levels with particular movie instances. Thus, at the most refined version of the model we can define the preferences of a person by either class-based dependency (the probability of enjoying documentary movies depends on whether the individual enjoys action movies) or instance-based dependency (the probability of enjoying *Terminator II* depends on whether the individual enjoys *The Hunt for Red October*). The latter model is essentially the same as the Bayesian network models learned by Breese et al. [2] in the context of collaborative filtering for TV programs.

In addition, the new flexibility in defining refined slot references allows us to make interesting combinations of these types of dependencies. For example, whether an individual enjoys a particular movie(e.g., *True Lies*) can be enough to predict whether she watches a whole other category of movies (e.g., James Bond movies).

5.6.4   Semantics

Using this definition, the semantics for PRM-CH are given by the following equation:

$$P(\mathcal{I} \mid \sigma_r, \Pi) = \prod_X \prod_{x \in \sigma_r(X)} P(x.\mathit{Class}) \prod_{A \in \mathcal{A}(X)} P(x.A \mid \mathrm{Pa}^{x.c}(x.A)). \tag{5.4}$$

As before, the probability of an instantiation of the database is the product of CPDs of the instance attributes; the key difference is that here, in addition to the skeleton determining the parents on an attribute, the subclass to which the object belongs determines which local probability model is used.

5.6.5   Coherence of Probabilistic Model

As in the case of PRMs with attribute uncertainty, we must be careful to guarantee that our probability distribution is in fact coherent. In this case, while the relational skeleton specifies which objects are related to which, it does not specify the subclass indicator for each object, so the mapping of formal to actual parents depends on the probabilistic choice for the subclass for the object. In addition, for refined slot references, the existence of the edge will depend on the subclass of the object. We will indicate edge existence by the coloring of an edge: a *black* edge exists in the graph, a *gray* edge may exist in the graph, and a *white* edge is invisible in the graph. As in previous sections, we define our coherence constraints using an instance dependency graph, relative to our PRM and relational skeleton.

Definition 5.25
The *colored instance dependency graph* for a CH-PRM Π_{CH} and a relational skeleton σ_r is a graph G_{σ_r}. The graph has the following nodes, for each class X and for each $x \in \sigma_r(X)$:

- A descriptive attribute node $x.A$, for every descriptive attribute $X.A \in \mathcal{A}(X)$;
- a subclass indicator node $x.\mathit{Class}$.

Let $\mathrm{Pa}^*(X.A) = \bigcup_{c \in \mathcal{C}[X]} \mathrm{Pa}^c(X.A)$. The dependency graph contains four types of edges. For each attribute $X.A$ (both descriptive attributes and the subclass indicator), we add the following edges:

- **Type I edges:** For every $x \in \sigma_r(X)$ and for each formal parent $X.B \in \mathrm{Pa}^*(X.A)$, we define an edge $x.B \to x.A$. This edge is black if the parents have not been specialized (which will be the case for the subclass indicator, $x.\mathit{Class}$, and possibly other attributes as well). All the other edges are colored gray.
- **Type II edges:** For every $x \in \sigma_r(X)$ and for each formal parent $X.\boldsymbol{K}.B \in \mathrm{Pa}^*(X.A)$, if $y \in x.\boldsymbol{K}$ in σ_r, we define an edge $y.B \to x.A$. If the CPD has been specialized, or if $\boldsymbol{K}$ contains any refined slot references this edge is colored *gray*; otherwise is is colored *black*. ∎

As before, type I edges correspond to intra-object dependencies and type II edges to inter-object dependencies. But since an object may be from any subclass, even though the relational skeleton specifies the objects to which it is related, until we know the subclass of an object, we do not know which of the local probability models applies. In addition, in the case where a parent of an object is defined via a refined slot reference, we also do not know the set of related objects until we know their subclasses. Thus, we add edges for every *possible* parent and color the edges used in defining parents gray. Type I and type II edges are gray when they are parents in a specialized CPD. In addition, type II edges may be gray if a refined slot reference is used in the definition of a parent.

At this point, the problem with our instance dependency graph is that there are some edges which are known to occur (the black edges) and some edges that may or may not exist (depending on the subclass of an object). How do we ensure our instance dependency graph is acyclic? In this case, we must ensure that the instance dependency graph is acyclic for any setting of the subclass indicators. Note that this is a probabilistic event. First, we extend our notion of acyclicity for our colored instance dependency graph.

Definition 5.26

A colored instance dependency graph is acyclic if, for any instantiation of the subclass indicators, there is an acyclic ordering of the nodes relative to the black edges in the graph. Given any a particular assignment of subclass indicators, we determine the black edges as follows:

- Given a subclass assignment $y.Class$, all of the edges involving this object are colored either black or white. Let $y.Class = d$. The edges for any parent nodes are colored black if they are defined by the CPD $\mathrm{Pa}^d(X.A)$, and white otherwise. In addition, the edges corresponding to any refined slot references, $\rho_{\langle d \rangle}(x, y)$, are set: If $y.Class = d$, the edge is colored black; otherwise it is painted white. ■

Based on this definition, we can specify conditions under which (5.4) specifies a coherent probability distribution.

Theorem 5.27

Let Π_{CH} be a PRM with class hierarchies whose colored dependency structure $\mathcal{S}$ is acyclic relative to a relational skeleton σ_r. Then Π_{CH} and σ_r define a coherent probability distribution over instantiations $\mathcal{I}$ that extend σ_r via (5.4).

As in the previous case of PRMs with attribute uncertainty and PRMs with structural uncertainty, we want to learn a model in one setting, and be assured that it will be acyclic for any skeleton we might encounter. Again we achieve this goal through our definition of class dependency graph. We do so by extending the class dependency graph to contain edges that correspond to the edges we defined in the instance dependency graph.

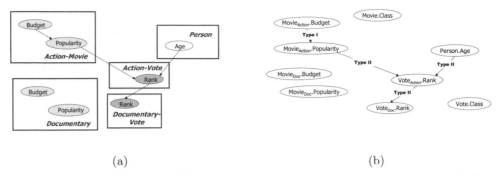

(a)   (b)

Figure 5.13 (a) A simple PRM with class hierarchies for the movie domain. (b) The class dependency graph for this PRM.

Definition 5.28
The *class dependency graph* for a PRM with class hierarchy Π_{CH} has the following set of nodes for each $X \in \mathcal{X}$:

- for each subclass $c \in \mathcal{C}[X]$ and attribute $A \in \mathcal{A}(X)$, a node $X_c.A$;
- a node for the subclass indicator $X.Class$;

and the following edges:

- **Type I edges:** For any node $X_c.A$ and formal parent $X_c.B \in \mathrm{Pa}^c(X_c.A)$ we have an edge $X_c.B \to X_c.A$.
- **Type II edges:** For any attribute $X_c.A$ and formal parent $X_c.\rho.B \in \mathrm{Pa}^c(X_c.A)$, where $\mathrm{Range}[\rho] = Y$, we have an edge $Y.B \to X_c.A$.
- **Type III edges:** For any attribute $X_c.A$, and for any direct superclass d, $c \prec d$, we add an edge $X_c.A \to X_d.A$. ∎

Figure 5.13 shows a simple class dependency graph for our movie example. The PRM-CH is given in figure 5.13(a) and the class dependency graph is shown in figure 5.13(b).

It is now easy to show that if this class dependency graph is acyclic, then the instance dependency graph is acyclic.

Lemma 5.29
If the class dependency graph is acyclic for a PRM with class hierarchies Π_{CH}, then for *any* relational skeleton σ_r, the colored instance dependency graph is acyclic.

And again we have the following corollary:

Corollary 5.30
Let Π_{CH} be a PRM with class hierarchies whose class dependency structure $\mathcal{S}$ is acyclic. For any relational skeleton σ_r, Π_{CH} and σ_r define a coherent probability distribution over instantiations $\mathcal{I}$ that extend σ_r via (5.4).

5.7 Inference in PRMs

An important aspect of any probabilistic representation is the support for making inferences; having made some observations, how do we condition on these observations and update our probabilistic model? Inference in PRMs supports many interesting patterns of reasoning. Oftentimes we can view the inference as influence flowing between the interrelated objects. Consider a simple example of inference about a particular student in our school PRM. A priori we may believe a student is likely to be smart. We may observe his grades in several courses and see that for the most part he received As, but in one class he received a C. This may cause us to slightly reduce our belief that the student is smart, but it will not change it significantly. However, if we find that most of the other students that took the course received high grades, we then may believe that the course is an easy course. Since it is unlikely that a smart student got a low grade in an easy course, our probability for the student being smart now goes down substantially.

There are several potential approaches for performing inference effectively in PRMs. In a few cases, particularly when the skeleton is small, or it results in a network with low tree width, we can do exact inference in the ground Bayesian network. In other cases, when there are certain types of regularities in the ground Bayesian network, we can still perform exact inference by carefully exploiting and reusing computations. And in cases where the ground Bayesian network is very large and we cannot exploit regularities in its structure, we resort to approximate inference.

5.7.1 Exact Inference

We can always resort to exact inference on the ground Bayesian Network, but the ground Bayesian Network may be very large and thus this inference may prove intractable. Under certain circumstances, inference algorithms can exploit the model structure to make inference tractable. Previous work on inference in structured probabilistic models [14, 19, 18] shows how effective inference can be done for a number of different structured probabilistic models. The algorithms make use of the structure imposed by the class hierarchy to decompose the distribution and effectively reuse computation.

There are two ways in which aspects of the structure can be used to make inference more efficient. The first structural aspect is the natural encapsulation of objects that occurs in a well-designed class hierarchy. Ideally, the interactions between objects will occur via a small number of object attributes, and the majority of interactions between attributes will be encapsulated within the class. This can provide a natural decomposition of the model suitable for inference. The complexity of the inference will depend on the "width" of the connections between objects; if the width is small, we are guaranteed an efficient procedure.

The second structural aspect that is used to make inference efficient is the fact that similar objects occur many times in the model. Pfeffer et al. [19] describe a recursive inference algorithm that caches the computations that are done for fragments of the model; these computations then need only be performed once; we can reuse them for another object occurring in the same context. We can think of this object as a generic object, which occurs repeatedly in the model. Exploiting these structural aspects of the model allow Pfeffer et al. [19] to achieve impressive speedups; in a military battlespace domain the structured inference was orders of magnitudes faster than the standard Bayesian Network exact inference algorithm.

5.7.2   Approximate Inference

Unfortunately the methods used in the inference algorithm above often are not applicable for the PRMs we study. In the majority of cases, there are no generic objects that can be exploited. Unlike standard Bayesian Network inference, we cannot decompose this task into separate inference tasks over the objects in the model, as they are typically all correlated. Thus, inference in the PRM requires inference over the ground network defined by instantiating a PRM for a particular skeleton.

In general, the ground network can be fairly complex, involving many objects that are linked in various ways. (For example, in some of our experiments, the networks involve hundreds of thousands of nodes.) Exact inference over these networks is clearly impractical, so we must resort to approximate inference. We use belief propagation (BP), a local message-passing algorithm, introduced by Pearl [17]. The algorithm is guaranteed to converge to the correct marginal probabilities for each node only for singly connected Bayesian networks. However, empirical results [16] show that it often converges in general networks, and when it does the marginals are a good approximation to the correct posterior.

We provide a brief outline of one variant of BP, and refer the reader to [20, 16, 15] for more details. Consider a Bayesian network over some set of nodes (which in our case would be the variables $x.A$). We first convert the graph into a *family graph*, with a node F_i for each variable V_i in the Bayesian network, containing V_i and its parents. Two nodes are connected if they have some variable in common. The CPD of V_i is associated with F_i. Let ϕ_i represent the factor defined by the CPD; i.e., if F_i contains the variables $V, Y_1, \ldots, Y_k$, then ϕ_i is a function from the domains of these variables to $[0, 1]$. We also define ψ_i to be a factor over V_i that encompasses our evidence about V_i: $\psi_i(V_i) \equiv 1$ if V_i is not observed. If we observe $V_i = v$, we have that $\psi_i(v) = 1$ and 0 elsewhere. Our posterior distribution is then $\alpha \prod_i \phi_i \times \prod_i \psi_i$, where α is a normalizing constant.

The BP algorithm is now very simple. At each iteration, all the family nodes simultaneously send messages to all others, as follows:

$$m_{ij}(F_i \cap F_j) \leftarrow \alpha \sum_{F_i - F_j} \phi_i \cdot \psi_i \cdot \prod_{k \in N(i) - \{j\}} m_{ki},$$

where α is a (different) normalizing constant and $N(i)$ is the set of families that are neighbors of F_i in the family graph. This process is repeated until the beliefs converge. At any point in the algorithm, our marginal distribution about any family F_i is $b_i = \alpha \cdot \phi_i \cdot \psi_i \cdot \prod_{k \in N(i)} m_{ki}$. Each iteration is linear in the number of edges in the Bayesian network. While the algorithm is not guaranteed to converge, it typically converges after just a few iterations. After convergence, the b_i give us approximate marginal distributions over each of the families in the ground network.

5.8 Learning

Next, we turn our attention to learning a PRM. In the learning problem, our input contains a relational schema that describes the basic vocabulary in the domain — the set of classes, the attributes associated with the different classes, and the possible types of relations between objects in the different classes. For simplicity, in the description that follows, we assume the training data consists of a fully specified instance of that schema; if there are missing values, then an expectation maximization (EM) algorithm is needed as well. We begin by describing learning PRMs with attribute uncertainty, next describe the extensions to support learning PRMs with structural uncertainty, and then describe support for learning PRMs with class hierarchies.

We assume that the training instance is given in the form of a relational database. Although our approach would also work with other representations (e.g., a set of ground facts completed using the closed-world assumption), the efficient querying ability of relational databases is particularly helpful in our framework, and makes it possible to apply our algorithms to large data sets.

There are two components of the learning task: parameter estimation and structure learning. In the parameter estimation task, we assume that the qualitative dependency structure of the PRM is known; i.e., the input consists of the schema and training database (as above), as well as a qualitative dependency structure $\mathcal{S}$. The learning task is only to fill in the parameters that define the CPDs of the attributes. In the structure learning task, the dependency structure is not provided (although the user can, if available, provide prior knowledge about the structure, e.g., in the form of constraints) and the goal is to extract an entire PRM, structure as well as parameters, from the training database alone. We discuss each of these problems in turn.

5.8.1 Parameter Estimation

We begin with learning the parameters for a PRM where the dependency structure is known. In other words, we are given the structure $\mathcal{S}$ that determines the set of parents for each attribute, and our task is to learn the parameters $\theta_{\mathcal{S}}$ that define the CPDs for this structure. Our learning is based on a particular training set, which we will take to be a complete instance $\mathcal{I}$. While this task is relatively straightforward, it is of interest in and of itself. In addition, it is a crucial component in the structure-learning algorithm described in the next section.

The key ingredient in parameter estimation is the likelihood function: the probability of the data given the model. This function captures the response of the probability distribution to changes in the parameters. The likelihood of a parameter set is defined to be the probability of the data given the model. For a PRM, the likelihood of a parameter set $\theta_{\mathcal{S}}$ is: $L(\theta_{\mathcal{S}} \mid \mathcal{I}, \sigma, \mathcal{S}) = P(\mathcal{I} \mid \sigma, \mathcal{S}, \theta_{\mathcal{S}})$. As usual, we typically work with the log of this function:

$$l(\theta_{\mathcal{S}} \mid \mathcal{I}, \sigma, \mathcal{S}) = \log P(\mathcal{I} \mid \sigma, \mathcal{S}, \theta_{\mathcal{S}})$$

$$= \sum_{X_i} \sum_{A \in \mathcal{A}(X_i)} \left[\sum_{x \in \sigma(X_i)} \log P(\mathcal{I}_{x.A} \mid \mathcal{I}_{\mathrm{Pa}(x.A)}) \right]. \tag{5.5}$$

The key insight is that this equation is very similar to the log-likelihood of data given a Bayesian network [11]. In fact, it is the likelihood function of the Bayesian network induced by the PRM given the skeleton. The main difference from standard Bayesian network parameter learning is that parameters for different nodes in the network are forced to be identical—the parameters are *shared* or *tied*.

5.8.1.1   *Maximum Likelihood Parameter Estimation*

We can still use the well-understood theory of learning from Bayesian networks. Consider the task of performing *maximum likelihood* parameter estimation. Here, our goal is to find the parameter setting $\theta_{\mathcal{S}}$ that maximizes the likelihood $L(\theta_{\mathcal{S}} \mid \mathcal{I}, \sigma, \mathcal{S})$ for a given $\mathcal{I}$, σ and $\mathcal{S}$. This estimation is simplified by the *decomposition* of log-likelihood function into a summation of terms corresponding to the various attributes of the different classes:

$$l(\theta_{\mathcal{S}} \mid \mathcal{I}, \sigma, \mathcal{S}) = \sum_{X_i} \sum_{A \in \mathcal{A}(X_i)} \left[\sum_{x \in \sigma(X_i)} \log P(\mathcal{I}_{x.A} \mid \mathcal{I}_{\mathrm{Pa}(x.A)}) \right]$$

$$= \sum_{X_i} \sum_{A \in \mathcal{A}(X_i)} \sum_{v \in \mathcal{V}(X.A)} \sum_{\mathbf{u} \in \mathcal{V}(\mathrm{Pa}X.A)} C_{X.A}[v, \mathbf{u}] \cdot \log \theta_{v \mid \mathbf{u}} \tag{5.6}$$

where $C_{X.A}[v, \mathbf{u}]$ is the number of times we observe $\mathcal{I}_{x.A} = v$ and $\mathcal{I}_{\mathrm{Pa}(x.A)} = \mathbf{u}$ Each of the terms in the above sum can be maximized independently of the rest. Hence, maximum likelihood estimation reduces to independent maximization problems, one for each CPD.

For many parametric models, such as the exponential family, maximum likelihood estimation can be done via *sufficient statistics* that summarize the data. In the case of multinomial CPDs, these are just the counts we described above, $C_{X.A}[v, \mathbf{u}]$, the number of times we observe each of the different values $v, \mathbf{u}$ that the attribute $X.A$ and its parents can jointly take.

An important property of the database setting is that we can easily compute sufficient statistics. To compute $C_{X.A}[v, v_1, \ldots, v_k]$, we simply query over the class

X and its parents' classes, and project onto the appropriate set of attributes. For example, to learn the parameters for the grade CPD from our school example, we can compute the sufficient statistics with the following SQL query:

SELECT grade, intelligence, difficulty, count(*)
FROM from registration, student, course
GROUP BY grade, intelligence, difficulty

In some cases, it is useful to materialize a view that can be used to compute the sufficient statistics. This is beneficial when the relationship between the child attribute and the parent attribute is many-one rather than one-one or one-many. For example, consider the dependence of attributes of **Student** on attributes of **Registration**. In our example PRM, a student's ranking depends on the student's grades. In this case we would construct a view using the following SQL query:

CREATE VIEW v1
SELECT student.*, **AVERAGE**(grade) **AS** ave_grade,
　　　AVERAGE(satisfaction) as ave_satisfaction
FROM student s, registration r
WHERE s.student_id = r.student

To compute the statistics we would then project on the appropriate attributes from view v1:

SELECT ranking, ave_grade, **COUNT**(*)
FROM v1
GROUP BY ranking, ave_grade

Thus both the creation of the view and the process of counting occurrences can be computed using simple database queries, and can be executed efficiently. The view creation for each combination of classes is done once during the full learning algorithm (we will see exactly at which point this is done in the next section when we describe the search). If the tables being joined are indexed on the appropriate set of foreign keys, the construction of this view is efficient: the number of rows in the resulting table is the size of the child attribute's table; in our example this is |Student|. Computing the sufficient statistics can be done in one pass over the resulting table. The size of the resulting table is simply the number of unique combinations of attribute values. We are careful to cache sufficient statistics so they are only computed once. In some cases, we can compute new sufficient statistics from a previously cached set of sufficient statistics; we make use of this in our algorithm as well.

5.8.1.2   *Bayesian Parameter Estimation*

In many cases, maximum likelihood parameter estimation is not robust: it overfits the training data. The Bayesian approach uses a prior distribution over the parameters to smooth the irregularities in the training data, and is therefore significantly more robust. As we will see in Section 5.8.2, the Bayesian framework also gives us a good metric for evaluating the quality of different candidate structures.

Roughly speaking, the Bayesian approach introduces a prior over the unknown parameters, and performs Bayesian conditioning, using the data as evidence, to compute a posterior distribution over these parameters. To apply this idea in our setting, recall that the PRM parameters θ_S are composed of a set of individual probability distributions $\theta_{X.A|\mathbf{u}}$ for each conditional distribution of the form $P(X.A \mid \mathrm{Pa}(X.A) = \mathbf{u})$. Following the work on Bayesian approaches for learning Bayesian networks [11], we make two assumptions. First, we assume *parameter independence*: the priors over the parameters $\theta_{X.A|\mathbf{u}}$ for the different $X.A$ and $\mathbf{u}$ are independent. Second, we assume that the prior over $\theta_{X.A|\mathbf{u}}$ is a *Dirichlet* distribution. Briefly, a Dirichlet prior for a multinomial distribution of a variable V is specified by a set of *hyperparameters* $\{\alpha[v] : v \in \mathcal{V}(V))\}$. A distribution on the parameters of $P(V)$ is Dirichlet if

$$P(\theta_V) \propto \prod_v \theta_v^{\alpha[v]-1}.$$

(For more details see [7].) If $X.A$ can take on k values, then the prior is

$$P(\theta_{X.A|\mathbf{u}}) = \mathrm{Dir}(\theta_{X.A|\mathbf{u}} \mid \alpha_1, \ldots, \alpha_k).$$

For a parameter prior satisfying these two assumptions, the posterior also has this form. That is, it is a product of independent Dirichlet distributions over the parameters $\theta_{X.A|\mathbf{u}}$. In other words,

$$P(\theta_{X.A|\mathbf{u}} \mid \mathcal{I}, \sigma, \mathcal{S}) = \mathrm{Dir}(\theta_{X.A|\mathbf{u}} \mid \alpha_{X.A}[v_1, \mathbf{u}] + C_{X.A}[v_1, \mathbf{u}], \ldots, \alpha_{X.A}[v_k, \mathbf{u}] + C_{X.A}[v_k, \mathbf{u}]).$$

Now that we have the posterior, we can compute the probability of new data. In the case where the new instance is conditionally independent of the old instances given the parameter values (which is always the case in Bayesian network models, but may not be true here), then the probability of the new data case can be conveniently rewritten using the expected parameters:

Proposition 5.31
Assuming multinomial CPDs, prior independence, and Dirichlet priors, with hyperparameters $\alpha_{X.A}[v, \mathbf{u}]$, we have that

$$E_\theta[P(X.A = v \mid \mathrm{Pa}(X.A) = \mathbf{u}) \mid \mathcal{I}] =$$
$$\frac{C_{X.A}[v, \mathbf{u}] + \alpha_{X.A}[v, \mathbf{u}]}{\sum_{i=1}^k C_{X.A}[v_i, \mathbf{u}] + \alpha_{X.A}[v_i, \mathbf{u}]}.$$

This suggests that the Bayesian estimate for θ_S should be estimated using this formula as well. Unfortunately, the expected parameter is not the proper Bayesian solution for computing probability of new data in the case where the new data instance is not independent of previous data given the parameters. Suppose that we want to use the posterior to evaluate the probability of an instance $\mathcal{I}'$ of another skeleton σ'. If there are two instances x and x' of the class X such that $v^{\mathcal{I}'}(\mathrm{Pa}(x.A)) = v^{\mathcal{I}'}(\mathrm{Pa}(x'.A))$, then we will be relying on the same multinomial parameter vector twice. Using the chain rule, we see that the second probability depends on the posterior of the parameters after seeing the training data, *and* the first instance. In other words, the probability of a relational database given a distribution over parameter values is not identical to the probability of the data set when we have a point estimate of the parameters (i.e., when we act as though we know their values). However if the posterior is sharply peaked (i.e., we have a strong prior, or we have seen many training instances), we can approximate the solution using the expected parameters of proposition 5.31. We use this approximation in our computation of the estimates for the parameters.

5.8.1.3   Structure Learning

We now move to the more challenging problem of learning a dependency structure automatically, as opposed to having it given by the user. There are three important issues that need to be addressed. We must determine which dependency structures are legal; we need to evaluate the "goodness" of different candidate structures; and we need to define an effective search procedure that finds a good structure.

5.8.1.4   Legal Structures

We saw in section 5.2.5.2 that we could construct a class dependency graph for a PRM, and the PRM defined a coherent probability distribution if the class dependency graph was stratified. During learning it is straightforward to maintain this structure, and consider only models whose dependency structure passes this test.

Maintaining a stratified class dependency graph   Given a stratified class dependency graph $G(V, E)$, we can check whether local changes to the structure destroy the stratification. The operations we are concerned with are ones which add an edge (u, v) into the structure (clearly deleting an edge cannot introduce a cycle). We can check whether a new edge will introduce a cycle in time $O(|V| + |E|)$.

Let $G(V, E)$ be our stratified class dependency graph and let $G'(V, E \cup \{(u, v)\})$ be the class dependency graph with edge (u, v) added. Clearly if there is a cycle in G', it must contain (u, v).

We can check whether the new edge introduces a cycle by checking to see if, using this edge, there is a path $u, v, \ldots, u$. This reduces to checking to see if there is a path in the graph from v to u. We can do a a simple depth-first search to explore the graph to check for a path in $O(|V| + |E|)$.

5.8.2   Evaluating Different Structures

Now that we know which structures are legal, we need to decide how to evaluate different structures in order to pick one that fits the data well. We adapt Bayesian *model selection* methods to our framework. We would like to find the MAP (maximum a posteriori) structure. Formally, we want to compute the posterior probability of a structure $\mathcal{S}$ given an instantiation $\mathcal{I}$. Using Bayes rule we have that

$$P(\mathcal{S} \mid \mathcal{I}, \sigma) \propto P(\mathcal{I} \mid \mathcal{S}, \sigma) P(\mathcal{S} \mid \sigma).$$

This score is composed of two parts: the prior probability of the structure, and the probability of the data assuming that structure.

The first component is $P(\mathcal{S} \mid \sigma)$, which defines a prior over structures. We assume that the choice of structure is independent of the skeleton, and thus $P(\mathcal{S} \mid \sigma) = P(\mathcal{S})$. In the context of Bayesian networks, we often use a simple uniform prior over possible dependency structures. Unfortunately, this assumption does not work in our setting. The problem is that there may be infinitely many possible structures.[2] In our genetics example, a person's genotype can depend on the genotype of his parents, or of his grandparents, or of his great-grandparents, etc. A simple and natural solution penalizes long indirect slot chains, by having $\log P(\mathcal{S})$ proportional to the sum of the lengths of the chains $\boldsymbol{K}$ appearing in $\mathcal{S}$.

The second component is the *marginal likelihood*:

$$P(\mathcal{I} \mid \mathcal{S}, \sigma) = \int P(\mathcal{I} \mid \mathcal{S}, \theta_{\mathcal{S}}, \sigma) P(\theta_{\mathcal{S}} \mid \mathcal{S}) \, d\theta_{\mathcal{S}}.$$

If we use a parameter-independent Dirichlet prior (as above), this integral decomposes into a product of integrals each of which has a simple closed-form solution. This is a simple generalization of the ideas used in the Bayesian score for Bayesian networks [12].

Proposition 5.32
If $\mathcal{I}$ is a complete assignment, and $P(\theta_{\mathcal{S}} \mid \mathcal{S})$ satisfies parameter independence and is a Dirichlet with hyperparameters $\alpha_{X.A}[v, \mathbf{u}]$, then the marginal likelihood of $\mathcal{I}$

---

2. Although there are only a finite number that are reasonable to consider for a given skeleton.

given $\mathcal{S}$ is

$$P(\mathcal{I} \mid \mathcal{S}, \sigma) =$$

$$\prod_i \prod_{A \in \mathcal{A}(X_i)} \left[\prod_{\mathbf{u} \in \mathcal{V}(()\mathrm{Pa}(X_i.A))} \mathrm{DM}(\{C_{X_i.A}[v, \mathbf{u}]\}, \{\alpha_{X_i.A}[v, \mathbf{u}]\}) \right], \qquad (5.7)$$

where $\mathrm{DM}(\{C[v]\}, \{\alpha[v]\}) = \frac{\Gamma(\sum_v \alpha[v])}{\Gamma(\sum_v (\alpha[v] + C[v]))} \prod_v \frac{\Gamma(\alpha[v] + C[v])}{\Gamma(\alpha[v])}$, and $\Gamma(x) = \int_0^\infty t^{x-1} e^{-t} dt$
is the *Gamma* function.

Hence, the marginal likelihood is a product of simple terms, each of which corresponds to a distribution $P(X.A \mid \mathbf{u})$ where $\mathbf{u} \in \mathcal{V}(\mathrm{Pa}(X.A))$. Moreover, the term for $P(X.A \mid \mathbf{u})$ depends only on the hyperparameters $\alpha_{X.A}[v, \mathbf{u}]$ and the sufficient statistics $C_{X.A}[v, \mathbf{u}]$ for $v \in \mathcal{V}(X.A)$.

The marginal likelihood term is the dominant term in the probability of a structure. It balances the complexity of the structure with its fit to the data. This balance can be seen explicitly in the asymptotic relation of the marginal likelihood to explicit penalization, such as the minimum description length (MDL) score (see, e.g., [11]).

Finally, we note that the Bayesian score requires that we assign a prior over parameter values for each possible structure. Since there are many (perhaps infinitely many) alternative structures, this is a formidable task. In the case of Bayesian networks, there is a class of priors that can be described by a single network [12]. These priors have the additional property of being *structure equivalent*, that is, they guarantee that the marginal likelihood is the same for structures that are, in some strong sense, equivalent. These notions have not yet been defined for our richer structures, so we defer the issue to future work. Instead, we simply assume that some simple Dirichlet prior (e.g., a uniform one) has been defined for each attribute and parent set.

5.8.3 Structure Search

Now that we have both a test for determining whether a structure is legal, and a scoring function that allows us to evaluate different structures, we need only provide a procedure for finding legal high-scoring structures. For Bayesian networks, we know that this task is NP-hard [3]. As PRM learning is at least as hard as Bayesian network learning (a Bayesian network is simply a PRM with one class and no relations), we cannot hope to find an efficient procedure that always finds the highest-scoring structure. Thus, we must resort to heuristic search.

As is standard in Bayesian network learning [11], we use a greedy local search procedure that maintains a "current" candidate structure and iteratively modifies it to increase the score. At each iteration, we consider a set of simple local transformations to the current structure, score all of them, and pick the one with the highest score. In the case where we are learning multinomial CPDs, the three operators we use are: *add edge*, *delete edge*, and *reverse edge*. In the case where we are learning tree CPDs, following [4], our operators consider only transformations to the CPD trees. The tree structure induces the dependency structure, as the parents of $X.A$ are simply those attributes that appear in its CPD tree. In this case, the two operators we use are: *split* — replaces a leaf in a CPD tree by an internal node with two leafs; and *trim* — replaces the subtree at an internal node by a single leaf.

The simplest heuristic search algorithm is a greedy hill-climbing search, using our score as a metric. We maintain our current candidate structure and iteratively improve it. At each iteration, we consider the appropriate set of local transformations to that structure, score all of them, and pick the one with highest score.

We refer to this simple algorithm as the greedy algorithm. There are several common variants to improve the robustness of hill-climbing methods. One is is to make use of random restarts to deal with local maxima. In this algorithm, when we reach a local maximum, we take some fixed number of random steps, and then we restart our search process. Another common approach is to make use of a tabulist, which keeps track of the most recent states visited, and allows only steps which do not return to a recently visited state. A more sophisticated approach is to make use of a simulated annealing style of algorithm which uses the following procedure: in the early phases of the search we are likely to take random steps (rather than the best step), but as the search proceeds (i.e., the temperature cools) we are less likely to take random steps and more likely to take the best greedy step. The algorithms we have used are either the simple greedy algorithm or a simple randomized algorithm.

Regardless of the specific heuristic search algorithm used, an important component of the search is the scoring of candidate structures. As in Bayesian networks, the decomposability property of the score has significant impact on the computational efficiency of the search algorithm. First, we decompose the score into a sum of *local scores* corresponding to individual attributes and their parents. (This local score of an individual attribute is exactly the logarithm of the term in square brackets in (5.7).) Now, if our search algorithm considers a modification to our current structure where the parent set of a single attribute $X.A$ is different, only the component of the score associated with $X.A$ will change. Thus, we need only reevaluate this particular component, leaving the others unchanged; this results in major computational savings.

However, there are still a very large number of possible structures to consider. We propose a heuristic search algorithm that addresses this issue. At a high level, the algorithm proceeds in phases. At each phase k, we have a set of potential parents $Pot_k(X.A)$ for each attribute $X.A$. We then do a standard structure search restricted to the space of structures in which the parents of each $X.A$ are in $Pot_k(X.A)$. The advantage of this approach is that we can precompute the view corresponding to $X.A, Pot_k(X.A)$; most of the expensive computations — the joins and the aggregation required in the definition of the parents — are precomputed in these views. The sufficient statistics for any subset of potential parents can easily be derived from this view. The above construction, together with the decomposability of the score, allows the steps of the search (say, greedy hill-climbing) to be done very efficiently.

The success of this approach depends on the choice of the potential parents. Clearly, a bad initial choice can result to poor structures. Following [8], which examines a similar approach in the context of learning Bayesian networks, we propose an iterative approach that starts with some structure (possibly one where each attribute does not have any parents), and select the sets $Pot_k(X.A)$ based on this structure. We then apply the search procedure and get a new, higher-scoring, structure. We choose new potential parents based on this new structure and reiterate, stopping when no further improvement is made.

It remains only to discuss the choice of $Pot_k(X.A)$ at the different phases. Perhaps the simplest approach is to begin by setting $Pot_1(X.A)$ to be the set of attributes in X. In successive phases, $Pot_{k+1}(X.A)$ would consist of all of $\mathrm{Pa}_k(X.A)$, as well as all attributes that are related to X via slot chains of length $< k$. Of course, these new attrributes may require aggregation; we may either specify the appropriate aggregator or search over the space of possible aggregators.

This scheme expands the set of potential parents at each iteration. In some cases, however, it may result in large set of potential parents. In such cases we may want to use a more refined algorithm that only adds parents to $Pot_{k+1}(X.A)$ if they seem to "add value" beyond $\mathrm{Pa}_k(X.A)$. There are several reasonable ways of evaluating the additional value provided by new parents. Some of these are discussed by Friedman et al. [8] in the context of learning Bayesian networks. These results suggest that we should evaluate a new potential parent by measuring the change of score for the family of $X.A$ if we add $\gamma(X.\boldsymbol{K}.B)$ to its current parents. We can then choose the highest scoring of these, as well as the current parents, to be the new set of potential parents. This approach would allow us to significantly reduce the size of the potential parent set, and thereby of the resulting view, while typically causing insignificant degradation in the quality of the learned model.

5.8.4 Learning PRMs with Structural Uncertainty

Next, we describe how to extend the basic PRM learning algorithm to deal with structural uncertainty. For PRMs with reference uncertainty, in addition we also attempt to learn the rules that govern the link models. For PRMs with existence uncertainty we learn the probability of existence of relationship objects.

5.8.4.1 Learning with Reference Uncertainty

The extension to scoring required to deal with reference uncertainty is not a difficult one. Once we fix the partitions defined by the attributes $\mathcal{P}[\rho]$, a CPD for S_ρ compactly defines a distribution over values of ρ. Thus, scoring the success in predicting the value of ρ can be done efficiently using standard Bayesian methods used for attribute uncertainty (e.g., using a standard Dirichlet prior over values of ρ).

The extension to search the model space for incorporating reference uncertainty involves expanding our search operators to allow the addition (and deletion) of attributes to partition definition for each reference slot. Initially, the partition of the range class for a slot $X.\rho$ is not given in the model. Therefore, we must also search for the appropriate set of attributes $\mathcal{P}[\rho]$. We introduce two new operators, **refine** and **abstract**, which modify the partition by adding and deleting attributes from $\mathcal{P}[\rho]$. Initially, $\mathcal{P}[\rho]$ is empty for each ρ. The **refine** operator adds an attribute into $\mathcal{P}[\rho]$; the **abstract** operator deletes one. As mentioned earlier, we can define the partition simply by looking at the cross product of the values for each of the partition attributes, or using a decision tree. In the case of a decision tree, **refine** adds a split to one of the leaves and **abstract** removes a split. These newly introduced operators are treated by the search algorithm in exactly the same way as the standard edge-manipulation operators: the change in the score is evaluated for each possible operator, and the algorithm selects the best one to execute.

We note that, as usual, the decomposition of the score can be exploited to substantially speed up the search. In general, the score change resulting from an operator ω is reevaluated only after applying an operator ω' that modifies the parent or partition set of an attribute that ω modifies. This is also true when we consider operators that modify the parent of selector attributes.

5.8.4.2 *Learning with Existence Uncertainty*

The extension of the Bayesian score to PRMs with existence uncertainty is straight forward; the exists attribute is simply a new descriptive attribute. The only new issue is how to compute sufficient statistics that include existence attributes $x.E$ without explicitly enumerating all the nonexistent entities. We perform this computation by counting, for each possible instantiation of $\text{Pa}(X.E)$, the number of potential objects with that instantiation, and subtracting the actual number of objects x with that parent instantiation.

Let $\mathbf{u}$ be a particular instantiation of $\text{Pa}(X.E)$. To compute $C_{X.E}[true, \mathbf{u}]$, we can use a standard database query to compute how many objects $x \in \sigma(X)$ have $\text{Pa}(x.E) = \mathbf{u}$. To compute $C_{X.E}[false, \mathbf{u}]$, we need to compute the number of *potential* entities. We can do this without explicitly considering each $(x_1, \ldots, x_k) \in \mathcal{I}(Y_1) \times \cdots \mathcal{I}(Y_k)$ by decomposing the computation as follows: Let ρ be a reference slot of X with $\text{Range}[\rho] = Y$. Let $\text{Pa}_\rho(X.E)$ be the subset of parents of $X.E$ along slot ρ and let $\mathbf{u}_\rho$ be the corresponding instantiation. We count the number of y consistent with $\mathbf{u}_\rho$. If $\text{Pa}_\rho(X.E)$ is empty, this count is simply $|\mathcal{I}(Y)|$. The product of these counts is the number of potential entities. To compute $C_{X.E}[false, \mathbf{u}]$, we simply subtract $C_{X.E}[true, \mathbf{u}]$ from this number.

No extensions to the search algorithm are required to handle existence uncertainty. We simply introduce the new attributes $X.E$, and integrate them into the search space. Our search algorithm now considers operators that add, delete, or reverse edges involving the exist attributes. As usual, we enforce coherence using the class dependency graph. In addition to having an edge from $Y.E$ to $X.E$ for every slot $\rho \in \mathcal{R}(X)$ whose range type is Y, when we add an edge from $Y.B$ to $X.A$, we add an edge from $Y.E$ to $X.E$ and an edge from $Y.E$ to $X.A$.

5.8.5 Learning PRM-CHs

We now turn to learning PRMs with class hierarchies. We examine two scenarios: in one case the class hierarchies are given as part of the input and in the other, in addition to learning the PRM, we also must learn the class hierarchy. The learning algorithms use the same criteria for scoring the models; however, the search space is significantly different.

5.8.6 Class Hierarchies Provided in the Input

We begin with the simpler learning with class hierarchies scenario, where we assume that the class hierarchy is given as part of the input. As in section 5.8, we restrict attention to fully observable data sets. Hence, we assume that, in our training set, the class of each object is given. Without this assumption, the subclass indicator attribute would play the role of a hidden variable, greatly complicating the learning algorithm.

As discussed above, we need a scoring function that allows us to evaluate different candidate structures, and a search procedure that searches over the space of possible structures. The scoring function remains largely unchanged. For each object x in each class X, we have the basic subclass c to which it belongs. For each attribute A of this object, the probabilistic model then specifies the subclass d of X from which c inherits the CPD of $X.A$. Then $x.A$ contributes only to the sufficient statistics for the CPD of $X_d.A$. With that recomputation of the sufficient statistics, the Bayesian score can now be computed unchanged.

Next we extend our search algorithm to make use of the subclass hierarchy. First, we extend our phased search to allow the introduction of new subclasses. Then, we introduce a new set of operators. The new operators allow us to refine and abstract the CPDs of attributes in our model, using our class hierarchy to guide us.

5.8.6.1 Introducing New Subclasses

New subclasses can be introduced at any point in the search. We may construct all the subclasses at the start of our search, or we may consider introducing them more gradually, perhaps at each phase of the search. Regardless of when the new subclasses are introduced, the search space is greatly expanded, and care must be taken to avoid the construction of an intractable search problem. Here we describe the mechanics of the introduction of the new subclasses.

For each new subclass introduced, each attribute for the subclass is associated with a CPD. A CPD can be marked as either "inherited" or "specialized." Initially, only the CPD for attributes of $X_\top$ are marked as specialized; all the other CPDs are inherited. Our original search operators — those that add and delete parents — can be applied to attributes at all levels of the class hierarchy. However, we only allow parents to be added and deleted from attributes whose CPDs have been specialized. Note that any change to the parents of an attribute is propagated to any descendents of the attribute whose CPDs are marked as inherited from this attribute.

Next, we introduce the operators Specialize and Inherit. If $X_c.A$ currently has an inherited CPD, we can apply Specialize($X_c.A$). This has two effects. First, it recomputes the parameters of that CPD to utilize only the sufficient statistics of the subclass c. To understand this point, assume that $X_c.A$ was being inherited from X_d prior to the specialization. The CPD of $X_d.A$ was being computed using all objects in $\mathcal{I}(X_d)$. After the change, the CPD will be computed using just the objects in $\mathcal{I}(X_c)$. The second effect of the operator is that it makes the CPD modifiable, in that we can now add new parents or delete them. The Inherit operator has the opposite effect.

In addition, when a new subclass is introduced, we construct new refined slot references that make use of the subclass. Let D be a newly introduced subclass of Y. For each reference slot ρ of some class X with range Y, we introduce a new refined slot reference $\rho_{\langle D \rangle}$. In addition, we add each reference slot of Y to D; however, we refine the domain from Y to D. In other words, if we have the new reference slot ρ', where $\text{Dom}[\rho'] = D$ and $\text{Range}[\rho'] = X$.

5.8.6.2 *Learning Subclass Hierarchies*

We next examine the case where the subclass hierarchies are not given as part of the input. In this case, we will learn them at the same time we are learning the PRM.

As above, we wish to avoid the problem of learning from partially observable data. Hence, we need to assume that the basic subclasses are observed in the training set. At first glance, this requirement seems incompatible with our task definition: if the class hierarchy is not known, how can we observe subclasses in the training data? We resolve this problem by defining our class hierarchy based on the standard class attributes. For example, movies might be associated with an attribute specifying the genre — action, drama, or documentary. If our search algorithm decides that this attribute is a useful basis for forming subclasses, we would define subclasses based in a deterministic way on its values. Another attribute might be the reputation of the director. The algorithm might choose to refine the class hierarchy by partitioning sitcoms according to the values of this attribute. Note that, in this case, the class hierarchy depends on an attribute of a related class, not the class itself.

We implement this approach by requiring that the subclass indicator attribute be a deterministic function of its parents. These parents are the attributes used to define the subclass hierarchy. In our example, Movie.*Class* would have as parents Movie.*Genre* and Movie.*Director.Reputation*. Note that, as the function defining the subclass indicator variable is required to be deterministic, the subclass is effectively observed in the training data (due to the assumption that all other attributes are observed).

We restrict attention to decision-tree CPDs. The leaves in the decision tree represent the basic subclasses, and the attributes used for splitting the decision tree are the parents of the subclass indicator variable. We can allow binary splits that test whether an attribute has a particular value, or, if we find it necessary, we can allow a split on all possible values of an attribute.

The decision tree gives a simple algorithm for determining the subclass of an object. In order to build the decision tree during our search, we introduce a new operator $\mathsf{Split}(X, c, X.\boldsymbol{K}.B)$, where c is a leaf in the current decision tree for $X.Class$ and $X.\boldsymbol{K}.B$ is the attribute on which we will split that subclass.

Note that this step expands the space of models that can be considered, but in isolation does not change the score of the model. Thus, if we continue to use a purely greedy search, we would never take these steps. There are several approaches for addressing this problem. One is to use some lookahead for evaluating the quality of such a step. Another is to use various heuristics for guiding us toward worthwhile splits. For example, if an attribute is the common parent of many other attributes within X_c, it may be a good candidate on which to split.

The other operators, Specialize and Inherit, remain the same; they simply use the subclasses defined by the decision tree.

5.9   Conclusion

In this chapter we have described a comprehensive framework for learning a statistical model from relational data. We have presented a method for the automatic construction of a PRM from an existing database. Our method learns a structured statistical model directly from the relational database, without requiring the data to be flattened into a fixed attribute-value format. We have shown how to perform parameter estimation, developed a scoring criterion for use in structure selection, and defined the model search space. We have also provided algorithms for guaranteeing the coherence of the learned model.

References

[1] C. Boutilier, N. Friedman, M. Goldszmidt, and D. Koller. Context-specific independence in Bayesian networks. In *Proceedings of the Conference on Uncertainty in Artificial Intelligence*, 1996.

[2] J. Breese, D. Heckerman, and C. Kadie. Empirical analysis of predictive algorithms for collaborative filtering. In *Proceedings of the Conference on Uncertainty in Artificial Intelligence*, 1998.

[3] D. Chickering. Learning Bayesian networks is NP-complete. In *Artificial Intelligence and Statistics*, 1996.

[4] D. Chickering, D. Heckerman, and C. Meek. A Bayesian approach to learning Bayesian networks with local structure. In *Proceedings of the Conference on Uncertainty in Artificial Intelligence*, 1997.

[5]   D. Cohn and T. Hofmann. The missing link—a probabilistic model of document content and hypertext connectivity. In *Proceedings of Neural Information Processing Systems*, 2001.

[6]   M. Craven, D. DiPasquo, D. Freitag, A. McCallum, T. Mitchell, K. Nigam, and S. Slattery. Learning to extract symbolic knowledge from the World Wide Web. In *Proceedings of the National Conference on Artificial Intelligence*, 1998.

[7]   M. H. DeGroot. *Optimal Statistical Decisions*. McGraw-Hill, New York, 1970.

[8]   N. Friedman, I. Nachman, and D. Peér. Learning of Bayesian network structure from massive datasets: The "sparse candidate" algorithm. In *Proceedings of the Conference on Uncertainty in Artificial Intelligence*, 1999.

[9]   L. Getoor. *Learning Statistical Models from Relational Data*. PhD thesis, Stanford University, Stanford, CA, 2001.

[10]   L. Getoor and J. Grant. PRL: A probabilistic relational language. *Machine Learning Journal*, 62(1-2):7–31, 2006.

[11]   D. Heckerman. A tutorial on learning with Bayesian networks. In M. I. Jordan, editor, *Learning in Graphical Models*, pages 301–354. MIT Press, Cambridge, MA, 1998.

[12]   D. Heckerman, D. Geiger, and D. Chickering. Learning Bayesian networks: The combination of knowledge and statistical data. *Machine Learning*, 20: 197–243, 1995.

[13]   D. Koller and A. Pfeffer. Probabilistic frame-based systems. In *Proceedings of the Conference on Uncertainty in Artificial Intelligence*, 1998.

[14]   D. Koller and A. Pfeffer. Object-oriented Bayesian networks. In *Proceedings of the Conference on Uncertainty in Artificial Intelligence*, 1997.

[15]   D. MacKay, R. McEliece, and J. Cheng. Turbo decoding as an instance of Pearl's belief propagation algorithm. *IEEE Journal on Selected Areas in Communication*, 16(2):140–152, 1997.

[16]   K. Murphy and Y. Weiss. Loopy belief propagation for approximate inference: An empirical study. In *Proceedings of the Conference on Uncertainty in Artificial Intelligence*, 1999.

[17]   J. Pearl. *Probabilistic Reasoning in Intelligent Systems*. Morgan Kaufmann, San Francisco, 1988.

[18]   A. Pfeffer. *Probabilistic Reasoning for Complex Systems*. PhD thesis, Stanford University, Stanford, CA, 2000.

[19]   A. Pfeffer, D. Koller, B. Milch, and K. Takusagawa. SPOOK: A system for probabilistic object-oriented knowledge representation. In *Proceedings of the Conference on Uncertainty in Artificial Intelligence*, 1999.

[20]   Y. Weiss. Correctness of local probability propagation in graphical models with loops. *Neural Computation*, 12(1):1–41, 2000.

6 Relational Markov Networks

Ben Taskar, Pieter Abbeel, Ming-Fai Wong, and Daphne Koller

One of the key challenges for statistical relational learning is the design of a representation language that allows flexible modeling of complex relational interactions. Many of the formalisms presented in this book are based on the directed graphical models (probabilistic relational models, probabilistic entity-relationship models, Bayesian logic programs). In this chapter, we present a probabilistic modeling framework that builds on undirected graphical models (also known as Markov random fields or Markov networks). Undirected models address two limitations of the previous approach. First, undirected models do not impose the acyclicity constraint that hinders representation of many important relational dependencies in directed models. Second, undirected models are well suited for discriminative training, where we optimize the conditional likelihood of the labels given the features, which generally improves classification accuracy. We show how to train these models effectively, and how to use approximate probabilistic inference over the learned model for collective classification and link prediction. We provide experimental results on hypertext and social network domains, showing that accuracy can be significantly improved by modeling relational dependencies.[1]

6.1 Introduction

We focus on supervised learning as a motivation for our framework. The vast majority of work in statistical classification methods has focused on "flat" data – data consisting of identically structured entities, typically assumed to be i.i.d. However, many real-world data sets are innately relational: hyperlinked webpages, cross-citations in patents and scientific papers, social networks, medical records, and more. Such data consists of entities of different types, where each entity type is

---

1. This chapter is based on work in [21, 22].

characterized by a different set of attributes. Entities are related to each other via different types of links, and the link structure is an important source of information.

Consider a collection of hypertext documents that we want to classify using some set of labels. Most naively, we can use a bag-of-words model, classifying each webpage solely using the words that appear on the page. However, hypertext has a very rich structure that this approach loses entirely. One document has hyperlinks to others, typically indicating that their topics are related. Each document also has internal structure, such as a partition into sections; hyperlinks that emanate from the same section of the document are even more likely to point to similar documents. When classifying a collection of documents, these are important cues that can potentially help us achieve better classification accuracy. Therefore, rather than classifying each document separately, we want to provide a form of *collective classification*, where we simultaneously decide on the class labels of all of the entities together, and thereby can explicitly take advantage of the correlations between the labels of related entities.

Another challenge arises from the task of predicting which entities are related to which others and what are the types of these relationships. For example, in a data set consisting of a set of hyperlinked university webpages, we might want to predict not just which page belongs to a professor and which to a student, but also which professor is which student's advisor. In some cases, the existence of a relationship will be predicted by the presence of a hyperlink between the pages, and we will have only to decide whether the link reflects an advisor-advisee relationship. In other cases, we might have to infer the very existence of a link from indirect evidence, such as a large number of coauthored papers.

We propose the use of a joint probabilistic model for an entire collection of related entities. Following the work of Lafferty et al. [13], we base our approach on discriminatively trained undirected graphical models, or *Markov networks* [17]. We introduce the framework of *relational Markov networks (RMNs)*, which compactly defines a Markov network over a relational data set. The graphical structure of an RMN is based on the relational structure of the domain, and can easily model complex patterns over related entities. For example, we can represent a pattern where two linked documents are likely to have the same topic. We can also capture patterns that involve groups of links: for example, consecutive links in a document tend to refer to documents with the same label. As we show, the use of an undirected graphical model avoids the difficulties of defining a coherent generative model for graph structures in directed models. It thereby allows us tremendous flexibility in representing complex patterns.

Undirected models lend themselves well to discriminative training, where we optimize the conditional likelihood of the labels given the features. Discriminative training, given sufficient data, generally provides significant improvements in classification accuracy over generative training (see [23]). We provide an effective parameter estimation algorithm for RMNs which uses conjugate gradient combined with approximate probabilistic inference (belief propagation [17, 14, 12]) for estimating the gradient. We also show how to use approximate probabilistic inference over the learned model for collective classification and link prediction. We provide experimental results on a webpage classification and social network task, showing significant gains in accuracy arising both from the modeling of relational dependencies and the use of discriminative training.

6.2 Relational Classification and Link Prediction

Consider hypertext as a simple example of a relational domain. A relational domain is defined by a schema, which describes entities, their attributes, and the relations between them. In our domain, there are two entity types: Doc and Link. If a webpage is represented as a bag of words, Doc would have a set of Boolean attributes Doc.*HasWord$_k$* indicating whether the word k occurs on the page. It would also have the label attribute Doc.*Label*, indicating the topic of the page, which takes on a set of categorical values. The Link entity type has two attributes: Link.*From* and Link.*To*, both of which refer to Doc entities.

In general, a *schema* specifies of a set of entity types $\mathcal{E} = \{E_1, \dots, E_n\}$. Each type E is associated with three sets of attributes: content attributes $E.\mathbf{X}$ (e.g., Doc.*HasWord$_k$*), label attributes $E.\mathbf{Y}$ (e.g., Doc.*Label*), and reference attributes $E.\mathbf{R}$ (e.g. Link.*To*). For simplicity, we restrict label and content attributes to take on categorical values. Reference attributes include a special unique key attribute $E.K$ that identifies each entity. Other reference attributes $E.R$ refer to entities of a single type $E' = Range(E.R)$ and take values in $Domain(E'.K)$.

An *instantiation* $\mathcal{I}$ of a schema $\mathcal{E}$ specifies the set of entities $\mathcal{I}(E)$ of each entity type $E \in \mathcal{E}$ and the values of all attributes for all of the entities. For example, an instantiation of the hypertext schema is a collection of webpages, specifying their labels, the words they contain, and the links between them. We will use $\mathcal{I}.\mathbf{X}$, $\mathcal{I}.\mathbf{Y}$, and $\mathcal{I}.\mathbf{R}$ to denote the content, label, and reference attributes in the instantiation $\mathcal{I}$; $\mathcal{I}.\mathbf{x}$, $\mathcal{I}.\mathbf{y}$, and $\mathcal{I}.\mathbf{r}$ to denote the values of those attributes. The component $\mathcal{I}.\mathbf{r}$, which we call an *instantiation skeleton* or *instantiation graph*, specifies the set of entities (nodes) and their reference attributes (edges). A hypertext instantiation graph specifies a set of webpages and links between them, but not their words or labels.

To address the link prediction problem, we need to make links first class citizens in our model. Following Getoor et al. [7], we introduce into our schema object types that correspond to links between entities. Each link object ℓ is associated with a tuple of entity objects $(o_1, \dots, o_k)$ that participate in the link. For example, a Hyperlink link object would be associated with a pair of entities — the linking page, and the linked-to page, which are part of the link definition. We note that link objects may also have other attributes; e.g., a hyperlink object might have attributes for the anchor words on the link.

As our goal is to predict link existence, we must consider links that exist and links that do not. We therefore consider a set of *potential* links between entities. Each potential link is associated with a tuple of entity objects, but it may or may not actually exist. We denote this event using a binary *existence* attribute *Exists*, which is *true* if the link between the associated entities exists and *false* otherwise. In our example, our model may contain a potential link ℓ for each pair of webpages, and the value of the variable $\ell.Exists$ determines whether the link actually exists or not. The link prediction task now reduces to the problem of predicting the existence attributes of these link objects.

6.3   Graph Structure and Subgraph Templates

The structure of the instantiation graph has been used extensively to infer its importance in scientific publications [5] and hypertext [10]. Several recent papers have proposed algorithms that use the link graph to aid classification. Chakrabarti et al. [2] use system-predicted labels of linked documents to iteratively relabel each document in the test set, achieving a significant improvement compared to a baseline of using the text in each document alone. A similar approach was used by Neville and Jensen [16] in a different domain. Slattery and Mitchell [19] tried to identify directory (or hub) pages that commonly list pages of the same topic, and used these pages to improve classification of university webpages. However, none of these approaches provide a coherent model for the correlations between linked webpages. Thus, they apply combinations of classifiers in a procedural way, with no formal justification.

Taskar et al. [20] suggest the use of *probabilistic relational models (PRMs)* for the collective classification task. PRMs [11, 6] are a relational extension to Bayesian networks [17]. A PRM specifies a probability distribution over instantiations consistent with a given instantiation graph by specifying a Bayesian network-like template-level probabilistic model for each entity type. Given a particular instantiation graph, the PRM induces a large Bayesian network over that instantiation that specifies a joint probability distribution over all attributes of all of the entities. This network reflects the interactions between related instances by allowing us to represent correlations between their attributes.

In our hypertext example, a PRM might use a naive Bayes model for words, with a directed edge between Doc.*Label* and each attribute Doc.*HadWord$_k$*; each of these attributes would have a *conditional probability distribution* $P($Doc.*HasWord$_k$* | Doc.*Label*) associated with it, indicating the probability that word k appears in the document given each of the possible topic labels. More importantly, a PRM can represent the interdependencies between topics of linked documents by introducing an edge from Doc.*Label* to Doc.*Label* of two documents if there is a link between them. Given a particular instantiation graph containing some set of documents and links, the PRM specifies a Bayesian network over all of the documents in the collection. We would have a probabilistic dependency from each document's label to the words on the document, and a dependency from each document's label to the labels of all of the documents to which it points. Taskar et al. [20] show that this approach works well for classifying scientific documents, using both the words in the title and abstract and the citation-link structure.

However, the application of this idea to other domains, such as webpages, is problematic since there are many cycles in the link graph, leading to cycles in the induced "Bayesian network," which is therefore not a coherent probabilistic model. Getoor et al. [8] suggest an approach where we do not include direct dependencies between the labels of linked webpages, but rather treat links themselves as random variables. Each two pages have a "potential link," which may or may not exist in the data. The model defines the probability of the link existence as a function of the labels of the two endpoints. In this link existence model, labels have no incoming edges from other labels, and the cyclicity problem disappears. This model, however, has other fundamental limitations. In particular, the resulting Bayesian network has a random variable for each potential link — N^2 variables for collections containing N pages. This quadratic blowup occurs even when the actual link graph is very sparse. When N is large (e.g., the set of all webpages), a quadratic growth is intractable. Even more problematic are the inherent limitations on the expressive power imposed by the constraint that the directed graph must represent a coherent generative model over graph structures. The link existence model assumes that the presence of different edges is a conditionally independent event. Representing more complex patterns involving correlations between multiple edges is very difficult. For example, if two pages point to the same page, it is more likely that they point to each other as well. Such interactions between many overlapping triples of links do not fit well into the generative framework.

Furthermore, directed models such as Bayesian networks and PRMs are usually trained to optimize the joint probability of the labels and other attributes, while the goal of classification is a discriminative model of labels given the other attributes. The advantage of training a model only to discriminate between labels is that it does not have to trade off between classification accuracy and modeling the joint distribution over nonlabel attributes. In many cases, discriminatively trained models are more robust to violations of independence assumptions and achieve higher classification accuracy than their generative counterparts.

In our experiments, we found that the combination of a relational language with a probabilistic graphical model provides a very flexible framework for modeling complex patterns common in relational graphs. First, as observed by Getoor et al. [7], there are often correlations between the attributes of entities and the relations in which they participate. For example, in a social network, people with the same hobby are more likely to be friends.

We can also exploit correlations between the *labels* of entities and the relation type. For example, only students can be teaching assistants in a course. We can easily capture such correlations by introducing cliques that involve these attributes. Importantly, these cliques are informative even when attributes are not observed in the test data. For example, if we have evidence indicating an advisor-advisee relationship, our probability that X is a faculty member increases, and thereby our belief that X participates in a teaching assistant link with some entity Z decreases.

We also found it useful to consider richer subgraph templates over the link graph. One useful type of template is a *similarity* template, where objects that share a certain graph-based property are more likely to have the same label. Consider, for example, a professor X and two other entities Y and Z. If X's webpage mentions Y and Z in the same context, it is likely that the X-Y relation and the Y-Z relation are of the same type; for example, if Y is Professor X's advisee, then probably so is Z. Our framework accomodates these patterns easily, by introducing pairwise cliques between the appropriate relation variables.

Another useful type of subgraph template involves *transitivity* patterns, where the presence of an A-B link and of a B-C link increases (or decreases) the likelihood of an A-C link. For example, students often assist in courses taught by their advisor. Note that this type of interaction cannot be accounted for by just using pairwise cliques. By introducing cliques over triples of relations, we can capture such patterns as well. We can incorporate even more complicated patterns, but of course we are limited by the ability of belief propagation to scale up as we introduce larger cliques and tighter loops in the Markov network.

We note that our ability to model these more complex graph patterns relies on our use of an undirected Markov network as our probabilistic model. In contrast, the approach of Getoor et al. [8] uses directed graphical models (Bayesian networks and PRMs [11]) to represent a probabilistic model of both relations and attributes. Their approach easily captures the dependence of link existence on attributes of entities. But the constraint that the probabilistic dependency graph be a directed acyclic graph makes it hard to see how we would represent the subgraph patterns described above. For example, for the transitivity pattern, we might consider simply directing the correlation edges between link existence variables arbitrarily. However, it is not clear how we would then parameterize a link existence variable for a link that is involved in multiple triangles. See [20] for further discussion.

6.4   Undirected Models for Classification

As discussed, our approach to the collective classification task is based on the use of undirected graphical models. We begin by reviewing *Markov networks*, a "flat" undirected model. We then discuss how Markov networks can be extended to the relational setting.

6.4.1   Markov Networks

We use $\mathbf{V}$ to denote a set of discrete random variables and $\mathbf{v}$ an assignment of values to $\mathbf{V}$. A Markov network for $\mathbf{V}$ defines a joint distribution over $\mathbf{V}$. It consists of a qualitative component, an undirected dependency graph, and a quantitative component, a set of parameters associated with the graph. For a graph G, a *clique* is a set of nodes $\mathbf{V}_c$ in G, not necessarily maximal, such that each $V_i, V_j \in \mathbf{V}_c$ is connected by an edge in G. Note that a single node is also considered a clique.

Definition 6.1

Let $G - (\mathbf{V}, E)$ be an undirected graph with a set of cliques $C(G)$. Each $c \in C(G)$ is associated with a set of nodes $\mathbf{V}_c$ and a *clique potential* $\phi_c(\mathbf{V}_c)$, which is a non-negative function defined on the joint domain of $\mathbf{V}_c$. Let $\Phi = \{\phi_c(\mathbf{V}_c)\}_{c \in C(G)}$. The Markov net (G, Φ) defines the distribution $P(\mathbf{v}) = \frac{1}{Z} \prod_{c \in C(G)} \phi_c(\mathbf{v}_c)$, where Z is the *partition function* — a normalization constant given by $Z = \sum_{\mathbf{v}'} \prod \phi_c(\mathbf{v}'_c)$. ∎

Each potential ϕ_c is simply a table of values for each assignment $\mathbf{v}_c$ that defines a "compatibility" between values of variables in the clique. The potential is often represented by a log-linear combination of a small set of *features*:

$$\phi_c(\mathbf{v}_c) = \exp\{\sum_i w_i f_i(\mathbf{v}_c)\} = \exp\{\mathbf{w}_c \cdot \mathbf{f}_c(\mathbf{v}_c)\} \ .$$

The simplest and most common form of a feature is the indicator function $f(\mathbf{V}_c) \equiv \delta(\mathbf{V}_c = \mathbf{v}_c)$. However, features can be arbitrary logical predicates of the variables of the clique, $\mathbf{V}_c$. For example, if the variables are binary, a feature might signify the parity or whether the variables are all the same value. More generally, the features can be real-valued functions, not just binary predicates. See further discussion of features at the end of section 6.4.

We will abbreviate log-linear representation as follows:

$$\log P(\mathbf{v}) = \sum_c \mathbf{w}_c \cdot \mathbf{f}_c(\mathbf{v}_c) - \log Z = \mathbf{w} \cdot \mathbf{f}(\mathbf{v}) - \log Z;$$

where $\mathbf{w}$ and $\mathbf{f}$ are the vectors of all weights and features.

For classification, we are interested in constructing discriminative models using *conditional Markov nets* which are simply Markov networks renormalized to model a conditional distribution.

Definition 6.2

Let $\mathbf{X}$ be a set of random variables on which we condition and $\mathbf{Y}$ be a set of target (or label) random variables. A *conditional Markov network* is a Markov network (G, Φ) which defines the distribution $P(\mathbf{y} \mid \mathbf{x}) = \frac{1}{Z(\mathbf{x})} \prod_{c \in C(G)} \phi_c(\mathbf{x}_c, \mathbf{y}_c)$, where $Z(\mathbf{x})$ is the partition function, now dependent on $\mathbf{x}$: $Z(\mathbf{x}) = \sum_{\mathbf{y}'} \prod \phi_c(\mathbf{x}_c, \mathbf{y}'_c)$. ∎

Logistic regression, a well-studied statistical model for classification, can be viewed as the simplest example of a conditional Markov network. In standard form, for $Y = \pm 1$ and $\mathbf{X} \in \{0, 1\}^n$ (or $\mathbf{X} \in \Re^n$), $P(y \mid \mathbf{x}) = \frac{1}{Z(\mathbf{x})} \exp\{y\mathbf{w} \cdot \mathbf{x}\}$. Viewing the model as a Markov network, the cliques are simply the edges $c_k = \{X_k, Y\}$ with potentials $\phi_k(x_k, y) = \exp\{y w_k x_k\}$. In this example, each feature is of the form $f_k(x_k, y) = y x_k$.

6.4.2   Relational Markov Networks

We now extend the framework of Markov networks to the relational setting. A *relational Markov network* specifies a conditional distribution over all of the labels

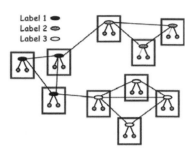

Figure 6.1   An unrolled Markov net over linked documents. The links follow a common pattern: documents with the same label tend to link to each other more often.

of all of the entities in an instantiation given the relational structure and the content attributes. (We provide the definitions directly for the conditional case, as the unconditional case is a special case where the set of content attributes is empty.) Roughly speaking, it specifies the cliques and potentials between attributes of related entities at a template level, so a single model provides a coherent distribution for any collection of instances from the schema.

For example, suppose that pages with the same label tend to link to each other, as in figure 6.1. We can capture this correlation between labels by introducing, for each link, a clique between the labels of the source and the target page. The potential on the clique will have higher values for assignments that give a common label to the linked pages.

To specify what cliques should be constructed in an instantiation, we will define a notion of a *relational clique template*. A relational clique template specifies tuples of variables in the instantiation by using a relational query language. For our link example, we can write the template as a kind of SQL query:

> SELECT doc1.Category, doc2.Category
> FROM Doc doc1, Doc doc2, Link link
> WHERE link.From = doc1.Key and link.To = doc2.Key

Note the three clauses that define a query: the FROM clause specifies the cross product of entities to be filtered by the WHERE clause and the SELECT clause picks out the attributes of interest. Our definition of clique templates contains the corresponding three parts.

Definition 6.3
A *relational clique template* $C = (\mathbf{F}, \mathbf{W}, \mathbf{S})$ consists of three components:

- $\mathbf{F} = \{F_i\}$ — a set of entity variables, where an entity variable F_i is of type $E(F_i)$.
- $\mathbf{W}(\mathbf{F.R})$ — a Boolean formula using conditions of the form $F_i.R_j = F_k.R_l$.
- $\mathbf{F.S} \subseteq \mathbf{F.X} \cup \mathbf{F.Y}$ — a selected subset of content and label attributes in $\mathbf{F}$. ∎

For the clique template corresponding to the SQL query above, $\mathbf{F}$ consists of *doc1*, *doc2*, and *link* of types Doc, Doc, and Link, respectively. $\mathbf{W(F.R)}$ is *link.From = doc1.Key* $\wedge$ *link.To = doc2.Key* and $\mathbf{F.S}$ is *doc1.Category* and *doc2.Category*.

A clique template specifies a set of cliques in an instantiation $\mathcal{I}$:

$$C(\mathcal{I}) \equiv \{c = \mathbf{f.S} : \mathbf{f} \in \mathcal{I}(\mathbf{F}) \wedge \mathbf{W(f.r)}\},$$

where $\mathbf{f}$ is a tuple of entities $\{f_i\}$ in which each f_i is of type $E(F_i)$; $\mathcal{I}(\mathbf{F}) = \mathcal{I}(E(F_1)) \times \ldots \times \mathcal{I}(E(F_n))$ denotes the cross product of entities in the instantiation; the clause $\mathbf{W(f.r)}$ ensures that the entities are related to each other in specified ways; and finally, $\mathbf{f.S}$ selects the appropriate attributes of the entities. Note that the clique template does not specify the nature of the interaction between the attributes; that is determined by the clique potentials, which will be associated with the template.

This definition of a clique template is very flexible, as the WHERE clause of a template can be an arbitrary predicate. It allows modeling complex relational patterns on the instantiation graphs. To continue our webpage example, consider another common pattern in hypertext: links in a webpage tend to point to pages of the same category. This pattern can be expressed by the following template:

```
SELECT doc1.Category, doc2.Category
FROM Doc doc1, Doc doc2, Link link1, Link link2
WHERE link1.From = link2.From and link1.To = doc1.Key
and link2.To = doc2.Key and not doc1.Key = doc2.Key
```

Depending on the expressive power of our template definition language, we may be able to construct very complex templates that select entire subgraph structures of an instantiation. We can easily represent patterns involving three (or more) interconnected documents without worrying about the acyclicity constraint imposed by directed models. Since the clique templates do not explicitly depend on the identities of entities, the same template can select subgraphs whose structure is fairly different. The RMN allows us to associate the same clique potential parameters with all of the subgraphs satisfying the template, thereby allowing generalization over a wide range of different structures.

Definition 6.4
A *relational Markov network* $\mathcal{M} = (\mathbf{C}, \Phi)$ specifies a set of clique templates $\mathbf{C}$ and corresponding potentials $\Phi = \{\phi_C\}_{C \in \mathbf{C}}$ to define a conditional distribution.

$$P(\mathcal{I}.\mathbf{y} \mid \mathcal{I}.\mathbf{x}, \mathcal{I}.\mathbf{r}) = \frac{1}{Z(\mathcal{I}.\mathbf{x}, \mathcal{I}.\mathbf{r})} \prod_{C \in \mathbf{C}} \prod_{c \in C(\mathcal{I})} \phi_C(\mathcal{I}.\mathbf{x}_c, \mathcal{I}.\mathbf{y}_c),$$

where $Z(\mathcal{I}.\mathbf{x}, \mathcal{I}.\mathbf{r})$ is the normalizing partition function:

$$Z(\mathcal{I}.\mathbf{x}, \mathcal{I}.\mathbf{r}) = \sum_{\mathcal{I}.\mathbf{y}'} \prod_{C \in \mathbf{C}} \prod_{c \in C(\mathcal{I})} \phi_C(\mathcal{I}.\mathbf{x}_c, \mathcal{I}.\mathbf{y}'_c). \quad \blacksquare$$

Using the log-linear representation of potentials, $\phi_C(\mathbf{V}_C) = \exp\{\mathbf{w}_C \cdot \mathbf{f}_C(\mathbf{V}_C)\}$, we can write

$$
\begin{aligned}
\log P(\mathcal{I}.\mathbf{y} \mid \mathcal{I}.\mathbf{x}, \mathcal{I}.\mathbf{r}) &= \sum_{C \in \mathbf{C}} \sum_{c \in C(\mathcal{I})} \mathbf{w}_C \cdot \mathbf{f}_C(\mathcal{I}.\mathbf{x}_c, \mathcal{I}.\mathbf{y}_c) - \log Z(\mathcal{I}.\mathbf{x}, \mathcal{I}.\mathbf{r}) \\
&= \sum_{C \in \mathbf{C}} \mathbf{w}_C \cdot \mathbf{f}_C(\mathcal{I}.\mathbf{x}, \mathcal{I}.\mathbf{y}, \mathcal{I}.\mathbf{r}) - \log Z(\mathcal{I}.\mathbf{x}, \mathcal{I}.\mathbf{r}) \\
&= \mathbf{w} \cdot \mathbf{f}(\mathcal{I}.\mathbf{x}, \mathcal{I}.\mathbf{y}, \mathcal{I}.\mathbf{r}) - \log Z(\mathcal{I}.\mathbf{x}, \mathcal{I}.\mathbf{r}),
\end{aligned}
$$

where

$$
\mathbf{f}_C(\mathcal{I}.\mathbf{x}, \mathcal{I}.\mathbf{y}, \mathcal{I}.\mathbf{r}) = \sum_{c \in C(\mathcal{I})} \mathbf{f}_C(\mathcal{I}.\mathbf{x}_c, \mathcal{I}.\mathbf{y}_c)
$$

is the sum over all appearances of the template $C(\mathcal{I})$ in the instantiation, and $\mathbf{f}$ is the vector of all $\mathbf{f}_C$.

Given a particular instantiation $\mathcal{I}$ of the schema, the RMN $\mathcal{M}$ produces an *unrolled* Markov network over the attributes of entities in $\mathcal{I}$. The cliques in the unrolled network are determined by the clique templates C. We have one clique for each $c \in C(\mathcal{I})$, and all of these cliques are associated with the same clique potential ϕ_C. In our webpage example, an RMN with the link feature described above would define a Markov net in which, for every link between two pages, there is an edge between the labels of these pages. Figure 6.1 illustrates a simple instance of this unrolled Markov network.

Note that we leave the clique potentials to be specified using arbitrary sets of feature functions. A common set is the complete table of indicator functions, one for each instantiation of the discrete-valued variables in the clique. However, this results in a large number of parameters (exponential in the number of variables). Often, as we encounter in our experiments, only a subset of the instantiations is of interest or many instantiations are essentially equivalent because of symmetries. For example, in an edge potential between labels of two webpages linked from a given page, we might want to have a single feature tracking whether the two labels are the same. In the case of triad cliques enforcing transitivity, we might constrain features to be symmetric functions with respect to the variables. In the presence of continuous-valued variables, features are often a predicate on the discrete variables multiplied by a continuous value. We do not prescribe a language for specifying features (as does Markov logic; see chapter 11), although in our implementation, we use a combination of logical formulae and custom-designed functions.

6.5   Learning the Models

We focus here on the case where the clique templates are given; our task is to estimate the clique potentials, or feature weights. Thus, assume that we are given a set of clique templates $\mathbf{C}$ which partially specify our (relational) Markov network, and our task is to compute the weights $\mathbf{w}$ for the potentials Φ. In the learning task, we are given some training set D where both the content attributes and the labels are observed. Any particular setting for $\mathbf{w}$ fully specifies a probability distribution $P_{\mathbf{w}}$ over D, so we can use the *likelihood* as our objective function, and attempt to find the weight setting that maximizes the likelihood (ML) of the labels given other attributes. However, to help avoid overfitting, we assume a prior over the weights (a zero-mean Gaussian), and use maximum a posteriori (MAP) estimation. More precisely, we assume that different parameters are a priori independent and define $p(w_i) = \frac{1}{\sqrt{2\pi\sigma^2}} \exp\left\{-w_i^2/2\sigma^2\right\}$. Both the ML and MAP objective functions are concave and there are many methods available for maximizing them. Our experience is that conjugate gradient performs fairly well for logistic regression and relational Markov nets. However, recent experience with conditional random fields (CRFs) suggests the L-BFGS method might be somewhat faster [18].

6.5.1   Learning Markov Networks

We first consider discriminative MAP training in the flat setting. In this case D is simply a set of i.i.d. instances; let d index over all labeled training data D. The discriminative likelihood of the data is $\prod_d P_{\mathbf{w}}(y_d \mid \mathbf{x}_d)$. We introduce the parameter prior, and maximize the log of the resulting MAP objective function:

$$\mathcal{L}(\mathbf{w}, D) = \sum_{d \in D} \left(\mathbf{w} \cdot \mathbf{f}(\mathbf{x}_d, y_d) - \log Z(\mathbf{x}_d)\right) - \frac{||\mathbf{w}||_2^2}{2\sigma^2} + C \ .$$

The gradient of the objective function is computed as

$$\nabla \mathcal{L}(\mathbf{w}, D) = \sum_{d \in D} \left(\mathbf{f}(\mathbf{x}_d, y_d) - \boldsymbol{E}_{P_{\mathbf{w}}}[\mathbf{f}(\mathbf{x}_d, Y_d)]\right) - \frac{\mathbf{w}}{\sigma^2} \ .$$

The last term is the shrinking effect of the prior and the other two terms are the difference between the expected feature counts and the empirical feature counts, where the expectation is taken relative to $P_{\mathbf{w}}$:

$$\boldsymbol{E}_{P_{\mathbf{w}}}[\mathbf{f}(\mathbf{x}_d, Y_d)] = \sum_{y'} \mathbf{f}(\mathbf{x}_d, y_d') P_{\mathbf{w}}(y_d' \mid \mathbf{x}_d) \ .$$

Thus, ignoring the effect of the prior, the gradient is zero when empirical and expected feature counts are equal.[2] The prior term gives the smoothing we expect from the prior: small weights are preferred in order to reduce overfitting. Note that the sum over y' is just over the possible categorizations for one data sample every time.

---

2. The solution of ML estimation with log-linear models is also the solution to the dual problem of maximum entropy estimation with constraints that empirical and expected feature counts must be equal [4].

6.5.2 Learning RMNs

The analysis for the relational setting is very similar. Now, our data set D is actually a single instantiation $\mathcal{I}$, where the same parameters are used multiple times — once for each different entity that uses a feature. A particular choice of parameters $\mathbf{w}$ specifies a particular RMN, which induces a probability distribution $P_{\mathbf{w}}$ over the unrolled Markov network. The product of the likelihood of $\mathcal{I}$ and the parameter prior define our objective function, whose gradient $\nabla \mathcal{L}(\mathbf{w}, \mathcal{I})$ again consists of the empirical feature counts minus the expected feature counts and a smoothing term due to the prior:

$$\mathbf{f}(\mathcal{I}.\mathbf{y}, \mathcal{I}.\mathbf{x}, \mathcal{I}.\mathbf{r}) - E_{\mathbf{w}}[\mathbf{f}(\mathcal{I}.\mathbf{Y}, \mathcal{I}.\mathbf{x}, \mathcal{I}.\mathbf{r})] - \frac{\mathbf{w}}{\sigma^2},$$

where the expectation $E_{P_{\mathbf{w}}}[\mathbf{f}(\mathcal{I}.\mathbf{Y}, \mathcal{I}.\mathbf{x}, \mathcal{I}.\mathbf{r})]$ is

$$\sum_{\mathcal{I}.\mathbf{y}'} \mathbf{f}(\mathcal{I}.\mathbf{y}', \mathcal{I}.\mathbf{x}, \mathcal{I}.\mathbf{r}) P_{\mathbf{w}}(\mathcal{I}.\mathbf{y}' \mid \mathcal{I}.\mathbf{x}, \mathcal{I}.\mathbf{r}) .$$

This last formula reveals a key difference between the relational and the flat case: the sum over $\mathcal{I}.\mathbf{y}'$ involves the exponential number of assignments to all the label attributes in the instantiation. In the flat case, the probability decomposes as a product of probabilities for individual data instances, so we can compute the expected feature count for each instance separately. In the relational case, these labels are correlated — indeed, this correlation was our main goal in defining this model. Hence, we need to compute the expectation over the joint assignments to all the entities together. Computing these expectations over an exponentially large set is the expensive step in calculating the gradient. It requires that we run inference on the unrolled Markov network.

6.5.3 Inference in Markov Networks

The inference task in our conditional Markov networks is to compute the posterior distribution over the label variables in the instantiation given the content variables. Exact algorithms for inference in graphical models can execute this process efficiently for specific graph topologies such as sequences, trees, and other low treewidth graphs. However, the networks resulting from domains such as our hypertext classification task are very large (in our experiments, they contain tens of thousands of nodes) and densely connected. Exact inference is completely intractable in these cases.

We therefore resort to approximate inference. There is a wide variety of approximation schemes for Markov networks, including sampling and variational methods. We chose to use *belief propagation*(BP) for its simplicity and relative efficiency and accuracy. BP is a local message passing algorithm introduced by Pearl [17] and later related to turbo-coding by McEliece et al. [14]. It is guaranteed to converge to the correct marginal probabilities for each node only for singly connected Markov networks. Empirical results [15] show that it often converges in general networks, and when it does, the marginals are a good approximation to the correct posteriors. As our results in section 6.6 show, this approach works well in our domain. We refer the reader to chapter 2 in this book for a detailed description of the BP algorithm.

6.6   Experimental Results

We present experiments with collective classification and link prediction, in both hypertext and social network data.

6.6.1   Experiments on WebKB

We experimented with our framework on the *WebKB* data set [3], which is an instance of our hypertext example. The data set contains webpages from four different computer science departments: Cornell, Texas, Washington, and Wisconsin. Each page has a label attribute, representing the type of webpage which is one of *course, faculty, student, project,* or *other*. The data set is problematic in that the category *other* is a grab bag of pages of many different types. The number of pages classified as *other* is quite large, so that a baseline algorithm that simply always selected *other* as the label would get an average accuracy of 75%. We could restrict attention to just the pages with the four other labels, but in a relational classification setting, the deleted webpages might be useful in terms of their interactions with other webpages. Hence, we compromised by eliminating all *other* pages with fewer than three outlinks, making the number of *other* pages commensurate with the other categories.[3] For each page, we have access to the entire HTML of the page and the links to other pages. Our goal is to collectively classify webpages into one of these five categories. In all of our experiments, we learn a model from three schools and test the performance of the learned model on the remaining school, thus evaluating the generalization performance of the different models.

Unfortunately, we cannot directly compare our accuracy results with previous work because different papers use different subsets of the data and different training/test splits. However, we compare to standard text classifiers such as naive Bayes, logistic regression, and support vector machines, which have been demonstrated to be successful on this data set [9].

---

3. The resulting category distribution is: course (237), faculty (148), other (332), research-project (82), and student (542). The number of remaining pages for each school are: Cornell (280), Texas (292), Washington (315), and Wisconsin (454). The number of links for each school are: Cornell (574), Texas (574), Washington (728) and Wisconsin (1614).

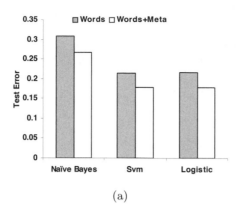
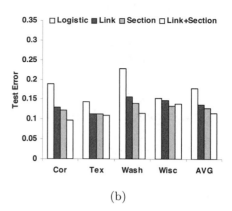

(a)   (b)

Figure 6.2 (a) Comparison of Naive Bayes, Svm, and Logistic on WebKB, with and without metadata features. (Only averages over the four schools are shown here.) (b) Flat versus collective classification on WebKB: flat logistic regression with metadata, and three different relational models: Link, Section, and a combined Section+Link. Collectively classifying page labels (Link, Section, Section+Link) consistently reduces the error over the flat model (logistic regression) on all schools, for all three relational models.

6.6.1.1 Flat Models

The simplest approach we tried predicts the categories based on just the text content on the webpage. The text of the webpage is represented using a set of binary attributes that indicate the presence of different words on the page. We found that stemming and feature selection did not provide much benefit and simply pruned words that appeared in fewer than three documents in each of the three schools in the training data. We also experimented with incorporating metadata: words appearing in the title of the page, in anchors of links to the page, and in the last header before a link to the page [24]. Note that metadata, although mostly originating from pages linking into the considered page, are easily incorporated as features, i.e., the resulting classification task is still flat feature-based classification. Our first experimental setup compares three well-known text classifiers — Naive Bayes, linear support vector machines [4] (Svm), and logistic regression (Logistic) — using words and metawords. The results, shown in figure 6.2(a), show that the two discriminative approaches outperform Naive Bayes. Logistic and Svm give very similar results. The average error over the four schools was reduced by around 4% by introducing the metadata attributes.

---

4. We trained one-against-others SVM for each category and during testing, picked the category with the largest margin.

6.6.1.2 Relational Models

Incorporating metadata gives a significant improvement, but we can take additional advantage of the correlation in labels of related pages by classifying them collectively. We want to capture these correlations in our model and use them for transmitting information between linked pages to provide more accurate classification. We experimented with several relational models. Recall that logistic regression is simply a flat conditional Markov network. All of our relational Markov networks use a logistic regression model locally for each page.

Our first model captures direct correlations between labels of linked pages. These correlations are very common in our data: courses and research projects almost never link to each other; faculty rarely link to each other; students have links to all categories but mostly to courses. The Link model, shown in figure 6.1, captures this correlation through links: in addition to the local bag of words and metadata attributes, we introduce a relational clique template over the labels of two pages that are linked.

A second relational model uses the insight that a webpage often has internal structure that allows it to be broken up into *sections*. For example, a faculty webpage might have one section that discusses research, with a list of links to all of the projects of the faculty member, a second section might contain links to the courses taught by the faculty member, and a third to his advisees. This pattern is illustrated in figure 6.3. We can view a section of a webpage as a fine-grained version of Kleinberg's hub [10] (a page that contains a lot of links to pages of a particular category). Intuitively, if we have links to two pages in the same section, they are likely to be on similar topics. To take advantage of this trend, we need to enrich our schema with a new relation Section, with attributes *Key*, *Doc* (the document in which it appears), and *Category*. We also need to add the attribute *Section* to Link to refer to the section it appears in. In the RMN, we have two new relational clique templates. The first contains the label of a section and the label of the page it is on:

    SELECT doc.Category, sec.Category
    FROM Doc doc, Section sec
    WHERE sec.Doc = doc.Key

The second clique template involves the label of the section containing the link and the label of the target page.

    SELECT sec.Category, doc.Category
    FROM Section sec, Link link, Doc doc
    WHERE link.Sec = sec.Key and link.To = doc.Key

The original data set did not contain section labels, so we introduced them using the following simple procedure. We defined a section as a sequence of three or more links that have the same path to the root in the HTML parse tree. In the training set, a section is labeled with the most frequent category of its links. There is a sixth

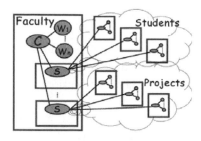

Figure 6.3   An illustration of the Section model.

category, *none*, assigned when the two most frequent categories of the links are less than a factor of 2 apart. In the entire data set, the breakdown of labels for the sections we found is: *course* (40), *faculty* (24), *other* (187), *research.project* (11), *student* (71), and *none* (17). Note that these labels are hidden in the test data, so the learning algorithm now also has to learn to predict section labels. Although not our final aim, correct prediction of section labels is very helpful. Words appearing in the last header before the section are used to better predict the section label by introducing a clique over these words and section labels.

We compared the performance of Link, Section, and Section+Link (a combined model which uses both types of cliques) on the task of predicting webpage labels, relative to the baseline of flat logistic regression with metadata. Our experiments used MAP estimation with a Gaussian prior on the feature weights with standard deviation of 0.3. Figure 6.2(b) compares the average error achieved by the different models on the four schools, training on three and testing on the fourth. We see that incorporating any type of relational information consistently gives significant improvement over the baseline model. The Link model incorporates more relational interactions, but each is a weaker indicator. The Section model ignores links outside of coherent sections, but each of the links it includes is a very strong indicator. In general, we see that the Section model performs slightly better. The joint model is able to combine benefits from both and generally outperforms all of the other models. The only exception is for the task of classifying the Wisconsin data. In this case, the joint Section+Link model contains many links, as well as some large tightly connected loops, so belief propagation did not converge for a subset of nodes. Hence, the results of the inference, which was stopped at a fixed arbitrary number of iterations, were highly variable and resulted in lower accuracy.

6.6.1.3   *Discriminative vs. Generative*

Our last experiment illustrates the benefits of discriminative training in relational classification. We compared three models. The Exists+Naive Bayes model is a completely generative model proposed by Getoor et al. [8]. At each page, a naive Bayes model generates the words on a page given the page label. A separate generative model specifies a probability over the existence of links between pages conditioned

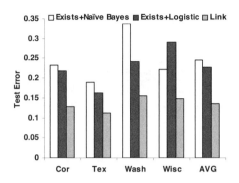

Figure 6.4 Comparison of generative and discriminative relational models. Exists+Naive Bayes is completely generative. Exists+Logistic is generative in the links, but locally discriminative in the page labels given the local features (words, meta-words). The Link model is completely discriminative.

on both pages' labels. We can also consider an alternative Exists+Logistic model that uses a discriminative model for the connection between page label and words — i.e., uses logistic regression for the conditional probability distribution of page label given words. This model has equivalent expressive power to the naive Bayes model but is discriminatively rather than generatively trained. Finally, the Link model is a fully discriminative (undirected) variant we have presented earlier, which uses a discriminative model for the label given both words and link existence. The results, shown in figure 6.4, show that discriminative training provides a significant improvement in accuracy: the Link model outperforms Exists+Logistic which in turn outperforms Exists+Naive Bayes.

As illustrated in table 6.1, the gain in accuracy comes at some cost in training time: for the generative models, parameter estimation is closed form while the discriminative models are trained using conjugate gradient, where each iteration requires inference over the unrolled RMN. On the other hand, both types of models require inference when the model is used on new data; the generative model constructs a much larger, fully connected network, resulting in significantly longer testing times. We also note that the situation changes if some of the data is unobserved in the training set. In this case, generative training also requires an iterative procedure (such as the expectation macimation algorihtm (EM)) where each iteration uses the significantly more expressive inference.

6.6.2 Experiments on extended WebKB

We collected and manually labeled a new relational data set inspired by WebKB [3]. Our data set consists of computer science department webpages from three schools: Stanford, Berkeley, and MIT. A total of 2954 pages are labeled into one of eight categories: faculty, student, research scientist, staff, research group, research project,

Table 6.1 Average train/test running times (seconds). All runs were done on a 700Mhz Pentium III. Training times are averaged over four runs on three schools each. Testing times are averaged over four runs on one school each.

	Links	Links+Section	Exists+NB
Training	1530	6060	1
Testing	7	10	100

course, and organization (organization refers to any large entity that is not a research group). *Owned pages*, which are owned by an entity but are not the main page for that entity, were manually assigned to that entity. The average distribution of classes across schools is: organization (9%), student (40%), research group (8%), faculty (11%), course (16%), research project (7%), research scientist (5%), and staff (3%).

We established a set of candidate links between entities based on evidence of a relation between them. One type of evidence for a relation is a hyperlink from an entity page or one of its owned pages to the page of another entity. A second type of evidence is a *virtual link*: We assigned a number of aliases to each page using the page title, the anchor text of incoming links, and email addresses of the entity involved. Mentioning an alias of a page on another page constitutes a virtual link. The resulting set of 7161 candidate links were labeled as corresponding to one of five relation types — advisor (faculty, student), member (research group/project, student/faculty/research scientist), teach (faculty/research scientist/staff, course), TA (student, course), part-of (research group, research project) — or "none," denoting that the link does not correspond to any of these relations.

The observed attributes for each page are the words on the page itself and the "metawords" on the page — the words in the title, section headings, anchors to the page from other pages. For links, the observed attributes are the anchor text, text just before the link (hyperlink or virtual link), and the heading of the section in which the link appears.

Our task is to predict the relation type, if any, for all the candidate links. We tried two settings for our experiments: with page categories observed (in the test data) and page categories unobserved. For all our experiments, we trained on two schools and tested on the remaining school.

Observed entity labels We first present results for the setting with observed page categories. Given the page labels, we can rule out many impossible relations; the resulting label breakdown among the candidate links is: none (38%), member (34%), part-of (4%), advisor (11%), teach (9%), TA (5%).

There is a huge range of possible models that one can apply to this task. We selected a set of models that we felt represented some range of patterns that manifested in the data.

Link-Flat is our baseline model, predicting links one at a time using multinomial logistic regression. This is a strong classifier, and its performance is competitive

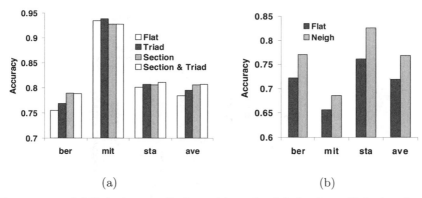

Figure 6.5 (a) Relation prediction with entity labels given. Relational models on average performed better than the baseline Flat model. (b) Entity label prediction. Relational model Neigh performed significantly better.

with other classifiers (e.g., support vector machines). The features used by this model are the labels of the two linked pages and the words on the links going from one page and its owned pages to the other page. The number of features is around 1000.

The relational models try to improve upon the baseline model by modeling the interactions between relations and predicting relations jointly. The Section model introduces cliques over relations whose links appear consecutively in a section on a page. This model tries to capture the pattern that similarly related entities (e.g., advisees, members of projects) are often listed together on a webpage. This pattern is a type of similarity template, as described in section 6.3. The Triad model is a type of transitivity template, as discussed in section 6.3. Specifically, we introduce cliques over sets of three candidate links that form a triangle in the link graph. The Section & Triad model includes the cliques of the two models above.

As shown in figure 6.2(a), both the Section and Triad models outperform the flat model, and the combined model has an average accuracy gain of 2.26%, or 10.5% relative reduction in error. As we only have three runs (one for each school), we cannot meaningfully analyze the statistical significance of this improvement.

As an example of the interesting inferences made by the models, we found a student-professor pair that was misclassified by the Flat model as none (there is only a single hyperlink from the student's page to the advisor's) but correctly identified by both the Section and Triad models. The Section model utilizes a paragraph on the student's webpage describing his or her research, with a section of links to research groups and the link to his or her advisor. Examining the parameters of the Section model clique, we found that the model learned that it is likely for people to mention their research groups and advisors in the same section. By capturing this trend, the Section model is able to increase the confidence of the student-advisor relation. The Triad model corrects the same misclassification in a different way. Using the same example, the Triad model makes use of the information that both the student and

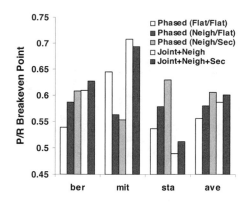

Figure 6.6   Relation prediction without entity labels. Relational models performed better most of the time, even though there are schools in which some models performed worse.

the teacher belong to the same research group, and the student TAed a class taught by his advisor. It is important to note that none of the other relations are observed in the test data, but rather the model bootstraps its inferences.

Unobserved entity labels When the labels of pages are not known during relations prediction, we cannot rule out possible relations for candidate links based on the labels of participating entities. Thus, we have many more candidate links that do not correspond to any of our relation types (e.g., links between an organization and a student). This makes the existence of relations a very low-probability event, with the following breakdown among the potential relations: none (71%), member (16%), part-of (2%), advisor (5%), teach (4%), TA (2%). In addition, when we construct a Markov network in which page labels are not observed, the network is much larger and denser, making the (approximate) inference task much harder. Thus, in addition to models that try to predict page entity and relation labels simultaneously, we also tried a two-phase approach, where we first predict page categories, and then use the predicted labels as features for the model that predicts relations.

For predicting page categories, we compared two models. The **Entity-Flat** model is a multinomial logistic regression that uses words and "metawords" from the page and its owned pages in separate "bags" of words. The number of features is roughly 10,000. The **Neighbors** model is a relational model that exploits another type of similarity template: pages with similar URLs often belong to the same category or tightly linked categories (research group/project, professor/course). For each page, two pages with URLs closest in edit distance are selected as "neighbors," and we introduced pairwise cliques between "neighboring" pages. Figure 6.5(b) shows that the **Neighbors** model clearly outperforms the **Flat** model across all schools, by an average of 4.9% accuracy gain.

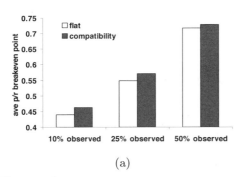 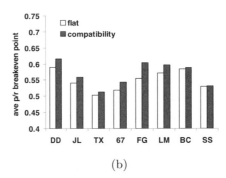

          (a)   (b)

Figure 6.7 (a) Average precision-recall breakeven point for 10%, 25%, 50% observed links. (b) Average precision-recall breakeven point for each fold of school residences at 25% observed links.

Given the page categories, we can now apply the different models for link classification. Thus, the Phased (Flat/Flat) model uses the Entity-Flat model to classify the page labels, and then the Link-Flat model to classify the candidate links using the resulting entity labels. The Phased (Neighbors/Flat) model uses the Neighbors model to classify the entity labels, and then the Link-Flat model to classify the links. The Phased (Neighbors/Section) model uses the Neighbors to classify the entity labels and then the Section model to classify the links.

We also tried two models that predict page and relation labels simultaneously. The Joint + Neighbors model is simply the union of the Neighbors model for page categories and the Flat model for relation labels given the page categories. The Joint + Neighbors + Section model additionally introduces the cliques that appeared in the Section model between links that appear consecutively in a section on a page. We train the joint models to predict both page and relation labels simultaneously.

As the proportion of the "none" relation is so large, we use the probability of "none" to define a precision-recall curve. If this probability is less than some threshold, we predict the most likely label (other than none); otherwise we predict the most likely label (including none). As usual, we report results at the precision-recall breakeven point on the test data. Figure 6.6 shows the breakeven points achieved by the different models on the three schools. Relational models, both phased and joint, did better than flat models on the average. However, performance varies from school to school and for both joint and phased models, performance on one of the schools is worse than that of the flat model.

6.6.3 Social Network Data

The data set we used has been collected by a portal website at a large university that hosts an online community for students [1]. Among other services, it allows students to enter information about themselves, create lists of their friends, and browse the social network. Personal information includes residence, gender, major, and year, as well as favorite sports, music, books, social activities, etc. We focused on the task of predicting the "friendship" links between students from their personal information and a subset of their links. We selected students living in sixteen different residences or dorms and restricted the data to the friendship links only within each residence, eliminating interresidence links from the data to generate independent training/test splits. Each residence has about fifteen to twenty-five students and an average student lists about 25% of his or her housemates as friends.

We used an eight-fold train-test split, where we trained on fourteen residences and tested on two. Predicting links between two students from just personal information alone is a very difficult task, so we tried a more realistic setting, where some proportion of the links is observed in the test data, and can be used as evidence for predicting the remaining links. We used the following proportions of observed links in the test data: 10%, 25%, and 50%. The observed links were selected at random, and the results we report are averaged over five folds of these random selection trials.

Using just the observed portion of links, we constructed the following flat features: for each student, the proportion of students in the residence that list him/her and the proportion of students he/she lists; for each pair of students, the proportion of other students they have as common friends. The values of the proportions were discretized into four bins. These features capture some of the relational structure and dependencies between links: Students who list (or are listed by) many friends in the observed portion of the links tend to have links in the unobserved portion as well. More importantly, having friends in common increases the likelihood of a link between a pair of students.

The Flat model uses logistic regression with the above features as well as personal information about each user. In addition to the individual characteristics of the two people, we also introduced a feature for each match of a characteristic; for example, both people are computer science majors or both are freshmen.

The Compatibility model uses a type of similarity template, introducing cliques between each pair of links emanating from each person. Similarly to the Flat model, these cliques include a feature for each match of the characteristics of the two potential friends. This model captures the tendency of a person to have friends who share many characteristics (even though the person might not possess them). For example, a student may be friends with several computer science majors, even though he is not a CS major himself. We also tried models that used transitivity templates, but the approximate inference with 3-cliques often failed to converge or produced erratic results.

Figure 6.7(a) compares the average precision-recall breakpoint achieved by the different models at the three different settings of observed links. Figure 6.7(b) shows the performance on each of the eight folds containing two residences each. Using a paired t-test, the Compatibility model outperforms Flat with p-values 0.0036, 0.00064, and 0.054 respectively.

6.7 Discussion and Conclusions

We propose an approach for collective classification and link prediction in relational domains. Our approach provides a coherent probabilistic foundation for the process of collective prediction, where we want to classify multiple entities and links, exploiting the interactions between the variables. We have shown that we can exploit a very rich set of relational patterns in classification, significantly improving the classification accuracy over standard flat classification.

We show that the use of a probabilistic model over link graphs allows us to represent and exploit interesting subgraph patterns in the link graph. Specifically, we have found two types of patterns that seem to be beneficial in several places. Similarity templates relate the classification of links or objects that share a certain graph-based property (e.g., links that share a common endpoint). Transitivity templates relate triples of objects and links organized in a triangle.

Our results use a set of relational patterns that we have discovered to be useful in the domains that we have considered. However, many other rich and interesting patterns are possible. Thus, in the relational setting, even more so than in simpler tasks, the issue of feature construction is critical. It is therefore important to explore the problem of automatic feature induction, as in [4].

Finally, we believe that the problem of modeling link graphs has numerous other applications, including analyzing communities of people and the hierarchical structure of organizations, identifying people or objects that play certain key roles, predicting current and future interactions, and more.

References

[1] L. Adamic, O. Buyukkokten, and E. Adar. A social network caught in the web. http://www.hpl.hp.com/shl/papers/social/, 2002.

[2] S. Chakrabarti, B. Dom, and P. Indyk. Enhanced hypertext categorization using hyperlinks. In *Proceedings of ACM International Conference on Management of Data*, 1998.

[3] M. Craven, D. DiPasquo, D. Freitag, A. McCallum, T. Mitchell, K. Nigam, and S. Slattery. Learning to extract symbolic knowledge from the World Wide Web. In *Proceedings of the National Conference on Artificial Intelligence*, 1998.

[4] S. Della Pietra, V. Della Pietra, and J. Lafferty. Inducing features of random fields. *IEEE Transactions on Pattern Analysis and Machine Intelligence*, 19 (4):380–393, 1997.

[5] L. Egghe and R. Rousseau. *Introduction to Informetrics*. Elsevier, Amsterdam, 1990.

[6] N. Friedman, L. Getoor, D. Koller, and A. Pfeffer. Learning probabilistic relational models. In *Proceedings of the International Joint Conference on*

Artificial Intelligence, 1999.

[7] L. Getoor, N. Friedman, D. Koller, and B. Taskar. Learning probabilistic models of relational structure. In *Proceedings of the International Conference on Machine Learning*, 2001.

[8] L. Getoor, E. Segal, B. Taskar, and D. Koller. Probabilistic models of text and link structure for hypertext classification. In *Proceedings of the IJCAI01 Workshop on Text Learning: Beyond Supervision*, 2001.

[9] T. Joachims. Transductive inference for text classification using support vector machines. In *Proceedings of the International Conference on Machine Learning*, 1999.

[10] J. M. Kleinberg. Authoritative sources in a hyperlinked environment. *Journal of the ACM*, 46(5):604–632, 1999.

[11] D. Koller and A. Pfeffer. Probabilistic frame-based systems. In *Proceedings of the National Conference on Artificial Intelligence*, 1998.

[12] F. Kschischang and B. Frey. Iterative decoding of compound codes by probability propagation in graphical models. *IEEE Journal of Selected Areas in Communications*, 16(2):219–230, 1998.

[13] J. Lafferty, A. McCallum, and F. Pereira. Conditional random fields: Probabilistic models for segmenting and labeling sequence data. In *Proceedings of the International Conference on Machine Learning*, 2001.

[14] R. McEliece, D. MacKay, and J. Cheng. Turbo decoding as an instance of Pearl's 'belief propagation' algorithm. *IEEE Journal on Selected Areas in Communications*, 16(2):140–152, 1998.

[15] K. P. Murphy, Y. Weiss, and M. I. Jordan. Loopy belief propagation for approximate inference: an empirical study. In *Proceedings of the Conference on Uncertainty in Artificial Intelligence*, 1999.

[16] J. Neville and D. Jensen. Iterative classification in relational data. In *Proceedings of the AAAI-2000 Workshop on Learning Statistical Models from Relational Data*, 2000.

[17] J. Pearl. *Probabilistic Reasoning in Intelligent Systems*. Morgan Kaufmann, San Francisco, 1988.

[18] F. Sha and F. Pereira. Shallow parsing with conditional random fields. In *Proceedings of Human Language Technology Conference and North American Chapter of the Association for Computational Linguistics*, 2003.

[19] S. Slattery and T. Mitchell. Discovering test set regularities in relational domains. In *Proceedings of the International Conference on Machine Learning*, 2000.

[20] B. Taskar, E. Segal, and D. Koller. Probabilistic classification and clustering in relational data. In *Proceedings of the International Joint Conference on Artificial Intelligence*, 2001.

[21] B. Taskar, P. Abbeel, and D. Koller. Discriminative probabilistic models for relational data. In *Proceedings of the Conference on Uncertainty in Artificial Intelligence*, 2002.

[22] B. Taskar, M. Wong, P. Abbeel, and D. Koller. Link prediction in relational data. In *Proceedings of Neural Information Processing Systems*, 2003.

[23] V. Vapnik. *The Nature of Statistical Learning Theory*. Springer-Verlag, New York, 1995.

[24] Y. Yang, S. Slattery, and R. Ghani. A study of approaches to hypertext categorization. *Journal of Intelligent Information Systems*, 18(2):219–241, 2002.

7 Probabilistic Entity-Relationship Models, PRMs, and Plate Models

David Heckerman, Chris Meek, Daphne Koller

In this chapter, we introduce a graphical language for relational data called the probabilistic entity-relationship (PER) model. The model is an extension of the entity-relationship model, a common model for the abstract representation of database structure. We concentrate on the directed version of this model—the directed acyclic probabilistic entity-relationship (DAPER) model. The DAPER model is closely related to the plate model and the probabilistic relational model (PRM), existing models for relational data. The DAPER model is more expressive than either existing model, and also helps to demonstrate their similarity. In addition to describing the new language, we discuss important facets of modeling relational data, including the use of restricted relationships, self relationships, and probabilistic relationships. Many examples are provided.

7.1 Introduction

For over a century, statistical modeling has focused primarily on "flat" data—data that can be encoded naturally in a single two-dimensional table having rows and columns. The disciplines of pattern recognition, machine learning, and data mining have had a similar focus. Notable exceptions include hierarchical models (e.g., [11]) and spatial statistics (e.g., [1]). Over the last decade, however, perhaps due to the ever-increasing volumes of data being stored in databases, the modeling of nonflat or *relational data* has increased significantly. During this time, several graphical languages for relational data have emerged including plate models (e.g.,[3, 9]) and probabilistic relational models (PRMs) (e.g., [5]). These models are to relational data what ordinary graphical models (e.g., directed acyclic graphs and undirected graphs) are to flat data.

In this chapter, we introduce a new graphical model for relational data—the probabilistic entity-relationship (PER) model. This model class is more expressive than either PRMs or plate models. We concentrate on a particular type of PER model—the directed acyclic probabilistic entity-relationship (DAPER) model—in which all probabilistic arcs are directed. It is this version of the PER model that is most similar to the plate model and the PRM. We define new versions of the plate model and the PRM such that their expressiveness is equivalent to the DAPER model, and then compare the new and old definitions. Consequently, we both demonstrate the similarity among the original languages as well as enhance their abilities to express conditional independence in relational data. Our hope is that this demonstration of similarity will foster greater communication and collaboration among statisticians who mostly use plate models and computer scientists who mostly use PRMs.

We in fact began this work with an effort to unify traditional PRMs and plate models. In the process, we discovered that it was important to distinguish between the concepts of entity and relationship (discussed in detail in the next section). We in turn discovered an existing language that does so—the entity-relationship (ER) model—a commonly used model for the abstract representation of database structure. We then extended this language to handle probabilistic relationships, creating the PER model.

We should emphasize that the languages we discuss are neither meant to serve as a database schema nor meant to be built on top of one. In practice, database schemata are built up over a long period of time as the needs of the database consumers change. Consequently, schemata for real databases are often not optimal or are completely unusable as the basis for statistical modeling. The languages we describe here are meant to be used as statistical modeling tools, independent of the schema of the database being modeled.

This work borrows heavily from concepts surrounding PRMs described in, e.g., Friedman et al. [5] and Getoor et al. [8]. Where possible, we use similar nomenclature, notation, and examples.

7.2   Background: Graphical Models

As mentioned, we shall concentrate on directed models in this chapter. Accordingly, we first review (ordinary) directed acyclic models.

A directed acyclic graphical (DAG) model for a finite set of attributes $\mathbf{X} = (X_1, \ldots, X_n)$ with joint distribution $p(\mathbf{x})$ has two components: (1) a directed acyclic graph—sometimes referred to as the *structure* of the model—that encodes a set of conditional independencies among the attributes, and (2) a collection of local distributions. The nodes in the directed acyclic graph are in one-to-one correspondence with the attributes in $\mathbf{X}$. To keep notation simple, we use X_i to refer to the node corresponding to attribute X_i. Whether X_i refers to an attribute or node will be clear from the context. The absence of arcs in the directed acyclic graph encode probabilistic independencies that allow the joint distribution for $\mathbf{X}$

to be written as

$$p(\mathbf{x}) = \prod_{i=1}^{n} p(x_i|\mathbf{pa}_i), \qquad (7.1)$$

where $\mathbf{pa}_i$ are the attributes corresponding to the parents of node X_i. The *local distributions* of the DAG model is the set of conditional probability distributions $p(x_i|\mathbf{pa}_i)$, $i = 1, \ldots, n$. Thus, a DAG model for $\mathbf{X}$ specifies the joint distribution for $\mathbf{X}$.

An example DAG model structure for attributes (X, Y, Z, W) is shown in figure 7.1(a). The structure (i.e., the missing arcs) encode the independencies: (1) X and Z are independent given Y, and (2) (Y, Z) and W are independent given X. We note that DAG models can be interpreted as a *generative model* for the data. In our example, we can generate a sample for (X, Y, Z, W) by first sampling X, then Y and W given X, and finally Z given Y.

As we shall see, when working with relational data, it is often necessary to express constraints or *restrictions* among attributes. Such restrictions can be encoded in a DAG model, which we review here.

As a simple example, suppose we have a generative story for binary (0/1) attributes X, Y, Z, and W that can be described by the DAG model structure shown in figure 7.1(a). In addition, suppose we know that at most two of these attributes take on the value 1. We can add this restriction to the model as shown in figure 7.1(b). Here, we have added a binary node named R. Associated with this node (not shown in the figure) is a local distribution wherein $R = 1$ with probability 1 when at most two of its parents take on value 1, and with probability zero otherwise. To encode the restriction, we set $R = 1$. Note that R is a *deterministic attribute*. That is, given the parents of R, R is known with certainty. As is commonly done in the graphical modeling literature, we indicate deterministic nodes with double ovals.[1]

Assuming that the restriction always holds—that is, R is always equal to 1—it is not meaningful to work with the joint distribution $p(x, y, z, w, r)$. Instead, the appropriate distribution to make inferences with is

$$p(\mathbf{x}|r = 1) = p(x)\ p(y|x)\ p(z|y)\ p(w|x)\ p(r = 1|x, y, z, w). \qquad (7.2)$$

Readers familiar with directed factor-graph models [4] will recognize that this distribution for (X, Y, Z, W) can be encoded by a directed factor-graph model in which node R is replaced by the factor $f(x, y, z, w) = p(r = 1|x, y, z, w)$. More generally, the factor-graph model is perhaps a more natural model for situations

---

1. DAG models can also be used to encode "soft" restrictions. For example, if we know that zero, one, two, three, and four of the attributes $\mathbf{X}$ take on the value 1 with probabilities p_0, p_1, p_2, p_3, and p_4, respectively, we can encode this soft restriction using the DAG model structure in figure 7.1(b) where R is no longer deterministic and has the appropriate local probability distribution.

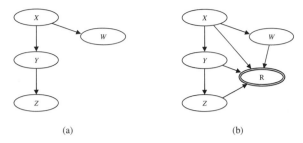

Figure 7.1 (a) A DAG model. (b) A similar DAG model with an added restriction among the attributes.

having both a generative component and restrictions. In this chapter, however, we use the DAG representation of restrictions so that we remain within the class of DAG models and thereby simplify the presentation.

7.3 The Basic Ideas

Before we describe languages for the statistical modeling of relational data, we begin with a description of a language for modeling the data itself. The language we discuss is the *entity-relationship (ER) model*, a commonly used abstract representation of database structure (e.g., [19]). The creation of an ER model is often the first step in the process of building a relational database. Features of anticipated data and how they interrelate are encoded in an ER model. The ER model is then used to create a relational schema for the database, which in turn is used to build the database itself.

It is important to note that an ER model is a representation of a database structure, not of a particular database that contains data. That is, an ER model can be developed prior to the collection of any data, and is meant to anticipate the data and the relationships therein.

When building ER models, we distinguish between entities, relationships, and attributes. An *entity* corresponds to a thing or object that is or may be stored in a database or data set[2]; a *relationship* corresponds to a specific interaction among entities; and an *attribute* corresponds to a variable describing some property of an entity or relationship. Throughout the chapter, we use examples to illustrate concepts.

Example 7.1
A university database maintains records on students and their IQs, courses and their difficulty, and the courses taken by students and the grades they receive.

---

2. In what follows, we make no distinction between a database and a data set.

In this example, we can think of individual students (e.g., john, mary) and individual courses (e.g., cs107, stat10) as entities.[3] Naturally, there will be many students and courses in the database. We refer to the set of students (e.g., {john,mary,...}) as an *entity set*. The set of courses (e.g., {cs107,stat10,...}) is another entity set. Most important, because an ER model can be built before any data is collected, we need the concept of an *entity class*—a reference to a set of entities without a specification of the entities in the set. In our example, the entity classes are Student and Course.

A relationship is a list of entities. In our example, a possible relationship is the pair (john, cs107), meaning that john took the course cs107. Using nomenclature similar to that for entities, we talk about relationship sets and relationship classes. A *relationship set* is a collection of like relationships—that is, a collection of relationships each relating entities from a fixed list of entity classes. In our example, we have the relationship set of student-course pairs. A *relationship class* refers to an unspecified set of like relationships. In our example, we have the relationship class Takes.

The IQ of john and the difficulty of cs107 are examples of *attributes*. We use the term *attribute class* to refer to an unspecified collection of like attributes. In our example, Student has the single attribute class Student.IQ and Course has the single attribute class Course.Diff. Relationships also can have attributes; and relationship classes can have attribute classes. In our example, Takes has the attribute class Takes.Grade.

An ER model for the structure of a database graphically depicts entity classes, relationships classes, attribute classes, and their interconnections. An ER model for Example 7.1 is shown in figure 7.2(a). The entity classes (Student and Course) are shown as rectangular nodes; the relationship class (Takes) is shown as a diamond-shaped node; and the attribute classes (Student.IQ, Course.Diff, and Takes.Grade) are shown as oval nodes. Attribute classes are connected to their corresponding entity or relationship class, and the relationship class is connected to its associated entity classes. (Solid edges are customary in ER models. Here, we use dashed edges so that we can later use solid edges to denote probabilistic dependencies.)

An ER model describes the potential attributes and relationships in a database. It says little about actual data. A *skeleton for a set of entity and relationship classes* is specification of the entities and relationships associated with a particular database. That is, a skeleton for a set of entity and relationship classes is a collection of corresponding entity and relationship sets. An example skeleton for our university database example is shown in figure 7.2(b).

An ER model *applied to a skeleton* defines a specific set of attributes. In particular, for every entity class and every attribute class of that entity class, an attribute is defined for every entity in the class; and for every relationship class and every at-

---

3. In a real database, longer names would be needed to define unique students and courses. We keep the names short in our example to make reading easier.

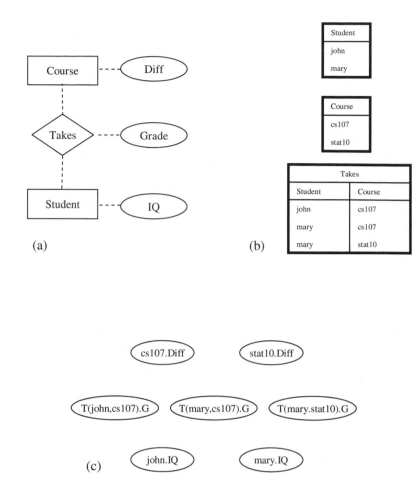

Figure 7.2   (a) An ER model depicting the structure of a university database. (b) An example skeleton for the entity and relationship classes in the ER model. (c) The attributes defined by the application of the ER model to the skeleton. The attribute names are abbreviated.

tribute class of that relationship class, an attribute is defined for every relationship in the class. The attributes defined by the ER model in figure 7.2(a) applied to the skeleton in figure 7.2(b) are shown in figure 7.2(c). In what follows, we use *ER model* to mean both the *ER diagram*—the graph in figure 7.2(a)—and the mechanism by which attributes are generated from skeletons.

A skeleton still says nothing about the values of attributes. An *instance for an ER model* consists of (1) a skeleton for the entity and relationship classes in that model, and (2) an assignment of a value to every attribute generated by the ER model and the skeleton. That is, an instance of an ER model is an actual database.

Let us now turn to the probabilistic modeling of relational data. To do so, we introduce a specific type of probabilistic ER model: the DAPER model. Roughly speaking, a DAPER model is an ER model with directed (solid) arcs among the attribute classes that represent probabilistic dependencies among corresponding attributes, and local distribution classes that define local distributions for attributes. Recall that an ER model applied to a skeleton defines a set of attributes. Similarly, a DAPER model applied to a skeleton defines a set of attributes as well as a DAG model for these attributes. Thus, a DAPER model can be thought of as a language for expressing conditional independence among unrealized attributes that eventually become realized given a skeleton.

As with the ER diagram and model, we sometimes distinguish between a *DAPER diagram*, which consists of the graph only, and the *DAPER model*, which consists of the diagram, the local distribution classes, and the mechanism by which a DAPER model defines a DAG model given a skeleton.

Example 7.2
In the university database (Example 7.1), a student's grade in a course depends both on the student's IQ and on the difficulty of the course.

The DAPER model (or diagram) for this example is shown in figure 7.3(a). The model extends the ER model in figure 7.2 with the addition of arc classes and local distribution classes. In particular, there is an *arc class* from Student.IQ to Takes.Grade and an arc class from Course.Diff to Takes.Grade. These arc classes are denoted as a solid directed arc. A local distribution class for Takes.Grade (not shown) represents the probabilistic dependence of grade on IQ and difficulty.

Just as we expand attribute classes in a DAPER model to attributes in a DAG model given a skeleton, we expand arc classes to arcs. In doing so, we sometimes want to limit the arcs that are added to a DAG model. In the current problem, for example, we want to draw an arc from attribute c.Diff for course c to attribute Takes(s, c').Grade for course c' and any student s, only when $c = c'$. This limitation is achieved by adding a *constraint* to the arc class—namely, the constraint course[Diff] = course[Grade] (see figure 7.3(a)). Here, the terms "course[Diff]" and "course[Grade]" refer to the entities c and c', respectively—the entities associated with the attributes at the ends of the arc.

The arc class from Student.IQ to Takes.Grade has a similar constraint: student[IQ] = student[Grade]. This constraint says that we draw an arc from attribute s.IQ for student s =student[IQ] to Takes(s', c).Grade for student s'=student[Grade] and any course c only when $s = s'$. As we shall see, constraints in DAPER models can be quite expressive—for example, they may include first-order expressions on entities and relationships.

Figure 7.3(c) shows the DAG (structure) generated by the application of the DAPER model in figure 7.3(a) to the skeleton in figure 7.3(b). (The attribute names in the DAG model are abbreviated.) The arc from stat10.Diff to Takes(mary,cs107).Grade, e.g., is disallowed by the constraint on the arc class from Course.Diff to Takes.Grade.

Regardless of what skeleton we use, the DAG model generated by the DAPER model in figure 7.3(a) will be acyclic. In general, as we show in section 7.7, if the attribute classes and arc classes in the DAPER diagram form an acyclic graph, then the DAG model generated from any skeleton for the DAPER model will be acyclic. Weaker conditions are also sufficient to guarantee acyclicity. We describe one in section 7.7.

In general, a *local distribution class* for an attribute class is a specification from which local distributions for attributes corresponding to the attribute class can be constructed, when a DAPER model is expanded to a DAG model. In our example, the local distribution class for Takes.Grade—written p(Takes.Grade|Student.IQ, Course.Diff)—is a specification from which the local distributions for Takes(s, c).Grade, for all students s and courses c, can be constructed. In our example, each attribute Takes(s, c).Grade will have two parents: s.IQ and c.Diff. Consequently, the local distribution class need only be a single local probability distribution. We discuss more complex situations in section 7.4.

Whereas most of this chapter concentrates on issues of representation, the problems of probabilistic inference, learning local distributions, and learning model structure are also of interest. For all of these problems, it is natural to extend the concept of an instance to that of a *partial instance*; an instance in which some of the attributes do not have values. A simple approach for performing probabilistic inference about attributes in a DAPER model given a partial instance is to (1) explicitly construct a ground graph, (2) instantiate known attributes from the partial instance, and (3) apply standard probabilistic inference techniques to the ground graph to compute the quantities of interest. One can improve upon this simple approach by utilizing the additional structure provided by a relational model—for example, by caching inferences in subnetworks. Koller and Pfeffer[15], for example, have done preliminary work in this direction. With regard to learning, note that from a Bayesian perspective, learning about both the local distributions and model structure can be viewed as probabilistic inference about (missing) attributes (e.g., parameters) from a partial instance. In addition, there has been substantial research on learning PRMs (e.g., [8]) and much of this work is applicable to DAPER models.

We shall explore PER models in much more detail in subsequent sections. Here, let us examine two alternate languages for relational data: plate models and PRMs.

Plate models were developed independently by Buntine[3] and the BUGS team (e.g., [9]) as a language for compactly representing graphical models in which there are repeated measurements. We know of no formal definition of a plate model, and so we provide one here. This definition deviates slightly from published examples of plate models, but it enhances the expressivity of such models while retaining their essence (see section 7.5).

According to our definition, plate and DAPER models are equivalent. The invertible mapping from a DAPER to a plate model is as follows. Each entity class in a DAPER model is drawn as a large rectangle—called a *plate*. The plate is labeled with the entity-class name. Plates are allowed to intersect or overlap. A relationship class for a set of entity classes is drawn at the named intersection of the plates corresponding to those entities. If there is more than one relationship

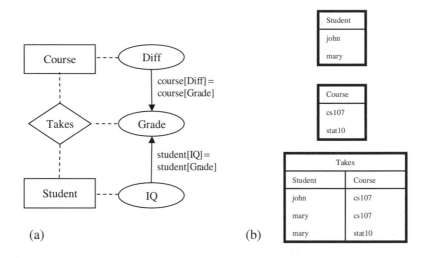

(a)   (b)

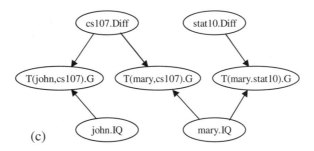

(c)

Figure 7.3 (a) A DAPER model showing that a student's grade in a course depends on both the student's IQ and the difficulty of the course. The solid directed arcs correspond to probabilistic dependencies. These arcs are annotated with constraints. (b) An example skeleton for the entity and relationship classes in the ER model (the same one shown in figure 6.2). (c) The DAG model (structure) defined by the application of the DAPER model to the ER skeleton.

class among the same set of entity classes, the plates are drawn such that there is a distinct intersection for each of the relationship classes. Attribute classes of an entity class are drawn as ovals inside the rectangle corresponding to the entity but outside any intersection. Attribute classes associated with a relationship class are drawn in the intersection corresponding to the relationship class. Arc classes and constraints are drawn just as they are in DAPER models. In addition, local distribution classes are specified just as they are in DAPER models.

The plate model corresponding to the DAPER model in figure 7.3(a) is shown in figure 7.4(a). The two rectangles are the plates corresponding to the Student and

Course entity classes. The single relationship class between Student and Course—Takes—is represented as the named intersection of the two plates. The attribute class Student.IQ is drawn inside the Student plate and outside the Course plate; the attribute class Course.Diff is drawn inside the Course plate and outside the Student plate; and the attribute class Takes.Grade is drawn in the intersection of the Student and Course plate. The arc classes and their constraints are identical to those in the DAPER model.

PRMs were developed in [5] explicitly for the purpose of representing relational data. The PRM extends the *relational model*—another commonly used representation for the structure of a database—in much the same way as the PER model extends the ER model. In this chapter, we shall define directed PRMs such that they are equivalent to DAPER models and, hence, plate models. This definition deviates from the one given by, e.g., [5], but enhances the expressivity of the language as previously defined (see section 7.6).

The invertible mapping from a DAPER model to a directed PRM (by our definition) takes place in two stages. First, the ER model component of the DAPER model is mapped to a relational model in a standard way (e.g., see [19]). In particular, both entity and relationship classes are represented as tables. Foreign keys—or what Getoor et al.[8] call *reference slots*—are used in the relationship-class tables to enocde the ER connections in the ER model. Attribute classes for entity and relationship classes are represented as attributes or columns in the corresponding tables of the relational model. Second, the probabilistic components of the DAPER model are mapped to those of the directed PRM. In particular, arc classes and constraints are drawn just as they are in the DAPER model.

The directed PRM corresponding to the DAPER model in figure 7.3(a) is shown in figure 7.4(b). (The local distribution for Takes.Grade is not shown.) The Student entity class and its attribute class Student.IQ appear in a table, as does the Course entity class and its attribute class Course.Diff. The Takes relationship and its attribute class Takes.Grade is shown as a table containing the foreign keys Student and Course. The arc classes and their constraints are drawn just as they are in the DAPER model.

7.4   Probabilistic Entity-Relationship Models

We now examine DAPER models in detail. After reviewing the fundamentals, we discuss the representation of restricted relationships, self relationships, and probabilistic relationships.

In what follows, we use the following conventions in our notation. We use either capitalized friendly names (e.g., Student, Course) or tokens (e.g., E) for entity classes. We use non capitalized friendly names or abbreviations (e.g., student[Grade], s) for corresponding entities. Similarly, we use capitalized friendly names (e.g., Takes) or tokens (e.g., R) for relationship classes. We use, e.g., $R(s, c)$ to say that entities s and c are a relationship associated with the relationship class

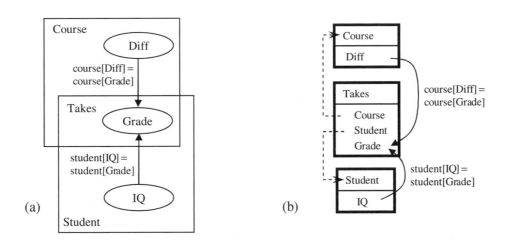

Figure 7.4   A plate model (a) and probabilistic relational model (b) corresponding to the DAPER model in Figure7.3(a).

R. We use X to refer to an arbitrary class when the distinction between an entity and relationship class is unimportant. We use expressions such as $X.A$ to represent an attribute class of class X, and $x.A$ to represent an (ordinary) attribute of entity x.

7.4.1   Fundamentals

A DAPER model can be viewed as a macro language—a language that, given a skeleton, expands to a DAG model. We use the term *ground graph* to refer to the structure of the DAG model created by the expansion of a DAPER model given a skeleton. An important part of this expansion is the drawing of arcs in the ground graph. Because the DAPER model is so compact, a mechanism is needed to constrain the drawing of arcs. Without such a mechanism, important conditional independence relations could not be expressed. As we have seen, this mechanism in a DAPER model takes the form of constraints on arc classes. To better understand how these constraints work, consider the following four related examples.

Example 7.3
A database contains diseases and symptoms for a given patient. Every disease is a potential cause of every symptom.

   The DAPER model for this example is shown in figure 7.5(a). The entity classes Disease and Symptom have attribute classes Disease.Present and Symptom.Present, respectively, and there are no relationship classes. In the diagram, the arc class from Disease.Present to Symptom.Present has no constraint. Because there is no constraint, the ground graph generated by the application of this DAPER model to any given skeleton is a full bipartite graph. The bipartite graph generated by the

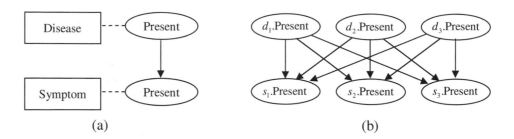

Figure 7.5   (a) A DAPER model for a complete bipartite graph between symptoms and diseases. (b) A ground graph (a DAG model structure) generated from the DAPER model given a skeleton with three diseases and three symptoms.

DAPER model applied to a skeleton in which there are three diseases and three symptoms is shown in figure 7.5(b).

We give this example first to emphasize that arc classes need not have constraints. Now, let us see what happens when we include such constraints.

Example 7.4

Extending example 7.3, suppose a physician has identified the possible causes of each symptom.

The DAPER model for example 7.4 is shown in figure 7.6(a). With respect to the model in figure 7.5(a), there is now the relationship class Causes, where Causes(d, s) is true if the physician has identified disease d as a possible cause of symptom s. Also new is the constraint Causes(d, s) on the arc class. This constraint says that, when we expand the DAPER model to a DAG model given a skeleton, we draw an arc from d.Present to s.Present only when Causes(d, s) holds. Note that, in the diagram we use "d" and "s" to refer to the entities associated with Disease.Present and Symptom.Present, respectively. In what follows, we will continue to make strong abbreviations as in this example, although such abbreviations are not required and may be undesirable for computer implementations of the PER language.

In the next two examples, we consider more complex constraints.

Example 7.5

Extending example 7.3 in a different way, suppose the physician has identified both primary (major) and secondary (minor) causes of disease.

The DAPER model for example 7.5 is shown in figure 7.7(a). There are now two relationship classes—Primary (1°) Causes and Secondary (2°) Causes—between the two entity classes, and the constraint is a disjunctive one: 1^oCauses$(d, s) \lor 2^o$Causes(d, s). This constraint says that, when the DAPER model is expanded to a DAG model given a skeleton, an arc is drawn from d.Present to s.Present only when d is a primary and/or secondary cause of s.

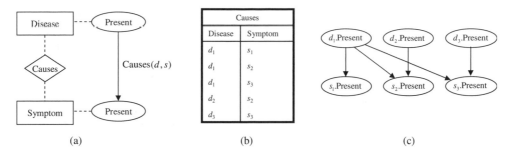

Figure 7.6 (a) A DAPER model for incomplete bipartite graph of diseases and symptoms. (b) A possible skeleton identifying diseases, symptoms, and potential causes of symptoms. (c) A DAG model resulting from the expansion of the DAPER model to the skeleton.

Example 7.6

Extending example 7.3 in a different way, suppose that both diseases and symptoms have category labels—labels drawn from the same set of categories. The possible causes of a symptom are diseases that have at least one category in common with that symptom.

The DAPER model for this example is shown in figure 7.7(b). Here, we have introduced a third entity class—Category—whose entities have relationships with Disease and Symptom. In particular, $R1(d, c)$ holds when disease d is in category c; and $R2(s, c)$ holds when symptom s is in category c. In this model, the arc class has the constraint $\exists c R1(d, c) \land R2(c, s)$, where c is an arbitrary entity in Category. Thus, when the DAPER model is expanded to a DAG given a skeleton, an arc will be drawn from d.Present to s.Present only when d and s share at least one category.

To understand how constraints are written and used in general, consider a DAPER model with an arc class from $X.A$ to $Y.B$. When this model is expanded to a ground graph given a skeleton, depending on the constraint, we might draw an arc from $x.A$ to $y.B$ for any x and y in the skeleton. To determine whether we do so, we look at the tail and head entities associated with this putative arc. The *tail entities* of the putative arc from $x.A$ to $y.B$ are the set of entities associated with x. If X is an entity class, then the tail entity is just the entity x. If X is a relationship class, then the tail entities are those entities in the relationship tuple x. Similarly, the *head entities* of this arc are the set of entities associated with y. For example, given the DAPER model and skeleton in figure 7.3 for the university database, the tail and head entities of the putative arc from john.IQ to Takes(john,cs107).Grade are (john) and (john,cs107), respectively. A *constraint* on the arc class from $X.A$ to $Y.B$ in a DAPER model is any first-order expression involving entities and relationship classes in the DAPER model such that the expression is bound when the tail and head entities are taken to be constants. To determine whether we draw an arc from $x.A$ to $y.B$, we evaluate the first-order expression using the tail and head entities of the putative arc. It must evaluate

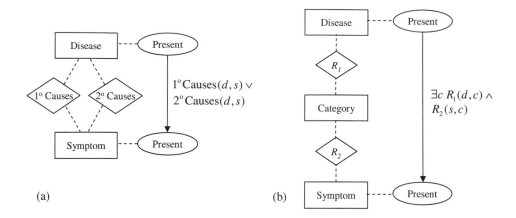

Figure 7.7   (a) A disjunctive constraint. (b) A constraint containing the existence quantifier.

to true or false. We draw the arc from $x.A$ to $y.B$ only if the expression is true. Continuing with the same university database example, let us determine whether to draw an arc from john.IQ to Takes(john,cs107).Grade. The relevant constraint— "student[IQ] = student[Grade]"—references the tail entity student[IQ] = john and the head entity student[Grade] = john. Thus, the expression evaluates to true and we draw the arc.

Next, let us consider the local distribution class. A *local distribution class* for attribute class $X.A$ is any specification from which the local distributions for attribute $x.A$, for any entity or relationship x in class X, may be constructed. In figure 7.3(c), each attribute for a student's grade in a course has two parents—one attribute corresponding to the difficulty of the course and another corresponding to the IQ of the student. Consequently, the local distribution class for Takes.Grade in the DAPER model can be a single (ordinary) local distribution. In general, however, a more complicated specification is needed. For example, in the ground graph of figure 7.6(c), the attribute s_1.Present has one parent, whereas the attributes s_2.Present and s_3.Present have two parents. Consequently, the local distribution class for Symptom.Present must be something more than a single local distribution.

In general, a local distribution class for $X.A$ may take the form of an enumeration of local distributions. In our example, we could specify a local distribution for every possible parent set of s.Present for every symptom s in every possible skeleton. Of course, such enumerations are cumbersome. Instead, a local distribution class is typically expressed as a canonical distribution such as noisy OR, logistic, or linear regression. Friedman et al.[5] refer to such specifications as *aggregators*.

So far, we have considered only DAPER models in which all attributes derive from attributes classes. In practice, however, it is often convenient to include (ordinary) attributes in a DAPER model. For example, in a Bayesian approach to learning the conditional probability distribution of Takes.Grade given Student.IQ and Course.Diff in example 7.2, we may add to the DAPER model an ordinary attribute θ corresponding to this uncertain distribution, as shown in figure 7.8(a). (If Grade is binary, e.g., θ would correspond to the parameter of a Bernoulli distribution.) The ground graph obtained from this DAPER model applied to the skeleton in figure 7.8(b) is shown in figure 7.8(c). Note that the attribute θ appears only once in the ground graph and that, because there is no annotation on the arc class from θ to Takes.Grade, there is an arc from θ to each grade attribute.

Although this view makes DAPER models easy to understand, formally, we do not allow such models to contain (ordinary) attributes. Instead, we specify that, for any DAPER model, (1) there is an entity class—Global—that is not drawn; (2) for any skeleton, this entity class has precisely one entity; and (3) every attribute class not connected explicitly to some visible entity class is connected to Global. This view is equivalent to the informal one just presented, but leads to simpler definitions and notation in our formal treatment of DAPER models in section 7.7.

7.4.2   Restricted Relationships

We now consider restricted relationships or, more precisely, restricted relationship classes. *A relationship class R in an ER (or PER) model is restricted* when some skeletons for the entity and relationship classes of the ER model are prohibited. In practice, many ER models contain restricted relationship classes; and graphical notation has been developed for common restrictions (e.g., [20]). Similarly, restricted relationship classes are an extremely useful tool for modeling with PER models. In this section, we consider several examples.

Example 7.7
A binary outcome O is measured on patients in multiple hospitals. Each patient is treated in exactly one hospital. It is believed that outcomes in any given hospital h are i.i.d. given Bernoulli parameter h.θ; and that these Bernoulli parameters are themselves i.i.d. across hospitals given hyperparameters α.

A DAPER model for this example is shown in figure 7.9(a). Here, entity classes Patient and Hospital are related by the relationship class In. The ground graph for a skeleton containing m hospitals and n_i patients in hospital i is shown in figure 7.9(b). This ground graph is the DAG model (structure) of what is often called a hierarchical model in the Bayesian literature (e.g., [7]).

In this example, the relationship class In is restricted in the sense that (patient,hospital) pairs are many to one—each patient is in exactly one hospital. This restriction is represented graphically by a curved arrowhead on the edge from In to Hospital in figure 7.9(a). The curved arrowhead is a standard notation in the language of ER models [20]; and we adopt this same notation for PER models. In general, given an ER or PER model with relationship class R connecting entity classes $E_1, \ldots, E_n$, if knowing entities in classes $E_1, \ldots, E_{i-1}, \ldots, E_{i+1}, \ldots, E_n$ uniquely determines entity E_i for any allowed skeleton, then a curved arrowhead is attached to the edge from R to E_i.

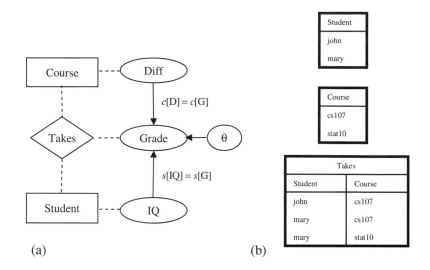

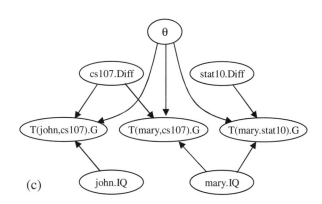

Figure 7.8 A modification to figure7.3 in which the local distribution for Takes.Grade given Student.IQ and Course.Diff is uncertain. (a) The DAPER model. (b) A skeleton (identical to the one in figure7.3). (c) The ground graph.

Note that, due to the many-to-one restriction in this problem, we could equivalently attach the attribute class O to In rather than to Patient. A DAPER model equivalent to the one in figure 7.9(a) is shown in figure 7.9(c).

Example 7.8
The occurrence of words in a document is used to infer its topic. The occurrence of words is mutually independent given document topic. Document topics are i.i.d. given multinomial parameters θ_t. The occurrence of word w in a document with topic t is i.i.d. given t and Bernoulli parameters $\theta_{w|t}$.

This example is commonly referred to a binary naive Bayes classification [18]. A DAPER model for this problem is shown in figure 7.10. The entity classes Document

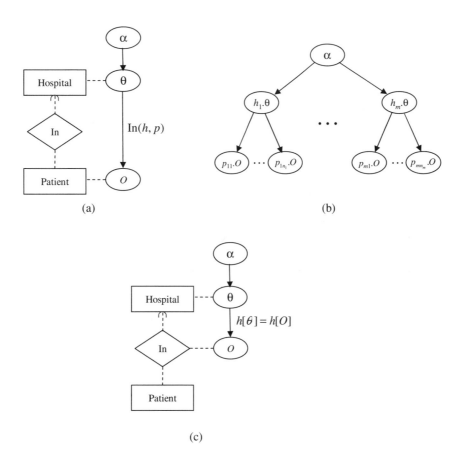

Figure 7.9 (a) A DAPER model for patient outcomes across multiple hospitals (example 7.7). (b) The ground graph (a hierarchical model structure) for a skeleton containing m hospitals and n_i patients in hospital i applied to the DAPER model in (a). (c) A DAPER model equivalent to the one in (a).

and Word are related by the single relationship class F. The attribute classes are Document.Topic representing the topic of a document, Word.$\theta_{w|t}$ representing the set of Bernoulli parameters $\theta_{w|t}$ for a word, and F(d, w).In representing whether word w is in document d. The relationship class F is restricted to be a `Full` relationship class. That is, in any allowed skeleton, all pairs (document,word) must be represented.[4] We indicate this restriction on the DAPER diagram by placing the annotation `Full` next to the relationship class. As we shall see in what follows, the `Full` restriction is useful in many situations.

---

4. In a practical database implementation, this relationship would be encoded sparsely, despite the Full restriction. That is, relationship (d, w) would be stored in the database only when word w appears in document d.

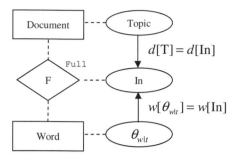

Figure 7.10   A DAPER model for binary naive Bayes document classification.

7.4.3   Self Relationships

Self relationships are relationships that relate like entities (and perhaps other entities as well). *A self-relationship class* is one that contains self relationships. Examples of self-relationship classes are common in databases: people are managers of other people, cities are near other cities, timestamps follow timestamps, and so on. ER models can represent self relationships in a natural manner. The extension to PER models is also straightforward, as we illustrate with the following three examples.

Example 7.9
In the university database example (example 7.2), a student's grade in a course depends on whether an advisor of the student is a friend of a teacher of the course.

The ER model for the data in this example is shown in figure 7.11(a). With respect to the ER model in figure 7.2(a), Professor is a new entity class and Advises, Teaches, and F are new relationship classes. Advises(p, s) means that professor p is an advisor of student s. Teaches(p, c) means that professor p teaches course c. (Students may have more than one advisor and courses may have more than one teacher.)

The relationship class F is introduced to model whether one professor is a friend of another. F is our first example of a self-relationship class—it contains relationships between professor pairs. The two dashed lines connecting F and the Professor entity class in the diagram indicate that F is a self-relationship class. F has one attribute class F.Friend, where the attribute F(p, p_f).Friend is true if professor p_f is a friend of professor p. Note that F has the `Full` constraint so that we can model whether any one professor is a friend of another. Also note that F(p_1, p_2).Friend may be true while F(p_2, p_1).Friend may be false.

The DAPER model for this example, including the new probabilistic relationship between F.Friend and Takes.Grade, is shown in figure 7.11(b). The constraint on the arc class from F.Friend to Takes.Grade is Teaches$(p, c) \wedge$ Advises(p_f, s). Thus, in any ground graph generated from this model, there is an arc from attribute F(p, p_f).Friend to attribute Takes(s, c).Grade whenever a teacher of the course is p

and an advisor of the student is p_f—precisely the additional dependence described in the example.

In the diagram, note that the relationship class F has the label "$F(p, p_f)$". The ordered pair (p, p_f) following F is introduced to unambiguously identify the different *roles* of the entity class in the self relationship. In this case, "p" and "p_f" refer to the roles of professor and professor's friend, respectively. This added notation in DAPER models is needed for the unambiguous specification of constraints. For example, suppose we had written the constraint on the arc class from F.Friend to Takes.Grade as $Teaches(p_f, c) \wedge Advises(p, s)$. This constraint means something different than the previous one—namely, that the student's grade depends on whether the course's *teacher* is a friend of the student's *advisor*.

Although not a standard convention for ER models, we allow an alternative representation for self relationships. Namely, we allow entity classes participating in a self-relationship class to be copied. The DAPER model in figure 7.11(b) drawn with this alternative convention is shown in figure 7.11(c). Here, there are two instances of the Professor entity class named "Professor (Teacher)" and "Professor (Advisor)". Note that copying allows us to annotate the role that each copy of the entity class plays in the self-relationship class. Models drawn with this copy convention are sometimes (but not always) more transparent. A similar convention is used in PRMs [5].

Example 7.10
A hidden Markov model (HMM) has hidden attributes slice.H, observed attributes slice.X, and uncertain parameters θ_h and $\theta_{x|h}$.

A DAPER model for such an HMM is shown in figure 7.12(a). The only entity class in the model is Slice. Its entities correspond to the time slices in the HMM. The only relationship class in the model—Next—is a restricted, self-relationship class. $Next(s, s_{+1})$ holds precisely when time slice s_{+1} immediately follows time slice s. Thus, Next is an example of a relationship class whose constraint induces a total order on its entities. We use `Order` to annotate this restriction. The attributes H and X correspond to the hidden and observed attributes in the HMM, respectively. The attribute classes θ_h and $\theta_{x|h}$ (connected to the Global entity class, which is not shown) represent the uncertain distributions.

Because arc classes can have constraints, DAPER models may contain arc classes that arc *self arcs*—arcs whose head and tail nodes are the same.[5] In this example, the self arc is used to represent the Markov chain of hidden attributes H. Another graphical model—Markov transition diagrams—uses self arcs in the much the same way. When a self arc appears in a DAPER model, it is not clear which way to draw arcs when expanding the model to a DAG model. In our example, do we draw arcs from $s.H$ to $s_{+1}.H$, or in the opposite direction? To remove the ambiguity, we use

---

5. We use the term "self arc" to refer both to arc classes and to arcs. The use will be clear from the context.

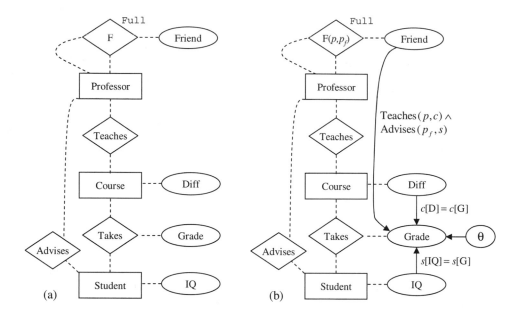

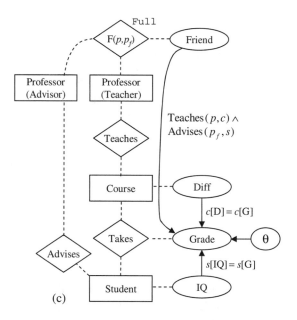

Figure 7.11   (a) An ER model showing Student, Course, and Professor entities and relationships among them. (b) A DAPER model showing that a student's grade in a course depends on whether the course's teacher likes the student's advisor. (c) The same model in (b) in which the Professor entity class has been copied.

bar–hat notation. In this example, the constraint is written $\text{Next}(\bar{s}, \hat{s}_{+1})$ indicating that the arc in drawn *from $s.H$ to $s_{+1}.H$.* In general, we use a bar and hat to denote head and tail entities, respectively.

When this DAPER model is expanded to a ground graph, the attribute $s_0.H$—where s_0 corresponds to the first time slice—has no parents. In contrast, the attribute $s.H$ where s corresponds to any other slice has one parent. Consequently, the local distribution class for Slice.H may be specified by two (ordinary) local distributions: $p(s_0.H)$ and $p(s_{i+1}.H|s_i.H)$ for $i > 0$.

A DAPER model using the copy convention for the HMM is shown in figure 7.12(b). Note that the attribute class Slice.X need be represented in only one copy of the entity class. The probabilistic dependencies between $s.H$ and $s.X$, for all slices s, are captured by the inclusion of X in one copy. Also note that, in this example and in any diagram where the copy convention is used, the bar–hat notation is not needed.

Example 7.11

A gene is transmitted through inheritance. The gene-allele frequencies θ are uncertain.

A DAPER model for this example is shown in figure 7.13(a). The model contains a single entity class Person and a single three-way, restricted, self relationship class Family. The relationship Family(p_c, p_m, p_f) holds when child p_c has mother and father p_m and p_f, respectively. The relationship class has the 2DAG constraint, meaning that each child has at most two parents and cannot be his or her own ancestor. The constraint on the single arc class indicates that only the gene of a child's mother and father influences the gene of the child. Note that the local distribution class for Gene has three components: (1) $p(\text{gene}|\text{no parents}) = \theta$, (2) $p(\text{gene}|\text{one parent})$, and (3) and $p(\text{gene}|\text{two parents})$. Figure 7.13(b) shows the same model in which the entity class Person appears three times.

When a DAPER model contains self relationships, its expansion can produce an invalid DAG model—in particular, one with a ground graph that contains directed cycles. For example, suppose we have a DAPER model where entity class E has a self-relationship class R, and $E.A$ has a self arc with no constraint. Then when we expand this model given a skeleton containing $R(e, e)$, the ground graph will contain the self arc from $e.A$ to $e.A$. In general, we need to ensure the ground graph is acyclic given all skeletons under consideration. In section 7.7, we describe sufficient conditions (including the absence of self relationships) that guarantee the acyclicity of ground graphs. In general, to determine whether the DAPER model produces only acyclic ground graphs for a given set of skeletons, one can check each ground graph individually.

7.4.4   Probabilistic Relationships

In many situations, relationships may be uncertain or random. In this section, we consider several examples and how they are represented with DAPER models.

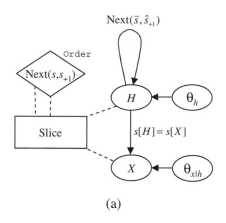

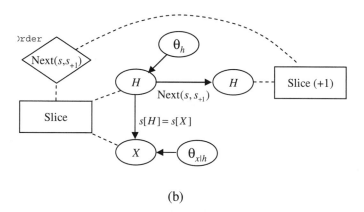

(b)

Figure 7.12   (a) The DAPER model representation of a hidden Markov model.
(b) The same model in which Slice is copied.

Example 7.12 Relationship Existence

A database contains academic papers and citations for a subset of those papers.
Using the citations we have, we model how the topics of two papers influence whether
one paper cites the other.[6]

If each paper in the database came with its citations, we could model this
database with the ER model shown in figure 7.14(a). Here, the single (copied) entity
class Paper has the self relationship Cites, where $\mathrm{Cites}(p_{cg}, p_{cd})$ holds when p_{cg} is the
citing paper and p_{cd} is the cited paper. In our example, however, we are uncertain
about the citations of papers whose citations have not been recorded. That is, we
are uncertain about the relationships in the relationship class Cites. To model this

---

6. We assume that citation lists for papers are missing at random.

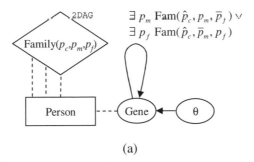

(a)

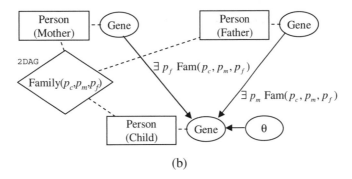

(b)

Figure 7.13   (a) The DAPER model for gene transmission through inheritance. (b) The same model in which Person is copied.

uncertainty, we use a DAPER model in which Cites is a `Full` relationship class with attribute class Cites.Exists, where $Cites(p_{cg}, p_{cd}).Exists$ is true when paper p_{cg} cites paper p_{cd}. In addition, to model how the topics of two papers influence this existence, we add the attribute class Paper.Topic and the arc classes as shown in figure 7.14(b).

In general, if we have a relationship class R that is uncertain, we model it in a DAPER model by making that relationship class `Full` and adding the attribute class R.Exists. Getoor et al. [8] discuss this type of uncertainty under the name *existence uncertainty* and use a similar mechanism to represent it in PRMs.

In many situations, relationship classes can be both probabilistic and restricted. In the remainder of this section, we consider two examples.

Example 7.13
Modifying example 7.12, we now know that the database was constructed such that it contains at most ten citations from the bibliography of any paper.[7]

---

7. We assume that citations above ten in number were censored at random.

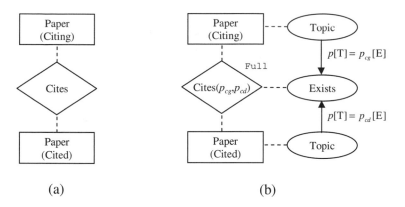

(a)   (b)

Figure 7.14   (a) An ER model for a citation database. (b) A DAPER model for the situation where citations are uncertain.

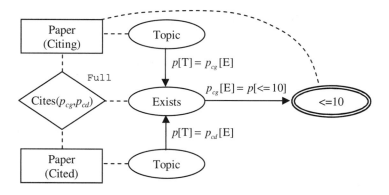

Figure 7.15   A DAPER model for the situation where citations are uncertain and limited to ten per paper.

The DAPER model in figure 7.15 shows the DAPER model for this example, where the Cites relationship class is both uncertain and restricted. As discussed in section 7.2, we encode the restrictions using instantiated deterministic nodes. With respect to figure 7.14(b), we have added a binary, attribute class *Paper.* $<= 10$. The double oval associated with this attribute class indicates that this attribute expands to deterministic attributes in a ground graph. In particular, a ground graph attribute $p. <= 10$ will have parents $\text{Cites}(p_{cg}, p_{cd}).Exists$, for all p_{cd}, and will be true exactly when ten or fewer of these parents are true. To encode the restriction, we set $p. <= 10$ to true for every p when performing inference in the ground graph.

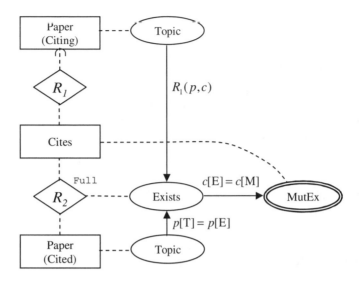

Figure 7.16   A DAPER model for the situation where only the cited papers are uncertain.

Example 7.14 Partial Relationship Existence
Modifying example 7.12 once again, the citation database now has a complete set of citations, but some of citations are so garbled that the identities of some of the cited papers are uncertain.

One way to think about this uncertainty is that the relationships $\text{Cites}(p_{cg}, p_{cd})$ are uncertain only in their second argument. Getoor et al. [8] refer to this uncertainty as *reference uncertainty* and present a special mechanism for representing it in PRMs. We take an alternative approach that uses only concepts that we have already discussed.

A DAPER model for this example is shown in figure 7.16. With respect to the DAPER model in figure 7.14(b), we have added the entity class Cites, and the relationship classes R_1 and R_2 between Paper and Cites. An entity pair in Cites corresponds to a citation—a citing and a cited paper. $R_1(p_{cg}, c)$ holds when paper p_{cg} is the citing paper in c, and $R_2(p_{cd}, c)$ holds when p_{cd} is the cited paper in c. The relationship class R_1 is a restricted (many-to-one) relationship class. In contrast, the relationship class R_2 is a probabilistic relationship class, restricted to be **Full**. The uncertainty in this relationship class is encoded with the attribute class R_2.Exists, where $R_2(p_{cd}, c)$.Exists is true precisely when citation c cites paper p_{cd}. To model the restriction that the possible cited papers of c are mutually exclusive, we first introduce the deterministic, attribute class Cites.MutEx. In any ground graph obtained from this DAPER model, $c.MutEx$ will be true exactly when one of its parents $R_2(p_{cd}, c)$.Exists is true. For any inference we perform with the ground graph, we set $c.MutEx$ to true for every citation c.

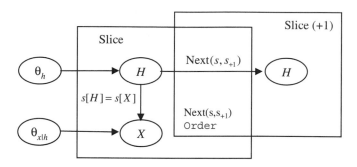

Figure 7.17   A plate model for an HMM corresponding to the DAPER model in figure7.12(b).

7.5   Plate Models

In this section, we revisit our definition of the plate model, give examples, and describe how our definition differs from previously published examples.

As discussed in section 7.3, we define the plate model by giving an invertible mapping from DAPER to plate model. Thus, the two model types are equivalent in the sense that they can represent the same conditional independence relationships for any given skeleton.

Summarizing the mapping from DAPER to plate model given in section 7.3, entity classes are drawn as large named rectangles called plates; a relationship class for a set of entity classes is drawn at the named intersection of the corresponding plates; attribute classes are drawn inside the rectangle corresponding to its entity or relationship class; and arc classes and constraints are drawn just as they are in DAPER models. For example, as we have discussed, the DAPER model in figure 7.3(a) has the corresponding plate model in figure 7.4(a). As another example, the DAPER model for the HMM shown in figure 7.12(b) has the corresponding plate model in figure 7.17. Note that, because plate models represent relationship classes as the intersection of plates, plates (corresponding to entity classes) must be copied when the model contains self-relationship classes.

The plate model corresponding to the DAPER model for the patient-hospital example in figure 7.3(a) is shown in figure 7.18(a). In this plate model, there are no attributes in the Patient plate outside the intersection. Thus, one can move the Patient plate fully inside the Hospital plate, yielding the diagram in figure 7.18(b). We allow this *nesting* in our framework. Furthermore, plates may be nested to an arbitrary depth. This convention corresponds to one found in published examples of plate models.

There are three differences between plate models as we have defined them and *traditional plate models*—plates models as they have been described in the literature. In all three cases, our definition provides a more expressive language.

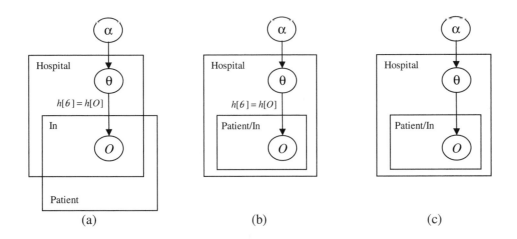

Figure 7.18 (a) A plate model corresponding to the DAPER model in figure7.12(a). (b) An equivalent plate model illustrating the graphical convention of nesting. (c) A traditional plate model, equivalent to the one in (b), in which the constraint $h[\theta] = h[O]$ is implicit.

One, in traditional plate models, an arc class emanating from an attribute class in a plate cannot leave that plate. Given this constraint, any arc class from attribute class $E.X$ must point either to attribute class $E.Y$ or to attribute class $R.Y$, where R is nested inside E.

Two, when a traditional plate model is expanded to a ground graph, arcs are drawn only between attributes corresponding to the same entity. To be more precise, consider a plate model containing the arc class from $E.X$ to $E.Y$. In a traditional plate model, the arc class implicitly has the constraint $e[X] = e[Y]$. Similarly, consider a plate model containing the arc class from $E.X$ to $R.Y$ where R is nested inside E, possibly many levels deep. Because R in nested inside E, for any relationship $r \in R$, the entities associated with r must uniquely determine an $e \in E$. Let $\boldsymbol{r}(e)$ be the set of the relationships r that uniquely determine e. Now, when this traditional plate model is expanded to a ground graph, arcs are drawn from $e.X$ to $r.Y$ only when $r \in \boldsymbol{r}(e)$. As an example, consider figure 7.18(c), which shows the traditional plate model for the patient–hospital example. Here, E=Hospital, R=In, and $\boldsymbol{r}(h) = \cup_p \{(h,p)\}$ for all hospitals h. Thus, the arc class from Hospital.θ to In$(h,p).O$ has the constraint $h[\theta] = h[O]$. This constraint is implicit (see figure 7.18(c)).

Three, traditional plate models contain no arc-class constraints other than the implicit ones just described.

The DAPER and plate model (as we have defined them) are equivalent. Nonetheless, in some situations, a DAPER model may be easier to understand than an equivalent plate model, and vice versa. When there are many entity and relationship classes (plates and intersections), DAPER models are often easier to understand.

In particular, drawing intersections when there are many plates can be difficult (although not impossible; see [10]). In contrast, when there are few entities and the nesting convention can be used, plates are often easier to understand.

7.6   Probabilistic Relational Models

In this section, we examine directed PRMs.

Recall that, as in the case of the plate model, we have specified an invertible mapping from a DAPER model to a directed PRM. Thus, DAPER models, plate models, and directed PRMs are equivalent. As described earlier, the mapping from a DAPER to directed PRM takes place in two stages: the ER model component of the DAPER model is mapped to a relational model, and then the probabilistic component of the DAPER model is mapped to the directed PRM. In the first stage, entity classes are mapped to tables; relationship classes are mapped to tables with foreign keys making the connections to entities; and attribute classes are mapped to attributes (columns) in relational tables. In the second stage, arc classes and constraints are drawn just as they are in the DAPER model.

There is one important difference between the directed PRM by our definition and the *traditional PRMs* as defined by Friedman et al.[5]. The difference is not in the relational-model component. The components for a PRM and traditional PRM are identical. Rather, the difference lies in how the probabilistic component is specified. In our PRM, the probabilistic component is a graphical augmentation of the relational model. In a traditional PRM, the probabilistic component takes the form of a list of arc classes. To illustrate this difference, compare the PRM in figure 7.4(b) with the corresponding traditional PRM in figure 7.19. In the latter figure, the arc classes pointing to Takes.Grade are specified in a separate list consisting of Takes.Course.Diff → Takes.Grade and Takes.Student.IQ → Takes.Grade.

The terms Takes.Course.Diff and Takes.Student.IQ are examples of what Friedman et al.[5] call *slot chains*. In general, a slot chain is a sequence of foreign key (or inverse foreign key) references. The linear nature of slot chains makes them less expressive than the first-order constraints in (our) PRMs. For example, in example 7.9 where a student's grade in a course depends on whether the course's teacher likes the student's advisor (example 7.9), there are two "relationship paths" from F.Friend to Student.Grade: one through Advises and one through Takes. This double path cannot be represented by a slot chain.

Getoor et al. [8] extend PRMs, allowing slot chains to mention probabilistic relationships. DAPER models are not so expressive. In the following section, we introduce contingent DAPER models that remove this limitation.

In practice, we find both DAPER models and PRMs easy to understand. Database designers who prefer ER models over relational models may prefer DAPER models over PRMs, and vice versa. We note, however, that the purpose of DAPER models and PRMs is not the implementation of mechanisms for data storage, but rather the modeling of probabilistic dependencies. Consequently, even

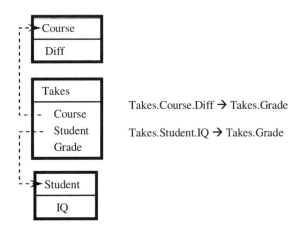

Figure 7.19 A traditional PRM corresponding to the model in figure7.4(b).

those who prefer to design databases with relational models may prefer the DAPER model for probabilistic modeling, as DAPER models make explicit the distinction between entities and relationships.

7.7 Technical Details

In this section, we formalize many of the concepts we have described. In addition, we state and prove a few relevant facts.

We use $\mathcal{E}$ and $\mathcal{R}$ to denote the set of entity and relationship classes, respectively. We use E and R (sometimes with subscripts) to denote an entity and relationship class, respectively, and X to denote an arbitrary class in $\mathcal{E} \cup \mathcal{R}$. We use $\sigma(E)$ and $\sigma(R)$ to denote an entity and relationship set, respectively, and $\sigma(X)$ to denote an arbitrary $\sigma(E)$ or $\sigma(R)$. We use e and r to denote a particular entity and relationship, respectively, and x to denote an arbitrary entity or relationship. We use $X.A$ to denote the attribute class A associated with class X, and $\mathcal{A}(X)$ to denote the set of attribute classes associated with class X. We use $x.A$ to denote an attribute associated with entity or relationship x, and $\mathcal{A}(x)$ to denote the set of attributes associated with x. Each attribute class and attribute is associated with a *domain*—a set of possible values. The domain of $x.A$ is the same as the domain of $X.A$ for every $x \in X$.

First, we define the ER model in the following series of definitions.

Definition 7.1
An *entity-relationship diagram for entity classes $\mathcal{E}$, relationship classes $\mathcal{R}$, and attribute classes $\mathcal{A}$* is a graph in which rectangular nodes correspond to entity classes, diamond nodes correspond to relationship classes, and oval nodes correspond to

attribute classes of entity or relationship classes. The node corresponding to a relationship class among entities $E_1, \ldots, E_n \in \mathcal{E}$ is connected to the nodes corresponding to these entities with a dashed edge. Attribute classes corresponding to an entity or relationship class are connected to this class with dashed edges.

Definition 7.2

A *skeleton for entity classes $\mathcal{E}$ and relationship classes $\mathcal{R}$*—denoted $\sigma_{\mathcal{E}\mathcal{R}}$—consists of (1) an entity set $\sigma(E)$ for every $E \in \mathcal{E}$ and (2) a relationship set $\sigma(R)$ for every $R \in \mathcal{R}$ that is consistent with any constraints imposed by the relationship classes.

Definition 7.3

An *entity-relationship model for entity classes $\mathcal{E}$, relationship classes $\mathcal{R}$, and attribute classes $\mathcal{A}$* is an ER diagram for $\mathcal{E}$, $\mathcal{R}$, and $\mathcal{A}$ that defines a set of (ordinary) attributes $\mathcal{A}(\sigma_{\mathcal{E}\mathcal{R}})$ for any skeleton $\sigma_{\mathcal{E}\mathcal{R}}$. In particular, attribute $x.A$ is in $\mathcal{A}(\sigma_{\mathcal{E}\mathcal{R}})$ if and only if there is an X in $\mathcal{E} \cup \mathcal{R}$ and an $x \in \sigma(X)$ such that A is in $\mathcal{A}(X)$.

Definition 7.4

An *entity-relationship instance for an ER model for $\mathcal{E}$, $\mathcal{R}$, and $\mathcal{A}$*—denoted $\mathcal{I}_{\mathcal{E}\mathcal{R}\mathcal{A}}$—consists of (1) a skeleton $\sigma_{\mathcal{E}\mathcal{R}}$ and (2) a value for every attribute in $\mathcal{A}(\sigma_{\mathcal{E}\mathcal{R}})$.

Now we consider domains wherein attributes may be probabilistic and define the DAPER model through the following series of definitions.

Definition 7.5

Given an entity or relationship class X with entity or relationship x, *the ordered set of entities $\boldsymbol{e}(x)$ associated with x* is as follows. If X is an entity class, then $\boldsymbol{e}(x) = (x)$. If X is a relationship class containing relationships $R(e_1, \ldots, e_n)$, then $\boldsymbol{e}(x) = (e_1, \ldots, e_n)$.

Note that the set $\boldsymbol{e}(x)$ is ordered to preserve roles associated with self-relationship classes.

Definition 7.6

Given an ER model with attribute classes $X.A$ and $Y.B$, *the constraint $\mathcal{C}_{AB}(\boldsymbol{e}(x), \boldsymbol{e}(y))$ for the ordered pair $(X.A, Y.B)$* is a first-order expression that is bound when the elements of $\boldsymbol{e}(x)$ and $\boldsymbol{e}(y)$ are taken as constants. The atoms of this expression have the form $R(e_1, \ldots, e_n)$ where R is a relationship class connected to entity classes $E_1, \ldots, E_n$ or a predefined relationship class such as equality, less than, greater than, and first.

Definition 7.7

A *directed probabilistic entity-relationship (DPER) diagram for entity classes $\mathcal{E}$, relationship classes $\mathcal{R}$, and attribute classes $\mathcal{A}$* consists of (1) an ER model for $\mathcal{E}$, $\mathcal{R}$, and $\mathcal{A}$, and (2) a set of *arc classes* drawn as solid directed arcs corresponding to probabilistic dependencies. There can be at most one arc class from attribute class $X.A$ to attribute class $Y.B$; and any arc class may have a constraint $\mathcal{C}_{AB}(\boldsymbol{e}(x), \boldsymbol{e}(y))$. The set of arc classes pointing to $X.A$ is the *parent class* of $X.A$, denoted $\mathcal{P}\mathcal{A}(X.A)$.

Definition 7.8

A *ground graph* for a DPER diagram and skeleton $\sigma_{\mathcal{E}\mathcal{R}}$ for $\mathcal{E}$, $\mathcal{R}$, and $\mathcal{A}$ is a directed graph constructed as follows. For every attribute in $\mathcal{A}(\sigma_{\mathcal{E}\mathcal{R}})$, there is a corresponding node in the graph. For any attribute $x.A \in \mathcal{A}(\sigma_{\mathcal{E}\mathcal{R}})$, its parent set $\mathbf{pa}(x.A)$ are those attributes $y.B \in \mathcal{A}(y)$ such that there is an arc class from $Y.B$ to $X.A$ and the expression $\mathcal{C}_{AB}(\mathbf{e}(x), \mathbf{e}(y))$ is true.

Definition 7.9

Given $\Sigma_{\mathcal{E}\mathcal{R}}$, a set of skeletons for $\mathcal{E}$, $\mathcal{R}$, and $\mathcal{A}$, a DPER diagram for $\mathcal{E}$, $\mathcal{R}$, and $\mathcal{A}$ is acyclic with respect to $\Sigma_{\mathcal{E}\mathcal{R}}$ if, for every $\sigma_{\mathcal{E}\mathcal{R}} \in \Sigma_{\mathcal{E}\mathcal{R}}$, the ground graph for the DPER diagram and $\sigma_{\mathcal{E}\mathcal{R}}$ is acyclic.

Theorem 7.10

If the probabilistic arcs of a DPER diagram for $\mathcal{E}$, $\mathcal{R}$, and $\mathcal{A}$ form an acyclic graph, then the DPER diagram is ayclic with respect to $\Sigma_{\mathcal{E}\mathcal{R}}$ for any $\Sigma_{\mathcal{E}\mathcal{R}}$.

Proof Suppose the theorem is false. Consider a cyclic ground graph for some skeleton. Denote the attributes in the cycle by $(x_1.A_1 \to x_2.A_2 \to \ldots \to x_n.A_n)$ where $x_1.A_1 = x_n.A_n$. For each attribute $x_i.A_i$ there is an associated attribute class $X_i.A_i$. From definition 7.8, we know that there must be an edge from $X_i.A_i \to X_{i+1}.A_{i+1}$. Because $X_1.A_1 = X_n.A_n$, there must be a cycle in the DPER diagram, which is a contradiction. Q.E.D.

Friedman et al.[5] prove something equivalent.

Definition 7.11

A *directed acyclic probabilistic entity-relationship (DAPER) model* for entity classes $\mathcal{E}$, relationship classes $\mathcal{R}$, attribute classes $\mathcal{A}$, and skeletons $\Sigma_{\mathcal{E}\mathcal{R}}$ consists of (1) an DPER diagram for $\mathcal{E}$, $\mathcal{R}$, and $\mathcal{A}$ that is acyclic with respect to every $\sigma_{\mathcal{E}\mathcal{R}} \in \Sigma_{\mathcal{E}\mathcal{R}}$, and (2) a *local distribution class*—denoted $P(X.A|\mathcal{PA}(X.A))$—for each attribute class $X.A$. Each local distribution class is a collection of information sufficient to determine a local distribution $p(x.A|\mathbf{pa}(x.A))$ for any $x.A \in \mathcal{A}(\sigma_{\mathcal{E}\mathcal{R}})$. For every $\sigma_{\mathcal{E}\mathcal{R}} \in \Sigma_{\mathcal{E}\mathcal{R}}$, the DAPER model specifies a DAG model for $\mathcal{A}(\sigma_{\mathcal{E}\mathcal{R}})$. The structure of this DAG model is the ground graph of the DPER diagram for $\sigma_{\mathcal{E}\mathcal{R}}$. The local distributions of this DAG model are the local distributions $p(x.A|\mathbf{pa}(x.A))$.

An immediate consequence of definition 7.11 is that, given $\mathcal{D}$, a DAPER model for $\mathcal{E}$, $\mathcal{R}$, $\mathcal{A}$, and $\Sigma_{\mathcal{E}\mathcal{R}}$ and a skeleton $\sigma_{\mathcal{E}\mathcal{R}} \in \Sigma_{\mathcal{E}\mathcal{R}}$, we can write the joint distribution for $\mathcal{A}(\sigma_{\mathcal{E}\mathcal{R}})$ as follows:

$$p(\mathcal{I}_{\mathcal{E}\mathcal{R}\mathcal{A}}|\sigma_{\mathcal{E}\mathcal{R}}, \mathcal{D}) = \prod_{X \in \mathcal{E} \cup \mathcal{R}} \prod_{x \in \sigma(X)} \prod_{A \in \mathcal{A}(X)} p(x.A|\mathbf{pa}(x.A)). \tag{7.3}$$

In the remainder of this section, we describe a condition weaker than the one in theorem 7.10 that guarantees the creation of acyclic ground graphs from a DPER model. In this discussion, we use $R(e_1, \ldots, e_n)$ to denote a particular relationship in a relationship set $\sigma(R)$.

Definition 7.12
A relationship class R is a *self-relationship class with respect to entity class E* if a relationship in R contains two or more references to entities in the entity class E.

Definition 7.13
A *projected pairwise self-relationship class* is obtained from a self-relationship class by projecting two of the entities in the relationships that are from the same entity class.

For example, the Family relationship class is a self-relationship class that can be projected into the Father-Child relationship class and the Mother-Child relationship class; and both are projected pairwise self-relationship classes.

Definition 7.14
Given skeleton $\sigma_{\mathcal{ER}}$ for $\mathcal{E}$ and $\mathcal{R}$, a relationship set $\sigma(R)$ for a self-relationship class R is *cyclic* if there exists a projected pairwise self-relationship class R' for some entity set E containing entities $e_1, \dots, e_n$ such that $R'(e_1, e_2), \dots, R'(e_{n-1}, e_n)$ and $R'(e_n, e_1)$. If a relationship set is not cyclic, it is *acyclic*.

Definition 7.15
An arc class in a DPER model is called a *self arc* if both the head and tail of the arc are the same attribute class. A self-arc class is *simple* if there is exactly one entity class associated with the attribute class associated with the self arc.

Theorem 7.16
If (1) the arc classes excluding the self arcs of the DPER diagram for $\mathcal{E}$, $\mathcal{R}$, and $\mathcal{A}$ form an acyclic graph, (2) every self arc class is simple and has a constraint with no disjunctions, no negations, and contains a self-relationship class for the entity class associated with the self arc, and (3) for every self-relationship class R, $\sigma(R)$ is acyclic for every $\sigma_{\mathcal{ER}} \in \Sigma_{\mathcal{ER}}$, then the DPER diagram is acyclic with respect to $\Sigma_{\mathcal{ER}}$.

Proof Suppose the theorem is false. Consider a ground graph G for some skeleton $\sigma_{\mathcal{ER}}$ containing a shortest cycle $(x_1.A_1, \dots, x_n.A_n)$ where $x_1.A_1 = x_n.A_n$. Suppose that the cycle contains at least two distinct attribute classes, that is, $X_i.A_i \neq X_{i+1}.A_{i+1}$. This implies that there must be a cycle in the DAPER diagram with the self-arc classes removed; however, from condition 1 and theorem 7.10 this cannot be the case. Therefore, all of the attribute classes in the cycle must be the same and must be included due to a single self-arc class. Due to condition (2), the cycle in the self-arc class must imply a cyclic self-relationship class but this contradicts condition (3). Q.E.D.

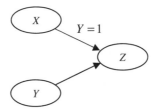

Figure 7.20 A contingent DAG model (structure) showing the context-specific independence X and Z are independent given $Y = 0$, but dependent given $Y = 1$.

7.8 Extensions and Future Work

In this chapter, we have concentrated on the DAPER model, a model that expands into a DAG model given a skeleton. In this section, we examine classes of PER models that expand into graphical models other than traditional DAG models. Many of the ideas here are preliminary and provide opportunities for future work.

An important limitation of traditional graphical models is their inability to represent context-specific independence. An example of such independence is the pair of independencies: (1) X and Z are independent given $Y = 0$, and (2) X and Z are dependent given $Y = 1$. Many extensions to graphical models have been developed that can represent particular classes of context-specific independence including decision-tree-DAG model hybrids (e.g., see [2]); contingent DAG models [6]; and similarity networks [12].

Let us consider a variation on contingent DAG models that uses notation slightly different from that in Fung and Shachter [6]. To understand this model class, consider the context-specific independence described in the previous paragraph: X and Z are independent given $Y = 0$, but dependent given $Y = 1$. Figure 7.20 shows a contingent DAG model (structure) for this independence. This contingent DAG model has a *state constraint* on the arc from Y to Z that reads $X = 1$. This constraint means that there is a dependence of Y on Z only when $X = 1$. In general, state constraints in contingent DAG models function much the way constraints do in DAPER models. In DAPER models, constraints are first-order expressions over entities that control the expansion to a DAG model. In contingent DAG models, state constraints are Boolean expressions over attribute–states that control the expression of conditional independence.

Now consider the contingent DAPER model—a model that expands to a contingent DAG model. The model is identical to an ordinary DAPER model except that arc classes are now annotated with an order pair. The first component of the ordered pair is a constraint just as is found in the ordinary DAPER model. The second component is a *state constraint class* that specifies the state constraints to be written during the expansion to a contingent DAG model. The state constraint class is a Boolean expression over attribute-states that may take head and tail entities as arguments.

Example 7.15 Identity Uncertainty
We have video images of multiple cars of different colors. We know how many cars there are and have zero or more observations of each car's color, but we are uncertain about what observations go with what cars.

Pasula and Russell[18] describe this example as having *identity uncertainty*. We can represent this example using the contingent DAPER model in figure 7.21(a). The two entity classes, Car and Observation, are related by the relationship class Of, where $Of(o, c)$ holds when observation o corresponds to car c. The probabilistic relationship Of has the many-to-one restriction: an observation is associated with exactly one car. As in previous examples, the many-to-one restriction is represented by the `Full` relationship class Of, together with the attribute class Of.Exists and the deterministic node MutEx (which is set to true). The arc class from Car.Color to Observation.Color is annotated with the ordered pair $(Of(o, c), Of(o, c).Exists = $ true). The first component says that we draw an arc from c.Color to o.Observation only when $Of(o, c)$ is true. (In this case, this constraint is vacuous because the relationship class F is `Full`.) The second component says that, when we draw such an arc, we add to it the state constraint $Of(o, c).Exists = $ true. Figure 7.21(b) shows the expansion of this contingent DAPER model to a contingent DAG model for a skeleton containing one car and two observations. Note that, because there is only one car, the MutEx nodes are redudant and can be omitted.

In this example, we know how many cars there are. If we do not, we can place a probability distribution on the number of cars and stipulate that the DAPER model in figure 7.21(a) should be applied to each possible number of cars.

Let us now discuss possibilities for relational modeling with undirected models. A commonly used (nonrelational) undirected model is the undirected graphical (UG) model. This model class has more than one definition—definitions that coincide only for positive distributions [17]. Here, we define a UG for attributes $\mathbf{X}$ with joint distribution $p(\mathbf{x})$ as a model having two components: (1) an undirected graph (the model structure) whose nodes are in one-to-one correspondence with $\mathbf{X}$, and (2) a collection of non-negative clique functions $\phi_m(\mathbf{x}_m)$, $m = 1, \ldots, M$, where m indexes the maximal cliques of the graph and $\mathbf{X}_m$ are the attributes in $\mathbf{X}$ in the mth maximal clique, such that

$$p(\mathbf{x}) = c \prod_{m=1}^{M} \phi_m(\mathbf{x}_m). \tag{7.4}$$

The term c is a normalization constant. As is the case for the DAG model, the UG model for $\mathbf{X}$ defines the joint distribution for $\mathbf{X}$. The clique functions are sometimes called *potentials*.

A UG model for (X, Y, Z) is shown in figure 7.22(a). The graph has a single maximal clique consisting of all three attributes, and hence represents an arbitrary distribution for these attributes.

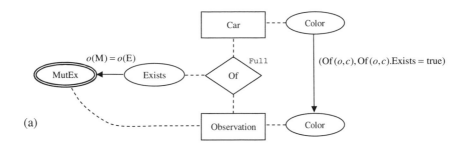

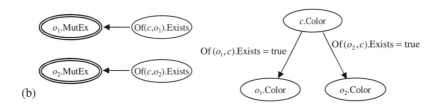

Figure 7.21   (a) A contingent DAPER model for example 7.15, an example of identity uncertainty. (b) A contigent DAG model resulting from the expansion of the model in (a) given a skeleton containing one car and two observations.

A related but more general undirected model is the hierarchical log-linear graphical (HLLG) model. An HLLG model is a model having two components: (1) an undirected hypergraph (the model structure) whose nodes are in one-to-one correspondence with $\mathbf{X}$, and (2) a collection of potentials $\phi_h(x_h)$, $h = 1, \ldots, H$, where h indexes the hyperarcs of the graph and $\mathbf{x}_h$ are the attributes in $\mathbf{X}$ of the hth hyperarc, such that

$$p(\mathbf{x}) = c \prod_{h=1}^{H} \phi_h(\mathbf{x}_h). \tag{7.5}$$

Again, an HLLG model for $\mathbf{X}$ defines the joint distribution for $\mathbf{X}$. In this chapter, we represent a hyperarc as a triangle connecting multiple nodes with undirected edges. For example, figure 7.22(b) shows an HLLG model with a single hyperedge.

By virtue of (7.4) and (7.5), both UG and HLLG model structures define factorization constraints on distributions. In this sense, HLLG models are more general than UG models. That is, given any UG model structure, there exists an HLLG model structure that can encode the same factorization constraints, but not vice versa. For example, the UG structure in figure 7.22(a) has the equivalent HLLG model structure shown in figure 7.22(b). In contrast, the HLLG model structure shown in figure 7.22(c) encodes the factorization constraint

$$p(x, y, z) = c \; \phi_1(x, y) \; \phi_2(y, z) \; \phi_3(x, z),$$

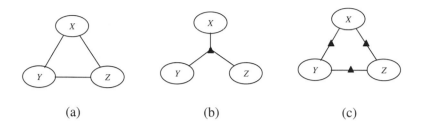

(a)   (b)   (c)

Figure 7.22 (a) A UG model structure. (b) An equivalent HLLG model structure. (c) An HLLG model that encodes pairwise interactions.

which cannot be represented by a UG model structure. Also, we note that the factorization constraints of any HLLG model can be encoded with a factor-graph model [16] in which all potentials are non-negative.

Turning to relational modeling, let us consider the hierarchical log-linear probabilistic entity-relationship (HELPER) model. A model in this class expands into an HLLG model. Like the DAPER model, a HELPER model is an extension of an ER model. In contrast to the DAPER model, the probabilistic component of a HELPER model is expressed as hyperedge classes and potential classes on those hyperedges. Hyperedge classes are expanded to an hyperedges according to constraints. These constraints, in turn, may be any first-order expression that is bound given the entities associated with the endpoints of the hyperedge.

Example 7.16
An arbitrary hierarchical log-linear graphical model with at most two-way interactions.

The HELPER diagram for this example is shown in figure 7.23(a). There is a single entity class Variable corresponding to the attributes in the hierarchical log-linear model, a single attribute class X, and a single self-relationship class Neigh, where Neigh(v_1, v_2) if $v_1.X$ and $v_2.X$ have a pairwise interaction. The only hyperedge class in the model is a self edge that connects Variable.X with itself. The constraint on this hyperedge class is such that $v_1.X$ and $v_2.X$ will be neighbors in the ground graph only when Neigh(v_1, v_2) holds. Note that the Neigh relationship class is restricted to be upper triangular so that the expanded graph has no self arcs and has at most one arc between any two attributes.

A sample skeleton for three attributes and the resulting hierarchical log-linear model is shown in figure 7.23(a) and b, respectively.

Whereas HLLG models have a natural relational counterpart, UG models do not. To understand this point, imagine a PER model that expands to a UG model. Such a model would need a mechanism for specifying potentials in the ground graph. Such potentials, however, are not defined until the maximal cliques of the ground graph are determined, and these cliques will depend on the skeleton used to expand the PER model.

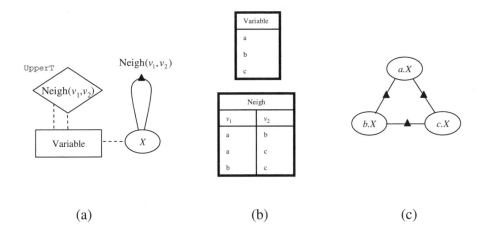

    (a)   (b)   (c)

Figure 7.23 (a) A HELPER model for an arbitrary hierarchical log-linear model with at most two-way interactions. (b) An example skeleton. (c) The hierarchical log-linear model resulting from the model in (a) applied to the skeleton in (b).

Finally, there are numerous classes of graphical models that we have not yet explored, including mixed directed and undirected models (e.g., see [17]); directed factor-graph models [4]; influence diagrams [14]; and dependency networks [13]. The development of PER models that expand to models in these classes also provides opportunities for research.

Acknowledgments

We thank David Blei, Tom Dietterich, Brian Milch, and Ben Taskar for useful comments.

References

[1] J. Besag. Spatial interaction and the statistical analysis of lattice systems. *Journal of the Royal Statistical Society*, 36:192—236, 1974.

[2] C. Boutlier, N. Friedman, M. Goldszmidt, and D. Koller. Context-specific independence in Bayesian networks. In *Proceedings of the Conference on Uncertainty in Artificial Intelligence*, 1996.

[3] W. Buntine. Operations for learning with graphical models. *Journal of Artificial Intelligence Research*, 2(159-225), 1994.

[4] B. Frey. Extending factor graphs so as to unify directed and undirected graphical models. In *Proceedings of the Conference on Uncertainty in Artificial*

Intelligence, 2003.

[5] N. Friedman, L. Getoor, D. Koller, and A. Pfeffer. Learning probabilistic relational models. In *Proceedings of the International Joint Conference on Artificial Intelligence*, 1999.

[6] R. Fung and R. Shachter. Contingent belief networks. 1990.

[7] A. Gelman, J. Carlin, H. Stern, and D. Rubin. *Bayesian Data Analysis*. Chapman and Hall, London, 1995.

[8] L. Getoor, N. Friedman, D. Koller, and B. Taskar. Learning probabilistic models of link structure. *Journal of Machine Learning Research*, 3:679–707, 2002.

[9] W. Gilks, A. Thomas, and D. Spiegelhalter. A language and program for complex Bayesian modeling. *The Statistician*, 43:169–177, 1994.

[10] J. Gill, J. Howse, S. Kent, and J. Taylor. Projections in Venn-Euler diagrams. In *Proceedings of the IEEE Symposium on Visual Languages*, 2000.

[11] I. Good. *The Estimation of Probabilities*. MIT Press, Cambridge, MA, 1965.

[12] D. Heckerman. *Probabilistic Similarity Networks*. MIT Press, Cambridge, MA, 1991.

[13] D. Heckerman, D. Chickering, C. Meek, R. Rounthwaite, and C. Kadie. Dependency networks for inference, collaborative filtering, and data visualization. *Journal of Machine Learning Research*, 1:49–75, 2000.

[14] R. Howard and J. Matheson. Influence diagrams. In *Readings on the Principles and Applications of Decision Analysis*, volume 2, pages 721—762. Strategic Decisions Group, Menlo Park, CA, 1981.

[15] D. Koller and A. Pfeffer. Object-oriented Bayesian networks. In *Proceedings of the Conference on Uncertainty in Artificial Intelligence*, 1997.

[16] F. Kschischang, B. Frey, and H. Loeliger. Factor graphs and the sum-product algorithm. *IEEE Transactions on Information Theory*, 47:498—519, 2001.

[17] S. Lauritzen. *Graphical Models*. Claredon Press, Oxford, UK, 1996.

[18] H. Pasula and S. Russell. Approximate inference in first-order probabilistic languages. In *Proceedings of the International Joint Conference on Artificial Intelligence*, 2001.

[19] J. Ullman and J. Widom. *A First Course in Database Systems*. Prentice Hall, Upper Saddle River, NJ, 2002.

8 Relational Dependency Networks

Jennifer Neville and David Jensen

Recent work on graphical models for relational data has demonstrated significant improvements in classification and inference when models represent the dependencies among instances. Despite its use in conventional statistical models, the assumption of instance independence is contradicted by most relational data sets. For example, in citation data there are dependencies among the topics of a paper's references, and in genomic data there are dependencies among the functions of interacting proteins. In this chapter we present relational dependency networks (RDNs), a graphical model that is capable of expressing and reasoning with such dependencies in a relational setting. We discuss RDNs in the context of relational Bayes networks and relational Markov networks and outline the relative strengths of RDNs—namely, the ability to represent cyclic dependencies, simple methods for parameter estimation, and efficient structure learning techniques. The strengths of RDNs are due to the use of *pseudo-likelihood* learning techniques, which estimate an efficient approximation of the full joint distribution. We present learned RDNs for a number of real-world data sets and evaluate the models in a prediction context, showing that RDNs identify and exploit cyclic relational dependencies to achieve significant performance gains over conventional conditional models.

8.1 Introduction

Many data sets routinely captured by businesses and organizations are relational in nature, yet until recently most machine learning research has focused on "flattened" propositional data. Instances in propositional data record the characteristics of homogeneous and statistically independent objects; instances in relational data record the characteristics of heterogeneous objects and the relations among those objects. Examples of relational data include citation graphs, the World Wide Web, genomic structures, fraud detection data, epidemiology data, and data on interrelated people, places, and events extracted from text documents.

The presence of *autocorrelation* provides a strong motivation for using relational techniques for learning and inference. Autocorrelation is a statistical dependency between the values of the same variable on related entities and is a nearly ubiquitous characteristic of relational data sets [14]. More formally, autocorrelation is defined with respect to a set of related instance pairs $P_R = \{(o_i, o_j) : o_i, o_j \in O\}$; it is the correlation between the values of a variable X on the instance pairs $(o_i.x, o_j.x)$ such that $(o_i, o_j) \in P_R$. Recent analyses of relational data sets have reported autocorrelation in the following variables:

- Topics of hyperlinked webpages [4, 39]
- Industry categorization of corporations that share board members [30]
- Fraud status of cellular customers who call common numbers [5]
- Topics of coreferent scientific papers [38, 29]
- Functions of proteins located together in a cell [28]
- Box office receipts of movies made by the same studio [14]
- Industry categorization of corporations that co-occur in news stories [1]
- Tuberculosis infection among people in close contact [10]

When relational data exhibit autocorrelation there is a unique opportunity to improve model performance because inferences about one object can inform inferences about related objects. Indeed, recent work in relational domains has shown that *collective inference* over an entire data set results in more accurate predictions than conditional inference for each instance independently [e.g., 4, 30, 21], and that the gains over conditional models increase as autocorrelation increases [16].

Joint relational models are able to exploit autocorrelation by estimating a joint probability distribution over an entire relational data set and collectively inferring the labels of related instances. Recent research has produced several novel types of graphical models for estimating joint probability distributions for relational data that consist of nonindependent and heterogeneous instances [e.g., 10, 39]. We will refer to these models as *probabilistic relational models* (PRMs).[1] PRMs extend traditional graphical models such as Bayesian networks to relational domains, removing the assumption of i.i.d. instances that underlies conventional learning techniques. PRMs have been successfully evaluated in several domains, including the World Wide Web, genomic data, and scientific literature.

Directed PRMs, such as relational Bayes networks[2] (RBNs) [10], can model autocorrelation dependencies if they are structured in a manner that respects the

---

1. Several previous papers [e.g., 8, 10] use the term *probabilistic relational model* to refer to a specific model that is now often called a *relational Bayesian network* [Koller, personal communication]. In this paper, we use PRM in its more recent and general sense.
2. We use the term *relational Bayesian network* to refer to Bayesian networks that have been upgraded to model relational databases. The term has also been used by Jaeger [13]

acyclicity constraint of the model. While domain knowledge can sometimes be used to structure the autocorrelation in an acyclic manner, often an acyclic ordering is unknown or does not exist. For example, in genetic pedigree analysis there is autocorrelation among the genes of relatives [20]. In this domain, the causal relationship is from ancestor to descendent so we can use the temporal parent-child relationship to structure the dependencies in an acyclic manner (i.e., parents' genes will never be influenced by the genes of their children). However, given a set of hyperlinked webpages, there is little information to use to determine the causal direction of the dependency between their topics. In this case, we can only represent an (undirected) correlation between the topics of two pages, not a (directed) causal relationship. The acyclicity constraint of directed PRMs precludes the learning of arbitrary autocorrelation dependencies and thus severely limits the applicability of these models in relational domains.

Undirected PRMs, such as relational Markov networks (RMNs) [39], can represent and reason with arbitrary forms of autocorrelation. However, research on these models has focused primarily on parameter estimation and inference procedures. The current RMN learning algorithm does not select features—model structure must be prespecified by the user. While in principle it is possible for RMN techniques to learn cyclic autocorrelation dependencies, inefficient parameter estimation makes this difficult in practice. Because parameter estimation requires multiple rounds of inference over the entire data set, it is impractical to incorporate it as a subcomponent of feature selection. Recent work on conditional random fields for sequence analysis includes a feature selection algorithm [24] that could be extended for RMNs. However, the algorithm abandons estimation of the full joint distribution and uses pseudo-likelihood estimation, which makes the approach tractable but removes some of the advantages of reasoning with the full joint distribution.

In this chapter, we outline relational dependency networks (RDNs), an extension of dependency networks (DNs) [11] for relational data. RDNs can represent and reason with the cyclic dependencies required to express and exploit autocorrelation during collective inference. In this regard, they share certain advantages of RMNs and other undirected models of relational data [4, 6]. Also, to our knowledge, RDNs are the first PRM capable of *learning* cyclic autocorrelation dependencies. RDNs offer a relatively simple method for structure learning and parameter estimation, which results in models that are easier to understand and interpret. In this regard they share certain advantages of RBNs and other directed models [37, 12]. The primary distinction between RDNs and other existing PRMs is that RDNs are an approximate model. RDN models approximate the full joint distribution and thus are not guaranteed to specify a coherent probability distribution. However, the quality of the approximation will be determined by the data available for learning—

---

to refer to Bayesian networks where the nodes correspond to relations and their values represent possible interpretations of those relations in a specific domain.

if the models are learned from large data sets, and combined with Monte Carlo inference techniques, the approximation should not be a disadvantage.

We start by reviewing the details of DNs for propositional data. Then we describe the general characteristics of PRM models and outline the specifics of RDN learning and inference procedures. We evaluate RDN learning and inference algorithms on both synthetic and real-world data sets, presenting learned RDNs for subjective evaluation and evaluating the models in a prediction context. Of particular note, all the real-world data sets exhibit multiple autocorrelation dependencies that were automatically discovered by the RDN learning algorithm. Finally, we review related work and conclude with a discussion of future directions.

8.2   Dependency Networks

Graphical models represent a joint distribution over a set of variables. The primary distinction between representations such as Bayesian networks and Markov networks and DNs is that DNs are an approximate representation. DNs approximate the joint distribution with a set of conditional probability distributions (CPDs) that are learned independently. This approach to learning results in significant efficiency gains over exact models. However, because the CPDs are learned independently, DN models are not guaranteed to specify a *consistent* joint distribution. This precludes DNs from being used to infer causal relationships and limits the applicability of exact inference techniques. Nevertheless, DNs can encode predictive relationships (i.e., dependence and independence), and Gibbs sampling inference techniques [e.g., 27] can be used to recover a full joint distribution, regardless of the consistency of the local CPDs.

8.2.1   DN Representation

Dependency networks are an alternative form of graphical model that approximate the full joint distribution with a set of conditional probability distributions that are each learned independently. A DN encodes probabilistic relationships among a set of variables $\mathbf{X}$ in a manner that combines characteristics of both undirected and directed graphical models. Dependencies among variables are represented with a bidirected graph $G = (V, E)$, where conditional independence is interpreted using graph separation, as with undirected models. However, as with directed models, dependencies are quantified with a set of conditional probability distributions P. Each node $v_i \in V$ corresponds to an $X_i \in \mathbf{X}$ and is associated with a probability distribution conditioned on the other variables, $P(v_i) = p(x_i | \mathbf{x} - \{x_i\})$. The parents of node i are the set of variables that render X_i conditionally independent of the other variables $(p(x_i | pa_i) = p(x_i | \mathbf{x} - \{x_i\}))$, and G contains a directed edge from each parent node v_j to each child node v_i $(e(v_j, v_i) \in E$ iff $X_j \in pa_i)$. The CPDs in P do not necessarily factor the joint distribution so we cannot compute the joint probability for a set of values $\mathbf{x}$ directly. However, given G and P, a joint distribution can be recovered through Gibbs sampling (see below for details). From the joint distribution, we can extract any probabilities of interest.

8.2.2   DN Learning

Both the structure and parameters of DN models are determined through learning the local CPDs. The DN learning algorithm learns a separate distribution for each variable X_i, conditioned on the other variables in the data (i.e., $\mathbf{X} - \{X_i\}$). Any conditional learner can be used for this task (e.g., logistic regression, decision trees). The CPD is included in the model as $P(v_i)$ and the variables selected by the conditional learner form the parents of X_i (e.g., if $p(x_i|\{\mathbf{x} - x_i\}) = \alpha x_j + \beta x_k$, then $pa_i = \{x_j, x_k\}$). The parents are then reflected in the edges of G appropriately. If the conditional learner is not selective (i.e., the algorithm does not select a subset of the features), the DN model will be fully connected (i.e., $pa_i = \mathbf{x} - \{x_i\}$). In order to build understandable DNs, it is desirable to use a selective learner that will learn CPDs that use a subset of the variables.

8.2.3   DN Inference

Although the DN approach to structure learning is simple and efficient, it can result in an inconsistent network, both structurally and numerically. In other words, there may be no joint distribution from which each of the CPDs can be obtained using the rules of probability. Learning the CPDs independently with a selective conditional learner can result in a network that contains a directed edge from X_i to X_j, but not from X_j to X_i. This is a structural inconsistency—X_i and X_j are dependent but X_j is not represented in the CPD for X_i. In addition, learning the CPDs independently from finite samples may result in numerical inconsistencies in parameter estimates, where the derived joint distribution does not sum to one. In practice, Heckerman et al. [11] show that DNs are nearly consistent if learned from large data sets because the data serves a coordinating function to ensure some degree of consistency among the CPDs. However, even when a DN is inconsistent, approximate inference techniques can still be used to estimate a full joint distribution and extract probabilities of interest. Gibbs sampling can be used to recover a full joint distribution, regardless of the consistency of the local CPDs, provided that each X_i is discrete and its CPD is positive [11].

8.3   Relational Dependency Networks

Several characteristics of DNs are particularly desirable for modeling relational data. First, learning a collection of conditional models offers significant efficiency gains over learning a full joint model. This is generally true, but is even more pertinent to relational settings where the feature space is very large. Second, networks that are easy to interpret and understand aid analysts' assessment of the utility of the relational information. Third, the ability to represent cycles in a network facilitates reasoning with autocorrelation, a common characteristic of relational data. In addition, whereas the need for approximate inference is a disadvantage of DNs for propositional data, due to the complexity of relational model graphs in practice, all PRMs use approximate inference.

RDNs extend DNs to work with relational data in much the same way that RBNs extend Bayesian networks and RMNs extend Markov networks. These extensions take a graphical model formalism and *upgrade* [17] it to a first-order logic representation with an entity-relationship model. We start by describing the general characteristics of PRMs and then discuss the details of RDNs in this context.

8.3.1   Probabilistic Relational Models

PRMs represent a joint probability distribution over the attributes of a relational data set. When modeling propositional data with a graphical model, there is a single graph G that comprises the model. In contrast, there are three graphs associated with models of relational data: the *data graph* G_D, the *model graph* G_M, and the *inference graph* G_I. These correspond to the *skeleton*, *model*, and *ground graph* as outlined in Heckerman et al. [12].

First, the relational data set is represented as a typed, attributed data graph $G_D = (V_D, E_D)$. For example, consider the data graph in figure 8.1(a). The nodes V_D represent objects in the data (e.g., authors, papers) and the edges E_D represent relations among the objects (e.g., author-of, cites).[3] Each node $v_i \in V_D$ and edge $e_j \in E_D$ is associated with a type $T(v_i) = t_{v_i}$ (e.g., paper, cited-by). Each item[4] type $t \in T$ has a number of associated attributes, $\mathbf{X^t} = (X_1^t, ..., X_m^t)$ (e.g., topic, year). Consequently, each object v_i and link e_j is associated with a set of attribute values determined by their type, $\mathbf{X_{v_i}^{t_{v_i}}} = (X_{v_i1}^{t_{v_i}}, ..., X_{v_im}^{t_{v_i}})$, $\mathbf{X_{e_j}^{t_{e_j}}} = (X_{e_j1}^{t_{e_j}}, ..., X_{e_jm'}^{t_{e_j}})$. A PRM model represents a joint distribution over the values of the attributes in the data graph, $\mathbf{x} = \{\mathbf{x_{v_i}^{t_{v_i}}} : v_i \in V, t_{v_i} = T(v_i)\} \cup \{\mathbf{x_{e_j}^{t_{e_j}}} : e_j \in E, t_{e_j} = T(e_j)\}$.

Next, the dependencies among attributes are represented in the model graph $G_M = (V_M, E_M)$. Attributes of an item can depend probabilistically on other attributes of the same item, as well as on attributes of other related objects or links in G_D. For example, the topic of a paper may be influenced by attributes of the authors that wrote the paper. Instead of defining the dependency structure over attributes of specific objects, PRMs define a generic dependency structure at the level of item types. Each node $v \in V_M$ corresponds to an X_k^t, where $t \in T \wedge X_k^t \in \mathbf{X^t}$. The set of attributes $\mathbf{X_k^t} = (X_{ik}^t : (v_i \in V \vee e_i \in E) \wedge T(i) = t)$ is tied together and modeled as a single variable. This approach of typing items and tying parameters across items of the same type is an essential component of PRM learning. It enables

---

3. We use rectangles to represent objects, circles to represent random variables, dashed lines to represent relations, and solid lines to represent probabilistic dependencies.
4. We use the generic term "item" to refer to objects or links.

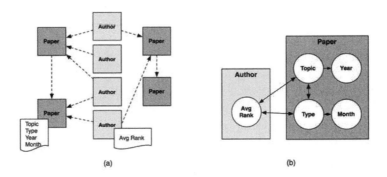

Figure 8.1 Example (a) data graph and (b) model graph.

generalization from a *single* instance (i.e., one data graph) by decomposing the data graph into *multiple* examples of each item type (e.g., all paper objects), and building a joint model of dependencies between and among attributes of each type.

As in conventional graphical models, each node is associated with a probability distribution conditioned on the other variables. Parents of X_k^t are either (1) other attributes associated with type t_k (e.g., paper *topic* depends on paper *type*), or (2) attributes associated with items of type t_j where items t_j are related to items t_k in G_D (e.g., paper *topic* depends on author *rank*). For the latter type of dependency, if the relation between t_k and t_j is one-to-many, the parent consists of a set of attribute values (e.g., author ranks). In this situation, current PRM models use aggregation functions to generalize across heterogeneous items (e.g., one paper may have two authors while another may have five). Aggregation functions are used to either map sets of values into single values, or to combine a set of probability distributions into a single distribution.

Consider the RDN model graph G_M in figure 8.1(b). It models the data in figure 8.1(a), which has two object types: paper and author. In G_M, each item type is represented by a plate, and each attribute of each item type is represented as a node. Edges characterize the dependencies among the attributes at the type level. The representation uses a modified plate notation—dependencies among attributes of the same object are contained inside the rectangle and arcs that cross the boundary of the rectangle represent dependencies among attributes of related objects. For example, $month_i$ depends on $type_i$, while $avgrank_j$ depends on the $type_k$ and $topic_k$ for all papers k related to author j in G_D.

There is a nearly limitless range of dependencies that could be considered by algorithms learning PRM models. In propositional data, learners model a fixed set of attributes intrinsic to each object. In contrast, in relational data, learners must decide how much to model (i.e., how much of the relational neighborhood around an item can influence the probability distribution of an item's attributes). For example, a paper's topic may depend on the topics of other papers written by its authors—but what about the topics of the references in those papers or the topics of other papers written by coauthors of those papers? Two common approaches to limiting search in the space of relational dependencies are (1) exhaustive search of all dependencies within a fixed-distance neighborhood (e.g., attributes of items up to k links away), or (2) greedy iterative-deepening search, expanding the search in the neighborhood in directions where the dependencies improve the likelihood.

Finally, during inference, a PRM uses a model graph G_M and a data graph G_D to instantiate an inference graph $G_I = (V_I, V_E)$ in a process sometimes called "rollout." The rollout procedure used by PRMs to produce G_I is nearly identical to the process used to instantiate sequence models such as hidden Markov models. G_I represents the probabilistic dependencies among all the variables in a single test set (here G_D is usually different from G'_D used for training). The structure of G_I is determined by both G_D and G_M—each item-attribute pair in G_D gets a separate, local copy of the appropriate CPD from G_M. The relations in G_D constrain the way that G_M is rolled out to form G_I. PRMs can produce inference graphs with wide variation in overall and local structure because the structure of G_I is determined by the specific data graph, which typically has nonuniform structure. For example, figure 8.2 shows the RDN from figure 8.1b rolled out over a data set of three authors and three papers, where P_1 is authored by A_1 and A_2, P_2 is authored by A_2 and A_3, and P_3 is authored by A_3. Notice that there are a variable number of authors per paper. This illustrates why current PRMs use aggregation in their CPDs—for example, the CPD for paper-type must be able to deal with a variable number of author ranks.

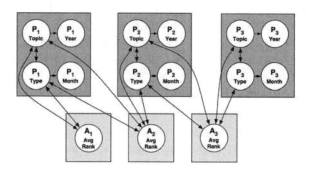

Figure 8.2   Example PRM inference graph.

8.3.2   RDN Representation

Relational dependency networks encode probabilistic relationships in a similar manner to DNs, extending the representation to a relational setting. RDNs use a bidirected model graph G_M with a set of conditional probability distributions P. Each node $v_i \in V_M$ corresponds to an $X_k^t \in \mathbf{X^t}$, $t \in T$ and is associated with a conditional distribution $p(x_k^t | pa_{x_k^t})$. Figure 8.1b illustrates an example RDN model graph for the data graph in figure 8.1a. The graphical representation illustrates the qualitative component (G_D) of the RDN—it does not depict the quantitative component (P) of the model, which consists of CPDs that use aggregation functions. Although conditional independence is inferred using an undirected view of the graph, bidirected edges are useful for representing the set of variables in each CPD. For example, in figure 8.1b the CPD for *Year* contains *Topic* but the CPD for *Topic* does not contain *Type*. This depicts any inconsistencies that result from the RDN learning technique.

8.3.3   RDN Learning

Learning a PRM model consists of two tasks: learning the dependency structure among the attributes of each object type, and estimating the parameters of the local probability models for an attribute given its parents. Relatively efficient techniques exist for learning both the structure and parameters of RBN models. However, these techniques exploit the requirement that the CPDs *factor* the full distribution—a requirement that imposes acyclicity constraints on the model and precludes the learning of arbitrary autocorrelation dependencies. On the other hand, although in principle it is possible for RMN techniques to learn cyclic autocorrelation dependencies, inefficiencies due to calculating the normalizing constant Z in undirected models make this difficult in practice. Calculation of Z requires a summation over all possible states **X**. When modeling the joint distribution of propositional data, the number of states is exponential in the number of attributes (i.e., $O(2^m)$). When modeling the joint distribution of relational data, the number of states is exponential in the number of attributes and *the number of instances*. If there are N objects, each with m attributes, then the total number of states is $O(2^{Nm})$. For any reasonable-size data set, a single calculation of Z is an enormous computational burden. Feature selection generally requires repeated parameter estimation while measuring the change in likelihood affected by each attribute, which would require recalculation of Z on each iteration.

The RDN learning algorithm uses a more efficient alternative—estimating the set of conditional distributions independently rather than jointly. This approach is based on *pseudo-likelihood* techniques [2], which were developed for modeling spatial data sets with similar autocorrelation dependencies. Pseudo-Likelihood estimation avoids the complexities of estimating Z and the requirement of acyclicity. In addition, this approach can utilize existing techniques for learning CPDs of relational data such as first-order Bayesian classifiers [7], structural logistic regression [35], or ACORA [34].

Instead of optimizing the log-likelihood of the full joint distribution, we optimize the pseudo-loglikelihood for each variable independently, conditioned on all other attribute values in the data:

$$PL(G_D; \theta) = \sum_{t \in T} \sum_{X_i^t \in X^t} \sum_{v \in T(v)} p(x_{vi}^t | pa_{x_{vi}^t}), \qquad (8.1)$$

Table 8.1　RDN learning algorithm

Learn RDN $(G_D, R, \mathbf{Q^t}, \mathbf{X^t})$:

$P \leftarrow \emptyset$

For each $t \in T$:

　　For each $X_k^t \in \mathbf{X^t}$:

　　　　Use R to learn a CPD for X_k^t given the attributes $\{X_{k' \neq k}^t\} \cup \mathbf{X^{t' \neq t}}$
　　　　in the relational neighborhood defined by Q^t.

　　　　$P \leftarrow P \cup CPD_{X_k^t}$

Use P to form G_M.

With this approach we give up the asymptotic efficiency guarantees of maximum likelihood estimators. However, under some general conditions the consistency of maximum pseudo-likelihood estimators can be established [9], which implies that, as sample size $\rightarrow \infty$, pseudo-likelihood estimators will produce unbiased estimates of the true parameters.

On the surface (8.1) may appear similar to the joint distribution specified by an RBN. However, the CPDs in the pseudo-likelihood are not required to factor the joint distribution of G_D. More specifically, when we consider the variable X_{vi}^t, we condition on the values of the parents $pa_{X_{vi}^t}$ regardless of whether the estimation of $pa_{X_{vi}^t}$ was conditioned on X_{vi}^t. The parents of X_{vi}^t may include the values of other attributes (e.g., $X_{vi'}^{t'}$ such that $t' \neq t$ or $i' \neq i$) or the values of the same variable on related items (e.g., $X_{v'i}^t$ such that $v' \neq v$).

The RDN learning algorithm is similar to the DN learning algorithm, except we use a relational probability estimation algorithm to learn a set of conditional models, maximizing the pseudo-likelihood for each variable separately. The algorithm input consists of

- G_D: a relational data graph
- R: a conditional relational learner
- $\mathbf{Q^t}$: a set of queries that specify the types T and limits the relational neighborhood that is considered in R for each T
- $\mathbf{X^t}$: a set of attributes for each item type

Table 8.3.3 outlines the learning algorithm in pseudocode. It cycles over each attribute of each item type and learns a separate CPD, conditioned on the other values in the training data. We discuss details of the subcomponents (querying and relational learners) next.

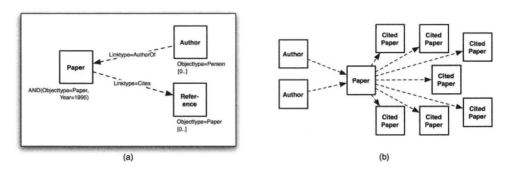

Figure 8.3 (a) Example QGraph query: Textual annotations specify match conditions on attribute values; numerical annotations (e.g., [0..]) specify constraints on the cardinality of matched objects (e.g., zero or more authors), and (b) matching subgraph.

8.3.3.1 Queries

The queries specify the relational neighborhoods that will be considered by the conditional learner R, and their structure defines a typing over instances in the database. Subgraphs are extracted from a larger graph database using the visual query language QGraph [3]. Queries allow for variation in the number and types of objects and links that form the subgraphs and return collections of all matching subgraphs from the database.

For example, consider the query in figure 8.3a.[5] The query specifies match criteria for a target item (paper) and its local relational neighborhood (authors and references). The example query matches all research papers that were published in 1995 and returns for each paper a subgraph that includes all authors and references associated with the paper. Figure 8.3b shows a hypothetical match to this query: a paper with two authors and seven references.

The query defines a typing over the objects of the database (e.g., people that have authored a paper are categorized as *authors*) and specifies the relevant relational context for the target item type in the model. For example, given this query the model R would model the distribution of a paper's attributes given the attributes of the paper itself and the attributes of its related authors and references. The queries are a means of restricting model search. Instead of setting a depth limit on the extent of the search, the analyst has a more flexible means with which to limit the search (e.g., we can consider other papers written by the paper's authors but not other authors of the paper's references).

___

5. We have modified the QGraph representation to conform to our convention of using rectangles to represent objects and dashed lines to represent relations.

8.3.3.2   *Conditional Relational Learners*

The conditional relational learner R is used for both parameter estimation and structure learning in RDNs. The variables selected by R are reflected in the edges of G appropriately. If R selects all of the available attributes, the RDN model will be fully connected.

In principle, any conditional relational learner can be used as a subcomponent to learn the individual CPDs. In this chapter, we discuss the use of two different conditional models—relational Bayesian classifiers (RBCs) [32] and relational probability trees (RPTs) [31].

Relational Bayesian classifiers RBCs extend Bayesian classifiers to a relational setting. RBC models treat heterogeneous relational subgraphs as a homogeneous set of attribute multisets. For example, when considering the references of a single paper the publication dates of those references form multisets of varying size (e.g., $\{1995, 1995, 1996\}$, $\{1975, 1986, 1998, 1998\}$). The RBC assumes each value of a multiset is independently drawn from the same multinomial distribution.[6] This approach is designed to mirror the independence assumption of the naive Bayesian classifier. In addition to the conventional assumption of attribute independence, the RBC also assumes attribute value independence within each multiset.

For a given item type T, the query scope specifies the set of item types $\mathbf{T_R}$ that form the relevant relational neighborhood for T. For example, in figure 8.3(a) $T = paper$ and $\mathbf{T_R} = \{paper, author, reference, authorof, cites\}$. To estimate the CPD for attribute X on items T (e.g., paper topic), the model considers all the attributes associated with the types in $\mathbf{T_R}$. RBCs are non-selective models so all the attributes are included as parents:

$$p(x|pa_x) \propto \prod_{t \in \mathbf{T_R}} \prod_{X_i^t \in X^t} \prod_{v \in T_R(x)} p(x_{vi}^t|x) \; p(x),$$

Relational probability trees RPTs are selective models that extend classification trees to a relational setting. RPT models also treat heterogeneous relational subgraphs as a set of attribute multisets, but instead of modeling the multisets as independent values drawn from a multinomial, the RPT algorithm uses aggregation functions to map a set of values into a single feature value. For example, when considering the publication dates of references of a research paper the RPT could construct a feature that tests whether the *average* publication date was after 1995. Figure 8.4 provides an example RPT learned on citation data.

The RPT algorithm automatically constructs and searches over aggregated relational features to model the distribution of the target variable X. The algorithm constructs features from the attributes associated with the types specified in the

---

6. Alternative constructions are possible but prior work [32] has shown this approach achieves superior performance over a wide range of conditions.

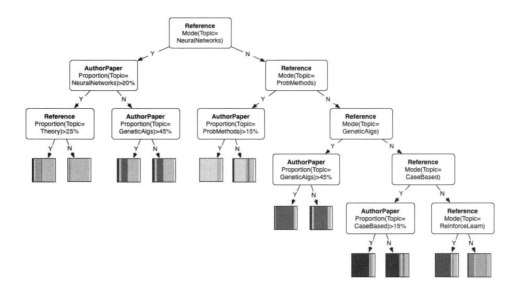

Figure 8.4   Example RPT to predict machine learning paper topic.

query. The algorithm considers four classes of aggregation functions to group multi-set values: *Mode, Count, Proportion, Degree*. For discrete attributes, the algorithm constructs features for all unique values of an attribute. For continuous attributes, the algorithm constructs features for a number of different discretizations, binning the values by frequency (e.g., *year* > 1992). Count, proportion, and degree features consider a number of different thresholds (e.g., *proportion*(A) > 10%). Feature scores are calculated using chi-square to measure correlation between the feature and the class. The algorithm uses prepruning in the form of a p-value cutoff and a depth cutoff to limit tree size. All experiments reported herein used $\alpha = 0.05/|attributes|$, *depth cutoff*=7, and considered ten thresholds and discretizations per feature.

The RPT learning algorithm adjusts for biases toward particular features due to degree disparity and autocorrelation in relational data [14, 15]. We have shown that RPTs build significantly smaller trees than other conditional models and achieve equivalent, or better, performance [31]. These characteristics of RPTs are crucial for learning understandable RDN models and have a direct impact on inference efficiency because smaller trees limit the size of the final inference graph.

8.3.4   RDN Inference

The RDN inference graph G_I is potentially much larger than the original data graph. To model the full joint distribution there must be a separate node (and CPD) for each attribute value in G_D. To construct G_I, the set of template CPDs in P is rolled out over the test-set data graph. Each item-attribute pair gets a separate, local copy of the appropriate CPD. Consequently, the total number of nodes in the inference graph will be $\sum_{v \in V_D} |\mathbf{X}^{\mathbf{T(v)}}| + \sum_{e \in E_D} |\mathbf{X}^{\mathbf{T(e)}}|$. Rollout facilitates generalization across data graphs of varying size—we can learn the CPD templates from one data graph and apply the model to a second data graph with a different number of objects by rolling out more CPD copies. This approach is analogous to other graphical models that tie distributions across the network and roll out copies of model templates (e.g., hidden Markov models).

We use Gibbs sampling for inference in RDN models. Gibbs sampling can be used to extract a unique joint distribution, regardless of the consistency of the model [11].

Table 8.3.4 outlines the inference algorithm. To estimate a joint distribution, we start by rolling out the model G_M onto the target data set G_D, forming the inference graph G_I. The values of all unobserved variables are initialized to values drawn from their prior distributions. Gibbs sampling then iteratively relabels each unobserved variable by drawing from its local conditional distribution, given the current state of the rest of the graph. After a sufficient number of iterations (*burnin*), the values will be drawn from a stationary distribution and we can use the samples to estimate probabilities of interest.

For prediction tasks we are often interested in the marginal probabilities associated with a single variable X (e.g., paper topic). Although Gibbs sampling may be a relatively inefficient approach to estimating the probability associated with a joint assignment of values of X (e.g., when $|X|$ is large), it is often reasonably fast to estimate the marginal probabilities for each X.

There are many implementation issues that can improve the estimates obtained from a Gibbs sampling chain, such as length of burn-in and number of samples. For the experiments reported in this chapter we used fixed-length chains of 2000 samples (each iteration relabels every value sequentially) with burn-in set at 100. Empirical inspection indicated that the majority of chains had converged by 500 samples.

8.4   Experiments

The experiments in this section demonstrate the utility of RDNs as a joint model of relational data. First, we use synthetic data to assess the impact of training-set size and autocorrelation on RDN learning and inference, showing that accurate models can be learned at reasonable data set sizes and that the model is robust to varying levels of autocorrelation. Next, we learn RDN models of three real-world data sets to illustrate the types of domain knowledge that the models discover automatically. In addition, we evaluate RDN models in a prediction context, where only a single attribute is unobserved in the test set, and report significant performance gains compared to two conditional models.

Table 8.2 RDN inference algorithm

Infer RDN $(G_D, G_M, P, iter, burnin)$:

$G_I(V_I, E_I) \leftarrow (\emptyset, \emptyset)$ \\ *form G_I from G_D and G_M*

For each $t \in T$ *in* G_M:

     For each $X_k^t \in \mathbf{X^t}$ *in* G_M:

         For each $v_i \in V_D$ *s.t.* $T(v_i) = t$:

             $V_I \leftarrow V_I \cup \{X_{v_i k}^t\}$

             For each $v_j \in V_D$ *s.t.* $X_{v_j} \in pa_{X_{v_i k}^t}$:

                 $E_I \leftarrow E_I \cup \{e_{ij}\}$

For each $v \in V_I$:   \\ *initialize Gibbs sampling*

     Randomly initialize x_v to an arbitrary value

$S \leftarrow \emptyset$ \\ *Gibbs sampling procedure*

For $i \in iter$:

     For each $v \in V_I$, in random order:

         Resample x_v' from $p(x_v | \mathbf{x} - \{x_v\})$

         $x_v \leftarrow x_v'$

         If $i > burnin$:

             $S \leftarrow S \cup \{\mathbf{x}\}$

Use samples S to estimate probabilities of interest

8.4.1 Synthetic Data Experiments

To explore the effects of training-set size and autocorrelation on RDN learning and inference, we generated homogeneous data graphs with autocorrelation due to an underlying (hidden) group structure. Each object has four Boolean attributes: X_1, X_2, X_3, and X_4. The data generation procedure uses a simple RDN where X_1 is autocorrelated (through objects one link away), X_2 depends on X_1, and the other two attributes have no dependencies. To generate data with autocorrelated X_1 values, we used manually specified conditional models for $p(X_1 | \mathbf{X_{1R}}, X_2)$.

We compare two different RDN models: RDN_{RBC} uses RBCs for the component model R; RDN_{RPT} uses RPT for R. The RPT performs feature selection, which may result in structural inconsistencies in the learned RDN. The RBC does not use feature selection so any deviation from the true model is due to numerical inconsistencies alone. Note that the two models do not consider identical feature spaces so we can only roughly assess the impact of feature selection by comparing RDN_{RBC} and RDN_{RPT} results.

8.4.1.1 RDN Learning

The first set of synthetic experiments examines the effectiveness of the RDN learning algorithm. Theoretical analysis indicates that, in the limit, the true parameters will

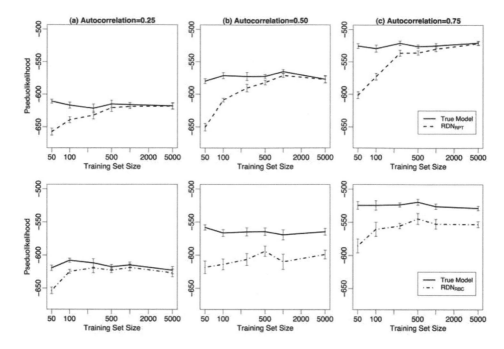

Figure 8.5 Evaluation of RDN learning.

maximize the pseudo-likelihood function. This indicates that the pseudo-likelihood function, evaluated at the learned parameters, will be no greater than the pseudo-likelihood of the true model (on average). To evaluate the quality of the RDN parameter estimates, we calculated the pseudo-likelihood of the testset data using both the true model (used to generate the data) and the learned models. If the pseudo-likelihood given the learned parameters approaches the pseudo-likelihood given the true parameters, then we can conclude that parameter estimation is successful. We also measured the standard error of the pseudo-likelihood estimate for a single test set using learned models from ten different training sets. This illustrates the amount of variance due to parameter estimation.

Figure 8.5 graphs the pseudo-loglikelihood of learned models as a function of training-set size for three levels of autocorrelation. Training-set size was varied at the levels $\{50, 100, 250, 500, 1000, 5000\}$. We varied $p(X_1 | \mathbf{X_1}_R, X_2)$ to generate data with approximate levels of autocorrelation corresponding to $\{0.25, 0.50, 0.75\}$. At each training set size (and autocorrelation level), we generated ten test sets. For each test set, we generated ten training sets and learned RDNs. Using each learned model, we measured the pseudo-likelihood of the test set (size 250) and averaged the results over the ten models.

Figure 8.5 plots the mean pseudo-likelihood of the test sets for both the learned models and the RDN used for data generation, which we refer to as *True Model*. The top row reports experiments with data generated from an RDN_{RPT}, where we learned RDN_{RPT} models. The bottom row reports experiments with data generated from an RDN_{RBC}, where we learned RDN_{RBC} models.

These experiments show that the learned RDN_{RPT} models are a good approximation to the true model by the time training-set size reaches 500, and that RDN learning is robust with respect to varying levels of autocorrelation. As expected, however, when training-set size is small, the RDNs are a better approximation for data sets with low levels of autocorrelation (see figure 8.5a).

There appears to be little difference between the RDN_{RPT} and RDN_{RBC} when autocorrelation is low, but otherwise the RDN_{RBC} needs significantly more data to estimate the parameters accurately. This may be in part due to the model's lack of selectivity, which necessitates the estimation of a greater number of parameters. However, there is little improvement even when we increase the size of the training sets to 10,000 objects. Furthermore, the discrepancy between the estimated model and the true model is greatest when autocorrelation is moderate. This indicates that the inaccuracies may be due to the naive Bayes independence assumption and its tendency to produce biased probability estimates [40].

8.4.1.2 RDN Inference

The second set of synthetic experiments evaluates the RDN inference procedure in a prediction context, where only a single attribute is unobserved in the test set. We generated data in the manner described above and learned RDNs for X_1. At each autocorrelation level, we generated ten training sets (size 500) and learned RDNs. For each training set, we generated ten test sets (size 250) and used the learned models to infer marginal probabilities for the class labels of the test-set instances. To evaluate the predictions, we report area under the ROC curve (AUC).[7] These experiments used the same levels of autocorrelation outlined above.

We compare the performance of three types of models. First, we measure the performance of RPT and RBC models. These are *conditional models* that reason about each instance independently and do not use the class labels of related instances. Next, we measure the performance of the two RDN models described above: RDN_{RBC} and RDN_{RPT}. These are *collective models* that reason about instances jointly, using the inferences about related instances to improve overall performance. Lastly, we measure performance of the two RDN models while allowing the true labels of related instances to be used during inference. This demonstrates the level of performance possible if the RDNs could infer the true labels of related instances with perfect accuracy. We refer to these as *ceiling models*: RDN_{RBC}^{ceil} and RDN_{RPT}^{ceil}.

Note that conditional models can reason about autocorrelation dependencies in a limited manner by using the attributes of related instances. For example, if there is a correlation between the words on a webpage and its topic, and the topics of hyperlinked webpages are autocorrelated, then we can improve the inference about

---

7. Squared-loss results are qualitatively similar to the AUC results reported in figure 8.6.

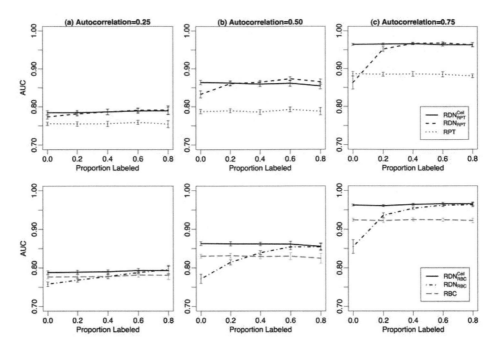

Figure 8.6   Evaluation of RDN inference.

a single page by modeling the contents of its neighboring pages. Recent work has shown that collective models are a low-variance means of reducing bias that work by modeling the autocorrelation dependencies directly [16]. Conditional models are also able to exploit autocorrelation dependencies through modeling the attributes of related instances, but variance increases dramatically as the number of attributes increases.

During inference we varied the number of known class labels in the test set, measuring performance on the remaining unlabeled instances. This serves to illustrate model performance as the amount of information seeding the inference process increases. We expect performance to be similar when other information seeds the inference process—for example, when some labels can be inferred from intrinsic attributes, or when weak predictions about many related instances serve to constrain the system. Figure 8.6 graphs AUC results for each of the models as the level of known class labels is varied.

In all configurations, RDN_{RPT} performance is equivalent, or better than, RPT performance. This indicates that even modest levels of autocorrelation can be exploited to improve predictions using RDN_{RPT} models. RDN_{RPT} performance is indistinguishable from that of RDN_{RPT}^{ceil} except when autocorrelation is high and there are no labels to seed inference. In this situation, there is little information to constrain the system during inference so the model cannot fully exploit the autocorrelation dependencies. When there is no information to anchor the predictions, there will be an identifiability problem—symmetric labelings that are highly au-

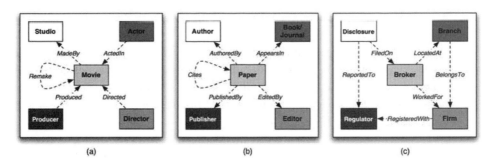

Figure 8.7 Data schema for (a) IMDb, (b) Cora, (c) NASD.

tocorrelated, but with opposite values, will be equally likely. In situations where there is little seed information, identifiability problems can bias RDN performance toward random.

In contrast, RDN_{RBC} performance is superior to RBC performance only when there is moderate to high autocorrelation and sufficient seed information. When autocorrelation is low, the RBC model is comparable to both the RDN_{RBC}^{ceil} and RDN_{RBC} models. Even when autocorrelation is moderate or high, RBC performance is still relatively high. Since the RBC model is low-variance and there are only four attributes in our data sets, it is not surprising that the RBC model is able to exploit autocorrelation to improve performance. What is more surprising is that RDN_{RBC} requires substantially more seed information than RDN_{RPT} in order to reach ceiling performance. This indicates that our choice of model should take test-set characteristics (e.g., number of known labels) into consideration.

8.4.2 Empirical Data Experiments

We learned RDN models for three real-world relational data sets to illustrate the types of domain knowledge that can be garnered, and evaluated the models in a prediction context, where the values of a single attribute are unobserved. Figure 8.7 depicts the objects and relations in each data set.

The first data set is drawn from the Internet Movie Database (IMDb: www.imdb.com). We collected a sample of 1382 movies released in the United States between 1996 and 2001, with their associated actors, directors, and studios. In total, this sample contains approximately 42,000 objects and 61,000 links.

The second data set is drawn from Cora, a database of computer science research papers extracted automatically from the web using machine learning techniques [25]. We selected the set of 4330 machine learning papers along with associated authors, cited papers, and journals. The resulting collection contains approximately 13,000 objects and 26,000 links. For classification, we sampled the 1669 papers published between 1993 and 1998.

The third data set is from the National Association of Securities Dealers (NASD) [33]. It is drawn from NASD's Central Registration Depository (CRD©) system, which contains data on approximately 3.4 million securities brokers, 360,000 branches, 25,000 firms, and 550,000 disclosure events. Disclosures record disciplinary information on brokers, including information on civil judicial actions, customer complaints, and termination actions. Our analysis was restricted to small and moderate-size firms with fewer than fifteen brokers, each of whom has an approved NASD registration. We selected a set of 10,000 brokers who were active in the years 1997-2001, along with 12,000 associated branches, firms, and disclosures.

8.4.2.1   RDN Models

The RDN models in figures 8.8, 8.9, and 8.10 continue with the RDN representation introduced in figure 8.1b. Each item type is represented by a separate plate. Arcs inside a plate represent dependencies among the attributes of a single object, and arcs crossing the boundaries of plates represent dependencies among attributes of related objects. An arc from x to y indicates the presence of one or more features of x in the conditional model learned for y. When the dependency is on attributes of objects more than a single link away, the arc is labeled with a small rectangle to indicate the intervening related-object type. For example, in figure 8.8 movie genre is influenced by the genres of other movies made by the movie's director, so the arc is labeled with a small D rectangle.

In addition to dependencies among attribute values, relational learners may also learn dependencies between the structure of relations (edges in G_D) and attribute values. *Degree* relationships are represented by a small black circle in the corner of each plate—arcs from this circle indicate a dependency between the number of related objects and an attribute value of an object. For example, in figure 8.8 movie receipts are influenced by the number of actors in the movie.

For each data set, we learned RDNs using queries that include all neighbors up to two links away in the data graph. For example in the IMDb, when learning a model of movie attributes we considered the attributes of associated actors, directors, producers, and studios, as well as movies related to those objects.

On the IMDb data, we learned an RDN model for ten discrete attributes including actor gender and movie opening weekend receipts ($> \$2$ million). Figure 8.8 shows the resulting RDN model. Four of the attributes—movie receipts, movie genre, actor birth year, and director first movie year—exhibit autocorrelation dependencies. Exploiting this type of dependency has been shown to significantly improve classification accuracy of RMNs compared to RBNs, which cannot model cyclic dependencies [39]. However, to exploit autocorrelation, RMNs must be instantiated with the appropriate clique templates—to date there is no RMN algorithm for *learning* autocorrelation dependencies. RDNs are the first PRM capable of learning cyclic autocorrelation dependencies.

On the Cora data, we learned an RDN model for seven attributes including paper topic (e.g., neural networks) and journal name prefix (e.g., IEEE). Figure 8.9

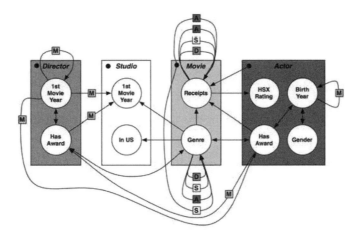

Figure 8.8   Internet Movie Database RDN.

shows the resulting RDN model. Again we see that four of the attributes exhibit autocorrelation. Note that when a dependency is on attributes of objects a single link away, the arc is unlabeled. For example, the unlabeled self-loops from paper variables indicates dependencies on the same variables in cited papers. In particular, the topic of a paper depends not only on the topics of other papers that it cites but also on the topics of other papers written by the authors. This model is a good reflection of our domain knowledge about machine learning papers.

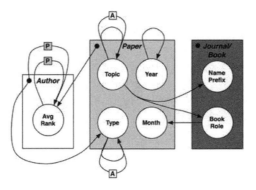

Figure 8.9   Cora machine learning papers RDN.

On the NASD data, we learned an RDN model for eleven attributes including broker is-problem and disclosure type (e.g., customer complaint). Figure 8.10 shows the resulting RDN model. Again we see that four of the attributes exhibit autocorrelation. Subjective inspection by NASD analysts indicates that the RDN has automatically uncovered statistical relationships that confirm the intuition of domain experts. These include temporal autocorrelation of risk (past problems are indicators of future problems) and relational autocorrelation of risk among brokers at the same branch—indeed, fraud and malfeasance are usually social phenomena, communicated and encouraged by the presence of other individuals who also wish to commit fraud [5]. Importantly, this evaluation was facilitated by the intrpretability of the RDN model—experts are more likely to trust, and make regular use of, models they can understand.

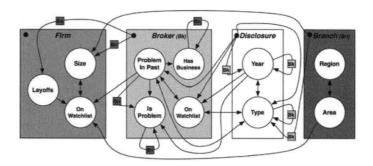

Figure 8.10   RDN for NASD data for 1999.

8.4.2.2   *Prediction*

We evaluated the learned models on prediction tasks in order to assess (1) whether autocorrelation dependencies among instances can be used to improve model accuracy, and (2) whether the RDN models, using Gibbs sampling, can effectively infer labels for a network of instances. To do this, we compared the same three classes of models used in section 8.4.1: RPTs and RBCs, RDNs, and ceiling RDNs.

Figure 8.11 shows AUC results for each of the models on the three prediction tasks. Figure 8.11a graphs the results of the RDN_{RPT} models, compared to the RPT conditional model. Figure 8.11b graphs the results of the RDN_{RBC} models, compared to the RBC conditional model. We used the following prediction tasks: movie receipts for IMDb, paper topic for Cora, and broker is-problem for NASD.

The graphs show the AUC for the most prevalent class, averaged over a number of training/test splits. We used temporal samples where we learned models on one year of data and applied the model to the subsequent year. We used two-tailed, paired t-tests to assess the significance of the AUC results obtained from the trials. The t-tests compare the RDN results to each of the other two models with a null hypothesis of no difference in the AUC.

When using the RPT as the conditional learner (figure 8.11(a), RDN performance is superior to RPT performance on all tasks. The difference is statistically significant for two of the three tasks. This indicates that autocorrelation is both present in the data and identified by the RDN models. The RPT can sometimes use attributes of related items to effectively represent and reason with autocorrelation dependencies.

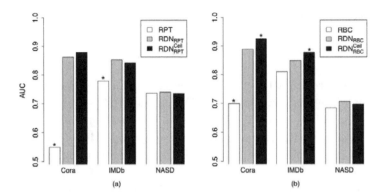

Figure 8.11 AUC results for (a) RDN_{RPT} and RPT models, and (b) RDN_{RBC} and RBC models. Asterisks denote model performance that is significantly different ($p < 0.10$) from RDN_{RPT} and RDN_{RBC}.

However, in some cases the attributes other than the class label contain little information about the class labels of related instances. This is the case for Cora— RPT performance is close to random because no other attributes influence paper topic (see figure 8.9). On all tasks, the RDN models achieve comparable performance to the ceiling models. This indicates that the RDN model achieved the same level of performance as if it had access to the true labels of related objects. On the NASD data, the RDN performance is slightly higher than that of the ceiling model. We note, however, that the ceiling model only represents a probabilistic ceiling— the RDN may perform better if an incorrect prediction for one object improves inferences about related objects.

Similarly, when using the RBC as the conditional learner (Figure 8.11(b)), the performance of RDN models is superior to the RBC models on all tasks and statistically significant for two of the tasks. However, the RDN models achieve comparable performance to the ceiling models on only one of the tasks. This may be another indication that RDN models combined with a non-selective conditional learner (e.g., RBCs) will experience increased variance during the Gibbs sampling process, and thus they may need more seed information during inference to achieve the near-ceiling performance. We should note that although the RDN_{RBC} models do not significantly outperform the RDN_{RPT} models on any of the tasks, the RDN_{RBC}^{Ceil} is significantly higher than RDN_{RPT}^{Ceil} for Cora and IMDb. This indicates that, when there is enough seed information, RDN_{RBC} models may achieve significant performance gains over RDN_{RPT} models.

8.5   Related Work

8.5.1   Probabilistic Relational Models

Probabilistic relational models are one class of models for density estimation in relational data sets. Examples of PRMs include RBNs and RMNs.

As outlined in section 8.3.1, learning and inference in PRMs involve a *data graph* G_D, a *model graph* G_M, and an *inference graph* G_I. All PRMs model data that can be represented as a graph (i.e., G_D). PRMs use different approximation techniques for inference in G_I (e.g., Gibbs sampling, loopy belief propagation [26]), but they all use a similar process for rolling out an inference graph G_I. Consequently, PRMs differ primarily with respect to the representation of the model graph G_M and how that model is learned.

The RBN learning algorithm [10] for the most part uses standard Bayesian network techniques for parameter estimation and structure learning. One notable exception is that the learning algorithm must check for "legal" structures that are guaranteed to be acyclic when rolled out for inference on arbitrary data graphs. In addition, instead of exhaustive search of the space of relational dependencies, the structure learning algorithm uses greedy iterative-deepening, expanding the search in directions where the dependencies improve the likelihood.

The strengths of RBNs include understandable knowledge representations and efficient learning techniques. For relational tasks, with a huge space of possible dependencies, *selective* models are easier to interpret and understand than *non-selective* models. Closed-form parameter estimation techniques allow for efficient structure learning (i.e., feature selection). Also because reasoning with relational models requires more space and computational resources, efficient learning techniques make relational modeling both practical and feasible.

The directed acyclic graph structure is the underlying reason for the efficiency of RBN learning. As discussed in section 8.1, the acyclicity requirement precludes the learning of arbitrary autocorrelation dependencies and limits the applicability of these models in relational domains. RDN models enjoy the strengths of RBNs (namely, understandable knowledge representation and efficient learning) without being constrained by an acyclicity requirement.

The RMN learning algorithm [39] uses maximum a posteriori parameter estimation with Gaussian priors, modifying Markov network learning techniques. The algorithm assumes that the clique templates are prespecified and thus does not search for the best structure. Because the user supplies a set of relational dependencies to consider (i.e., clique templates), it simply optimizes the potential functions for the specified templates.

RMNs are not hampered by an acyclicity constraint, so they can represent and reason with arbitrary forms of autocorrelation. This is particularly important for reasoning in relational data sets where autocorrelation dependencies are nearly ubiquitous and often cannot be structured in an acyclic manner. However, the tradeoff for this increased representational capability is a decrease in learning efficiency. Instead of closed form parameter estimation, RMNs are trained with conjugate gradient methods, where each iteration requires a round of inference. In large cyclic relational inference graphs, the cost of inference is prohibitively expensive—in particular, without approximations to increase efficiency, feature selection is intractable.

Similar to the comparison with RBNs, RDN models enjoy the strengths of RMNs but not their weaknesses. More specifically, RDNs are able to reason with arbitrary forms of autocorrelation without being limited by efficiency concerns during learning. In fact, the pseudo-likelihood estimation technique used by RDNs has been used recently to make feature selection tractable for conditional random field models [24].

8.5.2 Probabilistic Logic Models

A second class of models for density estimation consists of extensions to conventional logic programming that support probabilistic reasoning in first-order logic environments. We will refer to this class of models as *probabilistic logic models* (PLMs). Examples of PLMs include Bayesian logic programs [18] and Markov logic networks (MLNs) [36].

PLMs represent a joint probability distribution over the groundings of a first-order knowledge base. The first-order knowledge base contains a set of first-order formulae, and the PLM model associates a set of weights/probabilities with each of the formulae. Combined with a set of constants representing objects in the domain, PLM models specify a probability distribution over possible truth assignments to groundings of the first-order formulae. Learning a PLM consists of two tasks: generating the relevant first-order clauses, and estimating the weights/probabilities associated with each clause.

Within this class of models, MLNs are most similar in nature to RDNs. In MLNs, each node is a grounding of a predicate in a first-order knowledge base, and features correspond to first-order formulae and their truth-values. Learning an MLN consists of estimating the feature weights and selecting which features to include in the final structure. The input knowledge base defines the relevant relational neighborhood, and the algorithm restricts the search by limiting the number of distinct variables in a clause, using a weighted pseudo-likelihood scoring function for feature selection [19].

MLNs ground out to undirected Markov networks. In this sense, they are quite similar to RMNs, sharing the same strengths and weaknesses—they are capable of representing cyclic autocorrelation relationships but suffer from the complexity of full joint inference during learning, which decreases efficiency. Kok and Domingos [19] have recently demonstrated the promise of efficient pseudo-likelihood structure learning techniques. Our future work will investigate the performance tradeoffs between RDN and MLN approaches to pseudo-likelihood estimation for learning.

8.5.3   Collective Inference

Collective inference models exploit autocorrelation dependencies in a network of objects to improve predictions. Joint relational models, such as those discussed above, are able to exploit autocorrelation to improve predictions by estimating joint probability distributions over the entire graph and collectively inferring the labels of related instances.

An alternative approach to collective inference combines local individual classification models (e.g., RBCs) with a joint inference procedure (e.g., relaxation labeling). Examples of this technique include iterative classification [30], link-based classification [21], and probabilistic relational neighbor [22, 23]. These approaches to collective inference were developed in an ad hoc procedural fashion, motivated by the observation that they appear to work well in practice. RDN models formalize this approach in a principled framework—learning models locally (maximizing psuedolikelihood) and combining them with a global inference procedure (Gibbs sampling) to recover a full joint distribution. In this work we have demonstrated that autocorrelation is the reason behind improved performance in collective inference (see [16] for more detail) and explored the situations under which we can expect this type of approximation to perform well.

8.6   Discussion and Future Work

In this chapter we presented relational dependency networks, a new form of probabilistic relational model. We showed the RDN learning algorithm to be a relatively simple method for learning the structure and parameters of a probabilistic graphical model. In addition, RDNs allow us to exploit existing techniques for learning CPDs of relational data sets. Here we have chosen to exploit our prior work on RPTs, which construct parsimonious models of relational data, and RBCs, which are simple and surprisingly effective non-selective models. We expect the general properties of RDNs to be retained if other approaches to learning CPDs are used, given that those approaches learn accurate local models.

The primary advantage of RDN models is the ability to efficiently learn and reason with autocorrelation. Autocorrelation is a nearly ubiquitous phenomenon in relational data sets and the dependencies are often cyclic in nature. If a data set exhibits autocorrelation, and a model can learn the resulting dependencies, then we can exploit those dependencies to improve overall inferences by collectively inferring values for the entire set of instances simultaneously. The real and synthetic data experiments in this chapter show that collective inference with RDNs can offer significant improvement over conditional approaches when autocorrelation is present in the data. Except in rare cases, the performance of RDNs approaches the performance that would be possible if all the class labels of related instances were known. Because our analysis indicates that the amount of seed information may interact with the level of autocorrelation and local model characteristics to impact performance, future work will attempt to quantify these effects more formally.

We also presented learned RDNs for a number of real-world relational domains, demonstrating another strength of RDNs—their understandable and intuitive knowledge representation. Comprehensible models are a cornerstone of the knowledge discovery process, which seeks to identify novel and interesting patterns in large data sets. Domain experts are more willing to trust, and make regular use of, understandable models—particularly when the induced models are used to support additional reasoning. Understandable models also aid analysts' assessment of the utility of the additional relational information, potentially reducing the cost of information gathering and storage and the need for data transfer among organizations—increasing the practicality and feasibility of relational modeling.

Future work will compare RDN models to RMNs and MLNs in order to quantify the performance tradeoffs for using pseudo-likelihood functions rather than full likelihood functions for both parameter estimation and structure learning, particularly over data sets with varying levels of autocorrelation. Based on theoretical analysis of pseudo-likelihood estimation ([e.g., 9]), we expect there to be little difference when autocorrelation is low and increased variance when autocorrelation is high. If this is the case, there will need to be enough training data to withstand the increase in variance. Alternatively, bagging techniques may be a means of reducing variance with only a moderate increase in computational cost. In either case, the simplicity and relative efficiency of RDN methods are a clear win for learning models in relational domains.

Acknowledgments

We acknowledge the invaluable assistance of A. Shapira, and helpful comments from C. Loiselle. This effort is supported by DARPA and NSF under contract numbers IIS0326249 and HR0011-04-1-0013. The U.S. Government is authorized to reproduce and distribute reprints for governmental purposes notwithstanding any copyright notation hereon. The views and conclusions contained herein are those of the authors and should not be interpreted as necessarily representing the official policies or endorsements either expressed or implied of DARPA, NSF, or the U.S. Government.

References

[1]   A. Bernstein, S. Clearwater, and F. Provost. The relational vector-space model and industry classification. In *Proceedings of the IJCAI-2003 Workshop on Learning Statistical Models from Relational Data*, 2003.

[2]   J. Besag. Statistical analysis of non-lattice data. *The Statistician*, 24:3:179–195, 1975.

[3]   H. Blau, N. Immerman, and D. Jensen. A visual query language for relational knowledge discovery. Technical Report 01-28, University of Massachusetts Amherst, Computer Science Department, 2001.

[4]   S. Chakrabarti, B. Dom, and P. Indyk. Enhanced hypertext categorization using hyperlinks. In *Proceedings of ACM International Conference on Management of Data*, 1998.

[5]   C. Cortes, D. Pregibon, and C. Volinsky. Communities of interest. In *Proceedings of the International Symposium of Intelligent Data Analysis*, 2001.

[6]   P. Domingos and M. Richardson. Mining the network value of customers. In *International Conference on Knowledge Discovery and Data Mining*, 2001.

[7]   P. Flach and N. Lachiche. 1BC: A first-order Bayesian classifier. In *Proceedings of the International Conference on Inductive Logic Programming*, 1999.

[8]   N. Friedman, L. Getoor, D. Koller, and A. Pfeffer. Learning probabilistic relational models. In *Proceedings of the International Joint Conference on Artificial Intelligence*, 1999.

[9]   S. Geman and C. Graffine. Markov random field image models and their applications to computer vision. In *Proceedings of the International Congress of Mathematicians*, 1987.

[10]   L. Getoor, N. Friedman, D. Koller, and A. Pfeffer. Learning probabilistic relational models. In *Relational Data Mining*, pages 307–335. Springer-Verlag, 2001.

[11]   D. Heckerman, D. Chickering, C. Meek, R. Rounthwaite, and C. Kadie. Dependency networks for inference, collaborative filtering and data visualization. *Journal of Machine Learning Research*, 1:49–75, 2000.

[12]   D. Heckerman, C. Meek, and D. Koller. Probabilistic models for relational data. Technical Report MSR-TR-2004-30, Microsoft Research, 2004.

[13]   M. Jaeger. Relational Bayesian networks. In *Proceedings of the Conference on Uncertainty in Artificial Intelligence*, 1997.

[14]   D. Jensen and J. Neville. Linkage and autocorrelation cause feature selection bias in relational learning. In *Proceedings of the International Conference on Machine Learning*, 2002.

[15]   D. Jensen and J. Neville. Avoiding bias when aggregating relational data with degree disparity. In *Proceedings of the International Conference on Machine Learning*, 2003.

[16]   D. Jensen, J. Neville, and B. Gallagher. Why collective inference improves relational classification. In *International Conference on Knowledge Discovery and Data Mining*, 2004.

[17] K. Kersting. Representational power of probabilistic-logical models: From upgrading to downgrading. In *IJCAI-2003 Workshop on Learning Statistical Models from Relational Data*, 2003.

[18] K. Kersting and L. De Raedt. Basic principles of learning Bayesian logic programs. Technical Report 174, Institute for Computer Science, University of Freiburg, 2002.

[19] S. Kok and P. Domingos. Learning the structure of Markov logic networks. In *Proceedings of the International Conference on Machine Learning*, 2005.

[20] S. Lauritzen and N. Sheehan. Graphical models for genetic analyses. *Statistical Science*, 18:4:489–514, 2003.

[21] Q. Lu and L. Getoor. Link-based classification. In *Proceedings of the International Conference on Machine Learning*, 2003.

[22] S. Macskassy and F. Provost. A simple relational classifier. In *Proceedings of the 2nd Workshop on Multi-Relational Data Mining, KDD2003*, 2003.

[23] S. Macskassy and F. Provost. Classification in networked data: A toolkit and a univariate case study. Technical Report CeDER-04-08, Stern School of Business, New York University, 2004.

[24] A. McCallum. Efficiently inducing features of conditional random fields. In *Proceedings of the Conference on Uncertainty in Artificial Intelligence*, 2003.

[25] A. McCallum, K. Nigam, J. Rennie, and K. Seymore. A machine learning approach to building domain-specific search engines. In *Proceedings of the International Joint Conference on Artificial Intelligence*, 1999.

[26] K. Murphy, Y. Weiss, and M. Jordan. Loopy belief propagation for approximate inference: An empirical study. In *Proceedings of the Conference on Uncertainty in Artificial Intelligence*, 1999.

[27] R. Neal. Probabilistic inference using Markov chain Monte Carlo methods. Technical Report CRG-TR-93-1, Dept of Computer Science, University of Toronto, 1993.

[28] J. Neville and D. Jensen. Supporting relational knowledge discovery: Lessons in architecture and algorithm design. In *Proceedings of the Data Mining Lessons Learned Workshop, ICML2002*, 2002.

[29] J. Neville and D. Jensen. Collective classification with relational dependency networks. In *Proceedings of the Multi-Relational Data Mining Workshop, KDD2003*, 2003.

[30] J. Neville and D. Jensen. Iterative classification in relational data. In *AAAI-2000 Workshop on Learning Statistical Models from Relational Data*, 2000.

[31] J. Neville, D. Jensen, L. Friedland, and M. Hay. Learning relational probability trees. In *International Conference on Knowledge Discovery and Data Mining*, 2003.

[32]   J. Neville, D. Jensen, and B. Gallagher. Simple estimators for relational Bayesian classifers. In *Proceedings of the IEEE International Conference on Data Mining*, 2003.

[33]   J. Neville, O. Şimşek, D. Jensen, J. Komoroske, K. Palmer, and H. Goldberg. Using relational knowledge discovery to prevent securities fraud. In *International Conference on Knowledge Discovery and Data Mining*, 2005.

[34]   C. Perlich and F. Provost. Aggregation-based feature invention and relational concept classes. In *International Conference on Knowledge Discovery and Data Mining*, 2003.

[35]   A. Popescul, L. Ungar, S. Lawrence, and D. Pennock. Statistical relational learning for document mining. In *Proceedings of the IEEE International Conference on Data Mining*, 2003.

[36]   M. Richardson and P. Domingos. Markov logic networks. *Machine Learning Journal*, 62:107–136, 2006.

[37]   S. Sanghai, P. Domingos, and D. Weld. Dynamic probabilistic relational models. In *Proceedings of the International Joint Conference on Artificial Intelligence*, 2003.

[38]   B. Taskar, E. Segal, and D. Koller. Probabilistic classification and clustering in relational data. In *Proceedings of the International Joint Conference on Artificial Intelligence*, 2001.

[39]   B. Taskar, P. Abbeel, and D. Koller. Discriminative probabilistic models for relational data. In *Proceedings of the Conference on Uncertainty in Artificial Intelligence*, 2002.

[40]   B. Zadrozny and C. Elkan. Obtaining calibrated probability estimates from decision trees and naive Bayesian classifiers. In *Proceedings of the International Conference on Machine Learning*, 2001.

9 Logic-based Formalisms for Statistical Relational Learning

James Cussens

This chapter provides a selective overview of logic-based approaches to statistical relational learning. Issues of representation, inference, and learning are addressed with an emphasis on representation. A distinction is drawn between "directed" representations with connections to Bayesian nets and "undirected" ones related to Markov nets. Within directed representations a further distinction is made between using conditional probabilities and using logical rules to define probability distributions. Among the formalisms discussed are: the independent choice logic, probabilistic logic programming, and stochastic logic programs. The PRISM system is used to provide concrete examples of probabilistic inference and parameter estimation. The use of "possible worlds" to provide semantics is described and its role in connecting differing formalisms is analyzed.

9.1 Introduction

This chapter provides a high-level and selective overview of formalisms which incorporate both logic and probability. Naturally, the focus is on those formalisms which fall within the ambit of statistical relational learning (SRL) or which have influenced formalisms used for SRL. Learning (in the AI sense) is the central topic of this book, but in order to understand existing and potential learning algorithms for the formalisms discussed, it is necessary to understand what is represented by each formalism: we need to know what is to be learned before examining how to do the learning. Consequently, in this chapter there is a strong focus on issues of representation.

It is worth stating some important questions concerning logic and probability which will *not* be addressed here. First, "logic" in the general nontechnical sense of a method of rational reasoning includes probabilistic reasoning quite naturally since humans are required to reason in uncertain situations. Thus two of the historically most influential logic books include sections on probabilistic reasoning as a matter of course. The books concerned are the *Port-Royal Logic* [2] and *An Investigation of the Laws of Thought, on which are founded the Mathematical Theories of Logic and Probabilities* [4]. Here, however, we are not concerned with general issues in probabilistic reasoning, (dealing with conflicting evidence, probability kinematics, relations with other uncertainty calculi, etc). Instead both probability and logic will be treated as formalisms, i.e., in the narrow technical sense.

Secondly, there is a well-developed *logical interpretation of probability* found in the philosophical literature. The best-known advocates of this interpretation are Keynes [23] and Carnap [5]. The basic claim of this interpretation is that for *any* two propositions a and b there is an objective, logical relation of partial entailment between a and b which is measured by a unique conditional probability $P(b|a)$. See Howson and Urbach [18] for further details. This interpretation uses versions of the principle of indifference to "logically" infer such probability values. This approach is rejected in all the formalisms to be discussed: either the user defines probabilities or the probabilities are estimated from data. Whether these are the "right" probabilities is of no concern to the formalism.

9.1.1   Possible World Semantics

Although logic-based SRL formalisms reject Carnap's attempt to use logic to *determine* probabilities, his use of *possible worlds* to provide semantics for probabilistic statements is widely followed. Recall that to interpret terms and formulae of a (standard, nonprobabilistic) first-order language $\mathcal{L}$ it is necessary to consider $\mathcal{L}$-structures, also known as $\mathcal{L}$-interpretations, or more poetically, possible worlds. An $\mathcal{L}$-structure is a set (the *domain*) together with functions and relations. Each function (resp. predicate) symbol in the language has a corresponding function (resp. relation) on the domain. Standard (Tarskian) first-order semantics defines when a particular $\mathcal{L}$-formula is true in a particular $\mathcal{L}$-structure. For example, the formula *flies(tweety)* is true in a given $\mathcal{L}$-structure iff the individual which the constant *tweety* denotes is an element of the set which the predicate symbol *flies* denotes.

To explain possible world semantics for probabilistic statements we will follow the account of Halpern [17]. Using Halpern's notation, the probability that *flies(tweety)* is true is denoted by the term $w(flies(tweety))$.[1] The proposition that this probability is 0.8 is represented by the formula $w(flies(tweety)) = 0.8$.

As Halpern notes, it is not useful to ask whether a probabilistic statement such as $w(flies(tweety)) = 0.8$ is true in some particular $\mathcal{L}$-structure. In any given $\mathcal{L}$-structure, *tweety* either flies or does not. Instead we have to ask whether a *probability distribution over $\mathcal{L}$-structures* satisfies $w(flies(tweety)) = 0.8$ or not. A rigorous

---

1. Note on terminology: Throughout the rest of this chapter the term "the probability of F" (where F is a first-order formula) will be used as an abbreviation for "the probability that F is true."

account of how to answer this question is given by Halpern [17] but the basic idea is simple: a probability distribution μ over $\mathcal{L}$-structures—possible worlds—satisfies $w(flies(tweety)) = 0.8$ iff the set of worlds in which $flies(tweety)$ is true has probability 0.8 according to μ. Note that this means that $w(flies(tweety))$ is a *marginal* probability since it can be computed by summing over possible-world probabilities.

9.2 Representation

Probability-logic formalisms take one of two routes to defining probabilities. In the *directed* approach there is a nonempty set of formulae all of whose probabilities are explicitly stated: call these *probabilistic facts*, similarly to Sato [39]. Other probabilities are defined recursively with the probabilistic facts acting as base cases. A probability-logic model using the directed approach will be closely related to a recursive graphical model (Bayesian net). Most probability-logic formalisms fall into this category: for example, *probabilistic logic programming (PLP)* [30]; *probabilistic Horn abduction (PHA)* [36] and its later expansion the *independent choice logic (ICL)* [37]; *probabilistic knowledge bases (PKBs)* [31]; *Bayesian logic programs (BLPs)* (see chapter 10); *relational Bayesian networks (RBNs)* [20]; *stochastic logic programs (SLPs)* (see chapter 11) and the *PRISM* system [40].

The second, less common, approach is *undirected*, where no formula has its probability explicitly stated. *Relational Markov networks (RMNs)* (see chapter 6 and *Markov logic networks (MLNs)* (see chapter 12) are examples of this approach. In the undirected approach, the probability of each possible world is defined in terms of its "features," where each feature has an associated real-valued parameter. For example, in the case of MLN each feature is associated with a first-order formula: the value of the feature for a given world is simply the number of true ground instances of the formula in that world. Such approaches have much in common with undirected probabilistic models such as Markov networks. For example, to compute (perhaps conditional) probabilities of individual formulae, inference techniques from Markov networks can be used. See chapters 5 and 12, for further details.

9.2.1 Defining Random Variables Using Logic

Here we will focus on formalisms using the more common directed approach. The most basic requirement of such formalisms is to explicitly state that a given ground atomic formula has some probability of being true: a statement such as $w(flies(tweety)) = 0.8$ should be expressible. This is indeed the case for PLP, PHA/ICL, PKB, and PRISM. In all these cases, possible worlds semantics are explicitly invoked.

From a statistical point of view, asserting that $w(flies(tweety)) = 0.8$ amounts to viewing $flies(tweety)$ as a binary variable taking the values TRUE and FALSE. In many applications a restriction to binary variables would be be very inconvenient so a number of formalisms have machinery to allow a logical representation of random variables with n values for arbitrary finite n. For each such random variable this is done by stating that a set of n atomic formulae are mutually exclusive and exhaustive. Call such sets *alternatives* and call the determination of which formula is true in an alternative an *atomic choice*, following Poole [37]. In each possible world exactly one atomic choice is true. This approach is taken in PHA/ICL, PKB, and PRISM, and a similar one is used in PKB. Indeed, in these formalisms, alternatives are used even in the binary case, thus allowing a uniform logical representation of binary and nonbinary random variables. Rather than stating that $w(flies(tweety)) = 0.8$ we can write $w(flies(tweety, yes)) = 0.8$ and $w(flies(tweety, no)) = 0.2$, and state that $\{flies(tweety, yes), flies(tweety, no)\}$ is an alternative.

The PRISM system restricts the syntactic form of alternatives quite drastically as part of its *distribution condition* [40]. Each alternative is a set of atomic formulae of the form

$$\{msw(x, i, v_1), msw(x, i, v_2), \ldots, msw(x, i, v_m)\};$$

where x and i are the *switch name* and *trial-id* respectively, and msw is short for *mult-ary random switch*.[2] Translating to the language of random variables, $msw(x, i, v_j)$ is true in a world iff in that world the variable X_i takes the value v_j. For different trial-ids i, the random variables X_i are required to be i.i.d.

This restriction seems drastic, but since switch names can be structured logical terms, *in practice* no representational power is lost. Returning to tweety we could have the alternative

$$\{msw(flies(tweety), 1, yes), msw(flies(tweety), 1, no)\};$$

where the trial-id is effectively redundant, and now *flies* is a function symbol rather than a predicate symbol.

Since the distribution over values does not depend on the trial-id, this second argument is not present in actual PRISM code—it is implicit. Figure 9.1 gives the PRISM code for defining our tweety alternative. This code actually states that $\forall i \in \mathcal{N} : w(msw(flies(tweety), i, yes)) = 0.8 \land w(msw(flies(tweety), i, no)) = 0.2$, although for our example only $i = 1$ is needed.

```
values(flies(tweety),[yes,no]).
:- set_sw(flies(tweety),0.8+0.2).
```

Figure 9.1   PRISM code for tweety.

---

2. I have altered the notation slightly from that found in [40].

9.2.2 Using Logical Variables

Even at the rudimentary level of defining probabilities for atomic formulae some of the power of first-order methods is apparent. The basic point is that by using variables we can define probabilities for whole families of related atomic formulae. To take an example from Ngo and Haddaway [31], the PKB formula

$$P(nbrhd(X, bad)) = 0.3 \leftarrow in\_CALI(X)$$

makes up part of the definition of the distribution of random variables $nbrhd(X)$ for those X where $in\_CALI(X)$ is true. Informally, the formula says: "For those in California, there is probability 0.3 of living in a bad neighborhood." The formula $in\_CALI(X)$ is known as a *context literal*. Asserting that a context literal is true amounts to stating that it is true in all possible worlds, or equivalently, restricting the set of possible worlds under consideration to those where it is true. Thus the preceding formula can be translated into Halpern's syntax as

$$\forall x : w(nbrhd(x, bad)) = 0.3 \leftarrow w(in\_CALI(x)) = 1.$$

If, for example, we had that $w(in\_CALI(bob)) = 1$, meaning "it is certain that Bob lives in California," then it immediately follows that $w(nbrnd(bob, bad)) = 0.3$, meaning "Bob lives in a bad neighborhood with probability 0.3."

Such a mixture of probabilistic literals (i.e., $Pr(nbrnd(X, bad))$) and nonprobabilistic literals (i.e., $in\_CALI(X)$), where the latter states what is true in all worlds, is common. In PLP [30], stating what is true in all worlds is made explicit. The above formula would be written

$$nbrhd(X, bad) : [0.3, 0.3] \leftarrow in\_CALI(X) : [1, 1]$$

and would have the same informal intended meaning. As this example indicates, in PLP probability *intervals* are represented. To show the sort of formulae that can be expressed in PLP and what they mean, tables 9.1, 9.2 and 9.3 show three example PLP formulae, their informal meaning, and their representation in Halpern's notation, respectively.[3]

Table 9.1 PLP formulae

1.	$eastbound(train1) : [0.7, 0.9]$	$\leftarrow$	
2.	$bark(X) : [0.95, 1]$	$\leftarrow$	$dog(X) : [1, 1]$
3.	$not\_dog(X) : [1 - V_2, 1 - V_1]$	$\leftarrow$	$dog(X) : [V_1, V_2]$

---

3. Some of this material is taken from Cussens [6].

Table 9.2   Informal meanings for the PLP formulae in table 9.1

1.   The probability that train1 is eastbound is between 0.7 and 0.9.
2.   All dogs have a probability at least 0.95 of barking.
3.   If the probability that something is a dog lies between V_1 and V_2, then the probability that it is not a dog lies between $1 - V_2$ and $1 - V_1$.

Table 9.3   The PLP formulae in table 9.1 in Halpern's notation

1. $\qquad\qquad w(eastbound(train1)) \in [0.7, 0.9]$
2. $\qquad\qquad\quad \forall x : w(bark(x)) \in [0.95, 1] \quad \leftarrow \quad w(dog(x)) = 1$
3. $\quad \forall x, v_1, v_2 : not\_dog(x) \in [1 - v_2, 1 - v_1] \quad \leftarrow \quad w(dog(x)) \in [v_1, v_2]$

9.2.3   Logical Implication versus Conditional Probabilities

So far we have been looking mainly at formulae which directly define probabilities for atomic formulae. Directly stating all probabilities of interest is too restrictive and so formalisms provide mechanisms for defining probabilities which must be inferred rather than just "looked up."

For directed approaches, there are two basic ways in which this is done: using conditional probabilities and using logical rules. PKB [31], for example, focuses on the former approach allowing formulae such as

$$P(bglry(X, yes)|nbd(X, bad)) = 0.6 \leftarrow in\_CALI(X), \tag{9.1}$$

which corresponds to this statement in Halpern's notation:

$$\forall x : [w(bglry(x, yes) \wedge nbd(x, bad)) = 0.6 \times w(nbd(x, bad)) \leftarrow w(in\_CALI(x)) = 1],$$

which can be written in disjunctive form:

$$\forall x : [w(bglry(x, yes) \wedge nbd(x, bad)) = 0.6 \times w(nbd(x, bad)) \vee w(in\_CALI(x)) \neq 1]. \tag{9.2}$$

(All these formulae informally mean "For those living in California, the probability of being burgled if they live in a bad neighborhood is 0.6.") This approach implicitly defines a (possibly huge) Bayesian network (the *ground network*) where each node corresponds to a ground atomic formula. The conditional probability tables (CPTs) in the ground network are often defined with the help of combining rules such as noisy-or. The full ground network is never actually constructed. Instead only just enough of it is constructed to answer any given probabilistic query. This is a technique known as *knowledge-based model construction (KBMC)*.

The alternative approach is to use logical rules: statements of what is true in all worlds. But this raises a problem. From

$$w(flies(tweety)) = 0.8 \tag{9.3}$$

and the statement that $\forall x : happy(x) \leftarrow flies(x)$ is true in all worlds:

$$w(\forall x : happy(x) \leftarrow flies(x)) = 1, \tag{9.4}$$

we get not $w(happy(tweety)) = 0.8$ but merely $w(happy(tweety)) \geq 0.8$ (since *tweety* may be happy "for other reasons"). No specific probability is determined for $happy(tweety)$. There are two attitudes to this problem. The first is just to live with having mere bounds on probabilities. This is the approach taken by Boole [4] and Ng and Subrahmanian [30] and, using a propositional approach, Nilsson [32]. The second method is to invoke a version of the closed-world assumption (CWA), so that (9.4) is interpreted to mean

$$w(\forall x : happy(x) \leftrightarrow flies(x)) = 1$$

from which, together with (9.3), $w(happy(tweety)) = 0.8$ *does* follow. The CWA approach is taken in PHA/ICL [36, 37] and PRISM [40]. In both these formalisms there is a strict separation between the probabilistic facts—like $flies(tweety)$— whose probabilities are explicitly given, and formulae like $happy(tweety)$ whose probabilities have to be inferred from the probabilistic facts, the rules, and the CWA. This separation is achieved by syntactic restrictions on the rules so that no probabilistic fact can be inferred using the rules. The rules basically extend the distribution defined over the facts to the other atomic formulae. As Sato puts it:

> When a joint distribution P_F is given to a set F of facts in a logic program $DB = F \cup R$ where R is a set of rules, we can further extend it to a joint distribution P_{DB} over the set of least models of DB [39].

Further details on this point, and on the relation between PHA/ICL, PRISM, and SLPs are given by Cussens [9]. Two further points are worth mentioning. First, it is possible to combine conditional probability and rule-based methods, as shown by (9.1). In such cases it is important to distinguish between formulae in the antecedent of a rule and those in the conditional part of a conditional probability. For example, if in formula (9.1) we move the antecedent literal into the conditional part of the probability we get

$$P(bglry(X, yes)|nbd(X, bad), in\_CALI(X)) = 0.6, \tag{9.5}$$

which in Halpern's notation is

$$\begin{aligned}
\forall x : [\quad &w(bglry(x, yes) \wedge nbd(x, bad) \wedge in\_CALI(x)) = \\
&0.6 \times w(nbd(x, bad) \wedge in\_CALI(x)) \quad].
\end{aligned} \tag{9.6}$$

This results in a strictly stronger formula: (9.2) only impacts on those known to be Californians, whereas (9.6) states a conditional probability that applies to all individuals. Formally, (9.6) $\models$ (9.2) but (9.2) $\not\models$ (9.6). To see this abbreviate (9.6) to $\forall x : [p(x)]$ and (9.2) to $\forall x : [q(x) \lor w(in\_CALI(x)) \neq 1]$, then

$$
\begin{aligned}
(9.6) \quad &\equiv \quad \forall x : [\quad p(x) \quad & &] \\
&\Leftrightarrow \quad \forall x : [\quad p(x) \land (w(in\_CALI(x)) = 1 \quad & \lor \quad w(in\_CALI(x)) \neq 1) \quad &] \\
&\Leftrightarrow \quad \forall x : [\quad (p(x) \land w(in\_CALI(x)) = 1) \quad & \lor \quad (p(x) \land w(in\_CALI(x)) \neq 1) \quad &] \\
&\Leftrightarrow \quad \forall x : [\quad q(x) \quad & \lor \quad (p(x) \land w(in\_CALI(x)) \neq 1) \quad &] \\
&\Rightarrow \quad \forall x : [\quad q(x) \quad & \lor \quad w(in\_CALI(x)) \neq 1 \quad &] \\
&\equiv \quad (9.2)
\end{aligned}
$$

$$(9.7)$$

Secondly, although the connection to Bayesian networks is more direct when using conditional probabilities, it is also straightforward to encode Bayesian networks using the rule-based approach [36], since both cases share an underlying directedness.

9.2.4   Defining Joint Distributions

So far we have considered probabilities on the truth values of atomic formulae only. It is necessary to go further and have a mechanism for defining probabilities on (at least) conjunctions of atomic formulae. This defines the *joint* distribution over the truth values of atomic formulae. If each possible world has a conjunction that it alone satisfies, this will give us a complete distribution over possible worlds.

One approach is to assume independence in all cases where this is possible, an approach going back to Boole:

> The events whose probabilities are given are to be regarded as independent of any connexion but such as is either expressed, or necessarily implied, in the data ... ([4], pp. 256-7.)

Where alternatives (in the Poole sense) are used, it is clear that the atomic formulae in any given alternative are highly *dependent*. Equally, those formulae on either side of an implication must be dependent. However, we are at liberty to assume that formulae from different alternatives are independent and this is what is done in PHA/ICL and PRISM; indeed this is why the independent choice logic is so called. Note that this is only possible because these formalisms disallow "inferred probabilities," like *happy(tweety)*, from appearing in alternatives.

When a formalism (implicitly) defines a Bayesian network whose nodes are ground atomic formulae, then the probability of any conjunction is just the probability of the relevant joint instantiation of the Bayesian net in the normal way. A quite different way of combining Bayesian networks with logic is provided by *relational Bayesian networks* [20]. Each node in an RBN corresponds to a *relation*[4] instead of to an atomic formula. The possible values for a relation r are the possi-

---

4. This includes monadic relations such as *flies*.

ble interpretations of r. An interpretation for a relation r is a set of "true" ground atomic formulae with r as the predicate symbol: something that varies across possible worlds. For example, in one possible world the relation *mother* might have the interpretation

$$\{mother(gill, rob), mother(gill, jane), mother(dot, james)\},$$

whereas in another it might be

$$\{mother(gill, rob), mother(gill, jane), mother(alison, gill)\}.$$

Any joint instantiation of an RBN fixes an interpretation for all relations in the RBN and thus corresponds to some possible world. So an RBN defines a distribution over possible worlds. RBNs are, in fact, a special case of a more general class of models called *random relational structure models*. See Jaeger [19] for the full story.

9.2.5 Avoiding Possible World Semantics

Not all probability-logic formalisms are framed in terms of possible worlds. The hallmark of *Bayesian logic programs* [22] is a one-to-one mapping between ground atomic formulae and random variables *where there is no restriction on what these random variables might be.* In particular a random variable need not represent the probability with which the ground atomic formula *is true*; indeed it need not be binary. One advantage of this design decision is that continuous random variables can be represented. There is, however, a logical aspect to BLPs which has associated semantics. In BLPs, first-order clauses are used, together with combining rules, to define the *structure* of a BLP in much the same way that parent-child edges define the structure of a Bayesian network. Essentially, a ground instance of an atomic formula in the head of a clause corresponds to a child node, whereas those in the body are its parents. Using logical formulae to define the structure of a large (possibly infinite) Bayesian network in this way means that logical methods can be used to reason about the structure of the network. More on BLPs can be found in chapter 9 in this book.

The example of BLPs shows that it can be fruitful to use first-order logic as a convenient way of representing and manipulating data (and models) with complex structure, without too much concern about what the resulting probability distributions "mean." Much, but not all, of the work on SLPs [28, 7] takes this view, The easiest way to understand SLPs is by relating them to stochastic context-free grammars (SCFGs) as Muggleton [28] did in the original paper. In an SCFG each grammar rule has an associated probability. This provides a mechanism for probabilistically generating strings from the grammar: when there is a choice of grammar rules for expanding a nonterminal, one is chosen according to the probabilities. Any derivation in the grammar thus has a probability which is simply the product of the probabilities of all rules used in the derivation. The probability of any string is given by the sum of the probabilities of all derivations which generate that string. SLPs "lift" this basic idea to logic programs: probabilities are attached to first-order clauses, thus defining probabilities for proofs. SLPs are more complex than SCFGs since they are not generally context-free: not all sequences of clauses constitute a proof; some end in failure. There are different ways of dealing with this—one option is to use backtracking—which define different probability distributions [8]. More on SLPs can be found in chapter 10 of this book.

A "semantics-independent" approach appears pragmatic and flexible: is there not the problem that a formalism with possible-worlds semantics cannot model probability distributions over spaces other than possible worlds? In fact, the distinction between the two approaches is not so fundamental since, with a little imagination, any probability distribution can be viewed as one over some set of possible worlds. Conversely, having possible-worlds semantics certainly does not stop a formalism being applicable to real-world problems.

Moreover, imposing a possible-world semantics on a formalism can provide a useful "bridge" to related formalisms. For example, Cussens [9] provides a possible-worlds semantics to SLPs by translating SLPs into PRISM programs, the latter already having possible-world semantics. This amounts to mapping each proof to a possible world. A characterization of the sort of possible-world distributions thus defined is given by Sato and Kameya [40]. The connection between PHA/ICL and PRISM can then be used to connect SLPs with PHA/ICL.

9.3 Inference

Having defined a probability distribution in a logic-based formalism there remains the problem of computing probabilities to answer specific queries, such as "What's the probability that Tweety flies?" This problem is generally known as "inference" and the term is particularly apposite for a logic-based formalism, since for such formalisms it is possible to exploit nonprobabilistic logical inference to perform complex probabilistic computations. Here we will only consider inference for those formalisms (such as PHA/ICL and PRISM) which use logical implication to define probability distributions, since in such cases normal first-order inference can be used particularly directly to compute probabilities.

Consider, first, standard logical inference—using the first-order logical theory H in (9.8) by way of example. H defines possible output sequences (via the *hmm/2* predicate) for a hidden Markov model (HMM)whose parameters are yet to be defined. The HMM has two states (*s0* and *s1*) and two symbols in its output alphabet (*a* and *b*). Both states can emit both symbols and all four possible state transitions are possible. The only formula of any interest is the second which uses the *cons* function symbol to encode a nonempty sequence.

$$\forall s : hmm(s, null) \tag{9.8}$$
$$\forall s, x, y, t : hmm(s, cons(x, y)) \leftarrow emit(s, x), next(s, t), hmm(t, y)$$
$$emit(s0, a) \wedge emit(s0, b) \wedge emit(s1, a) \wedge emit(s1, b)$$
$$next(s0, s0) \wedge next(s0, s1) \wedge next(s1, s0) \wedge next(s1, s1)$$

Because the first-order language $\mathcal{L}$ used in (9.8) contains the function symbol *cons*, the language includes an infinite number of terms, and so there are an infinite number of groundings of the second universally quantified formula. However, to prove, for example, that the ground formula $hmm(s0, cons(a, cons(b, null)))$ follows from H it is not necessary to ground the formulae in H. In practice a theorem prover like Prolog [25] uses *unification* to partially instantiate formulae "on the fly" to establish a proof.

Recall that for PHA/ICL and PRISM there is a strict separation between the probabilistic facts for which probabilities are explicitly stated and all other formulae. To compute the probability of a formula F which is not a probabilistic fact, it suffices to find those conjunctions of facts which, together with the logical rules, entail F. Thanks to the ever-convenient CWA; $P(F)$ is then exactly the sum of the probabilities of these conjunctions. The key point is that finding the required conjunctions is a *purely logical* operation—abduction—and so algorithms and implementations for first-order logical inference can be used for it. The key importance of abduction is reflected in the name *probabilistic Horn abduction* [36].

To make this concrete, consider the PRISM program H' in figure 9.2. This is just a parameterized version of H, where, for simplicity, there is an implicit assumption that the initial state of the HMM is given. H' defines a distribution over a countably infinite set of possible worlds (each of which encodes a particular realization of the HMM). The facts are the (infinitely many) $msw/3$ atoms $msw(out(s0), 1, a)$, $msw(out(s0), 2, a), \ldots msw(tr(s1), 1, s0), msw(tr(s1), 2, s0), \ldots$ where the second argument has been suppressed as a programming convenience.

To compute the probability that, say, $hmm(s0, [a, b, a])$ is true, it is necessary to find conjunctions of facts the truth of which entail the truth of $hmm(s0, [a, b, a])$. Fortunately, we can use the PRISM built-in `probf/1` to explicitly show these, as displayed in figure 9.3. Figure 9.3 differs from the actual PRISM output in that the implicit second argument has been made explicit.

The first three lines of figure 9.3 state that $hmm(s0, [a, b, a])$ is true iff either

$$hmm(s0, [b, a]) \wedge msw(out(s0), 1, a) \wedge msw(tr(s0), 1, s0)$$

or

$$hmm(s1, [b, a]) \wedge msw(out(s0), 1, a) \wedge msw(tr(s0), 1, s1)$$

```
values(tr(S),[s0,s1,stop]).
:- set_sw(tr(s0),0.3+0.4+0.3).
:- set_sw(tr(s1),0.4+0.1+0.5).
values(out(S),[a,b]).
:- set_sw(out(s0),0.3+0.7).
:- set_sw(out(s1),0.6+0.4).

hmm(S,[X|Y]) :-
   msw(out(S),X),
   msw(tr(S),T),
   (
     T == stop, Y = []
   ;
     T \= stop, hmm(T,Y)
   ).
```

Figure 9.2 H': a PRISM encoding of a parameterized version of the hidden Markov model in (9.8).

```
| ?- probf(hmm(s0,[a,b,a])).

hmm(s0,[a,b,a])
   <=> hmm(s0,[b,a]) & msw(out(s0),1,a) & msw(tr(s0),1,s0)
     v hmm(s1,[b,a]) & msw(out(s0),1,a) & msw(tr(s0),1,s1)
hmm(s0,[b,a])
   <=> hmm(s0,[a]) & msw(out(s0),2,b) & msw(tr(s0),2,s0)
     v hmm(s1,[a]) & msw(out(s0),2,b) & msw(tr(s0),2,s1)
hmm(s1,[b,a])
   <=> hmm(s0,[a]) & msw(out(s1),3,b) & msw(tr(s1),3,s0)
     v hmm(s1,[a]) & msw(out(s1),3,b) & msw(tr(s1),3,s1)
hmm(s0,[a])
   <=> msw(out(s0),a) & msw(tr(s0),4,stop)
hmm(s1,[a])
   <=> msw(out(s1),a) & msw(tr(s1),4,stop)

yes
| ?- prob(hmm(s0,[a,b,a]),P).

P = 0.012429?
yes
```

Figure 9.3 Using abduction to compute a probability. The PRISM output has been altered so that the second argument on msw/3 is explicit.

is true. Note that these formulae are guaranteed to be mutually exclusive since $msw(tr(s0), 1, s0)$ and $msw(tr(s0), 1, s1)$ are defined to be alternatives. The next three lines state when $hmm(s0, [b, a])$ is true, and so on. It is not difficult to see that there are exactly eight mutually exclusive conjunctions of $msw/3$ facts which (together with the rules) entail $hmm(s0, [a, b, a])$. For example, one of these conjunctions is $msw(out(s0), 1, a)$, $msw(tr(s0), 1, s0)$, $msw(out(s0), 2, b)$, $msw(tr(s0), 2, s0)$, $msw(out(s0), 3, a)$, $msw(tr(s0), 4, stop)$. Since the $msw/3$ probabilistic facts are defined as independent, the probability of each conjunction is simply a product of the probabilities of the conjuncts. The probability of $hmm(s0, [a, b, a])$ is just the sum of these eight products, which, as figure 9.3 shows, happens to be 0.012429. Naturally, the sum is computed by dynamic programming similar to the variable elimination algorithm used in Bayesian networks. Sophisticated logic programming "tabling" technology can be exploited to do this elegantly and efficiently.

It should be stressed that this example of probabilistic inference was able to exploit the restrictions on PRISM programs that "all the probabilistic ground atoms in the body of each clause are probabilistically independent and the clauses defining a probabilistic predicate are probabilistically exclusive" [42], as well as the CWA. In other cases inference is much harder. For example, inference in PLP requires linear programming to deal with the inequalities involved and the linear program $LP(P)$ needed for a PLP program P "contains exponentially many linear programming variables w.r.t. the size of the Herbrand base of P" [29]. (The *Herbrand base* is the set of all ground atomic formulae expressible in the language used to define P.)

Naturally, one option for hard inference problems is to resort to approximate methods. For example, Angelopoulos and Cussens [1], used an SLP to represent a prior probability distribution over classification trees similarly to the way that the PRISM program above defined a distribution over HMM outputs. Since they adopt a Bayesian approach, learning reduces to probabilistic inference and so the key problem is to compute posterior probabilities: probabilities conditional on the observed data. Using exact inference to compute such probabilities (for example, the posterior class distribution for a test example) seems a hopeless task, so instead, the Metropolis-Hastings algorithm is used to sample from the posterior and thus to produce approximations to the desired probabilities.

9.4 Learning

Having considered how probability-logic formalisms represent probability distributions and how inference can be used to compute probabilities of interest, we can now turn to the issue of learning a model from data. As always, we consider the observed data as a sample generated by some unknown "true" model whose identity we wish to "learn" (or rather estimate). In some cases only the parameters of the model are unknown. In the general case both the structure and parameters of the true model are unknown. These two cases are considered in section 9.4.1 and section 9.4.2, respectively.

The paper by De Raedt and Kersting [10] provides an excellent overview of learning in probability-logic formalisms. The current section is complementary to De Raedt and Kersting's broad survey since, (1) for the sake of concreteness it examines parameter estimation in some detail for a particular formalism (PRISM) and (2) discusses the use of probabilities in pre-SRL inductive logic programming (ILP). An examination of pre-SRL ILP is useful since it seems likely that some of the techniques found there may be useful for more recent formalisms.

Before focusing on these two areas it is worth mentioning two key points about learning in probability-logic formalisms which are provided by De Raedt and Kersting [10].

- Much of the machinery for learning Bayesian networks can be used to learn directed probability-logic models such as BLPs. When first-order clauses are used for the structure of a directed model, then specialization and generalization of clauses corresponds to using a macro-operator for adding and deleting arcs in a Bayesian network. Parameter estimation for logical directed models corresponds to parameter estimation with tied parameters in a normal Bayesian network. This is because one first-order clause typically represents a collection of network fragments in the underlying Bayesian network via its ground instances.

- The probabilistic models associated with a PHA/ICL, PRISM, or SLP model depend on parameters associated with many predicates in the underlying logic program. This means that structure learning for such models is, in general, at least as hard as multiple-predicate learning / theory revision in ILP: which is known to be a hard problem. However, there exists work on learning SLPs in a restricted setting [27], and also work on applying grammatical inference techniques to learn SLPs [3].

As for other types of statistical inference, the key to learning in probability-logic formalisms is the likelihood function: the probability of the observed data as a function of the model. If the structure is fixed, then the likelihood is just a function of the model parameters. If a probability-logic formalism defines a distribution over possible worlds, then ideally we would like the data to be a collection of independent observations of possible worlds, each viewed as a sample drawn from the unknown "true" model. The probability of each world can then be computed using inference (section 9.3) and the likelihood of the data is just a product of these probabilities. In the case of alternative-based formalisms like PHA/ICL, PRISM, and SLPs, each data point would then be associated with a unique conjunction of atomic choices. Maximum likelihood estimation of the multinomial distribution over each alternative is then possible by simple counting in the normal way. A Bayesian approach using Dirichlet priors is equally simple.

However, in many cases each observation is a ground atomic formula, which is true in many worlds. This means the data-generating process is best viewed in terms of missing data: the "true" model generates a world, but we do not get to

```
hmm_out(X) :- hmm(s0,1,X).

hmm(S,N,[X|Y]) :-
  msw(out(S),X),
  msw(tr(S),T),
  (
    T == stop, Y = []
  ;
    T \= stop, NN is N+1, hmm(T,NN,Y)
  ).
```

Figure 9.4 PRISM program such that only one ground instance of $hmm\_out/1$ is true in each possible world

see this world, only some ground atomic formula that is true in it. The rest of the information required to determine the sampled world is missing. Unsurprisingly, the expectation maximization (EM) algorithm is generally used in such situations.

An alternative approach is presented by Kok and Domingos [24]. Here the data is contained in a (multitable) relational database. Each row in each table defines a ground atomic formula in the usual way. The entire database is equivalent to a conjunction of all these ground atomic formulae (so it is equivalent to a Datalog Prolog program). Using the CWA, this defines a unique world: all formulae which are not consequences of the conjunction are deemed false. (This unique world is the *minimal Herbrand model* of the associated Prolog program.) So, on the one hand we have only a single observation, but on the other it is an entire world that is observed. See Kok and Domingos [24] and chapter 11 this book for further details.

9.4.1 Parameter Estimation

To analyze parameter estimation, a modeling convention introduced by Sato and Kameya [40] will be adopted. There will be a *target predicate* such that in each possible world exactly one ground instance of this target predicate is true. This turns out not to be much of a restriction and simplifies the analysis greatly. For example, consider using PRISM to learn the parameters of the HMM of figure 9.2. The predicate $hmm/2$ is not a suitable target predicate, since any world in which all the following formulae are true—$msw(out(s0), 1, a)$, $msw(tr(s0), 1, s0)$, $msw(out(s0), 2, b)$, $msw(tr(s0), 2, s0)$, $msw(out(s0), 3, a)$, $msw(tr(s0), 4, stop)$— will also have $hmm(s0, [a, b, a])$, $hmm(s0, [b, a])$, and $hmm(s0, [a])$ true. This is illustrated by figure 9.3. Also, figure 9.2 as it stands is a conditional model— conditional on the initial state—since no distribution over the initial state has been defined. Changing the program to the one given in figure 9.4 and declaring that `hmm_out/1` is the target predicate— `target(hmm_out,1)` — is enough to fix both these problems. Now exactly one $hmm\_out/1$ formula will be true in each world.

However, each $hmm\_out/1$ formula will be true in many worlds, so that for maximum likelihood estimation of model parameters the EM algorithm is used. Fig-

```
| ?- learn([hmm_out([a,b,a,a]),hmm_out([b,b]),hmm_out([a,a,b])]).
..
Finished learning
        Number of iterations: 13.
        Final likelihood:-9.440724
        Total learning time: 0.01 seconds.
        All solution search time: 0.01 seconds.
        Total table space used: 6304 out of 240000000 bytes
Type show_sw to show the probability distributions.
yes
| ?- show_sw
Switch tr(s1): unfixed: s0 (0.235899) s1 (0.000014) stop (0.764086)
Switch out(s1): unfixed: a (0.254708) b (0.745291)
Switch tr(s0): unfixed: s0 (0.226177) s1 (0.773818) stop (0.000003)
Switch out(s0): unfixed: a (0.788360) b (0.211639)
```

Figure 9.5 EM learning with PRISM. (I have edited the output to reduce the precision of parameters.)

ure 9.5 shows a run of PRISM using the EM algorithm to estimate the parameters of the HMM using a data set of three examples. The algorithm was initialized with the values shown in figure 9.2. Abduction is used *once* to produce the data structure shown in figure 9.3. This can then be used in each iteration of the EM algorithm to compute the expected values required in the E-part of the EM algorithm.

So far a very simple and hopefully familiar example—HMM parameter estimation—has been used to explain parameter estimation in PRISM. Of course, there is no pressing reason to use SRL for this problem. The whole point of SRL is to address problems outside the remit of more standard approaches. So now consider a simple elaboration of the HMM learning problem which highlights some of the flexibility of a logic-based approach. Suppose that the HMM is *constrained* so that not all outputs from the HMM are permitted. This amounts to altering the definition of hmm_out/1 to

$$\text{hmm\_out(X) :- hmm(s0,1,X), constraint(X),} \qquad (9.9)$$

where the predicate *constraint*/1 is *any predicate* which can be defined using (clausal) first-order logic. Now there will be worlds in which no ground instance of the target predicate is true: these worlds will not be associated with a possible data point. To take a very simple example, if *constraint*/1 were defined thus:

constraint(X) :- X = [Y,Y|Z],

then the possible world illustrated by figure 9.3 would no longer entail $hmm\_out([a, b, a])$, since the first two elements differ. The distribution over ground instances of $hmm\_out/1$ is now a conditional one: conditional on the logically defined constraint being satisfied. This turns out to be an exponential-family distribution where the partition function Z is the probability that the constraint is true in a world sampled from the original, unconditional distribution.

It is still possible to use the EM algorithm to search for maximum likelihood estimates of the parameters of such a distribution; it is just that the generative characterization of this conditional distribution is more complicated. We assume, as always, that worlds are sampled from the true underlying distribution. If no ground instance of the target predicate is true in a sampled world, then that world is rejected and no data point is generated; otherwise the unique ground instance of the target predicate which is true in that world is added to the data. Viewing the observed data as being generated in this fashion we have an extra sort of missing data: the worlds which were entirely rejected. So the data is now *truncated* data. Fortunately, Dempster et al. [13] show that the EM algorithm is applicable even when the data has been truncated like this. The method was applied to SLPs by Cussens [7] under the name *failure-adjusted maximization (FAM)* and is used in the most recent version of the PRISM system [41].

9.4.2 Structure Learning

The structure of a probability-logic model is by definition some sort of first-order theory, frequently a set of first-order clauses, i.e., a logic program. ILP is the branch of machine learning concerned with inducing logic programs from data, so it is no surprise that ILP techniques are often used when learning the structure of probability-logic models from data.

Since its inception ILP has had no option but to induce de facto probabilistic models for the simple reason that deterministic, purely logical, rules rarely fit the data—however, the probabilistic aspect of induced rules has not always been properly formalized. In its simplest form, data for ILP is a set of true facts (positive examples) and a set of untrue facts (negative examples). The ideal is to find a set of clauses which, when added to an existing logic program (the background knowledge), entail all of the positives and none of the negatives. There is generally a bias for simple theories so that, for example, just returning the positive examples as the induced theory is decidedly suboptimal. In most real applications, this logical ideal is unreachable. So, instead of (hopelessly) searching for rules which fit the data exactly, many ILP systems search for *accurate* rules: ones which entail many more positives than negatives. Of course, training set accuracy can be an unreliable guide to true accuracy, so, for example, Bayesian estimates of true accuracy can be used Džeroski [14]. Bayesian estimation is available in the ALEPH system by using `mestimate` as the clause evaluation function, and setting the m parameter to define the underlying prior distribution. Each induced rule can now be returned with an associated parameter: its expected accuracy, or informally, its *probability*.

Using ILP to distinguish positives from negatives is most readily applicable to binary classification. In many other cases (particularly those where probability is explicitly represented) it is more appropriate to induce a logic program that *instantiates variables* to perform classification, regression [21], or more complex tasks akin to program synthesis. For example, figure 9.6 shows a clause induced using the ALEPH ILP system (from example input that comes with that system to demonstrate ILP learning of classification trees). The clause probabilistically classifies days according to whether they are suitable for playing or not by the simple expedient of "putting probability in the background." No negative examples

```
class(A,B) :-
    not (outlook(A,rain),windy(A,true)), outlook(A,sunny),
    humidity(A,C), lteq(C,70),
    random(B,[0.75-play,0.25-dont_play]).
```

Figure 9.6   Probabilistic classification rule induced by ALEPH.

are used to induce such a rule: the key is to declare that the class B is an output to be computed from the day A which is an input. In the ALEPH and Progol systems this is done with the declaration in figure 9.7.

```
:- modeh(1,class(+day,-class)).
```

Figure 9.7   ALEPH declaration that the `class/2` variable takes an input (indicated by the "+") of type `day` and generates an output (indicated by the "-") of type `class`.

It is possible to use an ILP algorithm to search for rules and then build some probabilistic model from these rules afterward. One option is to use a *combining rule* to compute probabilities for test examples entailed by more than one induced rule. (See chapter 9 for further details on combining rules.) Pompe and Kononenko [34] use a naive Bayes model to combine first-order classification rules with a later approach splitting induced first-order rules to better approximate the naive Bayes assumption [35]. This work is an example of the often used technique of viewing first-order rules (or parts of rules) as features for a nonlogical probabilistic model. If induced rules are going to be used eventually as the structural component of a probabilistic model, then naturally it is better that the algorithm searching for rules is designed to find rules suitable for this purpose.

A more thoroughly probabilistic approach is to use ILP techniques as subroutines in an algorithm that directly learns a probabilistic model from data. This is the approach taken by Dehaspe [11] with his MACCENT algorithm. The goal of MACCENT is to learn a conditional distribution giving a distribution over classes (C) for any given example (I). MACCENT uses the ILP framework of *learning from interpretations* where each example I is a Prolog program. There are thus connections to the approach of Kok and Domingos [24] mentioned earlier. The distribution is always a conditional exponential-family distribution of the form

$$p_\lambda(C|I) = \frac{1}{Z_\lambda(I)} \exp\left(\sum_{m=1}^{m=M} \lambda_m f_{j_m,k_m}(I,C)\right),$$

where each feature $f_{j,k}$ is a *Boolean clausal indicator function* defined using a class C_j and a Prolog query Q_k as follows:

$$f_{j,k}(I,C) = \begin{cases} 1 & \text{if } C = C_j \text{ and Prolog query } Q_k \text{ succeeds in instance } I \\ 0 & \text{otherwise} \end{cases}.$$

Both parameters λ_m and the features f_{j_m,k_m} are learned using an adaptation of the algorithm of Della Pietra et al. [12]. MACCENT searches the lattice of clausal indicator functions for good features using standard ILP search where these functions are ordered by logical generality (or more precisely θ-subsumption [33]).

9.5 Conclusion

In this chapter we have looked at the big three issues of representation, inference, and learning for probability-logic models, with a focus on representation. What is exciting about the current interest in SRL is that techniques for all three of these (often originating from different communities) are coming together to produce powerful techniques for learning from structured and relational data. (It is worth noting that there are initiatives with similar goals originating from the statistical community [16], although there logical approaches are not currently used.) The number of applications which involve such data are many: almost any real-world problem for which standard ILP is a reasonable choice—and many more besides—is also a target for SRL. To take just three recent examples, Frasconi et al. [15] applied a "declarative kernel" approach to (1) predicting mutagenicity, (2) information extraction, and (3) prediction of mRNA signal structure; Lodhi and Muggleton [26] applied failure-adjusted maximization to learn SLPs to model metabolic pathways and Riedel and Klein [38] learnt MLN based on discourse representation structures of a sentence to extract gene-protein interactions from annotated Medline abstracts.

References

[1] N. Angelopoulos and J. Cussens. Exploiting informative priors for Bayesian classification and regression trees. In *Proceedings of the International Joint Conference on Artificial Intelligence*, 2005.

[2] A. Arnauld and P. Nicole. *Port-Royal Logic*. Translated by Bobbs-Merrill, Indianapolis, IN, 1964.

[3] M. Bernard and A. Habrard. Learning stochastic logic programs. In *Proceedings of the Work-in-Progress Track at the International Conference on Inductive Logic Programming*, 2001.

[4] G. Boole. *An Investigation of the Laws of Thought, on which are founded the Mathematical Theories of Logic and Probabilities*. Reprint, Dover Publications, New York, NY, 1958.

[5] R. Carnap. *Logical Foundations of Probability*. University of Chicago Press, Chicago, 1950.

[6] J. Cussens. Bayesian inductive logic programming with explicit probabilistic bias. Technical Report PRG-TR-24-96, Oxford University Computing Laboratory, Oxford, UK, 1996.

[7] J. Cussens. Parameter estimation in stochastic logic programs. *Machine Learning*, 44(3):245–271, 2001.

[8] J. Cussens. Stochastic logic programs: Sampling, inference and applications. In *Proceedings of the Conference on Uncertainty in Artificial Intelligence*, 2000.

[9] J. Cussens. Integrating by separating: Combining probability and logic with ICL, PRISM and SLPs. APRIL project report, January 2005.

[10] L. De Raedt and K. Kersting. Probabilistic logic learning. *SIGKDD Explorations*, 5(1):31–48, 2003.

[11] L. Dehaspe. Maximum entropy modeling with clausal constraints. In *Inductive Logic Programming*, 1997.

[12] S. Della Pietra, V. Della Pietra, and J. Lafferty. Inducing features of random fields. *IEEE Transactions on Pattern Analysis and Machine Intelligence*, 19 (4):380–393, 1997.

[13] A. P. Dempster, N. M. Laird, and D. B. Rubin. Maximum likelihood from incomplete data via the *EM* algorithm. *Journal of the Royal Statistical Society, Series B*, 39(1):1–38, 1977.

[14] S. Džeroski. Handling Noise in Inductive Logic Programming. Master's thesis, Faculty of Electrical Engineering and Computer Science, University of Ljubljana, Ljubljana, Slovenia, 1991.

[15] P. Frasconi, A. Passerini, S. Muggleton, and H. Lodhi. Declarative kernels. Inductive Logic Programming, 2005.

[16] P. Green, N. Hjort, and S. Richardson, editors. *Highly Structured Stochastic Systems*. OUP, 2003.

[17] J. Halpern. An analysis of first-order logics of probability. *Artificial Intelligence*, 46:311–350, 1990.

[18] C. Howson and P. Urbach. *Scientific Reasoning: The Bayesian Approach*. Open Court, La Salle, Illinois, 1989.

[19] M. Jaeger. Relational Bayesian networks: A survey. *Electronic Transactions in Artificial Intelligence*, 6, 2002.

[20]   Manfred Jaeger. Relational Bayesian networks. In *Proceedings of the Conference on Uncertainty in Artificial Intelligence*, 1997.

[21]   A. Karalič and I. Bratko. First order regression. *Machine Learning*, 26(2-3): 147–176, 1997. ISSN 0885-6125.

[22]   K. Kersting and L. De Raedt. Bayesian logic programs. Technical Report 151, University of Freiburg, Freiburg, Germany, April 2001.

[23]   J. Keynes. *A Treatise on Probability*. Macmillan, London, 1921.

[24]   S. Kok and P. Domingos. Learning the structure of Markov logic networks. In *Proceedings of the International Conference on Machine Learning*, 2005.

[25]   J. Lloyd. *Foundations of Logic Programming*. Springer, Berlin, second edition, 1987.

[26]   H. Lodhi and S. Muggleton. Modelling metabolic pathways using stochastic logic programs-based ensemble methods. In *Proceedings of the International Conference on Computational Methods in System Biology*, 2004.

[27]   S. Muggleton. Learning the structure and parameters of stochastic logic programs. In *Inductive Logic Programming*, 2002.

[28]   S. Muggleton. Stochastic logic programs. In L. De Raedt, editor, *Advances in Inductive Logic Programming*, volume 32 of *Frontiers in Artificial Intelligence and Applications*, pages 254–264. IOS Press, Amsterdam, 1996.

[29]   R. Ng and V.S. Subrahmanian. A semantical framework for supporting subjective and conditional probabilities in deductive databases. *Journal of Automated Reasoning*, 10(2):191–235, 1993.

[30]   R. Ng and V.S. Subrahmanian. Probabilistic logic programming. *Information and Computation*, 101(2):150–201, 1992.

[31]   L. Ngo and P. Haddaway. Answering queries from context-sensitive probabilistic knowledge bases. *Theoretical Computer Science*, 171:147–171, 1997.

[32]   N. Nilsson. Probabilistic logic. *Artificial Intelligence*, 28:71–87, 1986.

[33]   Gordon D. Plotkin. A note on inductive generalization. *Machine Intelligence*, 5:153–163, 1970.

[34]   U. Pompe and I. Kononenko. Naive Bayesian classifier within ILP-R. In *Inductive Logic Programming*, 1995.

[35]   U. Pompe and I. Kononenko. Probabilistic first-order classification. In *Inductive Logic Programming*, 1997.

[36]   D. Poole. Probabilistic Horn abduction and Bayesian networks. *Artificial Intelligence*, 64(1):81–129, 1993.

[37]   D. Poole. The independent choice logic for modelling multiple agents under uncertainty. *Artificial Intelligence*, 94(1–2):5–56, 1997.

[38]   S. Riedel and E. Klein. Genic interaction extraction with semantic and syntactic chains. In *Proceedings of the Learning Language in Logic Workshop*, 2005.

[39]   T. Sato. A statistical learning method for logic programs with distribution semantics. In *Inductive Logic Programming*, 1995.

[40]   T. Sato and Y. Kameya. Parameter learning of logic programs for symbolic-statistical modeling. *Journal of Artificial Intelligence Research*, 15:391–454, 2001.

[41]   T. Sato, Y. Kameya, and N. Zhou. Generative modeling with failure in PRISM. In *Proceedings of the International Joint Conference on Artificial Intelligence*, 2005.

[42]   N. Zhou, T. Sato, and Y. Kameya. *A Reference Guide to PRISM Version 1.7*, March 2004.

10 Bayesian Logic Programming: Theory and Tool

Kristian Kersting and Luc De Raedt

Bayesian networks provide an elegant formalism for representing and reasoning about uncertainty. They are a probabilistic extension of propositional logic and, hence, inherit some of the limitations of propositional logic, such as the difficulties with representing objects and relations. In this chapter, we introduce Bayesian logic programs, which are an extension of Bayesian networks to overcome these limitations. Bayesian logic programs tightly integrate definite logic programs with Bayesian networks. The key idea underlying Bayesian logic programs is to establish a one-to-one mapping between ground atoms and random variables, and between the immediate consequence operator and the dependency relation. In doing so, Bayesian logic programs combine the advantages of both definite clause logic and Bayesian networks: notions of objects and relations, a separation of quantitative and qualitative aspects of the world, and a graphical representation.

10.1 Introduction

In recent years, there has been a significant interest in integrating probability theory with first-order logic and relational representations (see De Raedt and Kersting [5] for an overview). Muggleton [30] and Cussens [4] have upgraded stochastic grammars toward *stochastic logic programs*, Sato and Kameya [42] have introduced *probabilistic distributional semantics* for logic programs, and Domingos and Richardson [9] have upgraded Markov networks toward *Markov logic networks*. Another research stream including Poole's *independent choice logic* [38], Ngo and Haddawy's *Probabilistic-Logic Programs* [34], Jaeger's *relational Bayesian networks* [17], and Pfeffer's *probabilistic relational models* [37] concentrates on first-order logical and relational extensions of Bayesian networks.

Bayesian networks [36] are one of the most important, efficient, and elegant frameworks for representing and reasoning with probabilistic models. They have been applied to many real-world problems in diagnosis, forecasting, automated vision, sensor fusion, and manufacturing control [16]. A Bayesian network specifies a joint probability distribution over a finite set of random variables and consists of two components:

1. a *qualitative* or *logical* one that encodes the local influences among the random variables using a directed acyclic graph, and

2. a *quantitative* one that encodes the probability densities over these local influences.

Despite these interesting properties, Bayesian networks also have a major limitation, i.e., they are essentially propositional representations. Indeed, imagine modeling the localization of genes/proteins as was the task at the KDD Cup 2001 [3]. When using a Bayesian network, every gene is a single random variable. There is no way of formulating general probabilistic regularities among the localizations of the genes such as

the localization L *of gene* G *is influenced by the localization* L′ *of another gene* G′ *that interacts with* G.

The propositional nature and limitations of Bayesian networks are similar to those of traditional attribute-value learning techniques, which have motivated a lot of work on upgrading these techniques within inductive logic programming. This in turn also explains the interest in upgrading Bayesian networks toward using first-order logical representations.

Bayesian logic programs unify Bayesian networks with logic programming which allows the propositional character of Bayesian networks and the purely "logical" nature of logic programs to be overcome. From a knowledge representation point of view, Bayesian logic programs can be distinguished from alternative frameworks by having logic programs (i.e., definite clause programs, which are sometimes called "pure" Prolog programs), as well as Bayesian networks, as an immediate special case. This is realized through the use of a small but powerful set of primitives. Indeed, the underlying idea of Bayesian logic programs is to establish a one-to-one mapping between ground atoms and random variables, and between the *immediate consequence operator* and the *direct influence* relation. Therefore, Bayesian logic programs can also handle domains involving structured terms as well as continuous random variables.

In addition to reviewing Bayesian logic programs, this chapter

- contributes a *graphical representation* for Bayesian logic programs;
- its implementation in the Bayesian logic programs *tool* BALIOS; and
- shows how *purely logical predicates* as well as *aggregate function* are employed within Bayesian logic programs.

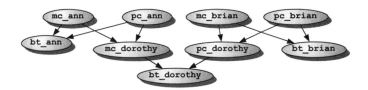

Figure 10.1   The graphical structure of a Bayesian network modeling the inheritance of blood types within a particular family.

The chapter is structured as follows. We begin by briefly reviewing Bayesian networks and logic programs in section 10.2. In section 10.3, we define Bayesian logic programs as well as their semantics. Afterward, in section 10.4, we discuss several extensions of the basic Bayesian logic programming framework. More precisely, we introduce a graphical representation for Bayesian logic programs and we discuss the effective treatment of logic atoms and of aggregate functions. In section 10.5, we sketch how to learn Bayesian logic programs from data. Before touching upon related work and concluding, we briefly present BALIOS, the engine for Bayesian logic programs.

10.2   On Bayesian Networks and Logic Programs

In this section, we first introduce the key concepts and assumptions underlying Bayesian networks and logic programs. In the next section we then show how these are combined in Bayesian logic programs. For a full and detailed treatment of each of these topics, we refer to [28] for logic programming or Prolog and to [18] for Bayesian networks.

We introduce Bayesian logic programs using an example from genetics which is inspired by [10]:

> It is a genetic model of the inheritance of a single gene that determines a person's X blood type bt(X). Each person X has two copies of the chromosome containing this gene, one, mc(Y), inherited from her mother m(Y, X), and one, pc(Z), inherited from her father f(Z, X).

We will use the following convention: x denotes a (random) variable, x a state, and **X** (resp. $\boldsymbol{x}$) a set of variables (resp. states). We will use **P** to denote a probability distribution, e.g., **P**(x), and P to denote a probability value, e.g., $P(\mathrm{x} = x)$ and $P(\mathbf{X} = \boldsymbol{x})$.

10.2.1   Bayesian Networks

A *Bayesian network* [36] is an augmented, directed acyclic graph, where each node corresponds to a random variable x_i and each edge indicates a *direct in-*

fluence among the random variables. It represents the joint probability distribution $\mathbf{P}(x_1, \ldots, x_n)$ over a fixed, finite set $\{x_1, \ldots, x_n\}$ of random variables. Each random variable x_i possesses a finite set $\mathbf{S}(x_i)$ of mutually exclusive states. Figure 10.1 shows the graph of a Bayesian network modeling our blood type example for a particular family. The familial relationship, which is taken from Jensen's *stud farm* example [19], forms the basis for the graph. The network encodes, e.g., that Dorothy's blood type is influenced by the genetic information of her parents Ann and Brian. The set of possible states of bt(dorothy) is $\mathbf{S}(\text{bt}(\text{dorothy})) = \{a, b, ab, 0\}$; the set of possible states of pc(dorothy) and mc(dorothy) are $\mathbf{S}(\text{pc}(\text{dorothy})) = \mathbf{S}(\text{mc}(\text{dorothy})) = \{a, b, 0\}$. The same holds for ann and brian. The direct predecessors of a node x, the parents of x, are denoted by $\mathbf{Pa}(x)$. For instance, $\mathbf{Pa}(\text{bt}(\text{ann})) = \{\text{pc}(\text{ann}), \text{mc}(\text{ann})\}$.

A Bayesian network stipulates the following conditional independence assumption.

Proposition 10.1 Independence Assumption of Bayesian Networks
Each node x_i in the graph is conditionally independent of any subset $\mathbf{A}$ of nodes that are not descendants of x_i given a joint state of $\mathbf{Pa}(x_i)$, i.e.,

$$\mathbf{P}(x_i \mid \mathbf{A}, \mathbf{Pa}(x_i)) = \mathbf{P}(x_i \mid \mathbf{Pa}(x_i)) \ .$$

For example, bt(dorothy) is conditionally independent of bt(ann) given a joint state of its parents $\{\text{pc}(\text{dorothy}), \text{mc}(\text{dorothy})\}$. Any pair $(x_i, \mathbf{Pa}(x_i))$ is called the *family* of x_i denoted as $\mathbf{Fa}(x_i)$; e.g., bt(dorothy)'s family is

$$(\text{bt}(\text{dorothy}), \{\text{pc}(\text{dorothy}), \text{mc}(\text{dorothy})\}) \ .$$

Because of the conditional independence assumption, we can write down the joint probability density as

$$\mathbf{P}(x_1, \ldots, x_n) = \prod_{i=1}^{n} \mathbf{P}(x_i \mid \mathbf{Pa}(x_i))$$

by applying the independence assumption 10.1 to the chain rule expression of the joint probability distribution. Thereby, we associate with each node x_i of the graph the conditional probability distribution $\mathbf{P}(x_i \mid \mathbf{Pa}(x_i))$, denoted as cpd($x_i$). The conditional probability distributions in our blood type domain are:

mc(dorothy)	pc(dorothy)	$\mathbf{P}(\text{bt}(\text{dorothy}))$
a	a	$(0.97, 0.01, 0.01, 0.01)$
b	a	$(0.01, 0.01, 0.97, 0.01)$
$\ldots$	$\ldots$	$\ldots$
0	0	$(0.01, 0.01, 0.01, 0.97)$

(similarly for ann and brian) and

mc(ann)	pc(ann)	$\mathbf{P}$(mc(dorothy))
a	a	$(0.98, 0.01, 0.01)$
b	a	$(0.01, 0.98, 0.01)$
$\cdots$	$\cdots$	$\cdots$
0	0	$(01, 0.01, 0.98)$

(similarly for pc(dorothy)). Further conditional probability tables are associated with the a priori nodes, i.e., the nodes having no parents:

$\mathbf{P}$(mc(ann))	$\mathbf{P}$(mc(ann))	$\mathbf{P}$(mc(ann))	$\mathbf{P}$(mc(ann))
$(0.38, 0.12, 0.50)$	$(0.38, 0.12, 0.50)$	$(0.38, 0.12, 0.50)$	$(0.38, 0.12, 0.50)$

10.2.2   Logic Programs

To introduce logic programs, consider figure 10.2, containing two programs, *grandparent* and *nat*. Formally speaking, we have that grandparent/2, parent/2 and nat/1 are *predicates* (with their *arity* i.e., number of arguments listed explicitly). Furthermore, jef, paul, and ann are *constants* and X, Y, and Z are *variables*. All constants and variables are also *terms*. In addition, there exist structured terms, such as s(X), which contains the *functor* s/1 of arity 1 and the term X. Constants are often considered as functors of arity 0. *Atoms* are predicate symbols followed by the necessary number of terms, e.g., parent(jef,paul), nat(s(X)), parent(X, Z), etc. We are now able to define the key concept of a (definite) *clause*. Clauses are formulae of the form A :-$B_1, \ldots, B_m$ where A and the B_i are logical atoms where all variables are understood to be universally quantified. For example, the clause grandparent(X, Y) :-parent(X, Z), parent(Z, Y) can be read as X is the grandparent of Y if X is a parent of Z and Z is a parent of Y. Let us call this clause c. We call grandparent(X, Y) the head(c) of this clause, and parent(X, Z), parent(Z, Y) the body(c). Clauses with an empty body, such as parent(jef, paul), are called *facts*. A (definite) clause program (or *logic program* for short) consists of a set of clauses. In figure 10.2, there are thus two logic programs, one defining grandparent/2 and one defining nat/1.

```
parent(jef,paul).                         nat(0).
parent(paul,ann).                         nat(s(X)) :- nat(X).
grandparent(X,Y) :- parent(X,Z), parent(Z,Y).
```

Figure 10.2   Two logic programs, *grandparent* and *nat*.

The set of variables in a term, atom, or clause E is denoted as $\mathrm{Var}(E)$, e.g., $\mathrm{Var}(c) = \{X, Y, Z\}$. A term, atom, or clause E is called *ground* when there is no variable occurring in E, i.e., $\mathrm{Var}(E) = \emptyset$. A *substitution* $\theta = \{V_1/t_1, \ldots, V_n/t_n\}$, e.g., $\{X/\mathrm{ann}\}$, is an assignment of terms t_i to variables V_i. Applying a substitution θ to a term, atom, or clause e yields the instantiated term, atom, or clause $e\theta$ where all occurrences of the variables V_i are simultaneously replaced by the term t_i, e.g., $c\theta$ is grandparent(ann, Y) :−parent(ann, Z), parent(Z, Y).

The *Herbrand base* of a logic program T, denoted as HB(T), is the set of all ground atoms constructed with the predicate, constant, and function symbols in the alphabet of T. For example, HB(*nat*) = {nat(0), nat(s(0)), nat(s(s(0))), ...} and

$$\text{HB}(grandparent) =$$
$$\{\text{parent(ann, ann)}, \text{parent(jef, jef)},$$
$$\text{parent(paul, paul)}, \text{parent(ann, jef)}, \text{parent(jef, ann)}, ...,$$
$$\text{grandparent(ann, ann)}, \text{grandparent(jef, jef)}, ...\}.$$

A *Herbrand interpretation* for a logic program T is a subset of HB(T). The *least Herbrand model* LH(T) (which constitutes the semantics of the logic program) consists of all facts $f \in$ HB(T) such that T logically entails f, i.e., $T \models f$. Various methods exist to compute the least Herbrand model. We merely sketch its computation through the use of the well-known *immediate consequence* operator T_B. The operator T_B is the function on the set of all Herbrand interpretations of B such that for any such interpretation $\mathcal{I}$ we have

$$T_B(\mathcal{I}) = \{\texttt{A}\theta \,|\text{there is a substitution } \theta \text{ and a clause } \texttt{A:−A}_1, \ldots, \texttt{A}_n \text{ in } B \text{ such}$$
$$\text{that } \texttt{A}\theta\texttt{:−A}_1\theta, \ldots, \texttt{A}_n\theta \text{ is ground and for } i = 1, \ldots, n : A_i\theta \in \mathcal{I}\}.$$

Now, for range-restricted clauses, the least Herbrand model can be obtained using the following procedure:

1:   Initialize LH := $\emptyset$
2:   **repeat**
3:       LH := T_B(LH)
4:   **until** LH does not change anymore

At this point the reader may want to verify that LH(*nat*) = HB(*nat*) and

$$\text{LH}(grandparent) =$$
$$\{\text{parent(jef, paul)}, \text{parent(paul, ann)}, \text{grandparent(jef, ann)}\}.$$

10.3   Bayesian Logic Programs

The logical component of Bayesian networks essentially corresponds to a propositional logic program. [1] Consider, for example, the program in figure 10.3. It encodes

---

1. Haddawy [14] and Langley [27] have a similar view on Bayesian networks. For instance, Langley does not represent Bayesian networks graphically but rather uses the notation of propositional definite clause programs.

```
pc(ann).
pc(brian).
mc(ann).
mc(brian).
mc(dorothy) :- mc(ann), pc(ann).
pc(dorothy) :- mc(brian), pc(brian).
bt(ann) :- mc(ann), pc(ann).
bt(brian) :- mc(brian), pc(brian).
bt(dorothy) :- mc(dorothy), pc(dorothy).
```

Figure 10.3 A propositional clause program encoding the structure of the blood type Bayesian network in figure 10.1.

the structure of the blood type Bayesian network in figure 10.1. Observe that the random variables in the Bayesian network correspond to logical atoms. Furthermore, the *direct influence* relation corresponds to the immediate consequence operator. Now, imagine another totally separated family, which could be described by a similar Bayesian network. The graphical structure and associated conditional probability distribution for the two families are controlled by the same intensional regularities. But these overall regularities cannot be captured by a traditional Bayesian network. So we need a way to represent these overall regularities.

Because this problem is akin to that with propositional logic and the structure of Bayesian networks can be represented using propositional clauses, the approach taken in Bayesian logic programs is to upgrade these propositional clauses encoding the structure of the Bayesian network to proper first-order clauses.

10.3.1 Representation Language

Applying the above-mentioned idea leads to the central notion of a Bayesian clause.

Definition 10.2 Bayesian Clause
A Bayesian (definite) clause c is an expression of the form $A \mid A_1, \ldots, A_n$ *where* $n \geq 0$, *the* $A, A_1, \ldots, A_n$ *are Bayesian atoms (see below) and all Bayesian atoms are (implicitly) universally quantified. When* $n = 0$, *c is called a Bayesian fact and expressed as* A.

So the differences between a *Bayesian clause* and a *logical clause* are:

1. the atoms $p(t_1, \ldots, t_1)$ and predicates $p/1$ arising are Bayesian, which means that they have an associated (finite[2]) set $\mathbf{S}(p/1)$ of possible states, and

2. we use "|" instead of ":−" to highlight the conditional probability distribution.

---

2. For the sake of simplicity we consider finite random variables, i.e., random variables having a finite set $\mathbf{S}$ of states. However, because the semantics rely on Bayesian networks, the ideas easily generalize to discrete and continuous random variables (modulo the restrictions well-known for Bayesian networks).

For instance, consider the Bayesian clause c bt(X)|mc(X), pc(X) where $\mathbf{S}(\mathtt{bt}/1) = \{a, b, ab, 0\}$ and $\mathbf{S}(\mathtt{mc}/1) = \mathbf{S}(\mathtt{pc}/1) = \{a, b, 0\}$. Intuitively, a Bayesian predicate p/1 generically represents a set of random variables. More precisely, each Bayesian ground atom g over p/1 represents a random variable over the states $\mathbf{S}(g) := \mathbf{S}(\mathtt{p}/1)$. For example, bt(ann) represents the blood type of a person named Ann as a random variable over the states $\{a, b, ab, 0\}$. Apart from that, most *logical* notions carry over to Bayesian logic programs. So we will speak of Bayesian predicates, terms, constants, substitutions, propositions, ground Bayesian clauses, Bayesian Herbrand interpretations, etc. For the sake of simplicity we will sometimes omit the term *Bayesian* as long as no ambiguities arise. We will assume that all Bayesian clauses c are range-restricted, i.e., $\mathrm{Var}(\mathrm{head}(c)) \subseteq \mathrm{Var}(\mathrm{body}(c))$. Range restriction is often imposed in the database literature; it allows one to avoid the derivation of nonground true facts (cf. section 10.2.2). As already indicated while discussing figure 10.3, a set of Bayesian clauses encodes the qualitative or structural component of the Bayesian logic programs. More precisely, ground atoms correspond to random variables, and the set of random variables encoded by a particular Bayesian logic program corresponds to its least Herbrand domain. In addition, the *direct influence* relation corresponds to the immediate consequence.

In order to represent a probabilistic model we also associate with each Bayesian clause c a conditional probability distribution cpd(c) encoding $\mathbf{P}(\mathrm{head}(c) \mid \mathrm{body}(c))$; cf. figure 10.4. To keep the exposition simple, we will assume that cpd(c) is represented as a table. More elaborate representations such as decision trees or rules would be possible too. The distribution cpd(c) generically represents the conditional probability distributions associated with each ground instance $c\theta$ of the clause c.

In general, one may have many clauses. Consider clauses c_1 and c_2

```
bt(X) | mc(X).
bt(X) | pc(X). \ ,
```

and assume corresponding substitutions θ_i that ground the clauses c_i such that $\mathrm{head}(c_1\theta_1) = \mathrm{head}(c_2\theta_2)$. In contrast to bt(X)|mc(X), pc(X), they specify cpd($c_1\theta_1$) and cpd($c_2\theta_2$), but not the desired distribution $\mathbf{P}(\mathrm{head}(c_1\theta_1) \mid \mathrm{body}(c_1) \cup \mathrm{body}(c_2))$. The standard solution to obtain the distribution required is so-called *combining rules*.

Definition 10.3 Combining Rule
A combining rule is a function that maps finite sets of conditional probability distributions $\{\mathbf{P}(\mathtt{A} \mid \mathtt{A_{i1}}, \ldots, \mathtt{A_{in_i}}) \mid i = 1, \ldots, m\}$ onto one (*combined*) conditional probability distribution $\mathbf{P}(\mathtt{A} \mid \mathtt{B_1}, \ldots, \mathtt{B_k})$ with $\{\mathtt{B_1}, \ldots, \mathtt{B_k}\} \subseteq \bigcup_{i=1}^{m} \{\mathtt{A_{i1}}, \ldots, \mathtt{A_{in_i}}\}$.

We assume that for each Bayesian predicate p/l there is a corresponding combining rule cr(p/l), such as *noisy_or* (see, e.g., [18]) or *average*. The latter assumes $n_1 = \ldots = n_m$ and $\mathbf{S}(\mathtt{A_{ij}}) = \mathbf{S}(\mathtt{A_{kj}})$, and computes the average of the distributions over $\mathbf{S}(\mathtt{A})$ for each joint state over $\bigotimes_j \mathbf{S}(\mathtt{A_{ij}})$; see also section 10.3.2.

By now, we are able to formally define Bayesian logic programs.

mc(X)	pc(X)	$\mathbf{P}(\mathtt{bt(X)})$
a	a	$(0.97, 0.01, 0.01, 0.01)$
b	a	$(0.01, 0.01, 0.97, 0.01)$
...	...	...
0	0	$(0.01, 0.01, 0.01, 0.97)$

m(Y, X)	mc(Y)	pc(Y)	$\mathbf{P}(\mathtt{mc(X)})$
true	a	a	$(0.98, 0.01, 0.01)$
true	b	a	$(0.01, 0.98, 0.01)$
...	...	...	...
false	a	a	$(0.33, 0.33, 0.33)$
...	...	...	...

m(ann, dorothy).
f(brian, dorothy).
pc(ann).
pc(brian).
mc(ann).
mc(brian).

mc(X)|m(Y, X), mc(Y), pc(Y).
pc(X)|f(Y, X), mc(Y), pc(Y).
bt(X)|mc(X), pc(X).

Figure 10.4 The Bayesian logic program *blood type* encoding our genetic domain. For each Bayesian predicate, the identity is the combining rule. The conditional probability distributions associated with the Bayesian clauses bt(X)|mc(X), pc(X) and mc(X)|m(Y, X), mc(X), pc(Y) are represented as tables. The other distributions are correspondingly defined. The Bayesian predicates m/2 and f/2 have as possible states $\{true, false\}$.

Definition 10.4 *Bayesian Logic Program*

A *Bayesian logic program B* consists of a (finite) set of Bayesian clauses. For each Bayesian clause c there is exactly one conditional probability distribution cpd(c), and for each Bayesian predicate p/l there is exactly one combining rule cr(p/l).

A Bayesian logic program encoding our blood type domain is shown in figure 10.4.

10.3.2 Declarative Semantics

Intuitively, each Bayesian logic program represents a (possibly infinite) Bayesian network, where the nodes are the atoms in the least Herbrand model of the Bayesian logic program. These declarative semantics can be formalized using the annotated *dependency graph*. The *dependency graph DG(B)* is that directed graph whose nodes correspond to the ground atoms in the least Herbrand model LH(B). It encodes the *direct influence* relation over the random variables in LH(B): *there is an edge from a node* x *to a node* y *if and only if there exists a clause* $c \in B$ *and a substitution* θ, *s.t.* y $= head(c\theta)$, x $\in body(c\theta)$ *and for all ground atoms* z *in* $c\theta$: z $\in LH(B)$. Figures 10.5 and 10.6 show the dependency graph for our *blood type* program. Here, mc(dorothy) *directly* influences bt(dorothy). Furthermore, defining the *influence* relation as the transitive closure of the *direct influence* relation, mc(ann) influences bt(dorothy).

The Herbrand base HB(B) constitute the set of all random variables we can talk about. However, only those atoms that are in the least Herbrand model LH(B) $\subseteq$ HB(B) will appear in the dependency graph. These are the atoms that are true in

```
m(ann,dorothy).
f(brian,dorothy).
pc(ann).
pc(brian).
mc(ann).
mc(brian).
mc(dorothy) | m(ann, dorothy),mc(ann),pc(ann).
pc(dorothy) | f(brian, dorothy),mc(brian),pc(brian).
bt(ann) | mc(ann), pc(ann).
bt(brian) | mc(brian), pc(brian).
bt(dorothy) | mc(dorothy),pc(dorothy).
```

Figure 10.5   The grounded version of the *blood type* Bayesian logic program of figure 10.4 where only clauses c with head$(c) \in$ LH(B) and body$(c) \subset$ LH(B) are retained. It (directly) encodes the Bayesian network as shown in figure 10.6. The structure of the Bayesian network coincides with the dependency graph of the *blood type* Bayesian logic program.

the logical sense, i.e., if the Bayesian logic program B is interpreted as a logical program. They are the so-called *relevant* random variables, the random variables over which a probability distribution is well-defined by B, as we will see. The atoms not belonging to the least Herbrand model are irrelevant. Now, to each node x in $DG(B)$ we associate the combined conditional probability distribution which is the result of applying the combining rule cr(p$/n$) of the corresponding Bayesian predicate p$/n$ to the set of cpd$(c\theta)$'s where head$(c\theta)$ = x and $\{$x$\} \cup$ body$(c\theta) \subseteq$ LH(B). Consider

```
cold.           fever | cold.
flu.            fever | flu.
malaria.        fever | malaria.    ,
```

where all Bayesian predicates have *true*, *false* as states, and *noisy_or* as combining rule. The dependency graph is

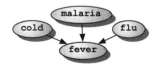

and *noisy or* $\{\mathbf{P}(\text{fever}|\text{flu}), \mathbf{P}(\text{fever}|\text{cold}), \mathbf{P}(\text{fever}|\text{malaria})\}$ is associated with fever (see [40], p. 444). Thus, if $DG(B)$ is acyclic and not empty, and every node in $DG(B)$ has a finite indegree then $DG(B)$ encodes a (possibly infinite) Bayesian network, because the least Herbrand model always exists and is unique. Consequently, the following independence assumption holds:

Proposition 10.5 Independence Assumption of Dependency Graph
Each node x is independent of its nondescendants given a joint state of its parents $\mathbf{Pa}(\text{x})$ in the dependency graph.

For instance, the dependency graph of the *blood type* program as shown in Figures 10.5 and 10.6 encodes that the random variable bt(dorothy) is independent of pc(ann) given a joint state of pc(dorothy), mc(dorothy). Using this assumption the following proposition (taken from [21]) holds:

Proposition 10.6 Semantics
Let B be a Bayesian logic program. If

1. $\mathrm{LH}(B) \neq \emptyset$,

2. $DG(B)$ is acyclic, and

3. each node in $DG(B)$ is influenced by a finite set of random variables,

then B specifies a unique probability distribution $\mathbf{P}_B$ over $\mathrm{LH}(B)$.

To see this, note that the least Herbrand $\mathrm{LH}(B)$ always exists, is unique, and countable. Thus, $DG(B)$ exists and is unique, and due to condition (3) the combined probability distribution for each node of $DG(B)$ is computable. Furthermore, because of condition (1) a total order π on $DG(B)$ exists, so that one can see B together with π as a stochastic process over $\mathrm{LH}(B)$. An induction argument over π together with condition (2) allows one to conclude that the family of finite-dimensional distributions of the process is projective (cf. [2]), i.e., the joint probability distribution over each finite subset $\mathbf{S} \subseteq \mathrm{LH}(B)$ is uniquely defined and $\sum_y \mathbf{P}(\mathbf{S}, \mathrm{x} = y) = \mathbf{P}(\mathbf{S})$. Thus, the preconditions of *Kolmogorov's theorem* [[2], p. 307] hold, and it follows that B given π specifies a probability distribution $\mathbf{P}$ over $\mathrm{LH}(B)$. This proves the proposition because the total order π used for the induction is arbitrary.

A program B satisfying the conditions (1), (2), and (3) of proposition 10.6 is called *well-defined*. A well-defined Bayesian logic program B specifies a joint distribution over the random variables in the least Herbrand model $\mathrm{LH}(B)$. As with Bayesian networks, the joint distribution over these random variables can be factored to

$$\mathbf{P}(\mathrm{LH}(B)) = \prod_{\mathrm{x}\in\mathrm{LH}(B)} \mathbf{P}(\mathrm{x}|\mathbf{Pa}(\mathrm{x})),$$

where the *parent* relation $\mathbf{Pa}$ is according to the dependency graph.

The *blood type* Bayesian logic program in figure 10.4 is an example of a well-defined Bayesian logic program. Its grounded version is shown in figure 10.5. It essentially encodes the original blood type Bayesian network of Figures 10.1 and 10.3. The only differences are the two predicates m/2 and f/2 which can be in one of the logical set of states *true* and *false*. Using these predicates and an appropriate set of Bayesian facts (the "extension") one can encode the Bayesian network for any family. This situation is akin to that in deductive databases, where the "intension" (the clauses) encodes the overall regularities and the "extension" (the facts) the specific context of interest. By interchanging the extension, one can swap contexts (in our case, families).

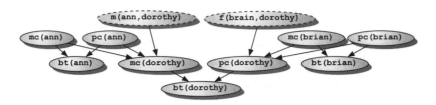

Figure 10.6   The structure of the Bayesian network represented by the grounded *blood type* Bayesian logic program in figure 10.5. The structure of the Bayesian network coincides with the dependency graph. Omitting the dashed nodes yields the original Bayesian network of figure 10.1.

10.3.3   Procedural Semantics

Clearly, any (conditional) probability distribution over random variables of the Bayesian network corresponding to the least Herbrand model can — in principle — be computed. As the least Herbrand model (and therefore the corresponding Bayesian network) can become (even infinitely) large, the question arises as to whether one needs to construct the full least Herbrand model (and Bayesian network) to be able to perform inferences. Here, inference means the process of answering probabilistic queries.

Definition 10.7 Probabilistic Query
A probabilistic query to a Bayesian logic program B is an expression of the form

$$\text{?- } \mathsf{q_1}, \ldots, \mathsf{q_n} \,|\, \mathsf{e_1} = e_1, \ldots, \mathsf{e_m} = e_m$$

where $n > 0$, $m \geq 0$. It asks for the conditional probability distribution

$$\mathbf{P}(\mathsf{q_1}, \ldots, \mathsf{q_n} \mid \mathsf{e_1} = e_1, \ldots, \mathsf{e_m} = e_m)$$

of the query variables $\mathsf{q_1}, \ldots, \mathsf{q_n}$ where $\{\mathsf{q_1}, \ldots, \mathsf{q_n}, \mathsf{e_1}, \ldots, \mathsf{e_m}\} \subseteq \mathrm{HB}(B)$.

To answer a probabilistic query, one fortunately does not have to compute the complete least Herbrand model. It suffices to consider the so-called support network.

Definition 10.8 Support Network
The *support network* N of a random variable $\mathsf{x} \in \mathrm{LH}(B)$ is defined as the induced subnetwork of

$$\{\mathsf{x}\} \cup \{\mathsf{y} \mid \mathsf{y} \in \mathrm{LH}(B) \text{ and } \mathsf{y} \text{ influences } \mathsf{x}\} \,.$$

The support network of a finite set $\{\mathsf{x_1}, \ldots, \mathsf{x_k}\} \subseteq \mathrm{LH}(B)$ is the union of the networks of each single $\mathsf{x_i}$.

For instance, the support network for $\mathsf{bt(dorothy)}$ is the Bayesian network shown in figure 10.6. The support network for $\mathsf{bt(brian)}$ is the subnetwork with root $\mathsf{bt(brian)}$, i.e.,

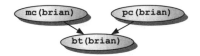

That the support network of a finite set $\mathbf{X} \subseteq \mathrm{LH}(B)$ is sufficent to compute $\mathbf{P}(\mathbf{X})$ follows from the following theorem (taken from [21]):

Theorem 10.9 Support Network

Let N be a possibly infinite Bayesian network, let $\mathbf{Q}$ be nodes of N, and $\mathbf{E} = \mathbf{e}$, $\mathbf{E} \subset N$, be some evidence. The computation of $\mathbf{P}(\mathbf{Q} \mid \mathbf{E} = \mathbf{e})$ does not depend on any node $\mathbf{x}$ of N which is not a member of the support network $N(\mathbf{Q} \cup \mathbf{E})$.

To compute the support network $N(\{\mathtt{q}\})$ of a single variable $\mathtt{q}$ efficiently, let us look at logic programs from a proof-theoretic perspective. From this perspective, a logic program can be used to prove that certain atoms or goals (see below) are logically entailed by the program. Provable ground atoms are members of the least Herbrand model.

Proofs are typically constructed using the SLD-resolution procedure which we will now briefly introduce. Given a goal $\mathtt{:\text{-}G_1, G_2 \dots, G_n}$ and a clause $\mathtt{G\text{:-}L_1, \dots, L_m}$ such that $\mathtt{G_1}\theta = \mathtt{G}\theta$, applying SLD resolution yields the new goal $\mathtt{:\text{-}L_1\theta, \dots, L_m\theta, G_2\theta \dots, G_n\theta}$. A *successful* refutation, i.e., a proof of a goal, is then a sequence of resolution steps yielding the empty goal, i.e. $\mathtt{:\text{-}}$. *Failed* proofs do not end in the empty goal. For instance, in our running example, $\mathtt{bt(dorothy)}$ is true, because of the following refutation:

$$\mathtt{:\text{-}bt(dorothy)}$$
$$\mathtt{:\text{-}mc(dorothy), pc(dorothy)}$$
$$\mathtt{:\text{-}m(ann, dorothy), mc(ann), pc(ann), pc(dorothy)}$$
$$\mathtt{:\text{-}mc(annn), pc(ann), pc(dorothy)}$$
$$\mathtt{:\text{-}pc(ann), pc(dorothy)}$$
$$\mathtt{:\text{-}pc(dorothy)}$$
$$\mathtt{:\text{-}f(brian, dorothy), mc(brian), pc(brian)}$$
$$\mathtt{:\text{-}mc(brian), pc(brian)}$$
$$\mathtt{:\text{-}pc(brian)}$$
$$\mathtt{:\text{-}}$$

Resolution is employed by many theorem provers (such as Prolog). Indeed, when given the goal $\mathtt{bt(dorothy)}$, Prolog would compute the above successful resolution refutation and answer that the goal is true.

The set of all proofs of $\mathtt{:\text{-}bt(dorothy)}$ captures all information needed to compute $N(\{\mathtt{bt(dorothy)}\})$. More exactly, the set of all ground clauses employed to prove $\mathtt{bt(dorothy)}$ constitutes the families of the support network $N(\{\mathtt{bt(dorothy)}\})$. For $\mathtt{:\text{-}bt(dorothy)}$, they are the ground clauses shown in figure 10.5. To build the

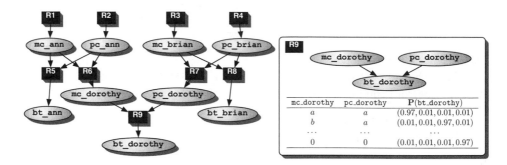

Figure 10.7 The rule graph for the *blood type* Bayesian network. On the right-hand side the local probability model associated with node R9 is shown, i.e., the Bayesian clause bt_dorothy|mc_dorothy, pc_dorothy with associated conditional probability table.

support network, we only have to gather all ground clauses used to prove the query variable and have to combine multiple copies of ground clauses with the same head using corresponding combining rules. To summarize, the support network $N(\{\mathbf{q}\})$ can be computed as follows:

1   Compute all proofs for :-q.
2   Extract the set S of ground clauses used to prove :-q.
3   Combine multiple copies of ground clauses h|b $\in S$ with the same head h using combining rules.

Applying this to :-bt(dorothy) yields the support network as shown in figure 10.6. Furthermore, the method can easily be extended to compute the support network for $\mathbf{P}(\mathbf{Q} \mid \mathbf{E} = \boldsymbol{e})$. We simply compute all proofs of :-q, q $\in \mathbf{Q}$, and :-e, e $\in \mathbf{E}$. The resulting support network can be fed into any (exact or approximative) Bayesian network engine to compute the resulting (conditional) probability distribution of the query. To minimize the size of the support network, one might also apply Schachter's Bayes-Ball algorithm [43].

10.4   Extensions of the Basic Framework

So far, we described the basic Bayesian logic programming framework and defined the semantics of Bayesian logic programs. Various useful extensions and modifications are possible. In this section, we discuss a *graphical representation*, efficient treatment of *logical atoms*, and *aggregate functions*. At the same time, we will also present further examples of Bayesian logic programs such as hidden Markov models (HMMs) [39] and probabilistic grammars [29].

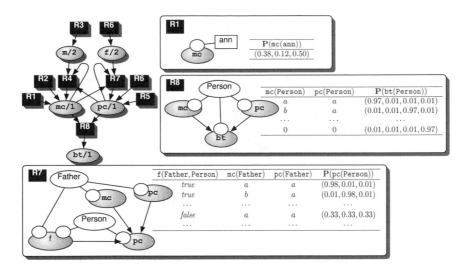

Figure 10.8 The graphical representation of the *blood type* Bayesian logic program. On the righthand side, some local probability models associated with Bayesian clause nodes are shown, e.g., the Bayesian clause *R7* pc(Person)|f(Father, Person), mc(Father), pc(Father) with associated conditional probability distribution. For the sake of simplicity, not all Bayesian clauses are shown.

10.4.1 Graphical Representation

Bayesian logic programs have so far been introduced using an adaptation of a logic programming syntax. Bayesian networks are, however, also graphical models and owe at least part of their popularity to their intuitively appealing graphical notation [20]. Inspired by Bayesian networks, we develop in this section a graphical notation for Bayesian logic programs.

In order to develop a graphical representation for Bayesian logic programs, let us first consider a more redundant representation for Bayesian networks: augmented bipartite (directed acyclic) graphs as shown in figure 10.7. In a bipartite graph, the set of nodes is composed of two disjoint sets such that no two nodes within the same set are adjacent. There are two types of nodes, namely

1. *gradient gray ovals* denoting random variables, and

2. *black boxes* denoting local probability models.

There is a box for each family $\mathbf{Fa}(\mathbf{x_i})$ in the Bayesian network. The incoming edges refer to the parents $\mathbf{Pa}(\mathbf{x_i})$; the single outgoing edge points to X_i. Each box is augmented with a Bayesian network fragment specifying the conditional probability distribution $\mathbf{P}(\mathbf{x_i}|\mathbf{Pa}(\mathbf{x_i}))$. For instance, in figure 10.7, the fragment associated with $R9$ specifies the conditional probability distribution of $\mathbf{P}(\text{bt}(\text{dorothy})|\text{mc}(\text{dorothy}), \text{pc}(\text{dorothy}))$. Interpreting this as a propositional

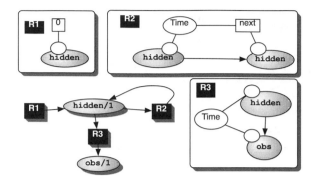

Figure 10.9   A dynamic Bayesian logic program modeling a hidden Markov model. The functor `next/1` is used to encode the discrete time.

Bayesian logic program, the graph can be viewed as a *rule graph* as known from database theory. Ovals represent Bayesian predicates, and boxes denote Bayesian clauses. More precisely, given a (propositional) Bayesian logic program B with Bayesian clauses $R_i \equiv \mathtt{h_i}|\mathtt{b_{i_1}}, \ldots, \mathtt{b_{i_m}}$, there are edges from from R_i to $\mathtt{h_i}$ and from $\mathtt{b_{i_j}}$ to R_i. Furthermore, to each Bayesian clause node, we associate the corresponding Bayesian clause as a Bayesian network fragment. Indeed, the graphical model in figure 10.7 represents the propositional Bayesian logic program of figure 10.5.

In order to represent first-order Bayesian logic programs graphically, we have to encode Bayesian atoms and their variable bindings in the associated local probability models. Indeed, logical terms can naturally be represented graphically. They form trees. For instance, the term $\mathtt{t(s(1,2),X)}$ corresponds to the tree

Logical variables such as X are encoded as white ovals. Constants and functors such as 1, 2, s, and t are represented as white boxes. Bayesian atoms are represented as gradient gray ovals containing the predicate name such as pc. Arguments of atoms are treated as placeholders for terms. They are represented as white circles on the boundary of the ovals (ordered from left to right). The term appearing in the argument is represented by an undirected edge between the white oval representing the argument and the "root" of the tree encoding the term (we start in the argument and follow the tree until reaching variables).

As an example, consider the Bayesian logic program in figure 10.8. It models the *blood type* domain. The graphical representation indeed conveys the meaning of the Bayesian clause $R7$: *the paternal genetic information* pc(Person) *of a person is influenced by the maternal* mc(M) *and the paternal* pc(M) *genetic information of the person's* Father.

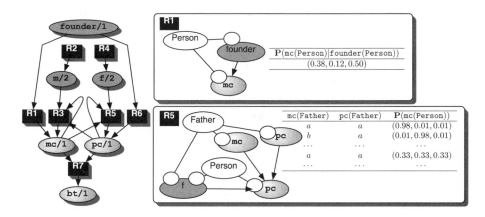

Figure 10.10 The *blood type* Bayesian logic program distinguishing between *Bayesian* (gradient gray ovals) and *logical* atoms (solid gray ovals).

As another example, consider figure 10.9 which shows the use of functors to represent dynamic probabilistic models. More precisely, it shows an HMM [39]. HMMs are extremely popular for analyzing sequential data. Application areas include computational biology, user modeling, speech recognition, empirical natural language processing, and robotics.

At each `Time`, the system is in a state `hidden(Time)`. The time-independent probability of being in some state at the next time `next(Time)` given that the system was in a state at `TimePoint` is captured in the Bayesian clause $R2$. Here, the next time point is represented as functor `next/1` . In HMMs, however, we do not have direct access to the states `hidden(Time)`. Instead, we measure some properties `obs(Time)` of the states. The measurement is quantified in Bayesian clause $R3$. The dependency graph of the Bayesian logic program directly encodes the well-known Bayesian network structure of HMMs:

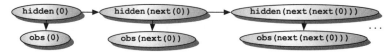

10.4.2 Logical Atoms

Reconsider the *blood type* Bayesian logic program in figure 10.8. The `mother/2` and `father/2` relations are not really *random* variables but *logical* ones because they are always in the same state, namely *true*, with probability 1, and can depend only on other logical atoms. These predicates form a kind of logical background theory. Therefore, when predicates are declared to be *logical*, one need not represent them in the conditional probability distributions. Consider the *blood type* Bayesian logic program in figure 10.10. Here, `mother/2` and `father/2` are declared to be *logical*. Consequently, the conditional probability distribution associated with the definition of, e.g., pc/1 takes only pc(Father) and mc(Father) into account but not f(Father, Person). It applies only to those substitutions for which f(Father, Person) is true, i.e., in the least Herbrand model. This can efficiently be checked using any Prolog engine. Furthermore, one may omit these logical atoms from the induced support network. More importantly, logical predicates provide the user with the full power of Prolog. In the *blood type* Bayesian logic program of figure 10.10, the logical background knowledge defines the founder/1 relation as

$$\text{founder(Person):-}\backslash\text{+(mother(\_, Person); father(\_, Person)).}$$

Here, $\backslash$+ denotes *negation*, the symbol _ represents an anonymous variable which is treated as a new, distinct variable each time it is encountered, and the semicolon denotes a *disjunction*. The rest of the Bayesian logic program is essentially as in figure 10.4. Instead of explicitly listing pc(ann), mc(ann), pc(brian), mc(brian) in the extensional part we have pc(P)|founder(P) and mc(P)|founder(P) in the intensional part.

The full power of Prolog is also useful to elegantly encode dynamic probabilistic models. Figure 10.11 (a) shows the generic structure of an HMM where the discrete time is now encoded as next/2 in the logical background theory using standard Prolog predicates:

$$\text{next(X, Y):-integer(Y), Y > 0, X is Y - 1.}$$

Prolog's predefined predicates (such as integer/1) avoid a cumbersome representation of the dynamics via the successor functor $0, \text{next}(0), \text{next}(\text{next}(0)), \ldots$ Imagine querying ?- obs(100) using the successor functor,

$$\text{?- obs(next(next(} \ldots \text{(next(0))} \ldots \text{))) .}$$

Whereas HMMs define probability distributions over regular languages, *probabilistic context-free grammars* (,s) [29] define probability distributions over context-free languages. Application areas of PCFGs include, e.g., natural language processing and computational biology. For instance, mRNA sequences constitute context-free languages. Consider, e.g., the following PCFG

$$\text{terminal([A|B], A, B).}$$
$$0.3 : \text{sentence(A, B):-terminal(A, a, C), terminal(C, b, B).}$$
$$0.7 : \text{sentence(A, B):-terminal(A, a, C), sentence(C, D), terminal(D, b, B).}$$

defining a distribution over $\{a^n b^n\}$. The grammar is represented as probabilistic *definite clause grammar* where the terminal symbols are encoded in the logical background theory via the first rule terminal([A|B], A, B) .

A PCFG defines a stochastic process with leftmost rewriting, i.e., refutation steps as transitions. Words, say *aabb*, are parsed by querying ?- sentence([a, a, b, b], []). The third rule yields ?- terminal([a, a, b, b], a, C), sentence(C, D), terminal(D, b, []). Applying the first rule yields ?- sentence([a, b, b], D), terminal(D, b, []) and the sec-

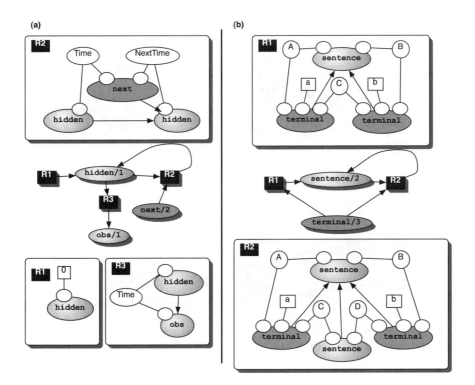

Figure 10.11 Two dynamic Bayesian logic programs. (a) The generic structure of a hidden Markov model more elegantly represented as in figure 10.9 using $\texttt{next}(\texttt{X},\texttt{Y}):-\texttt{integer}(\texttt{Y}),\texttt{Y}>0,\texttt{X is Y}-1..$ (b) A probabilistic context-free grammar over $\{a^n b^n\}$. The logical background theory defines $\texttt{terminal}/3$ as $\texttt{terminal}([\texttt{A}|\texttt{B}],\texttt{A},\texttt{B})$.

ond rule $\texttt{?-}\ \texttt{terminal}([\texttt{a},\texttt{b},\texttt{b}],\texttt{a},\texttt{C}),\texttt{terminal}(\texttt{C},\texttt{b},\texttt{D}),\texttt{terminal}(\texttt{D},\texttt{b},[])$. Applying the first rule three times yields a successful refutation. The probability of a refutation is the product of the probability values associated with clauses used in the refutation; in our case $0.7 \cdot 0.3$. The probability of *aabb* then is the sum of the probabilities of all successful refutations. This is also the basic idea underlying Muggleton's *stochastic logic programs* [30] which extend the PCFGs to definite clause logic.

Figure 10.11 (b) shows the $\{a^n b^n\}$ PCFG represented as a Bayesian logic program. The Bayesian clauses are the clauses of the corresponding *definite clause grammar*. In contrast to PCFGs, however, we associate a complete conditional probability distribution, namely $(0.3, 0.7)$ and $(0.7, 0.3; 0.0, 1.0)$ to the Bayesian clauses. For the query $\texttt{?-}\ \texttt{sentence}([\texttt{a},\texttt{a},\texttt{b},\texttt{b}],[])$, the following Markov chain is induced (omitting logical atoms):

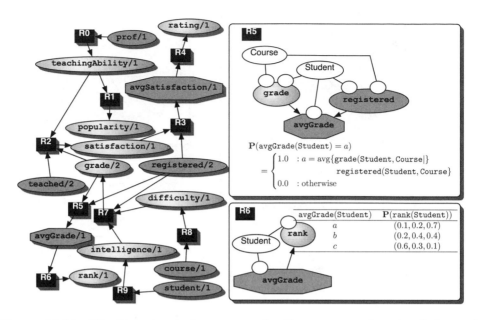

Figure 10.12 The Bayesian logic program for the *university* domain. Octagonal nodes denote aggregate predicates and atoms.

10.4.3 Aggregate Functions

An alternative to combining rules are *aggregate functions*. Consider the *university* domain due to [12]. The domain is that of a university, and contains professors, students, courses, and course registrations. Objects in this domain have several descriptive attributes such as `intelligence/1` and `rank/1` of a `student/1`. A student will typically be registered in several courses; the student's rank depends on the grades she receives in all of them. So we have to specify a probabilistic dependence of the student's rank on a multiset of course grades of size 1, 2, and so on.

In this situation, the notion of aggregation is more appropriate than that of a combining rule. Using combining rules, the Bayesian clauses would describe the dependence for a single course only. All information of how the rank probabilistically depends on the multiset of course grades would be "hidden" in the combining rule. In contrast, when using an aggregate function, the dependence is interpreted as a probabilistic dependence of `rank` on some *deterministically* computed aggregate property of the multiset of course grades. The probabilistic dependence is moved out of the combining rule.

To model this, we introduce *aggregate* predicates. They represent deterministic random variables, i.e., the state of an aggregate atom is a function of the joint state of its parents. As an example, consider the *university* Bayesian logic program as shown in figure 10.12. Here, `avgGrade/1` is an aggregate predicate, denoted as an octagonal node. As combining rule, the average of the parents' states is deterministically computed; cf. Bayesian clause $R5$. In turn, the student's `rank/1` probabilistically depends on her averaged rank; cf. $R6$.

The use of aggregate functions is inspired by *probabilistic relational models* [37]. As we will show in the related work section, using aggregates in Bayesian logic programs, it is easy to model probabilistic relational models.

10.5   Learning Bayesian Logic Programs

When designing Bayesian logic programs, the expert has to determine the structure of the Bayesian logic program by specifying the extensional and intensional predicates, and by providing definitions for each of the intensional predicates. Given this logical structure, the Bayesian logic program induces a Bayesian network whose nodes are the *relevant* random variables. It is well-known that determining the structure of a Bayesian network, and therefore also of a Bayesian logic program, can be difficult and expensive. On the other hand, it is often easier to obtain a set $D = \{D_1, \ldots, D_m\}$ of data cases, which can be used for learning.

10.5.1   The Learning Setting

For Bayesian logic programs, a data case $D_i \in D$ has two parts, a logical and a probabilistic part. The logical part of a data case is a Herbrand interpretation. For instance, the following set of atoms constitutes a Herbrand interpretation for the *blood type* Bayesian logic program.

$$\{\texttt{m(ann, dorothy)}, \texttt{f(brian, dorothy)}, \texttt{pc(ann)}, \texttt{mc(ann)}, \texttt{bt(ann)},$$
$$\texttt{pc(brian)}, \texttt{mc(brian)}, \texttt{bt(brian)}, \texttt{pc(dorothy)}, \texttt{mc(dorothy)}, \texttt{bt(dorothy)}\}$$

This (logical) interpretation can be seen as the least Herbrand model of an unknown Bayesian logic program. In general, data cases specify different sets of *relevant* random variables, depending on the given "extensional context." If we accept that the genetic laws are the same for different families, then a learning algorithm should transform such extensionally defined predicates into intensionally defined ones, thus compressing the interpretations. This is precisely what *inductive logic programming* techniques [31] do. The key assumption underlying any inductive technique is that the rules that are valid in one interpretation are likely to hold for other interpretations. It thus seems clear that techniques for *learning from interpretations* can be adapted for learning the logical structure of Bayesian logic programs.

So far, we have specified the logical part of the learning problem: we are looking for a set H of Bayesian clauses given a set D of data cases such that all data cases are a model of H. The hypotheses H in the space $\mathcal{H}$ of hypotheses are sets of Bayesian clauses. However, we have to be more careful. A candidate set $H \in \mathcal{H}$ has to be acyclic on the data, which implies that for each data case the induced Bayesian network has to be acyclic.

Let us now focus on the quantitative components. The quantitative component of a Bayesian logic program is given by the associated conditional probability distributions and combining rules. For the sake of simplicity, we assume that the combining rules are fixed. Each data case $D_i \in D$ has a probabilistic part that is a partial assignment of states to the random variables in D_i. As an example consider the following data case:

$$\{\mathtt{m}(\mathtt{ann}, \mathtt{dorothy}) = true, \mathtt{f}(\mathtt{brian}, \mathtt{dorothy}) = true, \mathtt{pc}(\mathtt{ann}) = a, \mathtt{mc}(\mathtt{ann}) = a,$$
$$\mathtt{bt}(\mathtt{ann}) = a, \mathtt{pc}(\mathtt{brian}) = a, \mathtt{mc}(\mathtt{brian}) = b, \mathtt{bt}(\mathtt{brian}) = ab,$$
$$\mathtt{pc}(\mathtt{dorothy}) = b, \mathtt{mc}(\mathtt{dorothy}) =?, \mathtt{bt}(\mathtt{dorothy}) = ab\},$$

where ? denotes an unknown state of a random variable. The partial assignments induce a joint distribution over the random variables. A candidate $H \in \mathcal{H}$ should reflect this distribution. In Bayesian networks the conditional probability distributions are typically learned using gradient descent or expectation maximization (EM) for a fixed structure of the Bayesian network. A scoring function $score_D(H)$ that evaluates how well a given structure $H \in \mathcal{H}$ matches the data is maximized.

To summarize, the learning problem is a probabilistic extension of the *learning from interpretations* setting from inductive logic programming and can be formulated as follows:

Given a set D of data cases, a set $\mathcal{H}$ of Bayesian logic programs and a scoring function $score_D$.

Find a candidate $H^* \in \mathcal{H}$ which is acyclic on the data cases such that the data cases $D_i \in D$ are models of H^* (in the logical sense) and H^* matches the data D best according to $score_D$.

Here, the best match refers to those parameters of the associated conditional probability distributions which maximize the scoring function.

The learning setting provides an interesting link between inductive logic programming and Bayesian network learning as we will show in the next section.

10.5.2   Maximum Likelihood Learning

Consider the task of performing *maximum likelihood* learning, i.e., $score_D(H) = \mathbf{P}(D|H)$. As in many cases, it is more convenient to work with the logarithm of this function, i.e., $score_D(H) = LL(D, H) := \log \mathbf{P}(D|H)$. It can be shown (see [22] for more details) that the likelihood of a Bayesian logic program coincides with the likelihood of the support network induced over D. Thus, learning Bayesian logic programs basically reduces to learning Bayesian networks. The main differences are the ways to estimate the parameters and to traverse the hypotheses space.

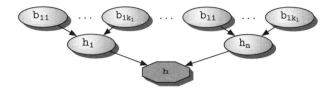

Figure 10.13 Decomposable combining rules can be expressed within support networks. The nodes h_i have the domain of h and cpd(c) associated. The node h becomes a deterministic node, i.e., its parameters are fixed. For example, for *noisy_or*, logical *or* is associated as function with h. Note that the h_i's are never observed; only h might be observed.

10.5.2.1   *Parameter Estimation*

The parameters of nonground Bayesian clauses have to be estimated. In order to adapt techniques traditionally used for parameter estimation of Bayesian networks such as the EM algorithm [7], combining rules are assumed to be *decomposable* [3] [15]. Decomposable combining rules can be completely expressed by adding extra nodes to the induced support network; cf. figure 10.13. These extra nodes are copies of the (ground) head atom which becomes a deterministic node. Now, each node in the support network is "produced" by exactly one Bayesian clause c, and each node derived from c can be seen as a separate "experiment" for the conditional probability distribution cpd(c). Therefore, the EM estimates the improved parameters as the following ratio:

$$\frac{\sum_{l=1}^{m} \sum_{\theta} \mathbf{P}(\text{head}(c\theta), \text{body}(c\theta) \mid D_l)}{\sum_{l=1}^{m} \sum_{\theta} \mathbf{P}(\text{body}(c\theta) \mid D_l)},$$

where θ denotes substitutions such that D_l is a model of $c\theta$.

10.5.2.2   *Traversing the Hypotheses Space*

Instead of adding, deleting, or flipping single edges in the support network, we employ refinement operators traditionally used in inductive logic programming to add, delete, or flip several edges in the support network at the same time. More specifically, according to some language bias — say we consider only functor-free and constants-free clauses — we use the two refinement operators $\rho_s : 2^{\mathcal{H}} \mapsto \mathcal{H}$ and $\rho_g : 2^{\mathcal{H}} \mapsto \mathcal{H}$. The operator $\rho_s(H)$ adds constant-free atoms to the body of a single clause $c \in H$, and $\rho_g(H)$ deletes constant-free atoms from the body of a single clause $c \in H$. Other refinement operators such as deleting and adding logically valid clauses, instantiating variables, and unifying variables are possible too; cf. [35].

---

3. Most combining rules commonly employed in Bayesian networks such as *noisy_or* are decomposable.

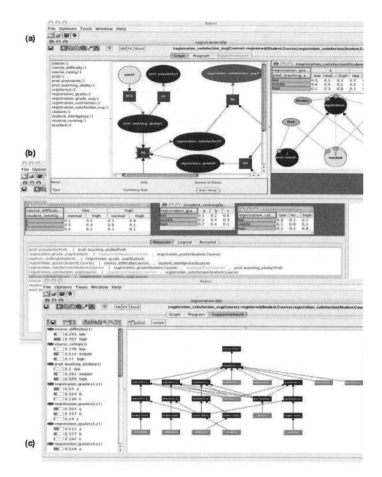

Figure 10.14 Balios—the engine for Bayesian logic programs. (a) Graphical representation of the *university* Bayesian logic program. (b) Textual representation of Bayesian clauses with associated conditional probability distributions. (c) Computed support network and probabilities for a probabilistic query.

Combining these ideas, a basic greedy hill-climbing algorithm for learning Bayesian logic programs can be sketched as follows. Assuming some data cases D, we take some H_0 as a starting point (for example, computed using some standard inductive logic programming system) and compute the parameters maximizing $LL(D, H)$. Then, we use $\rho_s(H)$ and $\rho_g(H)$ to compute the legal "neighbors" of H in $\mathcal{H}$ and score them. If $LL(D, H) < LL(D, H')$, then we take H' as new hypothesis. The process is continued until no further improvements in score are obtained.

10.6 Balios – The Engine for Basic Logic Programs

An engine for Bayesian logic programs featuring a graphical representation, logical atoms, and aggregate functions has been implemented in the BALIOS system [23], which is freely available for academic use at
`http://www.informatik.uni-freiburg.de/~kersting/profile/`. BALIOS is written in JAVA. It calls SICSTUS Prolog to perform logical inference and a Bayesian network inference engine to perform probabilistic inference. BALIOS features a GUI graphically representing Bayesian logic programs (figure 10.14), computing the most likely configuration, approximative inference methods (rejection, likelihood, and Gibbs sampling), and parameter estimation methods (hard EM, EM, and conjugate gradient).

10.7 Related Work

In the last ten years, there has been a lot of work done at the intersection of probability theory, logic programming, and machine learning [38, 14, 41, 30, 34, 17, 26, 1, 24, 9]; see [5] for an overview. Instead of giving a probabilistic characterization of logic programming such as [32], this research highlights the machine learning aspect and is known under the names of *statistical relational learning* (SRL) [11, 8], probabilistic logic learning (PLL) [5], or probabilistic inductive logic programming (PILP) [6]. Bayesian logic programs belong to the SRL line of research which extends Bayesian networks. They are motivated and inspired by the formalisms discussed in [38, 14, 34, 17, 10, 25]. We will now investigate these relationships in more detail.

Probabilistic logic programs [33, 34] also adapt a logic program syntax, the concept of the least Herbrand model to specify the relevant random variables, and SLD resolution to develop a query-answering procedure. Whereas Bayesian logic programs view atoms as random variables, probabilistic-logic programs view them as states of random variables. For instance,

$$P(\text{burglary}(\text{Person}, \text{yes}) \mid \text{neighbourhood}(\text{Person}, \text{average})) = 0.4$$

states that the a posteriori probability of a burglary in Person's house given that Person has an average neighborhood is 0.4. Thus, instead of conditional probability distributions, conditional probability values are associated with clauses.

Treating atoms as states of random variables has several consequences: (1) Exclusivity constraints such as

$$\text{false} \leftarrow \text{neighbourhood}(X, \text{average}), \text{neighbourhood}(X, \text{bad})$$

have to be specified in order to guarantee that random variables are always in exactly one state. (2) The inference procedure is exponentially slower in time for building the support network than that for Bayesian logic programs because there is a proof for each configuration of a random variable. (3) It is more difficult — if not impossible — to represent continuous random variables. (4) Qualitative, i.e., the logical component, and quantitative information, i.e., the probability values, are mixed. Just this separation of both information made the graphical representation for Bayesian logic programs possible.

Probabilistic and Bayesian logic programs are also related to Poole's framework of **probabilistic Horn abduction** [38], which is "a pragmatically-motivated simple logic formulation that includes definite clauses and probabilities over hypotheses" [38]. Poole's framework provides a link to abduction and assumption-based reasoning. However, as Ngo and Haddawy point out, probabilistic and therefore also Bayesian logic programs have not as many constraints on the representation language, represent probabilistic dependencies directly rather than indirectly, have a richer representational power, and their independence assumption reflects the causality of the domain.

Koller et. al. [10, 25] define **probabilistic relational models**, which are based on the well-known entity/relationship model. In probabilistic relational models, the random variables are the attributes. The relations between entities are deterministic, i.e., they are only true or false. Probabilistic relational models can be described as Bayesian logic programs.

Indeed, each attribute a of an entity type E is a Bayesian predicate $a(E)$ and each n-ary relation r is an n-ary logical Bayesian predicate r/n. Probabilistic relational models consist of a qualitative dependency structure over the attributes and their associated quantitative parameters (the conditional probability densities). Koller et. al. distinguish between two types of parents of an attribute. First, an attribute $a(X)$ can depend on another attribute $b(X)$, e.g., the professor's popularity depends on the professor's teaching ability in the *university* domain. This is equivalent to the Bayesian clause $a(X) \mid b(X)$. Second, an attribute $a(X)$ possibly depends on an attribute $b(Y)$ of an entity Y related to X, e.g., a student's grade in a course depends on the difficulty of the course. The relation between X and Y is described by a slot or logical relation $s(X, Y)$. Given these logical relations, the original dependency is represented by $a(X) \mid s(X, Y), b(Y)$. To deal with multiple ground instantiations of a single clause (with the same head ground atom), probabilistic relational models employ aggregate functions, as discussed earlier.

Clearly, probabilistic relational models employ a more restricted logical component than Bayesian logic programs do: it is a version of the commonly used entity/relationship model. Any entity/relationship model can be represented using a (range-restricted) definite clause logic. Furthermore, several extensions to treat *existential uncertainty*, *referential uncertainty*, and *domain uncertainty* exist. Bayesian logic programs have the full expressivity of definite clause logic and, therefore, of a universal Turing machine. Indeed, general definite clause logic (using functors) is undecidable. The functor-free fragment of definite clause logic, however, is decidable.

Jaeger [17] introduced **relational Bayesian networks**. They are Bayesian networks where the nodes are predicate symbols. The states of these random variables are possible interpretations of the symbols over an arbitrary, finite domain (here we only consider Herbrand domains), i.e., the random variables are set valued. The inference problem addressed by Jaeger asks for the probability that an interpretation contains a ground atom. Thus, relational Bayesian networks are viewed as Bayesian networks where the nodes are the ground atoms and have the domain $\{true, false\}$. [4] The key difference between relational Bayesian networks and Bayesian logic programs is that the quantitative information is specified by so-called probability formulae. These formulae employ the notion of combination functions, functions that map every finite multiset with elements from $[0, 1]$ into $[0, 1]$, as well as that of equality constraints. [5] Let $F(cancer)(x)$ be $noisy\_or\{comb_\Gamma\{exposed(x, y, z) \mid z; true\} \mid y; true\}$. This formula states that for any specific organ y, multiple exposures to radiation have a cumulative but independent effect on the risk of developing cancer of y. Thus, a probability formula not only specifies the distribution but also the dependency structure. Therefore and because of the computational power of combining rules, a probability formula is easily expressed as a set of Bayesian clauses: the head of the Bayesian clauses is the corresponding Bayesian atom and the bodies consist of all maximally generalized Bayesian atoms occurring in the probability formula. Now the combining rule can select the right ground atoms and simulate the probability formula. This is always possible because the Herbrand base is finite. For example, the clause `cancer(X) | exposed(X,Y,Z)` together with the right combining rule and associated conditional probability distribution models the example formula.

In addition to extensions of Bayesian networks, several other probabilistic models have been extended to the first-order or relational case: Sato [41] introduces *distributional semantics* in which ground atoms are seen as random variables over $\{true, false\}$. Probability distributions are defined over the ground facts of a program and propagated over the Herbrand base of the program using the clauses. Stochastic logic programs [30, 4], introduced by Muggleton, lift context-free probabilistic grammars to the first-order case. Production rules are replaced by clauses labeled with probability values. Recently, Domingos and Richardson [9] introduced Markov logic networks which upgrade Markov networks to the first-order case. The features of the Markov logic network are weights attached to first-order predicate logic formulae. The weights specify a bias for ground instances to be true in a logical model.

Finally, Bayesian logic programs are related — to some extent — to the **BUGS** language [13] which aims at carrying out Bayesian inference using Gibbs sampling.

---

4. It is possible, but complicated to model domains having more than two values.
5. To simplify the discussion, we will further ignore these equality constraints here.

It uses concepts of imperative programming languages such as for-loops to model regularities in probabilistic models. Therefore, the relation between Bayesian logic programs and BUGS is akin to the general relation between logical and imperative languages. This holds in particular for relational domains such as those used in this chapter. Without the notion of objects and relations among objects, family trees are hard to represent: BUGS uses traditional indexing to group together random variables (e.g. X_1, X_2, X_3 ... all having the same distribution), whereas Bayesian logic programs use definite clause logic.

10.8 Conclusions

We have described Bayesian logic programs, their representation language, their semantics, and a query-answering process, and briefly touched upon learning Bayesian logic programs from data.

Bayesian logic programs combine Bayesian networks with definite clause logic. The main idea of Bayesian logic programs is to establish a one-to-one mapping between ground atoms in the least Herbrand model and random variables. The least Herbrand model of a Bayesian logic program together with its direct influence relation is viewed as a (possibly infinite) Bayesian network. Bayesian logic programs inherit the advantages of both Bayesian networks and definite clause logic, including the strict separation of qualitative and quantitative aspects. Moreover, the strict separation facilitated the introduction of a graphical representation, which stays close to the graphical representation of Bayesian networks.

Indeed, Bayesian logic programs can naturally model any type of Bayesian network (including those involving continuous variables) as well as any type of pure Prolog program (including those involving functors). We also demonstrated that Bayesian logic programs can model HMMs and stochastic grammars, and investigated their relationship to other first-order extensions of Bayesian networks.

We have also presented the BALIOS tool, which employs the graphical as well as the logical notations for Bayesian logic programs. It is available at

http://www.informatik.uni-freiburg.de/~kersting/profile/.

and the authors invite the reader to employ it.

Acknowledgments

The authors thank Uwe Dick for implementing the BALIOS system. This research was partly supported by the European Union IST programme under contract number IST-2001-33053 and FP6-508861, APRIL I & II (**A**pplication of **Pr**obabilistic **I**nductive **L**ogic Programming).

References

[1] C. R. Anderson, P. Domingos, and D. S. Weld. Relational Markov models and their application to adaptive web navigation. In *International Conference on Knowledge Discovery and Data Mining*, 2002.

[2] Heinz Bauer. *Wahrscheinlichkeitstheorie, 4th edition.* Walter de Gruyter, Berlin, 1991.

[3] J. Cheng, C. Hatzis, M.–A. Krogel, S. Morishita, D. Page, and J. Sese. KDD Cup 2001 report. *SIGKDD Explorations*, 3(2):47 – 64, 2002.

[4] J. Cussens. Loglinear models for first-order probabilistic reasoning. In *Proceedings of the Conference on Uncertainty in Artificial Intelligence*, 1999.

[5] L. De Raedt and K. Kersting. Probabilistic logic learning. *ACM-SIGKDD Explorations: Special Issue on Multi-Relational Data Mining*, 5(1):31–48, 2003.

[6] L. De Raedt and K. Kersting. Probabilistic inductive logic programming. In *Proceedings of the International Conference on Algorithmic Learning Theory*, pages 19–36, 2004.

[7] A. P. Dempster, N. M. Laird, and D. B. Rubin. Maximum likelihood from incomplete data via the EM algorithm. *Journal of the Royal Statistical Society*, B 39:1–39, 1977.

[8] T. Dietterich, L. Getoor, and K. Murphy, editors. *Working Notes of the ICML-2004 Workshop on Statistical Relational Learning and its Connections to Other Fields (SRL-04)*, 2004.

[9] P. Domingos and M. Richardson. Markov Logic: A Unifying Framework for Statistical Relational Learning. In *Proceedings of the ICML-2004 Workshop on Statistical Relational Learning and its Connections to Other Fields*, pages 49–54, 2004.

[10] N. Friedman, L. Getoor, D. Koller, and A. Pfeffer. Learning probabilistic relational models. In *Proceedings of the International Joint Conference on Artificial Intelligence*, 1999.

[11] L. Getoor and D. Jensen, editors. *Working Notes of the IJCAI-2003 Workshop on Learning Statistical Models from Relational Data (SRL-03)*, 2003.

[12] L. Getoor, N. Friedman, D. Koller, and A. Pfeffer. Learning probabilistic relational models. In S. Džeroski and N. Lavrač, editors, *Relational Data Mining*, pages 307–335. Kluwer, 2001.

[13] W. R. Gilks, A. Thomas, and D. J. Spiegelhalter. A language and program for complex bayesian modelling. *The Statistician*, 43, 1994.

[14] P. Haddawy. Generating Bayesian networks from probabilistic logic knowledge bases. In *Proceedings of the Conference on Uncertainty in Artificial Intelligence*, 1994.

[15] D. Heckerman and J. Breese. Causal independence for probability assessment and inference using bayesian networks. Technical Report MSR-TR-94-08, Microsoft Research, Seattle, WA, 1994.

[16] D. Heckerman, A. Mamdani, and M. P. Wellman. Real-world applications of Bayesian networks. *Communications of the ACM*, 38(3):24–26, March 1995.

[17] M. Jaeger. Relational Bayesian networks. In *Proceedings of the Conference on Uncertainty in Artificial Intelligence*, 1997.

[18] F. V. Jensen. *Bayesian Networks and Decision Graphs*. Springer-Verlag, 2001.

[19] F. V. Jensen. *An Introduction to Bayesian Networks*. UCL Press Limited, 1996. Reprinted 1998.

[20] M. I. Jordan, editor. *Learning in Graphical Models*. MIT Press, Cambridge, MA, 1998.

[21] K. Kersting and L. De Raedt. Bayesian logic programs. Technical Report 151, University of Freiburg, Institute for Computer Science, Freiburg, Germany, April 2001.

[22] K. Kersting and L. De Raedt. Adaptive Bayesian Logic Programs. In *Proceedings of the International Conference on Inductive Logic Programming*, 2001.

[23] K. Kersting and U. Dick. Balios - The engine for Bayesian logic programs. In *Proceedings of the European Conference on Principles and Practice of Knowledege Discovery in Databases*, 2004.

[24] K. Kersting, T. Raiko, S. Kramer, and L. De Raedt. Towards discovering structural signatures of protein folds based on logical hidden Markov models. In *Proceedings of the Pacific Symposium on Biocomputing*, 2003.

[25] D. Koller. Probabilistic relational models. In *Proceedings of the International Conference on Inductive Logic Programming*, 1999.

[26] D. Koller and A. Pfeffer. Probabilistic frame-based systems. In *Proceedings of the National Conference on Artificial Intelligence*, 1998.

[27] P. Langley. *Elements of Machine Learning*. Morgan Kaufmann, San Fransisco, 1995.

[28] J. W. Lloyd. *Foundations of Logic Programming, 2nd edition*. Springer-Verlag, Berlin, 1989.

[29] C. H. Manning and H. Schütze. *Foundations of Statistical Natural Language Processing*. MIT Press, Cambridge, MA, 1999.

[30] S. Muggleton. Stochastic logic programs. In L. De Raedt, editor, *Advances in Inductive Logic Programming*, Amsterdam, 1996. IOS Press.

[31] S. Muggleton and L. De Raedt. Inductive logic programming: Theory and methods. *Journal of Logic Programming*, 19(20):629–679, 1994.

[32] R. Ng and V. S. Subrahmanian. Probabilistic logic programming. *Information and Computation*, 101(2):150–201, 1992.

[33] L. Ngo and P. Haddawy. Probabilistic logic programming and Bayesian networks. In *Algorithms, Concurrency and Knowledge: Proceedings of the Asian Computing Science Conference*, 1995.

[34] L. Ngo and P. Haddawy. Answering queries from context-sensitive probabilistic knowledge bases. *Theoretical Computer Science*, 171:147–177, 1997.

[35] S.-H. Nienhuys-Cheng and R. de Wolf. *Foundations of Inductive Logic Programming*. Springer-Verlag, 1997.

[36] J. Pearl. *Reasoning in Intelligent Systems: Networks of Plausible Inference, 2nd edition*. Morgan Kaufmann, San Fransisco, 1991.

[37] A. J. Pfeffer. *Probabilistic Reasoning for Complex Systems*. PhD thesis, Stanford University, 2000.

[38] D. Poole. Probabilistic Horn abduction and Bayesian networks. *Artificial Intelligence*, 64:81–129, 1993.

[39] L. R. Rabiner. A tutorial on hidden Markov models and selected applications in speech recognition. *Proceedings of the IEEE*, 77(2):257–286, 1989.

[40] S. J. Russell and P. Norvig. *Artificial Intelligence: A Modern Approach*. Prentice-Hall, Upper Saddle River, NJ, 1995.

[41] T. Sato. A statistical learning method for logic programs with distribution semantics. In *Proceedings of the International Conference on Inductive Logic Programming*, 1995.

[42] T. Sato and Y. Kameya. Parameter learning of logic programs for symbolic-statistical modeling. *Journal of Artificial Intelligence Research*, 15:391–454, 2001.

[43] R. D. Schachter. Bayes-Ball: The rational pasttime (for determining irrelevance and requisite information in belief networks and influence diagrams). In *Proceedings of the Conference on Uncertainty in Artificial Intelligence*, 1998.

11 Stochastic Logic Programs: A Tutorial

Stephen Muggleton and Niels Pahlavi

Stochastic logic programs (SLPs)provide a simple scheme for representing probability distributions over structured objects. Other papers have concentrated on technical issues related to the semantics and machine learning of SLPs. By contrast, this chapter provides a tutorial for the use of SLPs as a means of representing probability distributions over structured objects such as sequences, graphs, and plans.

11.1 Introduction

11.1.1 Logic Programs for Algorithms

Logic programs [5] provide a convenient way of describing computer algorithms in a compact and declarative fashion. A good example of this is the following Prolog [1] representation of the quick-sort algorithm.

```
quick_sort([],[]).
quick_sort([Head|Tail],Sorted) :-
        partition(Tail,Head,BeforeHead,AfterHead),
        quick_sort(BeforeHead,BeforeSorted).
        quick_sort(AfterHead,AfterSorted),
        append(BeforeSorted,[Head|AfterSorted],Sorted).
```

Here the key elements of the algorithm are captured in a few lines, showing the relationship between the various parts of the solution.

11.1.2 Logic Programs and Non-Determinism

An algorithm generally describes an entirely deterministic series of actions. However, apart from their use in describing algorithms logic programs can also describe processes involving non-deterministic choice. For instance, consider the following well-known logic program.

```
member(Element,[Element|_]).
member(Element,[_|List]) :-
        member(Element,List).
```

When provided with the goal *:- member(X,[b,a,c])*, a Prolog interpreter will give the following solutions.

```
X = b
X = a
X = c
```

Each of these three solutions is associated with one of the derivations of the given goal.

11.1.3   Probabilistic Non-Determinism

Consider the following non-deterministic logic program representation of the outcome of tossing a two-sided coin.

```
coin(head).
coin(tail).
```

This logic program can be interpreted as saying that when the coin is tossed it will either come up as heads or tails. However, the logic program does not state the frequency with which we can expect these two outcomes to occur. By associating probability labels with the clauses we get the following stochastic logic program (SLP) [9] representation of a fair coin (a coin with equal probability outcomes of heads and tails).

```
0.5: coin(head).
0.5: coin(tail).
```

Given the goal *:- coin(X)* we would now expect the outcomes $X = head$ and $X = tail$ to occur randomly with probability 0.5 in each case. Here we can view X as a random variable in the statistical sense.

11.2   Mixing Deterministic and Probabilistic Choice

We now consider two more complex representational problems. The first involves a simple game with probabilistic outcomes and the second a simplified version of the famous casino blackjack game. The first game is described below.

11.2.1 Simple Game of Chance

The game involves a player and a banker. The player starts with a quantity of N counters and the banker with M counters. Until the player chooses to stop he does the following repeatedly.

1. The player pays an entrance fee (F counters) to the banker.
2. The player rolls a six-sided dice and gets the value D.
3. The banker rewards the player with D counters.

11.2.2 Representing the Game as an SLP

Below we show how this game can be represented as an SLP. The form of SLP used below is known as an *impure* SLP. An impure SLP is one in which not every definite clause has a probability label. Those without a probability label are treated as normal logic program clauses. Let us start with the unlabeled part of the program.

```
play(State) :-
        act(stop(State,State)).
play(State) :-
        act(pay_entrance(State,State1)),
        act(dice_reward(State1,State2)),
        play(State2).
```

```
act(X) :- X.
```

Here we see the general playing strategy for the game. Every action such as *pay_entrance* and *dice_reward* is conducted by the predicate *act*. Each such action transforms one state into another. Play proceeds by recursing via the second clause until the stop action is taken using the first clause.

11.2.3 Representing the Actions

Next we show the way in which actions are represented.

```
stop([Player,Banker],_) :-
        Player1 is Player,
        Banker1 is Banker,
        write('Player = '), write(Player1), nl
        write('Banker = '), write(Banker1), nl
```

```
pay_entrance([Player,Banker],[Player-4,Banker+4]).
```

```
dice_reward([Player,Banker],[Player+D,Banker-D]) :-
        roll_dice(D).
```

The stop action simply prints out the playing state, which is represented as a two-element list consisting of the number of counters held by the *Player* and *Banker* respectively.

The *pay_entrance* action reduces the player's counters by *4* and increases the banker's counters by *4*.

The *dice_reward* action increases the player's counters by the value *D* of the rolled dice and decreases the banker's counters by *D*.

11.2.4   Representing the Dice

The dice represent the only probabilistic element of the game. A fair dice is represented as follows.

```
1/6: roll_dice(1).
1/6: roll_dice(2).
1/6: roll_dice(3).
1/6: roll_dice(4).
1/6: roll_dice(5).
1/6: roll_dice(6).
```

11.2.5   Simplified Blackjack Game

The end of this section will be dedicated to a more extended representational problem which involves a version of the blackjack game. After describing the game, we will show how we can represent it using the SLP framework and why this framework is efficient and adapted for this problem. Finally we will see how we could modify this version and the effect of such modifications on the corresponding SLP representation.

11.2.6   Description and Specifications

Our blackjack game model is very close to the real blackjack game, as described in Wikipedia [14]. We consider this version as a simplification of the real game in the sense that it does not include bets and money. It involves only one player and the player does not have any strategy.

Let us now describe the specifications of the game. Blackjack hands are scored by their point total. The hand with the highest total wins as long as it does not go over 21, which is called a "bust." Cards 2 through 10 are worth their face value, and face cards (Jack, Queen, King) are also worth 10. An ace counts as 11 unless it would bust a hand, in which case it counts as 1.

In our version there is only one player. His goal is to beat the dealer, by having the higher, unbusted hand. Note that if the player busts, he loses, even if the dealer also busts. If the player's and the dealer's hands have the same point value, this is known as a "push," and neither player nor dealer wins the hand.

The dealer deals the cards, in our version from one deck of cards. The dealer gives two cards to the player and to himself.

A two-card hand of 21 (an ace plus a ten-value card) is called a "blackjack" or a "natural," and is an automatic winner.

If the dealer has a blackjack and the player does not, the dealer wins automatically. If the player has a blackjack and the dealer does not, the player wins automatically. If the player and dealer both have blackjack, it is a tie (push). If neither side has a blackjack, in our version the strategy of the player is always to stand, then the dealer plays his hand. He must hit until he has at least 17, regardless of what the player has. The dealer may hit until he has a maximum of five cards in his hands.

The parameters of the game that could be modified, defining another version of the game are:

- the number of decks of cards;
- the maximum number of cards in a hand;
- the strategy of the player;
- the number of players.

11.2.7 Prolog Implementation of the Game

We show here how we can represent the game in Prolog. Such an implementation could lead to the SLP representation for several reasons. First, since SLPs lift the concept of logic programs, representing the game in Prolog allows us to translate it in order to obtain an SLP representation of the game. Secondly, it is interesting to see the difference of expressivity between logic programs and SLPs. Finally, the Prolog implementation permits us to experimentally verify the correctness of our representation.

Let us present the entry clause of the program.

```
game(Result,PScore,PHand,DScore,DHand) :-
  State0 = [[],[],[]],
  act(first_2_cards(State0,State1)),
  act(rest_of_game(State1,State2)),
  end_of_game(State2,Result,PScore,PHand,DScore,DHand).
```

```
act(X) :- X.
```

The general playing strategy has the same structure as for the simple game of chance described above. Indeed, every action such as `first_2_cards` and `rest_of_game` is conducted by the predicate `act`. Each such action transforms one state into another. The predicate `end_of_game` does not represent an action but calculates, given the final state of the game, the result, returning also the scores and the hands of the player and the dealer as its last arguments.

A playing state is represented as a list of three lists. The first list represents the player hand, the second the dealer hand, and the third all the cards already dealt.

The rest of the program defines each of the predicates which are mentioned in the body of the `clause`. For instance, let us present the definition of the predicate `rest_of_game`.

```
rest_of_game(State,State2) :-
  act(p_turn(State,State1)),
  act(d_turn(State1,State2)).
```

We need to introduce two other predicates; p_turn and d_turn. For instance, d_turn represents the dealer's turn after he has received his first two cards. In this phase he asks for extra cards until he stands. This corresponds to the following two clauses.

```
d_turn(State,State) :-
  d_stands(State).

d_turn(State,State2) :-
  \+ d_stands(State),
  act(d_deal_card(State,State1)),
  act(d_turn(State1,State2)).
```

The predicate d_deal_card represents the action of dealing a card to the dealer. Therefore, it requires taking a card from the deck of cards. Taking a card is represented by the following clause.

```
pick_card(Cards,Card) :-
  random_card(Card),
  non_member(Card,Cards).,
```

where

```
random_card((C,V)) :-
  repeat,
  random(1,5,C),
  random(1,14,V).
```

random is a build-in Prolog predicate which simulates the choice of a number between two bounds.

11.2.8   Representing the Blackjack Game as an SLP

SLP is the statistical relational learning (SRL) framework that is arguably the closest to logic programs in terms of declarativeness. Therefore SLP is the most expressive framework to translate the blackjack game into. Indeed, there are two type of clauses in the Prolog program that require two different types of treatment.

- The Prolog clauses without any random aspect are not modified in the SLP representation. Obviously we do not restrict ourselves to the notion of pure SLPs but instead we allow for impure SLP representations.

- The random aspects of the program are transformed in labeled clauses. However, taking a card from a deck of cards is the only probabilistic element of the game. Therefore, the Prolog implementation and the SLP representation of the blackjack game are virtually identical. The sole use of the predicate *random* is replaced by several labeled clauses expressing that taking a card from a deck is a random action. Let us show how the action of taking a card from the deck is translated:

Compared to the Prolog implementation of this action described above, the *random* predicates have to be replaced in the SLP representation by labeled clauses. The clause *choose_color* determines the color of the card and the clause *choose_value* determines the value of the card.

```
pick_card(Cards,Card) :-
  random_card(Card),
  non_member(Card,Cards).

random_card((C,V)) :-
  repeat,
  choose_color(C),
  choose_value(V).

0.25: choose_color(1).
0.25: choose_color(2).
0.25: choose_color(3).
0.25: choose_color(4).


0.07692308: choose_value(1).
0.07692308: choose_value(2).
0.07692308: choose_value(3).
0.07692308: choose_value(4).
0.07692308: choose_value(5).
0.07692308: choose_value(6).
0.07692308: choose_value(7).
0.07692308: choose_value(8).
0.07692308: choose_value(9).
0.07692308: choose_value(10).
0.07692308: choose_value(11).
0.07692308: choose_value(12).
0.07692308: choose_value(13).
```

Thus the SLP representation is almost as expressive as the Prolog program. Since SLPs are logically oriented, it is relatively easy to understand the rules of the game given the SLP representation.

11.2.9   Effect of Several Game Modifications

Let us now present how a modification in the parameters of the game description would affect this model.

- If we added other decks of cards, we would have to add an argument to the description of a card. A card would be defined as C=(Value,Color,Number_of_Deck). We would have to modify this in the relevant clauses but the number of these clauses is limited. We would also have to add a predicate `choose_deck` defined like `choose_color` and `choose_value`.

- If we allowed for more cards in a hand, we would only have to replace 5 by the new number in the definition of `d_stands`.

- If we wanted to assign a cleverer game strategy for the player, we would only have to modify the `p_stands` predicate.

- We would have to make more important changes if we wanted to change the number of players. Indeed, we would have to add equivalent predicates for all the predicates that model the actions of the players.

Thanks to its great expressivity and compactness, the SLP representation would not be modified much when changing the parameters of the game compared to other frameworks.

11.3   Stochastic Grammars

The initial inspiration for SLPs in [9] was the idea of lifting stochastic grammars to the expressive level of logic programs. In this section we show the relationship between stochastic grammars and SLPs.

11.3.1   Stochastic Automata

Stochastic automata, otherwise called hidden Markov models [11], have found many applications in speech recognition. An example is shown in figure 11.1. Stochastic automata are defined by a 5-tuple $A = \langle Q, \Sigma, q_0, F, \delta \rangle$. Q is a set of states. Σ is an alphabet of symbols. q_0 is the initial state and $F \subseteq Q$ ($F = \{q_2\}$ in figure 11.1) is the set of final states. $\delta : (Q \setminus F) \times \Sigma \to Q \times [0, 1]$ is a stochastic transition function which associates probabilities with labeled transitions between states. The sum of probabilities associated with transitions from any state $q \in (Q \setminus F)$ is 1.

In the following λ represents the empty string. The transition function $\delta^* : (Q \setminus F) \times \Sigma^* \to Q \times [0, 1]$ is defined as follows. $\delta^*(q, \lambda) = \langle q, 1 \rangle$. $\delta^*(q, au) = \langle q_{au}, p_a p_u \rangle$

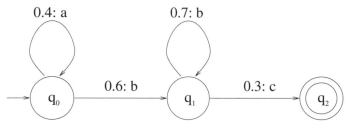

Figure 11.1   Stochastic automaton.

if and only if $\delta(q, a) = \langle q_a, p_a \rangle$ and $\delta^*(q_a, u) = \langle q_{au}, p_u \rangle$. The probability of u being accepted from state q in A is defined as follows. $Pr(u|q, A) = p$ if $\delta^*(q, u) = \langle q', p \rangle$ and $q' \in F$. $Pr(u|q, A) = 0$ otherwise.

Theorem 11.1
Probability of a string being accepted from a particular state Let $A = \langle Q, \Sigma, q_0, F, \delta \rangle$ be a stochastic automaton. For any $q \in Q$ the following holds.

$$\sum_{u \in \Sigma^*} Pr(u|q, A) = 1.$$

Proof Suppose the theorem is false. Either $q \in F$ or $q \notin F$. Suppose $q \in F$. Then by the definition of stochastic automata q has no outgoing transitions. Therefore by definition $Pr(u|q, A)$ is 1 for $u = \lambda$ and 0 otherwise, which is in accordance with the theorem. Therefore suppose $q \notin F$. Suppose in state q the transitions are $\delta(q, a_1) = \langle q, p_1 \rangle, \ldots, \delta(q, a_n) = \langle q, p_n \rangle$. Then each string u is accepted in proportions $p_1, \ldots, p_n$. according to its first symbol. That is to say, $\sum_{u \in \Sigma^*} Pr(u|q, A) = p_1 + .. + p_n$. But according to the definition of δ, $p_1 + \ldots + p_n = 1$, which means $\sum_{u \in \Sigma^*} Pr(u|q, A) = 1$. This contradicts the assumption and completes the proof. $\square$

If the probability of u being accepted by A is now defined as $Pr(u|A) = Pr(u|q_0, A)$, then the following corollary shows that A defines a probability distribution over Σ^*.

Corollary 11.2
Stochastic automata represent probability distributions Given stochastic automaton A,

$$\sum_{u \in \Sigma^*} Pr(u|A) = 1.$$

Proof Special case of theorem 11.1 when $q = q_0$. $\square$

The following example illustrates the calculation of probabilities of strings.

Example 11.1
Probabilities associated with strings For the automaton A in figure 11.1 we have $Pr(abbc|A) = 0.4 \times 0.6 \times 0.7 \times 0.3 = 0.0504$. $Pr(abac|A) = 0$.

$$0.4 : q_0 \rightarrow a q_0$$
$$0.6 : q_0 \rightarrow b q_1$$

$$0.7 : q_1 \rightarrow b q_1$$
$$0.3 : q_1 \rightarrow c q_2$$

$$1.0 : q_2 \rightarrow \lambda$$

Figure 11.2   Labelled production rule representation of stochastic automaton.

A can also be viewed as expressing a probability distribution over the language $L(A) = \{u : \delta^*(q_0, u) = \langle q, p \rangle \text{ and } q \in F\}$. The following theorem places bounds on the probability of individual strings in $L(A)$. The notation $|u|$ is used to express the length of string u.

Theorem 11.3
Probability bounds. Let $A = \langle Q, \Sigma, q_0, F, \delta \rangle$ be a stochastic automaton and let p_{min}, p_{max} be respectively the minimum and maximum probabilities of any transition in A. Let $u \in L(A)$ be a string.

$$p_{min}^{|u|} \leq Pr(u|A) \leq p_{max}^{|u|}.$$

Proof $Pr(u|A) = \prod_{i=1}^{|u|} p_i$, where p_i is the probability associated with the ith transition in A accepting u. Clearly each p_i is bounded below by p_{min} and above by p_{max}, and thus $p_{min}^{|u|} \leq Pr(u|A) \leq p_{max}^{|u|}$. $\square$

This theorem shows that (a) all strings in $L(A)$ have nonzero probability and (b) stochastic automata express probability distributions that decrease exponentially in the length of strings in $L(A)$.

11.3.2   Labeled Productions

Stochastic automata can be equivalently represented as a set of labeled production rules. Each state in the automaton is represented by a nonterminal symbol and each δ transition $\langle q, a \rangle \rightarrow \langle q', p \rangle$ is represented by a production rule of the form $p : q \rightarrow aq'$. Figure 11.2 is the set of labeled production rules corresponding to the stochastic automaton of figure 11.1. Strings can now be generated from this stochastic grammar by starting with the string q_0 and progressively choosing productions to rewrite the leftmost nonterminal randomly in proportion to their probability labels. The process terminates once the string contains no nonterminals. The probability of the generated string is the product of the labels of rewrite rules used.

$$0.5 : S \to \lambda$$
$$0.5 : S \to aSb$$

Figure 11.3 Stochastic context-free grammar

11.3.3 Stochastic Context-free Grammars

Stochastic context-free grammars [4] can be treated in the same way as the labeled productions of the last section. However, the following differences exist between the regular and context-free cases.

- To allow for the expression of context-free grammars the left-hand sides of the production rules are allowed to consist of arbitrary strings of terminals and nonterminals.

- Since context-free grammars can have more than one derivation of a particular string u, the probability of u is the sum of the probabilities of the individual derivations of u.

- The analogue of Theorem 11.3 holds only in relation to the length of the derivation, not the length of the generated string.

Example 11.2
The language $a^n b^n$ Figure 11.3 shows a stochastic context-free grammar G expressed over the language $a^n b^n$. The probabilities of generated strings are as follows. $Pr(\lambda|G) = 0.5$, $Pr(ab|G) = 0.25$, $Pr(aabb|G) = 0.125$.

11.4 Stochastic Logic Programs

Every context-free grammar can be expressed as a definite clause grammar [2]. For this reason the generalization of stochastic context-free grammars to SLPs is reasonably straightforward. First, a definite clause C is defined in the standard way as having the following form.

$$A \leftarrow B_1, \ldots, B_n,$$

where the atom A is the head of the clause and $B_1, \ldots, B_n$ is the body of the clause. C is said to be range restricted if and only if every variable in the head of C is found in the body of C. A *stochastic clause* is a pair $p : C$ where p is in the interval $[0, 1]$ and C is a range-restricted clause. A set of stochastic clauses P is called a *stochastic logic program* if and only if for each predicate symbol q in P the probability labels for all clauses with q in the head sum to 1.

$$0.5 : nate(0) \leftarrow$$
$$0.5 : nate(s(N)) \leftarrow nate(N)$$

Figure 11.4   Exponential distribution over natural numbers.

11.4.1   Stochastic SLD Refutations

For SLPs the stochastic refutation of a goal is analogous to the stochastic generation of a string from a set of labeled production rules. Suppose that P is an SLP. Then $n(P)$ will be used to express the logic program formed by dropping all the probability labels from clauses in P. A stochastic SLD procedure will be used to define a probability distribution over the Herbrand base of $n(P)$. The stochastic SLD derivation of atom a is as follows. Suppose $\leftarrow g$ is a unit goal with the same predicate symbol as a, no function symbols, and distinct variables. Next suppose that there exists an SLD refutation of $\leftarrow g$ with answer substitution θ such that $g\theta = a$. Since all clauses in $n(P)$ are range-restricted, θ is necessarily a ground substitution. The probability of each clause selection in the refutation is as follows. Suppose the first atom in the subgoal $\leftarrow g'$ can unify with the heads of stochastic clauses $p_1 : C_1, \ldots, p_n : C_n$, and stochastic clause $p_i : C_i$ is chosen in the refutation. Then the probability of this choice is $\frac{p_i}{p_1 + \ldots + p_n}$. The probability of the derivation of a is the product of the probability of the choices in the refutation. As with stochastic context-free grammars, the probability of a is then the sum of the probabilities of the derivations of a.

This stochastic SLD strategy corresponds to a distributional semantics [13] for P. That is, each atom a in the success set of $n(P)$ is assigned a nonzero probability (due to the completeness of SLD derivation). For each predicate symbol q the probabilities of atoms in the success set of $n(P)$ corresponding to q sum to 1 (the proof of this is analogous to theorem 11.1).

11.4.2   Polynomial Distributions

It is reasonable to ask whether theorem 11.3 extends in some form to SLPs. The distributions described in [10] include both those that decay exponentially over the length of formulae and those that decay polynomially. SLPs can easily be used to describe an exponential decay distribution over the natural numbers as follows.

Example 11.3
Exponential distribution Figure 11.4 shows a recursive SLP P which describes an exponential distribution over the natural numbers expressed in Peano arithmetic form. The probabilities of atoms are as follows. $Pr(nate(0)|P) = 0.5$, $Pr(nate(s(0))|P) = 0.25$, and $Pr(nate(s(s(0)))|P) = 0.125$. In general, $Pr(nate(N)|P) = 2^{-N-1}$.

$$1.0 : natp(N) \leftarrow nate(U), bin(U, N)$$

$$0.5 : bin(0, [1]) \leftarrow$$
$$0.5 : bin(s(U), [C|N]) \leftarrow coin(C), bin(U, N)$$

Figure 11.5 Polynomial distribution over natural numbers.

However, SLPs can also be used to define a polynomially decaying distribution over the natural numbers as follows.

Example 11.4

Polynomial distribution Figure 11.5 shows a recursive SLP P which describes a polynomial distribution over the natural numbers expressed in reverse binary form. Numbers are constructed by first choosing the length of the binary representation and then filling out the binary expression by repeated tossing of a fair coin. Since the probability of choosing a number N of length $log_2(N)$ is roughly $2^{-log_2(N)}$ and there are $2^{log_2(N)}$ such numbers, each with equal probability, $Pr(natp(N)|P) \approx 2^{-2log_2(N)} = N^{-2}$.

11.5 Learning Techniques

We will now briefly introduce the different existing learning techniques for SLP. We will begin with the description of data used for learning. We will then focus on studying the parameter estimation techniques and finally the structure learning, after having defined these notions.

11.5.1 Data Used

For SLP, as for stochastic context-free grammars, the evidence used for learning is facts or even clauses .

11.5.2 Parameter Estimation

The aim of parameter estimation is, given a set of examples, to infer the values λ^* of the parameters λ (which represent the quantitative part of the model) that best justify the set of examples. We will focus on the maximum likelihood estimation (MLE) which tries to find $\lambda^* = argmax_\lambda P(E|L, \lambda)$. Yet we cannot calculate exactly the MLE when data is missing, so the expectation maximization (EM) algorithm is the most commonly used technique.

As described in [12], "EM assumes that the parameters have been initialized (e.g., at random) and then iteratively perform the following two steps until convergence:

- E-Step: on the basis of the observed data and the present parameters of the model, compute a distribution over all possible completions of each partially observed data case.

- M-Step: Using each completion as a fully-observed data case weighted by its probability, compute the updated parameter using (weighted) frequency counting."

For SLP, one uses the *failure-adjusted maximization* (FAM) algorithm introduced by Cussens [3]. One has to learn the parameters thanks to the evidence, whereas the logical part of the SLP is given. The examples consist of atoms for a predicate p and are logically entailed by the SLP, since they are generated from the target SLP. In order to estimate the parameters, SLD trees are computed for each example. Each path from root to leaf is considered as one of the possible completions. Then, one weights the above completions with the product of probabilities associated with clauses that are used in the completions. Eventually, one obtains the improved estimates for each clause "by dividing the clause's expected counts by the sum of the expected counts of clauses for the same predicate."

11.5.3   Structure Learning

Given a set of examples E and a language bias B, which determines the set of possible hypotheses, one searches for a hypothesis $H^* \in B$ such that

- 1. H^* logically covers the examples E, i.e., $cover(H^*, E)$, and

- 2. the hypothesis H^* is optimal w.r.t. some scoring function scores, i.e., $H^* = argmax_{H \in B} = score(H, E)$.

The hypotheses are of the form (L, λ) where L is the logical part and λ the vector of parameters values defined in section 11.5.2.

The existing approaches use a heuristic search through the space of hypothesis. Hill-climbing or beam-search are typical methods that are applied until the candidate hypothesis satisfies the two conditions defined above. One applies refinement operators during the steps in the search space.

For SLPs, as described in [12], structure learning "involves applying a refinement operator at the *theory* level (i.e. considering multiple predicates) under entailment." It is theory revision in inductive logic programming. This problem being known as very hard, the only approaches have been restricted to learning missing clauses for a single predicate. Muggleton [7], introduced a two-phase approach that separates the structure learning aspects from the parameter estimation phase. In a more recent approach, Muggleton [8] presents an initial attempt to integrate both phases for single predicate learning.

11.6 Conclusion

Stochastic logic programs provide a simple scheme for representing probability distributions over structured objects. This chapter provides a tutorial for the use of SLPs as a means of representing probability distributions over structured objects such as sequences, graphs, and plans.

SLPs were initially applied to the problem of learning from positive examples only [6]. This required the implementation of the following function which defines the generality of an hypothesis.

$$g(H) = \sum_{x \in H} D_X(x).$$

The generality is thus the sum of the probability of all instances of hypothesis H. Clearly such a sum can be infinite. However, if a large enough sample is generated from D_X (implemented as an SLP), then the proportion of the sample entailed by H gives a good approximation of $g(H)$.

Acknowledgments

Our thanks for useful discussions on the topics in this chapter with James Cussens, Kristian Kersting, Jianzhong Chen, and Hiroaki Watanabe. This work was supported by the Esprit IST project "Application of Probabilistic Inductive Logic Programming II (APRIL II)" and the DTI Beacon project, "Metalog - Integrated Machine Learning of Metabolic Networks Applied to Predictive Toxicology."

References

[1] I. Bratko. *Prolog for Artificial Intelligence.* Addison-Wesley, London, 1986.

[2] W.F. Clocksin and C.S. Mellish. *Programming in Prolog.* Springer-Verlag, Berlin, 1981.

[3] J. Cussens. Parameter estimation in stochastic logic programs. *Machine Learning*, 44(3):245–271, 2001.

[4] K. Lari and S. J. Young. The estimation of stochastic context-free grammars using the inside-outside algorithm. *Computer Speech and Language*, 4:35–56, 1990.

[5] J.W. Lloyd. *Foundations of Logic Programming, 2nd edition.* Springer-Verlag, Berlin, 1987.

[6] S.H. Muggleton. Learning from positive data. In *Proceedings of the International Conference on Inductive Logic Programming*, 1997.

[7] S.H. Muggleton. Learning stochastic logic programs. *Electronic Transactions in Artificial Intelligence*, 4(041), 2000.

[8] S.H. Muggleton. Learning structure and parameters of stochastic logic programs. *Electronic Transactions in Artificial Intelligence*, 6, 2002.

[9] S.H. Muggleton. Stochastic logic programs. In L. de Raedt, editor, *Advances in Inductive Logic Programming*, pages 254–264. IOS Press, Amsterdam, 1996. URL `http://www.doc.ic.ac.uk/šhm/Papers/slp.pdf`.

[10] S.H. Muggleton and C.D. Page. A learnability model for universal representations. Technical Report PRG-TR-3-94, Oxford University Computing Laboratory, Oxford, UK, 1994.

[11] L.R. Rabiner. A tutorial on hidden Markov models and selected applications in speech recognition. *Proceedings of the IEEE*, 77(2):257–286, 1989.

[12] L. De Raedt and K. Kersting. Probabilistic logic learning. *ACM-SIGKDD Explorations*, 5(1):31–48, 2003.

[13] T. Sato. A statistical learning method for logic programs with distributional semantics. In *Proceedings of the Twelth International conference on logic programming*, pages 715–729, 1995.

[14] Wikipedia, 2006. Wikipedia's page on the Blackjack game, http://en.wikipedia.org/wiki/Blackjack.

12 Markov Logic: A Unifying Framework for Statistical Relational Learning

Pedro Domingos and Matthew Richardson

Interest in statistical relational learning (SRL) has grown rapidly in recent years. Several key SRL tasks have been identified, and a large number of approaches have been proposed. Increasingly, a unifying framework is needed to facilitate transfer of knowledge across tasks and approaches, to compare approaches, and to help bring structure to the field. We propose *Markov logic* as such a framework. Syntactically, Markov logic is indistinguishable from first-order logic, except that each formula has a weight attached. Semantically, a set of Markov logic formulae represents a probability distribution over possible worlds, in the form of a log-linear model with one feature per grounding of a formula in the set, with the corresponding weight. We show how approaches like probabilistic relational models, knowledge-based model construction, and stochastic logic programs can be mapped into Markov logic. We also show how tasks like collective classification, link prediction, link-based clustering, social network modeling, and object identification can be concisely formulated in Markov logic. Finally, we develop learning and inference algorithms for Markov logic, and report experimental results on a link prediction task.

12.1 The Need for a Unifying Framework

Many (if not most) real-world application domains are characterized by the presence of both uncertainty and complex relational structure. Statistical learning focuses on the former, and relational learning on the latter. Statistical relational learning (SRL) seeks to combine the power of both. Research in SRL has expanded rapidly in recent years, both because of the need for it in applications, and because statistical and relational learning have individually matured to the point where combining them is a feasible research enterprise. A number of key SRL tasks have been identified, including collective classification, link prediction, link-based clustering, social network modeling, object identification, and others. A large and growing number of

SRL approaches have been proposed, including knowledge-based model construction [55, 39, 29], stochastic logic programs [37, 9], PRISM [51], MACCENT [12], probabilistic relational models [17], relational Markov models [1], relational Markov networks [53], relational dependency networks [38], structural logistic regression [44], relational generation functions [7], constraint logic programming for probablistic knowledge (CLP($\mathcal{BN}$)) [50], and others.

While the variety of problems and approaches in the field is valuable, it makes it difficult for researchers, students, and practitioners to identify, learn, and apply the essentials. In particular, for the most part, the relationships between different approaches and their relative strengths and weaknesses remain poorly understood, and innovations in one task or application do not easily transfer to others, slowing down progress. There is thus an increasingly pressing need for a unifying framework, a common language for describing and relating the different tasks and approaches. To be most useful, such a framework should satisfy the following desiderata:

1. *The framework must incorporate both first-order logic and probabilistic graphical models.* Otherwise some current or future SRL approaches will fall outside its scope.

2. *SRL problems should be representable clearly and simply in the framework.*

3. *The framework must facilitate the use of domain knowledge in SRL.* Because the search space for SRL algorithms is very large even by AI standards, domain knowledge is critical to success. Conversely, the ability to incorporate rich domain knowledge is one of the most attractive features of SRL.

4. *The framework should facilitate the extension to SRL of techniques from statistical learning, inductive logic programming, probabilistic inference, and logical inference.* This will speed progress in SRL by taking advantage of the large extant literature in these areas.

In this chapter we propose *Markov logic* as a framework that we believe meets all of these desiderata. We begin by briefly reviewing the necessary background in Markov networks (section 12.2) and first-order logic (section 12.3). We then introduce Markov logic (section 12.4) and describe how several SRL approaches and tasks can be formulated in this framework (sections 12.5 and 12.6). Next, we show how techniques from logic, probabilistic inference, statistics and inductive logic programming can be used to obtain practical inference and learning algorithms for Markov logic (sections 12.7 and 12.8). Finally, we illustrate the application of these algorithms in a real-world link prediction task (section 12.9) and conclude (section 12.10).

12.2 Markov Networks

A *Markov network* (also known as a *Markov random field*) is a model for the joint distribution of a set of variables $X = (X_1, X_2, \ldots, X_n) \in \mathcal{X}$ [41]. It is composed of an undirected graph G and a set of potential functions ϕ_k. The graph has a node for each variable, and the model has a potential function for each clique in the graph. A potential function is a non-negative real-valued function of the state of the corresponding clique. The joint distribution represented by a Markov network is given by

$$P(X = x) = \frac{1}{Z} \prod_k \phi_k(x_{\{k\}}), \tag{12.1}$$

where $x_{\{k\}}$ is the state of the kth clique (i.e., the state of the variables that appear in that clique). Z, known as the *partition function*, is given by $Z = \sum_{x \in \mathcal{X}} \prod_k \phi_k(x_{\{k\}})$. Markov networks are often conveniently represented as *log-linear models*, with each clique potential replaced by an exponentiated weighted sum of features of the state, leading to

$$P(X = x) = \frac{1}{Z} \exp\left(\sum_j w_j f_j(x)\right). \tag{12.2}$$

A feature may be any real-valued function of the state. This chapter will focus on binary features, $f_j(x) \in \{0, 1\}$. In the most direct translation from the potential-function form (12.1), there is one feature corresponding to each possible state $x_{\{k\}}$ of each clique, with its weight being $\log \phi_k(x_{\{k\}})$. This representation is exponential in the size of the cliques. However, we are free to specify a much smaller number of features (e.g., logical functions of the state of the clique), allowing for a more compact representation than the potential-function form, particularly when large cliques are present. Markov Login Networks (MLNs) will take advantage of this.

Inference in Markov networks is #P-complete [49]. The most widely used method for approximate inference in Markov networks is Markov chain Monte Carlo (MCMC) [20], and in particular Gibbs sampling, which proceeds by sampling each variable in turn given its Markov blanket. (The Markov blanket of a node is the minimal set of nodes that renders it independent of the remaining network; in a Markov network, this is simply the node's neighbors in the graph.) Marginal probabilities are computed by counting over these samples; conditional probabilities are computed by running the Gibbs sampler with the conditioning variables clamped to their given values. Another popular method for inference in Markov networks is belief propagation [57].

Maximum likelihood or maximup a posteriori (MAP) estimates of Markov network weights cannot be computed in closed form, but, because the log-likelihood is a concave function of the weights, they can be found efficiently using standard gradient-based or quasi-Newton optimization methods [40]. Another alternative is iterative scaling [13]. Features can also be learned from data, by, for example, greedily constructing conjunctions of atomic features [13].

12.3 First-Order Logic

A *first-order knowledge base (KB)* is a set of sentences or formulae in first-order logic [18]. Formulae are constructed using four types of symbols: constants, variables, functions, and predicates. Constant symbols represent objects in the domain of interest (e.g., people: `Anna`, `Bob`, `Chris`, etc.). Variable symbols range over the objects in the domain. Function symbols (e.g., `MotherOf`) represent mappings from tuples of objects to objects. Predicate symbols represent relations among objects in the domain (e.g., `Friends`) or attributes of objects (e.g., `Smokes`). An *interpretation* specifies which objects, functions, and relations in the domain are represented by which symbols. Variables and constants may be *typed*, in which case variables range only over objects of the corresponding type, and constants can only represent objects of the corresponding type. For example, the variable x might range over people (e.g., Anna, Bob, etc.), and the constant C might represent a city (e.g, Seattle, Tokyo, etc.).

A *term* is any expression representing an object in the domain. It can be a constant, a variable, or a function applied to a tuple of terms. For example, `Anna`, x, and `GreatestCommonDivisor(x, y)` are terms. An *atomic formula* or *atom* is a predicate symbol applied to a tuple of terms (e.g., `Friends(x, MotherOf(Anna))`). Formulae are recursively constructed from atomic formulae using logical connectives and quantifiers. If F_1 and F_2 are formulae, the following are also formulae: $\neg F_1$ (negation), which is true iff F_1 is false; $F_1 \wedge F_2$ (conjunction), which is true iff both F_1 and F_2 are true; $F_1 \vee F_2$ (disjunction), which is true iff F_1 or F_2 is true; $F_1 \Rightarrow F_2$ (implication), which is true iff F_1 is false or F_2 is true; $F_1 \Leftrightarrow F_2$ (equivalence), which is true iff F_1 and F_2 have the same truth-value; $\forall x\ F_1$ (universal quantification), which is true iff F_1 is true for every object x in the domain; and $\exists x\ F_1$ (existential quantification), which is true iff F_1 is true for at least one object x in the domain. Parentheses may be used to enforce precedence. A *positive literal* is an atomic formula; a *negative literal* is a negated atomic formula. The formulae in a KB are implicitly conjoined, and thus a KB can be viewed as a single large formula. A *ground term* is a term containing no variables. A *ground atom* or *ground predicate* is an atomic formula all of whose arguments are ground terms. A *possible world* or *Herbrand interpretation* assigns a truth value to each possible ground predicate.

A formula is *satisfiable* iff there exists at least one world in which it is true. The basic inference problem in first-order logic is to determine whether a knowledge base KB *entails* a formula F, i.e., if F is true in all worlds where KB is true (denoted by $KB \models F$). This is often done by *refutation*: KB entails F iff $KB \cup \neg F$ is unsatisfiable. (Thus, if a KB contains a contradiction, all formulae trivially follow from it, which makes painstaking knowledge engineering a necessity.) For automated

Table 12.1 Example of a first-order knowledge base and MLN. `Fr()` is short for `Friends()`, `Sm()` for `Smokes()`, and `Ca()` for `Cancer()`

English	First-order logic	Clausal form	Wt
Friends of friends are friends	$\forall x \forall y \forall z \; \text{Fr}(x,y) \wedge$ $\text{Fr}(y,z) \Rightarrow \text{Fr}(x,z)$	$\neg\text{Fr}(x,y) \vee \neg\text{Fr}(y,z) \vee \text{Fr}(x,z)$	0.7
Friendless people smoke.	$\forall x \; (\neg(\exists y \, \text{Fr}(x,y)) \Rightarrow$ $\text{Sm}(x))$	$\text{Fr}(x,g(x)) \vee \text{Sm}(x)$	2.3
Smoking causes cancer.	$\forall x \; \text{Sm}(x) \Rightarrow \text{Ca}(x)$	$\neg\text{Sm}(x) \vee \text{Ca}(x)$	1.5
If two people are friends, either both smoke or neither does.	$\forall x \forall y \; \text{Fr}(x,y) \Rightarrow$ $(\text{Sm}(x) \Leftrightarrow \text{Sm}(y))$	$\neg\text{Fr}(x,y) \vee \text{Sm}(x) \vee \neg\text{Sm}(y),$ $\neg\text{Fr}(x,y) \vee \neg\text{Sm}(x) \vee \text{Sm}(y)$	1.1 1.1

inference, it is often convenient to convert formulae to a more regular form, typically *clausal form* (also known as *conjunctive normal form (CNF)*). A KB in clausal form is a conjunction of *clauses*, a clause being a disjunction of literals. Every KB in first-order logic can be converted to clausal form using a mechanical sequence of steps.[1] Clausal form is used in resolution, a sound and refutation-complete inference procedure for first-order logic [48].

Inference in first-order logic is only semidecidable. Because of this, knowledge bases are often constructed using a restricted subset of first-order logic with more desirable properties. The most widely used restriction is to *Horn clauses*, which are clauses containing at most one positive literal. The Prolog programming language is based on Horn clause logic [34]. Prolog programs can be learned from databases by searching for Horn clauses that (approximately) hold in the data; this is studied in the field of inductive logic programming (ILP) [32].

Table 12.1 shows a simple KB and its conversion to clausal form. Notice that, while these formulae may be *typically* true in the real world, they are not *always* true. In most domains it is very difficult to come up with non-trivial formulae that are always true, and such formulae capture only a fraction of the relevant knowledge. Thus, despite its expressiveness, pure first-order logic has limited applicability to practical AI problems. Many ad hoc extensions to address this have been proposed. In the more limited case of propositional logic, the problem is well solved by probabilistic graphical models. The next section describes a way to generalize these models to the first-order case.

---

1. This conversion includes the removal of existential quantifiers by Skolemization, which is not sound in general. However, in finite domains an existentially quantified formula can simply be replaced by a disjunction of its groundings.

12.4   Markov Logic

A first-order KB can be seen as a set of hard constraints on the set of possible worlds: if a world violates even one formula, it has zero probability. The basic idea in Markov logic is to soften these constraints: when a world violates one formula in the KB it is less probable, but not impossible. The fewer formulae a world violates, the more probable it is. Each formula has an associated weight that reflects how strong a constraint it is: the higher the weight, the greater the difference in log probability between a world that satisfies the formula and one that does not, other things being equal. We call a set of formulae in Markov logic a *Markov logic network*. MLNs define probability distributions over possible worlds [21] as follows.

Definition 12.1

An MLN L is a set of pairs (F_i, w_i), where F_i is a formula in first-order logic and w_i is a real number. Together with a finite set of constants $C = \{c_1, c_2, \ldots, c_{|C|}\}$, it defines a Markov network $M_{L,C}$ ((12.1) and (12.2)) as follows:

1. $M_{L,C}$ contains one binary node for each possible grounding of each predicate appearing in L. The value of the node is 1 if the ground atom is true, and 0 otherwise.

2. $M_{L,C}$ contains one feature for each possible grounding of each formula F_i in L. The value of this feature is 1 if the ground formula is true, and 0 otherwise. The weight of the feature is the w_i associated with F_i in L.

The syntax of the formulae in an MLN is the standard syntax of first-order logic [18]. Free (unquantified) variables are treated as universally quantified at the outermost level of the formula.

An MLN can be viewed as a *template* for constructing Markov networks. Given different sets of constants, it will produce different networks, and these may be of widely varying size, but all will have certain regularities in structure and parameters, given by the MLN (e.g., all groundings of the same formula will have the same weight). We call each of these networks a *ground Markov network* to distinguish it from the first-order MLN. From definition 12.1 and (12.1) and (12.2), the probability distribution over possible worlds x specified by the ground Markov network $M_{L,C}$ is given by

$$P(X=x) = \frac{1}{Z} \exp\left(\sum_i w_i n_i(x)\right) = \frac{1}{Z} \prod_i \phi_i(x_{\{i\}})^{n_i(x)}. \tag{12.3}$$

where $n_i(x)$ is the number of true groundings of F_i in x, $x_{\{i\}}$ is the state (truth values) of the atoms appearing in F_i, and $\phi_i(x_{\{i\}}) = e^{w_i}$. Notice that, although we defined MLNs as log-linear models, they could equally well be defined as products of potential functions, as the second equality above shows. This will be the most convenient approach in domains with a mixture of hard and soft constraints (i.e.,

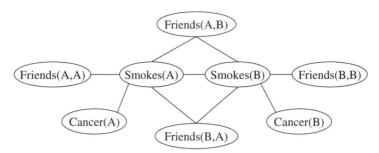

Figure 12.1 Ground Markov network obtained by applying the last two formulae in table 12.1 to the constants Anna(A) and Bob(B).

where some formulae hold with certainty, leading to zero probabilities for some worlds).

The graphical structure of $M_{L,C}$ follows from definition 12.1: there is an edge between two nodes of $M_{L,C}$ iff the corresponding ground atoms appear together in at least one grounding of one formula in L. Thus, the atoms in each ground formula form a (not necessarily maximal) clique in $M_{L,C}$. Figure 12.1 shows the graph of the ground Markov network defined by the last two formulae in table 12.1 and the constants Anna and Bob. Each node in this graph is a ground atom (e.g., Friends(Anna, Bob)). The graph contains an arc between each pair of atoms that appear together in some grounding of one of the formulae. $M_{L,C}$ can now be used to infer the probability that Anna and Bob are friends given their smoking habits, the probability that Bob has cancer given his friendship with Anna and whether she has cancer, etc.

Each state of $M_{L,C}$ represents a possible world. A possible world is a set of objects, a set of functions (mappings from tuples of objects to objects), and a set of relations that hold between those objects; together with an interpretation, they determine the truth-value of each ground atom. The following assumptions ensure that the set of possible worlds for (L, C) is finite, and that $M_{L,C}$ represents a unique, well-defined probability distribution over those worlds, irrespective of the interpretation and domain. These assumptions are quite reasonable in most practical applications, and greatly simplify the use of MLNs. For the remaining cases, we discuss below the extent to which each one can be relaxed.

Assumption 1
Unique names Different constants refer to different objects [18].

Assumption 2
Domain closure The only objects in the domain are those representable using the constant and function symbols in (L, C) [18].

Assumption 3
Known functions For each function appearing in L, the value of that function applied to every possible tuple of arguments is known, and is an element of C.

Table 12.2   Construction of all groundings of a first-order formula under assumptions 1–3

---

function Ground(F, C)
   inputs: F, a formula in first-order logic
          C, a set of constants
   output: G_F, a set of ground formulae
   calls: $CNF(F, C)$, which converts F to conjunctive normal form, replacing
          existentially quantified formulae by disjunctions of their groundings over C
$F \leftarrow CNF(F, C)$
$G_F = \emptyset$
for each clause $F_j \in F$
   $G_j = \{F_j\}$
   for each variable x in F_j
      for each clause $F_k(x) \in G_j$
         $G_j \leftarrow (G_j \setminus F_k(x)) \cup \{F_k(c_1), F_k(c_2), \ldots, F_k(c_{|C|})\}$,
            where $F_k(c_i)$ is $F_k(x)$ with x replaced by $c_i \in C$
   $G_F \leftarrow G_F \cup G_j$
for each ground clause $F_j \in G_F$
   repeat
      for each function $f(a_1, a_2, \ldots)$ all of whose arguments are constants
         $F_j \leftarrow F_j$ with $f(a_1, a_2, \ldots)$ replaced by c, where $c = f(a_1, a_2, \ldots)$
   until F_j contains no functions
return G_F

This last assumption allows us to replace functions by their values when grounding formulae. Thus the only ground atoms that need to be considered are those having constants as arguments. The infinite number of terms constructible from all functions and constants in (L, C) (the Herbrand universe of (L, C)) can be ignored, because each of those terms corresponds to a known constant in C, and atoms involving them are already represented as the atoms involving the corresponding constants. The possible groundings of a predicate in definition 12.1 are thus obtained simply by replacing each variable in the predicate with each constant in C, and replacing each function term in the predicate by the corresponding constant. Table 12.2 shows how the groundings of a formula are obtained given assumptions 1–3. If a formula contains more than one clause, its weight is divided equally among the clauses, and a clause's weight is assigned to each of its groundings.

Assumption 1 (unique names) can be removed by introducing the equality predicate (Equals(x, y), or x = y for short) and adding the necessary axioms to the MLN: equality is reflexive, symmetric, and transitive; for each unary predicate P, $\forall x \forall y\, x = y \Rightarrow (P(x) \Leftrightarrow P(y))$; and similarly for higher-order predicates and functions [18]. The resulting MLN will have a node for each pair of constants, whose value is 1 if the constants represent the same object and 0 otherwise; these nodes will be connected to each other and to the rest of the network by arcs representing the axioms above. Notice that this allows us to make probabilistic inferences about the equality of two constants. We have successfully used this as the basis of an approach to object identification (see section 12.6.5).

If the number u of unknown objects is known, assumption 2 (domain closure) can be removed simply by introducing u arbitrary new constants. If u is unknown but finite, assumption 2 can be removed by introducing a distribution over u, grounding the MLN with each number of unknown objects, and computing the probability of a formula F as $P(F) = \sum_{u=0}^{u_{max}} P(u)P(F|M_{L,C}^u)$, where $M_{L,C}^u$ is the ground MLN with u unknown objects. An infinite u requires extending MLNs to the case $|C| = \infty$.

Let $H_{L,C}$ be the set of all ground terms constructible from the function symbols in L and the constants in L and C (the "Herbrand universe" of (L, C)). Assumption 3 (known functions) can be removed by treating each element of $H_{L,C}$ as an additional constant and applying the same procedure used to remove the unique names assumption. For example, with a function $\texttt{G(x)}$ and constants $\texttt{A}$ and $\texttt{B}$, the MLN will now contain nodes for $\texttt{G(A)} = \texttt{A}$, $\texttt{G(A)} = \texttt{B}$, etc. This leads to an infinite number of new constants, requiring the corresponding extension of MLNs. However, if we restrict the level of nesting to some maximum, the resulting MLN is still finite.

To summarize, assumptions 1–3 can be removed as long as the domain is finite. We believe it is possible to extend MLNs to infinite domains (see Jaeger [27]), but this is an issue of chiefly theoretical interest, and we leave it for future work. In the remainder of this chapter we proceed under assumptions 1–3, except where noted.

A first-order KB can be transformed into an MLN simply by assigning a weight to each formula. For example, the clauses and weights in the last two columns of Table 12.1 constitute an MLN. According to this MLN, other things being equal, a world where n friendless people are nonsmokers is $e^{(2.3)n}$ times less probable than a world where all friendless people smoke. Notice that all the formulae in table 12.1 are false in the real world as universally quantified logical statements, but capture useful information on friendships and smoking habits, when viewed as features of a Markov network. For example, it is well-known that teenage friends tend to have similar smoking habits [35]. In fact, an MLN like the one in table 12.1 succinctly represents a type of model that is a staple of social network analysis [54].

It is easy to see that MLNs subsume essentially all propositional probabilistic models, as detailed below.

Proposition 12.2

Every probability distribution over discrete or finite precision numeric variables can be represented as a Markov logic network.

Proof Consider first the case of Boolean variables $(X_1, X_2, \ldots, X_n)$. Define a predicate of zero arity R_h for each variable X_h, and include in the MLN L a formula for each possible state of $(X_1, X_2, \ldots, X_n)$. This formula is a conjunction of n literals, with the hth literal being $R_h()$ if X_h is true in the state, and $\neg R_h()$ otherwise. The formula's weight is $\log P(X_1, X_2, \ldots, X_n)$. (If some states have zero probability, use instead the product form (see [12.3]), with $\phi_i()$ equal to the probability of the ith state.) Since all predicates in L have zero arity, L defines the same Markov network $M_{L,C}$ irrespective of C, with one node for each variable X_h.

For any state, the corresponding formula is true and all others are false, and thus (12.3) represents the original distribution (notice that $Z = 1$). The generalization to arbitrary discrete variables is straightforward, by defining a zero-arity predicate for each value of each variable. Similarly for finite-precision numeric variables, by noting that they can be represented as Boolean vectors. ∎

Of course, compact factored models like Markov networks and Bayesian networks can still be represented compactly by MLNs, by defining formulae for the corresponding factors (arbitrary features in Markov networks, and states of a node and its parents in Bayesian networks).[2]

First-order logic (with assumptions 1–3 above) is the special case of Markov logic obtained when all weights are equal and tend to infinity, as described below.

Proposition 12.3

Let KB be a satisfiable knowledge base, L be the MLN obtained by assigning weight w to every formula in KB, C be the set of constants appearing in KB, $P_w(x)$ be the probability assigned to a (set of) possible world(s) x by $M_{L,C}$, $\mathcal{X}_{KB}$ be the set of worlds that satisfy KB, and F be an arbitrary formula in first-order logic. Then:

1. $\forall x \in \mathcal{X}_{KB}\ \lim_{w \to \infty} P_w(x) = |\mathcal{X}_{KB}|^{-1}$
   $\forall x \notin \mathcal{X}_{KB}\ \lim_{w \to \infty} P_w(x) = 0$

2. For all F, $KB \models F$ iff $\lim_{w \to \infty} P_w(F) = 1$

Proof Let k be the number of ground formulae in $M_{L,C}$. By (12.3), if $x \in \mathcal{X}_{KB}$, then $P_w(x) = e^{kw}/Z$, and if $x \notin \mathcal{X}_{KB}$ then $P_w(x) \leq e^{(k-1)w}/Z$. Thus all $x \in \mathcal{X}_{KB}$ are equiprobable and $\lim_{w \to \infty} P(\mathcal{X} \setminus \mathcal{X}_{KB})/P(\mathcal{X}_{KB}) \leq \lim_{w \to \infty}(|\mathcal{X} \setminus \mathcal{X}_{KB}|/|\mathcal{X}_{KB}|)e^{-w} = 0$, proving part 1. By definition of entailment, $KB \models F$ iff every world that satisfies KB also satisfies F. Therefore, letting $\mathcal{X}_F$ be the set of worlds that satisfies F, if $KB \models F$, then $\mathcal{X}_{KB} \subseteq \mathcal{X}_F$ and $P_w(F) = \sum_{x \in \mathcal{X}_F} P_w(x) \geq P_w(\mathcal{X}_{KB})$. Since, from part 1, $\lim_{w \to \infty} P_w(\mathcal{X}_{KB}) = 1$, this implies that if $KB \models F$, then $\lim_{w \to \infty} P_w(F) = 1$. The inverse direction of part 2 is proved by noting that if $\lim_{w \to \infty} P_w(F) = 1$, then every world with nonzero probability must satisfy F, and this includes every world in $\mathcal{X}_{KB}$. ∎

In other words, in the limit of all equal infinite weights, the MLN represents a uniform distribution over the worlds that satisfy the KB, and all entailment queries can be answered by computing the probability of the query formula and checking whether it is 1. Even when weights are finite, first-order logic is "embedded" in Markov logic in the following sense. Assume without loss of generality that all weights are non-negative. (A formula with a negative weight w can be replaced by its negation with weight $-w$.) If the KB composed of the formulae in an

---

2. While some conditional independence structures can be compactly represented with directed graphs but not with undirected ones, they still lead to compact models in the form of Equation 12.3 (i.e., as products of potential functions).

MLN L (negated, if their weight is negative) is satisfiable, then, for any C, the satisfying assignments are the modes of the distribution represented by $M_{L,C}$. This is because the modes are the worlds x with maximum $\sum_i w_i n_i(x)$ (see [12.3]), and this expression is maximized when all groundings of all formulae are true (i.e., the KB is satisfied). Unlike an ordinary first-order KB, however, an MLN can produce useful results even when it contains contradictions. An MLN can also be obtained by merging several KBs, even if they are partly incompatible. This is potentially useful in areas like the Semantic Web [2] and mass collaboration [46].

It is interesting to see a simple example of how Markov logic generalizes first-order logic. Consider an MLN containing the single formula $\forall \mathtt{x}\ \mathtt{R}(\mathtt{x}) \Rightarrow \mathtt{S}(\mathtt{x})$ with weight w, and $C = \{\mathtt{A}\}$. This leads to four possible worlds: $\{\neg\mathtt{R}(\mathtt{A}), \neg\mathtt{S}(\mathtt{A})\}$, $\{\neg\mathtt{R}(\mathtt{A}), \mathtt{S}(\mathtt{A})\}$, $\{\mathtt{R}(\mathtt{A}), \neg\mathtt{S}(\mathtt{A})\}$, and $\{\mathtt{R}(\mathtt{A}), \mathtt{S}(\mathtt{A})\}$. From (12.3) we obtain that $P(\{\mathtt{R}(\mathtt{A}), \neg\mathtt{S}(\mathtt{A})\}) = 1/(3e^w + 1)$ and the probability of each of the other three worlds is $e^w/(3e^w + 1)$. (The denominator is the partition function Z; see section 12.2.) Thus, if $w > 0$, the effect of the MLN is to make the world that is inconsistent with $\forall \mathtt{x}\ \mathtt{R}(\mathtt{x}) \Rightarrow \mathtt{S}(\mathtt{x})$ less likely than the other three. From the probabilities above we obtain that $P(\mathtt{S}(\mathtt{A})|\mathtt{R}(\mathtt{A})) = 1/(1 + e^{-w})$. When $w \to \infty$, $P(\mathtt{S}(\mathtt{A})|\mathtt{R}(\mathtt{A})) \to 1$, recovering the logical entailment.

In practice, we have found it useful to add each predicate to the MLN as a unit clause. In other words, for each predicate $R(x_1, x_2, \ldots)$ appearing in the MLN, we add the formula $\forall x_1, x_2, \ldots\ R(x_1, x_2, \ldots)$ with some weight w_R. The weight of a unit clause can (roughly speaking) capture the marginal distribution of the corresponding predicate, leaving the weights of the non-unit clauses free to model only dependencies between predicates.

When manually constructing an MLN or interpreting a learned one, it is useful to have an intuitive understanding of the weights. The weight of a formula F is simply the log odds between a world where F is true and a world where F is false, other things being equal. However, if F shares variables with other formulae, as will typically be the case, it may not be possible to keep the truth-values of those formulae unchanged while reversing F's. In this case there is no longer a one-to-one correspondence between weights and probabilities of formulae.[3] Nevertheless, the probabilities of all formulae collectively determine all weights, if we view them as constraints on a maximum entropy distribution, or treat them as empirical probabilities and learn the maximum likelihood weights (the two are equivalent) [13]. Thus a good way to set the weights of an MLN is to write down the probability with which each formula should hold, treat these as empirical frequencies, and learn the weights from them using the algorithm in section 12.8. Conversely, the weights

---

3. This is an unavoidable side effect of the power and flexibility of Markov networks. In Bayesian networks, parameters are probabilities, but at the cost of greatly restricting the ways in which the distribution may be factored. In particular, potential functions must be conditional probabilities, and the directed graph must have no cycles. The latter condition is particularly troublesome to enforce in relational extensions [53].

in a learned MLN can be viewed as collectively encoding the empirical formula probabilities.

The size of ground Markov networks can be vastly reduced by having typed constants and variables, and only grounding variables to constants of the same type. However, even in this case the size of the network may be extremely large. Fortunately, many inferences do not require grounding the entire network, as we will see in section 12.7.

12.5   SRL Approaches

Because of the simplicity and generality of Markov logic, many representations used in SRL can be easily mapped into it. In this section, we informally do this for a representative sample of these approaches. The goal is not to capture all of their many details, but rather to help bring structure to the field. Further, converting these representations to Markov logic brings a number of new capabilities and advantages, and we also discuss these.

12.5.1   Knowledge-Based Model Construction

Knowledge-based model construction (KBMC) is a combination of logic programming and Bayesian networks [55, 39, 29]. As in Markov logic, nodes in KBMC represent ground predicates. Given a Horn KB, KBMC answers a query by finding all possible backward-chaining proofs of the query and evidence predicates from each other, constructing a Bayesian network over the ground predicates in the proofs, and performing inference over this network. The parents of a predicate node in the network are deterministic AND nodes representing the bodies of the clauses that have that node as head. The conditional probability of the node given these is specified by a combination function (e.g., noisy OR, logistic regression, arbitrary conditional probability table (CPT)). Markov logic generalizes KBMC by allowing arbitrary formulas (not just Horn clauses) and inference in any direction. It also sidesteps the thorny problem of avoiding cycles in the Bayesian networks constructed by KBMC, and obviates the need for ad hoc combination functions for clauses with the same consequent.

A KBMC model can be translated into Markov logic by writing down a set of formulae for each first-order predicate Pk(...) in the domain. Each formula is a conjunction containing Pk(...) and one literal per parent of Pk(...) (i.e., per first-order predicate appearing in a Horn clause having Pk(...) as the consequent). A subset of these literals are negated; there is one formula for each possible combination of positive and negative literals. The weight of the formula is $w = \log[p/(1-p)]$, where p is the conditional probability of the child predicate when the corresponding conjunction of parent literals is true, according to the combination function used. If the combination function is logistic regression, it can be represented using only a linear number of formulae, taking advantage of the fact that a logistic regression model is a (conditional) Markov network with a binary clique between each predictor and the response. Noisy OR can similarly be represented with a linear number of parents.

12.5.2 Other Logic Programming Approaches

Stochastic logic programs (SLPs) [37, 9] are a combination of logic programming and log-linear models. Puech and Muggleton [45] showed that SLPs are a special case of KBMC, and thus they can be converted into Markov logic in the same way. Like Markov logic, SLPs have one coefficient per clause, but they represent distributions over Prolog proof trees rather than over predicates; the latter have to be obtained by marginalization. Similar remarks apply to a number of other representations that are essentially equivalent to SLPs, like independent choice logic [43] and PRISM [51].

MACCENT [12] is a system that learns log-linear models with first-order features; each feature is a conjunction of a class and a Prolog query (clause with empty head). A key difference between MACCENT and Markov logic is that MACCENT is a classification system (i.e., it predicts the conditional distribution of an object's class given its properties), while an MLN represents the full joint distribution of a set of predicates. Like any probability estimation approach, Markov logic can be used for classification simply by issuing the appropriate conditional queries.[4] In particular, a MACCENT model can be converted into Markov logic simply by defining a class predicate (as in section 12.6.1), adding the corresponding features and their weights to the MLN, and adding a formula with infinite weight stating that each object must have exactly one class. (This fails to model the marginal distribution of the nonclass predicates, which is not a problem if only classification queries will be issued.) MACCENT can make use of deterministic background knowledge in the form of Prolog clauses; these can be added to the MLN as formulae with infinite weight. In addition, Markov logic allows uncertain background knowledge (via formulae with finite weights). As described in Subsection 12.6.1, MLNs can be used for collective classification, where the classes of different objects can depend on each other; MACCENT, which requires that each object be represented in a separate Prolog KB, does not have this capability.

Constraint logic programming is an extension of logic programming where variables are constrained instead of being bound to specific values during inference [31]. Probabilistic CLP generalizes SLPs to CLP [47], and CLP($\mathcal{BN}$) combines CLP with Bayesian networks [50]. Unlike in Markov logic, constraints in CLP($\mathcal{BN}$) are hard (i.e., they cannot be violated; rather, they define the form of the probability distribution).

---

4. Conversely, joint distributions can be built up from classifiers (e.g., [23]), but this would be a significant extension of MACCENT.

12.5.3   Probabilistic Relational Models

Probabilistic relational models (PRMs) [17] are a combination of frame-based systems and Bayesian networks. PRMs can be converted into Markov logic by defining a predicate $S(x, v)$ for each (propositional or relational) attribute of each class, where $S(x, v)$ means "The value of attribute S in object x is v." A PRM is then translated into an MLN by writing down a formula for each line of each (class-level) CPT and value of the child attribute. The formula is a conjunction of literals stating the parent values and a literal stating the child value, and its weight is the logarithm of $P(x|Parents(x))$, the corresponding entry in the CPT. In addition, the MLN contains formulae with infinite weight stating that each attribute must take exactly one value. This approach handles all types of uncertainty in PRMs (attribute, reference, and existence uncertainty).

As Taskar et al. [53] point out, the need to avoid cycles in PRMs causes significant representational and computational difficulties. Inference in PRMs is done by creating the complete ground network, which limits their scalability. PRMs require specifying a complete conditional model for each attribute of each class, which in large complex domains can be quite burdensome. In contrast, Markov logic creates a complete joint distribution from whatever number of first-order features the user chooses to specify.

12.5.4   Relational Markov Networks

Relational Markov networks (RMNs) use conjunctive database queries as clique templates [53]. They do not provide a language for defining features. As a result, by default RMNs require a feature for every possible state of a clique, making them exponential in clique size and limiting the complexity of dependencies they can model. Markov logic provides first-order logic as a powerful language for specifying features. Specifying the features also indirectly specifies the cliques, which can be very large as long as the number of relevant features (i.e., formulae) is tractable. Additionally, Markov logic generalizes RMNs by allowing uncertainty over arbitrary relations (not just attributes of individual objects). RMNs are trained discriminatively, and do not specify a complete joint distribution for the variables in the model. Discriminative training of MLNs is straightforward [52]. RMNs use MAP estimation with belief propagation for inference, which makes learning quite slow, despite the simplified discriminative setting; both pseudo-likelihood optimization and the discriminative training described in Singla and Domingos [52] are presumably much faster. To date, no structure-learning algorithms for RMNs have been proposed. MLN structure can be learned using standard inductive logic programming (ILP) techniques, as described later in this chapter, or by directly optimizing pseudo-likelihood, as described in Kok and Domingos [30].

12.5.5   Structural Logistic Regression

In structural logistic regression (SLR) [44], the predictors are the output of SQL queries over the input data. In the same way that a logistic regression model can be viewed as a discriminatively trained Markov network, an SLR model can be viewed as a a discriminatively trained MLN.[5]

12.5.6   Relational Dependency Networks

In a relational dependency network (RDN), each node's probability conditioned on its Markov blanket is given by a decision tree [38]. Every RDN has a corresponding MLN in the same way that every dependency network has a corresponding Markov network, given by the stationary distribution of a Gibbs sampler operating on it [23].

12.5.7   Plates and Probabilistic Entity Relationship Models

Large graphical models with repeated structure are often compactly represented using plates [4]. Markov logic allows plates to be specified using universal quantification. In addition, it allows individuals and their relations to be explicitly represented (see Cussens [8]), and context-specific independences to be compactly written down, instead of left implicit in the node models. More recently, Heckerman et al. [24] have proposed probabilistic entity relationship (ER) models, a language based on ER models that combines the features of plates and PRMs; this language can be mapped into Markov logic in the same way that ER models can be mapped into first-order logic. Probabilistic ER models allow logical expressions as constraints on how ground networks are constructed, but the truth-values of these expressions have to be known in advance; Markov logic allows uncertainty over all logical expressions.

12.5.8   BLOG

Milch et al. [36] have proposed a language, called BLOG (Bayesian Logic), designed to avoid making the unique names and domain closure assumptions. A BLOG program specifies procedurally how to generate a possible world, and does not allow arbitrary first-order knowledge to be easily incorporated. Also, it only specifies the structure of the model, leaving the parameters to be specified by external calls. BLOG models are directed graphs and need to avoid cycles, which substantially complicates their design. We saw in the previous section how to remove the unique names and domain closure assumptions in Markov logic. (When there are unknown objects of multiple types, a random variable for the number of each

---

5. Use of SQL aggregates requires that their definitions be imported into Markov logic.

type is introduced.) Inference about an object's attributes, rather than those of its observations, can be done simply by having variables for objects as well as for their observations (e.g., for books as well as citations to them). To date, no learning algorithms or practical inference algorithms for BLOG have been proposed.

12.6 SRL Tasks

Many SRL tasks can be concisely formulated in Markov logic, making it possible to see how they relate to each other, and to develop algorithms that are simultaneously applicable to all. In this section we exemplify this with five key tasks: collective classification, link prediction, link-based clustering, social network modeling, and object identification.

12.6.1 Collective Classification

The goal of ordinary classification is to predict the class of an object given its attributes. Collective classification also takes into account the classes of related objects (e.g., [6, 53, 38]). Attributes can be represented in Markov logic as predicates of the form $A(x,v)$, where A is an attribute, x is an object, and v is the value of A in x. The class is a designated attribute C, representable by $C(x,v)$, where v is x's class. Classification is now simply the problem of inferring the truth-value of $C(x,v)$ for all x and v of interest given all known $A(x,v)$. Ordinary classification is the special case where $C(x_i,v)$ and $C(x_j,v)$ are independent for all x_i and x_j given the known $A(x,v)$. In collective classification, the Markov blanket of $C(x_i,v)$ includes other $C(x_j,v)$, even after conditioning on the known $A(x,v)$. Relations between objects are represented by predicates of the form $R(x_i,x_j)$. A number of interesting generalizations are readily apparent; for example, $C(x_i,v)$ and $C(x_j,v)$ may be indirectly dependent via unknown predicates, possibly including the $R(x_i,x_j)$ predicates themselves.

12.6.2 Link Prediction

The goal of link prediction is to determine whether a relation exists between two objects of interest (e.g., whether Anna is Bob's Ph.D. advisor) from the properties of those objects and possibly other known relations (e.g., see Popescul and Ungar [44]). The formulation of this problem in Markov logic is identical to that of collective classification, with the only difference that the goal is now to infer the value of $R(x_i,x_j)$ for all object pairs of interest, instead of $C(x,v)$. The task used in our experiments is an example of link prediction (see section 12.9).

12.6.3 Link-Based Clustering

The goal of clustering is to group together objects with similar attributes. In model-based clustering, we assume a generative model $P(X) = \sum_C P(C) \, P(X|C)$, where X is an object, C ranges over clusters, and $P(C|X)$ is X's degree of membership in cluster C. In link-based clustering, objects are clustered according to their links (e.g., objects that are more closely related are more likely to belong to the same cluster), and possibly according to their attributes as well (e.g., see Flake et al. [16]). This problem can be formulated in Markov logic by postulating an unobserved predicate $C(x, v)$ with the meaning "x belongs to cluster v," and having formulas in the MLN involving this predicate and the observed ones (e.g., $R(x_i, x_j)$ for links and $A(x, v)$ for attributes). Link-based clustering can now be performed by learning the parameters of the MLN, and cluster memberships are given by the probabilities of the $C(x, v)$ predicates conditioned on the observed ones.

12.6.4 Social Network Modeling

Social networks are graphs where nodes represent social actors (e.g., people) and arcs represent relations between them (e.g., friendship). Social network analysis [54] is concerned with building models relating actors' properties and their links. For example, the probability of two actors forming a link may depend on the similarity of their attributes, and conversely two linked actors may be more likely to have certain properties. These models are typically Markov networks, and can be concisely represented by formulas like $\forall x \forall y \forall v \; R(x, y) \Rightarrow (A(x, v) \Leftrightarrow A(y, v))$, where x and y are actors, $R(x, y)$ is a relation between them, $A(x, v)$ represents an attribute of x, and the weight of the formula captures the strength of the correlation between the relation and the attribute similarity. For example, a model stating that friends tend to have similar smoking habits can be represented by the formula $\forall x \forall y \; \texttt{Friends}(x, y) \Rightarrow (\texttt{Smokes}(x) \Leftrightarrow \texttt{Smokes}(y))$ (table 12.1). As well as encompassing existing social network models, Markov logic allows richer ones to be easily stated (e.g., by writing formulas involving multiple types of relations and multiple attributes, as well as more complex dependencies between them).

12.6.5 Object Identification

Object identification (also known as record linkage, deduplication, and others) is the problem of determining which records in a database refer to the same real-world entity (e.g., which entries in a bibliographic database represent the same publication) [56]. This problem is of crucial importance to many companies, government agencies, and large-scale scientific projects. One way to represent it in Markov logic is by removing the unique names assumption as described in section 12.4, i.e., by defining a predicate $\texttt{Equals}(x, y)$ (or $x = y$ for short) with the meaning "x represents the same real-world entity as y." This predicate is applied both to records and their fields (e.g., "ICML" = "Intl. Conf. on Mach. Learn."). The dependencies between record matches and field matches can then be represented by formulas like $\forall x \forall y \ x = y \Leftrightarrow f_i(x) = f_i(y)$, where x and y are records and $f_i(x)$ is a function returning the value of the ith field of record x. We have successfully applied this approach to deduplicating the Cora database of computer science papers [52]. Because it allows information to propagate from one match decision (i.e., one grounding of $x = y$) to another via fields that appear in both pairs of records, it effectively performs collective object identification, and in our experiments outperformed the traditional method of making each match decision independently of all others. For example, matching two references may allow us to determine that "ICML" and "MLC" represent the same conference, which in turn may help us to match another pair of references where one contains "ICML" and the other "MLC." Markov logic also allows additional information to be incorporated into a deduplication system easily, modularly, and uniformly. For example, transitive closure is incorporated by adding the formula $\forall x \forall y \forall z \ x = y \wedge y = z \Rightarrow x = z$, with a weight that can be learned from data.

12.7   Inference

We now show how inference in Markov logic can be carried out. Markov logic can answer arbitrary queries of the form "What is the probability that formula F_1 holds given that formula F_2 does?" If F_1 and F_2 are two formulae in first-order logic, C is a finite set of constants including any constants that appear in F_1 or F_2, and L is an MLN, then

$$
\begin{aligned}
P(F_1 | F_2, L, C) &= P(F_1 | F_2, M_{L,C}) \\
&= \frac{P(F_1 \wedge F_2 | M_{L,C})}{P(F_2 | M_{L,C})} \\
&= \frac{\sum_{x \in \mathcal{X}_{F_1} \cap \mathcal{X}_{F_2}} P(X = x | M_{L,C})}{\sum_{x \in \mathcal{X}_{F_2}} P(X = x | M_{L,C})},
\end{aligned}
\tag{12.4}
$$

where $\mathcal{X}_{F_i}$ is the set of worlds where F_i holds, and $P(x | M_{L,C})$ is given by (12.3). Ordinary conditional queries in graphical models are the special case of (12.4) where all predicates in F_1, F_2, and L are zero-arity and the formulae are conjunctions. The question of whether a knowledge base KB entails a formula F in first-order logic is the question of whether $P(F | L_{KB}, C_{KB,F}) = 1$, where L_{KB} is the MLN obtained by assigning infinite weight to all the formulae in KB, and $C_{KB,F}$ is the set of all constants appearing in KB or F. The question is answered by computing $P(F | L_{KB}, C_{KB,F})$ by (12.4), with $F_2 = $ True.

Computing (12.4) directly will be intractable in all but the smallest domains. Since Markov logic inference subsumes probabilistic inference, which is #P-complete, and logical inference in finite domains, which is NP-complete, no better results can be expected. However, many of the large number of techniques for

Table 12.3 Network construction for inference in Markov logic

---

function ConstructNetwork(F_1, F_2, L, C)
    inputs: F_1, a set of ground atoms with unknown truth-values (the "query")
               F_2, a set of ground atoms with known truth-values (the "evidence")
               L, a Markov logic network
               C, a set of constants
    output: M, a ground Markov network
    calls: $MB(q)$, the Markov blanket of q in $M_{L,C}$
  $G \leftarrow F_1$
  while $F_1 \neq \emptyset$
    for all $q \in F_1$
      if $q \notin F_2$
        $F_1 \leftarrow F_1 \cup (MB(q) \setminus G)$
        $G \leftarrow G \cup MB(q)$
      $F_1 \leftarrow F_1 \setminus \{q\}$
  return M, the ground Markov network composed of all nodes in G, all arcs between
    them in $M_{L,C}$, and the features and weights on the corresponding cliques

---

efficient inference in either case are applicable to Markov logic. Because Markov logic allows fine-grained encoding of knowledge, including context-specific independences, inference in it may in some cases be more efficient than inference in an ordinary graphical model for the same domain. On the logic side, the probabilistic semantics of Markov logic allows for approximate inference, with the corresponding potential gains in efficiency.

In principle, $P(F_1|F_2, L, C)$ can be approximated using an MCMC algorithm that rejects all moves to states where F_2 does not hold, and counts the number of samples in which F_1 holds. However, even this is likely to be too slow for arbitrary formulae. Instead, we provide an inference algorithm for the case where F_1 and F_2 are conjunctions of ground literals. While less general than (12.4), this is the most frequent type of query in practice, and the algorithm we provide answers it far more efficiently than a direct application of (12.4). Investigating lifted inference (where queries containing variables are answered without grounding them) is an important direction for future work (see Jaeger [26] and Poole [42] for initial results). The algorithm proceeds in two phases, analogous to knowledge-based model construction [55]. The first phase returns the minimal subset M of the ground Markov network required to compute $P(F_1|F_2, L, C)$. The algorithm for this is shown in table 12.3. The size of the network returned may be further reduced, and the algorithm sped up, by noticing that any ground formula which is made true by the evidence can be ignored, and the corresponding arcs removed from the network. In the worst case, the network contains $O(|C|^a)$ nodes, where a is the largest predicate arity in the domain, but in practice it may be much smaller.

The second phase performs inference on this network, with the nodes in F_2 set to their values in F_2. Our implementation uses Gibbs sampling, but any inference method may be employed. The basic Gibbs step consists of sampling one ground atom given its Markov blanket. The Markov blanket of a ground atom is the set of ground predicates that appear in some grounding of a formula with it. The probability of a ground atom X_l when its Markov blanket B_l is in state b_l is

$$P(X_l\!=\!x_l|B_l\!=\!b_l) =$$
$$\frac{\exp(\sum_{f_i \in F_l} w_i f_i(X_l\!=\!x_l, B_l\!=\!b_l))}{\exp(\sum_{f_i \in F_l} w_i f_i(X_l\!=\!0, B_l\!=\!b_l)) + \exp(\sum_{f_i \in F_l} w_i f_i(X_l\!=\!1, B_l\!=\!b_l))}, \qquad (12.5)$$

where F_l is the set of ground formulae that X_l appears in, and $f_i(X_l = x_l, B_l\!=\!b_l)$ is the value (0 or 1) of the feature corresponding to the ith ground formula when $X_l = x_l$ and $B_l = b_l$. For sets of atoms of which exactly one is true in any given world (e.g., the possible values of an attribute), blocking can be used (i.e., one atom is set to true and the others to false in one step, by sampling conditioned on their collective Markov blanket). The estimated probability of a conjunction of ground literals is simply the fraction of samples in which the ground literals are true, after the Markov chain has converged. Because the distribution is likely to have many modes, we run the Markov chain multiple times. When the MLN is in clausal form, we minimize burn-in time by starting each run from a mode found using MaxWalkSat, a local search algorithm for the weighted satisfiability problem (i.e., finding a truth assignment that maximizes the sum of weights of satisfied clauses) [28]. When there are hard constraints (clauses with infinite weight), MaxWalkSat finds regions that satisfy them, and the Gibbs sampler then samples from these regions to obtain probability estimates.

12.8　Learning

We learn MLN weights from one or more relational databases. (For brevity, the treatment below is for one database, but the generalization to many is trivial.) We make a closed-world assumption [18]: if a ground atom is not in the database, it is assumed to be false. If there are n possible ground atoms, a database is effectively a vector $x = (x_1, \ldots, x_l, \ldots, x_n)$ where x_l is the truth value of the lth ground atom ($x_l = 1$ if the atom appears in the database, and $x_l = 0$ otherwise). Given a database, MLN weights can in principle be learned using standard methods, as follows. If the ith formula has $n_i(x)$ true groundings in the data x, then by Equation 12.3 the derivative of the log-likelihood with respect to its weight is

$$\frac{\partial}{\partial w_i} \log P_w(X\!=\!x) = n_i(x) - \sum_{x'} P_w(X\!=\!x')\, n_i(x'), \qquad (12.6)$$

where the sum is over all possible databases x', and $P_w(X = x')$ is $P(X = x')$ computed using the current weight vector $w = (w_1, \ldots, w_i, \ldots)$. In other words, the ith component of the gradient is simply the difference between the number of true groundings of the ith formula in the data and its expectation according to the current model. Unfortunately, counting the number of true groundings of a formula in a database is intractable, even when the formula is a single clause, as stated in the following proposition (due to Dan Suciu).

Proposition 12.4
Counting the number of true groundings of a first-order clause in a database is #P-complete in the length of the clause.

Proof Counting satisfying assignments of propositional monotone 2-CNF is #P-complete [49]. This problem can be reduced to counting the number of true groundings of a first-order clause in a database as follows. Consider a database composed of the ground atoms $R(0,1)$, $R(1,0)$, and $R(1,1)$. Given a monotone 2-CNF formula, construct a formula Φ that is a conjunction of predicates of the form $R(x_i, x_j)$, one for each disjunct $x_i \vee x_j$ appearing in the CNF formula. (For example, $(x_1 \vee x_2) \wedge (x_3 \vee x_4)$ would yield $R(x_1, x_2) \wedge R(x_3, x_4)$.) There is a one-to-one correspondence between the satisfying assignments of the 2-CNF and the true groundings of Φ. The latter are the false groundings of the clause formed by disjoining the negations of all the $R(x_i, x_j)$, and thus can be counted by counting the number of true groundings of this clause and subtracting it from the total number of groundings. ∎

In large domains, the number of true groundings of a formula may be counted approximately, by uniformly sampling groundings of the formula and checking whether they are true in the data. In smaller domains, and in our experiments below, we use an efficient recursive algorithm to find the exact count.

A second problem with (12.6) is that computing the expected number of true groundings is also intractable, requiring inference over the model. Further, efficient optimization methods also require computing the log-likelihood itself (12.3), and thus the partition function Z. This can be done approximately using a Monte Carlo maximum likelihood estimator (MC-MLE) [19]. However, in our experiments the Gibbs sampling used to compute the MC-MLEs and gradients did not converge in reasonable time, and using the samples from the unconverged chains yielded poor results.

A more efficient alternative, widely used in areas like spatial statistics, social network modeling, and language processing, is to optimize instead the pseudo-likelihood [3]

$$P_w^*(X\!=\!x) = \prod_{l=1}^{n} P_w(X_l\!=\!x_l | MB_x(X_l)), \tag{12.7}$$

where $MB_x(X_l)$ is the state of the Markov blanket of X_l in the data. The gradient of the pseudo-log-likelihood is

$$\frac{\partial}{\partial w_i} \log P_w^*(X\!=\!x) = \sum_{l=1}^{n} [n_i(x) - P_w(X_l\!=\!0|MB_x(X_l))\, n_i(x_{[X_l=0]})$$
$$-P_w(X_l\!=\!1|MB_x(X_l))\, n_i(x_{[X_l=1]})], \qquad (12.8)$$

where $n_i(x_{[X_l=0]})$ is the number of true groundings of the ith formula when we force $X_l = 0$ and leave the remaining data unchanged, and similarly for $n_i(x_{[X_l=1]})$. Computing this expression (or (12.7)) does not require inference over the model. We optimize the pseudo-log-likelihood using the limited-memory BFGS algorithm [33]. The computation can be made more efficient in several ways:

- The sum in (12.8) can be greatly sped up by ignoring predicates that do not appear in the ith formula.

- The counts $n_i(x)$, $n_i(x_{[X_l=0]})$, and $n_i(x_{[X_l=1]})$ do not change with the weights, and need only be computed once (as opposed to in every iteration of BFGS).

- Ground formulas whose truth-value is unaffected by changing the truth-value of any single literal may be ignored, since then $n_i(x) = n_i(x_{[X_l=0]}) = n_i(x_{[X_l=1]})$. In particular, this holds for any clause which contains at least two true literals. This can often be the great majority of ground clauses.

To combat overfitting, we penalize the pseudo-likelihood with a Gaussian prior on each weight.

When we know a priori which predicates will be evidence, MLN weights can also be learned discriminatively [52].

ILP techniques can be used to learn additional clauses, refine the ones already in the MLN, or learn an MLN from scratch. Here we use the CLAUDIEN system for this purpose [10]. Unlike most other ILP systems, which learn only Horn clauses, CLAUDIEN is able to learn arbitrary first-order clauses, making it well suited to Markov logic. Also, by constructing a particular language bias, we are able to direct CLAUDIEN to search for refinements of the MLN structure. Alternatively, MLN structure can be learned by directly optimizing pseudo-likelihood [30].

12.9   Experiments

We have empirically tested the algorithms described in the previous sections using a database describing the Department of Computer Science and Engineering at the University of Washington (UW-CSE). The domain consists of 12 predicates and 2707 constants divided into 10 types. Types include: publication (342 constants), person (442), course (176), project (153), academic quarter (20), etc. Predicates include: Professor(person), Student(person), Area(x, area) (with x ranging over publications, persons, courses, and projects), AuthorOf(publication, person), AdvisedBy(person, person), YearsInProgram(person, years), CourseLevel(course, level), TaughtBy(course, person, quarter), TeachingAssistant(course, person, quarter), etc. Additionally, there are 10 equality predicates: SamePerson (person, person), SameCourse(course, course), etc., which always have known, fixed values that are true iff the two arguments are the same constant.

Using typed variables, the total number of possible ground atoms (n in section 12.8) was 4,106,841. The database contained a total of 3380 tuples (i.e., there were 3380 true ground atoms). We obtained this database by scraping pages in the department's website (www.cs.washington.edu). Publications and AuthorOf relations were obtained by extracting from the BibServ database (www.bibserv.org) all records with author fields containing the names of at least two department members (in the form "last name, first name" or "last name, first initial").

We obtained a knowledge base by asking four volunteers to each provide a set of formulas in first-order logic describing the domain. (The volunteers were not shown the database of tuples, but were members of the department who thus had a general understanding about it.) Merging these yielded a KB of 96 formulas. The complete KB, volunteer instructions, database, and algorithm parameter settings are online at http://www.cs.washington.edu/ai/mln. Formulas in the KB include statements like: students are not professors; each student has at most one advisor; if a student is an author of a paper, so is her advisor; advanced students only TA courses taught by their advisors; at most one author of a given publication is a professor; students in phase I of the Ph.D. program have no advisor; etc. Notice that these statements are not always true, but are typically true.

For training and testing purposes, we divided the database into five subdatabases, one for each area: AI, graphics, programming languages, systems, and theory. Professors and courses were manually assigned to areas, and other constants were iteratively assigned to the most frequent area among other constants they appeared in some tuple with. Each tuple was then assigned to the area of the constants in it. Tuples involving constants of more than one area were discarded, to avoid train-test contamination. The subdatabases contained, on average, 521 true ground atoms out of a possible 58,457.

We performed leave-one-out testing by area, testing on each area in turn using the model trained from the remaining four. The test task was to predict the AdvisedBy(x, y) predicate given (a) all others (All Info) and (b) all others except Student(x) and Professor(x) (Partial Info). In both cases, we measured the average conditional log-likelihood of all possible groundings of AdvisedBy(x, y) over all areas, drew precision-recall curves, and computed the area under the curve. This task is an instance of link prediction, a problem that has been the object of much interest in statistical relational learning (see section 12.6). All KBs were converted to clausal form. Timing results are on a 2.8Ghz Pentium 4 machine.

12.9.1   Systems

In order to evaluate Markov logic, which uses logic and probability for inference, we wished to compare it with methods that use only logic or only probability. We were also interested in automatic induction of clauses using ILP techniques. This section gives details of the comparison systems used.

12.9.1.1 *Logic*

One important question we aimed to answer with the experiments is whether adding probability to a logical KB improves its ability to model the domain. Doing this requires observing the results of answering queries using only logical inference, but this is complicated by the fact that computing log-likelihood and the area under the precision-recall curve requires real-valued probabilities, or at least some measure of "confidence" in the truth of each ground atom being tested. We thus used the following approach. For a given knowledge base KB and set of evidence atoms E, let $\mathcal{X}_{KB \cup E}$ be the set of worlds that satisfy $KB \cup E$. The probability of a query atom q is then defined as $P(q) = \frac{|\mathcal{X}_{KB \cup E \cup q}|}{|\mathcal{X}_{KB \cup E}|}$, the fraction of $\mathcal{X}_{KB \cup E}$ in which q is true.

A more serious problem arises if the KB is inconsistent (which was indeed the case with the KB we collected from volunteers). In this case the denominator of $P(q)$ is zero. (Also, recall that an inconsistent KB trivially entails any arbitrary formula). To address this, we redefine $\mathcal{X}_{KB \cup E}$ to be the set of worlds which satisfies the maximum possible number of ground clauses. We use Gibbs sampling to sample from this set, with each chain initialized to a mode using WalkSat. At each Gibbs step, the step is taken with probability: 1 if the new state satisfies more clauses than the current one (since that means the current state should have 0 probability), 0.5 if the new state satisfies the same number of clauses (since the new and old state then have equal probability), and 0 if the new state satisfies fewer clauses. We then use only the states with the maximum number of satisfied clauses to compute probabilities. Notice that this is equivalent to using an MLN built from the KB and with all infinite equal weights.

12.9.1.2 *Probability*

The other question we wanted to answer with these experiments is whether existing (propositional) probabilistic models are already powerful enough to be used in relational domains without the need for the additional representational power provided by MLNs. In order to use such models, the domain must first be propositionalized by defining features that capture useful information about it. Creating good attributes for propositional learners in this highly relational domain is a difficult problem. Nevertheless, as a tradeoff between incorporating as much potentially relevant information as possible and avoiding extremely long feature vectors, we defined two sets of propositional attributes: order-1 and order-2. The former involves characteristics of individual constants in the query predicate, and the latter involves characteristics of relations between the constants in the query predicate.

For the order-1 attributes, we defined one variable for each (a, b) pair, where a is an argument of the query predicate and b is an argument of some predicate with the same value as a. The variable is the fraction of true groundings of this predicate in the data. Some examples of first-order attributes for AdvisedBy(Matt, Pedro) are: whether Pedro is a student, the fraction of publications that are published by Pedro, the fraction of courses for which Matt was a teaching assistant, etc.

The order-2 attributes were defined as follows: for a given (ground) query predicate $Q(q_1, q_2, \ldots, q_k)$, consider all sets of k predicates and all assignments of constants $q_1, q_2, \ldots, q_k$ as arguments to the k predicates, with exactly one constant per predicate (in any order). For instance, if Q is Advised − By(Matt, Pedro) then one such possible set would be {TeachingAssistant(_, Matt, _), TaughtBy(_, Pedro, _)}. This forms 2^k attributes of the example, each corresponding to a particular truth assignment to the k predicates. The value of an attribute is the number of times, in the training data the set of predicates have that particular truth assignment, when their unassigned arguments are all filled with the same constants. For example, consider filling the above empty arguments with "CSE546" and "Autumn_0304." The resulting set, {TeachingAssistant(CSE546, Matt, Autumn_0304), TaughtBy(CSE546, Pedro, Autumn_0304)} has some truth assignment in the training data (e.g., {True,True}, {True,False}, ...). One attribute is the number of such sets of constants that create the truth assignment {True,True}, another for {True,False}, and so on. Some examples of second-order attributes generated for the query AdvisedBy(Matt, Pedro) are: how often Matt is a teaching assistant for a course that Pedro taught (as well as how often he is not), how many publications Pedro and Matt have coauthored, etc.

The resulting 28 order-1 attributes and 120 order-2 attributes (for the All Info case) were discretized into five equal-frequency bins (based on the training set). We used two propositional learners: naive Bayes [14] and Bayesian networks [22] with structure and parameters learned using the VFBN2 algorithm [25] with a maximum of four parents per node. The order-2 attributes helped the naive Bayes classifier but hurt the performance of the Bayesian network classifier, so below we report results using the order-1 and order-2 attributes for naive Bayes, and only the order-1 attributes for Bayesian networks.

12.9.1.3 Inductive Logic Programming

Our original KB was acquired from volunteers, but we were also interested in whether it could have been developed automatically using ILP methods. As mentioned earlier, we used CLAUDIEN to induce a KB from data. CLAUDIEN was run with: local scope; minimum accuracy of 0.1; minimum coverage of 1, maximum complexity of 10; and breadth-first search. CLAUDIEN's search space is defined by its language bias. We constructed a language bias which allowed: a maximum of three variables in a clause; unlimited predicates in a clause; up to two non-negated appearances of a predicate in a clause, and two negated ones; and use of knowledge of predicate argument types. To minimize search, the equality predicates (e.g., SamePerson) were not used in CLAUDIEN, and this improved its results.

Besides inducing clauses from the training data, we were also interested in using data to automatically refine the KB provided by our volunteers. CLAUDIEN does not support this feature directly, but it can be emulated by an appropriately constructed language bias. We did this by, for each clause in the KB, allowing CLAUDIEN to (1) remove any number of the literals, (2) add up to v new variables, and (3) add up to l new literals. We ran CLAUDIEN for 24 hours on a Sun-Blade 1000 for each (v, l) in the set $\{(1, 2), (2, 3), (3, 4)\}$. All three gave nearly identical results; we report the results with $v = 3$ and $l = 4$.

12.9.1.4   Markov Logic

Our results compare the above systems to Markov logic. The MLNs were trained using a Gaussian weight prior with zero mean and unit variance, and with the weights initialized at the mode of the prior (zero). For optimization, we used the FORTRAN implementation of L-BFGS from Zhu et al. [58] and Byrd et al. [5], leaving all parameters at their default values, and with a convergence criterion (*ftol*) of 10^{-5}. Inference was performed using Gibbs sampling as described in section 12.7, with ten parallel Markov chains, each initialized to a mode of the distribution using MaxWalkSat. The number of Gibbs steps was determined using the criterion of DeGroot and Schervish [11][pp. 707 and 740-741]. Sampling continued until we reached a confidence of 95% that the probability estimate was within 1% of the true value in at least 95% of the nodes (ignoring nodes which are always true or false). A minimum of 1000 and maximum of 500,000 samples was used, with one sample per complete Gibbs pass through the variables. Typically, inference converged within 5000 to 100,000 passes. The results were insensitive to variation in the convergence thresholds.

12.9.2   Results

12.9.2.1   Training with MC-MLE

Our initial system used MC-MLE to train MLNs, with ten Gibbs chains, and each ground atom being initialized to true with the corresponding first-order predicate's probability of being true in the data. Gibbs steps may be taken quite quickly by noting that few counts of satisfied clauses will change on any given step. On the UW-CSE domain, our implementation took 4-5 ms per step. We used the maximum across all predicates of the Gelman criterion R [20] to determine when the chains had reached their stationary distribution. In order to speed convergence, our Gibbs sampler preferentially samples atoms that were true in either the data or the initial state of the chain. The intuition behind this is that most atoms are always false, and sampling repeatedly from them is inefficient. This improved convergence by approximately an order of magnitude over uniform selection of atoms. Despite these optimizations, the Gibbs sampler took a prohibitively long time to reach a reasonable convergence threshold (e.g., $R = 1.01$). After running for 24 hours (approximately 2 million Gibbs steps per chain), the average R-value across training sets was 3.04, with no one training set having reached an R-value less than 2 (other than briefly dipping to 1.5 in the early stages of the process). Considering this must be done iteratively as L-BFGS searches for the minimum, we estimate it would take anywhere from 20 to 400 days to complete the training, even with a weak convergence threshold such as $R = 2.0$. Experiments confirmed the poor quality of the models that resulted if we ignored the convergence threshold and limited the training process to less than ten hours. With a better choice of initial state, approximate counting, and improved MCMC techniques such as the Swendsen-Wang algorithm [15], MC-MLE may become practical, but it is not a viable option for training in the current version. (Notice that during learning MCMC is performed over the full ground network, which is too large to apply MaxWalkSat to.)

12.9.2.2 *Training with Pseudo-likelihood*

In contrast to MC-MLE, pseudo-likelihood training was quite fast. As discussed in section 12.8, each iteration of training may be done quite quickly once the initial clause and ground atom satisfiability counts are complete. On average (over the five test sets), finding these counts took 2.5 minutes. From there, training took, on average, 255 iterations of L-BFGS, for a total of 16 minutes.

12.9.2.3 *Inference*

Inference was also quite quick. Inferring the probability of all AdvisedBy(x, y) atoms in the All Info case took 3.3 minutes in the AI test set (4624 atoms), 24.4 in graphics (3721), 1.8 in programming languages (784), 10.4 in systems (5476), and 1.6 in theory (2704). The number of Gibbs passes ranged from 4270 to 500,000, and averaged 124,000. This amounts to 18 ms per Gibbs pass and approximately 200,000–500,000 Gibbs steps per second. The average time to perform inference in the Partial Info case was 14.8 minutes (vs. 8.3 in the All Info case).

12.9.2.4 *Comparison of Systems*

We compared twelve systems: the original KB (KB); CLAUDIEN (CL); CLAUDIEN with the original KB as language bias (CLB); the union of the original KB and CLAUDIEN's output in both cases (KB+CL and KB+CLB); an MLN with each of the above KBs (MLN(KB), MLN(CL), MLN(KB+CL), and MLN(KB+CLB)); naive Bayes (NB); and a Bayesian network learner (BN). Add-one smoothing of probabilities was used in all cases.

Table 12.4 summarizes the results, and figure 12.2 shows precision-recall curves for all areas (i.e., averaged over all AdvisedBy(x, y) predicates). MLNs are clearly more accurate than the alternatives, showing the promise of this approach. The purely logical and purely probabilistic methods often suffer when intermediate predicates have to be inferred, while MLNs are largely unaffected. Naive Bayes

Table 12.4 Experimental results for predicting `AdvisedBy(x, y)` when all other predicates are known (All Info) and when `Student(x)` and `Professor(x)` are unknown (Partial Info). CLL is the average conditional log-likelihood, and AUC is the area under the precision-recall curve. The results are averages over all atoms in the five test sets and their standard deviations. (See http://www.cs.washington.edu/ai/mln for details on how the standard deviations of the AUCs were computed.)

System	All Info		Partial Info	
	AUC	CLL	AUC	CLL
MLN(KB)	0.215±0.0172	−0.052±0.004	0.224±0.0185	−0.048±0.004
MLN(KB+CL)	0.152±0.0165	−0.058±0.005	0.203±0.0196	−0.045±0.004
MLN(KB+CLB)	0.011±0.0003	−3.905±0.048	0.011±0.0003	−3.958±0.048
MLN(CL)	0.035±0.0008	−2.315±0.030	0.032±0.0009	−2.478±0.030
MLN(CLB)	0.003±0.0000	−0.052±0.005	0.023±0.0003	−0.338±0.002
KB	0.059±0.0081	−0.135±0.005	0.048±0.0058	−0.063±0.004
KB+CL	0.037±0.0012	−0.202±0.008	0.028±0.0012	−0.122±0.006
KB+CLB	0.084±0.0100	−0.056±0.004	0.044±0.0064	−0.051±0.005
CL	0.048±0.0009	−0.434±0.012	0.037±0.0001	−0.836±0.017
CLB	0.003±0.0000	−0.052±0.005	0.010±0.0001	−0.598±0.003
NB	0.054±0.0006	−1.214±0.036	0.044±0.0009	−1.140±0.031
BN	0.015±0.0006	−0.072±0.003	0.015±0.0007	−0.215±0.003

performs well in AUC in some test sets, but very poorly in others; its CLLs are uniformly poor. CLAUDIEN performs poorly on its own, and produces no improvement when added to the KB in the MLN. Using CLAUDIEN to refine the KB typically performs worse in AUC but better in CLL than using CLAUDIEN from scratch; overall, the best-performing logical method is KB+CLB, but its results fall well short of the best MLNs. The general drop-off in precision at around 50% recall is attributable to the fact that the database is very incomplete, and only allows identifying a minority of the `AdvisedBy` relations. Inspection reveals that the occasional smaller drop-offs in precision at very low recalls are due to students who graduated or changed advisors after coauthoring many publications with them.

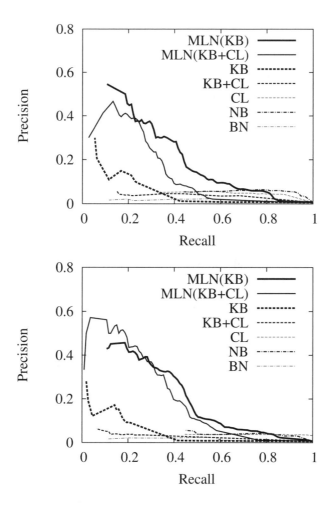

Figure 12.2 Precision and recall for all areas: All Info (upper graph) and Partial Info (lower graph).

12.10 Conclusion

The rapid growth in the variety of SRL approaches and tasks has led to the need for a unifying framework. In this chapter we propose *Markov logic* as a candidate for such a framework. Markov logic combines first-order logic and Markov networks and allows a wide variety of SRL tasks and approaches to be formulated in a common language. Initial experiments with an implementation of Markov logic have yielded good results. Software implementing Markov logic and learning and inference algorithms for it is available at http://www.cs.washington.edu/ai/alchemy.

Acknowledgments

We are grateful to Julian Besag, Vitor Santos Costa, James Cussens, Nilesh Dalvi, Alan Fern, Alon Halevy, Mark Handcock, Henry Kautz, Kristian Kersting, Tian Sang, Bart Selman, Dan Suciu, Jeremy Tantrum, and Wei Wei for helpful discussions. This research was partly supported by ONR grant N00014-02-1-0408 and by a Sloan Fellowship awarded to P. D. We used the VFML library in our experiments (http://www.cs.washington.edu/dm/vfml/).

References

[1]   C. Anderson, P. Domingos, and D. Weld. Relational Markov models and their application to adaptive Web navigation. In *Proceedings of the Eighth ACM SIGKDD International Conference on Knowledge Discovery and Data Mining*, pages 143–152, Edmonton, Canada, 2002. ACM Press.

[2]   T. Berners-Lee, J. Hendler, and O. Lassila. The Semantic Web. *Scientific American*, 284(5):34–43, 2001.

[3]   J. Besag. Statistical analysis of non-lattice data. *The Statistician*, 24:179–195, 1975.

[4]   W. Buntine. Operations for learning with graphical models. *Journal of Artificial Intelligence Research*, 2:159–225, 1994.

[5]   R. H. Byrd, P. Lu, and J. Nocedal. A limited memory algorithm for bound constrained optimization. *SIAM Journal on Scientific and Statistical Computing*, 16(5):1190–1208, 1995.

[6]   S. Chakrabarti, B. Dom, and P. Indyk. Enhanced hypertext categorization using hyperlinks. In *Proceedings of ACM International Conference on Management of Data*, 1998.

[7]   C. Cumby and D. Roth. Feature extraction languages for propositionalized relational learning. In *Proceedings of the IJCAI-2003 Workshop on Learning Statistical Models from Relational Data*, 2003.

[8]   J. Cussens. Individuals, relations and structures in probabilistic models. In *Proceedings of the IJCAI-2003 Workshop on Learning Statistical Models from Relational Data*, 2003.

[9]   J. Cussens. Loglinear models for first-order probabilistic reasoning. In *Proceedings of the Conference on Uncertainty in Artificial Intelligence*, 1999.

[10]   L. De Raedt and L. Dehaspe. Clausal discovery. *Machine Learning*, 26:99–146, 1997.

[11]   M. H. DeGroot and M. J. Schervish. *Probability and Statistics, 3rd edition*. Addison Wesley, Boston, 2002.

[12]   L. Dehaspe. Maximum entropy modeling with clausal constraints. In *Proceedings of the International Conference on Inductive Logic Programming*, 1997.

[13]   S. Della Pietra, V. Della Pietra, and J. Lafferty. Inducing features of random fields. *IEEE Transactions on Pattern Analysis and Machine Intelligence*, 19: 380–392, 1997.

[14]   P. Domingos and M. Pazzani. On the optimality of the simple Bayesian classifier under zero-one loss. *Machine Learning*, 29:103–130, 1997.

[15]   R.G. Edwards and A.G. Sokal. Generalization of the Fortuin-Kasteleyn-Swendsen-Wang representation and Monte Carlo algorithm. *Physics Review D*, 38:2009–2012, 1988.

[16]   G. W. Flake, S. Lawrence, and C. L. Giles. Efficient identification of Web communities. In *International Conference on Knowledge Discovery and Data Mining*, 2000.

[17]   N. Friedman, L. Getoor, D. Koller, and A. Pfeffer. Learning probabilistic relational models. In *Proceedings of the International Joint Conference on Artificial Intelligence*, 1999.

[18]   M. R. Genesereth and N. J. Nilsson. *Logical Foundations of Artificial Intelligence*. Morgan Kaufmann, San Mateo, CA, 1987.

[19]   C. J. Geyer and E. A. Thompson. Constrained Monte Carlo maximum likelihood for dependent data. *Journal of the Royal Statistical Society, Series B*, 54(3):657–699, 1992.

[20]   W. R. Gilks, S. Richardson, and D. J. Spiegelhalter, editors. *Markov Chain Monte Carlo in Practice*. Chapman and Hall, London, 1996.

[21]   J. Halpern. An analysis of first-order logics of probability. *Artificial Intelligence*, 46:311–350, 1990.

[22]   D. Heckerman, D. Geiger, and D. M. Chickering. Learning Bayesian networks: The combination of knowledge and statistical data. *Machine Learning*, 20:197–243, 1995.

[23]   D. Heckerman, D. M. Chickering, C. Meek, R. Rounthwaite, and C. Kadie. Dependency networks for inference, collaborative filtering, and data visualization. *Journal of Machine Learning Research*, 1:49–75, 2000.

[24]   D. Heckerman, C. Meek, and D. Koller. Probabilistic entity-relationship models, PRMs, and plate models. In *Proceedings of the ICML-2004 Workshop on Statistical Relational Learning and Its Connections to Other Fields*, 2004.

[25]   G. Hulten and P. Domingos. Mining complex models from arbitrarily large databases in constant time. In *International Conference on Knowledge Discovery and Data Mining*, 2002.

[26]   M. Jaeger. On the complexity of inference about probabilistic relational models. *Artificial Intelligence*, 117:297–308, 2000.

[27] M. Jaeger. Reasoning about infinite random structures with relational Bayesian networks. In *Proceedings of the International Conference on Principles of Knowledge Representation and Reasoning*, 1998.

[28] H. Kautz, B. Selman, and Y. Jiang. A general stochastic approach to solving problems with hard and soft constraints. In D. Gu, J. Du, and P. Pardalos, editors, *The Satisfiability Problem: Theory and Applications*, pages 573–586. American Mathematical Society, New York, 1997.

[29] K. Kersting and L. De Raedt. Towards combining inductive logic programming with Bayesian networks. In *Proceedings of the International Conference on Inductive Logic Programming*, 2001.

[30] S. Kok and P. Domingos. Learning the structure of Markov logic networks. In *Proceedings of the International Conference on Machine Learning*, 2005.

[31] J. Laffar and J.-L. Lassez. Constraint logic programming. In *Proceedings of the ACM Conference on Principles of Programming Languages*, 1987.

[32] N. Lavrač and S. Džeroski. *Inductive Logic Programming: Techniques and Applications*. Ellis Horwood, Chichester, UK, 1994.

[33] D. C. Liu and J. Nocedal. On the limited memory BFGS method for large scale optimization. *Mathematical Programming*, 45(3):503–528, 1989.

[34] J. W. Lloyd. *Foundations of Logic Programming*. Springer-Verlag, Berlin, 1987.

[35] E. Lloyd-Richardson, A. Kazura, C. Stanton, R. Niaura, and G. Papandonatos. Differentiating stages of smoking intensity among adolescents: Stage-specific psychological and social influences. *Journal of Consulting and Clinical Psychology*, 70(4), 2002.

[36] B. Milch, B. Marthi, and S. Russell. BLOG: Relational modeling with unknown objects. In *Proceedings of the ICML-2004 Workshop on Statistical Relational Learning and its Connections to Other Fields*, 2004.

[37] S. Muggleton. Stochastic logic programs. In L. De Raedt, editor, *Advances in Inductive Logic Programming*, pages 254–264. IOS Press, Amsterdam, 1996.

[38] J. Neville and D. Jensen. Collective classification with relational dependency networks. In *Proceedings of the Second International Workshop on Multi-Relational Data Mining*, 2003.

[39] L. Ngo and P. Haddawy. Answering queries from context-sensitive probabilistic knowledge bases. *Theoretical Computer Science*, 171:147–177, 1997.

[40] J. Nocedal and S. J. Wright. *Numerical Optimization*. Springer-Verlag, New York, NY, 1999.

[41] J. Pearl. *Probabilistic Reasoning in Intelligent Systems: Networks of Plausible Inference*. Morgan Kaufmann, San Francisco, 1988.

[42] D. Poole. First-order probabilistic inference. In *Proceedings of the International Joint Conference on Artificial Intelligence*, 2003.

[43] D. Poole. Probabilistic Horn abduction and Bayesian networks. *Artificial Intelligence*, 64:81–129, 1993.

[44] A. Popescul and L. H. Ungar. Structural logistic regression for link analysis. In *Proceedings of the Second International Workshop on Multi-Relational Data Mining*, 2003.

[45] A. Puech and S. Muggleton. A comparison of stochastic logic programs and Bayesian logic programs. In *Proceedings of the IJCAI-2003 Workshop on Learning Statistical Models from Relational Data*, 2003.

[46] M. Richardson and P. Domingos. Building large knowledge bases by mass collaboration. In *Proceedings of the International Conference on Knowledge Capture*, 2003.

[47] S. Riezler. *Probabilistic Constraint Logic Programming*. PhD thesis, University of Tubingen, Tubingen, Germany, 1998.

[48] J. A. Robinson. A machine-oriented logic based on the resolution principle. *Journal of the ACM*, 12:23–41, 1965.

[49] D. Roth. On the hardness of approximate reasoning. *Artificial Intelligence*, 82:273–302, 1996.

[50] V. Santos Costa, D. Page, M. Qazi, , and J. Cussens. CLP(BN): Constraint logic programming for probabilistic knowledge. In *Proceedings of the Conference on Uncertainty in Artificial Intelligence*, 2003.

[51] T. Sato and Y. Kameya. PRISM: A symbolic-statistical modeling language. In *Proceedings of the International Joint Conference on Artificial Intelligence*, 1997.

[52] P. Singla and P. Domingos. Discriminative training of Markov logic networks. In *AAAI Press*, 2005.

[53] B. Taskar, P. Abbeel, and D. Koller. Discriminative probabilistic models for relational data. In *Proceedings of the Conference on Uncertainty in Artificial Intelligence*, 2002.

[54] S. Wasserman and K. Faust. *Social Network Analysis: Methods and Applications*. Cambridge University Press, Cambridge, UK, 1994.

[55] M. Wellman, J. S. Breese, and R. P. Goldman. From knowledge bases to decision models. *Knowledge Engineering Review*, 7:35–53, 1992.

[56] W. Winkler. The state of record linkage and current research problems. Technical report, Statistical Research Division, US Census Bureau, 1999.

[57] J. S. Yedidia, W. T. Freeman, and Y. Weiss. Generalized belief propagation. In *Proceedings of Neural Information Processing Systems*, 2001.

[58] C. Zhu, R. H. Byrd, P. Lu, and J. Nocedal. Algorithm 778: L-BFGS-B, FORTRAN routines for large scale bound constrained optimization. *ACM Transactions on Mathematical Software*, 23(4):550–560, 1997.

13 BLOG: Probabilistic Models with Unknown Objects

Brian Milch, Bhaskara Marthi, Stuart Russell, David Sontag, Daniel L. Ong and Andrey Kolobov

Many AI problems, ranging from sensor data association to linguistic coreference resolution, involve making inferences about real-world objects that underlie some data. In many cases, we do not know the number of underlying objects or the mapping between observations and objects. This chapter presents a probabilistic modeling language, called Bayesian logic (BLOG), which allows such scenarios to be represented in a natural way. A well-formed BLOG model fully defines a distribution over model structures of a first-order logical language; these "possible worlds" can contain varying numbers of objects with varying relations among them. We show how to use a probabilistic form of Skolemization to express evidence about objects that were not initially known to exist. We also present a sampling-based approximate inference algorithm that does inference in finite time per sampling step on a large class of BLOG models, even those involving infinitely many random variables.

13.1 Introduction

Human beings and AI systems must convert sensory input into some understanding of what is going on in the world around them. That is, they must make inferences about the objects and events that underlie their observations. No prespecified list of objects is given; the agent must infer the existence of objects that were not known initially to exist.

In many AI systems, this problem of unknown objects is engineered away or resolved in a preprocessing step. However, there are important applications where the problem is unavoidable. *Population estimation*, for example, involves counting a population by sampling from it randomly and measuring how often the same object is resampled; this would be pointless if the set of objects were known in advance. *Record linkage*, a task undertaken by an industry of more than 300 companies, involves matching entries across multiple databases. These companies exist because of uncertainty about the mapping from observations to underlying objects. Finally, *multitarget tracking* systems perform *data association*, connecting, say, radar blips to hypothesized aircraft.

Probability models for such tasks are not new: Bayesian models for data association have been used since the 1960s [29]. The models are written in English and mathematical notation and converted by hand into special-purpose code. This can result in inflexible models of limited expressiveness—for example, tracking systems assume independent trajectories with linear dynamics, and record linkage systems assume a naive Bayes model for fields in records. It seems natural, therefore, to seek a *formal language* in which to express probability models that allow for unknown objects.

Recent achievements in the field of probabilistic graphical models [24] illustrate the benefits that can be expected from adopting a formal language: general-purpose inference algorithms, more sophisticated models, and techniques for automated model selection (structure learning). However, graphical models only describe fixed sets of random variables with fixed dependencies among them; they become awkward in scenarios with unknown objects. There has also been significant work on *first-order probabilistic languages* (FOPLs), which explicitly represent objects and the relations between them. We review some of this work in section 13.7. However, most FOPLs make the assumptions of *unique names*, requiring that the symbols or terms of the language all refer to distinct objects, and *domain closure*, requiring that no objects exist besides the ones referred to by terms in the language. These assumptions are inappropriate for problems such as multitarget tracking, where we may want to reason about objects that are observed multiple times or that are not observed at all. Those FOPLs that do support unknown objects often do so in limited and ad hoc ways. In this chapter, we describe Bayesian logic (BLOG) [19], a new language that compactly and intuitively defines probability distributions over outcomes with varying sets of objects.

We begin in section 13.2 with three example problems, each of which involves possible worlds with varying object sets and identity uncertainty. We show BLOG models for these problems and give initial, informal descriptions of the probability distributions that they define. Section 13.3 observes that the possible worlds in these scenarios are naturally viewed as model structures of *first-order logic*. It then defines precisely the set of possible worlds corresponding to a BLOG model. The key idea is a generative process that constructs a world by adding objects whose existence and properties depend on those of objects already created. In such a process, the existence of objects may be governed by many random variables, not just a single population size variable. Section 13.4 discusses exactly how a BLOG model specifies a probability distribution over possible worlds.

Section 13.5 solves a previously unnoticed "probabilistic Skolemization" problem: how to specify evidence about objects—such as radar blips—that one didn't know existed. Finally, section 13.6 briefly discusses inference in unbounded outcome spaces, stating a sampling algorithm and a completeness theorem for a large class of BLOG models and giving experimental results on one particular model.

13.2 Examples

In this section we examine three typical scenarios with unknown objects—simplified versions of the population estimation, record linkage, and multitarget tracking problems mentioned above. In each case, we provide a short BLOG model that, when combined with a suitable inference engine, constitutes a working solution for the problem in question.

Example 13.1

An urn contains an unknown number of balls—say, a number chosen from a Poisson distribution. Balls are equally likely to be blue or green. We draw some balls from the urn, observing the color of each and replacing it. We cannot tell two identically colored balls apart; furthermore, observed colors are wrong with probability 0.2. How many balls are in the urn? Was the same ball drawn twice?

```
1    type Color; type Ball; type Draw;

2    random Color TrueColor(Ball);
3    random Ball BallDrawn(Draw);
4    random Color ObsColor(Draw);

5    guaranteed Color Blue, Green;
6    guaranteed Draw Draw1, Draw2, Draw3, Draw4;

7    #Ball ~ Poisson[6]();

8    TrueColor(b) ~ TabularCPD[[0.5, 0.5]]();

9    BallDrawn(d) ~ Uniform({Ball b});

10   ObsColor(d)
11      if (BallDrawn(d) != null) then
12          ~ TabularCPD[[0.8, 0.2], [0.2, 0.8]](TrueColor(BallDrawn(d)));
```

Figure 13.1 BLOG model for balls in an urn (Example 13.1) with four draws.

The BLOG model for this problem, shown in Figure 13.1, describes a stochastic process for generating worlds. The first 4 lines introduce the types of objects in these worlds—colors, balls, and draws—and the functions that can be applied to these objects. For each function, the model specifies a *type signature* in a syntax similar to that of C or Java. For instance, line 2 specifies that TrueColor is a random function that takes a single argument of type Ball and returns a value of type Color. Lines

5–7 specify what objects may exist in each world. In every world, there are exactly two distinct colors, blue and green, and there are exactly four draws. These are the *guaranteed* objects. On the other hand, different worlds have different numbers of balls, so the number of balls that exist is chosen from a prior—a Poisson with mean 6. Each ball is then given a color, as specified on line 8. Properties of the four draws are filled in by choosing a ball (line 9) and an observed color for that ball (lines 10–12). The probability of the generated world is the product of the probabilities of all the choices made.

```
1    type Researcher; type Publication; type Citation;

2    random String Name(Researcher);
3    random String Title(Publication);
4    random Publication PubCited(Citation);
5    random String Text(Citation);

6    origin Researcher Author(Publication);

7    guaranteed Citation Cite1, Cite2, Cite3, Cite4;

8    #Researcher ~ NumResearchersPrior();
9    #Publication(Author = r) ~ NumPubsPrior();

10   Name(r) ~ NamePrior();
11   Title(p) ~ TitlePrior();

12   PubCited(c) ~ Uniform({Publication p});

13   Text(c) ~ NoisyCitationGrammar(Title(PubCited(c)),
14                                  Name(Author(PubCited(c)))));
```

Figure 13.2 BLOG model for Example 13.2 with four observed citations.

Example 13.2

We have a collection of citations that refer to publications in a certain field. What publications and researchers exist, with what titles and names? Who wrote which publication, and to which publication does each citation refer? For simplicity, we just consider the title and author-name strings in these citations, which are subject to errors of various kinds, and we assume only single-author publications.

Figure 13.2 shows a BLOG model for this example, based on the model in [23]. The BLOG model defines the following generative process. First, sample the total number of researchers from some distribution; then, for each researcher r, sample the number of publications by that researcher. Sample the researchers' names and publications' titles from appropriate prior distributions. Then, for each citation, sample the publication cited by choosing uniformly at random from the set of pub lications. Finally, generate the citation text with a "noisy" formatting distribution that allows for errors and abbreviations in the title and author names.

```
1   type Aircraft; type Blip;

2   random R6Vector State(Aircraft, NaturalNum);
3   random R3Vector ApparentPos(Blip);

4   nonrandom NaturalNum Pred(NaturalNum) = Predecessor;

5   origin Aircraft Source(Blip);
6   origin NaturalNum Time(Blip);

7   #Aircraft ~ NumAircraftPrior();

8   State(a, t)
9       if t = 0 then ~ InitState()
10      else ~ StateTransition(State(a, Pred(t)));

11  #Blip(Source = a, Time = t) ~ DetectionCPD(State(a, t));
12  #Blip(Time = t) ~ NumFalseAlarmsPrior();

13  ApparentPos(b)
14      if (Source(b) = null) then ~ FalseAlarmDistrib()
15      else ~ ObsCPD(State(Source(b), Time(b)));
```

Figure 13.3 BLOG model for Example 13.3.

Example 13.3

An unknown number of aircraft exist in some volume of airspace. An aircraft's state (position and velocity) at each time step depends on its state at the previous time step. We observe the area with radar: aircraft may appear as identical blips on a radar screen. Each blip gives the approximate position of the aircraft that generated it. However, some blips may be false detections, and some aircraft may not be detected. What aircraft exist, and what are their trajectories? Are there any aircraft that are not observed?

The BLOG model for this scenario (Figure 13.3) describes the following process: first, sample the number of aircraft in the area. Then, for each time step t (starting at $t = 0$), choose the state (position and velocity) of each aircraft given its state at time $t - 1$. Also, for each aircraft a and time step t, possibly generate a radar blip b with $Source(b) = a$ and $Time(b) = t$. Whether a blip is generated or not depends on the state of the aircraft—thus the number of objects in the world depends on certain objects' attributes. Also, at each step t, generate some false-alarm blips b' with $Time(b') = t$ and $Source(b') = null$. Finally, sample the position for each blip given the true state of its source aircraft (or using a default distribution for a false-alarm blip).

13.3   Syntax and Semantics: Possible Worlds

13.3.1   Outcomes as First-Order Model Structures

The possible outcomes for examples 12.1 through 12.3 are structures containing many related objects, with the set of objects and the relations among them varying from outcome to outcome. We will treat these outcomes formally as *model structures* of *first-order logic*. A model structure provides interpretations for the symbols of a first-order language; each sentence of the first-order language can be evaluated to yield a truth-value in each model structure.

In Example 13.1, the language has function symbols such as TrueColor(b) for the true color of ball b; BallDrawn(d) for the ball drawn on draw d; and Draw1 for the first draw. (Usually, first-order languages are described as having predicate, function, and constant symbols. For conciseness, we view all symbols as function symbols; predicates are just functions that return a Boolean value, and constants are just zero-ary functions.) To eliminate meaningless random variables, we use *typed* logical languages. Each BLOG model uses a language with a particular set of types, such as Ball and Draw. BLOG also has some built-in types that are available in all models, namely Boolean, NaturalNum, Integer, String, Real, and RkVector (for each $k \geq 2$). Each function symbol f has a *type signature* $(\tau_0, \ldots, \tau_k)$, where τ_0 is the return type of f and $\tau_1, \ldots, \tau_k$ are the argument types. The type Boolean receives special syntactic treatment: if the return type of a function f is Boolean, then terms of the form $f(t_1, \ldots, t_k)$ constitute atomic formulae, which can be combined using logical operators and placed inside quantifiers.

The logical languages used in BLOG are also *free*: a function is not required to apply to all tuples of arguments, even if they are appropriately typed [16]. For instance, in Example 13.3, the function Source usually maps blips to aircraft, but it is not applicable if the blip is a false detection. We adopt the convention that when a function is not applicable to some arguments, it returns the special value null. Any function that receives null as an argument also returns null, and an atomic formula that evaluates to null is treated as false.

The truth of any first-order sentence is determined by a *model structure* for the corresponding language. A model structure specifies the *extension* of each type and the *interpretation* for each function symbol:

Definition 13.1
A model structure ω of a typed, free, first-order language consists of an extension $[\tau]^\omega$ for each type τ, which may be an arbitrary set, and an interpretation $[f]^\omega$ for each function symbol f. If f has return type τ_0 and argument types $\tau_1, \ldots, \tau_k$, then $[f]^\omega$ is a function from $[\tau_1]^\omega \times \cdots \times [\tau_k]^\omega$ to $[\tau_0]^\omega \cup \{\mathsf{null}\}$.

Three model structures for the language used in Figure 13.1 are shown in Figure 13.4. Identity uncertainty arises because $[\mathsf{BallDrawn}]^\omega(\mathsf{Draw1})$ might be equal to $[\mathsf{BallDrawn}]^\omega(\mathsf{Draw2})$ in one structure (such as Figure 13.4(a)) but not

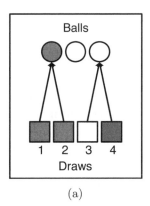
(a)

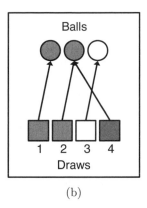
(b)

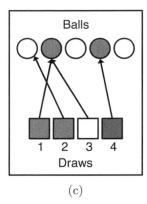
(c)

Figure 13.4 Three model structures for the language of Figure 13.1. Shaded circles represent balls that are blue; shaded squares represent draws where the drawn ball appeared blue (unshaded means green). Arrows represent the BallDrawn function from draws to balls.

another (such as Figure 13.4(b)). The set of balls, $[\text{Ball}]^{\omega}$, can also vary between structures, as Figure 13.4 illustrates. The purpose of a BLOG model is to define a probability distribution over such structures. Because any sentence can be evaluated as true or false in each model structure, a distribution over model structures implicitly defines the probability that φ is true for each sentence φ in the logical language.

13.3.2 Outcomes with Fixed Object Sets

We begin our formal discussion of BLOG semantics by considering the relatively simple case of models with fixed sets of objects. BLOG models for fixed object sets have five kinds of statements. A *type declaration*, such as the two statements on line 1 of Figure 13.3, introduces a type. A *random function declaration*, such as line 2 of Figure 13.3, specifies the type signature for a function symbol whose values will be chosen randomly in the generative process. A *nonrandom function definition*, such as the one on line 4 of Figure 13.3, introduces a function whose interpretation is fixed in all possible worlds. In our implementation, the interpretation is given by a Java class (`Predecessor` in this example). A *guaranteed object statement*, such as line 5 in Figure 13.1, introduces and names some distinct objects that exist in all possible worlds. For the built-in types, the obvious sets of guaranteed objects and constant symbols are predefined. The set of guaranteed objects of type τ in BLOG model M is denoted $G_M(\tau)$. Finally, for each random function symbol, a BLOG model includes a *dependency statement* specifying how values are chosen for that function. We postpone further discussion of dependency statements to section 13.4.

The first four kinds of statements listed above define a particular typed first-order language $\mathcal{L}_M$ for a model M. The set of *possible worlds* of M, denoted Ω_M, consists of those model structures of $\mathcal{L}_M$ where the extension of each type τ is $G_M(\tau)$, and all nonrandom function symbols (including guaranteed constants) have their given interpretations.

For each random function f and tuple of appropriately typed guaranteed objects $o_1, \ldots, o_k$, we can define a random variable (RV) $f[o_1, \ldots, o_k](\omega) \triangleq [f]^\omega(o_1, \ldots, o_k)$. For instance, in a simplified version of Example 13.1 where the urn contains a known set of balls $\{\mathsf{Ball1}, \ldots, \mathsf{Ball8}\}$ and we make four draws, the RVs are $\mathsf{TrueColor}[\mathsf{Ball1}], \ldots, \mathsf{TrueColor}[\mathsf{Ball8}]$, $\mathsf{BallDrawn}[\mathsf{Draw1}], \ldots, \mathsf{BallDrawn}[\mathsf{Draw4}]$, and $\mathsf{ObsColor}[\mathsf{Draw1}], \ldots, \mathsf{ObsColor}[\mathsf{Draw4}]$. The possible worlds are in one-to-one correspondence with full instantiations of these basic RVs. Thus, a joint distribution for the basic RVs defines a distribution over possible worlds.

13.3.3   Unknown Objects

In general, a BLOG model defines a generative process in which objects are added iteratively to a world. To describe such processes, we first introduce *origin function declarations*[1], such as lines 5–6 of Figure 13.3. Unlike other functions, origin functions such as Source or Time have their values set when an object is added. An origin function must take a single argument of some type τ (namely Blip in the example); it is then called a τ-origin function.

Generative steps that add objects to the world are described by *number statements*, such as line 11 of Figure 13.3:

```
#Blip(Source = a, Time = t) ~ DetectionCPD(State(a, t));
```

This statement says that for each aircraft a and time step t, the process adds some number of blips, and each of these added blips b has the property that $\mathsf{Source}(b) = a$ and $\mathsf{Time}(b) = t$. In general, the beginning of a number statement has the form

$$\#\tau(g_1 = x_1, \ldots, g_k = x_k),$$

where τ is a type, $g_1, \ldots, g_k$ are τ-origin functions, and $x_1, \ldots, x_k$ are logical variables. (For types that are generated ab initio with no origin functions, the empty parentheses are omitted, as in Figure 13.1.) The inclusion of a number statement means that for each appropriately typed tuple of objects $o_1, \ldots, o_k$, the generative process adds some random number (possibly zero) of objects q of type τ such that $[g_i]^\omega(q) = o_i$ for $i = 1, \ldots, k$. Note that the types of the generating objects $o_1, \ldots, o_k$ are the return types of $g_1, \ldots, g_k$.

Object generation can even be recursive: objects can generate other objects of the same type. For instance, consider a model of sexual reproduction in which every male–female pair of individuals produces some number of offspring. We could represent this with the number statement:

---

1. In [19] we used the term "generating function", but we have now adopted the term "origin function" because it seems clearer.

```
#Individual(Mother = m, Father = f)
        if Female(m) & !Female(f) then ~ NumOffspringPrior();
```

We can also view number statements more declaratively:

Definition 13.2

Let ω be a model structure of $\mathcal{L}_M$, and consider a number statement for type τ with origin functions $g_1, \ldots, g_k$. An object $q \in [\tau]^\omega$ *satisfies* this number statement applied to $o_1, \ldots, o_k$ in ω if $[g_i]^\omega(q) = o_i$ for $i = 1, \ldots, k$, and $[g]^\omega(q) = \mathsf{null}$ for all other τ-origin functions g.

Note that if a number statement for type τ omits one of the τ-origin functions, then this function takes on the value null for all objects satisfying that number statement. For instance, Source is null for objects satisfying the

false-detection number statement on line 12 of Figure 13.3:

```
#Blip(Time = t) ~ NumFalseAlarmsPrior();
```

Also, a BLOG model cannot contain two number statements with the same set of origin functions. This ensures that, in any given model structure, each object o has exactly one generation history, which can be found by tracing back the origin functions on o.

The set of possible worlds Ω_M is the set of model structures that can be constructed by M's generative process. To complete the picture, we must explain not only *how many* objects are added on each step, but also *what* these objects are. It turns out to be convenient to define the generated objects as follows: when a number statement with type τ and origin functions $g_1, \ldots, g_k$ is applied to generating objects $o_1, \ldots, o_k$, the generated objects are tuples $\{(\tau, (g_1, o_1), \ldots, (g_k, o_k), n) : n = 1, \ldots, N\}$, where N is the number of objects generated. Thus in Example 13.3, the aircraft are pairs $(\mathsf{Aircraft}, 1)$, $(\mathsf{Aircraft}, 2)$, etc., and the blips generated by aircraft are nested tuples such as $(\mathsf{Blip}, (\mathsf{Source}, (\mathsf{Aircraft}, 2)), (\mathsf{Time}, 8), 1)$. The tuple encodes the object's generation history; of course, it is purely internal to the semantics and remains invisible to the user.

Definition 13.3

The *universe* of a type τ in a BLOG model M, denoted $U_M(\tau)$, consists of the guaranteed objects of type τ as well as all nested tuples of type τ that can be generated from the guaranteed objects through finitely many recursive applications of number statements.

As the following definition stipulates, in each possible world the extension of τ is some subset of $U_M(\tau)$.

Definition 13.4

For a BLOG model M, the set of possible worlds Ω_M is the set of model structures ω of $\mathcal{L}_M$ such that

1. for each type τ, $G_M(\tau) \subseteq [\tau]^\omega \subseteq U_M(\tau)$;

2. nonrandom functions have the specified interpretations;

3. for each number statement in M with type τ and origin functions $g_1, \ldots, g_k$, and each appropriately typed tuple of generating objects $(o_1, \ldots, o_k)$ in ω, the set of objects in $[\tau]^\omega$ that satisfy this number statement applied to these generating objects is $\{(\tau, (g_1, o_1), \ldots, (g_k, o_k), n) \ : \ n = 1, \ldots, N\}$ for some natural number N;

4. for every type τ, each element of $[\tau]^\omega$ satisfies some number statement applied to some objects in ω.

Note that by part 3 of this definition, the number of objects generated by any given application of a number statement in world ω is a finite number N. However, a world can still contain infinitely many nonguaranteed objects if some number statements are applied recursively: then the world may contain tuples that are nested to depths $1, 2, 3, \ldots$, with no upper bound. Infinitely many objects can also result if number statements are triggered for every natural number, like the statements that generate radar blips in Example 13.3.

With a fixed set of objects, it was easy to define a set of basic RVs such that a full instantiation of the basic RVs uniquely identified a possible world. To achieve the same effect with unknown objects, we need two kinds of basic RVs:

Definition 13.5
For a BLOG model M, the set $\mathbf{V}_M$ of *basic random variables* consists of:

- for each random function f with type signature $(\tau_0, \ldots, \tau_k)$ and each tuple of objects $(o_1, \ldots, o_k) \in U_M(\tau_1) \times \cdots \times U_M(\tau_k)$, a *function application RV* $f[o_1, \ldots, o_k](\omega)$ that is equal to $[f]^\omega(o_1, \ldots, o_k)$ if $o_1, \ldots, o_k$ all exist in ω, and null otherwise;

- for each number statement with type τ and origin functions $g_1, \ldots, g_k$ that have return types $\tau_1, \ldots, \tau_k$, and each tuple of objects $(o_1, \ldots, o_k) \in U_M(\tau_1) \times \cdots \times U_M(\tau_k)$, a *number RV* $\#\tau[g_1 = o_1, \ldots, g_k = o_k](\omega)$ equal to the number of objects that satisfy this number statement applied to $o_1, \ldots, o_k$ in ω.

Intuitively, each step in the generative world-construction process determines the value of a basic variable. The crucial result about basic RVs is the following:

Proposition 13.6
For any BLOG model M and any complete instantiation of $\mathbf{V}_M$, there is at most one model structure in Ω_M consistent with this instantiation.

Some instantiations of $\mathbf{V}_M$ do not correspond to any possible world: for example, an instantiation for the urn-and-balls example where $\#\mathsf{Ball}[] = 2$, but $\mathsf{TrueColor}[(\mathsf{Ball}, 7)]$ is not null. Instantiations of $\mathbf{V}_M$ that correspond to a world are called *achievable*. Thus, to define a probability distribution over Ω_M, it suffices to define a joint distribution over the achievable instantiations of $\mathbf{V}_M$.

Now that we have seen this technical development, we can say more about the need to represent objects as tuples that encode generation histories. Equating objects with tuples might seem unnecessarily complicated, but it becomes very helpful when we define a Bayes net over the basic RVs (which we do in section 13.4.2). For instance, in the aircraft tracking example, the parent of ApparentPos [(Blip, (Source, (Aircraft, 2)), (Time, 8), 1)] is State [(Aircraft, 2), 8]. It might seem more elegant to assign numbers to objects as they are generated, so that the extension of each type in each possible world would be simply a prefix of the natural numbers. Specifically, we could number the aircraft arbitrarily, and then number the radar blips lexicographically by aircraft and time step. Then we would have basic RVs such as ApparentPos [23], representing the apparent aircraft position for blip 23. But blip 23 could be generated by any aircraft at any time step. In fact, the parents of ApparentPos [23] would have to include all the #Blip and State variables in the model. So defining objects as tuples yields a much simpler Bayes net.

13.4 Syntax and Semantics: Probabilities

13.4.1 Dependency Statements

Dependency and number statements specify exactly how the steps are carried out in our generative process. Consider the dependency statement for $\mathsf{State}(a, t)$ from Figure 13.3:

```
State(a, t)
    if t = 0 then ~ InitState()
    else ~ StateTransition(State(a, Pred(t)));
```

This statement is applied for every basic RV of the form State $[a, t]$ where $a \in U_M$ (Aircraft) and $t \in \mathbb{N}$. If $t=0$, the conditional distribution for State $[a, t]$ is given by the *elementary CPD* `InitState`; otherwise it is given by the elementary conditional probability distribution CPD `StateTransition`, which takes $\mathsf{State}(a, \mathsf{Pred}(t))$ as an argument. These elementary CPDs define distributions over objects of type R6Vector (the return type of State). In our implementation, elementary CPDs are Java classes with a method `getProb` that returns the probability of a particular value given a list of CPD arguments, and a method `sampleVal` that samples a value given the CPD arguments.

A dependency statement begins with a function symbol f and a tuple of logical variables $x_1, \ldots, x_k$ representing the arguments to this function. In a number statement, the variables $x_1, \ldots, x_k$ represent the generating objects. In either case, the rest of the statement consists of a sequence of *clauses*. When the statement is not abbreviated, the syntax for the first clause is

if *cond* **then** $\sim$ *elem-cpd*(*arg1*, ..., *argN*)

The *cond* portion is a formula of the first-order logical language $\mathcal{L}_M$ (containing no free variables other than $x_1, \ldots, x_k$) specifying the condition under which this clause should be used to sample a value for a basic RV. More precisely, if the possible world constructed so far is ω, then the applicable clause is the *first* one whose condition is satisfied in ω (assuming for the moment that ω is complete enough to determine the truth-values of the conditions). If no clause's condition is satisfied, or if the basic RV refers to objects that do not exist in ω, then the value is set by default to false for Boolean functions, null for other functions, and zero for number variables. If the condition in a clause is just "true," then the whole string "if true then" may be omitted.

In the applicable clause, each CPD argument is evaluated in ω. The resulting values are then passed to the elementary CPD. In the simplest case, the arguments are terms or formulae of $\mathcal{L}_M$, such as $\mathsf{State}(a, \mathsf{Pred}(t))$. An argument can also be a *set expression* of the form $\{\tau\ y : \varphi\}$, where τ is a type, y is a logical variable, and φ is a formula. The value of such an expression is the set of objects $o \in [\tau]^\omega$ such that ω satisfies φ with y bound to o. If the formula φ is just true it can be omitted: this is the case on line 9 of Figure 13.1, where we just see the expression $\{\mathsf{Ball}\ \mathsf{b}\}$. BLOG also includes other kinds of arguments to allow counting the number of elements in a set, aggregating a multiset of values, or passing in a set of pairs (o, w) where the o's are objects and the w's are nonuniform sampling weights.

We require that the elementary CPDs obey two rules related to nonguaranteed objects. First, if a CPD is defining a distribution over nonguaranteed objects, e.g., the Uniform CPD on line 9 of Figure 13.1), it should never assign positive probability to objects that do not exist in the partially completed world ω. To ensure this, we allow an elementary CPD to assign positive probability to a nonguaranteed object only if the object was passed in as part of a CPD argument (in Figure 13.1, $\{\mathsf{Ball}\ \mathsf{b}\}$ is passed in). Second, an elementary CPD cannot "peek" at the tuple representations of objects that are passed in: it must be invariant to permutations of the nonguaranteed objects.

13.4.2   Declarative Semantics

So far we have explained BLOG semantics procedurally, in terms of a generative process. To facilitate both knowledge engineering and the development of learning algorithms, we would like to have declarative semantics. The standard approach — which is used in most existing first-order regression systems (FOPLs) — is to say that a BLOG model defines a certain Bayesian network (BN) over the basic RVs. In this section we discuss how that approach needs to be modified for BLOG.

We will write σ to denote an instantiation of a set of RVs vars(σ), and σ_X to denote the value that σ assigns to X. If a BN is finite, then the probability it assigns to each complete instantiation σ is $P(\sigma) = \prod_{X \in \text{vars}(\sigma)} p_X(\sigma_X | \sigma_{\text{Pa}(X)})$, where p_X is the CPD for X and $\sigma_{\text{Pa}(X)}$ is σ restricted to the parents of X. In an infinite BN, we can write a similar expression for each *finite* instantiation σ that is closed under the parent relation (that is, $X \in \text{vars}(\sigma)$ implies $\text{Pa}(X) \subseteq \text{vars}(\sigma)$). If the

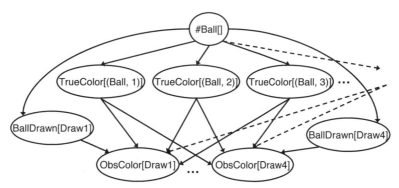

Figure 13.5 Bayes net for the BLOG model in Figure 13.1. The ellipses and dashed arrows indicate that there are infinitely many TrueColor [*b*] nodes.

BN is acyclic and each variable has finitely many ancestors, then these probability assignments define a unique distribution [14].

The difficulty is that in the BN corresponding to a BLOG model, variables often have infinite parent sets. For instance, the BN for Example 13.1 (shown partially in Figure 13.5) has an infinite number of basic RVs of the form TrueColor [*b*]: if it had only a finite number N of these RVs, it could not represent outcomes with more than N balls. Furthermore, each of these TrueColor [*b*] RVs is a parent of each ObsColor [*d*] RV, since if BallDrawn [*d*] happens to be *b*, then the observed color on draw *d* depends directly on the color of ball *b*. So the

ObsColor [*d*] nodes have infinitely many parents. In such a model, assigning probabilities to finite instantiations that are closed under the parent relation does not define a unique distribution: in particular, it tells us nothing about the ObsColor [*d*] variables.

We required instantiations to be closed under the parent relation so that the factors $p_X(\sigma_X | \sigma_{\mathrm{Pa}(X)})$ would be well-defined. But we may not need the values of *all* of X's parents in order to determine the conditional distribution for X. For instance, knowing BallDrawn [*d*] = (Ball, 13) and TrueColor [(Ball, 13)] = Blue is sufficient to determine the distribution for ObsColor [*d*]: the colors of all the other balls are irrelevant in this context. We can read off this context-specific independence from the dependency statement for ObsColor in Figure 13.1 by noting that the instantiation (BallDrawn [*d*] = (Ball, 13), TrueColor [(Ball, 13)] = Blue) determines the value of the sole CPD argument TrueColor(BallDrawn(*d*)). We say this instantiation *supports* the variable ObsColor [*d*] (see [20]).

Definition 13.7

An instantiation σ *supports* a basic RV V of the form $f[o_1, \ldots, o_k]$ or $\#\tau[g_1 = o_1, \ldots, g_k = o_k]$ if all possible worlds consistent with σ agree on (1) whether all the objects $o_1, \ldots, o_k$ exist, and, if so, on (2) the applicable clause in the dependency or number statement for V and the values for the CPD arguments in that clause.

Note that some RVs, such as #Ball [] in Example 13.1, are supported by the empty instantiation. We can now generalize the notion of being closed under the parent relation.

Definition 13.8
A finite instantiation σ is *self-supporting* if its instantiated variables can be numbered $X_1, \ldots, X_N$ such that for each $n \leq N$, the restriction of σ to $\{X_1, \ldots, X_{n-1}\}$ supports X_n.

This definition lets us give semantics to BLOG models in a way that is meaningful even when the corresponding BNs contain infinite parent sets. We will write $p_V(v \mid \sigma)$ for the probability that V's dependency or number statement assigns to the value v, given an instantiation σ that supports V.

Definition 13.9
A distribution P over Ω_M *satisfies* a BLOG model M if for every finite, self-supporting instantiation σ with $\text{vars}(\sigma) \subseteq \mathbf{V}_M$:

$$P(\Omega_\sigma) = \prod_{n=1}^{N} p_{X_n}(\sigma_{X_n} \mid \sigma_{\{X_1,\ldots,X_{n-1}\}}) \tag{13.1}$$

where Ω_σ is the set of possible worlds consistent with σ and $X_1, \ldots, X_N$ is a numbering of σ as in Definition 13.8.

A BLOG model is *well-defined* if there is exactly one probability distribution that satisfies it. Recall that a BN is well-defined if it is acyclic and each variable has a finite set of ancestors. Another way of saying this is that each variable can be "reached" by enumerating its ancestors in a finite, topologically ordered list. The well-definedness criterion for BLOG is similar, but deals with finite, self-supporting instantiations rather than finite, topologically ordered lists of variables. Because we are dealing with instantiations rather than variables, we need to make sure that they cover all possible worlds in addition to covering all basic variables.

Theorem 13.10
Let M be a BLOG model. Suppose that $\mathbf{V}_M$ is at most countably infinite,[2] and for each $V \in \mathbf{V}_M$ and $\omega \in \Omega_M$, there is a self-supporting instantiation that agrees with ω and includes V. Then M is well-defined.

Proof: We provide only a sketch of the proof here, deferring the full version to a more technical paper. First, since $\mathbf{V}_M$ is at most countably infinite, we can impose an arbitrary numbering (a bijection with some prefix of the natural numbers) on $\mathbf{V}_M$. This numbering is "global" in the sense that it does not depend on the instantiation of the random variables. Now, we define a sequence of auxiliary random variables $\{Y_n : 0 \leq n < |\mathbf{V}_M|\}$ on Ω_M as follows. Let

---

2. This is satisfied if the Real and R*k*Vector types are not arguments to random functions or return types of gorigin functions.

$Y_0(\omega) = X(\omega)$ where X is the first basic RV in the global ordering that is supported by the empty instantiation. For $n \geq 1$, let $\sigma_n(\omega)$ be the instantiation $(Y_0 = Y_0(\omega), \ldots, Y_{n-1} = Y_{n-1}(\omega))$. Then let $Y_n(\omega) = Z(\omega)$ where Z is the first basic RV in the global ordering that is supported by $\sigma_n(\omega)$, but has not already been used to define $Y_m(\omega)$ for any $m < n$. The important property of the sequence $\{Y_n\}$ is that any instantiation of $Y_0, \ldots, Y_{n-1}$ determines the CPD for Y_n. In other words, if we define our model in terms of $\{Y_n\}$, we get a standard BN in which each variable has finitely many ancestors.

However, we must show that this sequence $\{Y_n\}$ is well-defined. Specifically, we must show that for every $n < |\mathbf{V}_M|$ and every $\omega \in \Omega_M$, there exists a basic RV Z that is supported by $\sigma_n(\omega)$ and has not already been used to define $Y_m(\omega)$ for some $m < n$. This can be shown using the premise that for every $V \in \mathbf{V}_M$, there is a self-supporting instantiation consistent with ω that contains V.

We can use standard results from probability theory to show that there is a unique probability distribution over full instantiations of $\{Y_n\}$ such that each Y_n has the specified conditional distribution given all its predecessors. It remains to show that this distribution over instantiations corresponds to a unique distribution on Ω_M. First, we must show that each full instantiation of $\{Y_n\}$ corresponds to at most one possible world: this follows from Proposition 13.6, plus the fact that a full instantiation of $\{Y_n\}$ determines all the basic RVs. Second, we can show that the probability distribution we have defined over $\{Y_n\}$ is concentrated on instantiations that actually correspond to possible worlds — not instantiations that give RVs values of the wrong type, or give RVs non-null values in contexts where they must be null.

Finally, we need to check that this unique distribution on Ω_M indeed satisfies M. For finite, self-supporting instantiations σ that correspond to the auxiliary instantiations $\sigma_n(\omega)$ used in defining $\{Y_n\}$, the constraint is satisfied by construction. All other finite, self-supporting instantiations can be expressed as disjunctions of those "core" instantiations. From these observations, it is possible to show that (13.1) is satisfied for all finite, self-supporting instantiations. ∎

To check that the criterion of Theorem 13.10 holds for a particular example, we need to consider each basic RV. In Example 13.1, the number RV for balls is supported by the empty instantiation, so in every world it is part of a self-supporting instantiation of size one. Each TrueColor $[b]$ RV depends only on whether its argument exists, so these variables participate in self-supporting instantiations of size two. Similarly, each BallDrawn variable depends only on what balls exist. To sample an ObsColor $[d]$ variable, we need to know BallDrawn $[d]$ and TrueColor [BallDrawn $[d]$], so these variables are in self-supporting instantiations of size four. Similar arguments can be made for Examples 13.2 and 13.3. Of course, we would like to have an algorithm for checking whether a BLOG model is well-defined; the criteria given in Theorem 13.12 in section 13.6.2 are a first step in this direction.

13.5   Evidence and Queries

Because a well-defined BLOG model M defines a distribution over model structures, we can use arbitrary sentences of $\mathcal{L}_M$ as evidence and queries. But sometimes such sentences are not enough. In Example 13.3, the user observes radar blips, which are not referred to by any terms in the language. The user could assert evidence about the blips using existential quantifiers, but then how could he make a query of the form, "Did *this* blip come from the same aircraft as *that* blip?"

A natural solution is to allow the user to extend the language when evidence arrives, adding constant symbols to refer to observed objects. In many cases, the user observes some new objects, introduces some new symbols, and assigns the symbols to the objects in an uninformative order. To handle such cases, BLOG includes a special macro. For instance, given four radar blips at time 8, one can assert

```
{Blip r: Time(r) = 8} = {Blip1, Blip2, Blip3, Blip4};
```

This asserts that there are exactly four radar blips at time 8, and introduces new constants Blip1, . . . , Blip4 in one-to-one correspondence with those blips.

Formally, the macro augments the model with dependency statements for the new symbols. The statements implement sampling without replacement; for our example, we have

```
Blip1 ~ Uniform({Blip r : (Time(r) = 8)});
Blip2 ~ Uniform({Blip r : (Time(r) = 8) & (Blip1 != r)});
```

and so on. Once the model has been extended this way, the user can make assertions about the apparent positions of Blip1, Blip2, etc., and then use these symbols in queries.

These new constants resemble Skolem constants, but conditioning on assertions about the new constants is *not* the same as conditioning on an existential sentence. For example, suppose you go into a new wine shop, pick up a bottle at random, and observe that it costs \$40. This scenario is correctly modeled by introducing a new constant Bottle1 with a `Uniform` CPD. Then observing that Bottle1 costs at least \$40 suggests that this is a fancy wine shop. On the other hand, the mere *existence* of a \$40+ bottle in the shop does not suggest this, because almost every shop has *some* bottle at over \$40.

13.6   Inference

Because the set of basic RVs of a BLOG model can be infinite, it is not obvious that inference for well-defined BLOG models is even decidable. However, the generative process intuition suggests a rejection sampling algorithm. We present this algorithm not because it is particularly efficient, but because it demonstrates the decidability of inference for a large class of BLOG models (see Theorem 13.12 below) and illustrates several issues that any BLOG inference algorithm must deal with. At the end of this section, we present experimental results from a somewhat more efficient likelihood weighting algorithm.

13.6.1 Rejection sampling

Suppose we are given a partial instantiation e as evidence, and a query variable Q. To generate each sample, our rejection sampling algorithm starts with an empty instantiation σ. Then it repeats the following steps: enumerate the basic RVs in a fixed order[3] until we reach the first RV V that is supported by σ but not already instantiated in σ; sample a value v for V according to V's dependency statement; and augment σ with the assignment $V = v$. The process continues until all the query and evidence variables have been sampled. If the sample is consistent with the evidence e, then the program increments a counter N_q, where q is the sampled value of Q. Otherwise, it rejects this sample. After N accepted samples, the estimate of $P(Q = q \mid e)$ is N_q / N.

This algorithm requires a subroutine that determines whether a partial instantiation σ supports a basic RV V, and if so, returns a sample from V's conditional distribution. For a basic RV V of the form $f [o_1, \ldots, o_k]$ or $\#\tau [g_1 = o_1, \ldots, g_k = o_k]$, the subroutine begins by checking the values of the relevant number variables in σ to determine whether all of $o_1, \ldots, o_k$ exist. If some of these number variables are not instantiated, then σ does not support V. If some of $o_1, \ldots, o_k$ do not exist, the subroutine returns the default value for V. If they do all exist, the subroutine follows the semantics for dependency statements discussed in section 13.4.1. First, it iterates over the clauses in the dependency (or number) statement until it reaches a clause whose condition is either undetermined or determined to be true given σ (if all the conditions are determined to be false, then it returns the default value for V). If the condition is undetermined, then σ does not support V. If it is determined to be true, then the subroutine evaluates each of the CPD arguments in this clause. If σ determines the values of all the arguments, then the subroutine samples a value for V by passing those values to the `sampleVal` method of this clause's elementary CPD. Otherwise, σ does not support V.

To evaluate terms and quantifier-free formulae, we use a straightforward recursive algorithm. The base case looks up the value of a particular function application RV in σ; if this RV is not instantiated, the algorithm returns undetermined. To evaluate a formula, we evaluate its subformulae in order from left to right. We stop when we hit an undetermined subformula or when the value of the whole formula is determined. For example, to evaluate $\alpha \vee \beta$, we first evaluate α. If α is undetermined,

---

3. Each basic RV $f [o_1, \ldots, o_k]$ or $\#\tau [g_1 = o_1, \ldots, g_k = o_k]$ can be assigned a "depth" which is the maximum of the depths of nested tuples and the magnitudes of integers among its arguments $o_1, \ldots, o_k$. The number of RVs at each given depth is finite. Thus, we can enumerate first the RVs at depth 0, then those at depth 1, depth 2, etc.

we return "undetermined"; if α is true, we return true, and if α is false, we go on to evaluate β.[4]

It is more complicated to evaluate set expressions such as {Blip r: Time(r) = 8}, which can be used as CPD arguments. A naive algorithm for evaluating this expression would first enumerate all the objects of type Blip (which would require certain number variables to be instantiated), then select the blips r that satisfy $\text{Time}(r) = 8$. But Figure 13.3 specifies that there may exist some blips for each aircraft a and each natural number t: since there are infinitely many natural numbers, some worlds contain infinitely many blips. Fortunately, the number of blips r with $\text{Time}(r) = 8$ is necessarily finite: in every world there are a finite number of aircraft, and each one generates a finite number of blips at time 8. We have an algorithm that scans the formula within a set expression for *origin function restrictions* such as $\text{Time}(r) = 8$, and uses them to avoid enumerating infinite sets when possible. These restrictions may be either equality constraints, or inequalities that define a bounded set of natural numbers, such as $\text{Time}(r) < 12$. A similar method is used for evaluating quantified formulas.

13.6.2   Termination Criteria

In order to generate each sample, the algorithm above repeatedly instantiates the first variable that is supported but not yet instantiated, until it instantiates all the query and evidence variables. When can we be sure that this will take a finite amount of time? The first way this process could fail to terminate is if it goes into an infinite loop while checking whether a particular variable is supported. This happens if the program ends up enumerating an infinite set while evaluating a set expression or quantified formula. We can avoid this by ensuring that all such expressions in the BLOG model are finite once origin function restrictions are taken into account.

The sample generator also fails to terminate if it never constructs an instantiation that supports a particular query or evidence variable. To see how this can happen, consider calling the subroutine described above to sample a variable V. If V is not supported, the subroutine will realize this when it encounters a variable U that is relevant but not instantiated. Now consider a graph over basic variables where we draw an edge from U to V when the evaluation process for V hits U in this way. If a variable is never supported, then it must be part of a cycle in this graph, or part of a receding chain of variables $V_1 \leftarrow V_2 \leftarrow \cdots$ that is extended infinitely.

The graph constructed in this way varies from sample to sample: for instance, sometimes the evaluation process for ObsColor $[d]$ will hit TrueColor $[(\text{Ball}, 7)]$, and sometimes it will hit TrueColor $[(\text{Ball}, 13)]$. However, we can rule out cycles and

---

4. This left-to-right evaluation scheme does not always detect that a formula is determined: for instance, on $\alpha \vee \beta$, it returns "undetermined" if α is undetermined but β is true—even though $\alpha \vee \beta$ must be true in this case.

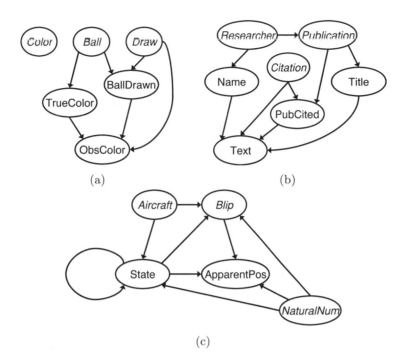

Figure 13.6 Symbol graphs for (a) the urn-and-balls model in Figure 13.1; (b) the bibliographic model in Figure 13.2; (c) the aircraft tracking model in Figure 13.3.

infinite receding chains in all these graphs by considering a more abstract graph over function symbols and types (along the same lines as the *dependency graph* of [15, 4]).

Definition 13.11

The *symbol graph* for a BLOG model M is a directed graph whose nodes are the types and random function symbols of M, where the parents of a type τ or function symbol f are

- the random function symbols that occur on the right-hand side of the dependency statement for f or some number statement for τ;
- the types of variables that are quantified over in formulae or set expressions on the right-hand side of such a statement;
- the types of the arguments for f or the return types of origin functions for τ.

The symbol graphs for our three examples are shown in Figure 13.6. If the sampling subroutine for a basic RV V hits a basic RV U, then there must be an edge from U's function symbol (or type, if U is a number RV) to V's function symbol (or type) in the symbol graph. This property, along with ideas from [20], allows us to prove the following:

Theorem 13.12

Suppose M is a BLOG model where

1. uncountable built-in types do not serve as function arguments or as the return types of origin functions;
2. each quantified formula and set expression ranges over a finite set once origin function restrictions are taken into account;
3. the symbol graph is acyclic.

Then M is well-defined. Also, for any evidence instantiation e and query variable Q, the rejection sampling algorithm described in section 13.6.1 converges to the posterior $P(Q|e)$ defined by the model, taking finite time per sampling step.

The criteria in Theorem 13.12 are very conservative: in particular, when we construct the symbol graph, we ignore all structure in the dependency statements and just check for the occurrence of function and type symbols. These criteria are satisfied by the models in Figures 13.1 and 13.2. However, the aircraft tracking model in Figure 13.3 does not satisfy the criteria because its symbol graph (Figure 13.6(c)) contains a self-loop from State to State. The criteria do not exploit the fact that State(a, t) depends only on State$(a, \text{Pred}(t))$, and the nonrandom function Pred is acyclic. Friedman et al. [4] have already dealt with this issue in the context of probabilistic relational models; their algorithm can be adapted to obtain a stronger version of Theorem 13.12 that covers the aircraft tracking model.

13.6.3   Experimental results

Milch et al. [20] describe a guided likelihood weighting algorithm that uses backward chaining from the query and evidence nodes to avoid sampling irrelevant variables. This algorithm can also be adapted to BLOG models. We applied this algorithm for Example 13.1, asserting that 10 balls were drawn and all appeared blue, and querying the number of balls in the urn. Figure 13.7(a) shows that when the prior for the number of balls is uniform over $\{1, \ldots, 8\}$, the posterior puts more weight on small numbers of balls; this makes sense because the more balls there are in the urn, the less likely it is that they are all blue. Figure 13.7(b), using a Poisson(6) prior, shows a similar but less pronounced effect.

Note that in Figure 13.7, the posterior probabilities computed by the likelihood weighting algorithm are very close to the exact values (computed by exhaustive enumeration of possible worlds with up to 170 balls). We were able to obtain this level of accuracy using runs of 20,000 samples with the uniform prior, and 100,000 samples using the Poisson prior. On a Linux workstation with a 3.2GHz Pentium 4 processor, the runs with the uniform prior took about 35 seconds (571 samples/second), and those with the Poisson prior took about 170 seconds (588 samples/second). Such results could not be obtained using any algorithm that constructed a single fixed BN, since the number of potentially relevant TrueColor $[b]$ variables is infinite in the Poisson case.

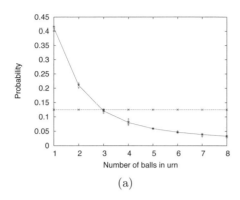 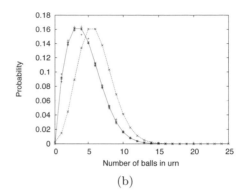

(a) (b)

Figure 13.7 Distribution for the number of balls in the urn (Example 13.1). Dashed lines are the uniform prior (a) or Poisson prior (b); solid lines are the exact posterior given that 10 balls were drawn and all appeared blue; and plus signs are posterior probabilities computed by five independent runs of 20,000 samples (a) or 100,000 samples (b).

13.7 Related Work

Gaifman [5] was the first to suggest defining a probability distribution over first-order model structures. Halpern [10] defines a language in which one can make statements about such distributions: for instance, that the probability of the set of worlds that satisfy Flies(Tweety) is 0.8. *Probabilistic logic programming* [22] can be seen as an application of this approach to Horn-clause knowledge bases. Such an approach only defines *constraints* on distributions, rather than defining a unique distribution.

Most FOPLs that define unique distributions fix the set of objects and the interpretations of (non-Boolean) function symbols. Examples include relational Bayesian networks [12] and Markov logic models [3]. Prolog-based languages such as probabilistic Horn abduction [26], PRISM [28], and Bayesian logic programs [14] work with *Herbrand models*, where the objects are in one-to-one correspondence with the ground terms of the language (a consequence of the unique names and domain closure assumptions).

There are a few FOPLs that allow explicit *reference uncertainty*, i.e., uncertainty about the interpretations of function symbols. Among these are two languages that use indexed RVs rather than logical notation: BUGS [7] and indexed probability diagrams (IPDs) [21]. Reference uncertainty can also be represented in probabilistic relational models (PRMs) [15], where a "single-valued complex slot" corresponds to an uncertain unary function. PRMs are unfortunately restricted to unary functions (attributes) and binary predicates (relations). Probabilistic entity-relationship models [11] lift this restriction, but represent reference uncertainty using relations (such as Drawn(d, b)) and special mutual exclusivity constraints, rather than with functions such as BallDrawn(d). Multientity Bayesian network logic (MEBN) [17] is similar to BLOG in allowing uncertainty about the values of functions with any number of arguments.

The need to handle unknown objects has been appreciated since the early days of FOPL research: Charniak and Goldman's plan recognition networks (PRNs) [2] can contain unbounded numbers of objects representing hypothesized plans. However, external rules are used to decide what objects and variables to include in a PRN. While each possible PRN defines a distribution on its own, Charniak and Goldman do not claim that the various PRNs are all approximations to some single distribution over outcomes.

Some more recent FOPLs do define a single distribution over outcomes with varying objects. IPDs allow uncertainty over the index range for an indexed family of RVs. PRMs and their extensions allow a variety of forms of uncertainty about the number (or existence) of objects satisfying certain relational constraints [15, 6] or belonging to each type [23]. However, there is no unified syntax or semantics for dealing with unknown objects in PRMs. MEBNs take yet another approach: an MEBN model includes a set of unique identifiers, for each of which there is an "identity" RV indicating whether the named object exists.

Our approach to unknown objects in BLOG can be seen as unifying the PRM and MEBN approaches. Number statements neatly generalize the various ways of handling unknown objects in PRMs: number uncertainty [15] corresponds to a number statement with a single origin function; existence uncertainty [6] can be modeled with two or more origin functions (and a CPD whose support is $\{0, 1\}$); and domain uncertainty [23] corresponds to a number statement with no origin functions. There is also a correspondence between BLOG and MEBN logic: the tuple representations in a BLOG model can be thought of as unique identifiers in an MEBN model. The difference is that BLOG determines which objects actually exist in a world using number variables rather than individual existence variables.

Finally, it is informative to compare BLOG with the IBAL language [25], in which a program defines a distribution over outputs that can be arbitrary nested data structures. An IBAL program could implement a BLOG-like generative process with the outputs viewed as logical model structures. But the declarative semantics of such a program would be less clear than the corresponding BLOG model.

13.8   Conclusions and Future Work

BLOG is a representation language for probabilistic models with unknown objects. It contributes to the solution of a very general problem in AI: intelligent systems must represent and reason about objects, but those objects may not be known a priori and may not be directly and uniquely identified by perceptual processes. Our approach defines generative models in which first-order model structures are created by adding objects and setting function values; everything else follows naturally from this design decision.

Much work remains to be done on BLOG. The inference algorithms presented in this chapter are not practical for any but the smallest examples. For real-world problems, we expect to employ Markov chain Monte Carlo (MCMC) techniques (see, e.g, Gilks et al. [8]), simulating a Markov chain over possible worlds. More precisely, these algorithms must use partial descriptions of possible worlds: in a model with infinitely many RVs, a world cannot be represented explicitly as a full instantiation. We plan to implement a general Gibbs sampling algorithm for BLOG models, using some of the same techniques as the BUGS system [7]. However, for models with unknown objects, we expect to obtain faster convergence with Metropolis-Hastings algorithms [18] using proposal distributions that split and merge objects [13]. For now, it appears that these proposal distributions will need to be designed by hand to propose reasonable splits and merges (e.g., merging publications with similar or identical titles), as was done in [23]. However, we have implemented a general Metropolis-Hastings inference engine for BLOG that maintains the state of the Markov chain and computes acceptance probabilities for any given proposal distribution. In the future, we plan to explore adaptive MCMC techniques (see, e.g., [9] and references therein).

Another important question is how to design BLOG models that will lead to accurate inferences from real-world data. For the citation matching problem, Pasula et al. [23] obtained state-of-the-art accuracy using reasonably simple prior distributions for publication titles and author names, estimated from BibTeX files and U.S. Census data (these results are competitive with the discriminative approach of Wellner et al. [31]). It is not so clear how to estimate the prior distributions for the numbers of objects of various types, such as researchers and publications. Pasula et al. [23] simply used a log-normal distribution, which has a very large variance. As an alternative to defining such a prior distribution, one could use the nonparametric version of BLOG proposed by Carbonetto et al. [1], which incorporates Dirichlet process mixture models.

Finally, perhaps the most interesting questions about BLOG have to do with learning. Parameter estimation, even from partially observed data, is conceptually straightforward: the sampling-based inference algorithms described above can serve as the basis for Monte Carlo expectation-maximization (EM) algorithms [30]. But learning the structure of BLOG models is an exciting open problem. In other statistical relational formalisms, techniques have been proposed for discovering dependencies that hold between attributes of related objects [4, 27]. We believe that extensions of these techniques can be applied to BLOG. The ultimate goal, however, is to develop algorithms that can hypothesize new attributes, new relations, and even new types of objects. BLOG provides a language in which such hypotheses can be expressed.

References

[1] P. Carbonetto, J. Kisyński, N. de Freitas, and D. Poole. Nonparametric Bayesian logic. In *Proceedings of the Conference on Uncertainty in Artificial Intelligence*, 2005.

[2] E. Charniak and R. P. Goldman. A Bayesian model of plan recognition. *Artificial Intelligence*, 64(1):53–79, 1993.

[3] P. Domingos and M. Richardson. Markov logic: A unifying framework for statistical relational learning. In *ICML Workshop on Statistical Relational Learning and Its Connections to Other Fields*, 2004.

[4] N. Friedman, L. Getoor, D. Koller, and A. Pfeffer. Learning probabilistic relational models. In *Proceedings of the International Joint Conference on Artificial Intelligence*, 1999.

[5] H. Gaifman. Concerning measures in first order calculi. *Israel Journal of Mathematics*, 2:1–18, 1964.

[6] L. Getoor, N. Friedman, D. Koller, and B. Taskar. Learning probabilistic models of relational structure. In *Proceedings of the International Conference on Machine Learning*, 2001.

[7] W. R. Gilks, A. Thomas, and D. J. Spiegelhalter. A language and program for complex Bayesian modelling. *The Statistician*, 43(1):169–177, 1994.

[8] W. R. Gilks, S. Richardson, and D. J. Spiegelhalter, editors. *Markov Chain Monte Carlo in Practice*. Chapman and Hall, London, 1996.

[9] H. Haario, E. Saksman, and J. Tamminen. An adaptive Metropolis algorithm. *Bernoulli*, 7:223–242, 2001.

[10] J. Y. Halpern. An analysis of first-order logics of probability. *Artificial Intelligence*, 46:311–350, 1990.

[11] D. Heckerman, C. Meek, and D. Koller. Probabilistic models for relational data. Technical Report MSR-TR-2004-30, Microsoft Research, Seattle, WA, 2004.

[12] M. Jaeger. Complex probabilistic modeling with recursive relational Bayesian networks. *Annals of Math and Artificial Intelligence*, 32:179–220, 2001.

[13] S. Jain and R. M. Neal. A split-merge Markov chain Monte Carlo procedure for the Dirichlet process mixture model. *Journal of Computational and Graphical Statistics*, 13:158–182, 2004.

[14] K. Kersting and L. De Raedt. Adaptive Bayesian logic programs. In *Proceedings of the International Conference on Inductive Logic Programming*, 2001.

[15] D. Koller and A. Pfeffer. Probabilistic frame-based systems. In *Proceedings of the National Conference on Artificial Intelligence*, 1998.

[16]   K. Lambert. Free logics, philosophical issues in. In E. Craig, editor, *Routledge Encyclopedia of Philosophy*. Routledge, London, 1998.

[17]   K. B. Laskey and P. C. G. da Costa. Of starships and Klingons: Bayesian logic for the 23rd century. In *Proceedings of the Conference on Uncertainty in Artificial Intelligence*, 2005.

[18]   N. Metropolis, A.W. Rosenbluth, M.N. Rosenbluth, A.H. Teller, and E. Teller. Equations of state calculations by fast computing machines. *Journal of Chemical Physics*, 21:1087–1092, 1953.

[19]   B. Milch, B. Marthi, S. Russell, D. Sontag, D. L. Ong, and A. Kolobov. BLOG: Probabilistic models with unknown objects. In *Proceedings of the International Joint Conference on Artificial Intelligence*, 2005.

[20]   B. Milch, B. Marthi, D. Sontag, S. Russell, D. L. Ong, and A. Kolobov. Approximate inference for infinite contingent Bayesian networks. In *Tenth International Workshop on Artificial Intelligence and Statistics*, 2005.

[21]   E. Mjolsness. Labeled graph notations for graphical models. Technical Report 04-03, School of Information and Computer Science, University of California, Irvine, 2004.

[22]   R. T. Ng and V. S. Subrahmanian. Probabilistic logic programming. *Information and Computation*, 101(2):150–201, 1992.

[23]   H. Pasula, B. Marthi, B. Milch, S. Russell, and I. Shpitser. Identity uncertainty and citation matching. In *Proceedings of Neural Information Processing Systems*, 2003.

[24]   J. Pearl. *Probabilistic Reasoning in Intelligent Systems, revised edition*. Morgan Kaufmann, San Francisco, 1988.

[25]   A. Pfeffer. IBAL: A probabilistic rational programming language. In *Proceedings of the International Joint Conference on Artificial Intelligence*, 2001.

[26]   D. Poole. Probabilistic Horn abduction and Bayesian networks. *Artificial Intelligence*, 64(1):81–129, 1993.

[27]   A. Popescul, L. H. Ungar, S. Lawrence, and D. M. Pennock. Statistical relational learning for document mining. In *Proceedings of the IEEE International Conference on Data Mining*, 2003.

[28]   T. Sato and Y. Kameya. Parameter learning of logic programs for symbolic-statistical modeling. *Journal of Artificial Intelligence Research*, 15:391–454, 2001.

[29]   R. W. Sittler. An optimal data association problem in surveillance theory. *IEEE Transactions on Military Electronics*, MIL-8:125–139, 1964.

[30]   G. C. G. Wei and M. A. Tanner. A Monte Carlo implementation of the EM algorithm and the poor man's data augmentation algorithms. *Journal of the American Statistical Association*, 85:699–704, 1990.

[31]   B. Wellner, A. McCallum, F. Peng, and M. Hay. An integrated, conditional model of information extraction and coreference with application to citation matching. In *Proceedings of the Conference on Uncertainty in Artificial Intelligence*, 2004.

14 The Design and Implementation of IBAL: A General-Purpose Probabilistic Language

Avi Pfeffer

This chapter describes IBAL, a high-level representation language for probabilistic AI. IBAL integrates several aspects of probability-based rational behavior, including probabilistic reasoning, Bayesian parameter estimation, and decision-theoretic utility maximization. IBAL is based on the functional programming paradigm, and is an ideal rapid prototyping language for probabilistic modeling. The chapter presents the IBAL language, and presents a number of examples in the language. It then discusses the semantics of IBAL, presenting the semantics in two different ways. Finally, the inference algorithm of IBAL is presented. Seven desiderata are listed for inference, and it is shown how the algorithm fulfils each of them.

14.1 Introduction

In a rational programming language, a program specifes a situation encountered by an agent; evaluating the program amounts to computing what a rational agent would believe or do in the situation. Rational programming combines the advantages of declarative representations with features of programming languages such as modularity, compositionality, and type systems. A system designer need not reinvent the algorithms for deciding what the system should do in each possible situation it encounters. It is sufficient to declaratively describe the situation, and leave the sophisticated inference algorithms to the implementors of the language.

One can think of Prolog as a rational programming language, focused on computing the beliefs of an agent that uses logical deduction. In the past few years there has been a shift in AI toward specifications of rational behavior in terms of probability and decision theory. There is therefore a need for a natural, expressive, general-purpose, and easy-to-program language for probabilistic modeling. This chapter presents IBAL, a probabilistic rational programming language. IBAL, pronounced "eyeball," stands for *Integrated Bayesian Agent Language*. As its name suggests, it integrates various aspects of probability-based rational behavior, including probabilistic reasoning, Bayesian parameter estimation, and decision-theoretic utility maximization. This chapter will focus on the probabilistic representation and reasoning capabilities of IBAL, and not discuss the learning and decision-making aspects.

High-level probabilistic languages have generally fallen into two categories. The first category is rule-based [19, 13, 5]. In this approach the general idea is to associate logic-programming-like rules with noise factors. A rule describes how one first-order term depends on other terms. Given a specific query and a set of observations, a Bayesian network (BN) can be constructed describing a joint distribution over all the first-order variables in the domain.

The second category of language is object-based [7, 8, 10]. In this approach, the world is described in terms of objects and the relationships between them. Objects have attributes, and the probabilistic model describes how the attributes of an object depend on other attributes of the same object and on attributes of related objects. The model specifies a joint probability distribution over the attributes of all objects in the domain.

This chapter explores a different approach to designing high-level probabilistic languages. IBAL is a functional language for specifying probabilistic models. Models in IBAL look like programs in a functional programming language. In the functional approach, a model is a description of a computational process. The process stochastically generates a value, and the meaning of the model is the distribution over the value generated by the process.

The functional approach, as embodied in IBAL, has a number of attractive features. First of all, it is an extremely natural way to describe a probabilistic model. To construct a model, one simply has to provide a description of the way the world works. Describing the generative process explicitly is the most direct way to describe a generative model. Second, IBAL is highly expressive. It builds on top of a Turing-complete programming language, so that every generative model that can reasonably be described computationally can be described in IBAL. Third, by basing probabilistic modeling languages on programming languages, we are able to enjoy the benefits of a programming language, such as a type system and type inference. Furthermore, by building on the technology of functional languages, we are able to utilize all their features, such as lambda abstraction and higher-order functions.

In addition, the use of a functional programming framework provides an elegant and uniform language with which to describe all aspects of a model. All levels of a model can be described in the language, including the low-level probabilistic dependencies and the high-level structure. This is in contrast to rule-based approaches, in which combination rules describe how the different rules fit together. It is also in contrast to object-based languages, in which the low-level structure is represented using conditional probability tables and a different language is used for high-level structure. Furthermore, PRMs use special syntax to handle uncertainty over the relational structure. This means that each such feature must be treated as a special case, with special purpose inference algorithms. In IBAL, special features are encoded using the language syntax, and the general-purpose inference algorithm is applied to handle them.

IBAL is an ideal rapid prototyping language for developing new probabilistic models. Several examples are provided that show how easy it is to express models in the language. These include well-known models as well as new models. IBAL has been implemented, and made publicly available at

`http:www.eecs.harvard.edu/~avi/IBAL`.

The chapter begins by presenting the IBAL language. The initial focus is on the features that allow description of generative probabilistic models. After presenting examples, the chapter presents the declarative semantics of IBAL.

When implementing a highly expressive reasoning language, the question of inference comes to the forefront. Because IBAL is capable of expressing many different frameworks, its inference algorithm should generalize the algorithms of those frameworks. If, for example, a BN is encoded in IBAL, the IBAL inference algorithm should perform the same operations as a BN inference algorithm. This chapter describes the IBAL inference algorithm and shows how it generalizes many existing frameworks, including Bayesian networks, hidden Markov models (HMMs), and stochastic context free grammars (SCFGs). Seven desiderata for a general-purpose inference algorithm are presented, and it is shown how IBAL's algorithm satisfies all of them simultaneously.

14.2 The IBAL Language

IBAL is a rich language. We first describe the core of the language which is used to build generative probabilistic models. Then we discuss how to encode observations in models. Finally we present some syntactic sugar that makes the language easier and more natural to use.

14.2.1 Basic Expressions

The basic program unit in IBAL is the *expression*. An expression describes a stochastic experiment that generates a value. Just as in a regular programming language an expression describes a computation that produces a value, so in IBAL an expression describes a computation that stochastically produces a value. IBAL provides constructs for defining basic expressions, and for composing expressions together to produce more complex expressions. In this section we provide an intuitive meaning for IBAL expressions in terms of stochastic experiments. We will provide precise semantics in section 14.4. The core of IBAL includes the following kinds of expressions.

Constant expressions A constant expression is a literal of one of the built-in primitive types, Boolean, integer and symbol. The symbol type contains symbolic constants, which can be any string value. For example, `true`, 6 and `'hello` are all constant expressions. A constant expression represents the experiment that always produces the given value.

Conditional expressions The expression `if` e_1 `then` e_2 `else` e_3 provides conditional choice between two possible outcomes. It corresponds to the experiment in which e_1 is evaluated; then, if the value of e_1 was `true`, e_2 is evaluated; otherwise e_3 is evaluated.

Stochastic choice The expression `dist [` p_1 `:` e_1 `,` ..., p_n `:` e_n `]` specifies a stochastic choice among the different possibilities $e_1, \ldots, e_n$. Each of the p_i is the probability of choosing the corresponding e_i. The expression corresponds to the experiment in which the ith branch is chosen with probability p_i, and then the expression e_i is evaluated.

Variable binding IBAL allows variables to be named and assigned a value, and then referred to later. This can be accomplished using an expression of the form `let` x `=` e_1 `in` e_2. Here x is the name of the variable being defined, e_1 is its definition, and e_2 is the expression in which x can appear. The simplest way to understand a `let` expression is that it corresponds to the experiment in which e_1 is evaluated, and then e_2 is evaluated, with the result of e_1 being used wherever x appears. The result of the entire `let` expression is the result of e_2.

Lambda abstraction IBAL provides lambda abstraction, allowing the definition of functions. The expression `lambda` $x_1, \ldots, x_n$ `->` e represents the function that takes arguments $x_1, \ldots, x_n$ whose body is e. Function definitions can also be recursive, using the syntax `fix` $f(x_1, \ldots, x_n)$ `->` e. Here f is the name of the function being defined, and the body e can refer to f. Both `lambda` and `fix` expressions correspond to experiments that always produce the functional value defined by the expression. The functional value is a closure consisting of argument names, a function body, and an environment in which to evaluate free variables.

Function application The expression $e_0(e_1, \ldots, e_n)$ represents function application. It corresponds to the experiment in which e_0 is evaluated, and its functional result is applied to the results of $e_1, \ldots, e_n$. Note that there may be uncertainty in e_0, the expression defining the function to be applied.

Tuple construction and access The expression $< x_1 : e_1, \ldots, x_n : e_n >$ constructs a tuple with components named $x_1, \ldots, x_n$. It corresponds to the experiment in which each of the e_i is evaluated and assigned to the component x_i. Once a tuple has been constructed, a component can be accessed using dot notation. The expression $e.x$ evaluates the expression e, and extracts component x from the result.

Comparison The expression e_1 `==` e_2 corresponds to the experiment in which e_1 and e_2 are evaluated. The result is `true` if the values of e_1 and e_2 are the same; otherwise it is `false`.

Example 14.1

It is important to note that in an expression of the form let $x = e_1$ in e_2 the variable x is assigned a specific value in the experiment; any stochastic choices made while evaluating e_1 are resolved, and the result is assigned to x. For example, consider

```
let z = dist [ 0.5 : true, 0.5 : false ] in
z & z
```

The value of z is resolved to be either **true** or **false**, and the same value is used in the two places in which z appears in z & z. Thus the whole expression evaluates to **true** with probability 0.5, not 0.25, which is what the result would be if z was reevaluated each time it appears. Thus the let construct provides a way to make different parts of an expression probabilistically dependent, by making them both mention the same variable. ∎

Example 14.2

This example illustrates the use of a higher-order function. It begins by defining two functions, one corresponding to the toss of a fair coin and one describing a toss of a biased coin. It then defines a higher-order function, whose return value is one of the first two functions. This corresponds to the act of deciding which kind of coin to toss. The example then defines a variable named c whose value is either the **fair** or **biased** function. It then defines two variables x and y to be different applications of the function contained in c. The variables x and y are conditionally independent of each other given the value of c. Note by the way that in this example the functions take zero arguments.

```
let fair = lambda () -> dist [ 0.5 : 'heads, 0.5 : 'tails ] in
let biased = lambda () -> dist [ 0.9 : 'heads, 0.1 : 'tails ] in
let pick = lambda () -> dist [ 0.5 : fair, 0.5 : biased ] in
let c = pick () in
let x = c () in
let y = c () in
<x:x, y:y> \ \ \bbox
```

14.2.2   Observations

The previous section presented the basic constructs for describing generative probabilistic models. Using the constructs above, one can describe any stochastic experiment that generatively produces values. The language presented so far can express many common models, such as BNs, probabilistic relational models, HMMs, dynamic Bayesian networks, and SCFGs. All these models are generative in nature. The richness of the model is encoded in the way the values are generated.

IBAL also provides the ability to describe conditional models, in which the generative probability distribution is conditioned on certain observations being satisfied. IBAL achieves this by allowing observations to be encoded explicitly in a model, at any point. An observation serves to condition the model on the observation being true.

An observation has the general syntax `obs` $x = v$ `in` e where x is a variable, v is a value, and e is an expression. Its meaning is the same as expression e, except that the value of variable x is conditioned to be equal to v. The variable x should have been defined earlier, as part of a `let` expression.

Example 14.3

Consider

```
let y = dist [ 0.5 : true, 0.5 : false ] in
let z =
  if y
  then dist [ 0.9 : true, 0.1 : false ]
  else dist [ 0.1 : true, 0.9 : false ] in
obs z = true in
y
```

Here, the distribution defined by the expression is the conditional distribution over y, given that z takes on the value `true`. ∎

14.2.3   Syntactic Sugar

In addition to the basic constructs described above, IBAL provides a good deal of syntactic sugar. The sugar does not increase the expressive power of the language, but makes it considerably easier to work with. The syntactic sugar is presented here, because it will be used in many of the later examples.

The `let` syntax is extended to make it easy to define functions. The syntax `let` $f(x_1, \ldots, x_n) = e$ is equivalent to `let` $f = $ `fix` $f(x_1, \ldots, x_n) = e$.

Thus far, every IBAL construct has been an expression. Indeed, everything in IBAL can be written as an expression, and presenting everything as expressions simplifies the presentation. A real IBAL program, however, also contains *definitions*. A *block* is a piece of IBAL code consisting of a sequence of variable definitions.

Example 14.4

For example, we can rewrite our coins example using definitions.

```
fair() = dist [ 0.5 : 'heads, 0.5 : 'tails ]
biased()  = dist [ 0.9 : 'heads, 0.1 : 'tails ]
pick() = dist [ 0.5 : fair, 0.5 : biased ]
c = pick()
x = c()
y = c()
```

The value of this block is a tuple containing a component for every variable defined in the block, i.e., `fair`, `biased`, `pick`, `c`, `x`, and `y`. ∎

Bernoulli and uniform random variables are so common that a special notation is created for them. The expression **flip** α is shorthand for **dist** $[\alpha : \texttt{true}, 1 - \alpha :$ **false**]. The expression **uniform** n is short for **dist** $[\frac{1}{n} : 0, \ldots, \frac{1}{n} : n - 1]$.

IBAL provides basic operators for working with values. These include logical operators for working with Boolean values and arithmetic operators for integer values. IBAL also provides an equality operator that tests any two values for equality. Operator notation is equivalent to function application, where the relevant functions are built in.

Dot notation can be used to reference nested components of variables. For example, **x.a.b** means the component named **b** of the component named **a** of the variable named **x**. This notation can appear anywhere a variable appears. For example, in an observation one can say **obs x.a = 'true in y**. This is equivalent to saying

```
let z = x.a in obs z = 'true in y.
```

Patterns can be used to match sets of values. A pattern may be

- an atomic value (Boolean, integer, or strong), that matches itself;
- the special pattern *, that matches any value;
- a variable, which matches any value, binding the variable to the matched value in the process;
- a tuple of patterns, which matches any tuple value such that each component pattern matches the corresponding component value.

For example, the pattern $< 2, *, \texttt{y} >$ matches value $< 2, \texttt{true}, \texttt{'h} >$, binding **y** to **'h** in the process. A pattern can appear in an observation. For example, **obs x = <2,*,y> in 'true** conditions the experiment on the value of **x** matching the pattern.

Patterns also appear in **case** expressions, which allow the computation to branch depending on the value of a variable. The general syntax of **case** expressions is

$$
\begin{aligned}
&\texttt{case } e_0 \texttt{ of}\\
&\#p_1 : e_1\\
&\ldots\\
&\#p_n : e_n
\end{aligned}
$$

where the p_i are patterns and the e_i are expressions. The meaning, in terms of a stochastic experiment, is to begin by evaluating e_0. Then its value is matched to each of the patterns in turn. If the value matches p_1, the result of the experiment is the result of e_1. If the value does not match p_1 through p_{i-1} and it does match p_i, then e_i is the result. It is an error for the value not to match any pattern. A **case** expression can be rewritten as a series of nested **if** expressions.

The **case** expression is useful for describing conditional probability tables as are used in BNs. In this case, the expression e_0 is a tuple consisting of the parents of the node, each of the patterns p_i matches a specific set of values of the parents, and the corresponding expression e_i is the conditional distribution over the node given the values of the parents. It is also possible to define a pattern that matches whenever a subset of the variables takes on specified values, regardless of the values of other variables. Such a pattern can be used to define conditional probability tables with context-specific independence, where only some of the parents are relevant in certain circumstances, depending on the values of other parents.

In addition to tuples, IBAL provides algebraic data types (ADTs) for creating structured data. An ADT is a data type with several variants. Each variant has a tag and a set of fields. ADTs are very useful in defining recursive data types such as lists and trees. For example, the list type has two variants. The first is `Nil` and has no fields. The second is `Cons` and has a field representing the head of the list and a further field representing the remainder of the list.

Example 14.5

Using the list type, we can easily define a stochastic context free grammar. First we define the `append` function that appends two lists. Then, for each nonterminal in the grammar we define a function corresponding to the act of generating a string with that non-terminal. For example,

```
append(x,y) =
  case x of
  # Nil -> y
  # Cons(a,z) -> Cons(a, append(z,y))
term(x) = Cons(x,Nil)
s() = dist [0.6:term('a);
            0.4:append(s(),t())]
t() = dist [0.9:term('b);
            0.1:append(t(),s())]
```

We can then examine the beginning of a string generated by the grammar using the `take` function:

```
take(n,x) =
  case(n,x) of
  # (0,_) -> Nil
  # (_,Nil) -> Nil
  # (_,Cons(y,z)) -> Cons(y,take(n-1,z))
```

∎

IBAL is a strongly typed language. The language includes **type** declarations that declare new types, and **data** declarations that define algebraic data types. The type system is based on that of ML. The type language will not be presented here, but it will be used in the examples, where it will be explained.

In some cases, it is useful to define a condition as being erroneous. For example, when one tries to take the head of an empty list, an error condition should result. IBAL provides an expression **error** s, where s is a string, to signal an error condition. This expression takes on the special value `ERROR:` *s*, which belongs to every type and can only be used to indicate errors.

Finally, IBAL allows comments in programs. A comment is anything beginning with a // through to the end of the line.

14.3 Examples

Example 14.6

Encoding a BN is easy and natural in IBAL. We include a definition for each variable in the network. A `case` expression is used to encode the conditional probability table for a variable. For example,

```
burglary = flip 0.01;

earthquake = flip 0.001;

alarm = case <burglary, earthquake> of
   # <false, false> : flip 0.01
   # <false, true> : flip 0.1
   # <true, false> : flip 0.7
   # <true, true> : flip 0.8
```

We can also easily encode conditional probability tables with structure. For example, we may want the `alarm` variable to have a noisy-or structure:

```
alarm = flip 0.01 // leak probability
  | earthquake & flip 0.1
  | alarm & flip 0.7
```

We may also create variables with context-specific independence. Context-specific independence is the case where a variable depends on a parent for some values of the other parents but not others. For example, if we introduce variables representing whether or not John is at home and John calls, John calling is dependent on the alarm only in the case that John is at home. IBAL's pattern syntax is very convenient for capturing context-specific independence. The symbol "*" is used as the pattern that matches all values, when we don't care about the value of a specific variable:

```
john_home = flip 0.5

john_calls = case <john_home, alarm> of
  # <false,*> : false
  # <true,false> : flip 0.001
  # <true,true> : flip 0.7
```

Example 14.7

Markov chains can easily be encoded in IBAL. Here we present an example where the states are integers. The sequence of chains produced by the model is represented as a `List`. The first line of the program defines the `List` data type:

```
data List [a] = Nil | Cons (a, List [a])
```

This declaration states that `List` is a parameterized type, taking on the type parameter `a`. That is, for any type `a`, `List [a]` is also a type. It then goes on to state that a `List [a]` can be one of two things: it can be `Nil`, or it can be the `Cons` of two arguments, the first of type `a` and the second of type `List [a]`.

Given a sequence of states represented as a `List`, it is useful to be able to examine a particular state in the sequence. The standard function `nth` does this.

```
nth (n,l) : (Int, List [a]) -> a =
  case l of
  # Cons (x,xs) : if n==0 then x else nth (n-1,xs)
  # Nil : error "Too short";
```

The first line of `nth` includes a typing rule. It states that `nth` is a function taking two arguments, where the first is an integer and the second is a `List [a]`, and returning a value of type `a`.

Next, we define the types to build up a Markov model. A Markov model consists of two functions, an initialization function and a transition function. The initialization function takes zero arguments and produces a state. The transition function takes a state argument and produces a state. Markov models are parameterized by the type of the state, which is here called `a`.

```
type Init [a] = () -> a;
type Trans [a] = (a) -> a;
type Markov [a] = < init : Init [a], trans : Trans [a] >;
```

Given a Markov model, we can realize it to produce a sequence of states.

```
realize (m) : (Markov [a]) -> List [a] =
  let f(x) = Cons (x, f(m.trans (x))) in
  f(m.init ());
```

Thus far, the definitions have been abstract, applying to every Markov model. Now we define a particular Markov model by supplying definitions for the initialization and transition functions. Note that the state here is integer, so the state space is infinite. The state can be any type whatsoever, including algebraic data types like lists or trees.

```
random_walk : Markov [Int] =
    < init : lambda () -> 0,
      trans : lambda (n) -> dist [ 0.5 : n++, 0.5 : n-- ] >;
```

It is easy to see how to generalize this example to HMMs by providing an observation function, and then specifying the observations using `obs` expressions. Then, combined with the previous example of BNs, we can generalize this to dynamic Bayesian networks [2]. ■

Example 14.8

One of the features of PRMs is *structural uncertainty*: uncertainty over the relational structure of the domain. One kind of structural uncertainty is *number uncertainty*, where we do not know how many objects an object is related to by a particular relation. In the development of the SPOOK system [17], a good deal of code was devoted to handling number uncertainty. In this example, we show how to encode number uncertainty in IBAL. By encoding it in IBAL, a lot of code is saved, and all the inference mechanisms for dealing with number uncertainty are essentially attained for free.

The main mechanism for representing number uncertainty in IBAL is a function `create` that creates a set consisting of a given number of objects of a certain kind. In addition to the number of objects, the function takes the function used to create individual objects as an argument:

```
create(n,f) =
  if n = 0
  then Nil
  else Cons(f(), create(n-1, f))
```

In this function, the argument `f` is a function that takes zero arguments. However, `create` can easily be used to create objects when the creating function takes arguments, by passing an intermediate function as follows. In the following code snippet, the `field` argument is the same for every course that is created, but the `prof` argument is different. We see here that the functional framework provides a great deal of flexibility in the way arguments are defined and passed to functions.

```
let f() =
  let p = prof(field1) in
  course(p, field)
in
create(5, f)
```

Once we have defined how to create sets of a given size, we can easily introduce uncertainty over the size. The number of objects to create is defined by its own expression, which may include `dist` or `uniform` expressions.

After creating a set, we want to be able to talk about properties of the set. PRMs use aggregate operators for this, and these can easily be encoded in IBAL. The following `count` function counts how many members of a set satisfy a given property. The first argument `p` is a predicate that takes an element of the set as argument and returns a Boolean.

```
count(p, s) =
  case s of
  # Nil : 0
  # Cons(x,xs) :
      if p x
      then 1 + count(p, xs)
      else count(p, xs)
```

In addition to `count`, we can easily define universal and existential quantifiers and other aggregates. ∎

Example 14.9

IBAL is an ideal language in which to rapidly prototype new probabilistic models. Here we illustrate using a recently developed kind of model, the *repetition model* [15]. A repetition model is used to describe a sequence of elements in which repetition of elements from earlier in the sequence is a common occurrence. It is attached to an existing sequence model such as an n-gram or an HMM. Here we describe the repetition HMM.

In a repetition HMM, there is a hidden state that evolves according to a Markov process, just as in an ordinary HMM. An observation is generated at each time point. With some probability ρ, the observation is generated from memory, meaning that a previous observation is reused for the current observation. With the remaining $1 - \rho$ probability, the observation is generated from the hidden state according to the observation model of the HMM. This model captures the fact that there is an underlying generative process as described by the HMM, but this process is sometimes superseded by repeating elements that have previously appeared. Repetition is a key element of music, and repetition models have successfully been applied to modeling musical rhythm.

To describe a repetition HMM in IBAL, we first need a function to select a random element from a sequence. The function `nth` takes an integer argument and selects the given element of the sequence. We then let the argument range uniformly over the length of the sequence, which is passed as an argument to the `select` function.

```
nth(n, seq) =
  case seq of
  # Cons(x,xs) :
      if n = 0
      then x
      else nth(n-1, xs)
  # Nil : error
```

```
select(length, seq) = nth(uniform length, seq)
```

Similarly to the way we defined Markov models earlier, a repetition HMM takes `init`, `trans`, and `obs` functions as arguments. The parameter ρ must be supplied. If we used all of IBAL's features it could be a learnable parameter. In our example we set it to 0.1. The generation process is described exceedingly simply. A function `sequence` generates the sequence of observations using a given memory of a given length, under the given model, beginning in a given state. The first thing it does is generate the new hidden state according to the transition model. Then it generates the observation using a `dist` expression on the parameter ρ. With probability ρ it selects the observation from memory; otherwise it uses the observation model. Finally, the entire sequence is put together by consing the current observation with the new sequence formed using the new memory from the new hidden state.

```
type Init [a] = () -> a;
type Trans [a] = (a) -> a;
type Obs [a,o] = (a) -> o;
type repetition_hmm [a,o] =
  < init : Init [a], trans : trans [a], obs : Obs [a,o] >;

param rho = [ 0.1, 0.9 ];

sequence(memory, length, model, state) =
  let h = model.trans(state) in
  let o = pdist rho [ select(length, memory), model.obs(h) ] in
  Cons(o, sequence(Cons(o, memory), length + 1, model, h))

repetition_hmm(model) =
  sequence(Nil, 0, model, state.init())
```

∎

In addition to these examples, IBAL can represent PRMs, and by extension dynamic PRMs [21]. Meanwhile, the decision-making constructs of IBAL allow the encoding of influence diagrams and Markov decision processes.

14.4 Semantics

In specifying the semantics of the language, it is sufficient to provide semantics for the core expressions, since the syntactic sugar is naturally induced from them. The semantics is distributional: the meaning of a program is specified in terms of a probability distribution over values.

14.4.1 Distributional Semantics

We use the notation $\mathcal{M}[e]$ to denote the meaning of expression e, under the distributional semantics. The meaning function takes as argument a probability distribution over environments. The function returns a probability distribution over values. We write $\mathcal{M}[e] \; \Delta \; v$ to denote the probability of v under the meaning of e

when the distribution over environments is Δ. We also use the notation $\mathcal{M}[e]\ \epsilon\ v$ to denote the probability of v under the meaning of e when the probability distribution over environments assigns positive probability only to ϵ.

We now define the meaning function for different types of expressions. The meaning of a constant expression is given by

$$\mathcal{M}[v]\ \Delta\ v' = \begin{cases} 1 & \text{if v' = v,} \\ 0 & \text{otherwise} \end{cases}$$

The probability that referring to a variable produces a value is obtained simply by summing over environments in which the variable has the given value:

$$\mathcal{M}[x]\ \Delta\ v = \sum_{\epsilon:\epsilon(x)=v} \Delta(\epsilon).$$

The meaning of an `if` expression is defined as follows. We first take the sum over all environments of the meaning of the expression in the particular environments. The reason we need to do this is because the meanings of the `if` clause and of the `then` and `else` clauses are correlated by the environment. Therefore we need to specify the particular environment before we can break up the meaning into the meanings of the subexpressions. Given the environments, however, the subexpressions become conditionally independent, so we can multiply their meanings together.

$$\mathcal{M}[\texttt{if } e_1 \texttt{ then } e_2 \texttt{ else } e_3]\ \Delta\ v = \sum_{\epsilon} \Delta(\epsilon) \left[\begin{array}{l} (\mathcal{M}[e_1]\ \epsilon\ \texttt{true})(\mathcal{M}[e_2]\ \epsilon\ v)+ \\ (\mathcal{M}[e_1]\ \epsilon\ \texttt{false})(\mathcal{M}[e_3]\ \epsilon\ v) \end{array} \right]$$

The distributional semantics of a `dist` expression simply states that the probability of a value under a `dist` expression is the weighted sum of the probability of the value under the different branches:

$$\mathcal{M}[\texttt{dist}[p_1 : e_1, \ldots, p_n : e_n]]\ \Delta\ v = \sum_i p_i(\mathcal{M}[e_i]\ \Delta\ v).$$

To define the meaning of an expression `let` $x = e_1$ `in` $e2$, we first define a probability distribution Δ' over extended environments that are produced by binding x with any possible value. The probability of an extended environment is the probability of the original environment that is being extended times the probability that e_1 will produce the given value in the original environment. We then define the meaning of the entire expression to be the meaning of e_2 under Δ'. The notation $\epsilon[x/v']$ indicates the environment produced by extending ϵ by binding x to v'.

$$\mathcal{M}[\texttt{let } x = e_1 \texttt{ in } e_2]\ \Delta\ v = \mathcal{M}[e_2]\ \Delta'\ v$$
$$\text{where } \Delta'(\epsilon') = \begin{cases} \Delta(\epsilon)(\mathcal{M}[e_1]\ \epsilon\ v') & \text{if } \epsilon' = \epsilon[x/v'] \\ 0 & \text{otherwise} \end{cases}$$

`lambda` and `fix` expressions are treated as constants whose values are closures. The only difference is that the closure specifies an environment, so we take the probability that the current environment is the closure environment.

$$
\mathcal{M}[\texttt{lambda } x_1, \ldots, x_n \to e] \; \Delta \; v = \begin{cases} \Delta(\epsilon) & \text{if } v = \left\{ \begin{array}{l} \text{args} = x_1, \ldots, x_n; \\ \text{body} = e; \\ \text{env} = \epsilon \end{array} \right\} \\ 0 & \text{otherwise} \end{cases}
$$

$$
\mathcal{M}[\texttt{fix } x_1, \ldots, x_n \to e] \; \Delta \; v = \begin{cases} \Delta(\epsilon) & \text{if } v = \left\{ \begin{array}{l} \text{args} = x_1, \ldots, x_n; \\ \text{body} = e; \\ \text{env} = \epsilon[f/v] \end{array} \right\} \\ 0 & \text{otherwise} \end{cases}
$$

The distributional semantics for function application is logically constructed as follows. We sum over all possible environments, and over all possible values $v_0, v_1, \ldots, v_n$, of the expression e_0 defining the function to be applied, and of the expressions $v_1, \ldots, v_n$ defining the arguments. We take the product of the probabilities of obtaining each v_i from e_i in the environment, and multiply by the probability that applying v_0 to $v_1, \ldots, v_n$ produces the value v. Here, applying v_0 to $v_1, \ldots, v_n$ means taking the meaning of the body of v_0 in an environment formed by extending the closure environment by binding each argument x_i to v_i.

$$
\mathcal{M}[e_0(e_1, \ldots, e_n)] \; \Delta \; v =
$$
$$
\sum_\epsilon \Delta(\epsilon) \sum_{v_0, v_1, \ldots, v_n} \left(\prod_{i=0}^n \mathcal{M}[e_i] \; \epsilon \; v_i \right) (\mathcal{M}[e] \; \epsilon'[x_1/v_1, \ldots, x_n/v_n] \; v)
$$
$$
\text{where } \{\text{args} = x_1, \ldots, x_n; \text{body} = e; \text{env} = \epsilon'\} = v_0
$$

The meaning of a tuple expression is given by

$$
\mathcal{M}[< x_1 : e_1, \ldots, x_n : e_n >] \; \Delta \; v =
$$
$$
\begin{cases} \sum_\epsilon \Delta(\epsilon) \prod_{i=1}^n \mathcal{M}[e_i] \; (\epsilon) \; v_i & \text{if } v = < x_1 : v_1, \ldots, x_n : v_n >, \\ 0 & \text{otherwise} \end{cases}
$$

The meaning of extracting a component from a tuple is

$$
\mathcal{M}[e.x] \; \Delta \; v = \sum_{v' : v'.x = v} \mathcal{M}[e] \; \Delta \; v'.
$$

Finally, the probability of a comparison being true is derived by taking the sum, over all possible values, of the probability that both expressions produce the value.

$$\mathcal{M}[e_1 == e_2]\, \Delta`v = \begin{cases} p & \text{if } v = \texttt{true} \\ 1 - p & \text{if } v = \texttt{false} \\ 0 & \text{otherwise} \end{cases}$$

$$\text{where } p = \sum_\epsilon \Delta(\epsilon) \sum_{v'} (\mathcal{M}[e_1]\, \epsilon\, v')(\mathcal{M}[e_2]\, \epsilon\, v')$$

The distributional semantics captures observations quite simply. The effect of an observation is to condition the distribution Δ over environments on the observation holding. When the probability that the observation holds is zero, the probability of the expression is defined to be zero.

$$\mathcal{M}[\texttt{obs } x = v' \texttt{ in } e]\, \Delta\, v = \begin{cases} \dfrac{\sum_{\epsilon : \epsilon(x) = v'} \Delta(\epsilon)(\mathcal{M}[e]\, \epsilon\, v)}{P(x = v')} & \text{if } P(x = v') > 0 \\ 0 & \text{if } P(x = v') = 0 \end{cases}$$

$$\text{where } P(x = v') = \sum_{\epsilon : \epsilon(x) = v'} \Delta(\epsilon)$$

14.4.2   Lazy Semantics

A very natural way to define a probabilistic model is to describe a generative model that generates possibly infinite values, and then to ask queries that only consider a finite portion of the values. For example, an SCFG may generate arbitrarily long strings. We may query the probability that a grammar generates a particular string. This requires looking at only a finite portion of the generated string, and a finite portion of the generation process.

We use lazy semantics in IBAL to get at the idea that only those parts of an expression that need to be evaluated in order to generate the result of the expression are evaluated. There are two places in particular where this applies. In a

$$\texttt{let } x_1 = e_1 \texttt{ in } e_2$$

expression, the subexpression e_1 is only evaluated if x is actually needed in evaluating e_2. More precisely, if e_1 defines a tuple, only those components of the tuple that are needed in e_2 are evaluated. In a function application

$$e_0(e_1, \ldots, e_n)$$

only those parts of the argument e_i are evaluated that are needed in evaluating the body of the function. The body of the function here could mean the body of any possible value of e_0 — if any value of e_0 requires a component of the argument, the component is evaluated.

Example 14.10
Consider the program

```
t() = Cons(flip 0.5, t())
```

```
g(x) =
  case x of
  # Cons(y,z) -> y

g(f())
```

The function `f()` defines an infinite sequence of *true* and *false* elements. The function `g()` then returns the first element in the sequence. When `g` is applied to `f`, the body of `g` specifies that only the first component of its argument is required. Therefore, when evaluating `f`, only its first component will be evaluated. That can be done by examining a single `flip`. ∎

The distributional semantics presented earlier is agnostic about whether it is eager or lazy. It simply presents a set of equations, and says nothing about how the equations are evaluated. Both eager and lazy interpretations are possible. The meaning of an expression under either interpretation is only well-defined when the process of evaluating it converges. The eager and lazy semantics do not necessarily agree. The eager semantics may diverge in some cases where the lazy semantics produces a result. However, if the eager semantics converges, the lazy semantics will produce the same result.

14.5 Desiderata for Inference

IBAL is able to capture many traditional kinds of representations, such as BNs, HMMs, and SCGGs. It can also express more recent models such as object-oriented Bayesian networks (OOBNs) and relational probability models [16]. For IBAL to be successful as a general-purpose language, the implementation should be designed to capture effective strategies for as many models as possible. This leads to the following desiderata. To be sure, this list is not complete. In particular, it does not consider issues to do with the time-space tradeoff. Nevertheless, it is a good set of goals, and no existing implementation is able to achieve all of them.

1. Exploit independence Independence and conditional independence are traditionally exploited by BNs. The inference algorithm should have similar properties to traditional BN algorithms when run on BN models.

2. Exploit low-level structure In BNs, the conditional probability distribution over a variable given its parents is traditionally represented as a table. Researchers have studied more compact representations, such as noisy-or and context-specific independence. Special-purpose inference algorithms have been designed for these structures [4, 20]. Because of IBAL's programming language constructs, it is easy to describe such structures — easier, in fact, than describing full conditional probability tables. The inference algorithm should be able to take a representation that elucidates the low-level structure and automatically provide benefits from exploiting the structure.

3. Exploit high-level structure Larger models can often be decomposed into weakly interacting components. It was discovered for OOBNs [17] that exploiting such high-level structure is a big win. In particular, the different components tend to be largely decoupled from one another, and they can be separated by a small interface that renders them conditionally independent of each other. IBAL represents high-level structure-using functions. The inference algorithm should take advantage of the decoupling of the internals of functions from the remainder of the model.

4. Exploit repetition Many frameworks such as SCFGs and HMMs involve many repeated computations. In IBAL, the same function can be applied many times, and this should be exploited to avoid repeated computation.

5. Exploit the query Often, one describes a very complex or infinite probabilistic model, but asks a query that only requires a small portion of the model. This is the process, for example, for SCFGs: the grammar can generate arbitrarily long sentences, but only a finite generation process is needed to generate a particular finite sentence. IBAL should use the query to consider only the parts of the generation process that are necessary for producing the result.

6. Exploit support of variables When a model contains variables, its behavior depends on their values. The *support* of a variable is the set of values it can take with positive probability. Taking the support into account can simplify inference, by restricting the set of inputs that need to be considered. It can turn a potentially infinite inference into a finite one.

7. Exploit evidence If we have observations in the program, they can be used to further limit the set of values variables can take, and to restrict the possible computations. For example, suppose we have a model in which a string is generated by a grammar that can generate arbitrarily long strings, and then observe that the string has length at most four. We can use this observation to restrict the portion of the grammar that needs to be examined.

14.6   Related Approaches

Previous approaches to inference in high-level probabilistic languages have generally fallen into four categories. On one side are approaches that use approximate inference, particularly Markov chain Monte Carlo methods. This is the approach used in BUGS [23] and the approach taken by Pasula and Russell in their first-order probabilistic logic [14]. While exact inference may be intractable for many models, and approximate strategies are therefore needed, the goal of this chapter is to push exact inference as far as possible.

The first generation of high-level probabilistic languages generally used the *knowledge-based model construction (KBMC)* approach (e.g. [19, 13, 10, 5]). In this approach, a knowledge base describes the general probabilistic mechanisms. These are combined with ground facts to produce a BN for a specific situation. A standard BN inference algorithm is then used to answer queries.

This approach generally satisfies only the first of the above desiderata. Since a BN is constructed, any independence will be represented in that network, and can be exploited by the BN algorithm. The second desideratum can also be satisfied, if a BN algorithm that exploits low-level structure is used, and the BN construction process is able to produce that structure. Since the construction process creates one large BN, any structure resulting from weakly interacting components is lost, so the third desideratum is not satisfied. Similarly, when there is repetition in the domain the large BN contains many replicated components, and the fourth desideratum is not satisfied. Satisfaction of the remaining desiderata depends on the details of the BN construction process. The most common approach is to grow the network using backward chaining, starting at the query and the evidence. If any of these lead to an infinite regress, the process will fail.

Sato and Kameya [22] present a more advanced version of this approach that achieves some of the aims of this paper. They use a tabling procedure to avoid performing redundant computations. In addition, their approach is query-directed. However they do not exploit low-level independence or weak interaction between objects, nor do they utilize observations or support.

More recent approaches take one of two tacks. The first is to design a probabilistic representation language as a programming language, whether a functional language [9, 18] or logic programming [12]. The inference algorithms presented for these languages are similar to evaluation algorithms for ordinary programming languages, using recursive descent on the structure of programs. The programming language approach has a number of appealing properties. First, the evaluation strategy is natural and familiar. Second, a programming language provides the fine-grained representational control with which to describe low-level structure. Third, simple solutions are suggested for many of the desiderata. For example, high-level structure can be represented in the structure of a program, with different functions representing different components. As for exploiting repetition, this can be achieved by the standard technique of *memoization*. When a function is applied to a given set of arguments, the result is cached, and retrieved whenever the same function is applied to the same arguments. Meanwhile, *lazy evaluation* can be used to exploit the query to make a computation simpler.

However, approaches based on programming languages have a major drawback. They do not do a good job of exploiting independence. Koller et al. [9] made an effort to exploit independence by maintaining a list of variables shared by different parts of the computation. The resulting algorithm is much more difficult to understand, and the solution is only partial. Given a BN encoded in their language, the algorithm can be viewed as performing variable elimination (VE) using a particular elimination order: namely, from the last variable in the program upward. It is well-known that the cost of VE is highly dependent on the elimination order, so the algorithm is exponentially more expensive for some families of models than an algorithm that can use any order.

In addition, while these approaches suggest solutions to many of the desiderata, actually integrating them into a single implementation is difficult. For example,

Koller et al. [9] suggested using both memoization and lazy evaluation, believing that since both were standard techniques their combination would be simple. In fact it turns out that implementing both simultaneously is considered extremely difficult![1] The final three desiderata are all variations on the idea that knowledge can be used to simplify computation. The general approach was captured by the term *evidence-finite computation* in [9]. However, this catchall term fails to capture the distinctions between the different ways knowledge can be exploited. A careful implementation of the algorithm in [9] showed that it achieved termination only in a relatively small number of possible cases. In particular it failed to exploit support and observations.

The final approach to high-level probabilistic inference is to use a structured inference algorithm. In this approach, used in object-oriented Bayesian networks and relational probabilistic models [17, 16], a BN fragment is provided for each model component, and the components are related to each other in various ways. Rather than constructing a single BN to represent an entire domain, inference works directly on the structured model, using a standard BN algorithm to work within each component. The approach was designed explicitly to exploit high-level structure and repetition. In addition, because a standard BN algorithm is used, this approach exploits independence. However, it does not address the final three desiderata. An anytime approximation algorithm [6] was provided for dealing with infinitely recursive models, but it is not an approximate inference algorithm.

In addition, this approach does not do as well as one might hope at exploiting low-level structure. One might rely on the underlying BN inference algorithm to exploit whatever structure it can. For example, if it is desired to exploit noisy-or structure, the representation should explicitly encode such structure, and the BN algorithm should take advantage of it. The problem with this approach is that it requires a special-purpose solution for each possible structure, and high-level languages make it easy to specify new structures. A case in point is the structure arising from quantification over a set of objects. In the SPOOK system [17], an object A can be related to a set of objects B, and the properties of A can depend on an aggregate property of B. If implemented naively, A will depend on each of the objects in B, so its conditional probability table will be exponential in the size of B. As shown in [17], the relationship between A and B can be decomposed in such a way that the representation and inference are linear in the size of B. Special purpose code had to be written in SPOOK to capture this structure, but it is easy to specify in IBAL, as described in example 14.8, so it would be highly beneficial if IBAL's inference algorithm can exploit it automatically.

14.7 Inference

14.7.1 Inference Overview

If we examine the desiderata of section 14.5, we see that they fall into two categories. Exploiting repetition, queries, support, and evidence all require avoiding unnecessary computation, while exploiting structure and independence require performing the necessary computation as efficiently as possible. One of the main insights gained during the development of IBAL's inference algorithm is that simultaneously trying to satisfy all the desiderata can lead to quite complex code. The inference process can be greatly simplified by recognizing the two different kinds of desiderata, and dividing the inference process into two phases. The first phase is responsible for determining exactly what computations need to be performed, while the second phase is responsible for performing them efficiently.

This division of labor is reminiscent of the symbolic probabilistic inference (SPI) algorithm for BN inference [11], in which the first phase finds a factoring of the probability expression, and the second phase solves the expression using the factoring. However, there is a marked difference between the two approaches. In SPI, the goal of the first phase is to find the order in which terms should be multiplied. In IBAL, the first phase determines which computations need to be performed, but not their order. That is left for the variable elimination algorithm in the second phase. Indeed, SPI could be used in the second phase of IBAL as the algorithm that computes probabilities.

The first phase of IBAL operates directly on programs, and produces a data structure called the *computation graph*. This rooted directed acyclic graph contains a node for every distinct computation to be performed. A computation consists of an expression to be evaluated, and the supports of free variables in the expression. The computation graph contains an edge from one node to another if the second node represents a computation for a subexpression that is required for the first node.

The second phase of the algorithm traverses the computation graph, *solving* every node. A solution for a node is a conditional probability distribution over the value of the expression given the values of the free variables, assuming that the free variables have values in the given supports. The solution is computed bottom up. To solve a node, the solutions of its children are combined to form the solution for the node.

On the surface, the design seems similar to that of the KBMC approaches. They both create a data structure, and then proceed to solve it. The IBAL approach shares with KBMC the idea of piggybacking on top of existing BN technology. However, the two approaches are fundamentally different. In KBMC, the constructed BN contains a node for every random variable occurring in the solution. By contrast, IBAL's computation graph contains a node for every *distinct*

---

1. Simon Peyton-Jones, personal communication.

computation that is performed during the solution process. If different random variables share the same computation, only one node is created. Secondly, the computation graph is not a BN. Rather, it is an intermediate data structure that guides the construction of many different BNs, and their combination to provide the solution to the query. Thirdly, traditional KBMC approaches typically do not utilize all the information available in the query, support, and evidence in constructing the BN, whereas IBAL uses all of these in constructing the computation graph.

14.7.2   First Phase

It is the task of the first phase to construct the computation graph, containing a node for every computation that has to be performed. At the end of the phase, each node will contain an expression to be evaluated, annotated with the supports of the free variables, and the support of the expression itself. The first phase begins by propagating observations to all subexpressions that they effect. The result of this operation is an annotated expression, where each expression is annotated with the effective observation about its result. When the computation graph is later constructed, the annotations will be used to restrict the supports of variables, and possibly to restrict the set of computations that are required. Thus the **seventh desideratum of exploiting evidence** is achieved. IBAL's observation propagation process is sound but not complete. For an SCFG, it is able to infer when the output string is finite that only a finite computation is needed to produce it. The details are omitted here.

14.7.2.1   *Lazy Memoization*

After propagating observations, the process of constructing the computation graph begins. In order not to construct any more than is necessary to answer the query, the graph is constructed lazily. In particular, whenever a `let x = ` e_1 ` in ` e_2 expression is encountered, the graph for e_2 is constructed to determine how much of `x` is required for e_2. Then only the required amount of the graph for e_1 is constructed. (Recall that a variable can have a complex value, so only part of its value may be required in another expression.) Similarly, when a function is applied to arguments, the graph for the arguments is constructed lazily. Since no node of the computation graph is constructed unless it has been determined that it is required for solving the query, the **fifth desideratum of exploiting the query** is achieved.

The **fourth desideratum of exploiting repetition** is achieved by avoiding repeated nodes in the graph. In particular, when a function is applied to arguments, the same node is used as long as (1) the supports of the required parts of the arguments are the same; (2) the required components of the output are the same; and (3) the observed evidence on the output is the same. This is quite a strong property. It requires that the same node be used when the supports of the arguments are the same, even if the arguments are defined by different expressions. It also stipulates that the supports only need to be the same on the required parts of the arguments.

Unfortunately, the standard technique of memoization does not interact well with lazy evaluation. The problem is that in memoization, when we want to create a new node in the computation graph, we have to check if there is an existing node for the same expression that has the same supports for the required parts of the arguments. But we don't know yet what the required parts of the arguments are, or what their supports are. Worse yet, with lazy evaluation, we may not yet know these things for expressions that already have nodes. This issue is the crux of the difficulty with combining lazy evaluation and memoization. In fact, no functional programming language appears to implement both, despite the obvious appeal of these features.

A new evaluation strategy was developed for IBAL to achieve both laziness and memoization together. The key idea is that when the graph is constructed for a function application, the algorithm speculatively assumes that an argument is not required. If it turns out that part of it is required, enough of the computation graph is created for the required part, and the graph for the application is reconstructed, again speculatively assuming that enough of the argument has been constructed. This process continues until the speculation turns out to be correct. At each point, we can check to see if there is a previously created node for the same expression that uses as much as we think is required of the argument. At no point will we create a node or examine part of the argument that is not required.

An important detail is that whenever it is discovered that an argument to the function is required, this fact is stored in the cache. This way, the speculative evaluation is avoided if it has already been performed for the same partial arguments. In general, the cache consists of a mapping from partial argument supports to either a node in the computation graph or to a note specifying that another argument is required.

For example, suppose we have a function

$$f(x,y,z) = \text{if } x \text{ then } y \text{ else } z$$

where the support of x is {true}, the support of y is {5,6}, and z is defined by a divergent function. We first try to evaluate f with no arguments evaluated. We immediately discover that x is needed, and store this fact in the cache. We obtain the support of x, and attempt to evaluate f again. Now, since x must be true, we discover that y is needed, and store this in the cache. We now attempt again to evaluate f with the supports of x and y, and since z is not needed, we return with a computation node, storing the fact that when x and y have the given supports, the result is the given node. The contents of the cache after the evaluation has completed are

$$
\begin{array}{lcl}
f(x,y,z) & \rightarrow & \text{Need } x \\
f(\{true\},y,z) & \rightarrow & \text{Need } y \\
f(\{true\},\{5,6\},z) & \rightarrow & \{5,6\}
\end{array}
$$

In subsequent evaluations of f, examining the cache will tell us to immediately evaluate the support of x, and if the support of x is {true}, we will immediately get the support of y, without any speculative computation required. If the support of y then turns out to be {5,6}, the result will be retrieved from the cache without any evaluation.

14.7.2.2 *Support Computation*

Aside from issues of laziness and memoization, the support computation is fairly straightforward, with the support of an expression being computed from the support of its subexpressions and its free variables. For example, to compute the support of dist $[e_1, ..., e_n]$, simply take the union of the supports of each of the e_i.

Some care is taken to use the supports of some subexpressions to simplify the computation of other subexpressions, so as to achieve the **sixth desideratum of exploiting supports**. The most basic manifestation of this idea is the application expression $e_1 e_2$, where we have *functional uncertainty*, i.e., uncertainty over the identity of the function to apply. For such an expression, IBAL first computes the support of e_1 to see which functions can be applied. Then, for each value f in the support of e_1, IBAL computes the support of applying f to e_2. Finally, the union of all these supports is returned as the support of $e_1 e_2$. For another example, consider an expression e of the form if e_1 else e_2 then e_3. A naive implementation would set the support of e to be the union of the supports of e_2 and e_3. IBAL is smarter, and performs a form of short-circuiting: if **true** is not in the support of e_1, the support of e_2 is not included in the support of e, and similarly for **false** and e_3.

14.7.3   Second Phase

In the second phase, the computation graph is solved from the bottom up. The solution for each node is generally not represented directly. Rather, it is represented as a set of *factors*. A factor *mentions* a set of variables, and defines a function from the values of those variables to real numbers. The variables mentioned by the factors in a solution include a special variable $*$ (pronounced "star") corresponding to the value of the expression, the free variables $\mathbf{X}$ of the expression, and other variables $\mathbf{Y}$. The solution specified by a set of factors $f_1, ..., f_n$ is $P(*|\mathbf{x}) = \frac{1}{Z} \sum_{\mathbf{y}} \prod_i f_i(*, \mathbf{x}, \mathbf{y})$, where Z is a normalizing factor.[2] The set of factors at any node are a compact, implicit representation of the solution at that node. It is up to the solution algorithm to decide which $\mathbf{Y}$ variables to keep around, and which to eliminate.

At various points in the computation, the algorithm eliminates some of the intermediate variables $\mathbf{Y}$, using VE [3] to produce a new set of factors over the remaining variables. The root of the computation graph corresponds to the user's

---

2. The f_i do not need to mention the same variables. The notation $f_i(*, \mathbf{x}, \mathbf{y})$ denotes the value of f_i when $*$, $\mathbf{x}$, and $\mathbf{y}$ are projected onto the variables mentioned by f_i.

query. At the root there are no free variables. To compute the final answer, all variables other than $*$ are eliminated using VE, all remaining factors are multiplied together, and the result is normalized. By using VE for the actual process of computing probabilities, the algorithm achieves the **first desideratum of exploiting independence**. The main point is that unlike other programming language-based approaches, IBAL does not try to compute probabilities directly by working with a program, but rather converts a program into the more manipulable form of factors, and rests on tried and true technology for working with them.

In addition, this inference framework provides an easy method to satisfy the **third desideratum of exploiting the high-level structure** of programs. As discussed in section 14.5, high-level structure is represented in IBAL using functions. In particular, the internals of a function are encapsulated inside the function, and are conditionally independent of the external world given the function inputs and outputs. From the point of view of VE, this means that we can safely eliminate all variables internal to the function consecutively. This idea is implemented by using VE to eliminate all variables internal to a function at the time the solution to the function is computed.

14.7.3.1 Microfactors

Most implementations of VE in BNs represent a factor as a table. A table consists of a sequence of rows, each row consisting of a complete assignment of values to the factor variables and a real number. This representation is incapable of capturing low-level structure, and it also does not closely match the form of IBAL programs. Therefore, in order to achieve the **second desideratum of exploiting low-level structure**, IBAL uses a more refined representation called *microfactors*. Microfactors have similarities to other representations used for exploiting low-level structure, such as partial functions [20] and algebraic decision diagrams [1], but they were developed to match the structure of IBAL programs as closely as possible.

The design of microfactors is motivated by several observations about IBAL programs. First, it is common for values of variables to map to zero. Consider a comparison $e_1 == e_2$. A microfactor is created mentioning variables Y_1 and Y_2 for the outcomes of e_1 and e_2, and $*$, the outcome of the expression. The only assignments that have positive probability are those where Y_1 and Y_2 are equal and $*$ is `true`, or Y_1 and Y_2 are unequal and $*$ is false. All others are zero. To take advantage of the common zeros, only positive cases are represented explicitly in a microfactor.

The second observation is that we often don't care about the value of a variable, as in the case of context-specific independence. For example, given the expression `if x then y else z`, we will not care about z if x is `true`. Similarly, a factor will often have the same value for all but a few values of a variable. Consider the expression `if x = 'a then y else z`. When translated into a factor, we obtain a function that is the same for all values of x except a. To take advantage of these cases, a row in a microfactor allows a variable to take on one of a set of values.

Sets of values are represented as either V or $\overline{V}$, where $V = \{v_1, \ldots, v_n\}$ is an explicitly enumerated set of elements. The notation $\overline{V}$ denotes the complement of V, with respect to the universe of possible values. These are called *Zariski sets*, after the Zariski topology in real analysis. We can use $\overline{\emptyset}$ to denote the situation where something holds for all values of a variable, and $\overline{\{v\}}$ when something holds for all but the one value v. Next, a row over a set of variables $X_1, \ldots, X_n$ associates each variable X_i with a Zariski set Z_i, notated $< X_1 : Z_1, \ldots, X_n : Z_n >$. A row represents the set of tuples $< X_1 = x_1, \ldots, X_n = x_n >$ such that $x_i \in Z_i$. A row is empty if any of the Z_i is $\emptyset$. A microfactor is a sequence of disjoint, but not necessarily covering rows, where each row is associated with a real number.

In order to implement VE, we need to define sum and product operations on microfactors. These in turn require intersection and difference operations on rows. Difference in turn is defined in terms of intersection and complements. Intersection is straightforward. Complement is more complex, and defined recursively. Because rows are not closed under complement, the complement operation returns a set of rows, whose union is the complement of the given row. These rows are guaranteed to be disjoint. Details of the operation are omitted.

To implement VE, we need multiplication and summation operators on factors. Multiplication is straightforward. For summation, an iterative process is used that guarantees that the resulting microfactor correctly represents the sum over the given variable in the original factor, and that its rows are disjoint. Again details are omitted.

14.7.3.2 Translating Programs into Microfactors

The next step in IBAL inference is to translate a program into a set of microfactors, and then perform VE. The goal is to produce factors that capture all the structure in the program, including both the independence structure and the low-level structure.

The translation is expressed through a set of rules, each of which takes an expression of a certain form and returns a set of microfactors. The notation $T[e]$ is used to denote the translation rule for expression e. Thus, for a constant expression $'v$ the rule is[3]

$$T['v] = \begin{array}{|c|c|} \hline * & \\ \hline v & 1 \\ \hline \end{array}.$$

The Boolean constants and `lambda` and `fix` expressions are treated similarly.

For a variable expression, $T[x]$, we need to make sure that the result has the same value as x. If x is a simple variable, whose values are symbols, the rule is as follows. Assuming $v_1, \ldots, v_n$ are the values in the support of x, this is achieved with the

---

3. For convenience, we omit the set brackets for singletons.

rule

$$T[x] = \begin{array}{|c|c|c|} \hline * & x & \\ \hline v_1 & v_1 & 1 \\ \hline \multicolumn{3}{c}{\cdots} \\ \hline v_n & v_n & 1 \\ \hline \end{array}.$$

Here, we exploit the fact that an assignment of values to variables not covered by any row has value 0.

If x is a complex variable with multiple fields, each of which is itself complex, we could use the above rule, considering all values in the cross-product space of the fields of x. However, that is unnecessarily inefficient. Rather, for each field a of x, we ensure separately that $*.a$ is equal to $x.a$. If a itself is complex, we break that equality up into fields. We end up with a factor like the one above for each simple chain c defined on x. If we let the simple chains be $c^1, \ldots, c^m$, and the possible values of c^i be $v_1^i, \ldots, v_{n^i}^i$, we get the rule

$$T[x] = \bigcup_{i=1}^{m} \begin{array}{|c|c|c|} \hline *.c^i & x.c^i & \\ \hline v_i^1 & v_i^1 & 1 \\ \hline \multicolumn{3}{c}{\cdots} \\ \hline v_{n^i}^1 & v_{n^i}^1 & 1 \\ \hline \end{array}.$$

The total number of rows according to this method is $\sum_{i=1}^{m} n^i$, rather than $\prod_{i=1}^{m} n^i$ for the product method.

Next we turn to variable definitions. Recall that those are specified in IBAL through a let expression of the form `let` $x = e_1$ `in` e_2. We need some notation: if $\boldsymbol{F}$ is a set of factors, $\boldsymbol{F}_{c^2}^{c^1}$ denotes the same set as $\boldsymbol{F}$, except that chain c^1 is substituted for c^2 in all the factors in $\boldsymbol{F}$. Now the rule for `let` is simple. We compute the factors for e_1, and replace $*$ with x. We then conjoin the factors for e_2, with no additional change. The full rule is[4] $T[\texttt{let } x = e_1 \texttt{ in } e_2] = T[e_1]_*^x \cup T[e_2]$.

For `if-then-else` expressions, we proceed as follows. First we define a primitive `prim_if` (x, y, z) that is the same as if but only operates on variables. Then we can rewrite

$$\texttt{if } e_1 \texttt{ then } e_2 \texttt{ else } e_3 =$$
$$\texttt{let } x = e_1 \texttt{ in}$$
$$\texttt{let } y = e_2 \texttt{ in}$$
$$\texttt{let } z = e_3 \texttt{ in}$$
$$\texttt{prim\_if } (x, y, z)$$

---

4. A fresh variable name is provided for the bound variable to avoid name clashes.

Now, all we need is a translation rule for `prim_if` and we can invoke the above `let` rule to translate all `if` expressions.[5] Let the simple chains on y and z be $c^1, \ldots, c^m$. (They must have the same set of simple chains for the program to be well typed.) Using the same notation as before for the possible values of these chains, a naive rule for `prim_if` is as follows:

$$T[\texttt{prim\_if}(x, y, z)] = \bigcup_{i=1}^{m}$$

$*.c^i$	x	$y.c^i$	$z.c^i$	
v_1^i	T	v_1^i	$\bar{\emptyset}$	1
		$\cdots$		
$v_{n^i}^i$	T	$v_{n^i}^i$	$\bar{\emptyset}$	1
v_1^i	F	$\bar{\emptyset}$	v_1^i	1
		$\cdots$		
$v_{n^i}^i$	F	$\bar{\emptyset}$	$v_{n^i}^i$	1

This rule exploits the context-specific independence (CSI) present in any `if` expression: the outcome is independent of either the `then` clause or the `else` clause given the value of the test. The CSI is captured in the $\bar{\emptyset}$ entries for the irrelevant variables. However, we can do even better. This rule unites $y.c^i$ and $z.c^i$ in a single factor. However, there is no row in which both are simultaneously relevant. We see that `if` expressions satisfy a stronger property than CSI. To exploit this property, the `prim_if` rule produces two factors for each c^i whose product is equal to the factor above.

$$T[\texttt{prim\_if}(x, y, z)] =$$

$$\bigcup_{i=1}^{m} \left\{ \quad , \quad \right\}$$

$*.c^i$	x	$y.c^i$	
v_1^i	T	v_1^i	1
	$\cdots$		
$v_{n^i}^i$	T	$v_{n^i}^i$	1
$\bar{\emptyset}$	F	$\bar{\emptyset}$	1

$*.c^i$	x	$z.c^i$	
v_1^i	F	v_1^i	1
	$\cdots$		
$v_{n^i}^i$	F	$v_{n^i}^i$	1
$\bar{\emptyset}$	T	$\bar{\emptyset}$	1

Note the last row in each of these factors. It is a way of indicating that the factor is only relevant if x has the appropriate value. For the first factor, if x has the value F, the factor has value 1 whatever the values of the other variables, and similarly for the other factor. The number of rows in the factors for c^i is two more than for the previous method, because of the "irrelevance rows." However, we have gained in that $y.c^i$ and $z.c^i$ are no longer in the same factor. Considering all the c^i, the moral graph for the second approach contains m fewer edges than for the first approach. Essentially, the variable x is playing the role of a separator for all the pairs $y.c^i$ and

---

5. In practice, if e_1, e_2, or e_3 are already variable expressions, we can omit the let expression defining x, y, or z and use them directly in the `prim_if`.

$z.c^i$. If we can avoid eliminating x until as late as possible, we may never have to connect many of the $y.c^i$ and $z.c^i$.

None of the expression forms introduced so far contained uncertainty. Therefore, every factor represented a zero-one function, in other words, a constraint on the values of variables. Intermediate probabilities are finally introduced by the dist expression, which has the form `dist` $[p_1 : e_1, \ldots, p_n : e_n]$. As in the case of `if`, we introduce a primitive `prim_dist` $(p_1, \ldots, p_n)$, which selects an integer from 1 to n with the corresponding probability. We also use `prim_case` which generalizes the `prim_if` above to take an integer test with n possible outcomes. We can then rewrite

$$\texttt{dist } [p_1 : e_1, \ldots, p_n : e_n] =$$

$$\texttt{let } x_1 = e_1 \texttt{ in}$$

$$\ldots$$

$$\texttt{let } x_n = e_n \texttt{ in}$$

$$\texttt{let } z = \texttt{ prim\_dist } (p_1, \ldots, p_n) \texttt{ in}$$

$$\texttt{prim\_case } (z, [x_1, \ldots, x_n])$$

To complete the specification, we only need to provide rules for `prim_dist` and `prim_case`. The `prim_dist` rule is extremely simple:

$$T[\texttt{prim\_dist}(p_1, \ldots, p_n)] =$$

*	
1	p_1
	$\ldots$
n	p_n

.

The `prim_case` rule generalizes the rule for `prim_if` above. It exploits the property that no two of the x_j can be relevant, because the dist expression selects only one of them. This technique really comes into its own here. If there are m different chains defined on the result, as before, and n different possible outcomes of the dist expression, the number of edges removed from the moral graph is $m * n$. The rule is

$$T[\texttt{prim\_case}(z, [x_1, \ldots, x_n])] =$$

$$\bigcup_{i=1}^{m} \bigcup_{j=1}^{n}$$

$*.c^i$	z	$x_j.c^i$	
v_1^i	j	v_1^i	1
	$\ldots$		
$v_{n^i}^i$	j	$v_{n^i}^i$	1
$\bar{\emptyset}$	$\{j\}$	$\bar{\emptyset}$	1

.

The rules for record construction and field access expressions are relatively simple, and are omitted. Observations are also very simple.

Next, we turn to the mechanism for applying functions. It also needs to be able to handle *functional uncertainty* — the fact that the function to be applied is itself defined by an expression, over whose value we have uncertainty. To start with, however, let us assume that we know which particular function we are applying to a certain set of arguments. For a function f, let $f.x_1, \ldots, f.x_n$ denote its formal arguments, and $f.b$ denote its body. Let $A[f, e_1, \ldots, e_n]$ denote the application of f to arguments defined by expressions $e_1, \ldots, e_n$. Then

$$A[f, e_1, \ldots, e_n] = T \left[\begin{array}{l} \mathtt{let}\, f.x_1 = e_1 \,\mathtt{in} \\ \cdots \\ \mathtt{let}\, f.x_n = e_n \,\mathtt{in} \\ f.b \end{array} \right].$$

By the `let` rule presented earlier, this will convert $f.b$ into a set of factors that mention the result variable $*$, the arguments $f.x_i$, and variables internal to the body of f. Meanwhile, each of the e_i is converted into a set of factors defining the distribution over $f.x_i$.

$$A[f, e_1, \ldots, e_n] = T[f.b] \cup \bigcup_i T[e_i]_*^{f.x_i}$$

To exploit encapsulation, we want to eliminate all the variables that are internal to the function call before passing the set of factors out to the next level. This can be achieved simply by eliminating all temporary variables except for those representing the $f.x_i$ from $T[f.b]$. Thus, a VE process is performed for every function application. The result of performing VE is a conditional distribution over $*$ given the $f.x_i$.[6]

Normally in VE, once all the designated variables have been eliminated, the remaining factors are multiplied together to obtain a distribution over the uneliminated variables. Here that is not necessary: performing VE returns a set of factors over the uneliminated variables that is passed to the next level up in the computation. Delaying the multiplication can remove some edges from the moral graph at the next level up.

Now suppose we have an application expression $e_0(e_1, \ldots, e_n)$. The expression e_0 does not have to name a particular function, and there may be uncertainty as to its value. We need to consider all possible values of the function, and apply each of those to the arguments. Let F denote the support of e_0. Then for each $f_i \in F$, we need to compute $A_i = A[f_i, e_1, \ldots, e_n]$ as above.

Now, we cannot simply take the union of the A_i as part of the application result, since we do not want to multiply factors in different A_i together. The different A_i represent the conditional distribution over the result for different function bodies. We therefore need to condition A_i on F being f_i. This effect is achieved as follows. Let $A_i^1, \ldots, A_i^m$ be the factors in A_i, and let $(r_1^j, p_1^j), \ldots, (r_{\ell^j}^j, p_{\ell^j}^j)$ be the rows in

---

6. There may also be variables that are free in the body of f and not bound by function arguments. These should also not be eliminated.

factor A_i^j. Then we can write

$$B_i = \bigcup_{j=1}^{m} \begin{array}{|c|c|c|} \hline F & *, f_i.x_1, \ldots, f_i.x_n & \\ \hline f_i & r_1^j & p_1^j \\ & \cdots & \\ f_i & r_{\ell j}^j & p_{\ell j}^j \\ \hline \overline{\{f_i\}} & \overline{\emptyset} \text{ for all} & 1 \\ \hline \end{array}$$

In words, each B_i^j is formed from the corresponding A_i^j in two steps. First, A_i^j is extended by adding a column for F, and setting its value to be equal to f_i. The effect is to say that when F is equal to f_i, we want A_i^j to hold. Then, a row is added saying that when F is unequal to f_i, the other variables can take on any value and the result will be 1. The effect is to say that A_i^j does not matter when $F \neq f_i$. We can now take the union of all the B_i. To complete the translation rule for function application, we just have to supply the distribution over F:

$$T[e_0(e_1, \ldots, e_n)] = \cup_i B_i \cup T[e_0]_*^F$$

14.8 Lessons Learned and Conclusion

The IBAL implementation represents the culmination of several years of investigation, that begin with the original "stochastic Lisp" paper [9] and continued with the SPOOK system [17]. A number of important lessons were learned from the process:

- Stochastic programming languages are surprisingly complex, and a sophisticated algorithm such as the one in this chapter is needed to implement them.
- As a corollary, a single mechanism is unlikely to achieve all the goals of inference in a complex system. The move to the two-phase approach greatly simplified the implementation, but was also an admission that the implementation had entered a new level of complexity.
- The design of the language and of the inference algorithm go hand in hand. The set of language constructs in IBAL was chosen to support the specific inference goals described in this chapter.
- Different approaches that are individually inadequate may each have something to contribute to the overall solution. Programming language evaluation approaches provide a natural way to work with programs, and were used in constructing the computation graph. SPOOK's approach of using local VE processes for different model components was used. Also, the KBMC approach of separating the model analysis and probability computation components was used, albeit in a very different way.

▪ Beware unexpected interactions between goals! Koller et al. [9] blithely declared that lazy evaluation and memoization would be used. In retrospect, combining the two mechanisms was the single most difficult thing in the implementation.

This chapter has presented the probabilistic inference mechanism for IBAL, a highly expressive probabilistic representation language. A number of apparently conflicting desiderata for inference were presented, and it was shown how IBAL's inference algorithm satisfies all of them. It is hoped that the development of IBAL provides a service to the community in two ways. First, it provides a blueprint for anyone who wants to build a first-order probabilistic reasoning system. Second, and more important, it is a general-purpose system that has been released for public use. In future it will hopefully be unnecessary for designers of expressive models to have to build their own inference engine. IBAL has succesfully been tried on BNs, HMMs (including infinite state-space models), stochastic grammars, and probabilistic relational models. IBAL has also been used successfully as a teaching tool in a probabilistic reasoning course at Harvard. Its implementation consists of approximately 10,000 lines of code. It includes over fifty test examples, all of which the inference engine is able to handle. IBAL's tutorial and reference manuals are both over twenty pages long.

Of course, there are many models for which the techniques presented in this chapter will be insufficient, and for which approximate inference is needed. The next step of IBAL development is to provide approximate inference algorithms. IBAL's inference mechanism already provides one way to do this. One can simply plug in any standard BN approximate inference algorithm in place of VE whenever a set of factors has to be simplified. However, other methods such as Markov chain Monte Carlo will change the way programs are evaluated, and will require a completely different approach.

References

[1] R. I. Bahar, E. A. Frohm, C. M. Gaona, G. D. Hachtel, E. Macii, A. Pardo, and F. Somenzi. Algebraic decision diagrams and their applications. In *IEEE/ACM International Conference on Computer-Aided Design*, 1993.

[2] T. Dean and K. Kanazawa. A model for reasoning about persistence and causation. *Computational Intelligence*, 5:142–150, 1989.

[3] R. Dechter. Bucket elimination : a unifying framework for probabilistic inference. In *Proceedings of the Conference on Uncertainty in Artificial Intelligence*, 1996.

[4] D. Heckerman and J. S. Breese. A new look at causal independence. In *Proceedings of the Conference on Uncertainty in Artificial Intelligence*, 1994.

[5] K. Kersting and L. de Raedt. Bayesian logic programs. In *Proceedings of the Work-In-Progress Track at the 10th International Conference on Inductive Logic Programming*, 2000.

[6]   D. Koller and A. Pfeffer. Semantics and inference for recursive probability models. In *Proceedings of the National Conference on Artificial Intelligence*, 2000.

[7]   D. Koller and A. Pfeffer. Object-oriented Bayesian networks. In *Uncertainty in Artificial Intelligence (UAI)*, 1997.

[8]   D. Koller and A. Pfeffer. Probabilistic frame-based systems. In *Proceedings of the National Conference on Artificial Intelligence*, 1998.

[9]   D. Koller, D. McAllester, and A. Pfeffer. Effective Bayesian inference for stochastic programs. In *Proceedings of the National Conference on Artificial Intelligence*, 1997.

[10]   K. B. Laskey and S. M. Mahoney. Network fragments: Representing knowledge for constructing probabilistic models. In *Proceedings of the Conference on Uncertainty in Artificial Intelligence*, 1997.

[11]   Z. Li and B. D'Ambrosio. Efficient inference in bayes' networks as a combinatorial optimization problem. *International Journal of Approximate Inference*, 11, 1994.

[12]   S. Muggleton. Stochastic logic programs. *Journal of Logic Programming*, 2001. Accepted subject to revision.

[13]   L. Ngo and P. Haddawy. Answering queries from context-sensitive probabilistic knowledge bases. *Theoretical Computer Science*, 1996.

[14]   H. Pasula and S. Russell. Approximate inference for first-order probabilistic languages. In *Proceedings of the International Joint Conference on Artificial Intelligence*, 2001.

[15]   A. Pfeffer. Repeated observation models. In *Proceedings of the National Conference on Artificial Intelligence*, 2004.

[16]   A. Pfeffer. *Probabilistic Reasoning for Complex Systems*. PhD thesis, Stanford Univeristy, 2000.

[17]   A. Pfeffer, D. Koller, B. Milch, and K. T. Takusagawa. SPOOK: A system for probabilistic object-oriented knowledge representation. In *Proceedings of the Conference on Uncertainty in Artificial Intelligence*, 1999.

[18]   D. Pless and G. Luger. Toward general analysis of recursive probability models. In *Proceedings of the Conference on Uncertainty in Artificial Intelligence*, 2001.

[19]   D. Poole. Probabilistic Horn abduction and Bayesian networks. *Artificial Intelligence Journal*, 64(1):81–129, 1993.

[20]   D. Poole and N. L. Zhang. Exploiting contextual independence in probabilistic inference. *Journal of Artificial Intelligence Research (JAIR)*, 2003.

[21]   S. Sanghai, P. Domingos, and D. Weld. Dynamic probabilistic relational models. In *Proceedings of the International Joint Conference on Artificial Intelligence*, 2003.

[22]   T. Sato and Y. Kameya. Parameter learning of logic programs for symbolic statistical modeling. *Journal of Artificial Intelligence Research*, 15:391–454, 2001.

[23]   D. J. Spiegelhalter, A. Thomas, N. Best, and W. R. Gilks. BUGS 0.5 : Bayesian inference using Gibbs sampling manual. Technical report, Institute of Public Health, Cambridge University, 1995.

15 Lifted First-Order Probabilistic Inference

Rodrigo de Salvo Braz, Eyal Amir and Dan Roth

Most probabilistic inference algorithms are specified and processed on a propositional level, even though many domains are better represented by first-order specifications that compactly stand for a class of propositional instantiations. In the last fifteen years, many algorithms accepting first-order specifications have been proposed. However, these algorithms still perform inference on a mostly propositional model, generated by the instantiation of first-order constructs. When this is done, the rich and useful first-order structure is not explicit anymore. This first-order representation and structure allow us to perform *lifted* inference, that is, inference on the first-order representation directly, manipulating not only individuals but also groups of individuals. This has the potential of greatly speeding up inference. We precisely define the problem and present an algorithm that generalizes variable elimination and manipulates first-order representations in order to perform lifted inference.

15.1 Introduction

Probabilistic inference algorithms are widely employed in artificial intelligence. Among those, graphical models such as Bayesian and Markov networks (BNs and MNs respectively) ([8]) are among the most popular. These models are specified by a set of conditional probabilities (for BNs) or factors, also called potential functions (for MNs). Both conditional probabilities and factors are defined over particular subsets of the available random variables, and map assignments of those random variables to positive real numbers (called *potentials* in MNs). For our purposes, it will be helpful to think of graphical models in general and simply consider conditional probabilities as a type of factor.

For example, in an application for document subject classification, one can specify a dependence between the random variables *subject_apple*, *word_mac* (which indicate that the subject of the document is "apple" and that the word "mac" is present in it) by defining a factor on their assignments. The higher the potential for a given assignment to these random variables, the more likely it will be in the joint distribution defined by the model.

A limitation of graphical models arises when the same dependence holds between different subsets of random variables. For example, we might declare the dependence above to hold also between *subject_microsoft, word_windows*. In traditional graphical models, we must use separate potential functions to do so, even though the dependence is the same. This brings redundancy to the model and possibly wasted computation. It is also an ad hoc mechanism since it does not cover other sets of random variables exhibiting the same dependence (in this case, some other company and product).

The root of this limitation is that graphical models are *propositional* (random variables can be seen as analogous to propositions in logic), that is, they do not allow quantifiers and parameterization of random variables by objects. A *first-order* or *relational* language, on the other hand, does allow for these elements. With such a language, we can specify a potential function that applies, for example, to *all* tuples of random variables obtained by instantiating X and Y in the tuple

$$subject(X), company(X), product(X, Y), word(Y). \tag{15.1}$$

This way we not only cover both cases presented before, but also unforeseen ones, with a single compact specification.

In the last fifteen years, many proposals for probabilistic inference algorithms accepting first-order specifications have been presented ([7, 6, 1, 4, 10, 11], among many others), most of which based on the theoretic framework of Halpern [5]. However, these solutions still perform inference at a mostly propositional level; they typically instantiate potential functions according to the objects relevant to the present query, thus obtaining a regular graphical model on propositional random variables, and then using a regular inference algorithm on this model. In domains with a large number of objects this may be both costly and essentially unnecessary. Suppose we have a medical application about the health of a large population, with a random variable per person indicating whether they are sick with a certain disease, and with a potential function representing the dependence between a person being sick and that person getting hospitalized. To answer the query "what is the probability that *someone* will be hospitalized?", an algorithm that depends on propositionalization will instantiate *a random variable per person*. However this is not necessary since one can calculate the same probability by reasoning about individuals on a general level, simply using the population size, in order to answer that query in a much shorter time. In fact, the latter calculation would not depend on the population size at all.

Naturally, it is possible to reformulate the problem so that it is solved in a more efficient manner. However, this would require manual devising of a process *specific* to the model or query in question. It is desirable to have an algorithm that can receive a *general* first-order model and *automatically* answer queries like these without computational waste.

A first step in this direction was given by Poole [9], which proposes a generalized version of the variable elimination algorithm [12] that is *lifted*, that is, deals with groups of random variables at a first-order level. The algorithm receives a specification in which parameterized random variables stand for all of their instantiations and then eliminates them in a way that is equivalent to, but much cheaper than, eliminating all their instantiations at once. For the parameterized potential function (15.1), for example, one can eliminate $product(X, Y)$ in a single step that would be equivalent to eliminating all of its instantiations.

The algorithm in Poole [9], however, applies only to certain types of models because it uses a single elimination operation that can only eliminate parameterized random variables containing all parameters present in the potential function (the method can eliminate $product(X, Y)$ from (15.1) but not $company(X)$ because the latter does not contain the parameter Y). As we will see later, Poole's algorithm uses the operation we call *inversion elimination*. In addition to inversion elimination, we have developed further operations (the main ones called *counting elimination* and *partial inversion*) that broaden the applicability of lifted inference to a greater extent ([2, 3]). These operations are combined to form the first-order variable elimination (FOVE) algorithm presented in this chapter. The cases to which lifted inference applies can be roughly summarized as those containing dependencies where the set of parameters of each parameterized random variable are disjoint or, when this is not the case, where there is a set of parameters whose instantiations create independent solvable cases. We specify these conditions in more detail when explaining the operations, and further discuss applicability in section 15.6. When no lifted inference operation applies to a specific part of a model, FOVE can still apply standard propositional methods to that part, assuring completeness and limiting propositional inference to only some parts of the model.

15.2 Language, Semantics and Inference problem

Like Markov networks, first-order probabilistic models (FOPMs) are essentially defined by a set of factors. However, unlike them, these factors are defined over *parameterized* random variables, and for this reason we call them **parfactors** (following [9]).

Given a universe of objects over which the parameters range, we can generate regular propositional factors from a parfactor by replacing its parameters by particular objects. A parfactor is therefore a compact representation of a set of regular factors, and a FOPM is a compact representation of a Markov network composed by all instantiations of all of its parfactors.

Based on the correspondence to logic concepts, we call a parameterized random variable an **atom**, and a parameter a **logical variable** (as opposed to *random* variables). We also call the functors of atoms **predicates**. Even though we informally refer to atoms as "parameterized random variables", they are not, technically speaking, random variables, but stand for classes of them. A ground atom, however, denotes a random variable. Sometimes we call random variables **ground** to emphasize their correspondence to ground atoms.

Logical variables are typed, with each type being a finite set of objects. We denote the **domain**, or **type**, of a logical variable X by D_X and its cardinality by $|X|$. In our examples, unless noted, all logical variables have the same type. Each predicate p also has its domain, D_p, which is the set of values that each of the random variables with that predicate can take.

Formally, a **parfactor** g is a tuple (ϕ_g, A_g, C_g), where ϕ_g is a potential function defined over atoms A_g to be instantiated by all substitutions of its logical variables satisfying a constraint C_g. A **constraint** is a pair (F, V) where F is an equational formula on logical variables and V is the set of logical variables to be instantiated (some of them may not be in the formula). We sometimes denote a constraint by its formula F alone, when the set of logical variables V is clear from context. Tautological formulas are represented by $\top$. For example, the parfactor $(\phi, (p(X), q(X, Y)), (X \neq a, \{X, Y\}))$ applies ϕ to all instantiations of $(p(X), q(X, Y))$ by substitutions of X and Y satisfying $X \neq a$. We denote the set of substitutions satisfying C by $[C]$.

While we are neutral as to how the potential functions are actually specified, logical formulas seem to be a convenient choice. For example, a weighted formula $0.7 : epidemic(D) \Rightarrow sick(P, D)$ might represent a potential function $\phi(epidemic(D), sick(P, D))$ with potential 0.7 for assignments in which the formula is true. This allows us to specify FOPMs by sets of weighted logical formulas that are intuitive and simple to read, and is the approach taken by Markov logic networks ([11]).

The **projection** $C_{|L}$ of a constraint $C = (F, V)$ **onto a set of logical variables** L is a constraint equivalent to $(\exists L' F, L)$ for $L' = V \setminus L$. Intuitively, $C_{|L}$ describes the conditions posed by C on L alone, that is, the possible substitutions on L that are part of substitutions in $[C]$. For example, $(X \neq a \wedge X \neq Y \wedge Y \neq b, \{X, Y\})_{|\{X\}} = (X \neq a, \{X\})$. FOVE uses a constraint solver which is able to solve several constraint problems, such as determining the number of solutions of a constraint and its projection onto sets of logical variables.

In certain contexts we wish to describe the class of random variables instantiated from an atom with constraints on its logical variables (for example, the set of random variables instantiated from $p(X, Y)$, with $X \neq a$). We call such pairs of atoms and constraints **constrained atoms**, or **c-atoms**. The **c-atoms of a parfactor** is the set of c-atoms formed by its atoms and its constraint.

Let α be a parfactor, c-atom, constraint or a set of those. We define $RV(\alpha)$ to be the set of (ground) random variables specified by α, and $\alpha\theta$ denotes the result of applying a substitution θ to α. $[C_g]$ is also denoted by Θ_g.

A FOPM is specified by a set of parfactors G and the types of its logical variables. Its semantics is a joint distribution defined on $RV(G)$ by the Markov network formed by all the instantiations of parfactors. Thus it is proportional to the product of all instantiated parfactors:

$$P(RV(G)) \propto \prod_{g \in G} \prod_{\theta \in \Theta_g} g\theta.$$

For convenience, we denote $\prod_{\theta \in \Theta_g} g\theta$ by $\Phi(g)$, and $\prod_{g \in G} \Phi(g)$ by $\Phi(G)$. Therefore we can write the above as $P(RV(G)) \propto \Phi(G)$.

The most important inference task in graphical models is marginalization. For FOPMs, it takes the following form: given a set of ground random variables Q, calculate

$$P(Q) \propto \sum_{RV(G) \setminus Q} \Phi(G), \qquad (15.2)$$

where the summation ranges over all assignments to $RV(G) \setminus Q$. Posterior probabilities can be calculated by representing evidence as additional parfactors on the evidence atoms.

The FOVE algorithm makes the simplifying assumption that the FOPM is **shattered** w.r.t the query Q. A set of c-atoms is **shattered** if the instantiations of any pair of its elements are either identical or disjoint. A parfactor, or set of parfactors, is shattered if the set of their c-atoms is shattered. A FOPM is shattered w.r.t. a query Q if the union of its c-atoms and those of the query is shattered. For example, we can have c-atoms $(p(X), X \neq a),(p(Y), Y \neq a)$ and $p(a)$ in a model, but not $p(Y)$ and $p(a)$, because $RV(p(a)) \subset RV(p(Y))$ but $RV(p(a)) \neq RV(p(Y))$. When a FOPM and query are not shattered, we can replace them by equivalent shattered FOPM and query through the process of **shattering**, detailed in section 15.5.2.

15.3   The First-Order Variable Elimination (FOVE) algorithm

Computing (15.2) directly is intractable since it would take exponential time in the number of random variables in $RV(G) \setminus Q$. This is the case even for the propositional case, which is the reason why algorithms have been developed that take advantage of independences represented in the model in order to compute marginals more efficiently. One of these algorithms is variable elimination (VE) [12]. First-order variable elimination (FOVE) is a first-order generalization of VE. While VE eliminates a random variable at a time, FOVE eliminates a c-atom, or set of c-atoms, at each step. By eliminating a c-atom, we implicitly eliminate all of its instantiations at the same time. Let E be a set of c-atoms to be eliminated from a FOPM with a set G of parfactors. Let $G_E, G_{\neg E} \subseteq G$ be the sets of parfactors depending and not depending on E, respectively. Then

$$\sum_{RV(G) \setminus Q} \Phi(G) = \sum_{(RV(G) \setminus RV(E)) \setminus Q} \Phi(G_{\neg E}) \sum_{RV(E)} \Phi(G_E).$$

We later show operations computing a parfactor g' such that $\sum_{RV(E)} \Phi(G_E) = \Phi(g')$. Once we have g', the right-hand side of the above is equal to

$$\sum_{(RV(G)\backslash RV(E))\backslash Q} \Phi(G_{\neg E})\Phi(g') = \sum_{(RV(G)\backslash RV(E))\backslash Q} \Phi(G_{\neg E} \cup \{g'\}) = \sum_{RV(G')\backslash Q} \Phi(G')$$

where $G' = G_{\neg E} \cup \{g'\}$. In other words, we have reduced the original marginalization to a smaller instance that does not include $RV(E)$. This is repeated until only Q is left.

A crucial difference between VE and FOVE is elimination ordering. VE eliminates random variables according to an ordering given a priori. In FOVE, eliminating certain c-atoms may require eliminating some other c-atoms first, so it may be the case that some c-atoms are not eliminable at all times (these conditions will be clarified later). Because parfactors and c-atoms are sometimes changed and reorganized during the algorithm, it is not a simple matter to choose an ordering in advance. Instead, the elimination ordering is dynamically determined.

Before we move on to explaining the operations for calculating $\sum_{RV(E)} \Phi(G_E) = \Phi(g')$, we mention that, in fact, they only calculate $\sum_{RV(E)} \Phi(g)$ for a single parfactor g. This is not a problem because the operation of **fusion**, covered in section 15.5.1, calculates g such that $\Phi(g) = \Phi(G)$ for any set of parfactors G.

15.3.1   Counting Elimination

We first show counting elimination on a specific example and later generalize it. Consider the summation

$$\sum_{RV(p(X))} \prod_{X,Y} \phi(p(X), p(Y)),$$

where p is a boolean predicate. (Note that the X used under the summation is not the same X used by the product. $RV(p(X))$ is shorthand for all assignments over the set $\{p(X) : X \in D_X\}$, so X is locally used. In fact, we could have written $RV(p(Y))$, or even $RV(p(Z))$, to the same effect. We choose to use X or Y to make the link with the atom in the parfactor more obvious.)

Counting elimination is based on the following insight: because a parfactor will typically only evaluate to a few different potentials, large groups of its instantiations will evaluate to the same potential. So the summation is rewritten

$$\sum_{RV(p(X))} \phi(0,0)^{|(0,0)|}\phi(0,1)^{|(0,1)|}\phi(1,0)^{|(1,0)|}\phi(1,1)^{|(1,1)|},$$

where $|(v_1, v_2)|$ indicates the number of possible choices for X and Y so that $p(X) = v_1$ and $p(Y) = v_2$ given the current assignment to $RV(p(X))$. These partition sizes can be calculated by a combinatorial, or counting, argument. Assume we know $\vec{N}_p$, a vector of integers that indicates how many random variables in $RV(p(X))$ are currently assigned a particular value, that is, $\vec{N}_{p,i} - |\{r \in RV(p(X)) : r = i\}|$

for each $i \in D_p$. Naturally, $\sum_i \vec{N}_{p,i} = |RV(p(X))|$. Then there are $\vec{N}_{p,v_1}$ possible values for X (so that $p(X) = v_1$) and $\vec{N}_{p,v_2}$ distinct possible values for Y (so that $p(Y) = v_2$), so $|(v_1, v_2)| = \vec{N}_{p,v_1} \vec{N}_{p,v_2}$.

We take advantage of the fact that the values $|(v_1, v_2)|$ do not depend on the particular assignments to $RV(p(X))$, but only on $\vec{N}_p$. This allows us to iterate over the *groups* of assignments with the same $\vec{N}_p$ and do the calculation for the entire group. We also take into account the group size, which is provided by the binomial coefficient of $\vec{N}_p$, $\binom{|RV(p(X))|}{\vec{N}_{p,0}}$ (or, equivalently, $\binom{|RV(p(X))|}{\vec{N}_{p,1}}$). We then have

$$\sum_{\vec{N}_p} \binom{|RV(p(X))|}{\vec{N}_{p,0}} \prod_{(v_1, v_2)} \phi(v_1, v_2)^{\vec{N}_{p,v_1} \vec{N}_{p,v_2}}$$

which has a number of terms linear in $|RV(p(X))|$, as opposed to the previous exponential number.

Counting elimination is not a universal method. The counting argument presented above requires that there be little interaction between the logical variables of atoms. If a parfactor is on $p(X,Y), q(X,Z)$, for example, the counting argument does not work because the choices for (X,Z) depend on the particular X chosen for $p(X)$; we can no longer compute number of choices using counters alone but need to know the particular assignment to $RV(p(X))$. Generally, under counting elimination, choices for one atom cannot constrain the choices for another atom (there are exceptions to this rule, as for example *just-different* atoms, presented in [3]).

We now give the formal account of counting elimination, starting with some preliminary definitions.

First, we define the notion of **independent atoms given a constraint**. Intuitively, this happens when choosing a substitution for the logical variables of one atom does not change the possible choices of substitutions for the other atom. Let $\bar{X}_1$ and $\bar{X}_2$ be two sets of logical variables such that $\bar{X}_1 \cup \bar{X}_2 \subseteq V$. $\bar{X}_1$ is *independent from* $\bar{X}_2$ *given* C if, for any substitution $\theta_2 \in [C_{|\bar{X}_2}]$, $C_{\lfloor \bar{X}_1} \Leftrightarrow (C\theta_2)_{|\bar{X}_1}$. $\bar{X}_1$ and $\bar{X}_2$ are *independent given* C if $\bar{X}_1$ is independent from $\bar{X}_2$ given C and vice-versa. Two *atoms* $p_1(\bar{X}_1)$ and $p_2(\bar{X}_2)$ are *independent given* C if $\bar{X}_1$ and $\bar{X}_2$ are independent given C.

Finally, we define **multinomial counters**. Let a be a c-atom with domain D_a. Then the *multinomial counter of* a, $\vec{N}_a$, is a vector where $\vec{N}_{a,j}$ indicates how many instantiations of a are assigned the j-th value in D_a. The *multinomial coefficient* $\vec{N}_a! = \frac{(\vec{N}_{a,1} + \cdots + \vec{N}_{a,|D_a|})!}{\vec{N}_{a,1}! \ldots \vec{N}_{a,|D_a|}!}$ is a generalization of binomial coefficients and indicates how many assignments to $RV(a)$ exhibit the particular value distribution counted by $\vec{N}_a$.

Counters can be applied to *sets* of c-atoms with the same general meaning. The set of multinomial counters for a set of c-atoms A is denoted $\vec{N}_A$, and the product $\prod_{a \in A} \vec{N}_a!$ of their multinomial coefficients is denoted $\vec{N}_A!$.

Theorem 15.1 Counting Elimination

Let g be a shattered parfactor and $E = \{E_1, \ldots, E_k\}$ be a subset of A_g such that $RV(E)$ is disjoint from $RV(A_g \setminus E)$, $A' = A_g \setminus E$ are all ground, and where each pair of atoms is independent given C_g. Then

$$\sum_{RV(E)} \prod_{\theta \in \Theta_g} \phi(A_g \theta) = \sum_{\vec{N}_E} \vec{N}_E! \prod_{v \in D_E} \phi(v, A')^{\prod_{i=1}^{k} \vec{N}_{E_i, v_i}}.$$

The theorem's proof reflects the argument given above. Counting elimination brings a significant computational advantage because iterating over assignments is exponential in $|RV(E)|$ while doing so over groups of assignments is only polynomial in it.

It is important to notice that E must contain all non ground c-atoms in g. Also, if all c-atoms in g are ground, E can be any subset of them and we will have a simple propositional summation, the same used in VE (counters over 1-random variable c-atoms reduce to ordinary assignments).

15.3.2 Inversion

Counting elimination requires a parfactor's atoms to be independent given its constraints. In particular, logical variables shared between atoms may render them dependent on each other. In some of these cases, the operation of *inversion* can be applied. In fact, even in cases in which counting elimination can be applied, it is advantageous to apply inversion first, if possible, for efficiency reasons.

Let us consider a couple of examples before we formalize inversion. Consider the following:

$$\sum_{RV(q(X,Y))} \prod_{XY} \phi(p(X), q(X, Y))$$

$$= \sum_{q(o_1, o_1)} \sum_{q(o_1, o_2)} \cdots \sum_{q(o_n, o_n)} \phi(p(o_1), q(o_1, o_1)) \phi(p(o_1), q(o_1, o_2)) \ldots \phi(p(o_n), q(o_n, o_n))$$

(by observing that $\phi(p(o_i), q(o_i, o_j))$ depends on $q(o_i, o_j)$ only)

$$= \sum_{q(o_1, o_1)} \phi(p(o_1), q(o_1, o_1)) \cdots \sum_{q(o_n, o_n)} \phi(p(o_n), q(o_n, o_n))$$

(by observing that only $\phi(p(o_i), q(o_i, o_j))$ depends on $q(o_i, o_j)$)

$$= \left(\sum_{q(o_1, o_1)} \phi(p(o_1), q(o_1, o_1)) \right) \ldots \left(\sum_{q(o_n, o_n)} \phi(p(o_n), q(o_n, o_n)) \right)$$

$$= \prod_{XY} \sum_{q(X, Y)} \phi(p(X), q(X, Y))$$

(by observing that only the summation is the same for all $q(X, Y)$)

$$= \prod_{XY} \phi'(p(X)).$$

Inversion works by establishing a one-to-one correspondence between parfactor instantiations and summations. If the summation were on the instantiations of $p(X)$, such correspondence would not be possible because there would be less summations ($|X|$ of them) than parfactor instantiations ($|X| * |Y|$ of them).

Another condition for inversion is that the c-atom being inverted not have different instances in the same instance of the parfactor. For example, we cannot use inversion on $p(X, Y)$ for a parfactor on $p(X, Y), p(Y, X)$ because for any pair of objects o_i, o_j, neither of the parfactor instantiations $p(o_i, o_j)$ and $p(o_j, o_i)$ can be factored out of the innermost of $\sum_{p(o_i, o_j)}$ and $\sum_{p(o_j, o_i)}$. This breaks the one-to-one correspondence between summations and instantiated parfactors.

In the case above, the resulting inner summation was propositional. Inversion resulting in propositional summations were called *inversion elimination* in our earlier work [2, 3]. In the next example, the inner summation is one computed by counting elimination.

Suppose we want to calculate

$$\sum_{RV(p(X,Y))} \prod_{X,Y,Z} \phi(p(X,Y), p(X,Z))$$
$$= \sum_{RV(p(X,Y))} \prod_{X} \prod_{Y,Z} \phi(p(X,Y), p(X,Z))$$
$$= \sum_{RV(p(o_1,Y))} \cdots \sum_{RV(p(o_n,Y))} \prod_{Y,Z} \phi(p(o_1,Y), p(o_1,Z)) \cdots \prod_{Y,Z} \phi(p(o_n,Y), p(o_n,Z))$$
$$= \Big(\sum_{RV(p(o_1,Y))} \prod_{Y,Z} \phi(p(o_1,Y), p(o_1,Z)) \Big) \cdots \Big(\sum_{RV(p(o_n,Y))} \prod_{Y,Z} \phi(p(o_n,Y), p(o_n,Z)) \Big)$$
$$= \prod_{X} \sum_{RV(p(X,Y))} \prod_{Y,Z} \phi(p(X,Y), p(X,Z))$$

Because X is now bound before the summation, it works as a constant (whose exact identity is irrelevant), and so it is not included in the counting argument. The counting argument now involves only Y and Z and is actually very similar to our original counting argument example. For that reason, the above is equal to $\prod_X \phi'()$, for ϕ' the result of counting elimination.

Inversions resulting in counting elimination problems only invert on a subset of the parfactor's logical variables. For this reason, they have been called *Partial inversions* in our previous work. Note however that, since propositional sums are a trivial case of counting elimination, both inversion operations can be unified into one. This is what we do in the formalization below.

15.3.2.1   *Uniform Solution Counting Partition (USCP)*

Before we present the theorem formalizing inversion, we touch a last issue. Consider the inversion of X resulting in the expression

$$\prod_{X} \sum_{RV(p(X,Y))} \prod_{Y \neq X, Z \neq X, Y \neq a, Z \neq a} \phi(p(X,Y), p(X,Z)).$$

The summation can be done by counting elimination since X is bound. However, it will depend on $|RV(p(X,Y))|$, but that depends on whether $X = a$ or not. One needs to split the expression according to cases $X = a$ and $X \neq a$:

$$\Big(\sum_{RV(p(a,Y))} \prod_{Y \neq a, Z \neq a} \phi(p(a,Y), p(a,Z)) \Big)$$
$$\times \Big(\prod_{X \neq a} \sum_{RV(p(X,Y))} \prod_{Y \neq X, Z \neq X, Y \neq a, Z \neq a} \phi(p(X,Y), p(X,Z)) \Big)$$

and then proceed as usual.

In general, one needs to consider the **uniform solution counting partition (USCP)** of the inverted logical variables with respect to an original constraint system. The USCP $U_L(C)$ of a set of logical variables L with respect to a constraint C is a set of constraints $\{C_1, \ldots, C_k\}$ such that $\{[C_i]\}_i$ forms a partition of $[C_{|L}]$ and

$$\forall i \cdot \forall \theta', \theta'' \in [C_i] \cdot |[C\theta']| = |[C\theta'']|,$$

that is, the number of solutions for the constraint conditioned on L is the same for each of the components C_i.

15.3.2.2   *Inversion Formalization*

Theorem 15.2 Inversion
Let g be a shattered parfactor, L a set of logical variables and E a set of c-atoms such that $RV(E)$ and $RV(A_g \setminus E)$ are disjoint. If

1. $\forall e_k, e_l \in E \cdot \forall \theta_i, \theta_j \in [C_{g|L}] \cdot \theta_i \neq \theta_j \Rightarrow RV(e_k\theta_i) \cap RV(e_l\theta_j) = \emptyset$.
2. $\forall \theta_i, \theta_j \in [C_{g|L}] \cdot \theta_i \neq \theta_j \Rightarrow RV(E\theta_i) \cap RV(E\theta_j) = \emptyset$.

then

$$\sum_{RV(E)} \Phi(g) = \prod_{C \in U_L(C_g)} \Phi(g_C),$$

where g_C is the parfactor $(\phi_{g'}, A_{g'}, C \wedge C_{g'})$ and using g' defined by the recursive computation $g'\theta = \sum_{RV(E\theta)} \Phi(g\theta)$, for θ an arbitrary element of $[C]$ (by the definition of USCP, it does not matter which).

Proof   Let $E = \{e_1, \ldots, e_n\}$, $[C_{g|L}] = \{\theta_1, \ldots, \theta_m\}$. Below, we decompose C_g into the part w.r.t. L and the remaining logical variables:

$$\sum_{RV(E)} \Phi(g) = \sum_{RV(E)} \prod_{\theta \in \Theta_g} \phi(A_g \theta)$$

$$= \sum_{RV(E)} \prod_{\theta \in [C_{g|L}]} \prod_{\theta' \in [C_g \theta]} \phi(A_g \theta \theta')$$

$$= \sum_{RV(e_1)} \cdots \sum_{RV(e_n)} \prod_{\theta \in [C_{g|L}]} \prod_{\theta' \in [C_g \theta]} \phi(A_g \theta \theta')$$

$$= \sum_{RV(e_1 \theta_1)} \cdots \sum_{RV(e_n \theta_1)} \cdots \sum_{RV(e_1 \theta_m)} \cdots \sum_{RV(e_n \theta_m)} \Big(\prod_{\theta' \in [C_g \theta_1]} \phi(A_g \theta_1 \theta') \Big) \ldots \Big(\prod_{\theta' \in [C_g \theta_m]} \phi(A_g \theta_m \theta') \Big)$$

$$= \Big(\sum_{RV(e_1 \theta_1)} \cdots \sum_{RV(e_n \theta_1)} \prod_{\theta' \in [C_g \theta_1]} \phi(A_g \theta_1 \theta') \Big) \ldots \Big(\sum_{RV(e_1 \theta_m)} \cdots \sum_{RV(e_n \theta_m)} \prod_{\theta' \in [C_g \theta_m]} \phi(A_g \theta_m \theta') \Big)$$

$$= \prod_{\theta \in [C_{g|L}]} \sum_{RV(e_1 \theta)} \cdots \sum_{RV(e_n \theta)} \Big(\prod_{\theta' \in [C_g \theta]} \phi(A_g \theta \theta') \Big)$$

$$= \prod_{\theta \in [C_{g|L}]} \sum_{RV(E\theta)} \Big(\prod_{\theta' \in [C_g \theta]} \phi(A_g \theta \theta') \Big)$$

$$= \prod_{C \in U_L(C_g)} \prod_{\theta \in [C]} \sum_{RV(E\theta)} \Phi(g\theta) = \prod_{C \in U_L(C_g)} \prod_{\theta \in [C]} \Phi(g_C \theta) = \prod_{C \in U_L(C_g)} \Phi(g_C).$$

Note that condition 1 is used to ensure the summations on $\sum_{RV(e_1 \theta_1)} \cdots \sum_{RV(e_n \theta_m)}$ are indeed distinct. Condition 2 ensures that the innermost products are on distinct sets of random variables and can therefore be factored out as shown.   ∎

15.3.3   The Algorithm

Figure 15.1 shows the main pseudocode for FOVE. The algorithm consists of successively choosing eliminations $(E, \{L_1, \ldots, L_k\})$, consisting of a collection of atoms E to eliminate after performing a series of inversions based on sets $L_1, \ldots, L_k$ of logical variables. A possible way of choosing eliminations is presented in figure 15.2. It is presented separately from the main algorithm for clarity, but because these two phases have many operations in common, actual implementations will typically integrate them more tightly.

There are potentially many ways to choose eliminations. The one we present starts by choosing an atom and checking if its inversion will produce a propositional summation, since this is the most efficient case. If not, we successively add atoms to E until G_E forms a parfactor where all atoms with logical variables are part of E (because counting elimination requires it). Then, for efficiency and to avoid shared logical variables between atoms, we try to determine as many inversions as possible, coded in the sequence $L_1, \ldots, L_k$, to be done before counting elimination (or explicit summation when counting cannot be done).

FUNCTION *FOVE*(G, Q)
G a set of parfactors, $Q \subseteq RV(G)$, G shattered against Q (section 15.5.2).
1. If $RV(G) = Q$, return G.
2. $(E, \{L_1, \ldots, L_k\}) \leftarrow CHOOSE\text{-}ELIMINATION(G, Q)$.
3. $g_E \leftarrow fs(G_E)$ (fusion, section 15.5.1).
4. $G' \leftarrow ELIMINATE(g_E, E)$.
5. Return $FOVE(G' \cup G_{\neg E}, Q)$.

FUNCTION *ELIMINATE*$(g, E, \{L_1, \ldots, L_k\})$
1. If $k = 0$ (no inversion)
   return $SUMMATION\text{-}WITHOUT\text{-}INVERSION(g, E)$.
2. $E_1 \leftarrow \{e \in E : LV(e) \cap L_1 \neq \emptyset\}$ (get inverted atoms).
3. Return $\bigcup_{C_1 \in U_L(C_g)} ELIMINATE\text{-}GIVEN\text{-}UNIFORMITY(g, E_1, C_1, \{L_2, \ldots, L_k\})$.

FUNCTION *ELIMINATE-GIVEN-UNIFORMITY*$(g, E_1, C_1, \{L_2, \ldots, L_k\})$
1. Choose $\theta_1 \in [C_1]$ (bind inverted logical variables arbitrarily).
2. $G' \leftarrow ELIMINATE(g\theta_1, E_1\theta_1, \{L_2, \ldots, L_k\})$.
3. $G'' \leftarrow \bigcup_{g'\theta_1 \in G'} (\phi_{g'}, A_{g'}, C_1 \wedge C_{g'})$.
4. Return $\bigcup_{g'' \in G''} SIMPLIFICATION(g'')$ (simplification, section 15.5.3).

FUNCTION *SUMMATION-WITHOUT-INVERSION*(g, E)
1. If $E = \{E_1, \ldots, E_k\}$ atoms are independent given C_g and $A_g \setminus E$ is ground
   return $(\sum_{\vec{N}_E} \vec{N}_E! \prod_v \phi_g(v, A_g \setminus E)^{\prod_{i=1}^k \vec{N}_{E_i, v_i}}, A_g \setminus E, \top)$ (counting, section 15.3.1).
2. Return $(\sum_{RV(E)} \prod_{\theta \in \Theta_g} \phi_g(A_g\theta_g), A_g \setminus E, C_g)$ (propositional elimination).

Notation:
- $LV(\alpha)$: logical variables in object α.
- $g\theta$: parfactor $(\phi_g, A_g\theta, C_g\theta)$.
- $U_L(C_g)$: USCP of L with respect to C_g (section 15.3.2.1).
- $C_{|L}$: constraints projected to a set of logical variables L.
- G_E: subset of parfactors G which depend on $RV(E)$.
- $G_{\neg E}$: subset of parfactors G which do not depend on $RV(E)$.
- $\top$: tautology constraint.

Figure 15.1   The FOVE algorithm.

15.4   An experiment

We use the implementation available at `http://l2r.cs.uiuc.edu/~cogcomp` to compare average run times between lifted and propositional inference (which produce the exact same results) for two different models while increasing the number

FUNCTION *CHOOSE-ELIMINATION*(G, Q)
1. Choose e from $A_G \setminus Q$.
2. $g \leftarrow fs(G_e)$ (fusion, section 15.5.1).
3. If $LV(e) = LV(g)$ and $\forall e' \in A_g$ $RV(e') \neq RV(e)$
   return $(\{e\}, LV(e))$ (inversion eliminable).
4. $E \leftarrow \{e\}$.
5. While $E \neq$ non-ground atoms of G_E
   $E \leftarrow E \cup$ non-ground atoms of G_E.
6. Return $(E, GET\text{-}SEQUENCE\text{-}OF\text{-}INVERSIONS(fs(G_E)))$.

FUNCTION *GET-SEQUENCE-OF-INVERSIONS*(g)
1. If there is no L_1 set of invertible logical variables in g (inversion, section 15.3.2)
   return $\emptyset$.
2. Choose $\theta_1 \in [C_{g|L_1}]$.
3. $\{L2, \dots, L_k\} \leftarrow GET\text{-}SEQUENCE\text{-}OF\text{-}INVERSIONS(g\theta_1)$.
4. Return $\{L_1, L_2, \dots, L_k\}$.

Figure 15.2 One possible way of choosing an elimination.

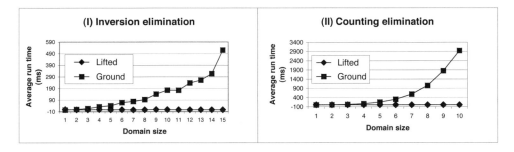

Figure 15.3 (I) Average run time for answering query $P(p)$ from a parfactor on $(p, q(X))$, using inversion elimination, with domain size $|X|$ being gradually increased. (II) Average run time for answering query $P(r)$ from a parfactor on $(p(X), p(Y), r)$, using counting elimination, with domain size $|X| = |Y|$ being gradually increased.

of objects in the domain. The first one, (I) in figure 15.3, answers the query $P(p)$ from a parfactor on $(p, q(X))$ and uses inversion elimination only. The inference in (II) answers query $P(r)$ from a parfactor on $(p(X), p(Y), r)$ and uses counting elimination only. In both cases propositional inference starts taking very long before any noticeable variation in lifted inference run times.

15.5   Auxiliary operations

15.5.1   Fusion

We have assumed in section 15.3 that we have operations to calculate $\sum_{RV(E)} \Phi(G_E)$, but elimination operations calculate $\sum_{RV(E)} \Phi(g)$, for g a *single* parfactor. *Fusion* bridges this gap by computing, for any set of parfactors G, a single parfactor $fs(G)$ such that $\Phi(G) = \Phi(fs(G))$.

Fusion works by replacing the constraints of all parfactor in the set by a single, common constraint which is the conjunction of them all. This guarantees that all parfactors get instantiated by the same set of substitutions on a single set of logical variables, which allows their products (in the expression for $\Phi(G)$) to be unified under a single product. Note that not all parfactors contain all the logical variables, and will be instantiated to the same ground factor by distinct substitutions (those agreeing on the logical variables present in the parfactor, but disagreeing on some of the others). In other words, some of the parfactors will have their number of instantiatiations increased by this unification. For this reason, we also exponentiate the potential function to the inverse of how many times the number of instantiations was increased, keeping the final result the same as before.

This is illustrated in the example below:

$$\left(\prod_{D,P} \phi_1(e(D), s(D, P))\right)\left(\prod_{D'} \phi_2(e(D'))\right) = \prod_{D,P,D'} \phi_1(e(D), s(D,P))\phi_2^{\frac{1}{|D,P|}}(e(D'))$$

$$= \prod_{D,P,D'} \phi_3(e(D), s(D, P), e(D')).$$

(note that logical variables in different parfactors must be standardized apart.) Formally, we have the fusion theorem below.

Theorem 15.3 Fusion
Let G be a set of parfactors. Define $C_G = \bigwedge_{g \in G} C_g$, $\Theta_G = [C_G]$ and $A_G = \bigcup_{g \in G} A_g$. Let $fs(G)$ be the parfactor $(\prod_{g \in G} \phi_g^{|\Theta_g|/|\Theta_G|}, A_G, C_G)$. Then $\Phi(G) = \Phi(fs(G))$.

Proof

$$\Phi(G) = \prod_{g \in G} \prod_{\theta \in \Theta_g} \phi_g(A_g\theta) = \prod_{g \in G} \prod_{\theta \in \Theta_G} \phi_g(A_g\theta)^{|\Theta_g|/|\Theta_G|}$$

$$= \prod_{\theta \in \Theta_G} \prod_{g \in G} \phi_g(A_g\theta)^{|\Theta_g|/|\Theta_G|} = \prod_{\theta \in \Theta_G} \phi_{fs(G)}(A_G\theta) = \Phi(fs(G))$$

∎

While the above is correct, it is rather unnatural to have $e(D)$ and $e(D')$ be distinct atoms. If a set of logical variables has the same possible substitutions, like D and D' here, we can do something better:

$$\left(\prod_{D,P}\phi_1(e(D),s(D,P))\right)\left(\prod_{D'}\phi_2(e(D'))\right) = \left(\prod_D\prod_P\phi_1(e(D),s(D,P))\right)\left(\prod_{D'}\phi_2(e(D'))\right)$$

$$= \prod_{D''}\left(\left(\prod_P\phi_1(e(D''),s(D'',P))\right)(\phi_2(e(D'')))\right)$$

$$= \prod_{D''}\left(\prod_P\phi_1(e(D''),s(D'',P))\phi_2(e(D''))^{\frac{1}{|P|}}\right)$$

$$= \prod_{D'',P}\phi_1(e(D''),s(D'',P))\phi_2^{\frac{1}{|P|}}(e(D''))$$

$$= \prod_{D'',P}\phi_3(e(D''),s(D'',P)).$$

Formally, this process is similar to inversion with respect to D''. However, it does require the additional previous step of unifying distinct logical variables (but with identical sets of possible substitutions) into a single one first (in the example, D and D' are replaced by D''). For lack of space we omit the details of this improvement.

15.5.2 Shattering

In section 15.3 we mentioned the need for *shattering*, which we now discuss in more detail. This need arises from c-atoms representing overlapping, but not identical, classes of random variables. Consider the following marginalization over parfactors g_1 and g_2 with potential functions ϕ_1 and ϕ_2 respectively:

$$\sum_{RV(p(X,Y))}\left(\prod_{X,Y}\phi_1(p(X,Y),q)\right)\prod_Y\phi_2(p(a,Y))$$

If we pick $E = p(a,Y)$, $G_E = \{g_1,g_2\}$. However, only some instantiations of g_1 depend on $p(a,Y)$ (the ones with $X = a$). Moreover, the operations we later talk about require any pair of c-atoms in G_E to represent either identical classes of random variables, or those classes to be disjoint. This is violated by $RV(p(a,Y))$ being a subset of $RV(p(X,Y))$. Picking $E = p(X,Y)$ also violates this requirement.

The solution is to **split** parfactor g_1 into two different parfactors. The union of instantiations of $(\phi_1,(p(X,Y),q),X\neq a)$ and $(\phi_1,(p(a,Y),q),\top)$ is identical to the set of instantiations of g_1, so the summation can be simply rewritten as

$$\sum_{RV(p(X,Y))}\left(\prod_{X,Y:X\neq a}\phi_1(p(X,Y),q)\right)\left(\prod_Y\phi_1(p(a,Y),q)\right)\prod_Y\phi_2(p(a,Y))$$

$$= \sum_{RV(p(X,Y):X\neq a)}\left(\prod_{X,Y:X\neq a}\phi_1(p(X,Y),q)\right)\sum_{p(a,Y)}\left(\prod_Y\phi_1(p(a,Y),q)\right)\prod_Y\phi_2(p(a,Y))$$

Now $E = p(a,Y)$ satisfies the operations' requirements. Picking $E = p(X,Y), X\neq a$ would work equally well.

Splitting parfactors is done by pairwise comparisons of atoms of the same predicate. We split parfactors $g_1 = (\phi_1, A_1, C_1)$ and $g_2 = (\phi_2, A_2, C_2)$ around atoms $a_1 \in A_1$ and $a_2 \in A_2$ by replacing them by parfactors $(\phi_1, A_1, C_1 \wedge a_1 = a_2)$, $(\phi_1, A_1, C_1 \wedge a_1 \neq a_2)$, $(\phi_2, A_2, C_2 \wedge a_1 = a_2)$ and $(\phi_2, A_2, C_2 \wedge a_1 \neq a_2)$, after standardizing apart their logical variables. In fact, we only need to keep those whose constraint is satisfiable. (This is why g_2 does not need to be broken in the example above – that would only produce itself and another parfactor with zero instantiations.) In particular, if $RV(a_1) = RV(a_2)$, we end up obtaining the original parfactors.

The uniformity requirement is met by **shattering** the FOPM in advance, that is, by successively splitting the parfactors of each pair of c-atoms, including the query atoms, until no overlapping non-identically grounded pair remains. The query atoms need to be involved in shattering because if a c-atom includes query and non-query random variables, it needs to be split so that the non-query ones can be eliminated.

As pointed out by Poole [9], splitting parfactors resembles the role of unification in first-order resolution, which determines the conditions for two atoms to match. In probabilistic inference, however, we are interested not only in the overlapping of atoms but also in the *residual* parfactors that originate from the matching. The reason for this difference is that the *number* of instantiations of a parfactor matters for the final joint distribution. In regular resolution, the original clauses are kept because their redundancy with the clauses resulting from resolution makes no difference, while here we need to discount them and replace the originals with the non-matching cases.

15.5.3   Irrelevant Logical Variable Simplification

Inversion often produces parfactors with constraints with logical variables not present in its atoms. The first inversion example produces the expression below. We can simplify it by observing that the actual value of Y is irrelevant inside the product. Only the number $|Y|$ of possible values for Y will make a difference. Therefore we can write

$$\prod_{XY} \phi'(p(X)) = \prod_{X} \phi'(p(X))^{|Y|} = \prod_{X} \phi''(p(X)).$$

15.6   Applicability of lifted inference

As explained in the previous sections, the lifted operations of FOVE are not always applicable, each of them requiring certain conditions to be satisfied in advance. Therefore a natural question is to what kinds of FOPMs we can apply FOVE in an exclusively lifted manner.

It is not clear at this point whether it is possible to tell in advance if a FOPM can be solved with lifted operations alone. The main reason for this is that lifted operations will be applied to parfactors resulting from previous operations, so we do not know them in advance. It may be that two parfactors satisfying the lifted operations conditions fuse to form one which does not. (This is similar to the fact that an elimination ordering is not computed in advance but only as the algorithm proceeds.)

As a summarization, the conditions for applying lifted operations to eliminate a set $RV(E)$ from a parfactor g are the following: for counting elimination, the atoms in g must be independent given its C_g; for inversion on $L \subseteq LV(g)$,

1. $\forall e_k, e_l \in E \cdot \forall \theta_i, \theta_j \in [C_{g|L}] \cdot \theta_i \neq \theta_j \Rightarrow RV(e_k\theta_i) \cap RV(e_l\theta_j) = \emptyset.$
2. $\forall \theta_i, \theta_j \in [C_{g|L}] \cdot \theta_i \neq \theta_j \Rightarrow RV(E\theta_i) \cap RV(E\theta_j) = \emptyset.$

When lifted operations do not apply, FOVE uses non-lifted operations to calculate $\sum_{RV(E)} G_E$. These non-lifted methods could be propositionalization, sampling etc, but with the advantage of being restricted to a subset of the model only.

15.7   Future Directions

There are several possible directions for further development of FOVE. One of the main ones is the incorporation of function symbols, both random (the color of an object, for example) and interpreted (summation over integers), which will greatly increase its expressivity and applicability.

In applications involving evidence over many objects (for example, the facts about all the words in an English document), shattering may take a long time because all parfactors have to be checked against it. The large number of objects involved may create the need for numerous parfactor splittings. This is unfortunate because often only some objects are truly relevant to the query. For example, analyzing only some words and phrases in a document will often be enough to determine its subject. Therefore a variant of FOVE that does only the necessary shattering, guided by the inference process, is of great interest.

Finally, lifted FOVE operations do not cover all possible cases and explicit summation may be required at times, so increasing their coverage is an important direction.

15.8   Conclusion

Intuitive descriptions of models very often include first-order elements. When these models are probabilistic, the dominant approach has been that of grounding the model to a propositional one and solving it with a regular propositional algorithm. This strategy loses the explicit representation of the model's first-order structure, which can be used to great computational advantage, and which is computationally hard to retrieve from the grounded model.

We presented FOVE, a first-order generalization of the popular VE propositional inference algorithm. Like VE, FOVE successively eliminates random variables from the model by summing them out while taking advantage of independences for efficiency. Unlike VE, FOVE directly manipulates first-order representations, eliminating c-atoms that stand for potentially large sets of random variables at once. This can in some cases exponentially (in the domain size) speed inference up.

There are important directions in which FOVE needs to be extended, such as incorporating function symbols, avoiding unnecessary shattering, and extending operations for as of yet uncovered cases. However FOVE is already applicable, and especially useful, in domains with large objects about which we have identical knowledge. More than that, it is a general framework to be expanded and help close the gap between logic and probabilistic reasoning.

Acknowledgments

This work was partly supported by Cycorp in relation to the Cyc technology, the Advanced Research and Development Activity (ARDA)'s Advanced Question Answering for Intelligence (AQUAINT) program, NSF grant ITR-IIS- 0085980, and a Defense Advanced Research Projects Agency (DARPA) grant HR0011-05-1-0040.

References

[1] V. S. Costa, D. Page, M. Qazi, and J. Cussens. CLP(BN): Constraint logic programming for probabilistic knowledge. In *Proceedings of the Conference on Uncertainty in Artificial Intelligence*, 2003.

[2] R. de Salvo Braz, E. Amir, and D. Roth. Lifted first-order probabilistic inference. In *Proceedings of the International Joint Conference on Artificial Intelligence*, 2005.

[3] R. de Salvo Braz, E. Amir, and D. Roth. MPE and partial inversion in lifted probabilistic variable elimination. In *National Conference on Artificial Intelligence*, 2006.

[4] N. Friedman, L. Getoor, D. Koller, and A. Pfeffer. Learning probabilistic relational models. In *Proceedings of the International Joint Conference on Artificial Intelligence*, 1999.

[5] J. Y. Halpern. An analysis of first-order logics of probability. In *Proceedings of the International Joint Conference on Artificial Intelligence*, 1990.

[6] K. Kersting and L. De Raedt. Bayesian logic programs. In *Proceedings of the Work-in-Progress Track at the 10th International Conference on Inductive Logic Programming*, 2000.

[7] L. Ngo and P. Haddawy. Probabilistic logic programming and Bayesian networks. In *Asian Computing Science Conference*, 1995.

[8] J. Pearl. *Probabilistic Reasoning in Intelligent Systems: Networks of Plausible Inference*. Morgan Kaufmann, San Mateo, CA, 1988.

[9] D. Poole. First-order probabilistic inference. In *Proceedings of the International Joint Conference on Artificial Intelligence*, 2003.

[10] D. Poole. Probabilistic Horn abduction and Bayesian networks. *Artificial Intelligence*, 64(1):81–129, 1993.

[11] M. Richardson and P. Domingos. Markov logic networks. Technical report, Department of Computer Science, University of Washington, 2004.

[12] N. L. Zhang and D. Poole. A simple approach to Bayesian network computations. In *Proceedings of the Tenth Biennial Canadian Artificial Intelligence Conference*, 1994.

16 Feature Generation and Selection in Multi-Relational Statistical Learning

Alexandrin Popescul and Lyle H. Ungar

Using rich sets of features generated from relational data often improves the predictive accuracy of regression models. The number of feature candidates, however, rapidly grows prohibitively large as richer feature spaces are explored. We present a framework, structural generalized linear regression (SGLR), which flexibly integrates feature generation with model selection allowing (1) augmentation of relational representation with cluster-derived concepts, and (2) dynamic control over the search strategy used to generate features. Clustering increases the expressivity of feature spaces by creating new concepts which contribute to the creation of new features, and can lead to more accurate models. Dynamic feature generation, in which decisions of which features to generate are based on the results of run-time feature selection, can lead to the discovery of accurate models with significantly less computation than generating all features in advance. We present experimental results supporting these claims in two multirelational document mining applications: document classification and link prediction.

16.1 Introduction

We present a statistical relational learning method, structural generalized linear regression (SGLR), for building predictive regression models from relational databases or domains with implicit relational structure such as collections of documents linked by citations or hyperlinks. In SGLR, features are dynamically generated by a refinement-graph style search over SQL queries, and tested for potential inclusion into a generalized linear regression model, such as linear, logistic, or Poisson regression. This approach has several advantages over more traditional logic-based inductive logic programming (ILP) methods. The tables resulting from SQL queries are easily aggregated in many ways, giving a rich space of quantitative, as well as Boolean features. The resulting regression models are typically more accurate than logical models. We also show how to automatically augment the original relational schema with additional derived features, facilitating the search for compound features.

SGLR, like several related methods [23, 18, 9, 27], searches a space of "feature generating expressions" to find those which generate new predictive features. In SGLR, a given relational database schema describing background data structures a search over database queries. Features are generated in two steps: a refinement-graph-like search of the space of SQL queries generates tables, which are then aggregated into real-valued features, which are tested for inclusion in a generalized linear model; i.e., each query generates a table, which in turn is aggregated to produce scalar feature candidates, from which statistically significant predictors are selected.

The initial relational schema is dynamically augmented with new relations containing concepts derived by clustering the data in the tables. For example, clustering documents by the words they contain or authors by venues they have published in gives new concepts – topics (document clusters) or communities (author clusters) – and new relations between the original items and the clusters they occur in (documents on a topic or authors in a community).

The main search is over the space of possible relational database queries, augmented to include aggregate or statistical operators, groupings, richer join conditions, and argmax-based queries. This search can be guided based on the types of predictive features discovered so far. We show below that a very simple "intelligent" search over the space of possible queries (and hence features) can result in discovery of predictive features with far less computation than static (e.g., breadth-first) search.

SGLR couples two elements helpful for successful learning:(1) a class of statistical models which outperforms logic-based models and (2) principled means of choosing what features to include in this model. Regression models are often more accurate than recursive partitioning methods such as C4.5 or FOIL-style logic descriptions. This difference is particularly apparent when there are vast numbers of potential features, many of which contribute some signal, for example, when words are included as features. Regression also allows us to use principled feature selection criteria such as Akaike information criterion (AIC), Bayes information criterion (BIC), and streaming feature selection (SFS) [4, 29, 33] to control against overfitting.

Figure 16.1 highlights the components of SGLR. Two main processes – relational feature generation and statistical modeling – are dynamically coupled into a single loop. Knowing the types of features selected so far by the statistical modeler allows the query generation component to guide its search, focusing on promising subspaces of the feature space. The search in the space of database queries involving one or more relations produces feature candidates one at a time for consideration by the statistical model selection component. The process results in a statistical model where each selected feature is the evaluation of a database query encoding a predictive data pattern in a given domain. We use logistic regression (or, equivalently, maximum entropy modeling). Features are tested sequentially for inclusion

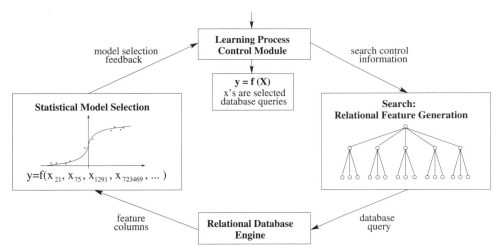

Figure 16.1   Learning process diagram.

in the regression model, and accepted if they are statistically significant after using a BIC [29] penalty to control against false discovery.

SGLR has several key characteristics which distinguish it from either pure probabilistic network modeling or ILP:

- The use of regression rather than logic allows the feature space to include statistical summaries or aggregates, and more expressive substitutions through nesting of intermediate aggregates (e.g., "How many times does this paper cite the most cited author in a conference to which it was submitted?").

- We use clustering to dynamically extend the set of relations generating new features. Clusters give better models of sparse data, improve scalability, and produce representations not possible with standard aggregates [12]. For example, one can cluster words based on co-occurrence in documents, giving "topics," or authors based on the number of papers they have published in the same venues, giving "communities." Once clusters are formed, they represent new relational concepts which are added to the relational database schema, and then used together with the original relations.

- We use relational database management systems and SQL rather than Prolog. Most real-world data lies in relational databases, with schemata and metainformation we can use. Relational database management systems incorporate decades of work on optimization, giving better scalability.

- Coupling generation and feature selection using discriminative modeling into a single loop gives a more flexible search than propositionalization Since the total number and type of features is not known in advance, the search formulation does lazy feature evaluation, allowing it to focus on more promising feature subspaces, giving higher time efficiency. Space efficiency is achieved by not storing pregenerated features, but rather considering them one by one as they are generated, and keeping only the few selected features.

We present results on two sets of tasks which use the data from CiteSeer (a.k.a. ResearchIndex), an online digital library of computer science papers [19]. CiteSeer contains a rich set of data, including paper titles, text of abstracts and documents, citation information, author names and affiliations, and conference or journal names. We represent CiteSeer as a relational database. For example, citation information is represented as a binary relation between citing and cited documents. Document authorship and publication venues of documents are also binary relations, while word counts can be represented as a ternary relation.

16.1.1   Invention of Cluster Relations

SGLR uses clustering to derive new relations and adds them to the database schema used in automatic generation of predictive features in statistical relational learning. Entities and relationships derived from clusters increase the expressivity of feature spaces by creating new first-class concepts. These concepts and relations are added to the database schema, and thus are considered (potentially in multiple combinations) during the search of the space of possible queries (figure 16.2). For example, in CiteSeer, papers can be clustered based on words or citations giving "topics," and authors can be clustered based on documents they coauthor giving "communities." In addition to simpler grouping (e.g., "Is this document on a given topic?"), such cluster-derived concepts become part of more complex feature expressions (e.g. "Does the database contain another document on the same topic and published in the same conference?"). The original database schema is implicitly used to decide which entities to cluster and what sources of attributes to use, possibly several per entity, creating alternative clusterings of the same objects. For example, documents can be clustered using words and, separately, using citations. Out of the large number of features generated, those which improve predictive accuracy are kept in the model, as decided by statistical feature selection criteria. Using cluster improves accuracy. Perhaps surprisingly, using cluster relations can also lead to a more rapid discovery of predictive features.

Cluster-relation invention as described here differs importantly from aggregation, which also creates new features from a relational representation [23, 26]. Aggregation allows one to summarize the information in a table returned from an SQL or logic query into scalar values usable by a regression model, for example, computing the *average* of a word count in all cited documents, or selecting a citing document with *max* number of incoming links. The clusters, on the other hand, create new relations in the database schema. The cluster relations are then used repeatedly to generate new queries and hence tables and features.

16.1.2   Dynamic Feature Generation

SGLR also supports *dynamic feature generation*, in which the order in which features are generated and evaluated is determined at run-time. Generating features is by far the most computationally demanding part of SGLR. In the example

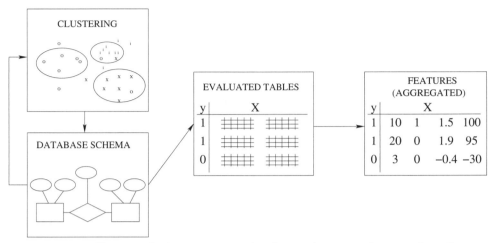

Figure 16.2   Cluster relations augment database schema used to produce feature candidates.

presented below, generating 100,000 features can take several CPU days due to the extensive SQL queries, particularly the joins. Dynamic feature generation can lead to discovery of predictive features with far less computation than generating all features in advance. When using the appropriate complexity penalties, one can still guarantee no overfitting, even when the order in which we generate features and test them for inclusion in the model is dynamically determined based on which features have so far been found to be predictive. This best first search often vastly reduces the number of computationally expensive feature evaluations.

Query expressions are assigned into multiple streams based on user-selected properties of the feature expressions; for example, based on the aggregate operator type. Since different sets of features are of different size (e.g., the number of different words is much greater than the number of journals or the number of topics), it is often easy to heuristically classify features into different streams. If feature generation has a known cost, this can also be taken into account. At each iteration, one of the streams is chosen to generate the next candidate feature, based on the expected utility of the streams features relative to those of other streams. For example, a simple and effective rule is to select the next query to be evaluated from the stream whose features have been included in the model in the highest percentage.

16.1.3   Chapter Overview

The following section describes the SGLR methodology in some detail, including how we cast feature generation as a search in the space of relational database queries, how cluster relations are created, and how the feature space is searched dynamically. Section 16.3 then describes two tasks using CiteSeer data which we use to test SGLR: classifying documents into their publication venues, conferences, or journals, and predicting the existence of a citation between two documents. The tasks serve as a proxy for a more general problem of learning from inherently relational and noisy network data, including social networks. Relations between documents, cited documents, authors, publication venues, and text can all be explored to discover predictive features. We show that adding new relations to the database can improve accuracy, and that dynamic search can achieve the same accuracy as its static alternative while generating far fewer features, and hence reducing the required CPU time. The final two sections discuss SGLR in the context of related work, and summarize some of its advantages.

16.2   Detailed Methodology

As described above, SGLR dynamically couples two main components: generation of feature candidates via a search in the space of queries to a relational database, and their selection for inclusion in a regression model using statistical model selection criteria. First, we give the high-level SGLR algorithm. Lines in italics are the parts that do cluster-relation generation. We deliberately leave the stopping criterion underspecified. Given the incremental nature of model building in SGLR, deciding when to stop will often depend on the available CPU time and on the accuracy achieved so far.

1: **while** more features needed **do**
2:      generate next SQL query expression using a refinement graph search
3:      query the database and retrieve a table
4:      *generate new cluster relations from the table*
5:      *augment the database with derived relations*
6:      apply aggregate operators to the table to produce a set of features
7:      test the new features for inclusion in the model
8: **end while**

16.2.1   Notation and Basic Concepts

The language of nonrecursive first-order logic formulae maps directly into SQL and relational algebra, (see e.g., [8]). Our implementation uses SQL for efficiency and connectivity with relational database engines.

Throughout this paper we use the following schema:

cites(FromDoc, ToDoc),
author(Doc, Auth),
published_in(Doc, Venue),
word_count(Doc, Word, Int).

Domains, or types, used here are different from the primitive SQL types. The specification of these domains in addition to the primitive SQL types is necessary to guide the search process more efficiently.

First-order expressions are treated as database queries resulting in a table of all satisfying solutions, rather than a single Boolean value. The extended notation supports aggregation over entire query results or over their individual columns. Aggregate operators are subscripted with the corresponding variable name if applied to an individual column, or are used without subscripts if applied to the entire table. For example, an average count of the word "learning" in documents cited by document d, is denoted as:

$$class'(d) \sim ave_C \left[cites(d, D), word\_count(D, learning, C) \right],$$

where $\sim$ denotes "modeled using," i.e., *the right hand side of the expression is a feature* to be tested for inclusion in the regression model, the response variable, or target concept, on the left-hand side of the expression. We use *prime* with the target relation to avoid confusion with recursive queries when, as in the features below, a background relation instance and the target relation are of the same type.

An example of a feature useful for predicting a citation link between two documents $d1$ and $d2$ is the number of documents they both cite.

$$cites'(d1, d2) \sim count \left[cites(d1, D), cites(d2, D) \right]$$

The target concept is binary, and the feature (the right-hand side of the expression) is a database query about both target documents $d1$ and $d2$:

16.2.2 Feature Generation: Search in the Space of Database Queries

16.2.2.1 *Refinement Graphs*

Relational feature generation is a search problem. We use top-down search of refinement graphs [30, 11], supplemented with aggregate operators. Figure 16.3 shows a fragment of the search space in the domain of document classification. Each node is a database query about a learning example d, and evaluates to a table of all satisfying solutions. Aggregate operators are then applied to produce multiple features.

SGLR uses the following variation of the refinement operator: it forms a join of a given query with a relation from the database schema, expanding the query into the nodes covering *all* possible configurations of equality conditions involving attributes in the new relation, such that (1) each refinement contains at least one equality condition between a new and an old attribute, (2) any attribute can be set equal to a constant of its type, and (3) the types are used to avoid equalities between attributes of different types. This refinement operator is complete. Not all refinements produced are the most general refinements of a given query; however, we

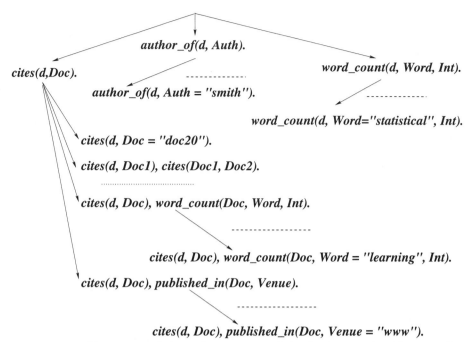

Figure 16.3   Fragment of the refinement graph in document classification domain

find that this definition can simplify pruning of equivalent subspaces by accounting only for the type and the number of relations in a query.

Table 16.1 presents the pseudocode of the refinement operator. After introducing notation with examples we walk over the pseudocode line by line. Evaluation of queries in the refinement graph nodes produces intermediate tables. Their aggregation is described in the next section.

R_i is a relation in a database schema **R**; for example: $cites(doc1 : Document, doc2 : Document)$ is a binary relation in the database. Its two attributes are $doc1$ and $doc2$, both of type *Document*. Attributes in a relation are denoted by a subscripted letter A. A query to be refined is q, for example:

```
SELECT DISTINCT *
FROM cites R1, cites R2
WHERE R1.doc1='d1' AND R2.doc1='d2' AND R1.doc2=R2.doc2
```

Q_{ref} is a set of refinements of query q, the variable which accumulates the result of the refinement function. S_{eq} is a set of equality conditions which form the conjunction in the *WHERE* clause of a refined query. $attrib(q)$ is a set of all attributes of relation instances in q:

```
{R1.doc1, R1.doc2, R2.doc1, R2.doc2}
```

$dom(A)$ are allowed constants of type A, e.g., containing all document IDs. $dom(A)$ must contain at least the target example constants identifying observations ($doc1$

Table 16.1 The refinement operator

---

refine(Query: q)

$Q_{ref} \leftarrow \{\}$
for each $R_i \in \mathbf{R}(i \in [1, n])$
    $S_{eq} \leftarrow \{\}$
    for each $A_j \in R_i$
        for each $A \in \{A_k | A_k \in attrib(q)\} \cup \{A_l | (A_l \text{ in } R_i) \wedge A_l \neq A_j\}$
            if($type(A_j) = type(A)$)
                $S_{eq} \leftarrow S_{eq} \cup \{norm(A_j = A)\}$
        for each $a \in dom(A_j)$
            $S_{eq} \leftarrow S_{eq} \cup \{norm(A_j = a)\}$
        for each $S \in 2^{S_{eq}}$
            if $\exists (A_i = A_j) \in S$ such that $A_i \in attrib(q) \vee A_j \in attrib(q)$
                $Q_{ref} \leftarrow Q_{ref} \cup \{q' | q'.WHERE =$
                $q.WHERE \cup \{S\} \wedge q'.FROM = q.FROM \cup \{R_i\}\}$
return Q_{ref}

---

and $doc2$, if they identify a target observation in the example above). In situations where generated features can include references to other constants, $dom(A)$ can include all values of A, or a subset, e.g., the entries with the highest correlation with the response variable or those above a count cutoff value. The following example of a query about the target pair $< d1, d2 >$ references other constants in the domain of document IDs; the query is nonempty when both $d1$ and $d2$ cite a particular document $d2370$:

```
SELECT DISTINCT *
FROM cites R1, cites R2
WHERE R1.doc1='d1' AND R2.doc1='d2' AND R1.doc2=R2.doc2
      AND R2.doc2='d2370'
```

$norm(A_i = A_j)$ alphanumerically orders A_i and A_j to avoid storing in S_{eq} equivalent entries $A_i = A_j$ and $A_j = A_i$. $type(A)$ is metatype of A, as is *Document* in the examples above, rather than an SQL type *String*. The set of equality conditions in query q is denoted by $q.WHERE$, e.g., a four-element set corresponding to the latter query example:

```
{R1.doc1='d1', R2.doc1='d2', R1.doc2=R2.doc2, R2.doc2='d2370'}
```

The refinement operator given in table 16.1 takes a query q as argument and returns the set of its refinements, Q_{ref}. Refinement of a given query starts by picking a relation instance in the database schema (loop starting at line 4). Adding this relation results in its Cartesian product with the view of q (not included in the refinement set), which forms a "template" to be filled by allowed configurations of equality conditions. For each attribute A_j in the newly added relation R_i (starting at line 6) we find other attributes in q or in R_i itself, such that their equality with A_j can be included in the conjunction of equality conditions. This has to take into account metatypes (line 8), e.g., an attribute of type *Document* cannot be checked for equality with an attribute of type *Author : taskar*. Entries in S_{eq} are normalized (line 9) alphabetically to avoid equivalent entries. Equality of A_j with target example identifiers (constants) are added to the set of equality conditions S_{eq}, as well as possibly other constants of the type of A_j (lines 12-14). At this point S_{eq} contains all possible terms which can enter in the conjunction of refinements of q when being joined with R_i. A refined query is formed for each subset of S_{eq} (starting at line 15) such that at least one of the equality conditions in the subset (S) involves an attribute in q, i.e., an attribute of an "old" relation instance already present in q. The process repeats for all relations R_i in the schema $\mathbf{R}$ (back to line 4). A node resulting in an empty table for each observation is not refined any further since its refinements will be empty too.

16.2.2.2   *Search Space Extension via Aggregate Operators*

As in predicate calculus, aggregates are not part of the abstract relational languages. Practical systems, however, implement them as additional features. SQL supports the use aggregates which produce real values, rather than the more limited Boolean features produced by logic-based approaches. Regression modeling makes full use of these real-valued features.

As we described above, a node in our refinement graph is a query evaluating into a table. These tables are in turn aggregated by multiple operators to produce features. We use the aggregate operators common in relational language extensions: *count*, *ave*, *max*, and *min*; binary logic-style features are included through the *empty* aggregate operator. Aggregate operators are applied to an entire table or to its columns, as appropriate given type restrictions, e.g., *ave* cannot be applied to a column of a categorical type. When aggregate operators are not defined, e.g., the average of an empty set, we use an interaction with a 1/0 (defined/not-defined) indicator variable. Table 16.2 presents pseudocode of the aggregation procedure at each search node (called for each observation i).

The use of aggregate operators in feature generation complicates pruning of the search space. We use a hash function of partially evaluated feature columns to avoid fully recomputing equivalent features. In general, determining equivalence among relational expressions is known to be NP-complete, although polynomial algorithms exist for restricted classes of expressions; see, e.g., [3, 22]. Equivalence determination based on the homomorphism theorem for "tableau" query formalism, essentially the class of conjunctive queries we consider before aggregation, is given in [1]. Optimizations could be done by better avoiding generation of equivalent queries. Children nodes in the refinement graph can, of course, reuse evaluations

Table 16.2 Aggregation of refinement graph views

---

aggregate(View: v)

v is the evaluation of a search node query per observation i
$\quad F \leftarrow \{\}$
$\quad$ for each $Aggr_i \in \mathbf{A}$ ($i \in [1, n]$)$\quad\quad$ // $\mathbf{A}$ is a set of aggregate operators
$\quad\quad$ if($defined(Aggr_i(v))$)$\quad\quad\quad\quad$ // applicability of $Aggr_i$ is determined by typing
$\quad\quad\quad F \leftarrow F \cup \{Aggr_i(v)\}$$\quad$ // e.g. "average" cannot be applied a categorical column
$\quad\quad$ for each column $C \in v$
$\quad\quad\quad$ if($defined(Aggr_i(C))$)
$\quad\quad\quad\quad F \leftarrow F \cup \{Aggr_i(C)\}$
return F

---

performed in their parent nodes; this considerably reduces computational burden at the expense of increased memory consumption.

16.3 Experimental Evaluation

16.3.1 Tasks and Data

We evaluate SGLR using data from CiteSeer (a.k.a. ResearchIndex), an online digital library of computer science papers [19]. CiteSeer includes text and titles of papers, citation information, author names, and conference or journal names. We represent CiteSeer as a relational database. For example, citation information is represented as a binary relation between citing and cited documents.

There are 1560 unique conferences and journals, 26,740 unique last names of authors, and 173,410 citations among our "universe" of 60,646 publication venues (conferences or journals) which could be extracted by matching with the DBLP database.[1] We limit the vocabulary to the 1000 most frequent words in the entire collection after Porter stemming and stop word removal to keep the data size to a manageable 6,894,712 `HasWord` relations denoting which words each document contains. These relations, and the number of instances are listed in table 16.3, along with the derived cluster relations which are later added to the database.

We explore two tasks using CiteSeer data: classifying documents into their publication venues and predicting the existence of a citation between two documents. The target concept pair in the two tasks are <Document, Venue> and <Document, Document> respectively. In both tasks, the search space contains queries based on

---

1. `http://dblp.uni-trier.de/`

Table 16.3   Sizes of the original and cluster-based relations

Relation	Size
PublishedIn(*doc*:Document, *vn*:Venue)	60,646
Author(*doc*:Document, *auth*:Person)	131,582
Citation(*from*:Document, *to*:Document)	173,410
HasWord(*doc*:Document, *word*:Word)	6,894,712
ClusterDocumentsByAuthors(*doc*:Document, *clust*:Clust0)	53,660
ClusterAuthorsByDocuments(*auth*:Person, *clust*:Clust1)	26,740
ClusterDocumentsByCitingDocuments(*doc*:Document,*clust*:Clust2)	31,603
ClusterDocumentsByCitedDocuments(*doc*:Document,*clust*:Clust3)	42,749
ClusterDocumentsByWords(*doc*:Document, *clust*:Clust4)	56,104
ClusterWordsByDocuments(*word*:Word, *clust*:Clust5)	1,000

several relations about documents, such as citation information, authorship, word content and publication venues of the document, and the response to be predicted is Boolean.

16.3.2   Cluster Creation

We use k-means (e.g., see [15]) to derive cluster relations; any other hard clustering algorithm could also be used. The results of clustering are represented by binary relations of the form <ClusteredEntity, ClusterID>.

Each many-to-many relation in the original schema can produce two distinct cluster relations (e.g., clusters of words by documents or of documents by words). Three out of the four relations in the schema presented above are many-to-many (PublishedIn is not); this results in six new cluster relations. Since the PublishedIn relation does not produce new clusters, nothing needs to be done to exclude the attributes of entities in the venue prediction training and test sets from participating in clustering. In link prediction, on the other hand, the relation corresponding to the target concept, Citation, does produce clusters, so in this case clustering is run without the links sampled for training and test sets.

k-means clustering requires the selection of k, the number of groups into which the entities are clustered. In the experiments presented here we fix k equal to 100 in all cluster relations except in ClusterWordsByDocuments, where only ten clusters were used because there are roughly an order of magnitude fewer clustered words than authors or documents. (This, since the vocabulary was limited to 1000 words.) The accuracy of resulting cluster-based models reported below could potentially be improved if one is willing to incur the cost of generating clusters with different values of k and testing the resulting features for model inclusion. One could also generate clusters from the rest of the tables generated as the space of queries is searched. For simplicity, we stuck to the first six such cluster relations. Table 16.3 summarizes the sizes of four original and the six derived cluster relations.

For clustering, we use the *tf-idf* vector-space cosine similarity [28]. The measure was originally designed for document similarity using word features, but we apply it here to broader types of data. In the formulae below, d stands for any object we want to cluster, and w are the attributes used to cluster d. For example, authors d can be clustered using the documents w they write. Below we refer to d's as documents and w's as words.

Each document d is viewed as a vector whose dimensions correspond to the words w's in the vocabulary; the vector elements are the *tf-idf* weights of the corresponding words, where $tfidf(w, d) = tf(w, d) \times idf(w)$. In the original formulation, "term frequency" $tf(w, d)$ is the number of times w occurs in d. In the experiments reported here we use *binary tf* indicating whether or not w occurs in d.[2] "Inverse document frequency" $idf(w) = \log \frac{|D|}{df(w)}$, where $|D|$ is the number of documents in a collection and $df(w)$ is the number of documents in which word w occurs at least once.

The similarity between two documents is then

$$sim(\mathbf{d_i}, \mathbf{d_j}) = \frac{\mathbf{d_i} \cdot \mathbf{d_j}}{||\mathbf{d_i}|| ||\mathbf{d_j}||},$$

where $\mathbf{d_i}$ and $\mathbf{d_j}$ are vectors with *tf-idf* coordinates as described above.

The cost of clustering is negligible compared to the cost of query evaluation, especially when one uses an efficient clustering algorithm. Linear-time algorithms are available using streaming methods [13], database methods [2, 32], or by exploiting regularities in the document citation structure [24].

16.3.3 Effect of Adding Cluster Relations

We compare models learned from the feature space generated from the four original noncluster relations with the models learned from the original four relations plus six derived cluster relations (clustersNO and clustersYES models). Models are learned with sequential feature selection using BIC [29], i.e., once each feature is generated, it is added to the model permanently if the BIC-penalized error improves, or is permanently dropped otherwise.

We use ten-fold reverse cross-validation to measure accuracy improvement from using cluster relations. All observations are split equally into ten sets. Each of the sets is used to train a model. Each of the models is tested on the remaining 90% of observations. This results in ten values per each tested level, which are used to derive error bounds. In venue prediction, there are 10,000 observations: 5000 positive examples of <Document,Venue> target pairs uniformly sampled from the relation PublishedIn, and 5000 negative examples where the document is uniformly sampled from the remaining documents, and the venue is uniformly

---

2. We use *binary tf* for consistency with the relation HasWord; we do not use counts in computing similarities since the original relation HasWord contains binary word occurrence data. Other derived cluster relations use naturally binary attributes.

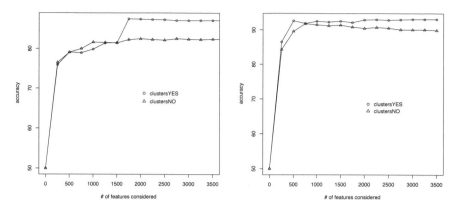

Figure 16.4   Learning curves: average test-set accuracy against the number of features generated from the training sets in ten-fold cross validation. *Left:* venue prediction, in each of ten runs $N_{train} = 1000$ and $N_{test} = 9000$. *Right:* link prediction, in each of ten runs $N_{train} = 500$ and $N_{test} = 4500$. Balanced positive/negative priors.

sampled from the domain of venues other than the true venue of the document. Positive example pairs are removed from the background relation `PublishedIn`, as well as the tuples involving documents sampled for the negative set. The size of the background relation `PublishedIn` decreases by 10,000 after removing training and test set tuples. In link prediction, the total number of observations is 5000: 2500 positive examples of `<Document,Document>` target pairs uniformly sampled from the `Citation` relation, and 2500 negative examples uniformly sampled from empty links in the citation graph. Positive example pairs are removed from the background relation `Citation`. The size of the background relation `Citation` reduces by 2500, the number of sampled positive examples.

A total of 3500 features are used in training each model. A numeric signature of partially evaluated features is maintained to avoid fully generating numerically equivalent features; note that this is different from avoiding syntactically equivalent nodes of the search space: two different queries can produce numerically equivalent feature columns, e.g., all zeros. Such repetition becomes common when feature generation progresses deeper in the search space.

Figure 16.4 presents test accuracy learning curves for models learned with and without cluster relations in venue prediction and link prediction respectively. Curve coordinates are averages over the runs in ten-fold cross validation. The learning curves show test-set accuracy changing with the number of features, in intervals of 250, generated and sequentially considered for model selection from the training set. The average test set accuracy of the cluster-based models after exploring the entire feature stream is 87.2% in venue prediction and 93.1% in link prediction, which is, respectively, 4.75 and 3.22 percentage points higher than the average accuracy of the models not using cluster relations.

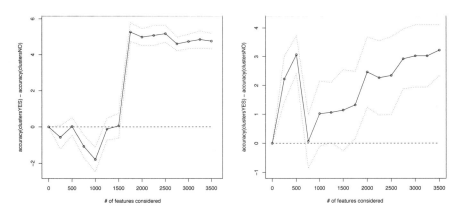

Figure   16.5 Mean   accuracy   difference: *accuracy*(*clustersYES*) −
accuracy(*clustersNO*) with 95% confidence intervals (bounds based on N=10
points, t-test distribution). *Left:* venue prediction. *Right:* link prediction

Figure 16.5 presents 95% confidence intervals of the difference in mean test accuracies of `clustersYES` and `clustersNO` models in venue prediction and link prediction respectively. In venue prediction, after exploring approximately half of the
feature stream, the improvement in accuracy by the cluster-based models is statistically significant at the 95% confidence level according to the t-test (confidence
intervals do not intersect with y=0). In the early feature generation, when considering the streams of about 1000 features, cluster-based models perform significantly
worse: at this phase, additional cluster-based features, while not yet significantly
improving accuracy, are delaying the discovery of significant noncluster-based features. In link prediction, while the significance of the improvement from cluster-
based features is reduced early in the stream, it continuously increases throughout
the rest of the stream. At the end of the stream the improvement in accuracy of the
cluster-based model is 3.22 percentage points, statistically significant at the 99.8%
confidence level. The highest accuracies (after seeing 750 features by `clustersNO`
and after seeing 3500 features by `clustersYES`) also statistically differ: the accuracy improvement in cluster-based models is 1.49 percentage points, significant at
the 99.9% confidence level.

The average number of features selected in ten `clustersYES` models is 32.0 in
venue prediction and 32.3 in link prediction, respectively; 27.9 and 31.8 features on
average were selected into `clustersNO` models from equally many feature candidates
(3500). The BIC penalty used here allows a small amount of overfitting (see
figure 16.4); more recent penalty methods such as SFS [33] avoid this problem.

The improved accuracy of the cluster-based model in venue prediction comes
mostly from a single cluster-based feature. This feature was selected in all cross-
validation runs. It is a binary cluster-based feature which is *on* for target docu-
ment/venue pair `<D,V>`, if a document `D1` exists in the cluster where `D` belongs
such that `D1` is published in the same venue as `D`. Using a logic-based notation, the

Table 16.4   Selected features which improve test accuracy by at least 1.0 percentage point. Target pair: `<D,V>`

FEATURE	MODEL
$size[publishedIn(\_, V)]$	BOTH
$exists[cites(D, D1), publishedIn(D1, V)]$	BOTH
$exists[cites(D1, D), publishedIn(D1, V)]$	BOTH
$exists[cites(D, D2), cites(D1, D2), publishedIn(D1, V)]$	BOTH
$exists[author(D, A), author(D1, A), publishedIn(D1, V)]$	BOTH
$exists[publishedIn(D1, V), docsByWords(D, C), docsByWords(D1, C)]$	CLUSTERSYES
$exists[cites(D, D3), cites(D3, D2), cites(D1, D2), publishedIn(D1, V)]$	CLUSTERSNO

feature is the following (abbreviated here `clustDocsByWords` by `topic`):[3]

$$exists[publishedIn(D1, V), topic(D, C), topic(D1, C)].$$

The following three cluster-based features were selected in more than five cross-validation runs (nine, nine and six times respectively) in the link prediction task (target: `<D1,D2>`):
$exists[docsByCitedDocs(D1, C), docsByCitedDocs(D2, C)]$,
$exists[docsByWords(D1, C), docsByWords(D2, C)]$,
$exists[docsByCitingDocs(D1, C), docsByCitingDocs(D2, C)]$.

Table 16.4 gives examples of features which improved test accuracy by at least 1 percentage point over the previous state of the venue prediction model in one of the cross-validation runs. The first five features, in the generated order, are in both `clustersYES` and `clustersNO` models. `D` and `V` are respectively document and venue in the target pair `<D,V>`.

The features in table 16.4 can be summarized as follows: document D is more likely to appear in a conference or journal V, if venue V publishes a lot of papers; if document D cites or is cited by another document published in the same venue V; if, more generally, document D is close in the citation graph to other documents published in V; if the author of D published another paper in the same venue V; and finally, in the case of the cluster-based model, if another document on the latent topic of D and published in V exists.

The cluster relations shown above led to higher classification accuracy. Another potential advantage, not shown experimentally, is that cluster-based features are generally cheaper to generate, since cluster relations contain fewer tuples than the original relations from which they were derived. This can lead to reduced computational costs per number of generated feature candidates.

---

3. Note that `D1` is always distinct from `D` as the tuple with publication venue of document `D` is removed from the background relation `PublishedIn`.

16.3.4 Dynamic Feature Generation

Up to this point, we presented models learned when doing the breadth-first search of the feature space. In this section we explore an alternative search strategy in which separate streams are used to generate queries (and hence features), and new queries are preferentially selected from those streams which have been most productive of useful features. The database query evaluation used in feature generation dominates the computational cost of our statistical relational learning methodology; thus, intelligently deciding which queries to evaluate can have a significant effect on total cost.

Feature generation in the SGLR framework consists of two steps: query expression generation and query evaluation. The former is cheap as it involves only syntactic operations on query strings; the latter is computationally demanding. The experiment is set up to test two strategies which differ in the order in which queries are evaluated. In both strategies, query *expressions* are generated by breadth-first search. The base-line, static, strategy evaluates queries in the same order the expressions appear in the search queue, while the alternative, dynamic strategy, enqueues queries into separate streams at the time its expression is generated, but chooses the next feature to be evaluated from the stream with the highest ratio:

$$(featuresAdded + 1)/(featuresTried + 1),$$

where $featuresAdded$ is the number of features selected for addition to the model, and $featuresTried$ is the total number of features tried by feature selection in this stream. Many other ranking methods could be used; this one has the virtue of being simple and, for the realistic situation in which the density of predictive features tends to decrease as one goes far into a stream, complete.

In the tests below, we use two streams. The first stream contains queries with aggregate operators `exists` and `count` over the entire table. The second stream contains features which are the counts of unique elements in individual columns. We stop the experiment when one of the streams is exhausted.

We report the difference in test-set accuracy between dynamic and static feature generation. In each of four data sets, the difference in accuracy is plotted against the number of features evaluated and considered by feature selection We also kept track of the CPU time required for each of these cases. The MySQL database engine was used. Data sets 1, 2, and 3 took roughly 20,000 seconds, while data set 4 took 40,000 seconds. In all four cases, plots of accuracy vs. CPU time used were qualitatively similar to the plots shown in figure 16.6.

In the experiments presented here, one of the two feature streams was a clear winner, suggesting the heuristic splitting feature was effective. When the choice of a good heuristic is difficult, dynamic feature generation, in the worst case, will split features into "equally good" streams, and will asymptotically lead to the same expected performance as the static feature generation by taking features from different streams with equal likelihood.

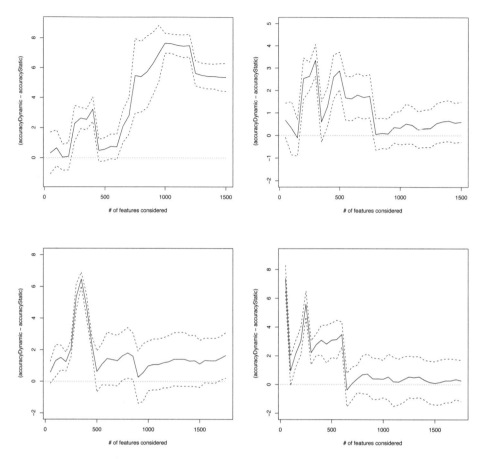

Figure 16.6   Test accuracy of the dynamic search minus test accuracy of the static search against the number of features considered. Errors: 95% confidence interval (ten-fold cross validation, in each of ten runs). In *row first* order: (a) Set 1 (venue prediction, with cluster relations), (b) set 2 (venue prediction, without cluster relations); (c) set 3 (link prediction, with cluster relations); (d) set 4 (link prediction, without cluster relations). $N_{train} = 1000$, $N_{test} = 9000$ in (a) and (b); $N_{train} = 500$, $N_{test} = 4500$ in (c) and (d)

The two-stream approach can be generalized to a multistream approach. For example, some streams can be formed based on the types of aggregate operators in query expressions, as we did here, and other streams can be formed based on the type of relations joined in a query, for example, split based on whether a query contains a cluster-derived relation, or a relation of the same type as the target concept. A query can be enqueued into one stream based on its aggregate operator, and into a different stream based on type of relation instances. The split of features into multiple streams need not be a disjoint partition. This method, if used with a check to avoid evaluation of a query which has been evaluated previously in a different stream, will not incur a significant increase in computational cost.

Another approach is to split features into multiple streams according to the sizes of their relation instances, which would serve as an estimate of evaluation time. This can lead to improvements for the following reasons: (1) out of two nearly collinear features a cheaper one will likely correspond to a simpler query and will be evaluated first, leading to approximately the same accuracy improvement as the second more expensive feature; and (2) there is no obvious correlation between the cost to evaluate a query and its predictive power. Therefore it can be expected that cheaper queries result in good features as likely as more expensive ones.

16.4   Related Work and Discussion

A number of approaches for modeling from relational representation have been proposed in the ILP community. Often, these approaches can be described as a "propositionalization," or as an "upgrade" depending on whether feature generation and modeling are integrated. Propositionalization [17] implies separation of modeling from relational feature generation. A logic theory learned with an ILP method can be used to produce binary features for a propositional learner. For example, Srinivasan and King [31] use linear regression to model features constructed from the clauses returned by Progol [21] to build predictive models in a chemical domain. Bernstein et al. [5] introduce a relational vector-space model for classification in domains with linked structure; a derived classifier based on known labels of linked neighbors is proposed in [20]. Decoupling feature construction from modeling, as done in propositionalization, retains the inductive bias of the technique used to construct features; i.e., better models potentially can be built if one allows a propositional learner itself to select its own features based on its own criteria. First-order regression system (FORS) [14] more closely integrates feature construction into regression modeling, but does so using a FOIL-like covering approach for feature construction. Additive, or cumulative, models, such as linear or logistic regression, have different criteria for feature usefulness; integrating feature construction and model selection into a single process is advocated in this context in [6, 25]. Coupling feature generation to model construction can also reduce computational costs by only generating features which will be tested for the model selection.

In contrast to propositionalization, upgrading usually implies that generation of relational features and their modeling are tightly coupled and driven by propositional learner's model selection criteria. SGLR shares these characteristics, and its simpler form, when no cluster-derived relations are used, is, in this sense, an "upgrade" of generalized linear models. TILDE [7] and WARMR [10] upgrade decision trees and association rules, respectively. S-CART [16] upgrades CART, a propositional algorithm for learning classification and regression trees. Dehaspe's MACCENT system [9] uses expected entropy gain from adding binary features to a maximum entropy classifier to direct a beam search over first-order clauses; it determines when to stop adding variables by testing the classifier on a held-out data set. Van Laer and De Raedt present an overview of upgrading in [18]. ILP gives one way to structure the search space; others can be used [27].

16.5   Conclusion

We presented structural generalized linear regression and used its logistic regression variant for analyzing document data from CiteSeer. SGLR combines the strengths of generalized linear regression modeling (e.g., linear, logistic, and Poisson) with the higher expressivity of features automatically generated from relational data sources. New, potentially predictive features and relations in the database are generated lazily, and selected with statistically rigorous criteria derived from the regression model being built. SGLR is applicable to large domains with complex, sparse and noisy data sources; these characteristics suggest focused, dynamic feature generation from rich feature spaces, regression modeling, rigorous feature selection, and the use of query and statistical optimizations, all of which contribute to the expressivity, accuracy, and scalability of SGLR.

SGLR is attractive in offering a factored architecture which allows one to plug in any additive statistical modeling tool and its corresponding feature selection criterion. This contrasts with recursive subdivision methods in which one cannot easily separate out search from modeling and feature selection. The factored architecture offers many advantages, including support for dynamic feature selection.

We showed how clustering can be used to derive new concepts and relations which augment database schema used in the automatic generation of predictive features in statistical relational learning. Clustering improves scalability through dimensionality reduction. More importantly, entities derived from clusters increase the expressivity of feature spaces by creating new first-class concepts which contribute to the creation of new features in more complex ways. For example, in CiteSeer, papers can be clustered based on words giving "topics." Associated with each cluster (or "concept") is a cluster relation (e.g., "on_topic") which then becomes part of more complex feature expressions such as $exists[publishedIn(D1, V), on\_topic(D, C), on\_topic(D1, C)]$. Such richer features result in more accurate models than those built only from the original relational concepts.

We also showed that dynamically deciding which features to generate can lead to the discovery of predictive features with substantially less computation than generating all features in advance, as done, for example, in propositionalization. Native statistical feature selection criteria can give run-time feedback for determining the order in which features are generated. Coupling feature generation to model construction can significantly reduce computational costs. Some ILP systems, such as Progol, also perform dynamic feature generation, albeit with logic models. Many problem domains should benefit from the SGLR or similar methods, including modeling of social networks, bioinformatics, disclosure control in statistical databases, and modeling of other hyperlinked domains, such as the web and databases of patents and legal cases.

References

[1] S. Abiteboul, R. Hull, and V. Vianu. *Foundations of Databases*. Addison-Wesley, Boston, 1995.

[2] R. Agrawal, J. Gehrke, D. Gunopulos, and P. Raghavan. Automatic subspace clustering of high dimensional data for data mining applications. In *Proceedings of ACM International Conference on Management of Data*, 1998.

[3] A. V. Aho, Y. Sagiv, and J. D. Ullman. Equivalences among relational expressions. *SIAM Journal of Computing*, 8(2):218–246, 1979.

[4] H. Akaike. Information theory and an extension of the maximum likelihood principle. In *Second International Symposium on Information Theory*, 1973.

[5] A. Bernstein, S. Clearwater, and F. Provost. The relational vector-space model and industry classification. In *IJCAI Workshop on Learning Statistical Models from Relational Data*, 2003.

[6] H. Blockeel and L. Dehaspe. Cumulativity as inductive bias. In *Workshop on Data Mining, Decision Support, Meta-Learning and ILP at PKDD*, 2000.

[7] H. Blockeel and L. De Raedt. Top-down induction of logical decision trees. *Artificial Intelligence*, 101(1-2):285–297, 1998.

[8] S. Ceri, G. Gottlob, and L. Tanca. *Logic Programming and Databases*. Springer-Verlag, Berlin, 1990.

[9] L. Dehaspe. Maximum entropy modeling with clausal constraints. In *Proceedings of the International Conference on Inductive Logic Programming*, 1997.

[10] L. Dehaspe and H. Toivonen. Discovery of frequent datalog patterns. *Data Mining and Knowledge Discovery*, 3(1):7–36, 1999.

[11] S. Dzeroski and N. Lavrac. An introduction to inductive logic programming. In Saso Dzeroski and Nada Lavrac, editors, *Relational Data Mining*, pages 48–73. Springer-Verlag, Berlin, 2001.

[12]   D. Foster and L. Ungar. A proposal for learning by ontological leaps. In *Proceedings of Snowbird Learning Conference*, Snowbird, UT, 2002.

[13]   S. Guha, N. Mishra, R. Motwani, and L. O'Callaghan. Clustering data streams. In *IEEE Symposium on Foundations of Computer Science*, 2000.

[14]   A. Karalic and I. Bratko. First order regression. *Machine Learning*, 26:147–176, 1997.

[15]   L. Kaufman and P. J. Rousseeuw. *Finding Groups In Data: An Introduction to Cluster Analysis*. Wiley-Interscience, Hoboken, NJ, 1990.

[16]   S. Kramer and G. Widmer. Inducing classification and regression trees in first order logic. In Saso Dzeroski and Nada Lavrac, editors, *Relational Data Mining*, pages 140–159. Springer-Verlag, Berlin, 2001.

[17]   S. Kramer, N. Lavrac, and P. Flach. Propositionalization approaches to relational data mining. In Saso Dzeroski and Nada Lavrac, editors, *Relational Data Mining*, pages 262–291. Springer-Verlag, Berlin, 2001.

[18]   W. Van Laer and L. De Raedt. How to upgrade propositional learners to first order logic: A case study. In Saso Dzeroski and Nada Lavrac, editors, *Relational Data Mining*, pages 235–261. Springer-Verlag, Berlin, 2001.

[19]   Steve Lawrence, C. Lee Giles, and Kurt Bollacker. Digital libraries and autonomous citation indexing. *IEEE Computer*, 32(6):67–71, 1999.

[20]   S. A. Macskassy and F. Provost. A simple relational classifier. In *KDD Workshop on Multi-Relational Data Mining*, 2003.

[21]   S. Muggleton. Inverse entailment and Progol. *New Generation Computing*, 13:245–286, 1995.

[22]   W. Nutt, Y. Sagiv, and S. Shurin. Deciding equivalences among aggregate queries. In *Proceedings of ACM International Conference on Principles of Database Systems*, 1998.

[23]   C. Perlich and F. Provost. Aggregation-based feature invention and relational concept classes. In *International Conference on Knowledge Discovery and Data Mining*, 2003.

[24]   A. Popescul, G. Flake, S. Lawrence, L. H. Ungar, and C. L. Giles. Clustering and identifying temporal trends in document databases. In *Proceedings of the IEEE Advances in Digital Libraries*, 2000.

[25]   A. Popescul, L. H. Ungar, S. Lawrence, and D. Pennock. Towards structural logistic regression: Combining relational and statistical learning. In *Proceedings of the Workshop on Multi-Relational Data Mining at KDD-2002*, Edmonton, Canada, 2002.

[26]   A. Popescul, L. H. Ungar, S. Lawrence, and D. Pennock. Statistical relational learning for document mining. In *Proceedings of the IEEE International Conference on Data Mining*, 2003.

[27] D. Roth and W. Yih. Relational learning via propositional algorithms: An information extraction case study. In *Proceedings of the International Joint Conference on Artificial Intelligence*, 2001.

[28] G. Salton and M.J. McGill. *Introduction to Modern Information Retrieval.* McGraw-Hill, New York, 1983.

[29] G. Schwartz. Estimating the dimension of a model. *Annals of Statistics*, 6 (2):461–464, 1978.

[30] E. Shapiro. *Algorithmic Program Debugging.* MIT Press, Cambridge, MA, 1983.

[31] A. Srinivasan and R. King. Feature construction with inductive logic programming: A study of quantitative predictions of biological activity aided by structural attributes. *Data Mining and Knowledge Discovery*, 3(1):37–57, 1999.

[32] T. Zhang, R. Ramakrishnan, and M. Livny. Birch: An efficient data clustering method for very large databases. In *Proceedings of ACM International Conference on Management of Data*, 1996.

[33] J. Zhou, B. Stine, D. Foster, and L. Ungar. Streaming feature selection using alpha investing. In *International Conference on Knowledge Discovery and Data Mining*, 2005.

17 Learning a New View of a Database: With an Application in Mammography

Jesse Davis, Elizabeth Burnside, Inês Dutra, David Page,
Raghu Ramakrishnan, Jude Shavlik and Vítor Santos Costa

Statistical relational learning (SRL) algorithms model joint probability distributions over relational databases. However, current SRL techniques that operate on databases are restricted to using only the fields and tables already in the database. Yet, database users often define additional fields or tables, known as views, that can be computed from the existing ones. We augment SRL algorithms by adding the ability to learn new fields. We present two different approaches to view learning. First, we develop a two-step approach where we search for all views of interest and then build a statistical model incorporating the selected views. Second, we describe SAYU-View, which integrates the view generation and model building steps. We motivate view learning in the context of creating an expert system for mammography. We show that view learning significantly improves the performance of the expert system.

17.1 Introduction

Statistical relational learning (SRL) focuses on algorithms for learning statistical models from relational databases. SRL advances beyond Bayesian network learning and related techniques by handling domains with multiple tables, by representing relationships between different rows of the same table, and by integrating data from several distinct databases. Currently, SRL techniques can learn joint probability distributions over the fields of a relational database with multiple tables. Nevertheless, SRL techniques are constrained to use only the tables and fields already in the database, without modification. In contrast, many human users of relational databases find it beneficial to define alternative *views* of a database—further fields or tables that can be computed from existing ones. This chapter shows that SRL algorithms also can benefit from the ability to define new views. Namely, it shows that view learning can be used for more accurate prediction of important fields in the original database.

We augment SRL algorithms by adding the ability to learn new fields, intentionally defined in terms of existing fields and intentional background knowledge. In database terminology, these new fields constitute a learned *view* of the database. We use inductive logic programming (ILP) to learn rules which intentionally define the new fields. We present two different methods to accomplish this goal. The first is a two-step approach where we search for all views of interest. This process is expensive and does not necessarily guarantee selecting the most useful view. The second framework, which we refer to as SAYU-View, has a tighter coupling between view generation and view usage. Our results show that view learning can result in significant benefits.

We present view learning in the specific application of creating an expert system in mammography. We chose this application for a number of reasons. First, it is an important practical application where there has been recent progress in collecting sizable amounts of data. Second, we have access to an expert-developed system. This provides a base reference against which we can evaluate our work [3]. Third, a large proportion of examples are negative. This distribution skew is often found in multi-relational applications. Last, our data consists of a single table. This allows us to compare our techniques against standard propositional learning. In this case, it is sufficient for view learning to extend an existing table with new fields, achieved by using ILP to learn rules for unary predicates. For other applications, it may be desirable to learn predicates of higher arity, which will correspond to learning a view with new tables rather than new fields only.

17.2   View Learning for Mammography

Offering breast cancer screening to the ever-increasing number of women over age 40 represents a great challenge. Cost-effective delivery of mammography screening depends on a consistent balance of high sensitivity and high specificity. It has been demonstrated that subspecialist, expert mammographers achieve this balance and perform significantly better than general radiologists [2, 34]. General radiologists have higher false-positive rates and hence biopsy rates, diminishing the positive predictive value for mammography [2, 34]. Unfortunately, despite the fact that specially trained mammographers detect breast cancer more accurately, there is a longstanding shortage of these individuals [10].

An expert system in mammography has the potential to help the general radiologist approach the effectiveness of a subspecialty expert, thereby minimizing both false-negative and false-positive results. Bayesian networks are probabilistic graphical models that have been applied to the task of breast cancer diagnosis from mammography data [17, 3, 5]. Bayesian networks produce diagnoses with probabilities attached. Because of their graphical nature, they are comprehensible to humans and useful for training. As an example, figure 17.1 shows the structure

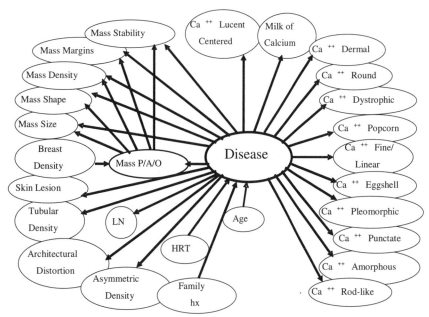

Figure 17.1   Expert Bayes net.

Table 17.1   The National Mammography Database schema, omitting some of the features

Patient	Abnormality	Date	Mass Shape	...	Mass Size	Location	Be/Mal
P1	1	5/02	Spic	...	0.03	RU4	B
P1	2	5/04	Var	...	0.04	RU4	M
P1	3	5/04	Spic	...	0.04	LL4	B
...	...	...	...	...	...	...	...

of a Bayesian network developed by a subspecialist, expert mammographer. For each variable (node) in the graph, the Bayes net has a conditional probability table giving the probability distribution over the values that the variable can take for each possible setting of its parents. The Bayesian network in figure 17.1 achieves accuracies higher than those of other systems and of general radiologists who perform mammograms, and commensurate with the performance of radiologists who specialize in mammography [3].

Table 17.1 shows the main table (with some fields omitted for brevity) in a large relational database of mammography abnormalities. The database schema is specified in the National Mammography Database (NMD) standard established by the American College of Radiology [1]. The NMD was designed to standardize data collection for mammography practices in the United States and is widely used for quality assurance. We omit a second, much smaller *biopsy* table, simply because we are interested in predicting—before the biopsy—whether an abnormality is benign or malignant. Note that the database contains one record per abnormality. By putting the database into one of the standard database "normal" forms, it would be possible to reduce some data duplication, but only a very small amount: the patient's age, status of hormone replacement therapy, and family history could be recorded once per *patient and date* in cases where multiple abnormalities are found on a single mammogram date. Such normalization would have no effect on our approach or results, so we choose to operate directly on the database in its defined form.

Figure 17.2 presents a hierarchy of the four types of learning that might be used for this task. Level 1 and level 2 are standard types of Bayesian network learning. Level 1 is simply learning the parameters for the expert-defined network structure. Level 2 involves learning the actual structure of the network in addition to its parameters. Notice that to predict the probability of malignancy of an abnormality, a Bayes net uses only the record for that abnormality. Nevertheless, data in other rows of the table may also be relevant: radiologists may also consider other abnormalities on the same mammogram or previous mammograms. For example, it may be useful to know that the same mammogram also contains another abnormality, with a particular size and shape; or that the same person had a previous mammogram with certain characteristics. Incorporating data from other rows in the table is not possible with existing Bayesian network learning algorithms and requires SRL techniques, such as probabilistic relational models [12]. Level 3 in figure 17.2 shows the state of the art in SRL techniques, illustrating how relevant fields from other rows (or other tables) can be incorporated into the network, using aggregation if necessary. Rather than using only the size of the abnormality under consideration, the new aggregate field allows the Bayes net to also consider the average size of all abnormalities found in the mammogram.

Presently, SRL is limited to using the original view of the database, that is, the original tables and fields, possibly with aggregation. Despite the utility of aggregation, simply considering only the existing fields may be insufficient for accurate prediction of malignancies. Level 4 in figure 17.2 shows the key capability that will be introduced and evaluated in this chapter: using techniques from rule learning to learn a new *view*. In this figure, the new view includes two new features utilized by the Bayes net that cannot be defined simply by aggregation of existing features. The new features are defined by two learned rules that capture "hidden" concepts potentially useful for accurately predicting malignancy, but that are not explicit in the given database tables. One learned rule states that a change in the shape of an abnormality at a location since an earlier mammogram may be indicative of a malignancy. The other says that an *increase* in the average of the sizes of the abnormalities may be indicative of malignancy. Note that both rules require

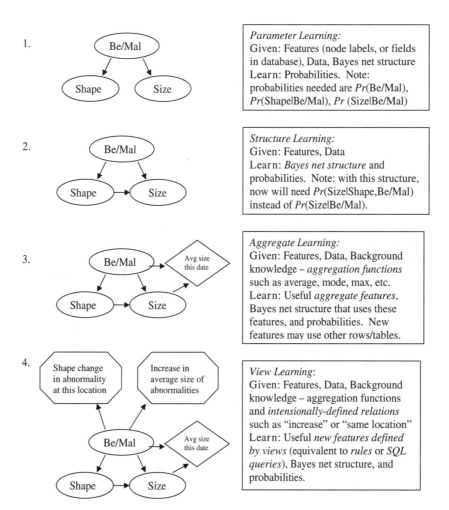

1.   *Parameter Learning:*
     Given: Features (node labels, or fields in database), Data, Bayes net structure
     Learn: Probabilities. Note: probabilities needed are *Pr*(Be/Mal), *Pr*(Shape|Be/Mal), *Pr* (Size|Be/Mal)

2.   *Structure Learning:*
     Given: Features, Data
     Learn: *Bayes net structure* and probabilities. Note: with this structure, now will need *Pr*(Size|Shape,Be/Mal) instead of *Pr*(Size|Be/Mal).

3.   *Aggregate Learning:*
     Given: Features, Data, Background knowledge – *aggregation functions* such as average, mode, max, etc.
     Learn: Useful *aggregate features*, Bayes net structure that uses these features, and probabilities. New features may use other rows/tables.

4.   *View Learning*:
     Given: Features, Data, Background knowledge – aggregation functions and *intensionally-defined relations* such as "increase" or "same location"
     Learn: Useful *new features defined by views* (equivalent to *rules* or *SQL queries*), Bayes net structure, and probabilities.

Figure 17.2 Hierarchy of learning types. Levels 1 and 2 are available through ordinary Bayesian network learning algorithms, level 3 is available only through state-of-the-art SRL techniques, and level 4 is described in this chapter.

reference to other rows in the table for the given patient, as well as intensional background knowledge to define concepts such as "increases over time." Neither rule can be captured by standard aggregation of existing fields.

Note that level 3 and level 4 learning would not be necessary if the database initially contained all the potentially useful fields capturing information from other relevant rows or tables. For example, the database might be initially constructed to contain fields such as "slope of change in abnormality size at this location over time," "average abnormality size on this mammogram," and so on. If humans can identify all such potentially useful fields beforehand and

define views containing these, then level 3 and level 4 learning are unnecessary. Nevertheless, the space of such *possibly* useful fields is quite large, and perhaps more easily searched by computer via level 3 and level 4 learning. Certainly in the case of the National Mammography Database standard [1], such fields were not available because they had not been defined and populated in the database by the domain experts, thus making level 3 and level 4 learning potentially useful.

17.3   Naive View Learning Framework

One can imagine a variety of approaches to perform view learning. As a first step, we apply existing technology to obtain a view learning capability. Any relational database can be naturally and simply represented using a subset of first-order logic [30]. ILP provides algorithms to learn rules, also expressed in logic, from such relational data [22], possibly together with background knowledge expressed as a logic program. ILP systems operate by searching a space of possible logical rules, looking for rules that score well according to some measure of fit to the data.

Our first learning framework works in two steps. First, we learn rules to predict whether an abnormality is malignant. We extend the original database by introducing the new rules as *additional features*. More precisely, each rule will correspond to a binary feature such that it takes the value *true* if the body, or condition, of the rule is satisfied, and *false* otherwise. We then run the Bayesian network structure learning algorithm, allowing it to use these new features in addition to the original features. Section 17.7 notes the relationship of the approach to earlier work on ILP for feature construction.

Below we show a simple rule learned by an ILP system. The rule covers 48 positive examples and 123 negative examples. This rule can now be used as a field in a new view of the database, and consequently as a new feature in the Bayesian network.

```
Abnormality A in mammogram M may be malignant if:
    A's tissue is not asymmetric,
    M contains another abnormality A2,
    A2's margins are spiculated, and
    A2 has no architectural distortion.
```

Note that the last two lines of the rule refer to other rows of the relational table for abnormalities in the database. Hence this rule encodes information not available to the current version of the Bayesian network [9].

17.4 Initial Experiments

The purposes of the experiments we conducted are twofold. First, we want to determine if using SRL yields an improvement compared to propositional learning. Secondly, we want to evaluate whether we see an improvement when moving up a level in the hierarchy outlined in figure 17.2. First, we try to learn a structure with just the original attributes (level 2) and see if that performs better than using the expert structure with trained parameters (level 1). Next, we add aggregate features to our network, representing summaries of abnormalities found either in a particular mammogram or for a particular patient. This corresponds to level 3 and we test whether this improves over levels 1 and 2. Finally, we investigate doing level 4 learning through the two-step algorithm and compare its performance to levels 1 through 3.

We experimented with a number of structure learning algorithms for Bayesian networks, including naive Bayes, tree-augmented nave (TAN) Bayes [11], and the sparse candidate algorithm [13]. However, we obtained the best results with the TAN algorithm in all experiments, so we will focus our discussion on TAN. In a TAN network, each attribute can have at most one other parent in addition to the class variable. The TAN model can be constructed in polynomial time with a guarantee that the model maximizes the log-likelihood of the network structure given the data set [14, 11].

17.4.1 Data and Methodology

We collected data for all screening and diagnostic mammography examinations that were performed at the Froedtert and Medical College of Wisconsin Breast Imaging Center between April 5, 1999 and February 9, 2004. It is important to note that the data consists of a radiologist's interpretation of a mammogram and not the raw image data. The radiologist reports conformed to the National Mammography Database (NMD) standard established by the American College of Radiology. From these reports, we followed the original network [3] to cull the 36 features deemed to be relevant by coauthor Burnside, an expert mammographer.

To evaluate and compare these approaches, we used stratified ten-fold cross-validation. We randomly divided the abnormalities into ten roughly equal-sized sets, each with approximately one-tenth of the malignant abnormalities and one-tenth of the benign abnormalities. When evaluating just the structure learning and aggregation, nine folds were used for the training set. When performing aggregation, we used binning to discretize the created features. We took care to only use the examples from the training set to determine the bin widths. When performing view learning, we had two steps in the learning process. In the first part, four folds of data were used to learn the ILP rules. The remaining five folds were used to learn the Bayes net structure and parameters.

When using cross-validation on a relational database, there exists one major methodological pitfall. Some of the cases may be related. For example, we may have multiple abnormalities for a single patient. Because these abnormalities are related (same patient), having some of these in the training set and others in the test set may cause us to perform better on those test cases than we would expect to perform on cases for other patients. To avoid such "leakage" of information into a training set, we ensured that all abnormalities associated with a particular patient were placed into the same fold for cross-validation. Another potential pitfall is that we may learn a rule that predicts an abnormality to be malignant based on properties of abnormalities in *later* mammograms. We ensured that we will never predict the status of an abnormality at a given date based on findings recorded for later dates.

17.4.2   Approach for Each Level of Learning

Level 1: Parameter learning We estimated the parameters of the expert structure from the data set using maximum likelihood estimates with Laplace correction. It has been previously noted that learning the parameters of the network improves performance over having expert-defined probabilities in each node [4].

Level 2: Structure learning The relational database for the mammography data contains one row for each abnormality described on a mammogram. Fields in this relational table include all those shown in the Bayesian network of figure 17.1. Therefore it is straightforward to use existing Bayesian network structure learning algorithms to learn a possibly improved structure for the Bayesian network.

Level 3: Aggregate learning We selected the numeric (e.g., the size of a mass) and ordered features (e.g., the density of a mass) in the database and computed aggregates for each of these features. In all, we determined that 27 of the 36 attributes were suitable for aggregation. We computed aggregates on both the patient and the mammogram level. On the patient level, we looked at all of the abnormalities for a specific patient. On the mammogram level, we only considered the abnormalities present on that specific mammogram. To discretize the averages, we divided each range into three bins. For binary features we used predefined bin sizes, while for the other features we attempted to get equal numbers of abnormalities in each bin. For aggregation functions we used maximum and average. The aggregation introduced $27 \times 4 = 108$ new features. The following paragraph presents further details of our aggregation process.

We used a three-step process to construct aggregate features. First, we chose a field to aggregate. Second, we selected an aggregation function. Third, we needed to decide over which rows to aggregate the feature, that is, which keys or links to follow. This is known as a slot chain in probabilistic relational models (PRM) terminology [12]. In our database, two such links exist. The patient ID field allows access to all the abnormalities for a given patient, providing aggregation on the

Patient	Abnormality	Date	Mass Shape	...	Mass Size	Location	Average Patient Mass Size	Average Mammogram Mass Size	Be/Mal
P1	1	5/02	Spic	...	0.03	RU4	0.0367	0.03	B
P1	2	5/04	Var	...	0.04	RU4	0.0367	0.04	M
P1	3	5/04	Spic	...	0.04	LL4	0.0367	0.04	B
...	...	...	...	...	...	...	...	...	...

Table 17.2 Database after aggregation on Mass Size field. Note the addition of two new fields, Average Patient Mass Size and Average Mammogram Mass Size, which represent aggregate features.

patient level. The second key is the combination of patient ID and mammogram date, which returns all abnormalities for a patient on a specific mammogram, providing aggregation on the mammogram level. To demonstrate this process, we will work though an example of computing an aggregate feature for patient 1 in the database given in figure 17.1. We will aggregate on the Mass Size field and use average as the aggregation function. Patient 1 has three abnormalities, one from a mammogram in May 2002 and two from a mammogram in May 2004. To calculate the aggregate on the patient level, we average the size for all three abnormalities, which is .0367. To find the aggregate on the mammogram level for patient 1, we have to perform two separate computations. First, we follow the link P1 and 5/02, which yields abnormality 1. The average for this key mammogram is simply .03. Second, we follow the link P1 and 5/04, which yields abnormalities 2 and 3. The average for these abnormalities is .04. Table 17.2 shows the database following construction of these aggregate features.

Level 4: View learning We used the ILP system Aleph [35] to implement level 4 learning. Aleph was asked to learn rules predictive of malignancy. We introduced three new intensional tables into Aleph's background knowledge to take advantage of relational information.

1. The `prior_Mammogram` relation connects information about any prior abnormality that a given patient may have.
2. The `same_Location` relation is a specification of the previous predicate. It adds the restriction that the prior abnormality must be in the same location as the current abnormality. Radiology reports include information about the location of abnormalities.

3. The `in_Same_Mammogram` relation incorporates information about other abnormalities a patient may have on the current mammogram.

By default, Aleph is set up to generate rules that would fully explain the examples. In contrast, our goal was to extract rules that would be beneficial as new views. The major problem in implementing level 4 learning was *how to select rules that would best complement level 3 information.* Clearly, Aleph's standard coverage algorithm was not designed for this application. Instead, we chose to first enumerate as many rules of interest as possible, and then chose interesting rules.

In order to obtain a varied set of rules, we ran Aleph under `induce_max` for each fold. `Induce_max` uses every positive example in each fold as a seed for the search. Also note that `induce_max` does not discard previously covered examples when scoring a new clause. Several thousand distinct rules were learned for each fold, with each rule covering many more malignant cases than (incorrectly covering) benign cases. We avoid the rule overfitting found by other authors [24] by doing breadth-first search for rules and by having a minimal limit on coverage.

Each seed generated anywhere from zero to tens of thousands of rules. Adding all rules would mean introducing thousands of often redundant features. We implemented the following algorithm:

1. We scanned all rules looking for duplicates and for rules that performed worse than a more general rule. This step significantly reduced the number of rules to consider.

2. We sorted rules according to their m-estimate.

3. We used a greedy algorithm that picks the rule with the highest m-estimate such that it covers an unexplained training example. Furthermore, each rule needs to cover a significant number of malignant cases. This step is similar to the standard ILP greedy covering algorithm, except that we do not follow the original order of the seed examples.

4. Last, we scanned the remaining rules, selecting those that covered a significant number of examples, and that were different from all previous rules, *even though these rules would not cover any new examples.*

It is important to note that the rule selection was an automated process. We picked the top fifty clauses in our experiments, obtained from practical considerations on the size of the Bayesian networks we would need to learn. The resulting views were added as new features to the database.

17.4.3   Results

We present the results of our first experiment, comparing levels 1 and 2, using both ROC and precision-recall curves. Figure 17.3 shows the ROC curve for these experiments, and figure 17.4 shows the precision-recall curves. Because of our skewed class distribution, due to the large number of benign cases, we prefer precision-recall curves over ROC curves because they better show the number of

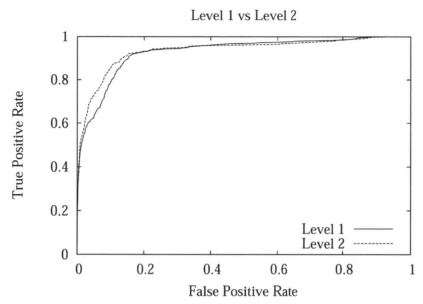

Figure 17.3 ROC curves for parameter learning (level 1) compared to structure learning (level 2).

"false alarms," or unnecessary biopsies. Therefore, we use precision-recall curves for the remainder of the results. Here, precision is the percentage of abnormalities that we classified as malignant that are truly cancerous. Recall is the percentage of malignant abnormalities that were correctly classified. To generate the curves, we pooled the results over all ten folds by treating each prediction as if it had been generated from the same model. We sorted the estimates and used all possible split points to create the graphs.

Figure 17.5 compares performance for all levels of learning. We can observe very significant improvements when adding multi-relational features. Aggregates provide the most benefit for higher recalls whereas rules help in the medium and low ranges of recall. We believe this is because ILP rules are more accurate than the other features, but have limited coverage.

Figure 17.6 shows the average area under the precision-recall curve for each level of learning that we defined in figure 17.2. We only consider recalls above 50%, as for this application radiologists would be required to perform at least at this level. We further use the paired t-test to compare the areas under the curve (recall ≥ 0.5) for every fold. We found improvement of level 2 over level 1 to be statistically significant with a 99% level of confidence. According to the paired t-test the improvement of level 3 presents an improvement over level 2 at the 97% confidence level. Furthermore, level 4 over level 2 is significant, using the area under the curve metric, at the 99% level. However, there is no significant difference between level 3 and level 4.

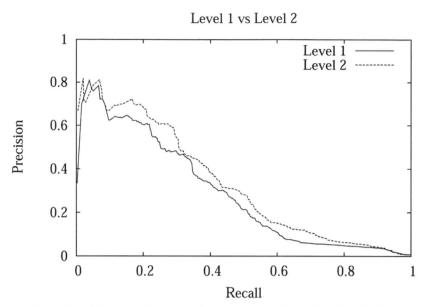

Figure 17.4 Precision-recall curves for parameter learning (level 1) compared to structure learning (level 2).

In this task, considering relational information is still crucial for improving performance since the relational approaches outperform the propositional methods. We mostly see significant improvement as we move the learning hierarchy outlined in figure 17.2. However, in this initial approach we see no significant difference between level 3 and level 4.

The process of generating the views in level 4 can be useful to the radiologist, as it identifies potentially interesting correlations between attributes. During our experiments, we presented coauthor Burnside with a set of 130 rules to review. She found several rules interesting, including the following:

```
Abnormality A in mammogram M for patient P is maligant if:
A has BI-RADS category 5,
A has a mass present,
A has a mass with high density,
P has a prior history of breast cancer,
P has an extra finding on same mammogram (B),
B has no pleomorphic microcalcifications,
B had no punctate calcifications.
```

This rule identified 42 malignant mammographic findings while only misclassifying 11 benign findings as cancer. The radiologist was intrigued by this rule because it suggests a hitherto unknown relationship between malignancy and high-density masses. In general, mass density was not previously thought to be a highly predictive feature, so this rule is valuable in its own right [6].

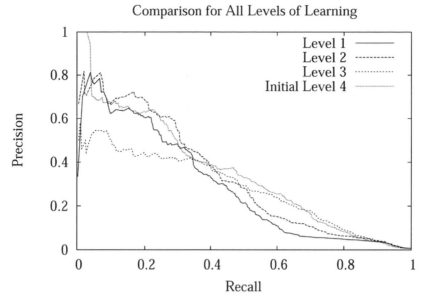

Figure 17.5   Precision-recall curves for each level of learning.

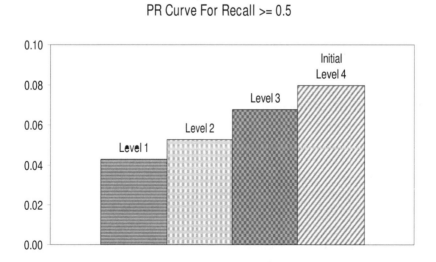

Figure 17.6   Area under the curve for recalls above 50%.

17.5   Integrated View Learning Framework

The initial methodology for level 4 follows a two-step process. In the first step, an ILP algorithm learns a set of rules. In the second step, the learned rules are added to the preexisting features to form a final model. This approach suffers from several weaknesses. First, we follow a brute-force approach to search for all *good* rules, but we have no way to evaluate which ones will actually improve the network. Second, the metric used to score the rules differs from the one we will ultimately use to evaluate the final model. Thus, we have no guarantee that the rule-learning process will select the rules that best contribute to the final classifier.

We propose an alternative approach, based on the idea of *constructing the classifier as we learn the rules* [8]. In the new approach, rules are scored by how much they improve the classifier, providing a tight coupling between rule generation and rule usage. We call this methodology *score as you use* or *SAYU*.

SAYU is closely related to nFOIL [20] and also to the work of Popescul et al. on structural logistic regression [29]. The relationships to these important works are discussed in section 17.7.

Our implementation of SAYU depends on both an ILP system and a propositional learner. Following the original work, we used Aleph as a rule proposer and TAN as our propositional learner.

Our algorithm works as follows. We randomly choose a seed example, and obtain its most specific, or *saturated* clause. We then perform a top-down breadth-first search of the subsumption lattice. We evaluate each clause by converting it to a binary feature, which is added to the current training set. We learn a new Bayes net incorporating this new feature, and score the network. If the new feature improves the score of the network, then we retain the feature in the network. If the feature degrades the performance of the network, it is discarded, and we revert back to the old classifier and continue searching. One other central difference exists with our algorithm compared to Aleph in that after the network accepts a rule, we randomly select a new seed. Thus, we are not searching for the best rule, but only the first rule that helps. However, nothing prevents the same seed from being selected multiple times during the search.

Finally, we need to define a scoring function. The main goal is to use the same scoring function for both learning and evaluation. Furthermore, we wish to be able to handle data sets that have a highly Skewed-class distribution. In the presence of skew, precision and recall are often used to evaluate classifier quality. In order to characterize how the algorithm performs over the whole precision-recall space, we follow Goadrich et al. [15], and adopt the area under the precision-recall curve as our scoring metric. When calculating the area under the precision-recall curve, we integrate from recall levels of 0.5 or greater. As we previously noted, a radiologist would have to achieve levels of recall in this range.

We have previously reported that SAYU performs on a par with level 3 and the initial approach to level 4. However, in these experiments we implemented SAYU

Input: Train Set T, Tune Set S, Stop Criteria
Output: A TAN Model
M = BuildTANClassifier(T);
$BestScore$ = AreaUnderPRCurve(M, S);
while *Stop criteria not met* **do**
    $done$ = false; *Choose* a positive example as a seed and saturate the example;
    repeat
        $NewFeature$ = Generate new clause according to saturated example;
        M_{new} = BuildTANClassifier($T \cup NewFeature$);
        $NewScore$ = AreaUnderPRCurve(M, $S \cup NewFeature$);
        if $NewScore \geq BestScore$ **then**
            $T = T \cup NewFeature$;
            $S = S \cup NewFeature$;
            $BestScore = NewScore$;
            $M = M_{new}$;
            $done$ = true;
        end
    until *not(done)*;
end
return M

Algorithm 1: SAYU-View Algorithm

Figure 17.7   The SAYU-View algorithm.

as a rule combiner only, not as a tool for view learning that *adds* fields to the existing set of fields (features) in the database [8]. We have modified SAYU to take advantage of the predefined features yielding a more integrated approach to view learning. We also report on a more natural design where SAYU starts from the level 3 network. We call this approach SAYU-View. Figure 17.7 gives pseudocode for the SAYU-View algorithm.

17.6   Further Experiments and Results

We use essentially the same methodology as described previously for the initial approach to view learning. On each round of cross-validation, we use four folds as a training set, five folds as a tuning set, and one fold as a test set. We only saturate examples from the training set. For SAYU-View, we use only the training set to learn the rules. The key difference between initial level 4 and SAYU-View is the following: for SAYU-View we use the training set to learn the structure and parameters of the Bayes net, and we use the tuning set to calculate the score of a network structure. Previously, we used the tune set to learn the network structure and parameters. In order to retain a clause in the network, the area under the precision-recall curve of the Bayes net incorporating the rule must achieve at least a 2% improvement over the area of the precision-recall curve of the best Bayes net.

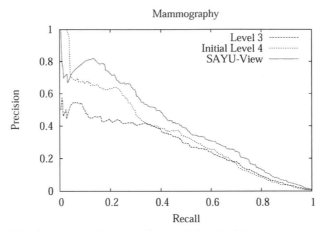

Figure 17.8   Precision-recall curves for each level of learning.

Within SAYU, the time to score a rule has increased. The Bayes net algorithm has to learn a new network topology and new parameters each time we score a rule (feature). Furthermore, inference must be performed to compute the score after incorporating a new feature. The SAYU algorithm is strictly more expensive than standard ILP as SAYU also has to prove whether a rule covers each example in order to create the new feature. To reflect the added cost, we use a time-based stop criterion for the new algorithm. This criterion is described in further detail in [8]. For each fold, we use the times from the baseline experiments in [8], so that our new approach to view learning takes the same time as the old approach. In practice, our settings resulted in evaluating around 20,000 clauses for each fold, requiring on average around four hours per fold on a Xeon 3MHz class machine.

Figure 17.8 includes a comparison of SAYU-View to level 3 and the initial approach to level 4. Again, we perform a two-tailed paired *t*-test on the area under the precision recall curve for levels of recall ≥ 0.5. SAYU-view performs significantly better than both these approaches at the 99% confidence level. Although we do not include the graph, SAYU-View performs significantly better than the SAYU-TAN (no initial features), also with a p-value < 0.01. SAYU-View also performs better than level 1 and level 2 with a p-value < 0.01. With the integrated framework for level 4, we now see significant improvement over lower levels of learning when we ascend the hierarchy defined in figure 17.2.

Figure 17.9 shows the average area under the precision-recall curve (AUCPR) for levels of recall ≥ 0.5 for level 3, the initial approach to level 4, and SAYU-View. The average AUCPR for SAYU-View yields a 30% increase in the average AUCPR over the initial approach to level 4. Furthermore, we see an increase in the average AUCPR of 53% over level 3. Another way to look at these results is the potential reduction of benign biopsies: procedures done on women without cancer. When detecting 90% of cancers (i.e., recall = 0.9), SAYU-View achieves a 35% reduction in benign biopsies over level 3 and a 39% reduction over the initial level 4 method

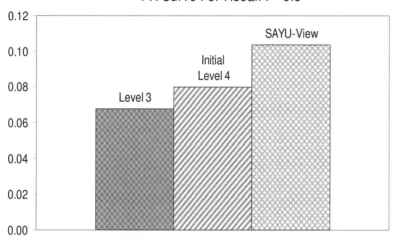

Figure 17.9 Area under the curve for recalls above 50%.

17.7 Related Work

Research in SRL has advanced along two main lines: methods that allow graphical models to represent relations, and frameworks that extend logic to handle probabilities. Along the first line, probabilistic relational models, or PRMs, introduced by Friedman et al., represent one of the first attempts to learn the structure of graphical models while incorporating relational information[12]. Recently Heckerman et al. have discussed extensions to PRMs and compared them to other graphical models[16]. A statistical learning algorithm for probabilistic logic representations was first given by Sato [33], and later Cussens [7] proposed a more general algorithm to handle log-linear models. Additionally, Muggleton [21] has provided learning algorithms for stochastic logic programs. The structure of the logic program is learned using ILP techniques, while the parameters are learned using an algorithm scaled up from that used for stochastic context-free grammars.

Newer representations garnering arguably the most attention are Bayesian logic programs (BLPs)[18], relational Markov networks (RMNs) [37], constraint logic programming with Bayes net constraints, or $CLP(\mathcal{BN})$ [32], and Markov logic networks (MLNs) [31]. MLNs are most similar to our approach. Nodes of MLNs are the ground instances of the literals in the rule, and the arcs correspond to the rules. One major difference is that, in our approach, nodes are the rules themselves. Although we cannot work at the same level of detail, our approach makes it straightforward to combine logical rules with other features, and we now can take full advantage of propositional learning algorithms.

The present work builds upon previous work on using ILP for feature construction. Such work treats ILP-constructed rules as Boolean features, re-represents each example as a feature vector, and then uses a feature-vector learner to produce a final classifier. To our knowledge, Pompe and Kononenko [25] were the first to apply naive Bayes to combine clauses. Other work in this category was by Srinivasan and King [36], who used rules as extra features for the task of predicting biological activities of molecules from their atom and bond structures. Popescul and Unger [26] use $k-means$ to derive cluster relations, which are then combined with the original features through structural regression. In a different vein, relational decision trees [23] use aggregation to provide extra features on a multi-relational setting, and are close to our level 3 setting. Knobbe et al. [19] proposed numeric aggregates in combination with logic-based feature construction for single attributes. Perlich and Provost discuss several approaches for attribute construction using aggregates over multi-relational features [24]. They also propose a hierarchy of levels of learning: feature vectors, independent attributes on a table, multidimensional aggregation on a table, and aggregation across tables. Some of these techniques in their hierarchy could be applied to perform view learning in SRL.

Another approach for a tight coupling between rule learning and rule usage is the recent work (done in parallel with ours) by Landwehr et al. [20]. That work presented a new system called nFOIL. We would like to highlight that several significant differences in the two pieces of work appear to be the following. First, nFOIL scores clauses by conditional log-likelihood rather than improvement in classifier accuracy or classifier AUC (area under ROC or precision-recall curve). Second, nFOIL can handle multiple-class classification tasks, which SAYU cannot. Third, the present chapter reports experiments on data sets with significant class skew, to which probabilistic classifiers are often sensitive. Fourth, this work looks at TAN opposed to naive Bayes. Finally, this work extends both [20] and [8] by giving the network an initial feature set.

Another related piece of work is that by Popescul *et al.* [28, 27, 29] on structural logistic regression. They use an ILP-like (refinement graph) search over rules, expressed as database queries, to define new features. Differences from the present work include their use of the new features within an logistic regression model rather than a graphical model, and the fact that they do not update the logistic regression model after adding each rule. A notable strength of their approach is that the rule-learning process itself can include aggregation.

17.8   Conclusions and Future Work

We presented a method for statistical relational learning which integrates learning from attributes, aggregates, and rules. Our example application shows benefits from the several levels of learning we proposed. Level 2, structure learning, clearly outperforms the expert structure. We further show that multi-relational techniques can achieve very significant improvements, even on a single table domain.

This chapter has shown that a simple form of view learning—treating rules induced by a standard ILP system as the additional features of a new view— yields improved performance over level 2 learning. Nevertheless, this improvement is roughly equal to that obtained by level 3 learning—by aggregation, as might be performed, for example, by a PRM. We have noted how this approach to view learning is quite similar to earlier work using ILP for feature construction.

A more interesting form of view learning, or level 4 learning, is SAYU-View, which closely integrates the ILP system and Bayesian network learning. It significantly improves performance over both level 3 learning and the simple form of view learning.

We believe many further improvements in view learning are possible. It makes sense to include aggregates in the background knowledge for rule generation. Alternatively, one can extend rules with aggregation operators, as proposed in recent work by Vens et al. [38]. We have found the rule selection problem to be nontrivial. Our greedy algorithm often generates too similar rules, and is not guaranteed to maximize coverage. We would like to approach this problem as an optimization problem weighing coverage, diversity, and accuracy.

Our approach of using ILP to learn new features for an existing table merely scratches the surface of the potential for view learning. A more ambitious approach would be to more closely integrate structure learning and view learning. A search could be performed in which each "move" in the search space is either to modify the probabilistic model or to refine the intentional definition of some field in the new view. Going further still, one might learn an intentional definition for an entirely new table. As a concrete example, for mammography one could learn rules defining a binary predicate that identifies "similar" abnormalities. Because such a predicate would represent a many-to-many relationship among abnormalities, a new table would be required.

SRL algorithms provide a substantial extension to existing statistical learning algorithms, such as Bayesian networks, by permitting statistical learning to be applied directly to relational databases with multiple tables. Nevertheless, the schemata for relational databases often are defined based on criteria other than effectiveness of learning. If a schema is not the most appropriate for a given learning task, it may be necessary to change it—by defining a new view—before applying other SRL techniques. View learning, as presented in this chapter, provides an automated capability to make such schema changes. Our approaches so far to view learning build on existing ILP technology. We believe ILP-based view learning can be greatly improved and extended, as outlined in the preceding paragraphs, for example to learn entirely new tables. Furthermore, many approaches to view learning outside of ILP remain to be explored.

Acknowledgments

Support for this research was partially provided by U.S. Air Force grant F30602-01-2-0571. Elizabeth Burnside is supported by a General Electric Research in Radiology Academic Fellowship. Inês Dutra and Vítor Santos Costa did this work while visiting the University of Wisconsin-Madison. Vítor Santos Costa was partially supported by the Fundação para a Ciência e Tecnologia. We thank Lisa Torrey, Mark Goadrich, Rich Maclin, Jill Davis, and Allison Holloway for reading over drafts of this chapter. We also thank the referees for their insightful comments.

References

[1]   American College of Radiology. Breast imaging reporting and data system (bi-rads), 2004. American College of Radiology.

[2]   M. Brown, F. Houn, E. Sickles, and L. Kessler. Screening mammography in community practice: Positive predictive value of abnormal findings and yield of follow-up diagnostic procedures. *American Journal of Roentgenology*, 165: 1373–1377, 1995.

[3]   E. Burnside, D. Rubin, and R. Shachter. A Bayesian network for screening mammography. In *American Medical Informatics Association*, pages 106–110, 2000.

[4]   E. Burnside, Y. Pan, C. Kahn, K. Shaffer, and D. Page. *Training a Probabilistic Expert System to Predict the Likelihood of Breast Cancer Using a Large Dataset of Mammograms (abstract)*. Radiological Society of North America, 2004.

[5]   E. Burnside, D. Rubin, and R. Shachter. Using a Bayesian network to predict the probability and type of breast cancer represented by microcalcifications on mammography. *Medinfo*, 2004:13–17, 2004.

[6]   E. Burnside, J. Davis, V. Santos Costa, I. Dutra, C. Kahn, J. Fine, and D. Page. Knowledge discovery from structured mammography reports using inductive logic programming. In *American Medical Informatics Association Symposium*, pages 96–100, 2005.

[7]   J. Cussens. Parameter estimation in stochastic logic programs. *Machine Learning*, 44(3):245–271, 2001.

[8]   J. Davis, E. Burnside, I. Dutra, D. Page, and V. Santos Costa. An integrated approach to learning Bayesian networks of rules. In *Proceedings of the European Conference on Machine Learning*, 2005.

[9]   J. Davis, E. Burnside, I. Dutra, D. Page, R. Ramakrishnan, V. Santos Costa, and J. Shavlik. View learning for statistical relational learning: With an application to mammography. In *Proceedings of the International Joint Conference on Artificial Intelligence*, 2005.

[10]   G. W. Eklund. Shortage of qualified breast imagers could lead to crisis. *Diagnostic Imaging*, 22:31–33, 2000.

[11]   N. Friedman, D. Geiger, and M. Goldszmidt. Bayesian networks classifiers. *Machine Learning*, 29:131–163, 1997.

[12]   N. Friedman, L. Getoor, D. Koller, and A. Pfeffer. Learning probabilistic relational models. In *Proceedings of the International Joint Conference on Artificial Intelligence*, 1999.

[13]   N. Friedman, I. Nachman, and D. Pe'er. Learning Bayesian network structure from massive datasets: The "sparse candidate" algorithm. In *Proceedings of the Conference on Uncertainty in Artificial Intelligence*, 1999.

[14]   D. Geiger. An entropy-based learning algorithm of Bayesian conditional trees. In *Proceedings of the National Conference on Artificial Intelligence*, 1992.

[15]   M. Goadrich, L. Oliphant, and J. Shavlik. Learning ensembles of first-order clauses for recall-precision curves: A case study in biomedical information extraction. In *Proceedings of the International Conference on Inductive Logic Programming*, 2004.

[16]   D. Heckerman, C. Meek, and D. Koller. Probabilistic entity-relationship models, prms, and plate models. Technical Report MSR-TR-2004-30, Microsoft Research, Seattle,WA, 2004.

[17]   C. Kahn, L. Roberts, K. Shaffer, and P. Haddawy. Construction of a Bayesian network for mammographic diagnosis of breast cancer. *Computers in Biology and Medicine*, 27:19–29, 1997.

[18]   K. Kersting and L. De Raedt. Basic principles of learning Bayesian logic programs. Technical report, Institute for Computer Science, University of Freiburg, Germany, 2002.

[19]   A. J. Knobbe, M. de Haas, and A. Siebes. Propositionalisation and aggregates. In *Proceedings of the European Conference on Principles and Practice of Knowledege Discovery in Databases*, 2001.

[20]   N. Landwehr, K. Kersting, and L. De Raedt. nFOIL: Integrating naive Bayes and FOIL. In *Proceedings of the National Conference on Artificial Intelligence*, 2005.

[21]   S. Muggleton. Learning stochastic logic programs. *Electronic Transactions in Artificial Intelligence*, 4(041), 2000.

[22]   S. Muggleton. Inductive logic programming. *New Generation Computing*, 8: 295–318, 1991.

[23]   J. Neville, D. Jensen, L. Friedland, and M. Hay. Learning relational probability trees. In *International Conference on Knowledge Discovery and Data Mining*, 2003.

[24]   C. Perlich and F. Provost. Aggregation-based feature invention and relational concept classes. In *International Conference on Knowledge Discovery and Data Mining*, 2003.

[25] U. Pompe and I. Kononenko. Naive Bayesian classifier within ILP-R. In L. De Raedt, editor, *Proceedings of the International Conference on Inductive Logic Programming*, 1995.

[26] A. Popescul and L. H. Ungar. Cluster-based concept invention for statistical relational learning. In *International Conference on Knowledge Discovery and Data Mining*, 2004.

[27] A. Popescul and L. H. Ungar. Statistical relational learning for link prediction. In *Workshop on Learning Statistical Models from Relational Data at IJCAI 2003*, 2003.

[28] A. Popescul, L. H. Ungar, S. Lawrence, and D. Pennock. Towards structural logistic regression: Combining relational and statistical learning. In *Workshop on Multi-Relational Data Mining at KDD*, 2002.

[29] A. Popescul, L. H. Ungar, S. Lawrence, and D. M. Pennock. Statistical relational learning for document mining. In *Proceedings of the IEEE International Conference on Data Mining*, 2003.

[30] R. Ramakrishnan and J. Gehrke. *Database Management Systems*. McGraw-Hill, New York, 2000.

[31] M. Richardson and P. Domingos. Markov logic networks. Technical report, Department of Computer Science, University of Washington, 2004.

[32] V. Santos Costa, D. Page, M. Qazi, and J. Cussens. CLP($\mathcal{BN}$): Constraint logic programming for probabilistic knowledge. In *Proceedings of the Conference on Uncertainty in Artificial Intelligence*, 2003.

[33] T. Sato. A statistical learning method for logic programs with distributional semantics. In *Proceedings of the International Conference on Inductive Logic Programming*, 1995.

[34] E. Sickles, D. Wolverton, and K. Dee. Performance parameters for screening and diagnostic mammography: specialist and general radiologists. *Radiology*, 224:861–869, 2002.

[35] A. Srinivasan. *The Aleph Manual*, 2001.

[36] A. Srinivasan and R. King. Feature construction with inductive logic programming: A study of quantitative predictions of biological activity aided by structural attributes. In *Proceedings of the International Conference on Inductive Logic Programming*, 1997.

[37] B. Taskar, P. Abbeel, and D. Koller. Discriminative probabilistic models for relational data. In *Proceedings of the Conference on Uncertainty in Artificial Intelligence*, 2002.

[38] C. Vens, A. Van Assche, H. Blockeel, and S. Džeroski. First order random forests with complex aggregates. In *Proceedings of the International Conference on Inductive Logic Programming*, 2004.

18 Reinforcement Learning in Relational Domains: A Policy-Language Approach

Alan Fern, SungWook Yoon, and Robert Givan

We study reinforcement learning in large relational Markov decision processes (MDPs). We introduce a new variant of approximate policy iteration (API) that replaces the usual value-function learning step with a learning step in policy space. This is advantageous in domains where good policies are easier to represent and learn than the corresponding value functions, which is often the case for the relational MDPs we are interested in. In order to apply API to such problems, we introduce a relational policy language and corresponding learner. In addition, we introduce a new bootstrapping routine for goal-based planning domains, based on random walks. Such bootstrapping is necessary for many large relational MDPs, where reward is extremely sparse, as API is ineffective in such domains when initialized with an uninformed policy. Our experiments show that the resulting system is able to find good policies for a number of classical planning domains and their stochastic variants by solving them as extremely large relational MDPs.

18.1 Introduction

Many planning domains are most most naturally represented in terms of objects and relations among them. Accordingly, AI researchers have long studied algorithms for planning and learning-to-plan in relational state and action spaces. These include, for example, "classical" STRIPS domains such as the blocks world and logistics.

A common criticism of such domains and algorithms is the assumption of an idealized, deterministic world model. This, in part, has led AI researchers to study planning and learning within a decision-theoretic framework, which explicitly handles stochastic environments and generalized reward-based objectives. However, most of this work is based on explicit or propositional state-space models, and so far has not demonstrated scalability to the large relational domains that are commonly addressed in classical planning.

Intelligent agents must be able to simultaneously deal with both the complexity arising from relational structure and the complexity arising from uncertainty. The primary goal of this research is to move toward such agents by bridging the gap between classical and decision-theoretic techniques.

In this chapter, we describe a straightforward and practical method for solving very large, relational Markov decision processes (MDPs). Our work can be viewed as a form of relational reinforcement learning (RRL) where we assume a strong simulation model of the environment. That is, we assume access to a black-box simulator, for which we can provide any (relationally represented) state/action pair and receive a sample from the appropriate next-state and reward distributions. The goal is to interact with the simulator in order to learn a policy for achieving high expected reward. It is a separate challenge, not considered here, to combine our work with methods for learning the environment simulator to avoid dependence on being provided such a simulator.

Dynamic-programming approaches to finding optimal control policies in MDPs [6, 25], using explicit (flat) state-space representations, break down when the state space becomes extremely large. More recent work extends these algorithms to use propositional [8, 11, 12, 9, 18, 21] as well as relational [10, 20] state-space representations. These extensions have significantly expanded the set of approachable problems, but have not yet shown the capacity to solve large classical planning problems such as the benchmark problems used in planning competitions [3], let alone their stochastic variants (see section 18.6 for example benchmarks). One possible reason for this is that these methods are based on calculating and representing value functions. For familiar STRIPS planning domains (among others), useful value functions can be difficult to represent compactly, and their manipulation becomes a bottleneck.

Most of the above techniques are purely deductive—that is, each value function is guaranteed to have a certain level of accuracy. Rather, in this work, we will focus on inductive techniques that make no such guarantees in practice. Existing inductive forms of approximate policy iteration (API) utilize machine learning to select compactly represented approximate value functions at each iteration of dynamic programming [7]. As with any machine learning algorithm, the selection of the hypothesis space, here a space of value functions, is critical to performance. An example space used frequently is the space of linear combinations of a human-selected feature set.

To our knowledge, there has been no previous work that applies any form of API to benchmark problems from classical planning, or their stochastic variants.[1]

---

1. Recent work in *relational reinforcement learning* has been applied to STRIPS problems with much simpler goals than typical benchmark planning domains, and is discussed below in section 18.7.

Again, one reason for this is the high complexity of typical value functions for these large relational domains, making it difficult to specify good value-function spaces that facilitate learning. Comparably, it is often much easier to compactly specify good policies, and accordingly good policy spaces for learning. This observation is the basis for recent work on inductive policy selection in relational planning domains, both deterministic [29, 33], and probabilistic [51]. These techniques show that useful policies can be learned using a policy-space bias described by a generic (relational) knowledge representation language. Here we incorporate those ideas into a novel variant of API that achieves significant success without representing or learning approximate value functions. Of course, a natural direction for future work is to combine policy-space techniques with value-function techniques, to leverage the advantages of both.

Given an initial policy, our approach uses the simulation technique of policy rollout [46] to generate trajectories of an improved policy. These trajectories are then given to a classification learner, which searches for a classifier, or policy, that "matches" the trajectory data, resulting in an approximately improved policy. These two steps are iterated until no further improvement is observed. The resulting algorithm can be viewed as a form of API where the iteration is carried out without inducing approximate value functions.

By avoiding value-function learning, this algorithm addresses the representational challenge of applying API to relational planning domains. However, another fundamental challenge is that, for nontrivial relational domains, API requires some form of bootstrapping. In particular, for most STRIPS planning domains the reward, which corresponds to achieving a goal condition, is sparsely distributed and unlikely to be reached by random exploration. Thus, initializing API with a random or uninformed policy, will likely result in no reward signal and hence no guidance for policy improvement. One approach to bootstrapping is to rely on the user to provide a good initial policy or heuristic that gives guidance toward achieving reward. Rather, in this work we develop a new automatic bootstrapping approach for goal-based planning domains which does not require user intervention.

Our bootstrapping approach is based on the idea of random-walk problem distributions. For a given planning domain, such as the blocks world, this distribution randomly generates a problem (i.e., an initial state and a goal) by selecting a random initial state and then executing a sequence of n random actions, taking the goal condition to be a subset of properties from the resulting state. The problem difficulty typically increases with n, and for small n (short random walks) even random policies can uncover reward. Intuitively, a good policy for problems with walk length n can be used to bootstrap API for problems with slightly longer walk lengths. Our bootstrapping approach iterates this idea, by starting with a random policy and very small n, and then gradually increasing the walk length until we learn a policy for very long random walks. Such long-random-walk policies clearly capture much domain knowledge, and can be used in various ways. Here, we show that empirically such policies often perform well on problems distributions from relational domains used in recent deterministic and probabilistic planning competitions.

Here, we give an evaluation of our system on a number of probabilistic and deterministic relational planning domains, including the AIPS-2000 competition benchmarks, and benchmarks from the hand-tailored track of the 2004 Probabilistic Planning Competition. The results show that the system is often able to learn policies in these domains that perform well for long-random-walk problems. In addition, these same policies often perform well on the planning-competition problem distributions, comparing favorably with the state-of-the-art planner Fast-Forward (FF) [24] in the deterministic domains. Our experiments also highlight a number of limitations of our current system, which point to interesting directions for future work.

The remainder of this chapter proceeds as follows. In section 18.2, we introduce our problem setup and then, in section 18.3, present our new variant of API. In sections 18.4 and 18.5, we describe an implemented instantiation of our API approach for relational planning domains. This includes a description of a generic policy language for relational domains, a classification learner for that language, and a novel bootstrapping technique for goal-based domains. Section 18.6 presents our empirical results, and finally sections 18.7 and 18.8 discuss related work and future directions.

18.2   Problem Setup

We formulate our work in the framework of MDPs. While our primary motivation is to develop algorithms for relational planning domains, we first describe our problem setup and approach for a general, action-simulator-based MDP representation. Later, in section 18.4, we describe a particular representation of planning domains as relational MDPs and the corresponding relational instantiation of our approach.

Following and adapting Kearns et al. [27] and Bertsekas and Tsitsiklis [7], we represent an MDP using a generative model $\langle S, A, T, R, I \rangle$, where S is a finite set of states, A is a finite, *ordered* set of actions, and T is a randomized "action-simulation" algorithm that, given state s and action a, returns a next state s' according to some unknown probability distribution $P_T(s'|s, a)$. The component R is a reward function that maps $S \times A$ to real numbers, with $R(s, a)$ representing the reward for taking action a in state s, and I is a randomized "initial-state algorithm" with no inputs that returns a state s according to some unknown distribution $P_0(s)$. We sometimes treat I and $T(s, a)$ as random variables with distributions $P_0(\cdot)$ and $P_T(\cdot|s, a)$ respectively.

For an MDP $M = \langle S, A, T, R, I \rangle$, a policy π is a (possibly stochastic) mapping from S to A. The *value function* of π, denoted $V^\pi(s)$, represents the expected, cumulative, discounted reward of following policy π in M starting from state s, and is the unique solution to

$$V^\pi(s) = E[R(s, \pi(s)) + \gamma V^\pi(T(s, \pi(s)))],$$

where $0 \leq \gamma < 1$ is the discount factor. The *Q-value function* $Q^\pi(s, a)$ represents the expected, cumulative, discounted reward of taking action a in state s and then following π, and is given by

$$Q^\pi(s, a) = R(s, a) + \gamma E[V^\pi(T(s, a))]. \tag{18.1}$$

We will measure the quality of a policy by the objective function $\overline{V}(\pi) = E[V^\pi(I)]$, giving the expected value obtained by that policy when starting from a randomly drawn initial state. A common objective in MDP planning and reinforcement learning is to find an optimal policy $\pi^* = \mathrm{argmax}_\pi \overline{V}(\pi)$. However, no automated technique, including the one we present here, has to date been able to guarantee finding an optimal policy in the relational planning domains we consider, in reasonable running time.

It is a well-known fact that given a current policy π, we can define a new improved policy

$$\mathcal{PI}^\pi(s) = \mathrm{argmax}_{a \in A} Q^\pi(s, a) \tag{18.2}$$

such that the value function of $\mathcal{PI}^\pi$ is guaranteed to (1) be no worse than that of π at each state s, and (2) strictly improve at some state when π is not optimal. *Policy iteration* is an algorithm for computing optimal policies by iterating policy improvement ($\mathcal{PI}$) from any initial policy to reach a fixed point, which is guaranteed to be an optimal policy. Each iteration of policy improvement involves two steps: (1) *policy evaluation*, where we compute the value function V^π of the current policy π, and (2) *policy selection*, where, given V^π from step 1, we select the action that maximizes $Q^\pi(s, a)$ at each state, defining a new improved policy.

18.3   Approximate Policy Iteration with a Policy Language Bias

Exact solution techniques, such as policy iteration, are typically intractable for large state space MDPs, such as those arising from relational planning domains. In this section, we introduce a new variant of API intended for such domains. First, we review a generic form of API used in prior work, based on learning approximate value functions. Next, motivated by the fact that value functions are often difficult to learn in relational domains, we describe our API variant, which avoids learning value functions and instead learns policies directly as state-action mappings.

18.3.1   API with Approximate Value Functions

API, as described in Bertsekas and Tsitsiklis [7], uses a combination of Monte Carlo simulation and inductive machine learning to heuristically approximate policy iteration in large state-space MDPs. Given a current policy π, each iteration of API approximates policy evaluation and policy selection, resulting in an approximately improved policy $\hat{\pi}$. First, the policy evaluation step constructs a training set of samples of V^π from a "small" but "representative" set of states. Each sample is computed using simulation, estimating $V^\pi(s)$ for the policy π at each state s by drawing some number of sample trajectories of π starting at s and then averaging the cumulative, discounted reward along those trajectories. Next, the policy selection step uses a function approximator (e.g., a neural network) to learn an approximation $\hat{V}^\pi$ to V^π based on the training data. $\hat{V}^\pi$ then serves as a representation for $\hat{\pi}$, which selects actions using sampled one-step lookahead based on $\hat{V}^\pi$, using

$$\hat{\pi}(s) = \arg\max_{a \in A} R(s,a) + \gamma E[\hat{V}^\pi(T(s,a))].$$

A common variant of this procedure learns an approximation of Q^π rather than V^π.

API exploits the function approximator's generalization ability to avoid evaluating each state in the state space, instead only directly evaluating a small number of training states. Thus, the use of API assumes that states and perhaps actions are represented in a factored form (typically, a feature vector) that facilitates generalizing properties of the training data to the entire state and action spaces. Note that in the case of perfect generalization (i.e., $\hat{V}^\pi(s) = V^\pi(s)$ for all states s), we have that $\hat{\pi}$ is equal to the exact policy improvement $\mathcal{PI}^\pi$, and thus API simulates exact policy iteration. However, in practice, generalization is not perfect, and there are typically no guarantees for policy improvement[2]—nevertheless, API often "converges" usefully [45, 47].

The success of the above API procedure depends critically on the ability to represent and learn good value-function approximations. For some MDPs, such as those arising from relational planning domains, it is often difficult to specify a space of value functions and learning mechanism that facilitate good generalization. For example, work in relational reinforcement learning [13] has shown that learning approximate value functions for classical domains, such as the blocks world, can be problematic.[3] In spite of this, it is often relatively easy to compactly specify good policies using a language for (relational) state-action mappings. This suggests that

---

2. Under very strong assumptions, API can be shown to converge in the infinite limit to a near-optimal policy [7].
3. In particular, the RRL work has considered a variety of value-function representation including relational regression trees, instance-based methods, and graph kernels, but none of them have generalized well over varying numbers of objects.

such languages may provide useful policy-space biases for learning in API. However, all prior API methods are based on approximating value functions and hence can not leverage these biases. With this motivation, we introduce a new form of API that directly learns policies without directly representing or approximating value functions.

18.3.2   Using a Policy Language Bias

A policy is simply a classifier that maps states to actions. Our API approach is based on this view, and is motivated by recent work that casts policy selection as a standard classification learning problem. In particular, given the ability to observe trajectories of a target policy, we can use machine learning to select a policy, or classifier, that mimics the target as closely as possible. This idea has been studied previously under the name "behavioral cloning" [44]. Khardon [30] studied this learning setting and provided PAC-like learnability results, showing that under certain assumptions, a small number of trajectories is sufficient to learn a policy whose value is close to that of the target. In addition, recent empirical work, in relational planning domains [29, 33, 51], has shown that by using expressive languages for specifying state-action mappings, good policies can be learned from sample trajectories of good policies.

These results suggest that, given a policy π, if we can somehow generate trajectories of an improved policy, then we can learn an approximately improved policy based on those trajectories. This idea is the basis of our approach. Figure 18.1 gives pseudocode for our API variant, which starts with an initial policy π_0 and produces a sequence of approximately improved policies. Each iteration involves two primary steps: First, given the current policy π, the procedure **Improved-Trajectories** (approximately) generates trajectories of the improved policy $\pi' = \mathcal{P}I^\pi$. Second, these trajectories are used as training data for the procedure **Learn-Policy**, which returns an approximation of π'. We now describe each step in more detail.

Step 1: Generating Improved-Trajectories Given a base policy policy π, the simulation technique of *policy rollout* [46, 7] computes an approximation $\hat{\pi}$ to the improved policy $\pi' = \mathcal{P}I^\pi$, where π' is the result of applying one step of policy iteration to π. Furthermore, for a given state s, policy rollout computes $\hat{\pi}(s)$ without the need to solve for π' at all other states, and thus provides a tractable way to approximately simulate the improved policy π' in large state-space MDPs. Often π' is significantly better than π, and hence so is $\hat{\pi}$, which can lead to substantially improved performance at a small cost. Policy rollout has provided significant benefits in a number of application domains, including, for example, backgammon [46], instruction scheduling [37], network congestion control [49], and solitaire [50].

Policy rollout computes $\hat{\pi}(s)$, the estimate of $\pi'(s)$, by estimating $Q^\pi(s,a)$ for each action a and then taking the maximizing action to be $\hat{\pi}(s)$ as suggested by (18.2). Each $Q^\pi(s,a)$ is estimated by drawing w trajectories of length h, where each trajectory is the result of starting at s, taking action a, and then following the

---

API $(n, w, h, M, \pi_0, \gamma)$

$\pi \leftarrow \pi_0$;

loop
   $T \leftarrow$ **Improved-Trajectories**(n, w, h, M, π);
   $\pi \leftarrow$ **Learn-Policy**(T);
until satisfied with π;   *// e.g. until change is small*

Return π;

Improved-Trajectories(n, w, h, M, π)

// training set size n, sampling width w,
// horizon h, MDP M, current policy π

$T \leftarrow \emptyset$;

repeat n times   *// generate n trajectories of improved policy*
   $t \leftarrow$ **nil**;
   $s \leftarrow$ state drawn from I; *// draw random initial state*
   for $i = 1$ to h
      $\langle \hat{Q}(s, a_1), \ldots, \hat{Q}(s, a_m) \rangle \leftarrow$ **Policy-Rollout**(π, s, w, h, H);
      $t \leftarrow t \cdot \langle s, \pi(s), \hat{Q}(s, a_1), \ldots, \hat{Q}(s, a_m)) \rangle$; *// concatenate sample to trajectory*
      $a \leftarrow$ action maximizing $\hat{Q}(s, a)$; *// action of the improved policy at state s*
      $s \leftarrow$ state sampled from $T(s, a)$; *// simulate action of improved policy*
   $T \leftarrow T \cup t$;
Return T;

Policy-Rollout (s, w, h, M, π)
// policy π, state s, sampling width w, horizon h, cost estimator H

for each action a_i in A
   $\hat{Q}(s, a_i) \leftarrow 0$;
   repeat w times   *// $\hat{Q}(s, a_i)$ is an average over w trajectories*
      $R \leftarrow R(s, a_i)$;
      $s' \leftarrow$ a state sampled from $T(s, a_i)$; *// take action a_i in s*
      for $i = 1$ to $h - 1$ *// take $h - 1$ steps of π, accumulating reward in R*
         $R \leftarrow R + \gamma^i R(s', \pi(s'))$;
         $s' \leftarrow$ a state sampled from $T(s', \pi(s'))$
      $\hat{Q}(s, a_i) \leftarrow \hat{Q}(s, a_i) + R$; *// include trajectory in average*
   $\hat{Q}(s, a_i) \leftarrow \frac{\hat{Q}(s, a_i)}{w}$;
Return $\langle \hat{Q}(s, a_1), \ldots, \hat{Q}(s, a_m) \rangle$

Figure 18.1 Pseudocode for our API algorithm. See section 18.4.3 for an instantiation of **Learn-Policy** called **Learn-Decision-List**.

actions selected by π for $h-1$ steps. The estimate of $Q^\pi(s, a)$ is then taken to be the average of the cumulative discounted reward along each trajectory. The *sampling width w* and *horizon h* are specified by the user, and control the tradeoff between increased computation time for large values, and reduced accuracy for small values.

The procedure **Improved-Trajectories** uses rollout to generate n length h trajectories of the improved policy $\hat{\pi}$, each trajectory beginning at a randomly drawn initial state. Rather than just recording the sequence of states encountered and actions selected by $\hat{\pi}$ along each trajectory, we store additional information that is used by our policy-learning algorithm. In particular, the ith element of a trajectory has the form $\langle s_i, \pi(s_i), \hat{Q}(s_i, a_1), \ldots, \hat{Q}(s_i, a_m) \rangle$, giving the ith state s_i along the trajectory, the action selected by the current (unimproved) policy at s_i, and the Q-value estimates $\hat{Q}(s_i, a)$ for each action. Thus each trajectory generated by **Improved-Trajectories** records for each state the action selected by $\hat{\pi}$ and the Q-values for all actions. Note that given the Q-value information for s_i the learning algorithm can determine the approximately improved action $\hat{\pi}(s)$, by maximizing over actions, if desired.

Step 2: Learn-Policy Intuitively, we want **Learn-Policy** to select a new policy that closely "matches" the training trajectories. In our experiments, we use relatively simple learning algorithms based on greedy search within a space of policies specified by a policy-language bias. In sections 18.4.2 and 18.4.3 we detail the policy-language learning bias used by our technique, and the associated learning algorithm. In Fern et al. [16] we provide a technical analysis of an idealized version of this algorithm, providing guidance regarding the number of training trajectories, horizon, and sampling width required to guarantee policy improvement with high probability. We note that by labeling each training state in the trajectories with the associated Q-values for each action, rather than simply with the best action, we enable the learner to make more informed tradeoffs, focusing on accuracy at states where wrong decisions have high costs, which was empirically useful. Also, the inclusion of $\pi(s)$ in the training data enables the learner to adjust the data relative to π, if desired—e.g., our learner uses a bias that focuses on states where large improvement appears possible.

Finally, we note that for API to be effective, it is important that the initial policy π_0 provide guidance toward improvement, i.e., π_0 must "bootstrap" the API process. For example, in goal-based planning domains π_0 should reach a goal from some of the sampled states. In section 18.5 we will discuss this important issue of bootstrapping and introduce a new bootstrapping technique.

18.4 API for Relational Planning

Our work is motivated by the goal of solving relational MDPs. In particular, we are interested in finding policies for relational MDPs that represent classical planning domains and their stochastic variants. Such policies can then be applied to any problem instance from a planning domain, and hence can be viewed as a form of domain-specific control knowledge.

In this section, we first describe a straightforward way to view classical planning domains (not just single problem instances) as relationally factored MDPs. Next, we describe our relational policy space in which policies are compactly represented as taxonomic decision lists. Finally, we present a heuristic learning algorithm for this policy space.

18.4.1   Planning Domains as MDPs

We say that an MDP $\langle S, A, T, R, I \rangle$ is *relational* when S and A are defined by giving a finite set of objects O, a finite set of predicates P, and a finite set of action types Y. A *fact* is a predicate applied to the appropriate number of objects, e.g., $\mathbf{on}(a, b)$ is a blocks-world fact. A state is a set of facts, interpreted as representing the "true" facts in the state. The state space S contains all possible sets of facts. An *action* is an action type applied to the appropriate number of objects, e.g., $\mathbf{putdown}(a)$, is a blocks-world action, and the action space A is the set of all such actions.

A classical planning domain describes a set of problem instances with related structure, where a problem instance gives an initial world state and goal. For example, the blocks world is a classical planning domain, where each problem instance specifies an initial block configuration and a set of goal conditions. Classical planners attempt to find solutions to specific problem instances of a domain. Rather, our goal is to "solve" entire planning domains by finding a policy that can be applied to all problem instances. As described below, it is straightforward to view a classical planning domain as a relational MDP where each MDP state corresponds to a problem instance.

State and Action Spaces Each classical planning domain specifies a set of action types Y, *world predicates* W, and possible world objects O. Together, Y and O define the MDP action space. Each state of the MDP corresponds to a single problem instance (i.e., a world state and a goal) from the planning domain by specifying both the current world and the goal. We achieve this by letting the set of relational MDP predicates be $P = W \cup G$, where G is a set of *goal predicates*. The set of goal predicates contains a predicate for each world predicate in W, which is named by prepending a "'g" onto the corresponding world predicate name (e.g., the goal predicate $\mathbf{gclear}$ corresponds to the world predicate $\mathbf{clear}$). With this definition of P we see that the MDP states are a set of goal and world facts, indicating the true world facts of a problem instance and the goal conditions. It is important to note, as described below, that the MDP actions will only change world facts and not goal facts. Thus, this large relational MDP can be viewed as a collection of disconnected sub-MDPs, where each sub-MDP corresponds to a distinct goal condition.

Reward Function Given an MDP state the objective is to reach another MDP state where the goal facts are a subset of the corresponding world facts—i.e., reach a world state that satisfies the goal. We will call such states *goal states* of the MDP.

For example, the MDP state

$$\{\textbf{on-table}(a), \textbf{on}(a, b), \textbf{clear}(b), \textbf{gclear}(b)\}$$

is a goal state in a blocks-world MDP, but would not be a goal state without the world fact **clear**(b). We represent the objective of reaching a goal state "quickly" by defining R to assign a reward of zero for actions taken in goal states and negative rewards for actions in all other states, representing the cost of taking those actions. Typically, for classical planning domains, the action costs are uniformly 1; however, our framework allows the cost to vary across actions.

Transition Function Each classical planning domain provides an action simulator (e.g., as defined by STRIPS rules) that, given a world state and action, returns a new world state. We define the MDP transition function T to be this simulator modified to treat goal states as terminal and to preserve without change all goal predicates in an MDP state. Since classical planning domains typically have a large number of actions, the action definitions are usually accompanied by preconditions that indicate the *legal actions* in a given state, where usually the legal actions are a small subset of all possible actions. We assume that T treats actions that are not legal as no-ops. For simplicity, our relational MDP definition does not explicitly represent action preconditions; however, we assume that our algorithms do have access to preconditions and thus only need to consider legal actions. For example, we can restrict rollout to only the legal actions in a given state.

Initial State Distribution Finally, the initial state distribution I can be any program that generates legal problem instances (MDP states) of the planning domain. For example, problem domains from planning competitions are commonly distributed with problem generators.

With these definitions, a good policy is one that can reach goal states via low-cost action sequences from initial states drawn from I. Note that here policies are mappings from problem instances to actions and thus can be sensitive to goal conditions. In this way, our learned policies are able to generalize across different goals. We next describe a language for representing such "generalized policies."

18.4.2   Taxonomic Decision List Policies

For single argument action types, many useful rules for planning domains take the form of "apply action type A to any object in class C" [33]. For example, in the blocks world a useful planning rule might be, "Pick up any clear block that belongs on the table but is not on the table," or in a logistics world, "Unload any object that is at its destination." This motivates the idea of using a formal class description language for representing such classes or sets of objects, and then learning policies that are represented via rules expressed in that language. In particular, if the selected class description language can compactly encode useful classes of objects, then we can learn rules for the policy by simply searching over short class descriptions.

This idea was first explored by Martin and Geffner [33] who introduced the use of decision lists of such rules, using description logic as a class description language. Their experiments in the deterministic blocks world showed promising results, highlighting the potential benefits of using class description languages to represent policies. With that motivation, we consider a policy space that is similar to the one used originally by Martin and Geffner, but generalized to handle multiple action arguments. Also, for historical reasons, rather than use description logic as our class description language, we use taxonomic syntax [35, 36], as described below.

Comparison Predicates For relational MDPs with world and goal predicates, such as those corresponding to classical planning domains, it is often useful for policies to compare the current state with the goal. To this end, we introduce a new set of predicates, called *comparison predicates*, which are derived from the world and goal predicates. For each world predicate p and corresponding goal predicate gp, we introduce a new comparison predicate cp that is defined as the conjunction of p and gp. That is, a comparison predicate fact is true if and only if both the corresponding world and goal predicates facts are true. For example, in the blocks world, the comparison predicate fact $\mathbf{con}(a, b)$ indicates that a is on b in both the current state and the goal—i.e., $\mathbf{on}(a, b)$ and $\mathbf{gon}(a, b)$ are true.

Taxonomic Syntax Taxonomic syntax provides a language for writing class expressions that represent sets of objects with properties of interest and serve as the fundamental pieces with which we build policies. Class expressions are built from the MDP predicates (including comparison predicates if applicable) and variables. In our policy representation, the variables will be used to denote action arguments, and at run-time will be instantiated by objects. For simplicity we only consider predicates of arity one and two, which we call *primitive classes* and relations, respectively. When a domain contains predicates of arity three or more, we automatically convert them to multiple auxiliary binary predicates. Given a list of variables $X = (x_1, \ldots, x_k)$, the syntax of class expressions is given by

$$C[X] ::= C_0 \mid x_i \mid \mathbf{a\text{-}thing} \mid \neg C[X] \mid (R \ C[X]) \mid (\min \ R)$$
$$R ::= R_0 \mid R^{-1} \mid R^*,$$

where $C[X]$ is a class expression, R is a relation expression, C_0 is a primitive class, R_0 is a primitive relation, and x_i is a variable in X. Note that, for classical planning domains, the primitive classes and relations can be world, goal, or comparison predicates. We define the *depth* $d(C[X])$ of a class expression $C[X]$ to be one if $C[X]$ is either a primitive class, **a-thing**, a variable, or $(\min \ R)$; otherwise we define $d(\neg C[X])$ and $d(R \ C[X])$ to be $d(C[X]) + 1$, where R is a relation expression and $C[X]$ is a class expression. For a given relational MDP we denote by $\mathcal{C}_d[X]$ the set of all class expressions $C[X]$ that have a depth of d or less.

The semantics of class expressions are given in terms of an MDP state s and a variable assignment $O = (o_1, \ldots, o_k)$, which assigns object o_i to variable x_i. The interpretation of $C[X]$ relative to s and O is a set of objects and is denoted by $C[X]^{s,O}$. A primitive class C_0 is interpreted as the set of objects for which the predicate symbol C_0 is true in s. For example, in the blocks world, the primitive class expressions **clear** and **gclear** represent the sets of blocks that are clear in the current world state and clear in the goal respectively. Likewise, a primitive relation R_0 is interpreted as the set of all object tuples for which the relation R_0 holds in s. For example, the primitive relation expression **on** represents the set of all pairs of blocks (o_1, o_2) such that o_1 is on o_2 in the current world state. The class expression **a-thing** denotes the set of all objects in s. The class expression x_i, where x_i is a variable, is interpreted to be the singleton set $\{o_i\}$.

The interpretation of compound expressions is given by

$$(\neg C[X])^{s,O} = \{o \mid o \notin C[X]^{s,O}\}$$
$$(R \; C[X])^{s,O} = \{o \mid \exists o' \in C[X]^{s,O} \text{ s.t. } (o', o) \in R^{s,O}\}$$
$$(min \; R)^{s,O} = \{o \mid \exists o' \text{ s.t. } (o, o') \in R^{s,O}, \nexists o' \text{ s.t. } (o', o) \in R^{s,O}\}$$
$$(R^*)^{s,O} = \mathbf{ID} \cup \{(o_1, o_v) \mid \exists o_2, \dots, o_{v-1} \text{ s.t. } (o_i, o_{i+1}) \in R^{s,O} \text{ for } 1 \le i < v\}$$
$$(R^{-1})^{s,O} = \{(o, o') \mid (o', o) \in R^{s,O}\},$$

where $C[X]$ is a class expression, R is a relation expression, and $\mathbf{ID}$ is the identity relation. Intuitively the class expression $(R \; C[X])$ denotes the set of objects that are related through relation R to some object in the set $C[X]$. For example, in the blocks world, the expression (**on on-table**) denotes the set of blocks that are currently on a block that is on the table. The expression $(R^* \; C[X])$ denotes the set of objects that are related through some "R chain" to an object in $C[X]$—this constructor is important for representing recursive concepts. For example, the expression (**on*** a), where a is a block, represents the set of blocks that are currently above a. The expression (min R) denotes the set of objects that are minimal under the relation R. For example, the expression (min **on**) represents the set of blocks that have no blocks above them, and are on some other block (i.e., the set of clear blocks).

The following class expressions are some examples of useful blocks-world concepts, given the primitive classes **clear**, **gclear**, **holding**, and **con-table**, along with the primitive relations **on**, **gon**, and **con**.

- (**gon^{-1} holding**) has depth two, and denotes the block that we want under the block being held.

- (**on*** (**on gclear**)) has depth three, and denotes the blocks currently above blocks that we want to make clear.

- (**con*** **con-table**) has depth two, and denotes the set of blocks in well-constructed towers.

- (**gon** (**con*** **con-table**)) has depth three, and denotes the blocks that belong on top of a currently well-constructed tower.

Decision-List Policies We represent policies as decision lists of *action-selection rules*. Each rule has the form $a(x_1, \dots, x_k) : L_1, L_2, \dots L_m$, where a is a k-argument action type, the L_i are *literals*, and the x_i are action-argument variables. We will denote the list of action-argument variables as $X = (x_1, \ldots, x_k)$. Each literal has the form $x \in C[X]$, where $C[X]$ is a taxonomic syntax class expression and x is an action-argument variable.

Given an MDP state s and a list of action-argument objects $O = (o_1, \ldots, o_k)$, we say that a literal $x_i \in C[X]$ is true given s and O iff $o_i \in C[X]^{s,O}$. We say that a rule $R = a(x_1, \ldots, x_k) : L_1, L_2, \ldots L_m$ allows action $a(o_1, \ldots o_k)$ in s iff each literal in the rule is true given s and O. Note that if there are no literals in a rule for action type a, then all possible actions of type a are allowed by the rule. A rule can be viewed as placing mutual constraints on the tuples of objects that an action type can be applied to. Note that a single rule may allow no actions or many actions of one type. Given a decision list of such rules we say that an action is allowed by the list if it is allowed by some rule in the list, and no previous rule allows any actions. Again, a decision list may allow no actions or multiple actions of one type. A decision list L for an MDP defines a policy $\pi[L]$ for that MDP. If L allows no actions in state s, then $\pi[L](s)$ is the least *legal* action in s; otherwise, $\pi[L](s)$ is the least (according to the action ordering) legal action that is allowed by L. It is important to note that since $\pi[L]$ only considers legal actions, as specified by action preconditions, the rules do not need to encode the preconditions, which allows for simpler rules and learning. In other words, we can think of each rule as implicitly containing the preconditions of its action type.

As an example of a taxonomic decision-list policy consider a simple blocks-world domain where the goal condition is always to clear off all of the red blocks. The primitive classes in this domain are **red**, **clear**, and **holding**, and the single relation is **on**. The following policy will solve any problem in the domain.

$$\textbf{putdown}(x_1) : x_1 \in \textbf{holding}$$
$$\textbf{pickup}(x_1) : x_1 \in \textbf{clear}, x_1 \in (\textbf{on}^*(\textbf{on red}))$$

The first rule will cause the agent to put down any block that is being held. Otherwise, if no block is being held, then find a block x_1 that is clear and is above a red block (expressed by $(\textbf{on}^*(\textbf{on red})))$ and pick it up.

18.4.3   Learning Taxonomic Decision Lists

For a given relational MDP, define $\mathcal{R}_{d,l}$ to be the set of action-selection rules that have a length of at most l literals and whose class expressions have depth at most d. Also, define $H_{d,l}$ to be the policy space defined by decision lists whose rules are from $\mathcal{R}_{d,l}$. Since the number of depth-bounded class expressions is finite there are a finite number of rules, and hence $H_{d,l}$ is finite, though exponentially large. Our implementation of **Learn-Policy**, as used in the main API loop, learns a policy in $H_{d,l}$ for user-specified values of d and l.

We use a Rivest-style decision-list learning approach [43]—an approach also taken by Martin and Geffner [33] for learning class-based policies. The primary difference between Martin and Geffner [33] and our technique is the method for selecting individual rules in the decision list. We use a greedy, heuristic search, while previous work used an exhaustive enumeration approach. This difference allows us to find rules that are more complex, at the potential cost of failing to find some good simple rules that enumeration might discover.

Recall from section 18.3, that the training set given to **Learn-Policy** contains trajectories of the rollout policy. Our learning algorithm, however, is not sensitive to the trajectory structure (i.e., the order of trajectory elements) and thus, to simplify our discussion, we will take the input to our learner to be a training set D that contains the union of all the trajectory elements. This means that for a trajectory set that contains n length h trajectories, D will contain a total of $n \cdot h$ training examples. As described in section 18.3, each training example in D has the form $\langle s, \pi(s), \hat{Q}(s, a_1), \ldots, \hat{Q}(s, a_m) \rangle$, where s is a state, $\pi(s)$ is the action selected in s by the previous policy, and $\hat{Q}(s, a_i)$ is the Q-value estimate of $Q^\pi(s, a_i)$. Note that in our experiments the training examples only contain values for the legal actions in a state.

Given a training set D, a natural learning goal is to find a decision-list policy that for each training example selects an action with the maximum estimated Q-value. This learning goal, however, can be problematic in practice as often there are several best (or close to best) actions as measured by the true Q-function. In such case, due to random sampling, the particular action that looks best according to the Q-value estimates in the training set is arbitrary. Attempting to learn a concise policy that matches these arbitrary actions will be difficult at best and likely impossible.

One approach [31] to avoiding this problem is to use statistical tests to determine the actions that are "clearly the best" (positive examples) and the ones that are "clearly not the best" (negative examples). The learner is then asked to find a policy that is consistent with the positive and negative examples. While this approach has shown some empirical success, it has the potential shortcoming of throwing away most of the Q-value information. In particular, it may not always be possible to find a policy that exactly matches the training data. In such cases, we would like the learner to make informed tradeoffs regarding suboptimal actions—i.e., prefer suboptimal actions that have larger Q-values. With this motivation, below we describe a cost-sensitive decision-list learner that is sensitive to the full set of Q-values in D. The learning goal is roughly to find a decision list that selects actions with large cumulative Q-values over the training set.

18.4.3.1   Learning Lists of Rules

We say that a decision list L *covers* a training example $\langle s, \pi(s), \hat{Q}(s, a_1), \ldots, \hat{Q}(s, a_m) \rangle$ if L suggests an action in state s. Given a set of training examples D, we search for a decision list that selects actions with high Q-value via an iterative set-covering approach carried out by **Learn-Decision-List**. Decision-list rules are constructed one at a time and in order until the list covers all of the training examples. Pseudocode for our algorithm is given in figure 18.2. Initially, the decision list is the null list and does not cover any training examples. During each iteration, we search for a

---

Learn-Decision-List (D, d, l, b)
// *training set D, concept depth d, rule length l, beam width b*
$L \leftarrow$ **nil**;
while (D is not empty)
    $R \leftarrow$ **Learn-Rule**(D, d, l, b);
    $D \leftarrow D - \{d \in d \mid R \text{ covers } d\}$;
    $L \leftarrow$ **Extend-List**(L, R); // *add R to end of list*
Return L;

Learn-Rule(D, d, l, b)
// *training set D, concept depth d, rule length l, beam width b*
for each action type a // *compute rule for each action type a*
    $R_a \leftarrow$ **Beam-Search**(D, d, l, w, a);
Return argmax_a**Hvalue**(R_a, D);

Beam-Search (D, d, l, w, a)
// *training set D, concept depth d, rule length l, beam width b, action type a*
$k \leftarrow$ arity of a;
$X \leftarrow (x_1, \ldots, x_k)$;   // *X is a sequence of action-argument variables*
$\text{L} \leftarrow \{(x \in C) \mid x \in X, C \in \mathcal{C}_d[X]\}$; // *set of depth bounded candidate literals*
$B_0 \leftarrow \{a(X) : \textbf{nil}\}$; $i \leftarrow 1$; // *initialize beam to a single rule with no literals*

loop
    $G = B_{i-1} \cup \{R \in \mathcal{R}_{d,l} \mid R = \textbf{Add-Literal}(R', l), R' \in B_{i-1}, l \in L\}$;
    $B_i \leftarrow$ **Beam-Select**(G, w, D); // *select best b heuristic values*
    $i \leftarrow i + 1$;
until $B_{i-1} = B_i$; // *loop until there is no more improvement in heuristic*
Return $\operatorname{argmax}_{R \in B_i}$**Hvalue**$(R, D)$ // *return best rule in final beam*

Figure 18.2   Pseudocode for learning a decision list in $H_{d,l}$ given training data D. The procedure **Extend-List**(L, R) simply adds rule R to the end of the decision list L. The procedure **Add-Literal**(R, l) simply returns a rule where literal l is added to the end of rule R. The procedure **Beam-Select**(G, w, D) selects the best b rules in G with different heuristic values. The procedure **Hvalue**(R, D) returns the heuristic value of rule R relative to training data D and is described in the text.

"high-quality" rule R with quality measured relative to the set of currently uncovered training examples. The selected rule is appended to the current decision-list, and the training examples newly covered by the selected rule are removed from the training set. This process repeats until the list covers all of the training examples. The success of this approach depends heavily on the function **Learn-Rule**, which selects a "good" rule relative to the uncovered training examples—typically a good rule is one that selects actions with the best (or close to best) Q-value and also covers a significant number of examples.

18.4.3.2   Learning Individual Rules

The input to the rule learner **Learn-Rule** is a set of training examples, along with depth and length parameters d and l, and a beam width b. For each action type a, the rule learner calls the routine **Beam-Search** to find a good rule R_a in $\mathcal{R}_{d,l}$ for action type a. **Learn-Rule** then returns the rule R_a with the highest value as measured by our heuristic, which is described later in this section.

For a given action type a, the procedure **Beam-Search** generates a beam $B_0, B_1 \ldots$, where each B_i is a set of rules in $\mathcal{R}_{d,l}$ for action type a. The sets evolve by specializing rules in previous sets by adding literals to them, guided by our heuristic function. Search begins with the most general rule $a(X) : \mathbf{nil}$, which allows any action of type a in any state. Search iteration i produces a set B_i that contains b rules with the highest *different* heuristic values among those in the following set[4]:

$$G = B_{i-1} \cup \{R \in \mathcal{R}_{d,l} \mid R = \mathbf{Add\text{-}Literal}(R', l), R' \in B_{i-1}, l \in L\},$$

where L is the set of all possible literals with a depth of d or less. This set includes the current best rules (those in B_{i-1}) and also any rule in $\mathcal{R}_{d,l}$ that can be formed by adding a new literal to a rule in B_{i-1}. The search ends when no improvement in heuristic value occurs, that is, when $B_i = B_{i-1}$. **Beam-Search** then returns the best rule in B_i according to the heuristic.

Heuristic Function For a training instance $\langle s, \pi(s), \hat{Q}(s, a_1), \ldots, \hat{Q}(s, a_m) \rangle$, following Harmon and Baird [22], we define the *Q-advantage* of taking action a_i instead of $\pi(s)$ in state s by $\Delta(s, a_i) = \hat{Q}(s, a_i) - \hat{Q}(s, \pi(s))$. Likewise, the Q-advantage of a rule R is the sum of the Q-advantages of actions allowed by R in s. Given a rule R and a set of training examples D, our heuristic function **Hvalue**(R, D) is equal to the number of training examples that the rule covers plus the sum of all the Q-advantages of the rule over those training examples.[5] Using Q-advantage rather than Q-value focuses the learner toward instances where a large improvement over the previous policy is possible. Naturally, one could consider using different weights for the coverage and Q-advantage terms, possibly tuning the weight automatically using validation data.

---

4. Since many rules in $\mathcal{R}_{d,l}$ are equivalent, we must prevent the beam from filling up with semantically equivalent rules. Rather than deal with this problem via expensive equivalence testing we take an ad hoc, but practically effective approach. We assume that rules do not coincidentally have the same heuristic value, so that ones that do must be equivalent. Thus, we construct beams whose members all have different heuristic values. We choose between rules with the same value by preferring shorter rules, then choose arbitrarily.

5. If the coverage term is not included, then covering a zero Q-advantage example is the same as not covering it. But zero Q-advantage can be good (e.g., the previous policy is optimal in that state).

18.5   Bootstrapping

There are two issues that are critical to the success of our API technique. First, API is fundamentally limited by the expressiveness of the policy language and the strength of the learner, which dictates its ability to capture the improved policy described by the training data at each iteration. Second, API can only yield improvement if **Improved-Trajectories** successfully generates training data that describes an improved policy. For large classical planning domains, initializing API with an uninformed random policy will typically result in essentially random training data, which is not helpful for policy improvement. For example, consider the MDP corresponding to the 20-block blocks world with an initial problem distribution that generates random initial and goal states. In this case, a random policy is unlikely to reach a goal state within any practical horizon time. Hence, the rollout trajectories are unlikely to reach the goal, providing no guidance toward learning an improved policy (i.e., a policy that can more reliably reach the goal).

Because we are interested in solving large domains such as this, providing "guiding inputs" to API is critical. In Fern et al. [15], we showed that by "bootstrapping" API with the domain-independent heuristic of the planner FF [24], API was able to uncover good policies for the blocks world, simplified logistics world (no planes), and stochastic variants. This approach, however, is limited by the heuristic's ability to provide useful guidance, which can vary widely across domains.

Here we describe a new bootstrapping procedure for goal-based planning domains, based on random walks, for guiding API toward good policies. Our planning system, which is evaluated in section 18.6, is based on integrating this procedure with API in order to find policies for goal-based planning domains. For non-goal-based MDPs, this bootstrapping procedure cannot be directly applied, and other bootstrapping mechanisms must be used if necessary. This might include providing an initial nontrivial policy, providing a heuristic function, or some form of reward shaping [34]. Below, we first describe the idea of random-walk distributions. Next, we describe how to use these distributions in the context of bootstrapping API, giving a new algorithm **LRW-API**.

18.5.1   Random-Walk Distributions

Throughout we consider an MDP $M = \langle S, A, T, R, I \rangle$ that correspond to goal-based planning domains, as described in section 18.4.1. Recall that each state $s \in S$ corresponds to a planning problem, specifying a world state (via world facts) and a set of goal conditions (via goal facts). We will use the terms "MDP state" and "planning problem" interchangeably. Note that, in this context, I is a distribution over planning problems. For convenience we will denote MDP states as tuples $s = (w, g)$, where w and g are the sets of world facts and goal facts in s respectively.

Given an MDP state $s = (w, g)$ and set of goal predicates G, we define $s|_G$ to be the MDP state (w, g') where g' contains those goal facts in g that are applications of a predicate in G. Given M and a set of *goal predicates* G, we define the *n-step random walk problem distribution* $\mathcal{RW}_n(M, G)$ by the following stochastic algorithm:

1. Draw a random state $s_0 = (w_0, g_0)$ from the initial state distribution I.

2. Starting at s_0 take n uniformly random actions, [6], giving a state sequence $(s_0, \ldots, s_n)$, where $s_n = (w_n, g_0)$ (recall that actions do not change goal facts). At each uniformly random action selection, we assume that an extra "no-op" action (that does not change the state) is selected with some fixed probability, for reasons explained below.

3. Let g be the set of goal facts corresponding to the world facts in w_n, so, e.g., if $w_n = \{\mathbf{on}(a, b), \mathbf{clear}(a)\}$, then $g = \{\mathbf{gon}(a, b), \mathbf{gclear}(a)\}$. Return the planning problem (MDP state) $(s_0, g)|_G$ as the output.

We will sometimes abbreviate $\mathcal{RW}_n(M, G)$ by $\mathcal{RW}_n$ when M and G are clear in context.

Intuitively, to perform well on this distribution a policy must be able to achieve facts involving the goal predicates that typically result after an n-step random walk from an initial state. By restricting the set of goal predicates G we can specify the types of facts that we are interested in achieving—e.g., in the blocks world we may only be interested in achieving facts involving the "on" predicate.

The random-walk distributions provide a natural way to span a range of problem difficulties. Since longer random walks tend to take us "further" from an initial state, for small n we typically expect that the planning problems generated by $\mathcal{RW}_n$ will become more difficult as n grows. However, as n becomes large, the problems generated will require far fewer than n steps to solve—i.e., there will be "more direct" paths from an initial state to the end state of a long random walk. Eventually, since S is finite, the problem difficulty will stop increasing with n.

A question raised by this idea is whether, for large n, good performance on $\mathcal{RW}_n$ ensures good performance on other problem distributions of interest in the domain. In some domains, such as the simple blocks world, [7], good random-walk performance does seem to yield good performance on other distributions of interest. In other domains, such as the grid world (with keys and locked doors), intuitively, a random walk is very unlikely to uncover a problem that requires unlocking a sequence of doors.

---

6. In practice, we only select random actions from the set of applicable actions in a state s_i, provided our simulator makes it possible to identify this set.

7. In the blocks world with large n, $\mathcal{RW}_n$ generates various pairs of random block configurations, typically pairing states that are far apart—clearly, a policy that performs well on this distribution has captured significant information about the blocks world.

We believe that good performance on long random walks is often useful, but is only addressing one component of the difficulty of many planning benchmarks. To successfully address problems with other components of difficulty, a planner will need to deploy orthogonal technology such as landmark extraction for setting subgoals [23]. For example, in the grid world, if we could automatically set the subgoal of possessing a key for the first door, a long random-walk policy could provide a useful macro for getting that key.

For the purpose of developing a bootstrapping technique for API, we limit our focus to finding good policies for long random walks. In our experiments, we define "long" by specifying a large walk length N. Theoretically, the inclusion of the "no-op" action in the definition of $\mathcal{RW}$ ensures that the induced random-walk Markov chain is aperiodic, and thus that the distribution over states reached by increasingly long random walks converges to a stationary distribution.[8] Thus $\mathcal{RW}_* = \lim_{n \to \infty} \mathcal{RW}_n$ is well-defined, and we take good performance on $\mathcal{RW}_*$ to be our goal.

18.5.2   Random-Walk Bootstrapping

For an MDP M, we define $M[I']$ to be an MDP identical to M only with the initial state distribution replaced by I'. We also define the *success ratio* $\mathrm{SR}(\pi, M[I])$ of π on $M[I]$ as the probability that π solves a problem drawn from I. Also treating I as a random variable, the *average length* $\mathrm{AL}(\pi, M[I])$ of π on $M[I]$ is the conditional expectation of the solution length of π on problems drawn from I given that π solves I. Typically the solution length of a problem is taken to be the number of actions; however, when action costs are not uniform, the length is taken to be the sum of the action costs. Note that for the MDP formulation of classical planning domains, given in section 18.4.1, if a policy π achieves a high $\overline{V}(\pi)$, then it will also have a high success ratio and low average cost.

Given an MDP M and set of goal predicates G, our system attempts to find a good policy for $M[\mathcal{RW}_N]$, where N is selected to be large enough to adequately approximate $\mathcal{RW}_*$, while still allowing tractable completion of the learning. Naively, given an initial random policy π_0, we could try to apply API directly. However, as already discussed, this will not work in general, since we are interested in planning domains where $\mathcal{RW}_*$ produces extremely large and difficult problems where random policies provide an ineffective starting point.

However, for very small n (e.g., $n = 1$), $\mathcal{RW}_n$ typically generates easy problems, and it is likely that API, starting with even a random initial policy, can reliably find a good policy for $\mathcal{RW}_n$. Furthermore, we expect that if a policy π_n performs well on $\mathcal{RW}_n$, then it will also provide "reasonably good," but perhaps not perfect, guidance on problems drawn from $\mathcal{RW}_m$ when m is only "moderately larger" than

---

8. The Markov chain may not be irreducible, so different initial states may give different stationary distributions; however, we only consider one initial state, described by I.

LRW-API $(N, G, n, w, h, M, \pi_0, \gamma)$

// *max random-walk length N, goal predicates G*
// *training set size n, sampling width w, horizon h,*
// *MDP M, initial policy π_0, discount factor γ.*

$\pi \leftarrow \pi_0; \quad n \leftarrow 1;$

loop

    if $\widehat{\mathrm{SR}}_\pi(n) > \tau$

        // *Find harder n-step distribution for π.*
        $n \leftarrow$ least $i \in [n, N]$ s.t. $\widehat{\mathrm{SR}}_\pi(i) < \tau - \delta$, or N if none;

    $M' = M[\mathcal{RW}_n(M, G)];$
    $T \leftarrow$ **Improved-Trajectories**$(n, w, h, M', \pi);$
    $\pi \leftarrow$ **Learn-Policy**$(T);$

until satisfied with π

Return $\pi;$

Figure 18.3 Pseudocode for **LRW-API**. $\widehat{\mathrm{SR}}_\pi(n)$ estimates the success ratio of π in planning domain D on problems drawn from $\mathcal{RW}_n(M, G)$ by drawing a set of problems and returning the fraction solved by π. Constants τ and δ are described in the text.

n. Thus, we expect to be able to find a good policy for $\mathcal{RW}_m$ by bootstrapping API with initial policy π_n. This suggests a natural iterative bootstrapping technique to find a good policy for large n (in particular, for $n = N$).

Figure 18.3 gives pseudocode for the procedure **LRW-API** which integrates API and random-walk bootstrapping to find a policy for the long-random-walk problem distribution. Intuitively, this algorithm can be viewed as iterating through two stages: first, finding a "hard enough" distribution for the current policy (by increasing n); and then finding a good policy for the hard distribution using API. The algorithm maintains a current policy π and current walk length n (initially $n = 1$). As long as the success ratio of π on RW_n is below the *success threshold* τ, which is a constant close to one, we simply iterate steps of approximate policy improvement. Once we achieve a success ratio of τ with some policy π, the if-statement increases n until the success ratio of π on $\mathcal{RW}_n$ falls below $\tau - \delta$. That is, when π performs well enough on the current n-step distribution we move on to a distribution that is "slightly" harder. The constant δ determines how much harder and is set small enough so that π can likely be used to bootstrap policy improvement on the harder distribution. (The simpler method of just increasing n by 1 whenever success ratio τ is achieved will also find good policies whenever this method does; however, this can take much longer, as it may run API repeatedly on a training set for which we already have a good policy.)

Once n becomes equal to the maximum walk length N, we will have $n = N$ for all future iterations. It is important to note that even after we find a policy with a good success ratio on $\mathcal{RW}_N$, it may still be possible to improve on the average length of the policy. Thus, we continue API on this distribution until we are satisfied with both the success ratio and average length of the current policy.

18.6   Relational Planning Experiments

In this section, we evaluate the **LRW-API** technique on relational MDPs corresponding to deterministic and stochastic classical planning domains. We first give results for a number of deterministic benchmark domains, showing promising results in comparison with the state-of-the-art planner FF [24], while also highlighting the limitations of our approach. Next, we give results for several stochastic planning domains, including those in the domain-specific track of the 2004 International Probabilistic Planning Competition (IPPC).

In all of our experiments, we use the policy learner described in section 18.4.3 to learn taxonomic decision-list policies. In all cases, the number of training trajectories is 100, and policies are restricted to rules with a depth bound d and length bound l. The discount factor γ was always one, and **LRW-API** was always initialized with a policy that selects random actions. We utilize a maximum-walk-length parameter $N = 10,000$ and set τ and δ equal to 0.9 and 0.1 respectively.

18.6.1   Deterministic Planning Experiments

We perform experiments in seven familiar STRIPS planning domains including those used in the AIPS-2000 Planning Competition, those used to evaluate TL-Plan in Bacchus and Kabanza [4], and the Gripper domain. Each domain has a standard problem generator that accepts parameters, which control the size and difficulty of the randomly generated problems. Below we list each domain and the parameters associated with them. A detailed description of these domains can be found in Hoffmann and Nebel [24]

- Blocks world (n) : the standard blocks worlds with n blocks
- Freecell (s, c, f, l) : a version of solitaire with s suits, c cards per suit, f freecells, and l columns
- Logistics (a,c,l,p) : the logistics transportation domain with p packages, l locations, c cities, and a airplanes
- Schedule (p) : a job shop scheduling domain with p parts
- Elevator (f, p) : elevator scheduling with f floors and p people
- Gripper (b) : a robotic gripper domain with b balls
- Briefcase (i) : a transportation domain with i items

18.6.1.1 LRW Experiments

Our first set of experiments evaluates the ability of **LRW-API** to find good policies for $\mathcal{RW}_*$. Here we utilize a sampling width of one for rollout, since these are deterministic domains. Recall that in each iteration of **LRW-API** we compute an (approximately) improved policy and may also increase the walk length n to find a harder problem distribution. We continued iterating **LRW-API** until we observed no further improvement. The training time per iteration is approximately five hours. Though the initial training period is significant, once a policy is learned it can be used to solve new problems very quickly, terminating in seconds with a solution when one is found, even for very large problems.

Figure 18.4 provides data for each iteration of **LRW-API** in each of the seven domains with the indicated parameter settings. The first column, for each domain, indicates the iteration number (e.g., the Blocks World was run for eight iterations). The second column records the walk length n used for learning in the corresponding iteration. The third and fourth columns record the success rate (SR) and average lenght (AL) of the policy learned at the corresponding iteration as measured on 100 problems drawn from $\mathcal{RW}_n$ for the corresponding value of n (i.e., the distribution used for learning). When this SR exceeds τ, the next iteration seeks an increased walk length n. The fifth and sixth columns record the SR and AL of the same policy, but measured on 100 problems drawn from the LRW target distribution $\mathcal{RW}_*$, which in these experiments is approximated by $\mathcal{RW}_N$ for $N = 10,000$.

So, for example, we see that in the Blocks World there are a total of eight iterations, where we learn at first for one iteration with $n = 4$, one more iteration with $n = 14$, four iterations with $n = 54$, and then two iterations with $n = 334$. At this point we see that the resulting policy performs well on $\mathcal{RW}_*$. Further iterations with $n = N$, not shown, showed no improvement over the policy found after iteration 8. In other domains, we also observed no improvement after iterating with $n = N$, and thus do not show those iterations. We note that all domains except Logistics (see below) achieve policies with good performance on $\mathcal{RW}_N$ by learning on much shorter $\mathcal{RW}_n$ distributions, indicating that we have indeed selected a large enough value of N to capture $\mathcal{RW}_*$, as desired.

18.6.1.2 General Observations

For several domains, our learner bootstraps very quickly from short random-walk problems, finding a policy that works well even for much longer random-walk problems. These include Schedule, Briefcase, Gripper, and Elevator. Typically, large problems in these domains have many somewhat independent subproblems with short solutions, so that short random walks can generate instances of all the different typical subproblems. In each of these domains, our best LRW policy is found in a small number of iterations and performs comparably to FF on $\mathcal{RW}_*$. We note that FF is considered a very good domain-independent planner for these domains, so we consider this a successful result.

iter. #	n	$\mathcal{RW}_n$ SR	AL	$\mathcal{RW}_*$ SR	AL	iter. #	n	$\mathcal{RW}_n$ SR	AL	$\mathcal{RW}_*$ SR	AL
Blocks World (20)						**Logistics (1,2,2,6)**					
1	4	0.92	2.0	0	0	1	5	0.86	3.1	0.25	11.3
2	14	0.94	5.6	0.10	41.4	2	45	0.86	6.5	0.28	7.2
3	54	0.56	15.0	0.17	42.8	3	45	0.81	6.9	0.31	8.4
4	54	0.78	15.0	0.32	40.2	4	45	0.86	6.8	0.28	8.9
5	54	0.88	33.7	0.65	47.0	5	45	0.76	6.1	0.28	7.8
6	54	0.98	25.1	0.90	43.9	6	45	0.76	5.9	0.32	8.4
7	334	0.84	45.6	0.87	50.1	7	45	0.86	6.2	0.39	9.1
8	334	0.99	37.8	1	43.3	8	45	0.76	6.9	0.31	11.0
FF				0.96	49.0	9	45	0.70	6.1	0.19	7.8
						10	45	0.81	6.1	0.25	7.6
Freecell (4,2,2,4)						...	...	...	...	...	...
1	5	0.97	1.4	0.08	3.6	43	45	0.74	6.4	0.25	9.0
2	8	0.97	2.7	0.26	6.3	44	45	0.90	6.9	0.39	9.3
3	30	0.65	7.0	0.78	7.0	45	45	0.92	6.6	0.38	9.4
4	30	0.72	7.1	0.85	7.0	FF				1	13
5	30	0.90	6.7	0.85	6.3						
6	30	0.81	6.7	0.89	6.6	**Schedule (20)**					
7	30	0.78	6.8	0.87	6.8	1	1	0.79	1	0.48	27
8	30	0.90	6.9	0.89	6.6	2	4	1	3.45	1	34
9	30	0.93	7.7	0.93	7.9	FF				1	36
FF				1	5.4						
						Briefcase (10)					
Elevator (20,10)						1	5	0.91	1.4	0	0
1	20	1	4.0	1	26	2	15	0.89	4.2	0.2	38
FF				1	23	3	15	1	3.0	1	30
						FF				1	28
Gripper (10)											
1	10	1	3.8	1	13						
FF				1	13						

Figure 18.4   Results for each iteration of **LRW-API** in seven deterministic planning domains. For each iteration, we show the walk length n used for learning, along with the success ratio (SR) and average length (AL) of the learned policy on both $\mathcal{RW}_n$ and $\mathcal{RW}_*$. Note that larger SR and smaller AL is better. The final policy shown in each domain performs above $\tau = 0.9$ SR on walks of length $N = 10,000$ (with the exception of Logistics), and further iteration does not improve the performance. For each benchmark we also show the SR and AL of the planner FF on problems drawn from $\mathcal{RW}_*$.

For two domains, Logistics[9] and Freecell, our planner is unable to find a policy with success ratio one on $\mathcal{RW}_*$. We believe that this is a result of the limited knowledge representation we allowed for policies for the following reasons. First, we ourselves cannot write good policies for these domains within our current policy language.[10] Second, the final learned decision lists for Logistics and Freecell contain a much larger number of more specific rules than the lists learned in the other domains. This indicates that the learner has difficulty finding general rules within the language restrictions that are applicable to large portions of training data, resulting in poor generalization. Third, the success ratio (not shown) for the sampling-based rollout policy, i.e., the improved policy simulated by **Improved-Trajectories**, is substantially higher than that for the resulting learned policy that becomes the policy of the next iteration. This indicates that **Learn-Decision-List** is learning a much weaker policy than the sampling-based policy generating its training data, indicating a weakness in either the policy language or the learning algorithm. For example, in the Logistics domain, at iteration 8, the training data for learning the iteration 9 policy is generated by a sampling rollout policy that achieves success ratio 0.97 on 100 training problems drawn from the same $\mathcal{RW}_{45}$ distribution, but the learned iteration 9 policy only achieves success ratio 0.70, as shown in the figure at iteration 9. Extending our policy language to incorporate the expressiveness that appears to be required in these domains will require a more sophisticated learning algorithm, which is a point of future work.

In the remaining domain, the Blocks World, the bootstrapping provided by increasingly long random walks appears particularly useful. The policies learned at each of the walk lengths 4, 14, 54, and 334 are increasingly effective on the target LRW distribution $\mathcal{RW}_*$. For walks of length 54 and 334, it takes multiple iterations to master the provided level of difficulty beyond the previous walk length. Finally, upon mastering walk length 334, the resulting policy appears to perform well for any walk length. The learned policy is modestly superior to FF on $\mathcal{RW}_*$ in success ratio and average length.

18.6.1.3 *Evaluation on the Original Problem Distributions*

In each domain we denote by π_* the best learned LRW policy—i.e., the policy, from each domain, with the highest performance on $\mathcal{RW}_*$, as shown in figure 18.4. Figure 18.5 shows the performance of π_*, in comparison to FF, on the original intended problem distributions for each of our domains. We measured the success ratio of both systems by giving a time limit of 100 seconds to solve a problem. Here we

---

9. In Logistics, the planner generates a long sequence of policies with similar, oscillating success ratios that are elided from the figure with ellipses for space reasons.
10. For example, in Logistics, one of the important concepts is "the set containing all packages on trucks such that the truck is in the packages goal city." However, the domain is defined in such a way that this concept cannot be expressed within the language used in our experiments.

Domain	Size	π_* SR	AL	FF SR	AL
Blocks	(20)	1	54	0.81	60
	(50)	1	151	0.28	158
Freecell	(4,2,2,4)	0.36	15	1	10
	(4,13,4,8)	0	—	0.47	112
Logistics	(1,2,2,6)	0.87	6	1	6
	(3,10,2,30)	0	—	1	158
Elevator	(60,30)	1	112	1	98
Schedule	(50)	1	175	1	212
Briefcase	(10)	1	30	1	29
	(50)	1	162	0	—
Gripper	(50)	1	149	1	149

Figure 18.5 Results on "standard" problem distributions for seven benchmarks. Success ratio (SR) and average length (AL) are provided for both FF and our policy learned for the LRW problem distribution. For a given domain, the same learned LRW policy is used for each problem size shown.

have attempted to select the largest problem sizes previously used in evaluation of domain-specific planners (either in AIPS-2000 or in Bacchus and Kabanza [4]), as well as show a smaller problem size for those cases where one of the planners we show performed poorly on the large size. In each case, we use the problem generators provided with the domains, and evaluate on 100 problems of each size.

Overall, these results indicate that our learned, reactive policies are competitive with the domain-independent planner FF. It is important to remember that these policies are learned in a domain-independent fashion, and thus **LRW-API** can be viewed as a general approach to generating domain-specific reactive planners. On two domains, Blocks World and Briefcase, our learned policies substantially outperform FF on success ratio, especially on large domain sizes. On three domains, Elevator, Schedule, and Gripper, the two approaches perform quite similarly on success ratio, with our approach superior in average length on Schedule but FF superior in average length on Elevator.

On two domains, Logistics and Freecell, FF substantially outperforms our learned policies on success ratio. We believe that this is partly due to an inadequate policy language, as discussed above. We also believe, however, that another reason for the poor performance is that the long-random-walk distribution $\mathcal{RW}_*$ does not correspond well to the standard problem distributions. This seems to be particularly true for Freecell. The policy learned for Freecell (4,2,2,4) achieved a success ratio of 93 % on $\mathcal{RW}_*$; however, for the standard distribution it only achieved 36%. This suggests that $\mathcal{RW}_*$ generates problems that are significantly easier than the standard distribution. This is supported by the fact that the solutions produced by FF on the standard distribution are on average twice as long as those produced on $\mathcal{RW}_*$. One likely reason for this is that it is easy for random walks to end up in dead states in Freecell, where no actions are applicable. Thus the random-walk distribution will typically produce many problems where the goals correspond to such dead states. The standard distribution on the other hand will not treat such dead states as goals.

18.6.2 Probabilistic Planning Experiments

Here we present experiments in three probabilistic domains that are described in the probabilistic planning domain language PPDDL [52].

- Ground Logistics (c, p) : a probabilistic version of logistics with no airplanes with c cities and p packages. The driving action has a probability of failure in this domain.

- Colored Blocks World (n) : a probabilistic blocks world with n colored blocks, where goals involve constructing towers with certain color patterns. There is a probability that moved blocks fall to the floor.

- Boxworld (c, p) : a probabilistic version of full logistics with c cities and p packages. Transportation actions have a probability of going in the wrong direction.

The Ground Logistics domain is originally from Boutilier et al. [10], and was also used for evaluation in Yoon et al. [51]. The Colored Blocks World and Boxworld domains are the domains used in the hand-tailored track of the International Planning Competition in which our LRW-API technique was entered. In the hand-tailored track, participants were provided with problem generators for each domain before the competition and were allowed to incorporate domain knowledge into the planner for use at competition time. We provided the problem generators to LRW-API and learned policies for these domains, which were then entered into the competition.

We have also conducted experiments in the other probabilistic domains from Yoon et al. [51], including variants of the blocks world and a variant of Ground Logistics, some of which appeared in Fern et al. [15]. However, we do not show those results here since they are qualitatively identical to the deterministic blocks world results described above and the Ground Logistics results we show below.

For our three probabilistic domains, we conducted LRW experiments using the same procedure as above. All parameters given to **LRW-API** were the same as above except that the sampling width used for rollout was set to $w = 10$, and τ was set to 0.85 in order to account for the stochasticity in these domains. The results of these experiments are shown in figure 18.6. These tables have the same form as figure 18.4, only the last row given for each domain now gives the performance of π_* on standard distribution, i.e., problems drawn from the domains problem generator.

iter. #	n	SR	$\mathcal{RW}_n$ AL	$\mathcal{RW}_*$ SR	AL
			Boxworld (10,5)		
1	10	0.73	4.3	0.03	61.5
2	10	0.93	2.3	0.13	58.4
3	20	0.91	4.4	0.17	55.9
4	40	0.96	6.1	0.31	50.4
5	170	0.62	30.8	0.25	52.2
6	170	0.49	37.9	0.17	55.7
7	170	0.63	29.3	0.21	55
8	170	0.63	29.1	0.18	55.3
9	170	0.48	36.4	0.17	55.3
Standard Distribution (15,15)				0	—
			Ground Logistics (3,4,4,3)		
1	5	0.95	2.71	0.17	168.9
2	10	0.97	2.06	0.84	17.5
3	160	1	6.41	1	7.2
Standard Distribution (5,7,7,20)				1	20
			Colored Blocks World (10)		
1	2	0.86	1.7	0.19	93.6
2	5	0.89	8.4	0.81	40.8
3	40	0.92	11.7	0.85	32.7
4	100	0.76	37.5	0.77	38.5
5	100	0.94	20.0	0.95	21.9
Standard Distribution (50)				0.95	123

Figure 18.6   Results for each iteration of **LRW-API** in three probabilistic planning domains. For each iteration, we show the walk length n used for learning, along with the success ratio (SR) and average length (AL) of the learned policy on both $\mathcal{RW}_n$ and $\mathcal{RW}_*$. For each benchmark, we show performance on the standard problem distribution of the policy whose performance is best on $\mathcal{RW}_*$.

For Boxworld, **LRW-API** is not able to find a good policy for $\mathcal{RW}_*$ or the standard distribution. Again, as for deterministic Logistics and Freecell, we believe that this is primarily because of the restricted policy language that is currently used by our learner. Here, as for those domains, we see that the decision-list learned for Boxworld contains many very specific rules, indicating that the learner was not able to generalize well beyond the training trajectories. For Ground Logistics, we see that **LRW-API** quickly finds a good policy for both $\mathcal{RW}_*$ and the standard distribution.

For Colored Blocks World, we also see that **LRW-API** is able to quickly find a good policy for both $\mathcal{RW}_*$ and the standard distribution. However, unlike the deterministic (uncolored) blocks world, here the success ratio is observed to be less than one, solving 95% of the problems. It is unclear why **LRW-API** is not able to find a "perfect" policy. It is relatively easy to hand-code a policy for Colored Blocks World using the language of the learner, hence inadequate knowledge representation is not the answer. The predicates and action types for this domain are not the same as those in its deterministic counterpart and other stochastic variants that we have previously considered. This difference apparently interacts badly with our learner's "search bias," causing it to fail to find a perfect policy. Nevertheless, these two results, along with the probabilistic planning results not shown here, indicate that when a good policy is expressible in our language, **LRW-API** can find good policies in complex relational MDPs. This makes **LRW-API** one of the few techniques that can simultaneously cope with the complexity resulting from stochasticity and from relational structure in domains such as these.

18.7 Related Work

Boutilier et al. [10] presented the first exact solution technique for relational MDPs based on structured dynamic programming. However, a practical implementation of the approach was not provided, primarily due to the need for the simplification of first-order logic formulae. These ideas, however, served as the basis for a logic programming-based system [28] that was successfully applied to blocks world problems involving "simple" goals and a simplified logistics world. This style of approach is inherently limited to domains where the exact value functions or policies can be compactly represented in the chosen knowledge representation. Unfortunately, this is not generally the case for the types of domains that we consider here, particularly as the planning horizon grows. Nevertheless, providing techniques such as these that directly reason about the MDP model is an important direction. Note that our API approach essentially ignores the underlying MDP model, and simply interacts with the MDP simulator as a black box.

An interesting research direction is to consider principled approximations of these techniques that can discover good policies in more difficult domains. This has been considered by Guestrin et al. [20], where a class-based MDP and value function representation was used to compute an approximate value function that could generalize across different sets of objects. Promising empirical results were shown in a multiagent tactical battle domain. Presently the class-based representation does not support some of the representation features that are commonly found in classical planning domains (e.g., relational facts such as **on**(a, b) that change over time), and thus is not directly applicable in these contexts. However, extending this work to richer representations is an interesting direction. Its ability to "reason globally" about a domain may give it some advantages compared to API.

Our approach is closely related to work in RRL [13], a form of online API that learns relational value-function approximations. Q-value functions are learned in the form of relational decision trees (Q-trees) and are used to learn corresponding policies (P-trees). The RRL results clearly demonstrate the difficulty of learning value-function approximations in relational domains. Compared to P-trees, Q-trees tend to generalize poorly and be much larger. RRL has not yet demonstrated scalability to problems as complex as those considered here—previous RRL blocks world experiments include relatively simple goals,[11] which lead to value functions that are much less complex than the ones here. For this reason, we suspect that RRL would have difficulty in the domains we consider precisely because of the value-function approximation step that we avoid; however, this needs to be experimentally tested.

We note, however, that our API approach has the advantage of using an unconstrained simulator, whereas RRL learns from "irreversible" world experience ("pure" reinforcment learning). By using a simulator, we are able to estimate the Q-values for *all* actions at each training state, providing us with rich training data. Without such a simulator, RRL is not able to directly estimate the Q-value for each action in each training state—thus, RRL learns a Q-tree to provide estimates of the Q-value information needed to learn the P-tree. In this way, value-function learning serves a more critical role when a simulator is unavailable. We believe that in many relational planning problems, it is possible to learn a model or simulator from world experience—in this case, our API approach can be incorporated as the planning component of RRL. Otherwise, finding ways to either avoid learning or to more effectively learn relational value functions in RRL is an interesting research direction.

Researchers in classical planning have long studied techniques for learning to improve planning performance. For a collection and survey of work on "learning for planning domains," see [39, 53]. Two primary approaches are to learn domain-specific control rules for guiding search-based planners (e.g., see [40, 48, 14, 26, 2, 1]), and, more closely related, to learn domain-specific reactive control policies [29, 33, 51].

Regarding the latter, our work is novel in using API to iteratively improve stand-alone control policies. Regarding the former, in theory, search-based planners can

---

11. The most complex blocks world goal for RRL was to achieve **on**(A, B) in an n block environment. We consider blocks world goals that involve all n blocks.

be iteratively improved by continually adding newly learned control knowledge—however, it can be difficult to avoid the utility problem [38], i.e., being "swamped" by low utility rules. Critically, our policy-language bias confronts this issue by preferring simpler policies. Our learning approach is also not tied to having a base planner (let alone tied to a single particular base planner), unlike most previous work. Rather, we only require a domain simulator.

The ultimate goal of such systems is to allow for planning in large, difficult problems that are beyond the reach of domain-independent planning technology. Clearly, learning to achieve this goal requires some form of bootstrapping and almost all previous systems have relied on the human for this purpose. By far, the most common human bootstrapping approach is "learning from small problems." Here, the human provides a small problem distribution to the learner, by limiting the number of objects (e.g., using two to five blocks in the blocks world), and control knowledge is learned for the small problems. For this approach to work, the human must ensure that the small distribution is such that good control knowledge for the small problems is also good for the large target distribution. In contrast, our long-random-walk bootstrapping approach can be applied without human assistance directly to large planning domains. However, as already pointed out, our goal of performing well on the LRW distribution may not always correspond well with a particular target problem distribution.

Our bootstrapping approach is similar in spirit to the bootstrapping framework of "learning from exercises"[41, 42]. Here, the learner is provided with planning problems, or "exercises," in order of increasing difficulty. After learning on easier problems, the learner is able to use its new knowledge, or "skills," in order to bootstrap learning on the harder problems. This work, however, has previously relied on a human to provide the exercises, which typically requires insight into the planning domain and the underlying form of control knowledge and planner. Our work can be viewed as an automatic instantiation of learning from exercises, specifically designed for learning LRW policies.

Our random-walk bootstrapping is most similar to the approach used in MICRO-HILLARY [17], a macrolearning system for problem solving. In that work, instead of generating problems via random walks starting at an initial state, random walks were generated "backward" from goal states. This approach assumes that actions are invertible or that we are given a set of "backward actions." When such assumptions hold, the backward random-walk approach may be preferable when we are provided with a goal distribution that does not match well with the goals generated by forward random walks. Of course, in other cases forward random walks may be preferable. MICRO-HILLARY was empirically tested in the $N \times N$ sliding-puzzle domain; however, as discussed in that work, there remain challenges for applying the system to more complex domains with parameterized actions and recursive structure, such as familiar STRIPS domains. To the best of our knowledge, the idea of learning from random walks has not been previously explored in the context of STRIPS planning domains.

Our API approach can be viewed as a type of "reduction" from planning or reinforcement learning to classification learning. That is, we solve an MDP by generating and solving a series of cost-sensitive classification problems. Recently, there have been several other proposals for reducing reinforcement learning to classification. The most closely related approach is by Lagoudakis and Parr [31], who also proposed a form of classification-based API. The primary difference is the form of the classification problem produced on each iteration. They generate standard multi-class classification problems, where the training data consists of states paired with either the best action (a positive example) or a nonbest action (negative example). Rather, we generate cost-sensitive classification problems where the training set consists of states paired with a cost vector that specifies the cost of selecting each action. The use of cost-sensitive classification allows a learner to make more informed tradeoffs when it is unable to find a rule that correctly selects the best action for all of the training data. Bagnell et al. [5] introduced a closely related algorithm for learning non-stationary policies in reinforcement learning. For a specified horizon time h, their approach learns a sequence of h policies. At each iteration, all policies are held fixed except for one, which is optimized by forming a classification problem via policy rollout[12]. Finally, Langford and Zadrozny [32] provide a formal reduction from reinforcement learning to classification, showing that ϵ-accurate classification learning implies near-optimal reinforcement learning. This approach uses an "optimistic" variant of sparse sampling to generate h classification problems, one for each horizon time step.

18.8   Summary and Future Work

We introduced a new variant of API that learns policies directly, without representing approximate value functions. This allowed us to utilize a relational policy language for learning compact policy representations. We also introduced a new API bootstrapping technique for goal-based planning domains. Our experiments show that the **LRW-API** algorithm, which combines these techniques, is able to find good policies for a variety of relational MDPs corresponding to classical planning domains and their stochastic variants. We know of no previous MDP technique that has been successfully applied to problems such as these.

Our experiments also pointed to a number of weaknesses of our current approach. First, our bootstrapping technique, based on long random walks, does not always correspond well to the problem distribution of interest. Investigating other automatic bootstrapping techniques is an interesting direction, related to the general problems of exploration and reward shaping in reinforcement learning. Second, we

---

12. Here the initial state distribution is dictated by the policies at previous time steps, which are held fixed. Likewise the actions selected along the rollout trajectories are dictated by policies at future time steps, which are also held fixed.

have seen that limitations of our current policy language and learner are partly responsible for some of the failures of our system. In such cases, we must either (1) depend on the human to provide useful features to the system, or (2) extend the policy language and develop more advanced learning techniques. Policy-language extensions that we are considering include various extensions to the knowledge representation used to represent sets of objects in the domain (in particular, for route finding in maps/grids), as well as non-reactive policies that incorporate search into decision making.

As we consider ever more complex planning domains, it is inevitable that our brute-force enumeration approach to learning policies from trajectories will not scale. Presently our policy learner, as well as the entire API technique, makes no attempt to use the definition of a domain when one is available. We believe that developing a learner that can exploit this information to bias its search for good policies is an important direction of future work. Recently, Gretton and Thiebaux [19] have taken a step in this direction by using logical regression (based on a domain model) to generate candidate rules for the learner. Developing tractable variations of this approach is a promising research direction. In addition, exploring other ways of incorporating a domain model into our approach and other "model-blind" approaches are critical. Ultimately, scalable AI planning systems will need to combine experience with stronger forms of explicit reasoning.

Acknowledgments

We thank Lin Zhu for originally suggesting the idea of using random walks for bootstrapping. This work was supported in part by NSF grants 9977981-IIS and 0093100-IIS.

References

[1] R. Aler, D. Borrajo, and P. Isasi. Using genetic programming to learn and improve control knowledge. *Artificial Intelligence*, 141(1-2):29–56, 2002.

[2] J. Ambite, C. Knoblock, and S. Minton. Learning plan rewriting rules. In *Proceedings of the International Conference on Artificial Intelligence Planning and Scheduling Systems*, 2000.

[3] F. Bacchus. The AIPS '00 planning competition. *AI Magazine*, 22(3)(3):57–62, 2001.

[4] F. Bacchus and F. Kabanza. Using temporal logics to express search control knowledge for planning. *Artificial Intelligence*, 16:123–191, 2000.

[5] J. Bagnell, S. Kakade, A. Ng, and J. Schneider. Policy search by dynamic programming. In *Proceedings of Neural Information Processing Systems*, 2003.

[6] R. Bellman. *Dynamic Programming*. Princeton University Press, Princeton, NJ, 1957.

[7] D. P. Bertsekas and J. N. Tsitsiklis. *Neuro-Dynamic Programming*. Athena Scientific, Nashua, NH, 1996.

[8] C. Boutilier and R. Dearden. Approximating value trees in structured dynamic programming. In *Proceedings of the International Conference on Machine Learning*, 1996.

[9] C. Boutilier, R. Dearden, and M. Goldszmidt. Stochastic dynamic programming with factored representations. *Artificial Intelligence*, 121(1-2):49–107, 2000.

[10] C. Boutilier, R. Reiter, and B. Price. Symbolic dynamic programming for first-order MDPs. In *Proceedings of the International Joint Conference on Artificial Intelligence*, 2001.

[11] T. Dean and R. Givan. Model minimization in Markov decision processes. In *Proceedings of the National Conference on Artificial Intelligence*, 1997.

[12] T. Dean, R. Givan, and S. Leach. Model reduction techniques for computing approximately optimal solutions for Markov decision processes. In *Proceedings of the National Conference on Artificial Intelligence*, 1997.

[13] S. Dzeroski, L. DeRaedt, and K. Driessens. Relational reinforcement learning. *Machine Learning*, 43:7–52, 2001.

[14] T. Estlin and R. Mooney. Multi-strategy learning of search control for partial-order planning. In *Proceedings of the National Conference on Artificial Intelligence*, 1996.

[15] A. Fern, S. Yoon, and R. Givan. Approximate policy iteration with a policy language bias. In *Proceedings of Neural Information Processing Systems*, 2003.

[16] A. Fern, S. Yoon, and R. Givan. Approximate policy iteration with a policy language bias: Solving relational Markov decision processes. *Journal of Artificial Intelligence Research*, to appear.

[17] L. Finkelstein and S. Markovitch. A selective macro-learning algorithm and its application to the NxN sliding-tile puzzle. *Journal of Artificial Intelligence Research*, 8:223–263, 1998.

[18] R. Givan, T. Dean, and M. Greig. Equivalence notions and model minimization in Markov decision processes. *Artificial Intelligence*, 147(1-2):163–223, 2003.

[19] C. Gretton and S. Thiebaux. Exploiting first-order regression in inductive policy selection. In *Proceedings of the Conference on Uncertainty in Artificial Intelligence*, 2004.

[20] C. Guestrin, D. Koller, C. Gearhart, and N. Kanodia. Generalizing plans to new environments in relational MDPs. In *Proceedings of the International Joint Conference on Artificial Intelligence*, 2003.

[21] C. Guestrin, D. Koller, R. Parr, and S. Venkataraman. Efficient solution algorithms for factored MDPs. *Journal of Artificial Intelligence Research*, 19: 399–468, 2003.

[22] M. Harmon and L. Baird. Residual advantage learning applied to a differential game. In *Proceedings of Neural Information Processing Systems*, 1995.

[23] J. Hoffman, J. Porteous, and L. Sebastia. Ordered landmarks in planning. *Journal of Artificial Intelligence Research*, 22:215–278, 2004.

[24] J. Hoffmann and B. Nebel. The FF planning system: Fast plan generation through heuristic search. *Journal of Artificial Intelligence Research*, 14:263–302, 2001.

[25] R. Howard. *Dynamic Programming and Markov Decision Processes*. MIT Press, Cambridge, MA, 1960.

[26] Y. Huang, B. Selman, and H. Kautz. Learning declarative control rules for constraint-based planning. In *International Conference on Machine Learning*, 2000.

[27] M. Kearns, Y. Mansour, and A. Ng. A sparse sampling algorithm for near-optimal planning in large Markov decision processes. *Machine Learning*, 49 (2–3):193–208, 2002.

[28] K. Kersting, M. Van Otterlo, and L. DeRaedt. Bellman goes relational. In *Proceedings of the International Conference on Machine Learning*, 2004.

[29] R. Khardon. Learning action strategies for planning domains. *Artificial Intelligence*, 113(1-2):125–148, 1999.

[30] R. Khardon. Learning to take actions. *Machine Learning*, 35(1):57–90, 1999.

[31] M. Lagoudakis and R. Parr. Reinforcement learning as classification: Leveraging modern classifiers. In *Proceedings of the International Conference on Machine Learning*, 2003.

[32] J. Langford and B. Zadrozny. Reducing t-step reinforcement learning to classification. *hunch.net/~jl/projects/reductions/RL_to_class/colt_submission.ps*, 2004.

[33] M. Martin and H. Geffner. Learning generalized policies in planning domains using concept languages. In *Proceedings of the International Conference on Principles of Knowledge Representation and Reasoning*, 2000.

[34] M. Mataric. Reward functions for accelarated learning. In *Proceedings of the International Conference on Machine Learning*, 1994.

[35] D. McAllester. Observations on cognitive judgements. In *Proceedings of the National Conference on Artificial Intelligence*, 1991.

[36] D. McAllester and R. Givan. Taxonomic syntax for first order inference. *Journal of the ACM*, 40(2):246–283, 1993.

[37] A. McGovern, E. Moss, and A. Barto. Building a basic block instruction scheduler using reinforcement learning and rollouts. *Machine Learning*, 49

(2/3):141–160, 2002.

[38]   S. Minton. Quantitative results concerning the utility of explanation-based learning. In *National Conference on Artificial Intelligence*, 1988.

[39]   S. Minton, editor. *Machine Learning Methods for Planning*. Morgan Kaufmann, San Fransisco, CA, 1993.

[40]   S. Minton, J. Carbonell, C. A. Knoblock, D. R. Kuokka, O. Etzioni, and Y. Gil. Explanation-based learning: A problem solving perspective. *Artificial Intelligence*, 40:63–118, 1989.

[41]   B. K. Natarajan. On learning from exercises. In *Annual Workshop on Computational Learning Theory*, 1989.

[42]   C. Reddy and P. Tadepalli. Learning goal-decomposition rules using exercises. In *Proceedings of the International Conference on Machine Learning*, 1997.

[43]   R. Rivest. Learning decision lists. *Machine Learning*, 2(3):229–246, 1987.

[44]   C. Sammut, S. Hurst, D. Kedzier, and D. Michie. Learning to fly. In *Proceedings of the International Conference on Machine Learning*, 1992.

[45]   G. Tesauro. Practical issues in temporal difference learning. *Machine Learning*, 8:257–277, 1992.

[46]   G. Tesauro and G. Galperin. On-line policy improvement using monte-carlo search. In *Conference on Advances in Neural Information Processing*, 1996.

[47]   J. Tsitsiklis and B. Van Roy. Feature-based methods for large scale DP. *Machine Learning*, 22:59–94, 1996.

[48]   M. Veloso, J. Carbonell, A. Perez, D. Borrajo, E. Fink, and J. Blythe. Integrating planning and learning: The PRODIGY architecture. *Journal of Experimental and Theoretical AI*, 7(1):81–120, 1995.

[49]   G. Wu, E. Chong, and R. Givan. Congestion control via online sampling. In *Infocom*, 2001.

[50]   X. Yan, P. Diaconis, P. Rusmevichientong, and B. Van Roy. Solitaire: Man versus machine. In *Proceedings of Neural Information Processing Systems*, 2004.

[51]   S. Yoon, A. Fern, and R. Givan. Inductive policy selection for first-order MDPs. In *Proceedings of the Conference on Uncertainty in Artificial Intelligence*, 2002.

[52]   H. Younes. Extending PDDL to model stochastic decision processes. In *Proceedings of the International Conference on Automated Planning and Scheduling Workshop on PDDL*, 2003.

[53]   T. Zimmerman and S. Kambhampati. Learning-assisted automated planning: Looking back, taking stock, going forward. *AI Magazine*, 24(2)(2):73–96, 2003.

19 Statistical Relational Learning for Natural Language Information Extraction

Razvan C. Bunescu and Raymond J. Mooney

Traditionally, information extraction (IE) systems treat separate potential extractions as independent. There are, however, cases when modeling the influences between different potential extractions could improve overall accuracy. In this chapter, we use the framework of relational Markov networks (RMNs) in order to model several specific relationships between candidate extractions. Inference and learning using this graphical model allow for "collective information extraction" in a way that exploits the mutual influence between possible extractions. Experiments on learning to extract protein names from biomedical abstracts demonstrate the advantage of this approach over existing IE methods.

19.1 Introduction

Understanding natural language presents many challenging problems that lend themselves to statistical relational learning (SRL). Historically, both logical and probabilistic methods have found wide application in natural language processing (NLP). NLP inevitably involves reasoning about an arbitrary number of entities (people, places, and things) that have an unbounded set of complex relationships between them. Representing and reasoning about unbounded sets of entities and relations has generally been considered a strength of predicate logic. However, NLP also requires integrating uncertain evidence from a variety of sources in order to resolve numerous syntactic and semantic ambiguities. Effectively integrating multiple sources of uncertain evidence has generally been considered a strength of Bayesian probabilistic methods and graphical models. Consequently, NLP problems are particularly suited for SRL methods that combine the strengths of first-order predicate logic and probabilistic graphical models. In this chapter, we review our recent work [4] on using relational Markov networks (RMNs) [30] for information extraction, the problem of identifying phrases in natural language text that refer to specific types of entities [7]. We use the expressive power of RMNs to represent and reason about several specific relationships between candidate entities and thereby collectively identify the appropriate set of phrases to extract. We present experiments on learning to extract protein names from biomedical text that demonstrate the advantage of this approach over existing information extraction methods.

The remainder of the chapter is organized as follows. In section 19.2, we review the history of logical and probabilistic approaches to NLP, and discuss the unique suitability of SRL for NLP. Section 19.3 introduces the problem of information extraction, followed by section 19.4, where we summarize our work on collective information extraction using RMNs. In section 19.5, we examine challenging problems for future research on SRL for NLP. In section 19.6, we present our conclusions.

19.2   Background on Natural Language Processing

Early research in NLP focused on symbolic techniques in which the knowledge required for understanding and generating language consisted of manually written production rules, semantic networks, or axioms in predicate logic [1]. The semantic analysis of language was a particular focus of NLP research in the 1970s, with researchers exploring tasks ranging from responding to commands and answering questions in a microworld [33] to answering database queries [34] and understanding short stories [26]. These early systems could perform impressive semantic interpretation and inference when understanding particular sentences or stories; however, they tended to require tedious amounts of application-specific knowledge engineering and were therefore quite brittle and not easily extended to new texts or new applications.

Disenchantment with the knowledge-engineering requirements and brittleness of symbolic, manually developed NLP systems grew. Meanwhile, researchers in speech recognition started to obtain promising results using statistical methods trained on large annotated corpora [16]. Eventually, statistical methods came to dominate speech recognition [15], and this development began to motivate the application of similar methods to other aspects of NLP, such as part-of-speech (POS) tagging [8].

During the early 1990s, research in computational linguistics underwent a dramatic paradigm shift. Statistical learning methods that automatically acquire knowledge for language processing from empirical data largely supplanted systems based on human knowledge engineering [14, 19]. However, in order to avoid the difficult problems of detailed semantic interpretation, NLP research focused on building robust systems for simpler tasks, such as POS tagging, syntactic parsing, wordsense disambiguation, and information extraction of specific types of entities.

Many of the methods used in statistical NLP are fundamentally SRL techniques since they perform some form of collective classification on unbounded length strings. Strings can be seen as simple instances of relational data where the individual items are characters, words, or tokens and the single relation "after" holds between adjacent items. Many NLP tasks, such as POS tagging, phrase chunking [24], and information extraction (e.g., named entity tagging), can be viewed as sequence labeling problems in which each word is assigned one of a small number of class labels. The label of each word typically depends on the labels of adjacent words in the sentence and collective inference must be performed to assign the overall most probable combination of labels to all of the words in the sentence. Statistical sequence models such as hidden Markov models (HMMs) [22] or conditional random fields (CRFs) [18] are used to model the data and some form of the Viterbi dynamic programming algorithm [31] is used to efficiently perform the collective classification. However, in order to develop systems that accurately and robustly perform natural language analysis, we believe that more advanced SRL methods are needed. In this chapter, we explore the application of an alternative SRL method to the natural language task of information extraction. We introduce the task in the following section and then present our recent SRL approach.

19.3 Information Extraction

Information extraction, locating references to specific types of items in natural language documents, is an important task with many practical applications. Typical examples include identifying various "named entities" such as names of people, companies, and locations. In this chapter, we consider the task of identifying names of human proteins in abstracts of biomedical journal articles. Figure 19.1 shows part of a sample abstract highlighting the protein names to be identified. This task is an important part of mining the scientific literature in order to build structured databases of existing biological knowledge. In particular, by mining 753,459 abstracts on the human organism from the Medline repository (http://www.ncbi.nlm.nih.gov/entrez/) we have extracted a database of 6580 interactions among 3737 human proteins. The details of this database have been published in the biological literature [23] and it is available on the web at http://bioinformatics.icmb.utexas.edu/idserve.

```
Production of nitric oxide ( NO ) in endothelial cells is regulated by direct
interactions of endothelial nitric oxide synthase ( eNOS ) with effector proteins such
as Ca2+ - calmodulin . Here we have ... identified a novel 34 kDa protein , termed
NOSIP ( eNOS interaction protein ) , which avidly binds to the carboxyl terminal
region of the eNOS oxygenase domain .
```

Figure 19.1 Medline abstract with all protein names emphasized.

In the simplest case, protein name identification can be treated as a sequence labeling problem in which each word (token) in the text is classified as either part of a protein name or not part of a protein name. As long as protein names are not immediately contiguous (a constraint consistently satisfied in the more than 1000 human-annotated abstracts we have examined), this labeling allows immediate recovery of all substrings constituting protein names. However, in practice, a larger set of word labels can result in more accurate extraction. In particular, we found that five word labels—Begin (the first word in a multiword name), End (the last word in a multiword name), Inside (an internal word in a multiword name), Single (a word corresponding to a single-word name), and Other (a word that is not part of a name)—gave the best empirical results by creating word classes with the most easily captured regularities.

In a recent follow-up to previously published experiments comparing a wide variety of information extraction learning methods (including HMM, support vector machines (SVMs), MaxEnt, and rule-based methods) on the task of tagging references to human proteins in Medline abstracts [6], CRFs were found to outperform competing techniques [23]. However, although CRFs capture the dependence between the labels of adjacent words, they do not adequately capture long-distance dependencies between potential extractions in different parts of a document. For example, in our protein-tagging task, repeated references to the same protein are common. If the context surrounding one occurrence of a phrase is very indicative of it being a protein, then this should also influence the tagging of another occurrence of the same phrase in a different context which is not typical of protein references. Consequently, more complex SRL methods that can capture such dependencies may result in more accurate information extraction. In the following section we show how RMNs can be used to model long-distance dependencies in the context of information extraction (for two recent alternative approaches, see the skip-chain CRFs introduced in [28] and the Gibbs sampling method from [11]).

19.4   Collective Information Extraction with RMNs

In this section, we present our research on using RMNs to collectively extract all of the entities in a particular document. In particular, we have tested our approach on the difficult problem of identifying names of human proteins in biomedical journal abstracts. Unlike proteins in some other organisms (e.g., yeast), human proteins have no standardized nomenclature, making them particularly difficult to recognize among the variety of entity types referenced in biomedical text. One important source of potential evidence is the correlations between the labels of repeated phrases inside a document, as well as between acronyms and their corresponding long form. In both cases, the mentioned phrases tend to have the same entity label. For example, figure 19.2 shows part of an abstract from Medline, an online database of biomedical articles. In this abstract, the protein referenced by *rpL22* is first introduced by its long name, *ribosomal protein L22*, followed by the short name, *rpL22*, within parentheses. The presence of the word *protein* is a very good indicator that the entire phrase *ribosomal protein L22* is a protein name. Also, *rpL22* is an acronym of *ribosomal protein L22*, which increases the likelihood that it too is a protein name. The same name *rpL22* occurs later in the abstract in contexts which do not indicate so clearly the entity type; however, we can use the fact that repetitions of the same name tend to have the same type inside the same document.

```
The control of human ribosomal    protein    L22 (rpL22 ) to enter into the nucleolus
and its ability to be assembled into the ribosome is regulated by its sequence .
The nuclear import of rpL22 depends on a classical nuclear localization signal
of four lysines at positions 13 - 16 . RpL22 normally enters the nucleolus via
a compulsory sequence of KKYLKK ( I - domain , positions 88 - 93 ) ... Once it
reaches the nucleolus , the question of whether rpL22 is assembled into the
ribosome depends upon the presence of the N - domain .
```

Figure 19.2   Medline abstract with all protein names emphasized.

The capitalization pattern of the name itself is another useful indicator; nevertheless it is not sufficient by itself, as similar patterns are also used for other types of biological entities such as cell types or amino acids. Therefore, correlations between the labels of repeated phrases, or between acronyms and their long form can provide additional useful information. Our intuition is that a method that could use this kind of information would show an increase in performance, especially when doing extraction from biomedical literature, where phenomena like repetitions and acronyms are pervasive. This type of document-level knowledge can be captured using relational Markov networks (RMNs), a version of undirected graphical models which have already been successfully used to improve the classification of hyperlinked webpages [30].

The rest of this section is organized as follows. In sections 19.4.1 and 19.4.2 we describe the input to our named entity extractor in terms of a set of candidate entities and their features. Subsequent sections introduce the RMN framework for entity recognition (representation, inference, and learning), ending with experimental results in section 19.4.8.

19.4.1   Candidate Entities

Typically, as described in section 19.3, entity recognition has been approached by classifying individual tokens. We [4] considered a different approach, where candidate phrases in a document are classified according to the desired set of entity types. An advantage of using phrase classification is that it allows for phrase-based features such as the text of the candidate phrase, or its similarity to dictionary entries. However, phrase classification requires an initial set of candidate entity phrases. Considering as candidate entities all contiguous word sequences from a document would lead to a quadratic number of phrases, which would adversely affect the time complexity of the extraction algorithm. For our task, there are various heuristics that can significantly reduce the size of the candidate set; two of these are listed below:

- **H1:** In general, named entities have limited length. Therefore, one simple way of creating the set of candidate phrases is to compute the maximum length of all annotated entities in the training set, and then consider as candidates all word sequences whose length is up to this maximum length. This is also the approach followed in SRV [12].

- **H2:** In the task of extracting protein names from Medline abstracts, we noticed that, like most entity names, almost all proteins in our data are base noun phrases (NPs) or parts of them. Therefore, such substrings are used to determine candidate entities. To avoid missing options, we adopt a very broad definition of base NP – a maximal contiguous sequence of tokens with their POS restricted to nouns, gerund verbs, past participle verbs, adjectives, numbers, and dashes. The complete set of POS tags is {*JJ, VBN, VBG, POS, NN, NNS, NNP, NNPS, CD, -*} (using the treebank notation [20]). Also, the last word (the head) of a base NP is constrained to be either a noun or a number. Candidate extractions then consist of base NPs, together with all their contiguous subsequences headed by a noun or number.

19.4.2   Entity Features

The set of features associated with each candidate is based on the feature templates introduced in [9], used there for training a reranking algorithm on the extractions returned by a maximum-entropy tagger. Many of these features use the concept of *word type*, which allows a different form of token generalization than POS tags. The *short type* of a word is created by replacing any maximal contiguous sequences of capital letters with A, of lowercase letters with "a", and of digits with "0." For example, the word *TGF-1* would be mapped to type *A-0*.

Consequently, each token position i in a candidate extraction provides three types of information: the word itself w_i, its POS tag t_i, and its short type s_i. The full set of feature types is listed in table 19.1, where we consider a generic candidate extraction as a sequence of $n + 1$ words $w_0 w_1 ... w_n$.

Each feature template instantiates numerous features. For example, the candidate extraction "HDAC1 enzyme" has the headword $HD=enzyme$, the short type $ST=A0\_a$, the prefixes $PF=A0$ and $PF=A0\_a$, and the suffixes $SF=a$ and $SF=A0\_a$. All other features depend on the left or right context of the entity. Feature values that occur less than three times in the training data are filtered out.

19.4.3   The RMN Framework for Entity Recognition

Given a collection of documents D, we associate with each document $d \in D$ a set of candidate entities $d.E$, in our case a restricted set of token sequences from the document as given by **H2** section 19.4.1. Each entity $e \in d.E$ is characterized by a

Table 19.1   Feature templates

Description	Feature Template	Description	Feature Template
Text / head	$w_0 w_1 ... w_n$ / w_n	Short type	$s_0 s_1 ... s_n$
Bigram left (4 bigrams)	$z_{-1} z_0$ where $z \in \{w, s\}$	Bigram right (4 bigrams)	$z_n z_{n+1}$ where $z \in \{w, s\}$
Trigram left (8 trigrams)	$z_{-2} z_{-1} z_0$ where $z \in \{w, s\}$	Trigram right (8 trigrams)	$z_n z_{n+1} z_{n+2}$ where $z \in \{w, s\}$
POS left	t_{-1}	POS right	t_{n+1}
Prefix (n+1 prefixes)	s_0 $s_0 s_1$ ... $s_0 s_1 ... s_{n+1}$	Suffix (n+1 suffixes)	s_n $s_{n-1} s_n$ ... $s_0 s_1 ... s_{n+1}$

predefined set of Boolean attributes $e.F$ section 19.4.2, the same for all candidate entities. One particular attribute is $e.label$ which is set to 1 if e is considered a valid extraction, and 0 otherwise. In this document model, labels are the only hidden variables, and the inference procedure will try to find a most probable assignment of values to labels, given the current model parameters and the values of all other variables.

Each document is associated with a *factor graph* [17], which is a bipartite graph containing two types of nodes:

- **Variable nodes** correspond directly to the labels of all candidate entities in the document.

- **Potential nodes** model the correlations between two or more entity attributes. For each such correlation, a *potential node* is created that is linked to all *variable nodes* involved. This is equivalent to creating a clique in the corresponding Markov random field.

The types of correlations captured by factor graphs (see figure 19.4 for some examples) are specified by matching *clique templates* against the entire set of candidate entities $d.E$. A clique template is a procedure that finds all subsets of entities satisfying a given constraint, after which, for each entity subset, it connects through a *potential node* all the *variable nodes* corresponding to a selected set of attributes. Formally, there is a set of clique templates C, with each template $c \in C$ specified by:

1. A matching operator M_c for selecting subsets of entities, $M_c(E) \subseteq 2^E$.

2. A selected set of features $S_c = \langle X_c, Y_c \rangle$, the same for all subsets of entities returned by the matching operator. X_c denotes the observed features, while Y_c refers to the hidden labels.

3. A clique potential ϕ_c which gives the compatibility of each possible configuration of values for the features in S_c, s.t. $\phi_c(s) \geq 0, \forall s \in S_c$.

Given a set E of nodes, $M_c(E)$ consists of subsets of entities whose attribute nodes S_c are to be connected in a clique. In previous applications of RMNs, the selected subsets of entities for a given template have the same size; however, some of our clique templates may match a variable number of entities. The set S_c may contain the same attribute from different entities. Usually, for each entity in a matching set, its label is included in S_c. All these will be illustrated with examples in sections 19.4.4 and 19.4.5 where the clique templates used in our model are described in detail.

Depending on the number of hidden labels Y_c selected by a clique c, we define two categories of clique templates:

- **Local templates** are all templates $c \in C$ for which $|Y_c| = 1$. They model the correlations between an entity's observed features and its label.

- **Global templates** are all templates $c \in C$ for which $|Y_c| > 1$. They capture influences between multiple entities from the same document.

After the factor graph model for a document d has been completed with potential nodes from all templates, the probability distribution over the random field of hidden entity labels $d.Y$ given the observed features $d.X$ is given by the Gibbs distribution:

$$P(d.Y|d.X) = \frac{1}{Z(d.X)} \prod_{c \in C} \prod_{G \in M_c(d.E)} \phi_C(G.X_c, G.Y_c), \tag{19.1}$$

where $Z(d.X)$ is the normalizing partition function:

$$Z(d.X) = \sum_Y \prod_{c \in C} \prod_{G \in M_c(d.E)} \phi_C(G.X_c, G.Y_c). \tag{19.2}$$

There are two problems that need to be addressed when working with RMNs:

1. **Inference** Usually, two types of quantities are needed from an RMN model:
   - The marginal distribution for a hidden variable, or for a subset of hidden variables in the graphical model.
   - The most probable assignment of values to all hidden variables in the model.

2. **Learning** As the structure of the RMN model is already defined by its clique templates, learning refers to finding the clique potentials that maximize the likelihood over the training data. Inference is usually performed multiple times during the learning algorithm, which means that an accurate, fast inference procedure is doubly important.

The actual algorithms used for inference and learning will be described in sections 19.4.6 and 19.4.7 respectively.

19.4.4   Local Clique Templates

As described in the previous section, the role of local clique templates is to model correlations between an entity's observed features (see table 19.1 and its label. For each binary feature f we introduce a local template LT_f. Given a candidate entity e, with the observed feature $e.f = 1$, the template LT_f creates a potential node linked to the variable node $e.label$. As an example, figure 19.3 shows that part of the factor graph which is generated around the entity label for "HDAC1 enzyme," with potential nodes for the head feature (HD), prefix features (PF) and suffix features (SF). Variable nodes are shown as empty circles and potential nodes are figured as black squares. The potential ϕ_f associated with all potential nodes created by template LT_f would consist in a 1×2 table, as $e.f$ is known to be 1, and $e.label$ has cardinality 2 (assuming only one entity type is to be extracted, we need only two values for the label attribute).

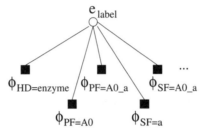

Figure 19.3   Factor graph for local templates.

19.4.5   Global Clique Templates

Global clique templates enable us to model hypothesized influences between entities from the same document. They create potential nodes connected to the label nodes of two or more entities. In our experiments we use three global templates:

- **Overlap template (OT)** No two entity names overlap in the text; i.e., if the span of one entity is $[s_1, c_1]$ and the span of another entity is $[s_2, e_2]$, and $s_1 \le s_2$, then $e_1 < s_2$.

- **Repeat template (RT)** If multiple entities in the same document are repetitions of the same name, their labels tend to have the same value (i.e., most of them are protein names, or most of them are not protein names). In section 19.4.5.2 we discuss situations in which repetitions of the same protein name are not tagged as proteins, and design an approach to handle this.

- **Acronym template (AT)** It is common convention that a protein is first introduced by its long name, immediately followed by its short form (acronym) in parentheses.

In figure 19.4 we show the factor graphs created by these global templates, each of which is explained in the following sections.

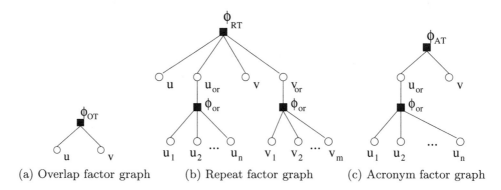

(a) Overlap factor graph   (b) Repeat factor graph   (c) Acronym factor graph

Figure 19.4   Factor graphs for global templates.

19.4.5.1   The Overlap Template

The definition of a *candidate extraction* from section 19.4.1 leads to many overlapping entities. For example, glutathione S - transferase is a base NP, and it generates five candidate extractions: glutathione, glutathione S, glutathione S - transferase, S - transferase, and transferase. If glutathione S - transferase has label-value 1, the other four entities should all have label-value 0, because they overlap with it.

This type of constraint is enforced by the overlap template by creating a potential node for each pair of overlapping entities and connecting it to their label nodes, as shown in figure 19.4(a). To avoid clutter, all entities in this and subsequent factor graphs stand for their corresponding labels. The potential function ϕ_{OT} is manually set so that at most one of the overlapping entities can have label-value 1, as illustrated in table 19.2.

Table 19.2   Overlap potential

ϕ_{OT}	$e_1.label = 0$	$e_1.label = 1$
$e_2.label = 0$	1	1
$e_2.label = 1$	1	0

Continuing with the previous example, because glutathione S and S - transferase are two overlapping entities, the factor graph model will contain an overlap potential node connected to the label nodes of these two entities.

19.4.5.2   The Repeat Template

We could specify the potential for the repeat template in a 2×2 table, this time leaving the table entries to be learned, given that assigning the same label to repetitions is not a hard constraint. However, we can do better by noting that the vast majority of cases where a repeated protein name is not also tagged as a protein happens when it is part of a larger phrase that *is* tagged. For example, "HDAC1 enzyme" is a protein name, therefore "HDAC1" is not tagged in this phrase, even though it may have been tagged previously in the abstract where it was not followed by "enzyme." We need a potential that allows two entities with the same text to have different labels if the entity with label-value 0 is inside another entity with label-value 1. But a candidate entity may be inside more than one "including" entity, and the number of including entities may vary from one candidate extraction to another. Using the example from section 19.4.5.1, the candidate entity glutathione is included in two other entities: glutathione S and glutathione S - transferase.

In order to instantiate potentials over a variable number of label nodes, we introduce a *logical OR clique template* that matches a variable number of entities. When this template matches a subset of entities $e_1, e_2, ..., e_n$, it will create an auxiliary OR entity e_{OR}, with a single attribute $e_{OR}.label$. The potential function ϕ_{OR} is manually set so that it assigns a nonzero potential only when $e_{OR}.label = e_1.label \vee e_2.label \vee ... \vee e_n.label$. The potential nodes are only created as needed, e.g., when the auxiliary OR entity is required by repeat and acronym clique templates.

Figure 19.4(b) shows the factor graph for a sample instantiation of the repeat template using the OR template. Here, u and v represent two same-text entities, u_1, $u_2, ... u_n$ are all entities that include u, and $v_1, v_2, ..., v_m$ are entities that include v. The potential function ϕ_{RT} can either be manually preset to prohibit unlikely label configurations, or it can be learned to represent an appropriate soft constraint. In our experiments, it was learned since this gave slightly better performance.

Following the previous example, suppose that the word glutathione occurs inside two base NPs in the same document, glutathione S - transferase and glutathione antioxidant system. Then the first occurrence of glutathione will be associated with the entity u, and correspondingly its including entities will be $u_1 =$ glutathione S and $u_2 =$ glutathione S - transferase. Similarly, the second occurrence of glutathione will be associated with the entity v, with the corresponding including entities $v_1 =$ glutathione antioxidant and $v_2 =$ glutathione antioxidant system.

19.4.5.3   The Acronym Template

One approach to the acronym template would be to use an extant algorithm for identifying acronyms and their long forms in a document, and then define a potential function that would favor label configurations in which both the acronym and its definition have the same label. One such algorithm is described by Schwartz and Hearst[27], achieving a precision of 96% at a recall rate of 82%. However, because this algorithm would miss a significant number of acronyms, we have decided to implement a softer version as follows: detect all situations in which a single word is enclosed between parentheses, such that the word length is at least 2 and it begins with a letter. Let v denote the corresponding entity. Let u_1, u_2, ..., u_n be all entities that end exactly before the open parenthesis. If this is a situation in which v is an acronym, then one of the entities u_i is its corresponding long form. Consequently, we use a logical OR template to introduce the auxiliary entity u_{OR}, and connect it to v's node label through an acronym potential ϕ_{AT}, as illustrated in figure 19.4(c).

For example, consider the phrase the antioxidant superoxide dismutase - 1 (SOD1). SOD1 satisfies our criteria for acronyms, thus it will be associated with the entity v in figure 19.4(c). The candidate long forms are u_1 = antioxidant superoxide dismutase - 1, u_2 = superoxide dismutase - 1, and u_3 = dismutase - 1.

19.4.6   Inference in Factor Graphs

In our setting, given the clique potentials, the inference step for the factor graph associated with a document involves computing the most probable assignment of values to the hidden labels of all candidate entities:

$$d.Y^* = arg \max_{d.Y} P(d.Y|d.X), \qquad (19.3)$$

where $P(d.Y|d.X)$ is defined as in (19.1). A brute-force approach is excluded, since the number of possible label configurations is exponential in the number of candidate entities. The sum-product algorithm [17] is a message-passing algorithm that can be used for computing the marginal distribution over the label variables in factor graphs without cycles, and with a minor change (replacing the sum operator used for marginalization with a max operator) it can also be used for deriving the most probable label assignment. In our case, in order to get an acyclic graph, we would have to use local templates only. However, it has been observed that the algorithm often converges in general factor graphs, and when it converges, it gives a good approximation to the correct marginals. The algorithm works by altering the belief at each label node by repeatedly passing messages between the node and all potential nodes connected to it [17].

19.4.7   Learning Potentials in Factor Graphs

Following a maximum likelihood estimation, we shall use the log-linear representation of potentials:

$$\phi_C(G.X_c, G.Y_c) = exp\{\mathbf{w_c}\mathbf{f_c}(G.X_c, G.Y_c)\}. \qquad (19.4)$$

Let $\mathbf{w}$ be the concatenated vector of all potential parameters $\mathbf{w_c}$. One approach to finding the maximum likelihood solution for $\mathbf{w}$ is to use a gradient-based method, which requires computing the gradient of the log-likelihood with respect to potential parameters $\mathbf{w_c}$. It can be shown that this gradient is equal with the difference between the empirical counts of $\mathbf{f_c}$ and their expectation under the current set of parameters **w**.

$$\nabla L(w, D) = \sum_{d \in D} f_c(d.X, d.Y) - \sum_{d \in D} \sum_{d.Y'} f_c(d.X, d.Y') P_w(d.Y'|d.X) \qquad (19.5)$$

The expectation in the second term is expensive to compute, since it requires summing over all possible configurations of candidate entity labels from a given document. To circumvent this complexity, we used the voted perceptron approach [13], which can be seen as approximating the full expectation of $\mathbf{f_c}$ with the $\mathbf{f_c}$ counts for the most likely labeling under the current parameters **w**.

$$\nabla L(w, D) \approx \sum_{d \in D} f_c(d.X, d.Y) - \sum_{d \in D} f_c(d.X, d.Y_w) \qquad (19.6)$$

The voted perceptron algorithm is detailed in table 19.3. At each step i in the

Table 19.3   The voted perceptron algorithm

Input: a set of documents D, number of epochs T, learning rate e.

set parameters $w_0 = 0$, counter $i = 0$
 for $t = 1...T$
      for every document $d \in D$
          $d.Y_i = arg\max_{d.Y'} P_{w_i}(d.Y'|d.X)$
          $w_{i+1} = w_i + e * [f(d.X, d.Y) - f(d.X, d.Y_i)]$
          $i = i + 1$

Output: $w = \frac{1}{T|D|} \sum_i w_i$

algorithm, inference is performed using the current parameters w_i, which results in the most likely labeling $d.Y_i$. The parameters are then updated based on the difference between the features counts computed on the ideal labeling $d.Y$ and those computed on the current most likely labeling $d.Y_i$. The final set of parameters is the average taken over the parameters at all steps i in the algorithm. In all our experiments, the perceptron was run for fifty epochs, with a learning rate set at 0.01.

19.4.8   Experimental Results

We have tested the RMN approach on two data sets that have been hand-tagged for human protein names. The first data set is Yapex[1] which consists of 200 Medline abstracts. The second dataset is Aimed[2], which consists of 225 Medline abstracts we previously annotated for evaluating systems that extract both human proteins and their interactions [6].

---

1. URL:www.sics.se/humle/projects/prothalt/
2. URL:ftp.cs.utexas.edu/mooney/bio-data/

We compared the performance of three systems:

- **LT-RMN** is the RMN approach using local templates and the overlap template.
- **GLT-RMN** is the full RMN approach, using all local and global templates.
- **CRF**, which uses a CRF for labeling token sequences. We used the CRF implementation from [21] with the set of tags and features employed by the maximum-entropy tagger described in [6].

All Medline abstracts were tokenized and then POS-tagged using the [2] tagger. Each extracted protein name in the test data was compared to the human-tagged data, with the positions taken into account. Two extractions are considered a match if they consist of the same character sequence in the same position in the text.

Results are shown in table 19.4, which presents the standard information extraction metrics of average *precision* (percentage of extracted names that are correct), *recall* (percentage of correct names that are extracted), and *F-measure* (harmonic mean of precision and recall) using ten-fold cross-validation.

Table 19.4 Information extraction performance on two human protein corpora

Yapex				Aimed			
Method	Precision	Recall	F-m	Method	Precision	Recall	F-m
LT-RMN	70.79	53.81	61.14	LT-RMN	81.33	72.79	76.82
GLT-RMN	69.71	65.76	67.68	GLT-RMN	82.79	80.04	81.39
CRF	72.45	58.64	64.81	CRF	85.37	75.90	80.36

In terms of F-measure, the use of global templates for modeling influences between possible entities from the same document significantly improves extraction performance over the local approach (a one-tailed paired *t*-test for statistical significance results in a *p*-value less than 0.01 on both data sets). There is also a small improvement over CRFs, with the results being statistically significant only for the Yapex data set, corresponding to a *p*-value of 0.02. As expected, GLT-RMN gave a consistently higher recall – additional protein names were extracted as a result of linking them to repetitions with more informative contexts.

We hypothesize that further improvements to the LT-RMN approach and a better inference algorithm would push the GLT-RMN performance even higher. In [3], based on a version of the junction tree algorithm that exploits the sparsity of the overlap potential, we show that exact inference for the LT-RMN case can be performed efficiently, with time complexity linear in terms of the number of candidate entities. In the same work, it is shown that if the candidate entities are given by the weak (but complete) heuristic H1, the new LT-RMN approach can be used for returning all text positions that are unlikely to belong to a named entity. This provides a general method for reducing the number of candidate extractions, which can replace the domain-dependent heuristic H2. The main drawback of this heuristic is that sometimes it may miss true entity names — its coverage is 95.6% on

Yapex and 97.1% on Aimed. As an example, H2 assumes that a candidate entity cannot contain parentheses; however the Yapex corpus contains a few entity names like V (1a) receptor, or interleukin 10 (IL-10) receptor, which violate this assumption. Instead, the local phrase model can be used to learn patterns like "allow a close parenthesis in an entity name if it is followed by the word *receptor*."

For the global model GLT-RMN, the inference procedure can be improved by using a tree-based message propagation schedule, also known as tree reparameterization (TRP) [32]. TRP has the advantage that if often converges in cases where the sum-product algorithm fails, requiring a considerably shorter time for convergence.

19.5 Future Research on SRL for NLP

There are a variety of promising directions for future research in applying SRL to NLP. With respect to information extraction, in addition to identifying entities, an important problem is extracting specific types of relations between entities. For example, in newspaper text, one can identify that an organization is located in a particular city or that a person is affiliated with a specific organization [35]; in biomedical text, one can identify that a protein interacts with another protein or that a protein is located in a particular part of the cell [5, 10]. SRL methods may be usefully applied to such problems since they require identifying relations between phrases that occur in different parts of a sentence or paragraph.

The complete task of natural language understanding incorporates a wide variety of interacting subtasks such as speech recognition, morphology, POS tagging, phrase chunking, syntactic parsing, word-sense disambiguation, semantic interpretation, anaphora (e.g. pronoun) resolution, and discourse processing. Each of these tasks requires disambiguating between numerous possibilities and resolving each of these ambiguities interacts in complex ways with many of the others. For example, when understanding the passage, "At the zoo, several men were showing a group of students various types of flying animals. Suddenly, one of the students hit the man with a bat," one must first use the context in the previous sentence to resolve the meaning of the word "bat" before being able to properly attach the misleading prepositional phrase "with a bat" to the man (NP) rather than to the hitting (verb phrase). SRL methods hold the promise of being able to integrate decisions at all levels of syntactic, semantic, and pragmatic processing in order to correctly interpret natural language. Several recent projects have taken the first steps in this direction. For example, Sutton et al. [29] present a dynamic version of a CRF that integrates POS tagging and NP chunking into one coherent process. Roth and Yi [25] present an information-extraction approach based on linear programming that integrates recognition of entities with the identification of relations between these entities. The ability of SRL techniques to integrate uncertain evidence from many interacting problems in order to collectively determine a globally coherent solution to all of them could help develop a complete, robust NLP system. However, such a system would create massive collective inference problems and would require efficient SRL methods that could scale to very large networks.

19.6   Conclusions

The area of natural language processing includes many problems that lend themselves to SRL methods. Most existing statistical methods in NLP, such as HMMs, sequence CRFs, and probabilistic context-free grammars are actually restrictive forms of SRL. More general SRL techniques have advantages over these existing methods and hold the promise of improving results on a number of difficult NLP problems. In this chapter, we have reviewed our research on applying SRL techniques to information extraction. By using RMNs to capture dependencies between distinct candidate extractions in a document, we achieved improved results on identifying names of proteins in biomedical abstracts compared to a traditional CRF. By using the ability of SRL to integrate disparate sources of evidence to perform collective inference over complex relational data, robust NLP systems that accurately resolve many interacting ambiguities can hopefully be developed.

Acknowledgments

This research was partially supported by the National Science Foundation under grants IIS-0325116 and IRI-9704943.

References

[1]   J. Allen. *Natural Language Understanding*. Benjamin/Cummings, Menlo Park, CA, 1987.

[2]   E. Brill. Transformation-based error-driven learning and natural language processing: A case study in part-of-speech tagging. *Computational Linguistics*, 21(4):543–565, 1995.

[3]   R. Bunescu. Learning for collective information extraction. Technical Report TR-05-02, Department of Computer Sciences, University of Texas at Austin, 2004.

[4]   R. Bunescu and R. J. Mooney. Collective information extraction with relational Markov networks. In *Proceedings of the Annual Meeting of the Association for Computational Linguistics*, 2004.

[5]   R. Bunescu and R. J. Mooney. Subsequence kernels for relation extraction. In *Proceedings of the Conference on Neural Information Processing Systems*, 2005.

[6]   R. Bunescu, R. Ge, R. Kate, E. Marcotte, R. J. Mooney, A. Kumar Ramani, and Y. Wah Wong. Comparative experiments on learning information extrac-

tors for proteins and their interactions. *Artificial Intelligence in Medicine (Special Issue on Summarization and Information Extraction from Medical Documents)*, 33(2):139–155, 2005.

[7] C. Cardie. Empirical methods in information extraction. *AI Magazine*, 18(4): 65–79, 1997.

[8] Kenneth W. Church. A stochastic parts program and noun phrase parser for unrestricted text. In *Proceedings of the Conference on Applied Natural Language Processing*, 1988.

[9] M. Collins. Ranking algorithms for named-entity extraction: Boosting and the voted perceptron. In *Proceedings of the Annual Meeting of the Association for Computational Linguistics*, 2002.

[10] M. Craven and J. Kumlien. Using multiple levels of learning and diverse evidence sources to uncover coordinately controlled genes. In *Proceedings of the International Conference on Intelligent Systems for Molecular Biology*, 1999.

[11] J. Finkel, T. Grenager, and C. Manning. Incorporating non-local information into information extraction systems by Gibbs sampling. In *Proceedings of the Annual Meeting of the Association for Computational Linguistics*, 2005.

[12] D. Freitag. Information extraction from HTML: Application of a general learning approach. In *Proceedings of the National Conference on Artificial Intelligence*, 1998.

[13] Y. Freund and R. Schapire. Large margin classification using the perceptron algorithm. *Machine Learning*, 37:277–296, 1999.

[14] J. Hirschberg. Every time I fire a linguist, my performance goes up, and other myths of the statistical natural language processing revolution. Presented at the National Conference on Artificial Intelligence, 1998.

[15] F. Jelinek. *Statistical Methods for Speech Recognition*. MIT Press, Cambridge, MA, 1998.

[16] F. Jelinek. Continuous speech recognition by statistical methods. *Proceedings of the IEEE*, 64(4):532–556, 1976.

[17] F. R. Kschischang, B. Frey, and H.-A. Loeliger. Factor graphs and the sum-product algorithm. *IEEE Transactions on Information Theory*, 47(2):498–519, 2001.

[18] J. Lafferty, A. McCallum, and F. Pereira. Conditional random fields: Probabilistic models for segmenting and labeling sequence data. In *Proceedings of the International Conference on Machine Learning*, 2001.

[19] C. Manning and H. Schütze. *Foundations of Statistical Natural Language Processing*. MIT Press, Cambridge, MA, 1999.

[20] M. Marcus, B. Santorini, and M. Marcinkiewicz. Building a large annotated corpus of English: The Penn treebank. *Computational Linguistics*, 19(2):313–330, 1993.

[21] A. McCallum. Mallet: A machine learning for language toolkit. http://mallet.cs.umass.edu, 2002.

[22] L. Rabiner. A tutorial on hidden Markov models and selected applications in speech recognition. *Proceedings of the IEEE*, 77(2):257–286, 1989.

[23] A. Ramani, R. Bunescu, R. J. Mooney, and E. Marcotte. Consolidating the set of known human protein-protein interactions in preparation for large-scale mapping of the human interactome. *Genome Biology*, 6(5):r40, 2005.

[24] L. Ramshaw and M. Marcus. Text chunking using transformation-based learning. In *Proceedings of the Third Workshop on Very Large Corpora*, 1995.

[25] D. Roth and W. Yih. A linear programming formulation for global inference in natural language tasks. In *Proceedings of the Conference on Natural Language Learning*, 2004.

[26] R. Schank and C. Riesbeck. *Inside Computer Understanding: Five Programs plus Miniatures*. Lawrence Erlbaum and Associates, Hillsdale, NJ, 1981.

[27] A. Schwartz and M. Hearst. A simple algorithm for identifying abbreviation definitions in biomedical text. In *Proceedings of the Eighth Pacific Symposium on Biocomputing*, 2003.

[28] C. Sutton and A. McCallum. Collective segmentation and labeling of distant entities in information extraction. In *ICML Workshop on Statistical Relational Learning and Its Connections to Other Fields*, 2004.

[29] C. Sutton, K. Rohanimanesh, and A. McCallum. Dynamic conditional random fields: Factorized probabilistic models for labeling and segmenting sequence data. In *Proceedings of the International Conference on Machine Learning*, 2004.

[30] B. Taskar, P. Abbeel, and D. Koller. Discriminative probabilistic models for relational data. In *Proceedings of the Conference on Uncertainty in Artificial Intelligence*, 2002.

[31] A. Viterbi. Error bounds for convolutional codes and an asymptotically optimum decoding algorithm. *IEEE Transactions on Information Theory*, 13 (2):260–269, 1967.

[32] M. Wainwright, T. Jaakkola, and A. Willsky. Tree-based reparameterization framework for approximate estimation on graphs with cycles. In *Proceedings of the Conference on Neural Information Processing Systems*, 2001.

[33] T. Winograd. *Understanding Natural Language*. Academic Press, Orlando, FL, 1972.

[34] W. A. Woods. Lunar rocks in natural English: Explorations in natural language question answering. In Antonio Zampoli, editor, *Linguistic Structures Processing*. Elsevier North-Holland, New York, 1977.

[35] D. Zelenko, C. Aone, and A. Richardella. Kernel methods for relation extraction. *Journal of Machine Learning Research*, 3:1083–1106, 2003.

20 Global Inference for Entity and Relation Identification via a Linear Programming Formulation

Dan Roth and Wen-tau Yih

Natural language decisions often involve assigning values to sets of variables, representing low-level decisions and context-dependent disambiguation. In most cases there are complex relationships among these variables representing dependencies that range from simple statistical correlations to those that are constrained by deeper structural, relational, and semantic properties of the text.

In this chapter we study a specific instantiation of this problem in the context of identifying named entities and relations between them in free-form text. Given a collection of discrete random variables representing outcomes of learned local predictors for entities and relations, we seek an optimal global assignment to the variables that respects multiple constraints, including constraints on the type of arguments a relation can take, and the mutual activity of different relations.

We develop a linear programming formulation to address this global inference problem and evaluate it in the context of simultaneously learning named entities and relations. We show that global inference improves stand-alone learning; in addition, our approach allows us to efficiently incorporate expressive domain and task-specific constraints at decision time, resulting, beyond significant improvements in the accuracy, in "coherent" quality of the inference.

20.1 Introduction

In a variety of AI problems there is a need to learn, represent, and reason with respect to definitions over structured and relational data. Examples include learning to identify properties of text fragments such as functional phrases and named entities, identifying relations such as "A is the assassin of B" in text, learning to classify molecules for mutagenicity from atom-bond data in drug design, learning to identify 3D objects in their natural surrounding, and learning a policy to map goals to actions in planning domains.

Learning to make decisions with respect to natural language input is a prime source of examples for the need to represent, learn, and reason with structured and relational data [12, 13, 16, 18]. Natural language tasks presents several challenges to statistical relational learning (SRL). It is necessary (1) to represent structured domain elements in the sense that their internal (hierarchical) structure can be encoded, and learning functions in these terms can be supported, and (2) it is essential to represent concepts and functions relationally, in the sense that different data instantiations may be abstracted to yield the same representation, so that evaluation of functions over different instantiations will produce the same output. Moreover, beyond having to deal with structured *input*, in many natural language understanding tasks there is a rich relational structure also on the *output* of predictors. Natural language decisions often depend on the outcomes of several different but mutually dependent predictions. These predictions must respect some constraints that could arise from the nature of the data or from domain-specific conditions. For example, in part-of-speech (POS)tagging, a sentence must have at least one verb, and cannot have three consecutive verbs. These facts can be used as constraints. In named entity recognition, "no entities overlap" is a common constraint used in various works [37]. When predicting whether phrases in sentences represent entities and determining their type, the relations between the candidate entities provide constraints on their allowed (or plausible) types, via selectional restrictions.

While the classifiers involved in these global decisions need to exploit the relational structure in the input [30], we will not discuss these issues here, and will focus here instead on the task of inference with the classifiers' outcomes. Namely, this work is concerned with the *relational structure over the outcomes of predictors*, and studies natural language inferences which exploit the global structure of the problem, aiming at making decisions which depend on the outcomes of several different but mutually dependent classifiers.

Efficient solutions to problems of this sort have been given when the constraints on the predictors are *sequential* [25, 15]. These solutions can be categorized into the following two frameworks. The first, which we call *learning global models*, trains a probabilistic model under the constraints imposed by the domain. Examples include variations of hidden Markov models (HMMs), conditional models, and sequential variations of Markov random fields (MRFs) [21]. The other framework, *inference with classifiers* [28], views maintaining constraints and learning component classifiers as separate processes. Various local classifiers are trained without the knowledge of the global output constraints. The predictions are taken as input to an inference procedure which is given these constraints and then finds the best global prediction. In addition to the conceptual simplicity and modularity of this approach, it is more efficient than the global training approach, and seems to perform better experimentally in some tasks [37, 26, 32].

Typically, efficient inference procedures in both frameworks rely on dynamic programming (e.g., Viterbi), which works well for sequential data. However, in many important problems, the structure is more general, resulting in computationally intractable inference. Problems of these sorts have been studied in computer vision, where inference is generally performed over low-level measurements rather than over higher-level predictors [22, 3].

This work develops a novel *inference with classifiers* approach. Rather than being restricted to sequential data, we study a fairly general setting. The problem is defined in terms of a collection of discrete random variables representing binary relations and their arguments; we seek an optimal assignment to the variables in the presence of the constraints on the binary relations between variables and the relation types. Following ideas that were developed recently in the context of approximation algorithms [8], we model inference as an optimization problem, and show how to cast it in a linear programming (LP) formulation. Using existing numerical packages, which are able to solve very large LP problems in a very short time[1], inference can be done very quickly.

Our approach could be contrasted with other approaches to sequential inference or to general MRF approaches [21, 35]. The key difference is that in these approaches, the model is learned globally, under the constraints imposed by the domain. Our approach is designed to address also cases in which some of the local classifiers are learned (or acquired otherwise) in other contexts and at other times, or incorporated as background knowledge. That is, some components of the global decision need not, or cannot, be trained in the context of the decision problem. This way, our approach allows the incorporation of constraints into decisions in a dynamic fashion and can therefore support task-specific inference. The significance of this is clearly shown in our experimental results.

We develop our model in the context of natural language inference and evaluate it here on the problem of *simultaneously* recognizing named entities and relations between them.

For instance, in the sentence `J. V. Oswald was murdered at JFK after his assassin, R. U. KFJ shot...`, we want to identify the *kill (KFJ, Oswald)* relation. This task requires making several local decisions, such as identifying named entities in the sentence, in order to support the relation identification. For example, it may be useful to identify that Oswald and KFJ are *people*, and JFK is a *location*. This, in turn, may help to identify that a *kill* action is described in the sentence. At the same time, the relation *kill* constrains its arguments to be *people* (or at least, not to be *location*s) and helps to enforce that Oswald and KFJ are likely to be *people*, while JFK may not.

In our model, we first learn a collection of "local" predictors, e.g., entity and relation identifiers. At decision time, given a sentence, we produce a global decision

---

1. For example, CPLEX [11] is able to solve a linear programming problem of 13 million variables within 5 minutes.

that optimizes over the suggestions of the classifiers that are active in the sentence, known constraints among them and, potentially, domain-specific or task-specific constraints relevant to the current decision. Although a brute-force algorithm may seem feasible for short sentences, as the number of entity variables grows, the computation becomes intractable very quickly. Given n entities in a sentence, there are $O(n^2)$ possible binary relations between them. Assume that each variable (entity or relation) can take l labels ("none" is one of these labels). Thus, there are l^{n^2} possible assignments, which is too large to explicitly enumerate even for a small n.

When evaluated on simultaneous learning of named entities and relations, our approach not only provides a significant improvement in the predictors' accuracy; more importantly, it provides *coherent* solutions. While many statistical methods make "incoherent" mistakes (i.e., inconsistency among predictions) that no human ever makes, as we show, our approach improves also the *quality* of the inference significantly.

The rest of the chapter is organized as follows. Section 20.2 formally defines our problem and section 20.3 describes the computational approach we propose. Experimental results are given in section 20.5, including a case study that illustrates how our inference procedure improves the performance. We introduce some common inference methods used in various text problems as comparison in section 20.6, followed by some discussions and conclusions in section 20.7.

20.2   The Relational Inference Problem

We consider the relational inference problem within the *reasoning with classifiers* paradigm, and study a specific but fairly general instantiation of this problem, motivated by the problem of recognizing named entities (e.g., persons, locations, organization names) and relations between them (e.g. work_for, located_in, live_in). Conceptually, the entities and relations can be viewed, taking into account the mutual dependencies, as shown in figure 20.1, where the nodes represent entities (e.g., phrases) and the links denote the binary relations between the entities. Each entity and relation has several properties. Some of the properties, such as words inside the entities and POS tags of words in the context of the sentence, are easy to acquire. However, other properties like the semantic types (i.e., class labels, such as "people" or "locations") of phrases are difficult. Identifying the labels of entities and relations is treated here as a learning problem. In particular, we learn these target properties as functions of all other properties of the sentence.

To describe the problem in a formal way, we first define sentences and entities as follows.

Definition 20.1 Sentence and Entities
A sentence S is a linked list which consists of words w and entities $\mathcal{E}$. An entity can be a single word or a set of consecutive words with a predefined boundary. Entities in a sentence are labeled as $\mathcal{E} = \{E_1, E_2, \cdots, E_n\}$ according to their order, and

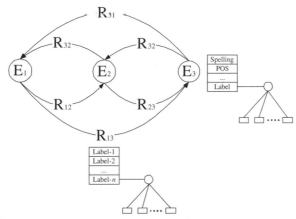

Figure 20.1 A conceptual view of entities and relations.

they take values (i.e., labels) that range over a set of entity types $\mathcal{L_E}$. The value assigned to $E_i \in \mathcal{E}$ is denoted $f_{E_i} \in \mathcal{L_E}$.

Notice that determining the entity boundaries is also a difficult problem – the *segmentation* (or *phrase detection*) problem [1, 25]. Here we assume it is solved and given to us as input; thus we only concentrate on classification.

$$\boxed{\text{Dole}}\text{'s wife ,}\boxed{\text{Elizabeth}}\text{, is a native of}\boxed{\text{Salisbury , N.C.}}$$
$$\quad\textbf{E1}\qquad\qquad\qquad\textbf{E2}\qquad\qquad\qquad\qquad\textbf{E3}$$

Figure 20.2 A sentence that has three entities.

Example 20.1
The sentence in figure 20.2 has three entities: $E_1 =$ "Dole", $E_2 =$ "Elizabeth," and $E_3 =$ "Salisbury, N.C."

A relation is defined by the entities that are involved in it (its arguments). Note that we only discuss binary relations.

Definition 20.2 Relations
A (binary) relation $R_{ij} = (E_i, E_j)$ represents the relation between E_i and E_j, where E_i is the first argument and E_j is the second. In addition, R_{ij} can range over a set of entity types $\mathcal{L_R}$. We use $\mathcal{R} = \{R_{ij}\}_{\{1 \leq i,j \leq n; i \neq j\}}$ as the set of binary relations on the entities $\mathcal{E}$ in a sentence. Two special functions $\mathcal{N}^1$ and $\mathcal{N}^2$ are used to indicate the argument entities of a relation R_{ij}. Specifically, $E_i = \mathcal{N}^1(R_{ij})$ and $E_j = \mathcal{N}^2(R_{ij})$.

Note that in this definition, the relations are directed (e.g., there are both R_{ij} and R_{ji} variables). This is because the arguments in a relation often take different roles and have to be distinguished. Examples of this sort include *work_for*, *located_in* and *live_in.* If a relation variable R_{ij} is predicted as a mutual relation (e.g., *spouse_of*), then the corresponding relation R_{ji} should be also assigned the same label. This additional constraint can be easily incorporated in our inference framework. Also notice that we simplify the definition slightly by not considering self-relations (e.g., R_{ii}). This can be relaxed if this type of relations appears in the data.

Example 20.2
In the sentence given in figure 20.2, there are six relations between the entities: R_{12} = ("Dole", "Elizabeth"), R_{21} = ("Elizabeth," "Dole"), R_{13} = ("Dole," "Salisbury, N.C."), R_{31} = ("Salisbury, N.C.," "Dole"), R_{23} = ("Elizabeth," "Salisbury, N.C."), and R_{32} = ("Salisbury, N.C.," "Elizabeth")

We define the types (i.e., classes) of relations and entities as follows.

Definition 20.3 Classes
We denote the set of predefined entity classes and relation classes as $\mathcal{L}_\mathcal{E}$ and $\mathcal{L}_\mathcal{R}$ respectively. $\mathcal{L}_\mathcal{E}$ has one special element, *other_ent*, which represents any unlisted entity class. Similarly, $\mathcal{L}_\mathcal{R}$ also has one special element, *other_rel*, which means the involved entities are irrelevant or the relation class is undefined.

When it is clear from the context, we use E_i and R_{ij} to refer to the entity and relation, as well as their types (class labels). Note that each relation and entity variable can take only one class according to definition 20.3. Although there may be different relations between two entities, it seldom occurs in the data. Therefore, we ignore this issue for now.

Example 20.3
Suppose $\mathcal{L}_\mathcal{E}$ = { *other_ent, person, location* } and $\mathcal{L}_\mathcal{R}$ = { *other_rel, born_in, spouse_of* }. For the entities in figure 20.2, E_1 and E_2 belong to *person* and E_3 belongs to *location*. In addition, relation R_{23} is *born_in*, R_{12} and R_{21} are *spouse_of*. Other relations are *other_rel*.

Given a sentence, we want to predict the labels of a set $\mathcal{V}$ which consists of two types of variables – entities $\mathcal{E}$ and relations $\mathcal{R}$. That is, $\mathcal{V} = \mathcal{E} \cup \mathcal{R}$. However, the class label of a single entity or relation depends not only on its local properties but also on the properties of other entities and relations. The classification task is somewhat difficult since the predictions of entity labels and relation labels are mutually dependent. For instance, the class label of E_1 depends on the class label of R_{12} and the class label of R_{12} also depends on the class label of E_1 and E_2. While we can assume that all the data is annotated for training purposes, this cannot be assumed at evaluation time. We may presume that some local properties, such as the words or POS tags, are given, but none of the class labels for entities or relations are.

To simplify the complexity of the interaction within the graph but still preserve the characteristic of mutual dependency, we abstract this classification problem in the following probabilistic framework. First, the classifiers are trained independently and used to estimate the probabilities of assigning different labels given the observation (that is, the easily classified properties in it). Then, the output of the classifiers is used as a conditional distribution for each entity and relation, given the observation. This information, along with the constraints among the relations and entities, is used to make global inference.

In the task of entity and relation recognition, there exist some constraints on the labels of corresponding relation and entity variables. For instance, if the relation is *live_in*, then the first entity should be a *person*, and the second entity should be a *location*. The correspondence between the relation and entity variables can be represented by a bipartite graph. Each relation variable R_{ij} is connected to its first entity E_i, and second entity E_j. We define a set of constraints on the outcomes of the variables in $\mathcal{V}$ as follows.

Definition 20.4   *Constraints*

A constraint is a function that maps a relation label and an entity label to either 0 or 1 (contradict or satisfy the constraint). Specifically, $\mathcal{C}^1 : \mathcal{L}_\mathcal{R} \times \mathcal{L}_\mathcal{E} \rightarrow \{0,1\}$ constrains values of the first argument of a relation. $\mathcal{C}^2$ is defined similarly and constrains values of the second argument.

Note that while we define the constraints here as Boolean functions, our formalism allows us to associate weights with constraints and to include statistical constraints [32]. Also note that we can define a large number of constraints, such as $\mathcal{C}^R : \mathcal{L}_\mathcal{R} \times \mathcal{L}_\mathcal{R} \rightarrow \{0,1\}$ which constrain the labels of two relation variables. For example, we can define a set of constraints on a mutual relation *spouse_of* as $\{(spouse\_of, spouse\_of) = 1, (spouse\_of, l_r) = 0, \text{ and } (l_r, spouse\_of) = 0$ for any $l_r \in \mathcal{L}_\mathcal{R}$, where $l_r \neq spouse\_of\}$. By enforcing these constraints on a pair of symmetric relation variables R_{ij} and R_{ji}, the relation class *spouse_of* will be assigned to either both R_{ij} and R_{ji} or none of them. [In fact, as will be clear in section 20.3, the language used to describe constraints is very rich – linear (in)equalities over $\mathcal{V}$.]

We seek an inference algorithm that can produce a coherent labeling of entities and relations in a given sentence. Furthermore, it optimizes an objective function based on the conditional probabilities or other confidence scores estimated by the entity and relation classifiers, subject to some natural constraints. Examples of these constraints include whether specific entities can be the argument of specific relations, whether two relations can occur together among a subset of entity variables in a sentence, and any other information that might be available at the inference time. For instance, suppose it is known that entities A and B represent the same location; one may like to incorporate an additional constraint that prevents an inference of the type: "C lives in A; C does not live in B."

We note that a large number of problems can be modeled this way. Examples include problems such as chunking sentences [25], coreference resolution and sequencing problems in computational biology, and the recently popular problem of semantic role labeling [5, 6]. In fact, each of the components of our problem here, namely the separate task of recognizing named entities in sentences and the task of recognizing semantic relations between phrases, can be modeled this way. However, our goal is specifically to consider interacting problems at different levels, resulting in more complex constraints among them, and exhibit the power of our method.

20.3   Integer Linear Programming Inference

The most direct way to formalize our inference problem is using MRFs [9]. Rather than doing that, for computational reasons, we first use a fairly standard transformation of MRFs to a discrete optimization problem (see [19] for details). Specifically, under weak assumptions we can view the inference problem as the following optimization problem, which aims at minimizing the objective function that is the sum of the following two cost functions.

Assignment cost   This is the cost of deviating from the assignment of the variables $\mathcal{V}$ given by the classifiers. The specific cost function we use is defined as follows: Let l be the label assigned to variable $u \in \mathcal{V}$. If the posterior probability estimation is $p = P(f_u = l|\bar{x})$, where $\bar{x}$ represents the input feature vector, then the assignment cost $c_u(l)$ is $-\log p$.

Constraint cost   This is the cost imposed by breaking constraints between neighboring nodes. The specific cost function we use is defined as follows: Consider two entity nodes E_i, E_j and their corresponding relation node R_{ij}; that is, $E_i = \mathcal{N}^1(R_{ij})$ and $E_j = \mathcal{N}^2(R_{ij})$. The constraint cost indicates whether the labels are consistent with the constraints. In particular, we use: $d^1(f_{E_i}, f_{R_{ij}})$ is 0 if $(f_{R_{ij}}, f_{E_i}) \in \mathcal{C}^1$; otherwise, $d^1(f_{E_i}, f_{R_{ij}})$ is ∞ [2]. Similarly, we use d^2 to force the consistency of the second argument of a relation.

Since we are looking for the most probable global assignment that satisfies the constraints, the overall cost function we optimize for a global labeling f of all variables is

$$C(f) = \sum_{u \in \mathcal{V}} c_u(f_u) + \sum_{R_{ij} \in \mathcal{R}} \left[d^1(f_{R_{ij}}, f_{E_i}) + d^2(f_{R_{ij}}, f_{E_j}) \right] \qquad (20.1)$$

Unfortunately, this combinatorial problem (20.1) is computationally intractable even when placing assumptions on the cost function [19]. The computational approach we adopt is to develop a *linear programming* formulation of the problem, and then solve the corresponding *integer linear programming* (ILP) problem[3]. Our LP formulation is based on the method proposed by Chekuri et al. [8]. Since the objective function (20.1) is not a linear function in terms of the labels, we introduce

---

2. In practice, we use a very large number (e.g., 9^{15}).
3. In this chapter, ILP only means *integer linear programming*, not inductive logic programming.

new binary variables to represent different possible assignments to each original variable; we then represent the objective function as a linear function of these binary variables.

Let $x_{\{u,i\}}$ be an indicator variable, defined to be 1 if and only if variable u is labeled i and 0 otherwise, where $u \in \mathcal{E}, i \in \mathcal{L}_\mathcal{E}$ or $u \in \mathcal{R}, i \in \mathcal{L}_\mathcal{R}$. For example, $x_{\{E_1,person\}} = 1$ when the label of entity E_1 is *person*; $x_{\{R_{23},spouse\_of\}} = 0$ when the label of relation R_{23} is not *spouse_of*. Let $x_{\{R_{ij},r,E_i,e_1\}}$ be an indicator variable representing whether relation R_{ij} is assigned label r and its first argument, E_i, is assigned label e_1. For instance, $x_{\{R_{12},spouse\_of,E_1,person\}} = 1$ means the label of relation R_{12} is *spouse_of* and the label of its first argument, E_1, is *person*. Similarly, $x_{\{R_{ij},r,E_j,e_2\}} = 1$ indicates that R_{ij} is assigned label r and its second argument, E_j, is assigned label e_2. With these definitions, the optimization problem can be represented as the following integer linear program.

$$\min \sum_{E \in \mathcal{E}} \sum_{e \in \mathcal{L}_\mathcal{E}} c_E(e) \cdot x_{\{E,e\}} + \sum_{R \in \mathcal{R}} \sum_{r \in \mathcal{L}_\mathcal{R}} c_R(r) \cdot x_{\{R,r\}}$$

$$+ \sum_{\substack{E_i,E_j \in \mathcal{E} \\ E_i \neq E_j}} \left[\sum_{r \in \mathcal{L}_\mathcal{R}} \sum_{e_1 \in \mathcal{L}_\mathcal{E}} d^1(r,e_1) \cdot x_{\{R_{ij},r,E_i,e_1\}} + \sum_{r \in \mathcal{L}_\mathcal{R}} \sum_{e_2 \in \mathcal{L}_\mathcal{E}} d^2(r,e_2) \cdot x_{\{R_{ij},r,E_j,e_2\}} \right],$$

subject to:

$$\sum_{e \in \mathcal{L}_\mathcal{E}} x_{\{E,e\}} = 1 \quad \forall E \in \mathcal{E} \tag{20.2}$$

$$\sum_{r \in \mathcal{L}_\mathcal{R}} x_{\{R,r\}} = 1 \quad \forall R \in \mathcal{R} \tag{20.3}$$

$$x_{\{E,e\}} = \sum_{r \in \mathcal{L}_\mathcal{R}} x_{\{R,r,E,e\}} \quad \begin{aligned} &\forall E \in \mathcal{E}, e \in \mathcal{L}_\mathcal{E}, \\ &\forall R \in \{R : E = \mathcal{N}^1(R) \ \text{or} \ E = \mathcal{N}^2(R)\} \end{aligned} \tag{20.4}$$

$$x_{\{R,r\}} = \sum_{e \in \mathcal{L}_\mathcal{E}} x_{\{R,r,E,e\}} \quad \forall R \in \mathcal{R}, r \in \mathcal{L}_\mathcal{R}, E = \mathcal{N}^1(R) \tag{20.5}$$

$$x_{\{R,r\}} = \sum_{e \in \mathcal{L}_\mathcal{E}} x_{\{R,r,E,e\}} \quad \forall R \in \mathcal{R}, r \in \mathcal{L}_\mathcal{R}, E = \mathcal{N}^2(R) \tag{20.6}$$

$$x_{\{E,e\}} \in \{0,1\} \quad \forall E \in \mathcal{E}, e \in \mathcal{L}_\mathcal{E} \tag{20.7}$$

$$x_{\{R,r\}} \in \{0,1\} \quad \forall R \in \mathcal{R}, r \in \mathcal{L}_\mathcal{R} \tag{20.8}$$

$$x_{\{R,r,E,e\}} \in \{0,1\} \quad \forall R \in \mathcal{R}, r \in \mathcal{L}_\mathcal{R}, E \in \mathcal{E}, e \in \mathcal{L}_\mathcal{E} \tag{20.9}$$

Equations (20.2) and (20.3) require that each entity or relation variable can only be assigned one label. Equations (20.4), (20.5), and (20.6) assure that the assignment to each entity or relation variable is consistent with the assignment to its neighboring variables. Equations (20.7), (20.8), and (20.9) are the integral constraints on these binary variables.

There are several advantages of representing the problem in an LP formulation. First of all, linear (in)equalities are fairly general and are able to represent many types of constraints (e.g., the decision time constraint in the experiment in section 20.5). More importantly, an ILP problem at this scale can be solved very quickly using current numerical packages, such as Xpress-MP [42] or CPLEX [11]. We introduce the general strategies of solving an ILP problem here.

20.4   Solving Integer Linear Programming

To solve an ILP problem, a straightforward idea is to *relax* the integral constraints. That is, replacing (20.7), (20.8), and (20.9) with

$$x_{\{E,e\}} \geq 0 \qquad \forall E \in \mathcal{E}, e \in \mathcal{L}_{\mathcal{E}} \tag{20.10}$$

$$x_{\{R,r\}} \geq 0 \qquad \forall R \in \mathcal{R}, r \in \mathcal{L}_{\mathcal{R}} \tag{20.11}$$

$$x_{\{R,r,E,e\}} \geq 0 \qquad \forall R \in \mathcal{R}, r \in \mathcal{L}_{\mathcal{R}}, E \in \mathcal{E}, e \in \mathcal{L}_{\mathcal{E}}, \tag{20.12}$$

If linear programming relaxation (LPR) returns an integer solution, then it is also the optimal solution to the ILP problem. In fact, it can be shown that the optimal solution of a linear program is always integral if the coefficient matrix of its standard form is *unimodular* [34].

Definition 20.5
A matrix $\mathbf{A}$ of rank m is called *unimodular* if all the entries of $\mathbf{A}$ are integers, and the determinant of every square submatrix of $\mathbf{A}$ of order m is in 0,+1,-1.

Theorem 20.6   Veinott and Dantzig
Let $\mathbf{A}$ be an (m,n)-integral matrix with full row rank m. Then the polyhedron $\{\mathbf{x}|\mathbf{x} \geq 0; \mathbf{A}\mathbf{x} = \mathbf{b}\}$ is integral for each integral vector $\mathbf{b}$, if and only if $\mathbf{A}$ is unimodular.

Theorem 20.6 indicates that if a linear program is in its standard form, then regardless of the cost function and the integral vector $\mathbf{b}$, the optimal solution is an integer point if and only if the coefficient matrix $\mathbf{A}$ is unimodular.

When LPR returns a noninteger solution, the ILP problem is usually handled by one of the two strategies: *rounding* and *search*.

The goal of *rounding* is to find an integer point that is close to the noninteger solution. Under some conditions of the cost function, which do not hold in our problem, a well-designed rounding algorithm can be shown that the rounded solution is a good approximation to the optimal solution [19, 8]. Nevertheless, in general, the outcomes of the rounding procedure may not even be a legitimate solution to the problem.

To find the optimal solution of an ILP problem, a *search* approach based on the idea of *branch and bound* divides an ILP problem into several LP subproblems, and uses the noninteger solutions returned by an LP solver to reduce the search space.

When LPR finds a noninteger solution, it splits the problem on the noninteger variable. For example, suppose variable x_i is fractional in a noninteger solution to the ILP problem $\min\{cx : x \in S, x \in \{0,1\}^n\}$, where S is the linear constraints. The ILP problem can be split into two sub-LPR problems, $\min\{cx : x \in S \cap \{x_i = 0\}\}$ and $\min\{cx : x \in S \cap \{x_i = 1\}\}$. Since any feasible solution provides an upper bound and any LPR solution generates a lower bound, the search tree can be effectively cut.

One technique that is often combined with *branch and bound* is *cutting plane*. When a noninteger solution is given by LPR, it adds a new linear constraint that makes the noninteger point infeasible, while still keeping the optimal integer solution in the feasible region. As a result, the feasible region is closer to the ideal polyhedron, which is the convex hull of feasible integer solutions. The most well-known cutting plane algorithm is Gomory's fractional cutting plane method [41], for which it can be shown that only a finite number of additional constraints are needed. Moreover, researchers developed different cutting plane algorithms for different types of ILP problems. One example is [40], which only focuses on binary ILP problems.

In theory, a search-based strategy may need several steps to find the optimal solution. However, LPR always generates integer solutions for *all* the (thousands of) cases we have experimented with, even though the coefficient matrix in our problem is not unimodular.

20.5 Experiments

We describe below two sets of experiments on the problem of simultaneously recognizing entities and relations. In the first, we view the task as a knowledge acquisition task – we let the system read sentences and identify entities and relations among them. Given that this is a difficult task which may require quite often information beyond the sentence, we consider also a "forced decision" task, in which we simulate a question-answering situation – we ask the system, say, "Who killed whom?" and evaluate it on identifying correctly the relation and its arguments, given that it is known that somewhere in this sentence this relation is active. In addition, this evaluation exhibits the ability of our approach to incorporate task specific constraints at decision time. At the end of this section, we will also provide a case study to illustrate how the inference procedure corrects mistakes both in entity and relation predictions.

20.5.1 Data Preparation

We annotated the named entities and relations in some sentences from the TREC documents. In order to effectively observe the interaction between relations and entities, we chose 1437 sentences[4] that have at least one active relation. Among those sentences, there are 5336 entities, and 19,048 pairs of entities (binary relations). Entity labels include 1685 *persons*, 1968 *locations*, 978 *organizations*, and 705 *other_ent*. Relation labels include 406 *located_in*, 394 *work_for*, 451 *orgBased_in*, 521 *live_in*, 268 *kill*, and 17,007 *other_rel*. Note that most pairs of entities have no active relations at all. Therefore, relation *other_rel* significantly outnumbers others. Examples of each relation label and the constraints between a relation variable and its two entity arguments are shown in table 20.1.

Table 20.1   Relations of interest and the corresponding constraints

Relation	Entity1	Entity2	Example
located_in	loc	loc	(New York, US)
work_for	per	org	(Bill Gates, Microsoft)
orgBased_in	org	loc	(HP, Palo Alto)
live_in	per	loc	(Bush, US)
kill	per	per	(Oswald, JFK)

20.5.2   Tested Approaches

In order to focus on the evaluation of our inference procedure, we assume the problem of *segmentation* (or *phrase detection*) [1, 25] is solved, and the entity boundaries are given to us as input; thus we only concentrate on their classifications.

We evaluate our LP-based inference procedure by observing its effect in different approaches of combining the entity and relation classifiers. The first approach is to train entity and relation classifiers *separately*. In particular, the relation classifier does not know the labels of its entity arguments, and the entity classifier does not know the labels of relations in the sentence, either. For the entity classifier, one set of features is extracted from words within a size 4 window around the target phrase. They are (1) words, POS tags, and conjunctions of them; and (2) bigrams and trigrams of the mixture of words and tags. In addition, some other features are extracted from the target phrase, which are listed in table 20.2.

For the relation classifier, there are three sets of features:

1. features similar to those used in the entity classification are extracted from the two argument entities of the relation;

2. conjunctions of the features from the two arguments;

3. some patterns extracted from the sentence or between the two arguments.

---

4. The   data   used   here   is   available   by   following   the   data   link   from `http://L2R.cs.uiuc.edu/~cogcomp/`

5. We collected names of famous places, people, and popular titles from other data sources in advance.

Table 20.2 Some features extracted from the target phrase

Symbol	Explanation
icap	the first character of a word is capitalized
acap	all characters of a word are capitalized
incap	some characters of a word are capitalized
suffix	the suffix of a word is "ing," "ment," etc.
bigram	bigram of words in the target phrase
len	number of words in the target phrase
place[5]	the phrase is/has a known place's name
prof[5]	the phrase is/has a professional title (e.g., Lt.)
name[5]	the phrase is/has a known person's name

Table 20.3 Some patterns used in relation classification

Pattern	Example
arg_1 , arg_2	San Jose, CA
arg_1 , $\cdots$ a $\cdots$ arg_2 *prof*	John Smith, a Starbucks manager $\cdots$
in/at arg_1 in/at/, arg_2	Officials in Perugia in Umbria province said $\cdots$
arg_2 *prof* arg_1	CNN reporter David McKinley $\cdots$
arg_1 $\cdots$ native of $\cdots$ arg_2	Elizabeth Dole is a native of Salisbury, N.C.
arg_1 $\cdots$ based in/at arg_2	$\cdots$ a manager for Kmart based in Troy, Mich. said $\cdots$

Some features in category 3 are "the number of words between arg_1 and arg_2 ," "whether arg_1 and arg_2 are the same word," or "arg_1 is the beginning of the sentence and has words that consist of all capitalized characters," where arg_1 and arg_2 represent the first and second argument entities respectively. Table 20.3 presents some patterns we use.

The learning algorithm used is a regularized variation of the Winnow update rule incorporated in SNoW [29, 31, 4], a multiclass classifier that is specifically tailored for large-scale learning tasks. SNoW learns a sparse network of linear functions, in which the targets (entity classes or relation classes, in this case) are represented as linear functions over a common feature space. While SNoW can be used as a classifier and predicts using a winner-take-all mechanism over the activation value of the target classes, we can also rely directly on the raw activation value it outputs, which is the weighted linear sum of the active features, to estimate the posteriors. It can be verified that the resulting values provide a good source of probability estimation. We use softmax [2] over the raw activation values as conditional probabilities. Specifically, suppose the number of classes is n, and the raw activation values of class i is act_i. The posterior estimation for class i is derived by the following equation

$$p_i = \frac{e^{act_i}}{\sum_{1 \le j \le n} e^{act_j}}.$$

In addition to the *separate* approach, we also test several pipeline models, which we denote $E \to R$, $R \to E$ and $E \leftrightarrow R$. The $E \to R$ approach first trains the basic entity classifier (E), which is identical to the entity classifier in the *separate* approach. Its predictions on the two entity arguments of a relation are then used conjunctively as additional features (e.g., *person–person* or *person–location*) in learning the relation classifier (R). Similarly, $R \to E$ first trains the relation classifier (R); its output is then used as additional features in the entity classifier (E). For example, the additional feature could be "this entity is predicted as the first argument of a *work_for* relation." The $E \leftrightarrow R$ model is the combination of the above two. It uses the entity classifier in the $R \to E$ model and the relation classifier in the $E \to R$ model as its final classifiers.

Although the true labels of entities and relations are known during training, only the *predicted* labels are available during evaluation on new data (and in testing). Therefore, rather than training the second-stage pipeline classifiers on the available *true* labels, we train them on the *predictions* of the previous stage classifiers. This way, at test time the classifiers are being evaluated on data of the same type they were trained on, making the second-stage classifier more tolerant to the mistakes [6]. The need to train pipeline classifiers this way has been observed multiple times in natural language processing (NLP) research, and we also have validated it in our experiments. For example, when the relation classifier is trained using the true entity labels, the performance is usually worse than when training it using the predicted entity labels.

The last approach, *omniscient*, tests the conceptual upper bound of this entity-relation classification problem. It also trains the two classifiers separately. However, it assumes that the entity classifier knows the *correct* relation labels, and similarly the relation classifier knows the *right* entity labels as well. This additional information is then used as features in training and testing. Note that this assumption is unrealistic. Nevertheless, it may give us a hint on how accurately the classifiers with global inference can achieve. Finally, we apply the LP-based inference procedure to the above five models, and observe how it improves the performance.

20.5.3   Results

We test the aforementioned approaches using five fold cross-validation. For each approach, we also perform a paired t-test on its F_1 scores before and after inference. Tables 20.4 and 20.5 show the performance of each approach in *recall, precision*, and F_1.

The results show that the inference procedure consistently improves the performance of the five models, both in entities and relations. One interesting observation

---

6. In order to derive similar performance in testing, ideally the previous stage classifier should be trained using a different corpus. We didn't take this approach because of data scarcity.

Table 20.4 Results of the entity classification in different approaches. Experiments are conducted using five fold cross-validation. Numbers in boldface indicate that the p-values are smaller than 0.1. Symbols $\dagger$ and $\ddagger$ indicate significance at 95% and 99% levels respectively. Significance tests were computed with a two-tailed paired t-test.

Approach	person			location			organization		
	Rec	Prec	F_1	Rec	Prec	F_1	Rec	Prec	F_1
Separate	89.5	89.8	89.4	87.0	91.5	89.0	67.6	91.3	77.0
Separate w/ Inf	90.5	90.6	90.4	88.6	91.8	**90.1**	71.0	91.2	**79.4**
E → R	89.5	89.8	89.4	87.0	91.5	89.0	67.6	91.3	77.0
E → R w/ Inf	89.7	90.1	**89.7**†	87.0	91.7	89.1	69.0	91.2	78.0
R → E	89.1	88.7	88.6	88.1	89.8	88.9	71.4	89.3	78.7
R → E w/ Inf	88.6	88.6	88.3	88.2	89.4	88.7	72.1	88.5	79.0
E ↔ R	89.1	88.7	88.6	88.1	89.8	88.9	71.4	89.3	78.7
E ↔ R w/ Inf	89.5	89.1	**89.0**	88.7	89.7	**89.1**	72.0	89.5	79.2
Omniscient	94.9	93.7	94.2	92.4	96.6	94.4	88.1	93.5	90.7
Omniscient w/ Inf	96.1	94.2	**95.1**‡	94.0	97.0	**95.4**	88.7	94.9	91.7

is that the *omniscient* classifiers, which know the correct entity or relation labels, can still be improved by the inference procedure. This demonstrates the effectiveness of incorporating constraints, even when the learning algorithm may be able to learn them from the data.

One of the more significant results in our experiments, we believe, is the improvement in the *quality* of the decisions. As mentioned in section 20.1, incorporating constraints helps to avoid inconsistency in classification. It is interesting to investigate how often such mistakes happen without global inference, and see how effective the global inference is.

For this purpose, we define the *quality* of the decision as follows. For a relation variable and its two corresponding entity variables, if the labels of these variables are predicted correctly and the relation is active (i.e., not *other_rel*), then we count it as a *coherent* prediction. *Quality* is then the number of *coherent* predictions divided by the sum of *coherent* and *incoherent* predictions. When the inference procedure is not applied, 5% to 25% of the predictions are incoherent. Therefore, the quality is not always good. On the other hand, our global inference procedure takes the natural constraints into account, so it never generates incoherent predictions. If the relation classifier has the correct entity labels as features, a good learner should learn the constraints as well. As a result, the quality of *omniscient* is almost as good as *omniscient with inference*.

Another experiment we performed is the *forced decision* test, which boosts the F_1 score of the "kill" relation to 86.2%. In this experiment, we assume that the system knows which sentences have the "kill" relation at the decision time, but it does not know which pair of entities have this relation. We force the system to determine

Table 20.5   Results of the relation classification in different approaches. Experiments are conducted using five-fold cross-validation. Numbers in boldface indicates that that the p-values are smaller than 0.1. Symbols $\dagger$ and $\ddagger$ indicate significance at 95% and 99% levels respectively. Significance tests were computed with a two-tailed paired t-test.

Approach	located_in			work_for			orgBased_in		
	Rec	Prec	F_1	Rec	Prec	F_1	Rec	Prec	F_1
Separate	53.0	43.3	45.2	41.9	55.1	46.3	35.6	85.4	50.0
Separate w/ Inf	51.6	56.3	**50.5**‡	40.1	74.1	**51.2**	35.7	90.8	50.8
E $\rightarrow$ R	56.4	52.5	50.7	44.4	60.8	51.2	42.1	77.8	54.3
E $\rightarrow$ R w/ Inf	55.7	53.2	50.9	42.9	72.1	**53.5**†	42.3	78.0	54.5
R $\rightarrow$ E	53.0	43.3	45.2	41.9	55.1	46.3	35.6	85.4	50.0
R $\rightarrow$ E w/ Inf	53.0	49.8	**49.1**†	41.6	67.5	**50.4**	36.6	87.1	51.2
E $\leftrightarrow$ R	56.4	52.5	50.7	44.4	60.8	51.2	42.1	77.8	54.3
E $\leftrightarrow$ R w/ Inf	55.7	53.9	51.3	42.3	72.0	**53.1**	41.6	79.8	54.3
Omniscient	62.9	59.5	57.5	50.3	69.4	58.2	50.3	77.9	60.9
Omniscient w/ Inf	62.9	61.9	**59.1**	50.3	79.2	**61.4**†	50.9	81.7	**62.5**‡

Approach	live_in			kill		
	Rec	Prec	F_1	Rec	Prec	F_1
Separate	39.7	61.7	48.0	81.5	75.3	77.6
Separate w/ Inf	41.7	68.2	**51.4**†	80.8	82.7	81.4
E $\rightarrow$ R	50.0	58.9	53.5	81.5	73.0	76.5
E $\rightarrow$ R w/ Inf	50.0	57.7	53.0	80.6	77.2	78.3
R $\rightarrow$ E	39.7	61.7	48.0	81.5	75.3	77.6
R $\rightarrow$ E w/ Inf	40.6	64.1	49.4	81.5	79.7	80.1
E $\leftrightarrow$ R	50.0	58.9	53.5	81.5	73.0	76.5
E $\leftrightarrow$ R w/ Inf	49.0	59.1	53.0	81.5	77.5	**79.0**†
Omniscient	56.1	61.7	58.2	81.4	76.4	77.9
Omniscient w/ Inf	57.3	63.9	**59.9**	81.4	79.9	79.9

which of the possible relations in a sentence (i.e., which pair of entities) has this "kill" relation

by adding the following linear inequality.

$$\sum_{R \in \mathcal{R}} x_{\{R, kill\}} \geq 1$$

This is equivalent to saying that at least one of the relation variables in the sentence should be labeled as "kill." Since this additional constraint only applies to on the sentences in which the "kill" relation is active, the inference results of other sentences are not changed. Note that it is a realistic situation (e.g., in the context of question answering) in that it adds an external constraint, not present at the time of learning the classifiers, and it evaluates the ability of our inference algorithm to cope with it. The results exhibit that our expectations are correct.

20.5.4 Case Study

Although tables 20.4 and 20.5 clearly demonstrate that the inference procedure improves the performance, it is interesting to see *how* it corrects the mistakes by examining a specific case. The following sentence is taken from a news article in our corpus. The eight entities are in boldface, labeled E_1 to E_8.

> At the proposal of the **Serb Radical Party**$_{|E_1}$, the Assembly elected political **Branko Vojnic**$_{|E_2}$ from **Beli Manastir**$_{|E_3}$ as its speaker, while **Marko Atlagic**$_{|E_4}$ and Dr. **Milan Ernjakovic**$_{|E_5}$, **Krajina**$_{|E_6}$ **Serb Democratic Party**$_{|E_7}$ (**SDS**$_{|E_8}$) candidates, were elected as deputy speakers.

Table 20.6 shows the probability distribution estimated by the basic classifiers, the predictions before and after the inference, along with the true labels. Table 20.7 provides this information for the relation variables. Because the values of most of them are *other_rel*, we only show a small set of them here.

Table 20.6 Example: Inference effect on entities' predictions: the true labels, the predictions before and after inference, and the probabilities estimated by the basic classifiers.

	Label	before Inf.	after Inf.	other	person	loc.	org
E_1	Org	Org	Org	0.21	0.13	0.06	**0.60**
E_2	Per	Other	Other	**0.46**	0.16	0.33	0.05
E_3	Loc	Loc	Loc	0.29	0.25	**0.31**	0.15
E_4	Per	Other	Other	**0.37**	0.20	0.33	0.10
E_5	*Per*	*Loc*	*Per*	0.10	0.31	**0.36**	0.23
E_6	Loc	Loc	Loc	0.24	0.05	**0.61**	0.10
E_7	*Org*	*Per*	*Org*	0.15	**0.41**	0.03	0.40
E_7	Org	Org	Org	0.35	0.17	0.11	**0.37**

In this example, the inference procedure corrects two variables – E_5 (Milan Ernjakovic) and E_7 (Serb Democratic Party). If we examine the probability distribution of these two entity variables in table 20.6, it is easy to see that the classifier has difficulty deciding whether E_5 is a person's name or location, and whether E_7 is a person or organization. The strong belief that there is a *work_for* relation between these two entities (see the row R_{57} in table 20.7) enables the inference procedure to correct this mistake. In addition, several relation predictions are also corrected from *work_for* to *other_rel* because they lack the support of the entity classifier.

Note that not every mistake can be rectified, as several *work_for* relations are misidentified as *other_rel*. This may be due to the fact that the relation *other_rel* can take any types of entities as its arguments. In some rare cases, the inference

Table 20.7 Example: Inference effect on relations' predictions: the true labels, the predictions before and after inference, and the probabilities estimated by the basic classifiers.

	Label	before Inf.	after Inf.	other_rel	located_in	work_for	org_in	live_in	kill
R_{23}	kill	other_rel	other_rel	**0.66**	0.10	0.03	0.03	0.11	0.08
R_{37}	*other_rel*	*work_for*	*other_rel*	0.38	0.07	**0.41**	0.02	0.10	0.02
R_{47}	work_for	other_rel	other_rel	**0.65**	0.05	0.19	0.02	0.06	0.03
R_{48}	work_for	other_rel	other_rel	**0.83**	0.06	0.03	0.02	0.04	0.03
R_{51}	other_rel	work_for	work_for	0.36	0.06	**0.42**	0.01	0.13	0.02
R_{52}	*other_rel*	*work_for*	*other_rel*	0.24	0.15	**0.28**	0.04	0.22	0.07
R_{56}	*other_rel*	*work_for*	*other_rel*	0.23	0.16	**0.35**	0.01	0.22	0.02
R_{57}	work_for	work_for	work_for	0.26	0.07	**0.44**	0.01	0.21	0.02
R_{58}	work_for	other_rel	other_rel	**0.58**	0.06	0.14	0.02	0.17	0.02
R_{67}	work_for	other_rel	other_rel	**0.67**	0.06	0.19	0.02	0.05	0.01
R_{68}	work_for	other_rel	other_rel	**0.76**	0.09	0.04	0.04	0.05	0.02

procedure may change a correct prediction to a wrong label. However, since this seldom happens, the overall performance is still improved after inference.

One interesting thing to notice is the efficiency of this ILP inference in practice. Using a Pentium III 800MHz machine, it takes less than 30 seconds to process all the 1437 sentences (5336 entity variables and 19,048 relation variables in total).

20.6 Comparison with Other Inference Methods

In this section, we provide a broader view of inference methods and place the ILP approach described in this chapter in this context. Our approach to the problem of learning with structured output decouples learning and inference stages. As mentioned earlier, this is not the only approach. In other approaches (e.g., [39, 36]), training can be done globally, coupled with the inference. Coupling training and inference has multiple effects on performance and time complexity, which we do not discuss here (but see [32, 26] for some comparative discussion) as we concentrate on the inference component. Inference is the problem of determining the *best* global output $\hat{\mathbf{y}} \in \mathcal{F}(\mathbf{Y})$ given model parameters $\boldsymbol{\lambda}$, according to some cost function f, where $\mathbf{Y}$ is the output space and $\mathcal{F}(\mathbf{Y}) \subseteq \mathbf{Y}$ is the subset of $\mathbf{Y}$ that satisfy some constraints. Formally, if $\mathbf{x}$ represents the input data, then $\hat{\mathbf{y}}$ is decided as follows:

$$\hat{\mathbf{y}} = \operatorname{argmax}_{\mathbf{y} \in \mathcal{F}(\mathbf{Y})} f(\mathbf{x}, \mathbf{y}; \boldsymbol{\lambda}).$$

The efficiency and tractability of the inference procedure dictate the feasibility of the whole framework. However, whether there exists an efficient and exact inference algorithm highly depends on the problem's structure. Polynomial-time algorithms usually do not exist when there are complex constraints among the output variables (just like the entity/relation problem described in this chapter). In this section, we briefly introduce several common inference algorithms in various text-processing problems, and contrast them with our ILP approach.

20.6.1 Exact Polynomial-time Methods

Most polynomial-time inference methods are based on dynamic programming. For linear chain structures, the Viterbi algorithm and its variations are the most popular. For tree structures, different cubic-time algorithms have been proposed. Although replacing these algorithms with the ILP approach does not necessarily make the inference more efficient in practice, as we show below, the ILP framework does provide these polynomial-time algorithms an easy way to incorporate additional "declarative" constraints, which may not be possible to express within the original inference algorithm. We describe these methods here and sketch how they can be formulated as an integer linear programming problem.

20.6.1.1 *The Viterbi Algorithm*

Linear-chain structures are often used for sequence labeling problems, where the task is to decide the label of each token. For this problem, HMMs [27], conditional sequential models and other extensions [25], and conditional random fields [21] are commonly used. While the first two methods learn the state transition between a pair of consecutive tokens, conditional random fields relax the directionality assumption and train the potential functions for the size-1 (i.e., a single token) and size-2 (a pair of consecutive tokens) cliques. In both cases, the Viterbi algorithm is usually used to find the most probable sequence assignment.

We describe the Viterbi algorithm in the linear-chain conditional random fields setting as follows. Suppose we need to predict the labels of a sequence of tokens, $t_0, t_1, \cdots, t_{m-1}$. Let $\mathcal{Y}$ be the set of possible labels for each token, where $|\mathcal{Y}| = m$. A set of $m \times m$ matrices $\{M_i(\mathbf{x}) | i = 0, \ldots, n-1\}$ is defined over each pair of labels $y', y \in \mathcal{Y}$

$$M_i(y', y | \mathbf{x}) = \exp(\sum_j \lambda_j f_j(y', y, \mathbf{x}, i)),$$

where λ_j are the model parameters and f_j are the features. By augmenting two special nodes y_{-1} and y_n before and after the sequence with labels start and end respectively, the sequence probability is

$$p(\mathbf{y} | \mathbf{x}, \boldsymbol{\lambda}) = \frac{1}{Z(\mathbf{x})} \prod_{i=0}^{n} M_i(y_{i-1}, y_i | \mathbf{x}).$$

$Z(\mathbf{x})$ is a normalization factor that can be computed from the M_i's but is not needed in evaluation. We only need to find the label sequence $\mathbf{y}$ that maximizes the product of the corresponding elements of these $n + 1$ matrices. The Viterbi algorithm is the standard method that computes the most likely label sequence given the observation. It *grows* the optimal label sequence incrementally by scanning the matrices from position 0 to n. At step i, it records all the optimal sequences ending at a label $y, \forall y \in \mathcal{Y}$ (denoted by $\mathbf{y}_i^*(y)$), and also the corresponding product $P_i(y)$. The recursive function of this dynamic programming algorithm is

1. $P_0(y) = M_0(\text{start}, y|\mathbf{x})$ and $\mathbf{y}_0^*(y) = y$.
2. for $1 \leq i \leq n$, $\mathbf{y}_i^*(y) = \mathbf{y}_{i-1}^*(\hat{y}).(y)$ and $P_i(y) = \max_{y' \in \mathcal{Y}} P_{i-1}(y')M(y', y|\mathbf{x})$, where $\hat{y} = \text{argmax}_{y' \in \mathcal{Y}} P_{i-1}(y')M(y', y|\mathbf{x})$ and "." is the concatenation operator.

The optimal sequence is therefore $\mathbf{y}_{n-1}^* = [\mathbf{y}_n^*]_{0..n-1}$, which is the best path to the end symbol but taking only position 0 to position $n-1$.

The solution that Viterbi outputs is in fact the shortest path in the graph constructed is as follows. Let n be the number of tokens in the sequence, and m be the number of labels each token can take. The graph consists of $nm + 2$ nodes and $(n-1)m^2 + 2m$ edges. In addition to two special nodes start and end that denote the start and end positions of the path, the label of each token is represented by a node v_{ij}, where $0 \leq i \leq n-1$, and $0 \leq j \leq m-1$. If the path passes node v_{ij}, then label j is assigned to token i. For nodes that represent two adjacent tokens $v_{(i-1)j}$ and $v_{ij'}$, where $0 \leq i \leq n$, and $0 \leq j, j' \leq m-1$, there is a directed edge $x_{i,jj'}$ from $v_{(i-1)j}$ to $v_{ij'}$, with the cost $-\log(M_i(jj'|\mathbf{x}))$.

Obviously, the path from start to end will pass exactly one node on position i. That is, exactly one of the nodes $v_{i,j}, 0 \leq j \leq m-1$, will be picked. Figure 20.3 illustrates the graph. Suppose that $\mathbf{y} = y_0 y_1 \cdots y_{n-1}$ is the label sequence determined by the path. Then

$$\text{argmin}_{\mathbf{y}} - \sum_{i=0}^{n-1} \log(M_i(y_{i-1}y_i|\mathbf{x})) = \text{argmax}_{\mathbf{y}} \prod_{i=0}^{n-1} M_i(y_{i-1}y_i|\mathbf{x}).$$

Namely, the nodes in the shortest path are exactly the labels returned by the Viterbi algorithm.

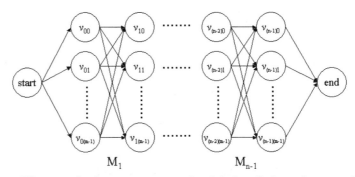

Figure 20.3   The graph that represents the labels of the tokens and the state transition (also known as the *trellis* in hidden Markov models).

The Viterbi algorithm can still be used when the matrix is slightly modified to incorporate simple constraints. For example, in the task of information extraction, if the label of a word is the *beginning* of an entity (B), *inside* an entity (I), or *outside* any entity (O), a token label O immediately followed by a label I is not a valid labeling. The constraint can be incorporated by changing the corresponding transitional probability or matrix entries to 0 [10, 20]. However, more general, nonMarkovian constraints cannot be resolved using the same trick.

Recently, Roth and Yih [32] proposed a different inference approach based on ILP to replace the Viterbi algorithm. The basic idea there is to use integer linear programming to find the shortest path in the trellis (e.g., figure 20.3). Each edge of the graph is represented by an indicator variable to represent whether this edge is in the shortest path or not. The cost function can be written in terms of a linear function of these indicator variables. In this ILP, linear (in)equalities are added to enforce that the values of these indicator variables represent a legitimate path. This ILP can be solved simply by LP relaxation because the coefficient matrix is totally unimodular. However, the main advantage of this new setting is its ability to allow more general constraints that can be encoded either in linear (in)equalities or in the cost function. Interested readers may see [32] for more details.

20.6.1.2   *Constraint Satisfaction with Classifiers*

A second efficient inference algorithm for linear sequence tasks that has been used successfully for natural language and information extraction problems is *constraint satisfaction with classifiers* (CSCL) [25]. This method was first proposed for shallow parsing – identifying atomic phrases (e.g., base noun phrases) in a given sentence. In that case, two classifiers are first trained to predict whether a word **opens** (O) a phrase or **closes** (C) a phrase. Since these two classifiers may generate inconsistent predictions, the inference task has to decide which OC pairs are indeed the boundaries of a phrase.

We illustrate their approach by the following example. Suppose a sentence has six tokens, $t_1, \cdots, t_6$, as indicated in figure 20.4. The classifiers have identified three opens (O) and three closes (C) in this sentence (i.e., the open and close brackets). Among the OC pairs (t_1, t_3), (t_1, t_5), (t_1, t_6), (t_2, t_3), (t_2, t_5), (t_2, t_6), (t_4, t_5), (t_4, t_6), the inference procedure needs to decide which of them are the predicted phrases, based on the cost function. In addition, the chosen phrases should not overlap or embed with each other. Let the predicate "this pair is selected as a phrase" be represented by an indicator variable $x_i \in X$, where $|X| = 8$ in this case. They associate a cost function $c : X \to R$ with each variable (where the value $c(x_i)$ is determined as a function of the corresponding OC classifiers), and try to find a solution that minimizes the overall cost, $\sum_{i=1}^{n} c(x_i) x_i$.

This problem can be reduced elegantly to a shortest path problem by the following graph construction. Each open and close word is represented by an O node and a C node. For each possible OC pair, there is a direct link from the corresponding open

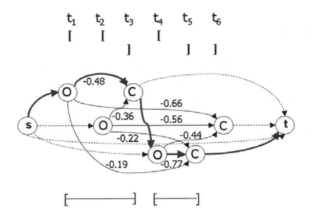

Figure 20.4 Identifying phrases in a sentence using the constraints satisfaction with classifiers (CSCL) approach, courtesy of Vasin Punyakanok.

node O to the close node C. Finally, one source (s) node and one target (t) node are added. Links are added from s to each O and from each C to t. The cost of an OC link is $-p_i$, where p_i is the probability that this OC pair represents a phrase, estimated by the O and C classifiers.

Because the inference process is also done by finding the shortest path in the graph, the ILP framework described in [32] is applicable here as well.

20.6.1.3 Clause Identification

The two efficient approaches mentioned above can be generalized beyond the sequential structure, to tree structures. Cubic-time dynamic algorithms are often used for inference in various tree-structure problems, such as parsing [17] or clause identification [38]. As an example, we discuss the inference approach proposed by Carreras et al. [7], in the context of clause identification. Clause identification is a partial parsing problem. Given a sentence, a clause is defined as a sequence of words that contains a subject and a predicate [38]. In the following example sentence taken from the Penn yreebank [23], each pair of corresponding parentheses represents a clause. The task is thus to identify all the clauses in the sentence.

(The deregulation of railroads and trucking companies (that (began in 1980)) enabled (shippers to bargain for transportation).)

Although the problem looks similar to shallow parsing, the constraints between the clauses are weaker – clauses may not overlap, but a clause can be embedded in another. Formally speaking, let w_i be the ith word in a sentence of n words. A clause can be defined as a pair of numbers (s, t), where $1 \leq s \leq t \leq n$, which represents the word sequence $w_s, w_{s+1}, \ldots, w_t$. Given two clauses $c_1 = (s_1, t_1)$ and $c_2 = (s_2, t_2)$, we say that these two clauses overlap iff $s_1 < s_2 \leq t_1 < t_2$ or $s_2 < s_1 \leq t_2 < t_1$.

Similarly to the approach presented throughout this chapter, in [7, 6], this problem is solved by combining learning and inference. Briefly speaking, each candidate clause $c = (s, t)$ in the targeted sentence is associated with a score, $score(c)$, estimated by the classifiers. Let $\mathbf{C}$ be the set of all possible clauses in the given sentence, $\mathcal{F}(\mathbf{C})$ all possible subsets of $\mathbf{C}$ that satisfy the nonoverlapping constraint. Then the *best* clause prediction is defined as

$$\mathbf{c}^* = \mathrm{argmax}_{\mathbf{c} \in \mathcal{F}(\mathbf{C})} \sum_{c \in \mathbf{c}} score(c).$$

Carreras et al. [7] proposed a dynamic programming algorithm to solve this inference problem. In this algorithm, two 2D matrices are maintained: `best-split[s,t]` stores the optimal clause predictions in $w_s, w_{s+1}, \ldots, w_t$; `score[s,t]` is the score of the clause (s, t). By filling the table recursively, the optimal clause prediction can be found in $O(n^3)$ time.

As in the previous cases discussed in this section, it is clear that this problem can be represented as an ILP. Each candidate clause (s, t) can be represented by an indicator variable $x_{s,t}$. The cost function is the sum of the score times the corresponding indicator variable, namely $\sum(score(s, t) \cdot x_{s,t})$. Suppose clause candidates (s_1, t_1) and (s_2, t_2) overlap. The nonoverlapping constraint can be enforced by adding a linear inequality, $x_{s_1, t_1} + x_{s_2, t_2} \leq 1$.

20.6.2 Generic Methods – Search

As discussed above, exact polynomial time algorithms exist for specific constraint structures; however, the inference problem typically becomes computationally intractable when additional constraints are introduced, or more complex structures are needed. A common computational approach to the inference problem in this case is *search*. Following the definition in [33], search is used to find a legitimate state transition path from the initial state to a goal state while trying to minimize the cost. The problem can be treated as consisting of four components: state space, operators (the legitimate state transitions), goal-test (a function that examines whether a goal state is reached), and path-cost-function (the cost function of the whole path). Figure 20.5 depicts a generic search algorithm.

To solve the entity-relation problem described in this chapter, we can define the state space as the set of all possible labels of the entities and relations (namely, $\mathcal{L}_\mathcal{E}$ and $\mathcal{L}_\mathcal{R}$), plus "*undecided.*" In the initial state, the values of all the variables are "*undecided.*" A legitimate operator changes an entity or relation variable from "*undecided*" to one of the possible labels, subject to the constraints. The goal-test evaluates whether every variable has been assigned a label, and the path-cost is the sum of the assignment cost of each variable.

The main advantage of inference using search is its generality. The cost function need not be linear. The constraints can also be fairly general: as long as the decision

Algorithm 1
generic-search(problem, enqueue-func)

>   nodes ← MakeQueue(MakeNode(init-state(problem)))
>   while (node is not empty)
>   node ← RemoveFront(nodes)
>   if (goal-test(node)) then return node
>   next ← Operators(node)
>   nodes ← enqueue-func(problem, nodes, next)
>   end
>   return failure

end

Figure 20.5   The generic search algorithm, adapted from [33].

on whether a state violates constraints can be evaluated efficiently, they can be used to define the operators.

The main disadvantage, however, is that there is no guarantee of optimality. Despite this weakness, it has been shown that *search* is a successful approach in some tasks empirically. For instance, Moore [24] applied beam search to find the best word alignment given a linear model learned using voted perceptron. Recently, Daumé and Marcu [14] demonstrated an approximate large margin method for learning structured output, where the key inference component is search.

In contrast, our ILP approach may or may not be able to replace this search mechanism, depending on the specific cost function. Nevertheless, in several real-world problems, we observed that our ILP method may not be slower than search, but is guaranteed to find the optimal solution.

20.7   Conclusion

We presented a linear-programming based approach for global inference in cases where decisions depend on the outcomes of several different but mutually dependent classifiers. Even in the presence of a fairly general constraint structure, deviating from the sequential nature typically studied, this approach can find the optimal solution efficiently.

Contrary to general search schemes (e.g., beam search), which do not guarantee optimality, the LP approach provides an efficient way of finding the optimal solution. The key advantage of the LP formulation is its generality and flexibility; in particular, it supports the ability to incorporate classifiers learned in other contexts, "hints" supplied, and decision-time constraints, and reason with all these

for the best global prediction. In sharp contrast with the typically used pipeline framework, our formulation does not blindly trust the results of some classifiers, and therefore is able to overcome mistakes made by classifiers with the help of constraints.

Our experiments have demonstrated these advantages by considering the interaction between entity and relation classifiers. In fact, more classifiers can be added and used within the same framework. For example, if coreference resolution is available, it is possible to incorporate it in the form of constraints that force the labels of the coreferred entities to be the same (but, of course, allowing the global solution to reject the suggestion of these classifiers). Consequently, this may enhance the performance of entity-relation recognition and, at the same time, correct possible coreference resolution errors. Another example is to use chunking information for better relation identification; suppose, for example, that we have available chunking information that identifies Subj+Verb and Verb+Object phrases. Given a sentence that has the verb "murder," we may conclude that the subject and object of this verb are in a "kill" relation. Since the chunking information is used in the global inference procedure, this information will contribute to enhancing its performance and robustness, relying on having more constraints and overcoming possible mistakes by some of the classifiers. Moreover, in an interactive environment where a user can supply new constraints (e.g., a question-answering situation) this framework is able to make use of the new information and enhance the performance at decision time, without retraining the classifiers. As we have shown, our formulation supports not only improved accuracy but also improves the "coherent" quality of the decisions. We believe that it has the potential to be a powerful way for supporting natural language inference.

Acknowledgments

Most of this research was done when Wen-tau Yih was at the University of Illinois at Urbana-Champaign. This research was supported by NSF grants CAREER IIS-9984168 and ITR IIS-0085836, an ONR MURI award and by the Advanced Research and Development Activity (ARDA)'s Advanced Question Answering for Intelligence (AQUAINT) program.

References

[1] S. Abney. Parsing by chunks. In R. Berwick, S. Abney, and C. Tenny, editors, *Principle-Based Parsing: Computation and Psycholinguistics*, pages 257–278. Kluwer, Dordrecht, Netherlands, 1991.

[2] C. Bishop. *Neural Networks for Pattern Recognition*. Oxford University Press, Oxford, UK, 1995.

[3] Y. Boykov, O. Veksler, and R. Zabih. Fast approximate energy minimization via graph cuts. *IEEE Transactions on Pattern Analysis and Machine Intelligence*, 23(11):1222–1239, 2001.

[4] A. Carlson, C. Cumby, J. Rosen, and D. Roth. The SNoW learning architecture. Technical Report UIUCDCS-R-99-2101, University of Illinois at Urbana-Champaign Computer Science Department, May 1999.

[5] X. Carreras and L. Màrquez. Introduction to the CoNLL-2004 shared tasks: Semantic role labeling. In *Proceedings of the Conference on Natural Language Learning*, 2004.

[6] X. Carreras and L. Màrquez. Introduction to the CoNLL-2005 shared task: Semantic role labeling. In *Proceedings of the Conference on Natural Language Learning*, 2005.

[7] X. Carreras, L. Màrquez, V. Punyakanok, and D. Roth. Learning and inference for clause identification. In *Proceedings of the European Conference on Machine Learning*, 2002.

[8] C. Chekuri, S. Khanna, J. Naor, and L. Zosin. Approximation algorithms for the metric labeling problem via a new linear programming formulation. In *Symposium on Discrete Algorithms*, 2001.

[9] R. Chellappa and A. Jain. *Markov Random Fields: Theory and Application.* Academic Press, April 1993.

[10] H. Chieu and H. Ng. A maximum entropy approach to information extraction from semi-structure and free text. In *Proceedings of the National Conference on Artificial Intelligence*, 2002.

[11] CPLEX. ILOG, Inc. http://www.ilog.com/products/cplex/, 2003.

[12] C. Cumby and D. Roth. Relational representations that facilitate learning. In *Proceedings of the International Conference on Principles of Knowledge Representation and Reasoning*, 2000.

[13] C. Cumby and D. Roth. On kernel methods for relational learning. In *Proceedings of the International Conference on Machine Learning*, 2003.

[14] H. Daumé III and D. Marcu. Learning as search optimization: Approximate large margin methods for structured prediction. In *Proceedings of the International Conference on Machine Learning*, 2005.

[15] T. Dietterich. Machine learning for sequential data: A review. In *Structural, Syntactic, and Statistical Pattern Recognition*, pages 15–30. Springer-Verlag, 2002.

[16] Y. Even-Zohar and D. Roth. A classification approach to word prediction. In *Proceedings of the Annual Meeting of the North American Association of Computational Linguistics*, 2000.

[17] M. Johnson. PCFG models of linguistic tree representations. *Computational Linguistics*, 24(4):613–632, 1998.

[18] R. Khardon, D. Roth, and L. G. Valiant. Relational learning for NLP using linear threshold elements. In *Proceedings of the International Joint Conference on Artificial Intelligence*, 1999.

[19] J. Kleinberg and E. Tardos. Approximation algorithms for classification problems with pairwise relationships: Metric labeling and markov random fields. In *IEEE Symposium on Foundations of Computer Science*, 1999.

[20] T. Kristjannson, A. Culotta, P. Viola, and A. McCallum. Interactive information extraction with constrained conditional random fields. In *Proceedings of the National Conference on Artificial Intelligence*, 2004.

[21] J. Lafferty, A. McCallum, and F. Pereira. Conditional random fields: Probabilistic models for segmenting and labeling sequence data. In *Proceedings of the International Conference on Machine Learning*, 2001.

[22] A. Levin, A. Zomet, and Y. Weiss. Learning to perceive transparency from the statistics of natural scenes. In *Proceedings of Neural Information Processing Systems*, 2002.

[23] M. P. Marcus, M. A. Marcinkiewicz, and B. Santorini. Building a large annotated corpus of English: the Penn treebank. *Computational Linguistics*, 19(2):313–330, 1993.

[24] R. C. Moore. A discriminative framework for bilingual word alignment. In *Proceedings of the Conference on Empirical Methods in Natural Language Processing*, 2005.

[25] V. Punyakanok and D. Roth. The use of classifiers in sequential inference. In *Proceedings of Neural Information Processing Systems*, 2001.

[26] V. Punyakanok, D. Roth, W. Yih, and D. Zimak. Learning and inference over constrained output. In *Proceedings of the International Joint Conference on Artificial Intelligence*, 2005.

[27] L.R. Rabiner. A tutorial on hidden Markov models and selected applications in speech recognition. *Proceedings of the IEEE*, 77(2), February 1989.

[28] D. Roth. Reasoning with classifiers. In *Proceedings of the European Conference on Machine Learning*, 2002.

[29] D. Roth. Learning to resolve natural language ambiguities: A unified approach. In *Proceedings of the National Conference on Artificial Intelligence*, 1998.

[30] D. Roth and W. Yih. Relational learning via propositional algorithms: An information extraction case study. In *Proceedings of the International Joint Conference on Artificial Intelligence*, 2001.

[31] D. Roth and W. Yih. Probabilistic reasoning for entity and relation recognition. In *Proceedings of the International Conference on Computational Linguistics*, 2002.

[32] D. Roth and W. Yih. Integer linear programming inference for conditional random fields. In *Proceedings of the International Conference on Machine Learning*, 2005.

[33] S. Russell and P. Norvig. *Artificial Intelligence: A Modern Approach*. Prentice Hall, Upper Saddle River, NJ, 1995.

[34]   A. Schrijver. *Theory of Linear and Integer Programming.* Wiley Interscience Series in Discrete Mathmatics. John Wiley & Sons, Hoboken, NJ, 1986.

[35]   B. Taskar, P. Abbeel, and D. Koller. Discriminative probabilistic models for relational data. In *Proceedings of Uncertainty in Artificial Intelligence*, 2002.

[36]   B. Taskar, D. Klein, M. Collins, D. Koller, and C. Manning. Max-margin parsing. In *Proceedings of the Conference on Empirical Methods in Natural Language Processing*, 2004.

[37]   E. F. Tjong Kim Sang and F. De Meulder. Introduction to the CoNLL-2003 shared task: Language-independent named entity recognition. In *Proceedings of the Conference on Natural Language Learning*, 2003.

[38]   E. F. Tjong Kim Sang and H. Déjean. Introduction to the CoNLL-2001 shared task: Clause identification. In Walter Daelemans and Rémi Zajac, editors, *Proceedings of the Conference on Natural Language Learning*, pages 53–57, 2001.

[39]   I. Tsochantaridis, T. Hofmann, T. Joachims, and Y. Altun. Support vector machine learning for interdependent and structured output spaces. In *Proceedings of the International Conference on Machine Learning*, 2004.

[40]   X. Wang and A. Regan. A cutting plane method for integer programming problems with binary variables. Technical Report UCI-ITS-WP-00-12, University of California, Irvine, 2000.

[41]   L. Wolsey. *Integer Programming.* John Wiley & Sons, Hoboken, NJ, 1998.

[42]   Xpress-MP. Dash Optimization. http://www.dashoptimization.com/products.html, 2003.

Contributors

Pieter Abbeel
Computer Science Department
Stanford University
abbeel@cs.stanford.edu

Eyal Amir
Department of Computer Science
University of Illinois, Urbana-Champaign
eyal@cs.uiuc.edu

Rodrigo de Salvo Braz
Department of Computer Science
University of Illinois, Urbana-Champaign
braz@uiuc.edu

Razvan C. Bunescu
Department of Computer Sciences
University of Texas, Austin
razvan@cs.utexas.edu

Elizabeth Burnside
Department of Radiology
Department of Biostatistics and Medical Informatics
University of Wisconsin, Madison
es.burnside@hosp.wisc.edu

Vítor Santos Costa
COPPE/Sistemas
Universidade Federal do Rio de Janeiro, Brazil
vitor@cos.ufrj.br

James Cussens
Department of Computer Science &
York Centre for Complex Systems Analysis
University of York, UK
jc@cs.york.ac.uk

Jesse Davis
Department of Computer Science
University of Wisconsin, Madison
jdavis@cs.wisc.edu

Luc De Raedt
Institute for Computer Science, Machine Learning Lab
Albert-Ludwigs-Universität Freiburg, Germany
deraedt@informatik.uni-freiburg.de

Pedro Domingos
Department of Computer Science and Engineering
University of Washington
pedrod@cs.washington.edu

Inês Dutra
COPPE/Sistemas
Universidade Federal do Rio de Janeiro, Brazil
ines@cos.ufrj.br

Sašo Džeroski
Department of Knowledge Technologies
Jožef Stefan Institute, Slovenia
Saso.Dzeroski@ijs.si

Alan Fern
School of Electrical Engineering and Computer Science
Oregon State University
afern@eecs.orst.edu

Nir Friedman
School of Computer Science and Engineering
Hebrew University, Israel
nir@cs.huji.ac.il

Lise Getoor
Computer Science Department
University of Maryland, College Park
getoor@cs.umd.edu

Robert Givan
School of Electrical and Computer Engineering
Purdue University
givan@purdue.edu

David Heckerman
Microsoft Research Redmond
heckerma@microsoft.com

David Jensen
Computer Science Department
University of Massachusetts, Amherst
jensen@cs.umass.edu

Kristian Kersting
Institute for Computer Science, Machine Learning Lab
Albert-Ludwigs-Universität Freiburg, Germany
kersting@informatik.uni-freiburg.de

Daphne Koller
Computer Science Department
Stanford University
koller@cs.stanford.edu

Andrey Kolobov
Computer Science Division
University of California, Berkeley
karayaone@rambler.ru

Bhaskara Marthi
Computer Science Division
University of California, Berkeley
bhaskara@cs.berkeley.edu

Andrew McCallum
Department of Computer Science
University of Massachusetts, Amherst
mccallum@cs.umass.edu

Chris Meek
Microsoft Research Redmond
meek@microsoft.com

Brian Milch
Computer Science Division
University of California, Berkeley
milch@cs.berkeley.edu

Raymond J. Mooney
Department of Computer Sciences
University of Texas, Austin
mooney@cs.utexas.edu

Stephen Muggleton
Department of Computing,
Imperial College London, UK
shm@doc.ic.ac.uk

Jennifer Neville
Computer Science Department
University of Massachusetts, Amherst
jneville@cs.umass.edu

Daniel L. Ong
Computer Science Division
University of California, Berkeley
dlong@ocf.berkeley.edu

David Page
Department of Biostatistics and Medical Informatics
University of Wisconsin, Madison
page@biostat.wisc.edu

Niels Pahlavi
Department of Computing,
Imperial College London, UK

Avi Pfeffer
Division of Engineering and Applied Sciences
Harvard University
avi@eecs.harvard.edu

Alexandrin Popescul
Department of Computer and Information Science
University of Pennsylvania
popescul@cis.upenn.edu

Raghu Ramakrishnan
Department of Computer Science
University of Wisconsin, Madison
raghu@cs.wisc.edu

Matthew Richardson
Microsoft Research Redmond
mattri@microsoft.com

Dan Roth
Department of Computer Science
University of Illinois, Urbana-Champaign
danr@uiuc.edu

Stuart Russell
Computer Science Division
University of California, Berkeley
russell@cs.berkeley.edu

Jude Shavlik
Department of Computer Science
University of Wisconsin, Madison
shavlik@cs.wisc.edu

David Sontag
Department of Electrical Engineering and Computer Science
Massachusetts Institute of Technology
dsontag@csail.mit.edu

Charles Sutton
Department of Computer Science
University of Massachusetts, Amherst
casutton@cs.umass.edu

Ben Taskar
Department of Computer and Information Science
University of Pennsylvania
taskar@cis.upenn.edu

Lyle H. Ungar
Department of Computer and Information Science
University of Pennsylvania
ungar@cis.upenn.edu

Ming-Fai Wong
Computer Science Department
Stanford University
mingfai.wong@cs.stanford.edu

Wen-tau Yih
Machine Learning and Applied Statistics Group
Microsoft Research Redmond
scottyih@microsoft.com

SungWook Yoon
School of Electrical and Computer Engineering
Purdue University
sy@purdue.edu

Index

An online index is available on the book webage at
`http://www.cs.umd.edu/srl-book/index.htm`